ISBN: 9781313641210

Published by:
HardPress Publishing
8345 NW 66TH ST #2561
MIAMI FL 33166-2626

Email: info@hardpress.net
Web: http://www.hardpress.net

THE POSTAGE STAMPS

OF THE

UNITED STATES

BY

JOHN N. LUFF

NEW YORK:

THE SCOTT STAMP & COIN CO., LTD.

1902.

CONTENTS.

	PAGE
Introductory,	3
Historical Notes,	5
The Postmasters' Stamps,	9
Alexandria, Va.,	12
Annapolis, Md,,	13
Baltimore, Md.,	15
Boscawen, N. H.,	20
Brattleboro, Vt.,	21
Lockport, N. Y.,	26
Millbury, Mass.,	27
New Haven, Conn.,	29
New York, N. Y.,	32
Philadelphia, Pa.,	38
Pittsfield, Mass.,	39
Providence, R. I.,	40
St. Louis, Mo.,	45
Washington, D. C.,	52
Worcester, Mass.,	54
Madison, Fla.,	55
Government Issues,	57
Issue of 1847,	59
Issue of 1851-55,	65
Issue of 1857-60,	75
Issues of 1861-66,	81
Issue of 1861,	81
" " 1863,	90
" " 1866,	91
Issue of 1867,	97
Issue of 1869,	108
Issue of 1870,	119
Issues of 1873-75,	130
Issue of 1879,	144
Issues of 1881-88,	147
Issue of 1881-82,	147
" " April 10th, 1882,	149
" " October 1st, 1883,	151
" " June 15th, 1887,	153

CONTENTS.

	PAGE.
Issues of 1887-88,	155
Issue of 1890,	160
Issue of 1893,	170
Issue of 1894-95,	179
Issue of 1898 (Trans-Mississippi Series),	191
Issue of 1898,	196
Issue of 1901 (Pan-American Series),	200
Carriers' Stamps,	202
The Baltimore Carriers' Stamps,	207
The Boston Carriers' Stamps,	211
The Charleston Carriers' Stamps,	215
The Louisvile Carriers' Stamps,	222
The New York Carriers' Stamps,	225
The Philadelphia Carriers' Stamps,	233
Wells, Fargo & Co.'s Pony Express Stamps,	238
The Franklin Carriers' Stamp,	244
The Eagle Carriers' Stamp,	248
Special Delivery Stamps,	250
Official Stamps (Issue of 1873),	256
Official Stamps (Issue of 1879),	274
Newspaper and Periodical Stamps (Issue of 1865),	289
" " " " (Issue of 1875),	294
" " " " (Issue of 1879),	303
" " " " (Issue of 1894),	318
" " " " (Issue of 1895),	320
Postage Due Stamps,	329
Issue of 1879,	329
Issues of 1894-95,	336
Provisional Issues,	341
Reprints, Re-Issues and Special Printings,	343
Issue of 1847,	346
" " 1857,	348
" " 1861.	349
" " 1869,	350
" " 1870,	351
" " 1882,	354
" " 1883,	354
Carriers' Stamps,	355
Official Stamps,	356
Newspaper and Periodical Stamps,	359
Postage Due Stamps,	364
Official Seals,	365
Appendix,	375
Addenda,	401
Errata,	403
Index,	405

INTRODUCTORY.

The first of the series of articles which constitute this work, and which it is now my pleasure to present in a more permanent form, appeared in the *American Journal of Philately* for June, 1897.

Philatelists had, for some time, felt the need of a new history of the postage stamps of the United States, as the only work on this subject, which was then extant, had been written many years before and, in spite of its numerous excellent features, had become obsolete. The discoveries of recent years had increased the interest in the stamps of this country, enlarged the field of collecting and given us new literary material which it was desirable to gather into some permanent form.

I had frequently been urged to undertake this task but had hesitated on account of its magnitude, fully realizing the amount of research and labor involved in properly placing such a work before the public. However, I, at last, decided to undertake the work and have carried it out to the best of my ability. I must leave it to my readers to decide what measure of success has attended my efforts.

The difficulties attending the study of the stamps of the United States are great, especially in the case of the early issues. Of the postmasters' and carriers' stamps there are practically no records, either public or private. The men who issued or handled the stamps have most of them passed away. Those who remain can recall but little and human memory is proverbially fallible. To find the best and most reliable data we must turn to the earlier philatelic publications and from these sources I have drawn freely.

Even in the case of the government issues we can obtain but little information. Until 1894 the stamps were not printed by the government but by contractors. The official records seldom show more than the quantities of stamps received and distributed. Even these records are usually inaccessible, except in the shape of the annual reports of the Postmaster-General, which are, as a rule, merely perfunctory lists of the number of stamps of each value distributed in each year and supply very little that we wish to know of design paper, colors and the numerous details which are of interest to philatelists.

In preparing this work I have spared neither time nor pains and, thanks to the liberality of my publishers, expenditure for material and investigation has not been stinted. The various chapters have now been carefully corrected and amplified. I have tried to include every interesting detail and every item which might be of value. I fear I have sometimes given extracts and statistics that make dull reading, but it has seemed necessary to include them for the sake of completeness.

Of regular issues by the government, the adhesive stamps only will be considered. The envelope stamps occupy a field by themselves and there are already extant several very complete and elaborate works devoted to them. But, among the provisional issues by postmasters and the carriers' stamps, envelopes will be described. They are few in number and their inclusion is desirable for the sake of historical completeness.

It is fitting that I should express here my obligation to many others, both collectors and dealers, for their valued assistance. They have placed at my disposal their collections and stocks and have aided me in other ways. It was originally my intention to make individual mention of those who assisted me. I now find that I have a long list of such friends, yet I fear that I may have failed to note some names Rather than risk a seeming, though unintentional neglect, I deem it best to say that I am indebted to many of those best known in philately in this country and in Europe, and to many others whose names are not so familiar but whose good will was the equal of any. To all I offer my sincere thanks.

HISTORICAL NOTES.

The first efforts towards establishing a postal system in what is now the United States were made by the colonies of Massachussetts and Pennsylvania; by the former in 1676 and by the latter in 1683. The head offices were located in Boston and Philadelphia. These systems were designed for the convenience of the colonies establishing them, rather than for the benefit of the North American colonies in general. **Early postal Arrangements.**

The mother country seems to have given no favorable attention to the needs of the colonies in the direction of postal communication until 1692 and the project remained unfruitful for nearly twenty years after that date. In the annual report of the Postmaster-General, dated November 29th, 1851, we read:

"As early as 1677, upon the petition of several merchants of Boston (Massachussetts), Mr. John Hayward, scrivener, was appointed by the court, 'to take in and convey letters according to their direction.'

This was probably the first post office and mail service authorized in America. Local and imperfect arrangements for the conveyance of mails were afterwards made, at different periods, in several of the colonies, until 1710, when the British Parliament passed an act authorizing the British Postmaster-General 'to keep one chief letter office in New York, and other chief letter offices in each of her Majesty's provinces or colonies in America.' Deputy Postmasters-General for North America were subsequently and from time to time appointed by the Postmaster-General in England, and Doctor Benjamin Franklin was so appointed in 1755. He was removed in 1774.

On the 26th of July, 1775, the Continental Congress determined 'that a Postmaster-General be appointed for the United Colonies,' and to allow him 'a salary of one thousand dollars per annum for himself and three hundred and forty dollars per annum for a secretary and comptroller.' On proceeding to the election of Postmaster General, 'Benjamin Franklin, Esq., was unanimously chosen.'

The Articles of Confederation of 1778 gave to the United States in Congress assembled 'the sole and exclusive right and power of establishing and regulating post offices, from one State to another throughout all the United States, and exacting such postage on the papers passing through the same as may be requisite to defray the expenses of an office.' The little progress made during the period of the Confederation shows that this power was too limited to be useful, and when the increase of the mail service before the adoption of the constitution of the United States is compared with its subsequent extension one cannot fail to perceive that the prosperity, efficiency, and value of this department are chiefly to be ascribed to the national government founded under the constitution of the Union.

The first Congress assembled under our present constitution passed 'An act for the temporary establishment of a post office' approved September 22, 1789. This act directed the appointment of a Postmaster General, and was to continue in force until the end of the next session of Congress. Under this provision Samuel Osgood, of Massachussetts, was appointed by President Washington, Postmaster-General of the United States, and this was the first appointment to that office. * * *

The earliest reliable statistics of the General Post Office are those for the year 1790, when the number of post offices was seventy-five ; the extent of the post routes 1,875 miles; and the revenues of the department $37,935."

To those who are interested in the early history and gradual develope-
ment of our postal system, I recommend the perusal of an article by Mr.
James Rees in the *American Journal of Philately* for April, 1876.

The rates of postage were at first excessively high. In 1816 they were
considerably reduced. From that date until the Act of March 3rd, 1845,

Rates of Postage which established uniform postage throughout the United States, the rate for
a single letter varied from 6 cents to 25 cents, according to distance, the latter
sum carrying a letter only 400 miles. Double and triple letters were charged
in proportion. A single letter was not one of a certain weight, but a single
sheet of paper, folded and addressed on the back. Two sheets of paper or a
sheet and a cover constituted a double letter.

The Act of March 3rd, 1845, established rates of postage as follows:

"For every single letter in manuscript or paper of any kind by or upon which information shall be asked for or communicated in writing or by marks or signs, conveyed in the
mail, for any distance under three hundred miles, five cents; and for any distance over three
hundred miles, ten cents; and for a double letter there shall be charged double these rates;
and for a treble letter, treble these rates; and for a quadruple letter, quadruple these rates;
and every letter or parcel not exceeding half an ounce in weight shall be deemed a single
letter, and every additional weight of half an ounce, or additional weight of less than half
an ounce, shall be charged with an additional single postage. And all drop letters or letters
placed in any post-office, not for transmission through the mail, but for delivery only, shall
be charged with postage at the rate of two cents each."

Circulars were charged two cents each. Newspapers were charged
according to size. A sheet under certain dimensions was charged one cent
for a distance less than one hundred miles and one and one half cents for a
greater distance. For a sheet larger than the regulation size the rate was
two cents. Pamphlets and magazines were charged two and one half cents
each.

Any one who studies the early issues of this country, the issues of postmasters, carriers and the local posts, or any of the records of the time, soon
notices that in its early days the post office department was never a leader

Post Office not a but always a follower. It allowed others to make all experiments, reforms
Leader. and improvements, and then copied or took up their work. It was only when
local posts had demonstrated that lower rates were profitable or had drawn
to themselves the patronage of the public, through rapid or more frequent
service, that the government granted similar improvements.

A very interesting account of the early postal laws and of the private
posts is given by Mr. James Leslie, U. S. Consul at Nice, in the *Stamp
Collectors Magazine*, for Nov. 1, 1863. In view of the fact that Mr Leslie

Early Postal Laws was evidently thoroughly conversant with his subject and that he wrote at
and Private Posts. the time that the various changes in the postal laws had finally brought the
government service into effective working form and enabled it to supersede
the private posts, I think a liberal quotation from his article may be of
interest:

"The proper explanation of the many local postage stamps issued in the United States
is only to be found in a thorough review of the postal laws passed by the United States'
Congress and in a careful study of the various changes wrought by these successive legislative acts in the mode of distribution of letters and in the rates of postage. * * *
The agitation in favor of and final adoption in England of the penny-postage system,
excited a corresponding interest and movement in the United States in favor of a reduction
of what were felt to be, in comparison with British rates, extortionate postal charges. As
happens with all political reforms, it took time to develope public sentiment and to draw the

attention of Congress to this important subject. The government rates for carrying letters were deemed so onerous that, in the fall of 1844,* private parties undertook to transport letters on their own account between points where they felt sure that money could be earned at lower rates. And, although such attemps to defraud the post-office revenues were in direct contravention of existing laws, popular sentiment, impressed with the idea of getting a better service at a lower price, winked at the law's infractions ; and, although the violations of the law were carried on with comparatively little secrecy, the perpetrators were never reached or, at any rate, were never punished. * * *

The successful efforts of these private carriers soon commenced to tell upon the postal revenues, and, as the natural consequence, the post-office department was compelled to propose the remedy so clamorously called for by public opinion. By the Act of March 3, 1845, Congress at one sweep abolished the previous dear rates, as well as the annoying scale of varying distances ; and, whilst substituting the weight-standard, reduced at the same time the rate for a single letter to 5 cents for any distance under three thousand miles, and 10 cents for all distances over three thousand miles. By the provisions of the same act, drop-letters (by which was meant letters for delivery in the same town where posted, as distinguished from letters intended for transportation to other towns) were made chargeable with a tax of 2 cents, *prepayment being optional*.

It must be borne in mind that, in addition to all the rates just mentioned, the post-office carriers were entitled to charge upon all letters, without exception, delivered at one's residence, a fee of 2 cents for delivery. This last item of revenue formed the entire compensation of the carriers, who, deeming themselves underpaid, were unwilling to make more than two deliveries a day – one in the morning, and another in the afternoon. It will be seen that, under this arrangement, the entire tax levied upon a drop-letter, carried a few squares' distance, and delivered at one's residence, was 4 cents, or only 1 cent less than the sum charged for transporting a similar letter nearly three thousand miles !

It is to this important fact, and *to the want of frequent deliveries* in large cities and towns, that we may legitimately trace the creation of the numerous private post companies. In all the chief towns, these companies established a system of letter-boxes, from which letters were collected and delivered five or six times a day, and at one-half or even one-fourth the rates charged by the Government. The usual price was 1 cent or 2 cents. At first in the principal cities, when there was no competition, the price was two cents. Later, as rivalry started up in the private postal service, some of the companies lowered the price to one cent. In some of the smaller cities, where the distances travelled over by the carriers were comparatively short, the price was never higher than one cent. Hence almost every city had its one, or, as in Philadelphia or New York, its half-dozen local posts ; and hence why, upon the stamps employed by these companies, the usual designations of value will be found to be one and two cents. * * *

It was not in fact, till 1847, that the American Congress decided upon the introduction of postage stamps. The eleventh section of the Act of March 3, 1847, provides as follows :

'Section XI. That to facilitate the transportation of letters in the mail the Postmaster-General be authorized to prepare postage stamps which, when attached to any letter or packet, shall be evidence of the payment of the postage chargeable on such letter.'

An important innovation upon the system of postal regulations was introduced into the Act, passed March 3, 1851. Whilst still leaving the prepayment of letters optional, this new law reduced the rate for letters under three thousand miles to 3 cents, *if prepaid;* whilst, if not prepaid, the old rate of 5 cents was collected. * * *

The continued success of the private posts at this period caused the insertion of a provision in this same Act of 1851, authorizing the Postmaster-General to establish ' post routes within the cities or towns'; to reduce the total charge, inclusive of delivery-fee, upon drop-letters to two cents ; and to provide for collecting and conveying to the chief office of the general post letters intended for transportation to other cities, – the latter duty having been previously monopolized by the private carriers. This explains a great many of the local stamps bearing such inscriptions as the following : ' *To the Mail, one cent*'; *Post-Office Despatch* '; *Government City Despatch* '; and also, the one issued by the Post-office Department, viz, the blue oval stamp, with vignette of an eagle rising, and the inscription, ' *U. S. P. O. Despatch, prepaid one cent* '

But, notwithstanding the provisions of the Act of 1851 referred to, the post office officials were slow to exercise the authority granted. Though the price on drop-letters was reduced to only 2 cents, still the rapid and frequent deliveries, which the public had become accustomed to from the private companies, were not yet supplied by the Post-office Department ; the government post office carriers refusing to make more than the traditional two daily deliveries, unless they were assured a remunerative salary, which should not be dependent upon the number of letters, more or less, which they delivered. * * *

By the Act of June 15, 1860, a still further reduction was made in the fee for the

---

*NOTE.—Mr. Leslie's date may be set back nearly three years, since we now know that Greig's City Despatch Post was established in the city of New York on Jan. 1st, 1812. It is claimed that Hale's post was in operation at a still earlier date, but did not use stamps.

delivery of letters ; the rate collected by the carriers on *all* letters, whether received from abroad or mailed in the city itself, being one cent. A special appropriation of money was also made, to make up the loss to the carriers consequent upon this reduction, by substituting a fixed salary for these officials. And yet nothing was said in the Act as to the *compulsory* prepayment of this delivery-fee of 1 cent. In reality that question remained an open one until the present year. By the Act of March 3, 1863, the question was definitely settled. It provides for frequent deliveries (which can now be easily carried out, since the carriers have regular fixed salaries); it compels prepayment on all drop-letters, upon which the rate is made two cents (a step backwards, it may be remarked, *en passant*); and abolishes all delivery tax upon letters coming from other towns. The law took effect on the 1st of July, and this accounts for the introduction of the new 2 cents adhesive label, and the 2 cents envelope, both with the effigy of President Jackson.

The question of the right of private carriers to transport letters within the municipal limits of the cities was settled authoritatively in 1861, by the United States Court for the Eastern District of Pennsylvania, in a suit brought by the government against Messrs. Kochersperger & Co., successors to D. O. Blood & Co., of Philadelphia. The Court decided that, by the language of the Post-Office Act of March 3, 1851 (already previously quoted), the 'streets' of cities and towns were made 'post-routes', and that the Government alone had power to transport letters over them. This decision, happily commended to popular approval by the tardy awakening of the post-office officials to increased energy and enter-prise, was the death blow to the local companies Though the Government did not com-mence suit against all the parties, the decision in the one case had served as a sufficient warning ; and, at the present time, private-posts and local stamps in the United States may be considered amongst the things of the past."

THE POSTMASTERS' STAMPS.

This most interesting group of stamps, representing the earliest official attempts to meet the requirements of the public and lead the way for proper governmental supply and control of postage stamps, presents many difficulties to the philatelic student and writer.

Previous to the introduction of adhesive stamps, letters were marked "PAID" or "DUE," either with pen and ink or hand stamps of various designs. Sometimes the words sufficed but usually the amount of the postage and the date were added. The three may be found separately applied and also combined in one hand-stamp. The varieties of type are numerous.

Use of Marks.

As has been previously remarked, the introduction of adhesive postage stamps in Europe was followed by a demand for similar conveniences in this country. But the Government was slow to accede to popular wishes and did not yield until the example had been set by the local posts and by issues of a semi-private nature on the part of certain postmasters.

The first adhesive stamp used in this country was issued by the City Despatch Post, otherwise known as Greig's Post, established in New York City, January 1st, 1842. This proved such an annoyance to the Government that it was suppressed and in its place the United States City Despatch Post was established. Perhaps it would be more correct to say that this post was bought out, since its proprietor, Alex. M. Greig, was given the position of letter carrier.

First Local Stamp.
First Carriers' Stamp.

It is said that the Act of March 3rd, 1845, as originally prepared, contained provisions for the prepayment of postage and the use of adhesive stamps on letters to foreign countries. But neither provision was contained in the Act, as passed.

Between the passage of the Act of March 3d, 1845, establishing the uniform rates of 5 and 10 cents, and that of the Act of March 3rd, 1847, by which the Postmaster General was at last authorized to issue postage stamps, the postmasters in several cities had postage stamps prepared and sold them to the public. It is probable that this action was prompted by a desire to accommodate their customers and to increase the receipts of their offices, by offering facilities in competition with those of the private posts. They usually sold their stamps at a slight advance over the face value, in order to re-imburse themselves for the expense of manufacture. It is possible that the limited use of several of these stamps may be, to some extent, due to this premium.

With one exception—that of a few of the stamps of the New York Postmaster, which were sent experimentally to other cities—these stamps had no currency outside of the city in which they were issued. They were recognized by the postmaster who issued them, as marks of postage prepaid, when placed on letters mailed at his office; but no other postmaster would accept them as such, if placed on letters deposited in his office. The stamps, to another office than that of issue, merely took the place of the word "PAID," in fact that word was usually impressed on the letters or used as a cancellation for the adhesive stamps. The stamps would carry letters from the office of issue to any other office but they would not carry a reply, since each postmaster would only recognize the label or mark for which postage had been paid to him.

Stamps available
only at issuing
office.

It is interesting to note, on many of the postmaster's stamps, a survival of the early custom of vouching for the prepayment of postage by means of the postmaster's signature. The New York Postmaster or his deputies placed their initials on the stamps of that city. Mr. Mitchell of New Haven wrote his name on each stamp. The Postmaster of Alexandria numbered his stamps. The stamps of Brattleboro bear a facsimile of the Postmaster's initials, and on those from Baltimore the signature is reproduced in full.

Signatures on
Stamps.

While, previous to March, 1847, there was no law authorizing the Postmaster General to issue stamps or to sanction their issue by others, there does not seem to have been any law forbidding such issue. If the stamps of the various postmasters were brought to the attention of the Postmaster General he appears to have paid no heed to them, probably regarding them as private contracts between the postmasters and their customers and in no way detrimental to the interest of the Government, since the accounts were made up from the letters handled and the postage paid on them and not from the sales of the stamps.

It is noteworthy that these stamps usually bear the words "Post Office" and the name of the city in which they were issued. Only those in authority would have dared to place these words upon the stamps. Their face values, five and ten cents, were the established government rates for service under and over 3,000 miles and were too high for local letters. They were clearly intended for more extended use than the local service of the cities in which they were issued. The workmanship of many of them is superior to that of the stamps of the local posts, indicating that their projectors felt warranted in incurring considerable expense in their production.

These unofficial issues have at least the implied sanction of the authorities, since nothing was done, before March, 1847, to stop their use. Not only was their passage through the mails observed and allowed but wide publicity was given to them through the press. This unspoken consent, added to the fact that they were issued by those holding authority from the Government, gives them a semi-official character. Their position in philately is extremely interesting if not unique.

A Postmaster's
Stamp officially
recognized.

In one instance the stamps of a postmaster received official recognition. In the *Metropolitan Philatelist* for March, 1894, Mr. F. W. Hunter says of the stamps issued by Robert H. Morris, the Postmaster of New York:

"During the year 1846, Mr. Morris sold the 5c black New York to the postmasters of Boston, Washington, Albany and Philadelphia. My informant is not positive of the stamps being used in Philadelphia, but at all events the stamps were sold to the postmaster for use in that city. Cave Johnson, the Postmaster-General of the United States under President James K. Polk, authorized and directed the sale of the stamps to the Postmasters of the above mentioned cities. The stamps were only to be sold for letters directed to New York City. When affixed to letters they were to be treated as unpaid by their respective postmasters and forwarded to New York and when there the letters were considered as " PAID " by the postal authorities in that city. This was done for a short time. solely as an experiment to test the practicability of use of postage stamps throughout the United States."

The first of the postmasters to issue stamps was Robert H. Morris, Postmaster of New York. A number of other offices quickly followed his example. It seems best to consider these stamps in the alphabetical order of the offices issuing them.

ALEXANDRIA, VA,

Date of Issue.
This stamp was issued about 1846, the earliest known cancellation being Sept. 9th, 1846.

Daniel Bryan was Postmaster at Alexandria from 1845 to 1847. Tiffany's *History of the Postage Stamps of the United States* gives the name "Brien" but I am informed by Mr. W. F. Lambert, of Alexandria, that the correct spelling is "Bryan."

Historical.
The first known copy of this stamp was found by the late John K. Tiffany in his family correspondence. It was described in *Le Timbre Poste* for March, 1873. The stamp is on the original cover, to which it is attached by a wafer. The letter is dated July 10th, 1847. This stamp still remains in Mr. Tiffany's collection.

A second copy is described in the *Philatelic Monthly* for August, 1879 The description agrees with that of the copy previously known. The letter bears the date of Sept. 9th, 1846. This specimen is now the property of a Philadelphia collector.

Within a few years a third copy has been found and has passed into the collection of Mr. Thos. J. Shryock.

These three are all that are known up to this date. The first and third are cut round. I have been unable to learn what is the shape of the second one.

The first two copies bear the regular dated cancellation of Alexandria, the word "Paid" and a large figure "5" in a rectangle, all hand-stamped in red. The third copy is not on the cover.

Design and Paper.
The stamps are type-set and are impressed by hand on thin, colored, wove paper. In addition Mr. Shryock's copy bears "No. 45" written in black ink in the space between "5" and "POST OFFICE." Probably each copy was similarly numbered. Diameter, 27mm.

ADHESIVE STAMP.

Buff Wove Paper.

Imperforate.

1846.   5 cents black

ANNAPOLIS, MD.

This envelope was issued by Martin F. Revell, Postmaster at Annapolis from 1844 to 1849. The exact date of issue is not known but it is probably 1846.

Date of Issue.

The device is suggestive of a seal and is 18½mm, in diameter. The "5" and "PAID" apparently constitute part of the stamp. It is printed in dull carmine-red in the upper right corner of a white envelope which measures 120x71mm.

Design.

The design is very deeply impressed, so much so that portions of it show distinctly on the back flaps This would probably not have been the case had the envelope contained a letter and been hand-stamped after being deposited in the post office. The cancellation mark, on the contrary, does not show on the back. These points are of some value, as tending to confirm the genuine provisional nature of the envelope. From the character of the work and the deep impression I believe the device and "5" "PAID" to have been printed on a press, rather than hand-stamped, and all at one impression

The only known copy of the Annapolis envelope is in the collection of Mr. W. A. Castle, to whose courtesy I owe the privilege of first describing it.

The following documents supply the history of the stamp, so far as it is now known :

NEW YORK, Sept 3, 1895.

To whom it may Concern :

Sometime in January, 1895, during our Mr. G. A. Burger's stay in the city of Philadelphia, he received permission to look through the old correspondence of the firm of Carstairs.

Documents.

Among other rare envelopes and stamps he found a small white envelope stamped "Post-Office, Annapolis, Md." with Eagle in center and "5" "Paid," on the upper right hand of the envelope in red, and the regular Annapolis post mark on the left side of the envelope in blue.

From information which we received in Annapolis from Jas. Revell, son of the Postmaster there from 1844-49, we are convinced that this is a postmaster's provisional stamped envelope, like the New Haven.

We guarantee it to be a genuine original stamped envelope.

BURGER & Co.

CIRCUIT COURT FOR ANNE ARUNDEL COUNTY,

Annapolis, Md., April 25. 1895.

> A pen and ink sketch
>
> of the
>
> Annapolis envelope

An envelope with the above address and stamp has been presented to me for identification. I have quite a distinct recollection of the stamp "Annapolis, Md., 20 Mar." as having been used by my father (now dec'd) in the Annapolis P. O., of which he was Postmaster some time prior to 1849. The stamp with eagle center has also a very familiar appearance and carries me back many years, when I was quite a lad, going to college (St. John's, Annapolis), often assisting my father, Martin F. Revell, in the office. I am decidedly of the opinion and such is my strong impression that these stamped envelopes, with eagle center in stamp and marked "paid", were sold by my father for the convenience of the public.

JAS. REVELL,

Associate Judge of 5th Judicial Court of Maryland.

Reference List.

ENVELOPE.

White Wove Paper.

Size : 12ᴄx71mm.

1846?   5 cents carmine-red

Since the foregoing was written, in June, 1897, I have not been able to obtain any further information about this envelope or confirmation of the claim that it is a postmaster's provisional. Collectors, as a whole, appear to be skeptical and unwilling to accept it.

Hand-stamps.

Mr. B. V. Jenkins has shown me a folded letter-sheet (not an envelope) which has this seal stamped, in dark blue ink, in the upper left corner of the address side. In the upper right corner is stamped a figure "2", in the same ink. There is no cancellation mark or date of use. The paper is a pale gray-blue. Mr. Crawford Capen has shown me a similar letter sheet which is dated March 24th, 1848. I am told that there are others in existence and that all bear evidence that the seal was applied after mailing, thus making it merely a postmark.

A Questionable Adhesive.

I have also been shown what pretends to be an Annapolis adhesive stamp. This is stamped in dark blue on bluish paper, exactly like the letter sheet just described. It is affixed to a cover which bears the word "PAID" and a postmark dated "May 21", but neither touches the would-be stamp. There is nothing to prove that this bit of paper was used as a stamp, nor, on the other hand, is there any positive evidence to the contrary. Yet I cannot overcome the conviction that it is a fraud, and I must confess that, at this writing, I look with great doubt upon all the so-called Annapolis provisionals.

BALTIMORE, MD.

These stamps were issued by James Madison Buchanan, who was post-master at Baltimore from 1845 to 1849. The earliest cancellation which I have seen is March 18th, 1846 and the latest March 27th, 1847, but I am told Date of Issue. the stamps were in use as late as 1849. It is said that there is a record in the Baltimore post office which describes these stamps and states that they were on bluish paper, and were first used early in 1846. This might be thought to indicate the priority of issue of the stamps on bluish paper, but the dates of letters bearing the stamps show that both colors of paper were in use concurrently.

The attention of collectors was first called to the Baltimore stamps by the following communication, published in *The Philatelist* for February, 1875: **Historical.**

" To the Editor of *The Philatelist*,

DEAR SIR :—I have the honor to give you the following description of a stamp recently discovered in this city, among the old papers in a vault of one of the oldest banking houses in the city. It was on a letter from New Orleans in 1845 or 1846. The envelope was unfortunately destroyed. The stamp is narrow oblong ; inscribed JAMES M. BUCHANAN above; 5 CENTS, below. A penstroke is drawn through the name. It is impressed on thin laid white paper, and attached to the envelope by two wafers. The cancellation is blue.

At the same time and place were found six St. Louis, four of the 5c and two of the 10c. Also sixty ' New York Post Office,' and about a hundred 5 and 10c United States 1847.

Yours respectfully,

WASHINGTON, U. S. A." T. C. BOURNE.

Two things attract our attention in this letter; first, the writer's mistake in attributing the stamp to New Orleans; and second, the statement that it was on white laid paper. We do not know, to day, any copy of this stamp on laid paper.

The stamps were printed from an engraved plate, probably of copper. The surface of the plate was divided by thin vertical and horizontal lines into rectangles, about 53 to 54mm. long by 16 to 17mm. high. The design is very **Design.** simple, being merely a fac-simile of the postmaster's signature, with the value below it. The signature is from 47 to 50¼mm. in length, the "5 Cents" from 20 to 22¾mm. and the "10 Cents" from 24 to 25mm.

It has been surmised that both values were engraved on one plate but this appears scarcely probable. The number of stamps on the plate or plates

is not known. As in the case of all hand-engraved plates, each stamp differs
from the others. I have found eleven varieties of the 5 cents and three of the
Varieties and Arrangement. 10 cents. These are shown in the accompanying photogravure (Plate A).
The differences consist in the lengths of the signature and value, their relative
positions, and the shape and shading of the numerals and periods. On
referring to the photogravure it will be seen that the first stamp in the left
hand vertical row is undoubtedly from the upper left corner of the sheet.
The margin of the second stamp in that row shows it to belong on that side
of the sheet. For the same reason it is evident that the first and second
stamps in the right hand vertical row came from that side of the sheet, while
the margins of the third stamp locate it in the lower right corner. Since this
illustration was made I have seen a copy of the third stamp in the first row
which has a broad margin at the right. In the middle row the two stamps
cancelled by crossed diagonal lines form an unsevered pair. It will also be
observed that the first of the ten cent stamps has a margin at the left. This
is as far as I have been able to attain toward the restoration of the arrangement of the stamps on the plates.

It is reasonable to assume that plates like these, on which each stamp
was separately engraved, would be of limited size. The relatively large
number of copies with margins confirms this theory. I anticipate that the
plate of the five cents contained about fifteen to twenty-five stamps, and that
of the ten cents a still smaller number.

I have recently been told that an old gentleman, living in Baltimore,
has a photograph of an original sheet of the Buchanan stamps. Others say
it is a photograph of a sketch or tracing of such a sheet. My efforts to
obtain more definite information about this have, so far, proved unfruitful.

Refererence List.   ADHESIVE STAMPS.

Wove Paper.

Imperforate.

1846.   5 cents black on white, 11 varieties
                   5 cents black on bluish, 11 varieties
                   10 cents black on white, 3 varieties
                   10 cents black on bluish, 3 varieties

The covers bearing the Baltimore stamps have usually the regular
dated cancellation mark of the city, the word "PAID" and a large figure "5
Cancellations. or "10" in an oval. An illustration of the latter marks will be found at the
head of the paragraphs describing the envelopes. They are usually hand-
stamped in blue and frequently one or more of them touches the stamp. The
stamps have often an additional cancellation of pen strokes.

A year or two ago several of the philatelic papers announced the
discovery of a 5 cent Baltimore stamp on violet paper. Examination showed
Counterfeit. this to be merely a poor imitation, copied from an illustration in a stamp
catalogue, and only about one half the size of the genuine stamp. It ought
not to have deceived the most casual observer and is only mentioned here
because of the somewhat extended notice given to it by the philatelic press.

This illustration represents an adhesive frank which Postmaster Buchanan is said to have sold at five cents each and recognized, when affixed to letters, as indicating postage prepaid. The frank consists of his autograph, written in black ink, on a small rectangle of white paper. The signature is 114mm. long and the paper measures 125x26mm. **Design.**

I have seen only one copy. It was affixed to a letter sheet (apparently before the sheet was folded), so that it passed diagonally across the lower left corner of the address side and folded over upon the back flaps. The cover was cancelled "Baltimore, May 17," and had the "PAID" and "5" in an oval which were in regular use at that office. All these marks were in blue. The cover bore also the date "1846," written in pencil. This, I was told, was the date of the letter which was formerly within the cover.

This specimen has a well authenticated history. In 1846 the crew of a shipwrecked French vessel was brought into Baltimore. At that date there was no French consul in that city but the functions of the consul at Philadelphia extended to Baltimore. The consul, Monsieur d'Hauterive, was informed that these sailors were destitute and wished to be sent home. He despatched an agent to Baltimore to make proper investigations, take testimony and report to him. This agent used the copy of the frank which I have described. **Historical.**

ADHESIVE STAMP. **Reference List.**

White Wove Paper

Imperforate.

May 17th, 1846.   (5 cents) black

While the date of use is later than that known on some copies of the Baltimore stamps which are described at the beginning of this chapter, I am inclined to think that it was issued earlier than those stamps and was the successor of the stamped envelopes.

Concerning this stamp we have but scant information. It is believed to have been issued by the Baltimore postmaster about 1848.

The only known copy is on the original cover, addressed to Mr. Samuel Lynch, Jeweller, Hillsboro, N. C. It was found by Mr. F. W. Hunter in examining the correspondence of the addressee, and now adorns a celebrated collection in Paris. The envelope bears the regular cancellation mark of the

city of Baltimore. The date is somewhat indistinct but appears to be April 12. The year, as usual, is not given on the cover. It is, however, supplied by the letter and is 1848. There are also the cancellation " PAID " and figure " 10 " in an oval, hand-stamped in blue, as previously described for this city. None of these, however, touch the stamp, which is cancelled by two pen strokes. The word " PAID " is also written on the envelope. The stamp measures 23x25mm. The use of the postmaster's stamps after the appearance of the Government issue of 1847 is not unknown ; both the Baltimore and the St. Louis stamps have been reported as used after that date.

ADHESIVE STAMP.

Yellowish White Wove Paper.

Imperforate.

April 12th, 1848.   10 (cents) black

The reader will kindly remember that this stamp is chronicled " for what it is worth," and without guarantee or even an expression of personal opinion. There is always the possibility that it is merely an ornamental label which some one has affixed to the cover through a whim or to deceive.

The postmaster of Baltimore also issued stamped envelopes. They are simple affairs, being ordinary envelopes of the period, bearing the written

signature of the postmaster, or a hand-stamped fac-simile of it, in the upper right corner ; below this are the word " PAID " and large numeral in an oval, which latter marks were in regular use in the post office to indicate prepayment of postage. The impressions are in blue for the 5 cents and red for the 10 cents. The hand stamped signatures are usually in black though sometimes in blue. They appear to have been made with ordinary writing ink. One copy is known on which the word " PAID " is placed above the signature.

The single envelopes each bear one accountant's check mark, while those with the double impression of the " 5 " have two checks.

I have seen only one copy of the envelope with written signature. It

is dated Sept. 22, 1845. The signature is in black ink.

Of the envelopes with hand-stamped signature the only date of use which I have been able to secure is Nov. 24. The year is not given but is, presumably, 1845.

All the Baltimore envelopes are of a high degree of rarity and I believe only one specimen of each variety of the ten cents red has been discovered.

From the dates of use it would appear that the envelopes were issued in advance of the adhesive stamps.

ENVELOPES.

1845.

5 (cents) blue on manila, signature written
5 (cents) blue on white   "   hand-stamped
5 (cents) blue on buff   "   "
5 (cents) blue on salmon   "   "
5x5 (cents) blue on white   "   "
5x5 (cents) blue on buff   "   "
10 (cents) red on white   "   "
10 (cents) red on buff   "   "

BOSCAWEN, N. H.

PAID
5
CENTS

This stamp is believed to have been issued in 1846 by the Postmaster of Boscawen, N. H. The postmaster from 1845 to 1851 was Worcester Webster, a relative of the celebrated Daniel Webster.

Design.

The stamp is of the most primitive nature. It appears to have been produced from a few carelessly set type and is hand-stamped in dull blue ink on thin, yellowish white, hand-made paper, in quality like coarse tissue paper. The word "PAID" measures 13x3mm., "CENTS" is 17½x3mm., and the numeral is 6½mm. high and 6mm. wide. The only copy known is in the collection of Mr. H. E. Deats. It is on a small white envelope, addressed to Concord, N. H. The stamp is uncancelled. In the upper left corner is written—presumably by the postmaster, as was the custom of the period— "Boscawen, N. H., Dec. 13," in two lines.

The following letter accompanies this cover:

PLAINFIELD, N. J, Feb. 28, 1894.

Historical.

MR. H. E. DEATS,

DEAR SIR :—Permit me to enclose for your inspection a few philatelic gems. * * * The old and very curious envelope I have owned for the past 29 years and came into possession of it at the general post-office in Washington, D. C. through Mr. Wm. M. Ireland, who was then chief clerk and the Third Asst. P. M General. As you will see, the mailing office, Boscawen, was written on the corner, as was the custom of P. M's in those days, when no cancellation stamp was used. It performed its duty as a postal envelope and I do not doubt but it is as genuine as any of the provisional issues of the period before stamps were issued. * * * Yours truly,

H. H. LOWRIE, A. P. A.

Inquiries made in Boscawen have failed to supply any further information.

Reference List.

ADHESIVE STAMP.

Yellowish White Wove Paper.

Imperforate.

18—.   5 cents dull blue

It will perhaps not be amiss to remind ourselves at this point that, at the period which we are considering, the salaries of the postmasters depended on the cash receipts of their offices. They were, therefore, anxious to have as many letters as possible sent prepaid. This may explain, the issue of stamps in comparatively small towns, as well as the quite expensive designs provided by some of the postmasters.

BRATTLEBORO, VT.

This stamp was issued by Frederick N. Palmer, who was postmaster at Brattleboro from July, 1845, to November, 1848. The issue was probably made in the summer of 1846. In the collection of Mr. C. F. Bishop there is **Date of Issue.** a copy of the stamp on the original cover. The enclosed letter is dated August 27th, 1846, and the writer says: "I pay this just to show you the stamp. It is against my principles, you know." From this we may infer that the stamp was a novelty and probably had very recently appeared.

From the character of the engraving and impression we conclude that the material of the plate was copper. The stamps measure 21x14mm. Each **Engraving and** was separately engraved and, consequently, differs slightly from the others. **Arrangement.** Spaces about 1mm. wide divided the stamps from each other and, likewise, the rows. Through the middle of these spaces were drawn thin lines of color. There were not, however, any such lines on the outer sides of the stamps. It has long been understood that the plate contained ten stamps, arranged in two horizontal rows of five, with the imprint "Eng^d. by Thos. Chubbuck, Bratt^o.." below the middle stamp of the bottom row. This arrangement will be discussed in a later paragraph. The autographic initials in the center of each stamp are, of course, those of the postmaster. The stamps were printed in black on thick buff wove paper.

The history of the Brattleboro stamp is entertainingly set forth in the philatelic magazines. In the *American Journal of Philately*, dated January **Historical.** 20th, 1869, appeared an article by Dr. J. A. Petrie, in which was included the following letter:

NEWTON CORNER, MASS., Dec. 10th, 1868.

DEAR SIR:—You are mistaken in saying that the stamps about which you inquire have never been described.

I received about two years ago a little paper printed in Vermont (I now forget by **Letter of Post-** whom and in what exact locality), devoted to the subject of postage stamps. **master Palmer.**

It mentioned the private stamp issued by me as P. M. at Brattleboro.

This paper was sent me in a letter by a person who was *very* desirous to obtain the original plate from which they were printed.

I was appointed sometime during the first year of Mr. Polk's administration ; Hon. Cave Johnson, P. M. General.

Mr. Polk was elected in 1845.*

---

*The writer means inaugurated.

The stamps were issued, I think, during my first year as P. M., and I suppose them to be the very first P. O. stamps issued in this country.

It was a strictly private thing, neither ordered or repudiated by the P. O. Department, and in my account with the Department made no difference.

My object in issuing it was to accommodate the people and save myself labor in making and collecting quarterly bills, almost everything at that time being either charged or forwarded without prepayment.

I was disappointed in the effect, having still to charge the *stamps* and collect my bills.

I retained the office during the balance of Mr. Polk's term, and used the stamps more or less during my connection with the office.

The canceling with red ink was uniform, though much a matter of choice.

As to the number issued, I should say only five or six hundred as an experiment.

They were engraved by Mr. Thomas Chubbuck, then of Brattleboro, now of Spring-field, Mass., who wrote me about a year since inquiring about the original plate.

The plate was laid aside and I have never been able to find it, though it may yet come to light.

I have none of the stamps by me, have not seen one for a great while, and think I could scarcely describe it correctly.

Yours, &c.,

To J. A. PETRIE, M. D.,   F. N. PALMER, M. D.
    Elizabeth, N. J.

Cancellations.

This article also gives a description of the stamps and says they were printed from a steel plate and that "they are, so far as I have been able to find, cancelled with a stroke of red ink drawn in part across them." The "cancelling with red ink," mentioned by Mr. Palmer, was probably the familiar cancellation "PAID" which, as far as is known, was stamped in red on all postally used copies. The obliteration by a pen mark of red writing ink was quite another affair, as will shortly be made evident.

In the *Stamp Collector's Magazine* for November, 1870, we find an interesting article by Mr. L. H. Bragg. He begins by quoting a note which appeared in No. 3 of the *Stamp Collector's Record*, published at Albany, N. Y., February 15th, 1865. This was, doubtless, the paper to which Mr. Palmer intended to refer, and the description of the stamps given by it was probably the first to appear in print, at least in a philatelic publication. The writer summarizes all references to the stamp, which had appeared to that date, and gives a brief digest of the articles. None of this is sufficiently new or interesting to repeat. He continues :

Interview with Mr. Chubbuck.

So much for the public history of the stamp to the present date. Now for the results of my own investigations. On the 2nd of last September, I called upon Mr. Thomas Chub-buck, at his office in Springfield, stated to him the gist of the facts I have here detailed at length, and learned the full particulars of his own connection with the matter. He went to Boston in 1845, and remained there until June 13, 1848, and being something of a musical amateur, he formed the acquaintance of postmaster Palmer, who was then a music teacher ; hence it came about that he was one day persuaded to engrave "the Brattleboro stamp." The chief object of the postmaster in issuing the stamp, as Mr Chubbuck recollects it, was to turn an honest penny, in this wise : By Act of March 3, 1845, uniform rates of 5 cents and 10 cents, for letter postage under and over 3,000 miles, respectively, were established, but prepayment was left at the option of the senders. Now, as his own official salary was proportionate to the cash receipts of his office, it was for each postmaster's interest to have as many as possible of the letters deposited at his office *prepaid ;* and Mr. Palmer's idea was that the novelty of these stamps would induce many to prepay their letters with them who otherwise would not attend to that then rather uncommon duty. Especially as he sold his stamps on credit to those with whom he had private or official business accounts, did he expect that this would be likely to be the case.

As the correspondent of the *Journal* shows, the use of the stamp did not (as the *Record* claimed) abrogate the necessity of branding "Paid 5 cents" upon each letter prepaid with it, the same as upon each one prepaid with coin ; and it was to this old-established "paid" mark, and not to the presence of the stamp itself, that the outside postmasters gave attention when taking account of letters received from Brattleboro Regarding the length of time that the stamps were in use, Mr. Chubbuck was quite confident that Dr. Palmer was in error in stating that he "employed them occasionally up to the end of his official term" (March 3, 1849), as he (Mr. C.) distinctly recollects that the postmaster burned all the unsold stamps in his possession immediately on the appearance of the 5 and 10 cent " U. S. post-office " stamps issued under authority of the Act of March 3, 1847. Thus on the one hand is shown the error of the *Record* in supposing the stamp to have been prepared and used as a temporary substitute for the current " Franklin 5," when the supply of the latter chanced to be exhausted ; and on the other, the error of Dr. Petrie, in supposing it to have been used continuously until March, 1849. The latter writer, too, probably makes an erroneous inference in placing 1845 as the date of issue. Mr. Chubbuck had no memoranda by which he could recall the exact date of delivering the stamps to the postmaster, as his cash account showed that he collected the bill for his services ("seven and a half dollars, for engraving the plate ; one dollar and a half, for printing 500 stamps ; total, nine dollars") at the time of his leaving town, June, 1848. He is inclined to believe, however, that as he did not go to Brattleboro until May 30, 1845, and did not form the acquaintance of Dr. Palmer, until sometime afterwards, he could not have engraved the stamps before the opening of 1846. Another indication in this direction is the fact, that as Dr. Palmer was not appointed until "sometime during the year" which began March 4, 1845—perhaps not till toward the end of the calendar year,—he would not be likely to think of doing so novel a thing as to issue a postage stamp until he had become well settled in office. I think, then, that it is reasonable to conclude that the life of the Brattleboro stamp was of less than twelve months' duration, divided pretty equally between the years 1846 and 1847.

Dr. Palmer states that but few were used, as would naturally be the case in so modest a village, in so short an interval ; and Mr. Chubbuck adds, that the balance in stock of the original 500 impressions were burned in 1847. Hence, as the most persistent searching has failed to bring to light the original plate, it is no wonder that the very existence of the stamp has been called in question ; and it is undoubted that the few impressions in existence are, and always will be, among the very rarest of authentic postal labels. The editor's hint may be counted for certain—that there will never be "an invasion of Brattleboros,"—for the "large portion of the issue hidden in some surprisingly out-of-the-way nook," for some "enterprising dealer to discover," does not exist.

Unsold stamps burned in 1847.

A small portion of the issue, however, does exist, and that portion is now in my own possession. The copper-plate prepared by Mr Chubbuck contained eight stamps each intended to be identical with the other, but showing under the microscope minute differences in the lines and shadings. Besides the regular border of each stamp, a fine line was drawn on the plate on each side of the stamps where they met, in order to separate each one, much as the marks of perforation separate the stamps of a sheet now. Hence, by paying careful attention to these lines on a single detached stamp, one could decide the exact part of the plate of which it was the impression. The eight stamps of the plate were engraved quite closely together, and the outer margins, though not broad, were so much broader than the inner one as to be at once noticeable. Upon this narrow outer margin, at the bottom of the stamp next the left corner one, on the lower row, was the imprint, in minute characters, ENG^{D.} BY THOS. CHUBBUCK, BRATT^{O.} The general appearance of each stamp was described with tolerable correctness in the notice quoted from the *Record*, and the cut which heads this article renders further notice of it unnecessary. It may be remarked, however, that the paper of the stamp was rather a deep shade of buff than an actual brown.

Now, on the day when the engraver delivered these 500 stamps, together with the eight-faced plate, to the postmaster, he bethought himself that he should like to preserve a specimen copy of his work, and so, with the postmaster's consent, he laid aside a sheet of eight, and afterwards stuck the same, with red wafers, into his general scrap book. Before removing the stamps from the office, however, though his friend protested against the formal security against fraud, he took the latter's pen and obliterated them, by drawing a red-ink stroke through the left upper corner of each stamp on the sheet. Seven of these stamps, on the afternoon of my visit to Mr. Chubbuck, were found lying loosely among his other scraps and specimens, and were quickly transferred to me. The fate of the eighth is uncertain, the engraver having the impression that he had laid it away by itself as a specimen.

Significance of the red pen marks.

The rank held by the stamp is fortunately not a matter of doubt. It is of exactly the same nature as the better-known provisional "post-office" issues of New York, Providence and St. Louis Like them, it was issued on the postmaster's private responsibility, to assist in the public, official duties of his office ; and, like them, it was superseded by the 5 cent and 10 cent "U. S. post-office" issues of 1847. Dr. Palmer's supposition, that his was the first post-office stamp issued in America, is, very possibly, a mistaken one, as Mr. Chubbuck well remembered the "big head" stamp of New York, and was under the impression that the idea of issuing the Brattleboro stamp was derived from the success of this.

In conclusion, it is worth noticing that the inscription "POST-OFFICE" instead of "POSTAGE," on the first regular issue of government stamps, was probably derived from that upon the provisional issues,—the idea being that the stamps of the "U. S.", or general "post-office," would serve alike for the "New York," "Providence," "St. Louis," "Brattleboro," and all other "post-offices" within the national domain.

Here we have an explanation of the red pen marks. It may be well to remark, at this point, that in the illustration of a restored plate which accompanies this book, numbers 3, 4, 5, 6, 7, 8 and the single copy below the plate were all cancelled by a pen-stroke in red ink and, doubtless, came from the sheet kept by Mr. Chubbuck. Traces of these marks may be seen on some of the varieties, on others it was not retained in the photograph.

In the *American Journal of Philately* for November 20th, 1870, is published a letter from Dr. J. A. Petrie in which he refers to the foregoing

Corrections.

article. After indulging in some little journalistic amenities he says, referring to Mr. Bragg: " He states that there were only 500 of the Brattleboro stamps printed when the fact is 500 impressions of the plate were worked off, making 4,000 stamps. Mr. Chubbuck moved from Boston, his former home, to Brattleboro, and not as L. H. B. has it, from Brattleboro to Boston.''

Following this, there appeared in the same journal, under the date of January 20th, 1871, an article by Mr. J. W. Scott. At the head of this article is a group of ten rectangles, intended to show the arrangement of the stamps on the plate. The second space is occupied by a wood cut which is a very tolerable reproduction of the variety of the stamp which filled that position on the plate. The writer says:

" In the January number of Volume II of this paper, we gave the full history or all that was then known concerning the Brattleboro' stamp, but since then an American writer· in the *Stamp Collector's Magazine* has thrown new light on the subject, which has opened the way for further discoveries, concerning this interesting stamp. The article in question is also valuable for pointing out some errors in Dr. Palmer's statement, which the writer erroneously attributes to Dr. Petrie, but unfortunately nearly all his own statements are incorrect.

Upon seeing the paper on the Brattleboro' stamp. in the *Stamp Collector's Magazine*, in which the writer stated he had a sheet of seven varieties. our publishers being determined to secure the sheet at any cost, immediately wrote the possessor, offering to pay more than any one else, whatever the price might be, but that gentleman having already given another party the refusal of them, at what he considered a high figure, they were compelled to purchase of the new owner, at four times the price the discoverer realized ; directly upon seeing the sheet we were struck with the curious appearance of the engraver's imprint, which instead of being at either end or in the middle, was under the second from the end ; upon examining the back we clearly saw traces of the wafers mentioned in L. H. B's letter,—of these there were one at each corner of the left hand and one above the stamp that the imprint was under ; if the sheet had been stuck down in this way, the two right hand ones would have been loose and liable to turn up, which to say the least was a strange manner of fixing them in a book. These circumstances were sufficient evidence to us that the sheet had originally consisted of *ten varieties*, but we certainly should not have stated it here unless we could prove it beyond doubt. The Brattleboro' in our own collection, which was obtained from one formed in New Brunswick, and was cancelled by a red pen-mark, was at once con-
Reconstruction of the sheet.
sulted, and was found to be *different to any on the sheet*, and to have a wide margin on the left end *which corresponded to the margin on three sides of the sheet* Letters despatched to two collectors, who were known to have Brattleboro' cancelled by red, in a few days brought the desired stamps and also the owners. The stamps were placed together and found to fit exactly, each one being different. Photographs of the complete sheet were then taken (which by the way will be presented to any one who gets up a club of ten subscribers to the *Journal*, and to *no* one else under any consideration), and the stamps distributed to their respective owners, in all probability never to be replaced."

As nearly as can be determined from this article, the block of seven stamps there described contained numbers 3, 4, 5, 7, 8, 9 and 10 of the plate and numbers 1, 2 and 6 were added to complete it.

After reading this article I made search among collectors for a copy of the photograph mentioned and succeeded in obtaining one. Unfortunately, it was so badly faded as to be useless for reproduction. After the inevitable losses in that process, there would remain nothing legible. However, the lettering and stronger lines were still sufficiently distinct to enable me, on comparing a stamp with the photograph, to readily determine its original position. If the reader will refer to the illustration (Plate B), he will at once perceive that an excellent guide is offered by the shape and position of the dash underneath the initials of the postmaster. I decided to restore the plate by means of fresh photographs of the several varieties, taken from stamps kindly loaned me by friends. In this, I succeeded all too well, since I have obtained photographs of eleven varieties, all undoubtedly genuine, when the plate is supposed to have contained only ten. I had just secured the ten varieties shown in the old photograph, when Mr. Francis C. Foster kindly sent me a specimen from his collection, the celebrated copy on which he squandered the large sum of sixty cents. Behold! it was an eleventh variety. There appears to be no question of its absolute genuineness. The character of the engraving, impression and paper preclude any possibility of doubt on this point. In addition it bears Mr. Chubbuck's red pen-mark. The ink of this mark is, by-the-bye, of a peculiar dull rose or magenta shade, not easily mistaken when once seen.

Discovery of an eleventh variety.

 Having this eleventh type, the question naturally arises, where does it belong? Mr. Scott distinctly says that the stamps from which his original photograph was made fitted together, that one had a broad margin at the left and that the engraver's imprint was under the middle stamp of the lower row. I have seen stamp number 5 in the plate with a broad margin at the right. It, therefore, seems probable that these two rows were complete as shown in the illustration. Were there then other rows on the plate? If so, they must have been placed in another group or pane, since certain of the stamps in the group of ten have margins at top or bottom wider than the space between the two rows, thus proving there were no stamps immediately adjacent to them. The eleventh variety also has a wide margin at the bottom. Assuming that there were other rows of the stamps, I have sought to find further varieties that differed from what we may call the original ten. But, though I have seen duplicates of many of the ten, I have been unable to advance beyond this puzzling eleventh variety. It has been suggested that a single stamp was first engraved as a sample. This, proving satisfactory, was used as a guide for the group of ten, which was subsequently engraved on the same plate. The impressions for the postmaster were probably taken from the ten only, but a few sheets, such as that saved by Mr. Chubbuck, may have shown the eleventh stamp. I regret that I must leave the subject in this unsettled condition.

ADHESIVE STAMP.

Reference List.

Thick Buff Wove Paper.

Imperforate.

Aug. (?) 1846. 5 cents black. 11 varieties

LOCKPORT, N. Y.

This stamp is practically without a history. There are no records or traditions of its issue. The only copy known to exist was found in Lockport among the correspondence of an old firm. It was purchased by the Scott Stamp and Co., Ltd., from the finder, a gentleman well and favorably known to them. They have every reason to believe in the *bona-fides* of the finder and the authenticity of the stamp. It was affixed to a double sheet of letter-paper. The sheet having been folded, it was addressed on the first or outer side to Robert Monell, Esq., Geneva, N. Y. On the second page was the letter, dated March 18, 1846, and signed by Holmes & Moss. The reply was written on the third page. The sheet was then refolded and addressed to Messrs. Holmes & Moss, Lockport, N. Y. On this side it bears the postmark "Geneva, N. Y., Mch. 24." Thus the stamp returned to its place of origin. As a rule, we do not expect to find the postmasters stamps in the cities in which they were issued but in other cities, to which they have franked letters. This copy now adorns a celebrated European collection. Hezekiah W. Scovell was postmaster at Lockport in 1846.

Design.
The double-lined oval with the name of the place measures 32x23mm. and is hand-stamped in dull red on a small piece of coarse wove paper, buff in color and 34x25mm. in dimensions. By a second operation the word "PAID", 16x4mm., is stamped in the upper part of the inner oval, in ink of the same shade. Below this is the numeral "5", in manuscript, in black ink. The stamp is cancelled by crossed penstrokes of black. The postmark and word "PAID" are impressed on the cover in red. The latter mark is identical with the same word on the stamps and might be supposed to be a cancellation in both instances but, as one agrees in shade with the postmark and the other with the stamp, it is probable that the latter constitutes part of the stamp.

Reference List.

ADHESIVE STAMP.

Buff Wove Paper.

Imperforate.

1846.   5 cents red and black

MILLBURY, MASS.

Colonel Asa H. Waters was postmaster at Millbury, from January 18th, 1836, to November 10th, 1848. During that period the stamp illustrated above was issued. The earliest cancellation known is July 18th, 1846. The stamps were made from a roughly cut wood block and printed one at a time on a hand-press. They are 22mm. in diameter. The portrait was apparently intended to represent Washington. It has been claimed that there are two varieties of this stamp, but I have failed to discover more than one, though I have examined either the original or a photograph of every known copy but one.

Date of Issue.
Design.

The usual cancellation of the Millbury stamp is the word "PAID" in red. The letters bear in addition a large figure " 5 " in a circle and the dated cancellation of the city. It is interesting to note that in the cancellation the name is spelled " Milbury."

Col. Waters was, at the time of his postmastership, largely interested in manufactures and left the work of the post-office in the hands of his deputies. To one of them, Henry Waterman, we owe the stamp.

Historical.

Seeing the stamps of the New York Post Office he perceived their utility and, in order that his own town might enjoy a similar convenience, had the block cut in Boston and a supply of stamps printed from it.

The first copy of this stamp was discovered in a bound volume of letters in the library of the American Antiquarian Society at Worcester, Mass. For a long time only three copies were known, but in recent years several more have been found, including a perfect unused copy with full gum, which is now in the collection of M. La Renotière (Ferrary).

The following letter, which I reproduce by permission of Mr. H. E. Deats, may interest philatelists:

MILLBURY, Jan. 24, 1885.

MR. PAINE.

DEAR SIR :—On referring to my commission as P. M. at Millbury, I find it dated Jan. 18th, 1836, and signed by Amos Kendall, P. M. General.

It has this endorsement :   '' Resigned to Henry Waterman, Nov. 10, 1848, A. H. W.'

In all the years I held the office I never had much to do with the details but relied mostly on my deputies. Waterman was the last and best and I got him appointed in my place. He was a jeweller by trade, quite ingenious, and I have an impression he did get up some kind of P. M. stamp, but too slight to state positively. He came from Providence, R. I., whither he returned many years ago and I believe is living there still. If so, he could probably give you more satisfactory information than I can.

Turning to my file of letters—some of which date back sixty odd years—I find postage marked from 6¼ to 25 cents according to distance, up to 1845. I find on the letters a '' 5 '' in a circle and I find several in years following stamped in the same way '' 5 '' or '' 10.'' The first affixed stamp I have found is on a letter dated '' Grafton, March 21, 1849.'' Being P. M. most of my letters came '' FREE.''

I wish to enquire why this eager pursuit of a 5 cent Millbury P. O. stamp of 1845— for which several advertisements have appeared in papers   What's up?

Very respectfully yours,
Asa H. Waters.

Nothing is now known of the block from which the stamps were printed and we may assume that it has been destroyed.

Reference List.

ADHESIVE STAMP.

Gray-blue Wove Paper.

Imperforate.

1846.   5 cents black

NEW HAVEN, CT.

These envelopes were issued by E. A. Mitchell, who was postmaster at New Haven from 1844 to 1852.

Colors.

Nearly all the envelopes were supplied by the customers. Most of them were white, though other colors are known. They were hand-stamped in red or blue and signed in ink of a contrasting color, either blue, red or black. The design is 31mm. high and 26mm. wide.

In the *American Journal of Philately* for May 20th, 1871, there appeared an interesting account of these envelopes and the following letter from Mr. Mitchell:

New Haven, Ct., May 15, 1871.

J. A. Petrie, M D.,
    Dr. Sir :—

Yours of the 6th and 13th are at hand. Being extensively engaged in business, I have but little spare time to devote to the postage stamp matter. My object in getting up this stamp was simply to accommodate the public, as I charged no profit. The postage was uniform, 5c for all distances, and weight, I think, half ounce ; same as at present, but prepaid.

Historical.

As no letters could be paid after business hours or Sundays, these were convenient for that purpose as well as others.

Many brought their own envelopes, and I only charged 5c, for the postage.

The business of the office was so limited, that, to prevent objection by the P. O. Department, or forgery, I signed each one.

The stamp (or die) is a small hand-stamp, and was made by F. P. Gorham, then the principal engraver of New Haven, but now deceased. I considered the whole matter at the time, of so little importance, that many minor facts in the case are entirely gone from my mind. I think all were printed on white envelopes, and stamped in red ink and signed in blue ink Red ink (vermilion) was used as the office ink in stamping the letters, and think that must have been the color.

It is possible that buff envelopes were used for a few, but probably not.

I have no way of knowing how many were printed, or when commenced and ended, as all my papers and accounts of current business of the office are destroyed. The amount sold were few and probably not over 2,000 all together. They being done by hand and with no motive of profit, they were not generally offered for sale. I was appointed Post-Master Sept. 12th, 1844, and was succeeded by John B. Robertson in 1852.

I cannot state the cost of the plate.

The plate or stamp is a single short hand-stamp. The stamp is of brass. There was only one denomination that being 5c. The impression was always on envelopes. I had not thought of the stamp since leaving the Post office until I received a letter from Mr. Brown; and after hunting up the stamp, I printed a few myself and sent him, writing on them, "canceled" Thinking possibly there might be some objection by the P. O. Department to my striking off impressions, I enclosed a copy to the P. M. Gen'l, giving a short history of it, and asking if there would be any objection to my furnishing some to friends and stamp collectors. Unlike his predecessors, C. A. Wickliffe, Cave Johnson and Mr. Collamer, under whom I served, who always required any respectful letter to be answered, he has not given me any reply ; this is my reason for writing cancelled on those sent Mr. Brown.

So far I have not had over 20 impressions issued. If I had any on hand when I left the office they were destroyed, as stamps came in use the latter part of my term. I have had three applications for the die, and am offered as high as $100 for it. Parties also want a stereotype plate made, and others want 1,000 of the impressions

As the original purpose was not to make money, so I shall *positively refuse* to sell any impressions, or sell the stamp.

. As the stamp seems to possess a centenial kind of value quite unanticipated by me, I have decided to place it in possession of the New Haven Colonial Historical Society.

I shall in a few days have a pad ready so that I can print a few perfect impressions, when I will send you a few more

I have not as yet heard of any of the old envelopes coming to light. As all originals had my own signature, of course I cannot furnish lots to dealers, even if I wished.

I am yours,

E. A. MITCHELL.

The New Haven envelope was first described by Mr. Wm. Brown in the *Curiosity Cabinet* for May, 1871. Mr. Brown had found a copy, cut square, in a collection which he purchased and which afterwards proved to have been stolen from a prominent lawyer of New Haven. The rightful owner presented Mr. Brown with the stamp In describing these envelopes and their history he wrote: "Some of the post-offices refused to recognize them and reported the facts to the Department. As, however, the stamps could only be used at the New Haven office and were sent as prepaid matter, properly entered on the New Haven post bill, there could be no loss to the Government, and the Department, taking a liberal view of the subject, authorized their continuance." I very much doubt that these envelopes were ever "authorized" and would suggest that "allowed" would probably be the more correct word.

The first copy found.

A second copy of the envelope was found in 1886 by Mr. R. C. Fagan, of Middletown, Conn. This was entire but the stamp was badly faded. It passed into the hands of Mr. C. H. Mekeel who, by the advice of a friend, treated it with sulphate of iron, which effectually obliterated all of it but the signature. A third copy was purchased by Mr. E. B. Sterling in June, 1892, at a sale of autographs. For this copy Mr. Sterling paid the very moderate sum of ten cents. These are all the copies of which we have any published accounts. But several other copies are known to exist in collections.

Other copies.

The reprints were made on several occasions The first lot, about twenty impressions, was made in 1871 for Mr. W. P. Brown. They were in dull blue, on thick hard white paper, with the signature and word "copy" written in lilac-rose ink One specimen is known without the word "copy." Shortly after the first reprinting a second lot was struck off for Dr. J. A. Petrie. There were about thirty in this lot. The impressions were in carmine-red, slightly paler than the originals. Most of them were signed in dark blue ink, but a few copies are known with the signature in black. The paper is the same as that of the first reprints. At a later period a third and larger lot were printed for Mr. N. F. Seebeck. These are in dull red on soft yellowish

Reprints.

white paper. None of these last reprints were signed but copies are known with a forged signature. The reprints were not made on envelopes but only on pieces of paper. They may be distinguished from the originals by the colors and by slight differences in the signature.

Accepting Mr. Mitchell's expressed intention, collectors have for many years believed the original die to be in the possession of the New Haven Colonial Historical Society. But Mr. H. E. Deats has proven this to be incorrect and has definitely located the die. From correspondence, kindly placed at my disposal by Mr. Deats, I reproduce the following letter:

Present location of the die.

April 13, 1897.

H. E. DEATS, ESQ.,
    Flemington, N. J.

DEAR SIR :—Referring further to the matter of the "New Haven Stamp" I find that the original die, together with some signed reprints, are in the possession of Mr. Edward Mitchell, the only grandson of the Mr. Mitchell, formerly postmaster here.

The die and reprints were handed down to the present Mr. Mitchell on the death of his father, the only son of Postmaster Mitchell, and are regarded by the family as sort of an heirloom which money would not tempt them to part with.

Mr. Peats, a friend of mine, who for many years prior to the death of Postmaster Mitchell was his confidential man. having the care of his most important matters, tells me that for a long time he himself had the care of this die, and did at the time the reprints were printed and signed in 1872, and that he knows that the die in Mr. Mitchell's possession now is the original.   Respectfully yours,
                                                              J. ENGLISH.

It is to be hoped, should this die ever pass from the possession of Mr. Mitchell's family, it will be into the care of some Society which will guard it from any further use for reprinting.

ENVELOPES.

Reference List.

1845.   5 (cents) deep carmine on white, signature in violet-red
                        5 (cents) deep carmine on white, signature in dull blue
                        5 (cents) deep carmine on pale blue, signature in black
                        5 (cents) gray-blue on orange-buff, signature in black
                        5 (cents) blue-black on buff, signature in blue

REPRINTS.

1871.   5 (cents) dull blue on white, signature in lilac-rose
                        5 (cents) dull blue on white, signature and "copy" in
                                lilac-rose
                        5 (cents) carmine-red on brownish-buff, signature in dark
                                blue
                        5 (cents) carmine-red on white, signature in dark blue
                        5 (cents) carmine-red on white, signature in black
                        5 (cents) carmine-red on white, without signature
                        5 (cents) red on white, without signature
                        5 (cents) red on yellowish-white, without signature

New York, N. Y.

These stamps were issued during the postmastership of Robert H. Morris, which extended from May 21st, 1845 until 1849. They rightly stand at the head of the provisional issues by postmasters.

The stamps were printed from a steel plate made by Rawdon, Wright & Hatch. It has been stated that this plate contained one hundred impressions, arranged in ten rows of ten. I cannot find any foundation for this claim, beyond a tradition that some one remembers having seen a quantity of the stamps in strips of ten. We know from sheets of postmasters stamps, carriers, locals, etc., that the custom of the period was to make much smaller plates.

Size of the plate.

The following copies of accounts have been obtained from the records of the manufacturers:

POSTMASTER R. H. MORRIS.

1845.

July 12.	Engraving steel plate of Post Office stamps,	$40.00
"	Printing 1,000 impressions,	10.00
"	167 sheets paper and gumming do. @ 3c,	5.01
		$55.01

Delivered July 12, 1845,	30 impressions.
" " 14, "	20 "
" " 15, "	120 "
' " 16, "	270 "
" Aug. 28, "	200 "
" Sept. 17, "	200 "
" Oct. 3, "	126 "
Total,	966 impressions.

POSTMASTER R. H. MORRIS.

Printing 2,590 sheets Post Office stamps from Nov. 25, 1845, to Jan. 7 1847,	$25.90
431 sheets paper and gumming @ 3c,	12.93
	$38.83

Nov. 25, 1845,		400 impressions.
		500 "
		500 "
		50 "
		187 "
		150 "
		100 "
		100 "
		400 "
		103 "
Jan. 7, 1847,		100 "
	Total,	2,590 impressions.
July 12 to Oct. 3, 1845,		966 "
	Grand total,	3,556 impressions.

These records are apparently transferred from other books and the dates between November 25th, 1845 and January 7th, 1847, are missing. There are no further charges against Postmaster Morris.

The usual charge, at that date, was one hundred dollars for a plate containing one hundred stamps. The rate for smaller plates was higher in proportion, to cover the cost of the design and die. It would seem a reasonable assumption that the charge of forty dollars would represent the price of a plate containing twenty-five stamps.

Since Messrs. Rawdon, Wright & Hatch used 598 sheets for 3,556 impressions, it becomes evident that each sheet was cut into six pieces. The small difference of 5⅓ sheets may, doubtless, be attributed to spoiled impressions. I am informed by Mr. H. G. Mandel, an expert of the first rank upon all subjects of stamp manufacture, that, at the period we are considering, a *large* sheet of paper measured 28x22 inches. Such a sheet would cut into six pieces 9⅓x11 inches. And such a piece would take an impression from a plate of twenty-five stamps, five rows of five stamps each, and leave a good margin all around. It is also possible that the sheets of paper were smaller than 28x22 inches.

Finally, 3,556 impressions from a plate containing twenty-five stamps would give a total of 88,900 stamps. In view of the limited correspondence of the day and the very general practice of sending letters marked "PAID," this quantity of stamps would appear to be ample for the length of time they were in use.

There are a number of minor varieties, caused by touching up the plate and by defective transfers. The most prominent variety is that known as the "double line at bottom," the engraver having drawn an extra frame line on that side. It is said that this variety occurs three times on the sheet. In the collection of Mr. G. E. Jones there is a vertical pair with wide margins at the left and bottom, showing it to be from the lower left corner of the sheet. The upper stamp of the pair has the extra line. We can thus determine the position of one copy of this variety. Another prominent variety is caused by a misplaced transfer and shows the outlines of "FIVE CENTS" repeated across the face of the letters. An interesting account of the minor varieties will be found in an article by Mr. F. W. Hunter, published in the *Metropolitan Philatelist* for March, 1894. Mr. H. E. Deats has endeavored to reconstruct the original sheet by means of pairs showing the different varieties but, so far, he has not succeeded.

Minor varietie

Paper. The stamps are found on a variety of papers. The commonest is a thin wove, of a pale bluish or grayish tint. The stamps on white paper are much less frequently met with and those on deep gray-blue paper are decidedly scarce. In addition to the several shades of wove paper, copies are known on ribbed and pelure paper and also a few which show portions of a water-mark of large Roman capitals. This is, doubtless, a papermaker's watermark. I have seen part of the letter " J," the top of an " E " or " F " and upright strokes which might belong to a variety of letters.

　　　1　　　　　　　II　　　　　　III　　　　　IV　　　　　V

Initials on the stamps. The stamps are usually endorsed with the initials of the postmaster or one of his assistants. It is said that at first the stamps were sold unsigned. I have seen such copies, on white and bluish papers, cancelled July 18th and 21st, 1845. It will be observed that these dates are close to that on which the stamps were issued. Fearing that they might be counterfeited, it was decided to authenticate the stamps by the endorsement of the postmaster. Mr. Morris undertook to do this but soon found that it required too much of his time and delegated the work to his assistants. It is believed that he signed only two sheets, on two succeeding days. On one sheet the initials " R. H. M." (I) read from top to bottom of the stamp in a slightly diagonal line. On the other sheet the direction of the endorsement is reversed and reads from bottom to top. The majority of the stamps are signed "A. C. M." (II, III, IV) horizontally across the face. These are the initials of Alonzo Castle Monson, brother-in-law of Robert H. Morris. A similar endorsement (v) was made by Marciana Monson, brother of A. C. Monson. It is possible that W. C. R. Engrist, Mr. Morris' private secretary, and other clerks may have endorsed some of the stamps. The endorsements were always in red ink.

　　　The stamps were cancelled in various ways: with pen strokes in blue or red ink, the word " PAID," the circular date marks of the office, a circle crossed by parallel lines, and the letters " U. S." in an octagon. All the hand-stamped cancellations were in red.

Die and Plates. It is not known what became of the original plate. The records of Rawdon, Wright & Hatch and their successors, the American Bank Note Co., are silent on this point. The original die is understood to be in the custody of the latter company. About 1862 a new plate was made from this die for George A. Hussey, of Hussey's Post. He was an obliging gentleman who supplied large quantities of locals and other stamps to the trade. When originals were not obtainable he made good the deficiency with reprints, or, rather than disappoint his customers, had new plates and stones made, that he might furnish the stamps required. These productions have been called by harsh names in later years, but perhaps the critics failed to appreciate the gentleman's intentions.]

Sheets from the new plate have nine stamps, arranged in three rows of three. Each differs very slightly from the others, the most prominent variety being the middle stamp in the lower row, which has the white stock shaded by crossed diagonal lines. From this plate reprints were struck in black on deep blue and white papers. Owing to irregular contraction of the paper after printing the reprints differ in size from each other and also from the originals. The originals measure 20½x28mm. The reprints on blue paper measure 20½x28½mm. and those on white paper 20x28½mm. The stamps on the original plate are 1½mm. apart, while those on the reprint plate are separated by 2½mm. Other impressions were struck in blue, green, red and brown on white paper. As there were no originals in these colors these impressions are, at best, only proofs.

From the copy book of Mr. R. H. Morris—kindly loaned me by Mr. Monson Morris—I quote the following interesting letter:

POST OFFICE, NEW YORK, July 12, 1845.
MY DEAR SIR:—I have adopted a stamp which I sell at 5 cents each. The accompanying is one. I prefer losing the cost of making them to having it insinuated that I am speculating out of the public. Your office of course will not officially notice my stamp, but will be governed only by the post office stamp of prepayment. Should there by any accident be deposited in your office a letter directed to the City of New York with one of my stamps upon it, you will mark the letter unpaid the same as though no stamp was upon it, though when it reaches my office I shall deliver it as a paid letter. In this manner the accounts of the offices will be kept as now, there can be no confusion, and as each office is the judge of its own stamps there will be no danger from counterfeits.
ROBT. H. MORRIS, P. M.
To P. M. Boston, Philadelphia, Albany, Washington.

This shows plainly the expectations and intentions of the New York postmaster. I am told that, in the files of the Post Office Department at Washington, there are letters from postmasters, asking if the New York stamp was a postage stamp and that the reply to these inquiries was in the affirmative. But on referring to a quotation on page 11, it will be seen that sometime in the next year the New York stamps were sent, by order of the Postmaster-General, to the above cities, to be used as a test of the practicability of postage stamps. I have seen copies on the original covers, mailed in Boston on February 1st and April 11th, 1846.

ADHESIVE STAMPS.

Imperforate.

Wove Paper.

July 12th, 1845.   5 cents black on bluish
5 cents black on gray-blue
5 cents black on white
5 cents black on yellowish white

Varieties:

5 cents black on bluish.   Without signature
5 cents black on gray-blue.   "   "
5 cents black on white   "   "
5 cents black on yellowish white "   "

Watermarked Paper.

5 cents black on bluish

Ribbed Paper.

5 cents black on bluish

Pelure Paper.

5 cents black on bluish

Variety :

5 cents black on bluish. Without signature

Reprints.

Wove Paper.

1862 (?)   5 cents black on deep blue

5 cents black on white

Envelopes.

Mr. Morris also issued envelopes but their design is uncertain, since no copy is known to have been preserved. The only description we have of them is given in the *New York Express*. On July 7th, 1845, its Washington correspondent, writing under date of the 2nd, says:

Historical.

"It was suggested in New York to Mr. Morris, your postmaster, that he might accommodate the public very much by selling stamped envelopes, as the law does not authorize the sale of stamps on the English plan. When he was here he laid the subject before the Postmaster-General, who has to-day decided that the postmaster can do this. The envelopes are to be marked with the amount of postage thereon, say 5 or 10 or more cents, as the case may be, and the initials of the postmaster are to be superadded, and then the envelopes can be sold. The object is to facilitate the payment of prepaid letters. Postmasters can intercharge envelopes whenever they can agree to do so among themselves."

In the same journal for July 8th, 1845, we find the following editorial:

FREE STAMPED ENVELOPES.—When the bill for cheap postage was before Congress, it contained a clause authorizing the sale of stamps on the plan of the English system. The provision was, however, stricken out, leaving the public only the old method of prepaying letters during the business hours of the post office. A suggestion was made to our new postmaster. Mr. Morris, that the public convenience would be very much promoted if he would sell envelopes which would pass free through his office. By this measure letters could be sent at any hour of the night to the post-office, and the postage paid, where the writer desired it, by enclosing it in a free envelope. The postmaster proposed to sell stamps at five cents each, but this not having been sanctioned by Congress, we should think would not be the best way ; and as the public convenience demands something of the kind, we are glad to learn that he has prepared envelopes of the kind referred to, some of which we have seen. They are marked FIVE CENTS and under these words is the name R H. MORRIS. For letters over one ounce they will be marked according to the post-office rates, in the same way. These envelopes will be sold by the postmaster at six and a quarter cents each, or sixteen for a dollar of the common kind and the common size. This will be as cheap or cheaper than they can be bought in small quantities at the stationers. A thin envelope will contain two letters and be subject only to a single postage. Envelopes of various sizes will also be furnished, and of fine quality when desired by the purchaser. The plan, we hear, has also been adopted by the postmaster at Washington, D. C., and has met the approval of the Postmaster-General. We think it is one not only of convenience to the public, but that it will add to the revenue of the department very considerably.

Again I quote from Mr. Morris' copy book:

POST OFFICE, NEW YORK, July 30, 1845.

MY DEAR SIR :—Yours of the 28th, marked 'private," was duly received.

Letter of Postmaster Morris to the Postmaster General.

I at first contemplated issuing envelopes with my name on them and selling them at the usual cost of the envelope and the postage upon it, and indeed, at the earnest solicitation of one or two friends, I prepared some, of which I sold in all about two dollars worth. I afterwards, upon mature reflection, determined I would not continue to do so, for the reason, among others, that I was unwilling to expose myself to the imputation that, while ostensibly I was selling them for the accommodation of the public, I was in reality doing it for the pecuniary profit of the difference between what envelopes could be purchased for by the quantity and what I should sell them for at retail. I therefore adopted instead of the envelope a stamp, one of which is on the envelope herewith. These stamps I dispose of at their face. I make nothing by them except such as may be lost or destroyed, but, on the contrary, have to pay for the plate and the impressions.

I have adopted this plan first for the accommodation of the public and second to enable me practically to judge of the benefits of it, that you might make a representation to the next Congress, and procure, if desirable, a law authorizing government stamps and, I hope, a system of prepayment of letters I intended to have made this explanation to you before this. I have, however, been so occupied that I have neglected to do so and your letter reminded me of my duty.

Very sincerely and respectfully yours,

Hon. CAVE JOHNSON,   ROBT H. MORRIS, P. M.
    P. M Genl., Washington.

In view of the foregoing statements it cannot be doubted that en-velopes were issued by the postmaster at New York. The quantity was very limited, not exceeding forty. They were marked " FIVE CENTS " and possibly " TEN CENTS " and " R. H. Morris." Beyond this we have no information. The *American Journal of Philately* for January 1888, lists them as " 5 cents black." I have been unable to find any authority for calling the color black and should, on the contrary, expect them to be stamped in red, as that was the color in use in the New York post-office at that date for cancellations and other hand-stamps. The signature of the postmaster may have been in red or black ink, as both colors were in use in the office. The former was the color used in signing the stamps. The *Express* speaks of the envelopes as of "the common kind and the common size," from which we may infer that they were the ordinary buff envelopes of the period.

Design and colors. (margin note)

ENVELOPES.

Reference List. (margin note)

July 7th, 1845.   5 cents————on————

Philadelphia, Pa.

The claim that stamps were issued by George F. Lehman, postmaster at Philadelphia from 1845 to 1849, is based on nothing more substantial than tradition. No copy of anything which might have served as a postmaster's stamp, or which was in use at the date of the provisional issues by the post-masters of other cities, is known to-day. The carriers stamps are, of course, excepted from these remarks.

The claim that something in the nature of stamps was used in Philadelphia was first made in the *American Journal of Philately* for November 20th, 1871. In an article by "Cosmopolitan," on page 125, we find the following :

" Another discovery, no less important than the last, has been made lately, viz.: a provisional stamp for the City of Philadelphia. For particulars of the emanation of this stamp, I am indebted to a gentleman occupying a prominent position in the General Post Office, who was engaged in the Philadelphia Post Office at the time the stamp was first issued. The exact date of its issue cannot be definitely ascertained, but it was during the administration of Dr. Geo. F. Lehman, postmaster of Philadelphia, between 1845 and 1849. It can hardly be called a stamp proper, as Dr Lehman had simply an arrangement by which parties, who might be compelled to mail letters after the close of the office, could have the necessary stamps placed on them by the clerks and charged to their accounts or collected by the carriers. In most cases this was a band in which the letters were enclosed and endorsed by the parties. But in other cases there were small slips *printed* and pasted on one corner of the letters. There were several varieties of them used, but, unfortunately, the most careful search has revealed no specimens as yet. There is no possible doubt but that they were actually used and in numbers, as my informant recollects them from 1845 until 1849 and even afterwards."

So far as I am aware, subsequent research has not added to our knowledge of or revealed the existence of a Philadelphia postmaster's stamp.

PITTSFIELD, MASS.

Again we have no positive proof in the shape of existing stamps, though the postmaster is credited with having issued them.

Tiffany's *History of the Postage Stamps of the United States* says on this subject:

"A short notice published in one of the Springfield, Mass., papers, in the summer of 1874, asserts that in overhauling the vaults of the Berkshire Mutual Fire Insurance Company of Pittsfield, a number of stamps were found that were issued by the Pittsfield postmaster, in 1846-47. Phineas Allen was postmaster of Pittsfield at the time. No further information concerning these stamps has rewarded inquiry."

At my request Mr. W. C. Stone has very kindly searched the files of the various Springfield papers for the summer of 1874, but has failed to find the article referred to by Mr. Tiffany. It would appear either that there was a mistake in the date given or that the article was in some Pittsfield or Berkshire County paper. Mr. Stone, however, found mention of the Insurance Co. having moved into new quarters in July 1874, and it is probable that the stamps were found at the time of this removal.

Mr. Stone also sends me the following extract from the *American Philatelic Magazine* for March 1888:

THE STAMPS OF THE PITTSFIELD POSTMASTER.

The first notice that I had of the above stamps was in reading Mr. Tiffany's history and of course became very interested in them. My search through the back files of local news in the *Springfield* (Mass) *Republican* rewarded me with the following :

"While overhauling the vaults of the Berkshire Mutual Fire Insurance Company, a number of stamps were found which were issued by the postmaster, Mr. Phineas Allen, in 1846."

The stamps spoken of excited no little curiosity, for the weekly papers of the time (1874), reviewed them and the stamps passed through several hands and are still in town. I asked an old resident and a newspaper man regarding them and he said he thought the design was that of a post rider. He has promised me more news later and I hope to be able to present an illustration in an early number.

W. F. JILLSON.

Unfortunately no further numbers of the magazine were ever issued and a few years ago Mr. Jillson was drowned, thus depriving us of the benefit of any additional information he may have acquired.

Further efforts to secure information about the Pittsfield stamps have been unrewarded.

PROVIDENCE, R. I.

Welcome B. Sayles was appointed postmaster at Providence by President James K. Polk in 1844. He was reappointed by President Franklin Pierce and served ten or twelve years in all. In various philatelic articles the postmaster's name has been erroneously given as Welcome P. Sayles and H. B. Sayles.

In 1846, Postmaster Sayles issued postage stamps of five and ten cents face value. They were engraved on copper by George W. Babcock and **Engraving and Printing.** printed by Henry A. Hidden & Co. The engraving of the plate has hitherto been credited to Henry A. Hidden, though the statement has occasionally been questioned. Mr. J. Frank Read of Providence talked with Mr. Babcock some years ago about the Providence stamps and learned the facts, as here given. From about 1835 to 1865 Mr. Babcock did most of the fine plate work and engraving in Providence. Neither Henry A. Hidden nor his brother James did engraving of this quality, but they had the largest printing establishment in the city, and printed the majority of the bills for the state banks and copper and steel plate work for corporations, manufacturers, etc.

The stamps are printed on hard, yellowish-white, hand-made paper. The paper is usually quite thin, but Mr. H. E. Deats has a sheet on decidedly **Paper.** thick paper, though of the same quality and making as the ordinary sheets. Variation in thickness was not at all unusual in the hand-made papers of fifty years ago, the stipulation usually being for a certain weight to the ream, any excess or shortage being corrected by the use of sheets purposely made very thin or very thick.

As will be seen from the illustration (Plate B), the plate contained twelve stamps, arranged in four rows of three stamps each. The stamp in the upper right corner had a face value of ten cents, all the others being of five cents. As the stamps were engraved directly on the plate, each differs from the others in minor details. From rulings on the plate it is evident that the original intention was to make it larger, but this was abandoned and only the twelve stamps were engraved.

For many years the plate was believed to be in the custody of the State Treasury or of the Rhode Island Historical Society and statements to this effect were repeatedly made in philatelic publications. The incorrectness of these statements was shown in September, 1893, by the sale of the plate to the Bogert & Durbin Co. by Lycurgus Sayles of Providence. With the plate were sold 32 complete sheets, and 61 single copies of the five cent and 18 of the ten cent stamps. The price paid has been stated at $2,500 to $3,000.

Lycurgus Sayles was a nephew of the former postmaster, Welcome B. Sayles. After the latter retired from the postmastership he practiced law. One day in 1854 he was having a sort of house cleaning in his office, examining and destroying many packages of old letters and papers. One package he handed to his nephew with the remark: "Here, you had better take this. It is some of my old postmaster's stamps, and the plate they were made from." Mr. Sayles placed the package in a pigeon hole in the top of an old-fashioned desk he was then using, and there it remained until, in 1893, he was shown one of the stamps by a Providence collector, and learned that they were of value and the plate much desired. Whereupon he searched for and found the plate and, as has been stated, subsequently sold it.

The original printing of the Providence stamps appears to have been quite extensive, as, at various times, large numbers of the sheet have been held by stamp dealers. But the gradual destruction which is always going on among philatelic treasures, has had its effect and to-day the number of sheets is comparatively limited. Most of the unused stamps may be traced to one source of supply. They came from John Hagen, one of the three letter carriers of the city under Postmaster Sayles.

On this subject Mr. E. B Hanes writes me: "About 1850 the Providence post office was removed from Westminster Street to Market Square. At that time it required only a very few carriers to serve the city. One of them, named John Hagen, whom I afterwards well knew, told me that Mr. Sayles, the postmaster, had a very large quantity of the stamps printed, as he had no doubt of their general use. There were, at the time of the removal, several square packages of full sheets, which the postmaster told Hagan he could have. So Hagan carried them home as playthings for his children. I knew these young Hagans and was their play-fellow and, before the days of stamp collecting, these bundles of Providence stamps were used as foot balls and other implements of play."

Mrs. Hagan afterwards used the majority of these sheets to paper a small room in the attic of their house. Such sheets as remained were gradually dispersed and, when a demand arose for more, many were removed from the attic walls and sold.

The sheets were orginally gummed with a very thin gum which was almost white and quite smooth. It did not extend to the edges of the sheets nor discolor the paper. Mr. Deats' sheet on thick paper has this gum. The sheets without gum which are occasionally seen may probably be assigned to those removed from the walls of the Hagan attic. It is said that Fred Hagan, son of John Hagan, brought a quantity of these sheets to New York about 1890 and had them regummed. This gum is yellowish, crackly and full of

Discovery of the Plate.

Historical

Gum.

spots of thicker gum. It usually does not extend to the edges of the sheet and, as a rule, turns the paper quite yellowish.

Used copies of the five cent stamp are quite rare and, so far as I am aware, the ten cents is not known in this condition. It has even been asserted **Cancelled copies.** that the Providence stamps were never in use. But cancelled copies on the original covers are not unknown and it must be remembered that of the loose stamps, which had remained in the postmaster's hands and were sold with the plate, there were 61 five cents and 18 ten cents, which would indicate that a number of sheets had been cut up, the majority of the five cent stamps sold, and the ten cents left on hand. All the used copies which I have seen were cancelled by a "v" shaped mark, made with a pen and black ink. The covers also bear the dated postmark of the city, the word "PAID" and a figure "5." All these are hand-stamped in red. The only dates of use of which I have a memorandum are August 25th and November 14th, 1846.

After the purchase of the plate it was carefully cleaned, and the corrosion removed by Livermore & Knight, of Providence, and proofs on thick card board struck from it, in blue, red, green, brown and black.

As soon as it was known that the plate of the Providence stamps had passed into the hands of dealers the possibility of reprinting became a subject **Reprints.** of discussion. In spite of the fact that the owners claimed that no reimpressions had been made, beyond the proofs just mentioned, there were persistent, though unconfirmed, rumors of reprints. Probably many of the assertions were founded on the report that, about the time the plate was sold, diligent search was made, in and near Providence, for old hand-made paper, such as was used for state bank bills and similar securities. This paper was identical with that on which the Providence stamps were printed. Small quantities of it were known to be held by individuals and old firms and sales of it were said to have been made.

It was not until 1898 that the existence of the reprints was finally admitted. We now know that there were two reprintings. The first was probably made soon after the purchase of the plate and is on the old paper just referred to. There are three varieties of this paper. The first is thick hard and white. The second is also thick and hard but it is of a yellowish tone and coarser quality. The third is thin and soft and has rose colored fibres in its substance. A second and much larger lot of reprints was made in 1898. Before this reprinting took place the face of the plate was electroplated with steel. These last reprints were made on a thin hard white wove paper, apparently hand-made, of close grain and decidedly modern character. A single sheet was printed in green. All the reprints are without gum. The impression is never as strong as that of the originals and the ink has a grayish tint. On the reverse of each sheet is printed in large fancy capitals

B	O	G
E	R	T
D	U	R
B	I	N

These letters are in a gold-bronze ink which is said to be indelible and they are so arranged that one letter falls on the back of each stamp. It is much to be regretted that there was not placed on the face of each stamp on the plate some small dot or mark by which the true character of the reprints would always be readily apparent. It is yet more regrettable that they were ever made at all.

ADHESIVE STAMPS.   Reference List.

Imperforate.

Yellowish White Wove Paper,

1846.   5 cents black, gray-black. 11 varieties
                  10 cents black, gray-black

REPRINTS.

Thick Hard White Paper.

1893.   5 cents gray-black. 11 varieties
                  10 cents gray-black

Thick Hard Yellowish White Paper.

                  5 cents gray-black. 11 varieties
                  10 cents gray-black

Thin Soft White Paper with Colored Fibres.

                  5 cents gray-black. 11 varieties
                  10 cents gray-black

Thin Hard White Paper.

1898.   5 cents gray-black. 11 varieties
                  10 cents gray-black
                  5 cents green. 11 varieties
                  10 cents green

There are a number of counterfeits of these stamps. Many of them come to us from Europe but the most dangerous were made in this country. Concerning these counterfeits Mr. C. W. Bowen, to whom I am indebted for   Counterfeits. much valuable information about the Providence stamps, writes me: "About forty years ago (the exact date cannot be given) Mr. C. A. Pabodie of this city was asked by some one—he cannot now remember who—to make an engraving similar to that from which two stamps, which the applicant gave him, were printed. This he did. The party took the plate and the only record remaining in the hands of Mr. P. is a proof which was made before the plate was delivered."

Mr. Pabodie was a member of the firm of Pabodie & Thompson. The proof shows that the counterfeit die—for such it was, rather than a plate— was made in imitation of the first and second stamps in the right hand vertical row of the original plate. This die was undoubtedly made for George A. Hussey, who had at least two lithographic stones made by transfers from it. One stone bore one hundred reproductions of the five cents, arranged in ten rows of ten. The other bore ninety reproductions, in ten rows of nine. The transfers on the second stone were equally divided between the five and

ten cents, but they were arranged without any regularity and one of ten cents
was placed tête bêche. Some of these counterfeits were printed on a thin
yellowish white paper, quite like that of the originals. There were also impressions on a variety of colored and fancy papers. These and much other
trash were printed for Hussey by Thomas Wood, 2½ Murray Street, New
York.

The counterfeits are not such as need deceive any one at all careful or
who compares them with a reproduction of an original sheet. The originals
measure 28x20mm., the counterfeits are usually a trifle larger or smaller,
according to the paper on which they are printed.

ST. LOUIS, MO.

TYPE I.   TYPE II.   TYPE III.

TYPE I.   TYPE II.   TYPE III.

TYPE I.   TYPE II.

The St. Louis stamps were issued in November, 1845 by John M. Wimer, who received his appointment as postmaster in that year. His name has been given by various writers as Hymer and Wymer, but Wimer is correct. Date of Issue. The exact date of issue of the stamps is not known but it was probably about November 1st, as the *Missouri Republican* of the 5th published the following notice:

LETTER STAMPS.—Mr. Wimer, the postmaster, has prepared a set of letter stamps, or rather marks, to be put upon letters, indicating that the postage has been paid. In this he has copied after the plan adopted by the postmaster of New York and other cities. These stamps are engraved to represent the Missouri Coat of Arms, and are five and ten cents. They are so prepared that they may be stuck upon a letter like a wafer and will prove a great convenience to merchants and all those having many letters to send post paid, as it saves all trouble of paying at the post-office. They will be sold as they are sold in the East, viz : sixteen five-cent stamps and eight ten-cent stamps for a dollar. We would recommend merchants and others to give them a trial.

On November 13th, 1845, the same paper published a second notice, as follows:

POST-OFFICE STAMPS.—Mr. Wimer, the postmaster, requests us to say that he will furnish nine ten-cent stamps and eighteen five-cent stamps for one dollar, the difference being required to pay for the printing of the stamps.

In the collection of Mr H. E. Deats is a copy of the ten cent stamp, cancelled Nov. 20th, 1845. This is the earliest cancellation known on any of these stamps.

The stamps were engraved on copper by J. M. Kershaw, at that date the leading engraver in St. Louis and proprietor of the Western Card and **Engraving and** Seal Engraving Establishment. The designs, adapted from the arms of the **Arrangement.** State of Missouri, were engraved on a small thin copper plate, such as was used for visiting cards. The designs were arranged in two vertical rows, three five cents in the left row and three ten cents in the right. They vary slightly in size, measuring 17¾ to 18¼x22 to 22½mm. Being separately engraved, each differs in minor details from the others. The varieties of the five cents may be readily distinguished by the ornaments in the upper corners or the **Varieties.** position of the bears relative to the vertical frame lines. In type I, the haunches of both bears touch the frame lines. In type II, the bear at the right touches the frame but that at the left is about ¾mm. from it. And in type III, neither bear touches the frame. The most readily noted marks on the ten cents are the curved dashes below the words "POST OFFICE." On type I there are three dashes below the words, on type II three pairs of dashes and on type III similar pairs of dashes with rows of dots between them. The first arrangement of the types is usually called plate I, though more properly it is the first state of the plate, as only one plate was ever used.

It may be well to remark here that until 1895 the correct arrangement of the types on the plate was not known. With the limited material at command previous to that date, philatelists had attempted to restore the arrangement and, under the circumstances, had succeeded very well, since only types I and III of the five cents were transposed. In nearly all the articles on the St. Louis stamps, written previous to 1895, the types of the five cents which we now call I, II and III were called C. B. and A. The types of the ten cents were correctly arranged.

The majority of the St. Louis stamps appear to have been used by two large firms of that city or by people connected with them. These firms were Crow & McCreery, wholesale dry goods merchants, and William Nisbet & Co., bankers. When these stamps were in use the great trade and mail route between the cities of the eastern coast and New Orleans was via the Ohio and Mississippi rivers. Louisville, Ky., was an important point on this route and was connected with St. Louis by a line of fast steamers.

The two firms above mentioned were in the habit of sending to their correspondents in Louisville bulky letters, containing drafts, other letters to be forwarded, etc. On these heavy letters the postage was, of course, large.

In the celebrated find of St. Louis stamps, which was made in Louisville in the summer of 1895, were many covers bearing stamps representing postage from twenty-five to fifty cents. We may infer that the desirability

of stamps of higher face value than ten cents was early apparent. The simplest and least expensive way of providing such stamps was by altering the
existing plate. Accordingly two of the five cent stamps, types I and II,
were changed to twenty cents. The stamps furnish evidence that this was
accomplished in the customary way, *i. e.*, by placing the plate face downward on a hard surface and hammering on the reverse of the parts to be
altered until the face was driven flush at those points. The new numerals
were then engraved and any damage to the surrounding parts repaired.
Evidence of damage in this driving up of the surface is seen in the broken
frame lines above the numerals on the twenty cent stamps and in the missing
paw of the right-hand bear on type II of that value. The latter stamp also
shows a good example of retouching in the dashes under "Saint" and
"Louis." Being altered from types I and II of the five cents, the characteristic marks of those types will serve to distinguish the twenty cent stamps.
This altered or second state of the plate is usually referred to as plate II.

    Apparently it was soon found that the demand for the twenty cent
stamps was not as great as had been anticipated, while, on the other hand,
the number of five cent stamps supplied by printings from the altered plate
was disproportionate and insufficient, in view of the number required for
ordinary letters. So the plate was again changed, the numerals on the twenty
cent stamps being erased and fives engraved in their place. These new
numerals differ somewhat from those which originally occupied the position.
In type I re-engraved the "5" is fully twice as far from the top frame line as
in the original state. It is correspondingly nearer the garter surrounding the
arms. In the first state several fine shading lines pass between the lower part
of the "5" and the garter but in the re-engraved stamp the heavy shading of
the numeral almost touches the garter. In the re-engraved stamp the four
dashes under "Saint" and "Louis" have disappeared, except about one-half
of the upper dash under each word. In type II re-engraved the ornament
in the flag of the "5" is a diamond instead of a triangle, the diamond in the
bow is much longer than in the first state, and the ball of the numeral,
originally blank, now contains a large dot. At the right of the shading of
the "5" is a short curved line, which is evidently a remnant of the "o" of
"20". The paw of the bear on the right, which was obliterated in making
the first alteration, has now been restored. It is heavily outlined but only
lightly shaded.

    There are many other points of difference between the re-engraved
types and the originals but those I have indicated are the most prominent
and will suffice to distinguish them.

    At the time of the second alteration of the plate type III of the five
cents was slightly retouched. Evidence of this retouching is most easily
found in the ball of the "5", which now contains a large dot in place of the
almost imperceptible one in the early state of the type.

    The third and last state of the plate is commonly called plate III.

    The first printing consisted of 500 impressions on greenish-gray wove
paper. This printing was, of course, from the plate in its original state. The
second printing took place early in 1846. Stamps from this printing are

Alterations of the
Stamps.

Retouch of five
cents.

Printing and
Paper.

known cancelled in March of that year. Again 500 impressions were printed, this time from the plate in the second state and on paper of two colors, greenish-gray and lilac-gray. Probably only a small quantity of paper of the first color was used, as only two copies of the twenty cent stamps are known on that paper. The third printing, made from the plate in the third state, is believed to have taken place in January, 1847. The earliest cancellation known on stamps of this printing is Feb. 5th, 1847. For this printing an almost pelure paper, very hard and transparent, was used. The color is a cold gray. The extreme scarcity of stamps on this paper would indicate that but few of them were used, though it is believed that, as on previous occasions, 500 sheets were printed.

What became of the remainder of the last printing, of the probable remainder of twenty cent stamps from the previous printing, and of the plate, **Remainders and Plate.** are unsettled questions. They may have been destroyed when the Government issue of 1847 appeared or when the post-office building was demolished. The household effects of Mr. Wimer were lost by the sinking of a steamboat on the Mississippi river, during the war, and may have included the plate and remainders. Lastly, they may have been among his private papers, which were siezed by the Government, in 1865, at the time of his arrest as a suspected Confederate. Whatever their fate, there seems to be little doubt that they no longer exist.

Reference List.

ADHESIVE STAMPS.

Imperforate.

Greenish Wove Paper.

Nov., 1845.	5 (cents) black, 3 varieties
	10 (cents) black, 3 "
1846.	20 (cents) black, 2 "

Lilac-Gray Wove Paper.

1846.	5 (cents) black, 1 variety
	10 (cents) black, 3 varieties
	20 (cents) black, 2 "

Gray Pelure Paper.

1847.	5 (cents) black, 3 varieties
	10 (cents) black, 3 "

Probably no stamps have provoked more discussion and articles in the philatelic magazines than those of St. Louis. For many years philatelists were of divided opinion regarding the twenty cent stamps—the majority holding that they were frauds—and their genuineness was not established to the satisfaction of all until the Louisville find.

The first mention of a St. Louis stamp is found in the *Stamp Collectors' Magazine* for November, 1863. In "Addenda to Mount Brown's Catalogue **Historical.** of Postage Stamps," under the head of "United States of America" and the subhead "Labels of Private Offices," we find this brief record:

"Saint Louis Post-Office (device supported by bears), black, imp., rect., 10c."

This description, together with an equally brief description of the New York and Providence stamps, is repeated in the number for the following month, in an article on "United States Local Postage Stamps."

The author of the article expresses the opinion that the stamps of the three cities are not private locals but issues by the Government postmasters in anticipation of the regular issues of the Post Office Department. He calls attention to their bearing the names of the cities and the words "Post Office" (which private individuals would scarcely dare usurp), to their values, which were too high for local letters but correct for the Government rates under and over 3,000 miles, and to their superiority in workmanship to the local stamps.

The stamp referred to in these two articles was the 10c, type II.

The five cents was first known to collectors in Europe in June, 1864, as may be seen by referring to the *Stamp Collectors' Magazine* for 1870, page 29. This was type III. This value was first mentioned in print in 1865, in *Kline's Manual*.

A second variety of the ten cents (type I), was discovered by Mr. L. W. Durbin and reported in the *American Journal of Philately* for April, 1869. In September of the same year Mr. E. L. Pemberton described type II of the five cents in *The Philatelist*.

In an article in the *American Journal of Philately* for January, 1870, Mr. J. W. Scott described, for the first time, type I of the five cents, type III of the ten cents and the two types of the twenty cents, noting the fact that they were altered from types of the five cents.

During this time the leading philatelists of the day had been carrying on in the magazines an animated discussion on the question of the genuineness of the stamps. The announcement of the twenty cent value gave new vigor to the contest.

In the *Stamp Collectors' Magazine* for January, 1871, Mr. E. L. Pemberton described an investigation he had made of the St. Louis stamps. He began his study with a very unfavorable opinion of the twenty cents and of certain of the papers. But—having gotten together thirteen five cents, twelve ten cents and the three copies of the twenty cents then known—he, after careful study, announced his unqualified belief in their genuineness. In view of the comparatively limited number of specimens at his command, the accuracy of Mr. Pemberton's conclusions is remarkable. He placed the shades of the paper in their correct order of issue, described accurately the three states of the plate, the retouching of type III of the five cents, the re-engraving of type II of that value and expressed his belief in the existence of a similar re-engraving of type I, though he had not found a copy of the stamp. In fact, fully twenty-four years before we were ready to accept the information, he told us nearly all of the technical details which we know to-day. We have only been able to add the description of type I re-engraved and to correct the positions of types I and II, which he had transposed, a mistake most pardonable when we remember that at that time only one pair of these stamps was known and he had not the advantage of seeing it.

In spite of the ability of this article and the high repute of its author, the leading philatelists declined to accept the twenty cent stamps

Remarkable study by E. L. Pemberton.

as genuine and paid no attention to the retouched and re-engraved fives.

In the fall of 1894, Mr. John K. Tiffany made an exhaustive study of the St. Louis stamps and published his conclusions in the *Philatelic Journal of America* for December of that year. He, like Mr. Pemberton, began in doubt and ended in belief. In this article the re-engraving of type I of the five cents is described for the first time.

The great find at Louisville.

But the great find of St. Louis stamps, made in the summer of 1895, was more convincing than any theories or arguments and served to put at rest any lingering doubts as to their genuineness. In this find were included a strip of two twenties and a five cents, strips of three of both the five and ten cents, horizontal pairs of five and ten, twenty and ten, etc., etc.; thus locating positively the varieties in the several states of the plate.

Approximate number in existence.

Previous to 1869 very few copies of the St. Louis stamps were known, probably not more than twenty. In that year Mr. J. W. Scott purchased a lot consisting of about 50 five cents, 100 ten cents and 3 twenty cents. A few years later about 20 five and ten cents (including a pair of the former value) came from the banking house of Messrs. Riggs at Washington. About 1889 Mr. G. B. Calman purchased from the firm of J. & J. Stuart & Co., of New York some 25 specimens of the five and ten cents, most of which were on the pelure paper. A few odd copies had also been discovered in various places including a fourth copy of the twenty cents. Last of all came the Louisville find consisting of 75 five cents, 46 ten cents and 16 twenty cents. This enumeration enables us to approximate the number of St. Louis stamps in existence.

Counterfeits.

I have seen two counterfeits of the five cent St. Louis stamps which might readily deceive anyone who did not take the trouble to compare them with copies known to be genuine or with photographs. Both are in imitation of type III and printed on a paper which reproduces fairly well the greenish-gray of that used for the originals.

The more dangerous of the counterfeits may be distingushed by the following points: There are three dots instead of four above the diamond in the bow of the numeral "5." The curved line following the outline of the numeral does not extend far enough to the left at the bottom. The lettering on the garter and the scroll below the bear is too well done, note especially the "E" of "WE". The first curved line below the lettered scroll terminates on the right between the "I" and "C" of "OFFICE." On the originals this line stops over the "I." Also on the originals there is a mark, caused by a slip of the engravers tool, at the left of the upper curve of the "S" of "POST" and a similar mark crossing the inner frame line above and to the left of the "S" of "SAINT." There are no such marks on the counterfeit.

In March 1868 the *Stamp Collectors' Magazine* published illustrations of the five cents (type III) and ten cents (type II). The second of the two counterfeits is made either from a careful reproduction of the illustration in that magazine or from the cut itself. The following marks will serve to distinguish this counterfeit: There is a heavy shading at the right of the numeral "5." The four dashes below "SAINT" and "LOUIS" are much too long, especially the lower three, which are little more than dots in the originals. Immediately above " LOUIS " in the originals is a long curved line, which is missing in the counterfeit. On the latter also the first curved line below the scroll on which the bears stand is much too long, beginning between the "o" and "s" of "POST" and ending between the "1" and " C " of "OFFICE," while on the originals it begins between the "s" and "T" and ends over the " 1."

I anticipate that the companion illustration in the *Stamp Collectors' Magazine*, has been used to produce counterfeits of the ten cents but I have not seen them.

The pretended two-cent St. Louis stamp, which we occasionally find in old collections, is of quite a different design from that of the regular values and is entirely fraudulent.

Two-cent Stamp.

WASHINGTON, D. C.

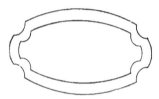

Date of Issue.

Historical.

Col. Charles K. Gardiner, postmaster at Washington from March 31st, 1845 to June 30th, 1849, issued stamped envelopes of five and ten cents face value, but unfortunately, no copies have been preserved.

The *New York Express* for July 8th, 1845, in an article on the envelopes issued by the New York Postmaster, says: "The plan, we hear, has also been adopted by the Postmaster at Washington, D. C., and has met the approval of the Postmaster-General."

Mr. C. F. Rothfuchs found in the daily papers of Washington, published on the 23rd and 25th of July, 1845, the following:

INTERESTING TO CITIZEN AND SOJOURNERS IN WASHINGTON —Upon inquiry at the city post office, we learn that Col. Gardiner has had franked (or rather prepaid) envelopes prepared, which do away with the necessity of personal application at the delivery window when one wishes to pay postage on sending off a letter. They are for sale at the post office at the following rates; which barely pay the cost, after deducting the sum chargeable on each for postage, viz :

18	envelopes to enclose letters charged at 5 cents for					$1.00
9	"	"	"	"	"	.50
1	"	"	"	"	"	.06¼
9	"	"	"	"	10 cents	1.00
4	"	"	"	"	10 "	.50
1	"	"	"	"	5 "	

This plan, it will be recollected, has been adopted in the northern cities, to the great advantage of the public, and its introduction here will save our fellow citizens many a long and hitherto indispensable trudge, in this metropolis of magnificent distances.

In reply to a request for further information Mr. Rothfuchs writes me:

"On the Washington, D. C., Postmaster's stamp I have spent considerable time without success, not even locating one. I have interviewed many of the old residents but could not find any one who remembered it. I finally discovered the man who carried the mail between Washington and Alexandria, Va., during the time the stamp was in use. He said that he

remembered it ; that it was an envelope with printing at one corner. And he
made a draft like this " (see cut at head of this chapter) " which he said was
the design. He did not remember if Col. Gardiner's signature was on it or
not. So far none have been located to my knowledge and the design above
is the only information I have received."

From the shape of the design it would appear a reasonable inference
that the name of the city and the value were placed between the curved lines
and the signature of the postmaster in the center.

ENVELOPES.

July, 1845.   5 cents ———— on ————
                    10 cents ———— on ————

WORCESTER, MASS.

Again we are confronted by the fact that stamps were prepared and sold by the postmaster of a city but that none, so far as we know, are now in existence.

Maturin L. Fisher, was postmaster at Worcester from 1839 to 1849.

Historical. Our information concerning the stamps is largely supplied by the following paragraph in the *National Aegis*, published in Worcester, September 2nd, 1846 :

POST OFFICE STAMPS.—The postmaster has issued postage stamps of the denomination of five and ten cents. They are very convenient, and will save the trouble of making change at the post office, and will enable people to send prepaid letters at times when the office is closed. To cover the expense of engraving and printing, these stamps are sold at five per cent. advance upon the regular rates of postage.

Postmaster Fisher and the clerks connected with the post office at that period, as well as most of the older inhabitants, are now dead. Though friends have, at my request, made personal efforts and enlisted the public press, they have been unable to obtain any further information.

Reference List.   ADHESIVE STAMPS.

1846.   5 cents ———
                  10 cents ———

MADISON, FLA.

The so-called Madison stamp has been catalogued as a provisional issue of the Confederate States. If it were a stamp at all, it would belong among the United States postmaster's stamps, since it was issued by a postmaster holding office under the government of the United States and not under the Confederacy. While I do not regard it as being anything more than a label, I deem it appropriate to refer briefly to it here.

The stamp (for convenience we will call it by that name) was first mentioned in the *American Journal of Philately* for March 1872. It is there illustrated, from the copy in the Philbrick collection, and described as Historical. type set, printed in gold bronze on blue wove foolscap paper, and having the value spelled "CNETS" instead of "CENTS." The article embodies the following letter from the former postmaster of Madison :

"SIR :—Your letter of May 20th has been received. I regret not having any stamp used by me while postmaster at Madison during the existence of the Confederacy. I can, however, give you, I think, a pretty correct idea of their appearance, as represented in the following figure, which is about the size and shape. Having a printing press at command, stamped the foregoing figure, and before the ink became dry, sprinkled yellow bronze on it, which gave the stars and border the appearance of gold. Ordinary foolscap paper was used. All the fractional currency in circulation disappeared about that time, and it was difficult to make change ; indeed almost impossible to conduct the post office, having no United States postage stamps, as my supply was exhausted soon after the assemblage of the Confederate Congress at Montgomery, Ala., and under whose authority I was instructed to conduct the offices, under the rules of the United States government, and pay over all moneys due to that Government, until I would be commissioned postmaster under the Confederate States, if I saw proper to accept it, which would happen soon ; and believing my allegiance due to the Confederacy, I was loth to apply for stamps to the United States, and determined to mail letters paid in money only. Therefore the stamps were issued by me for the purpose of making change, and sold in quantities to suit the business part of the community, so that any letter found in the letter-box with my stamp on it had evidence of having been paid for, and was accordingly stamped ' Paid in Money,' in accordance with the laws regulating the United States post offices, and charged in the way-bills as paid in money forwarded to the distributing offices, and every cent due to the United States was paid in money on account of the mails by me. The stamps were never credited beyond the reach of the post-offices at Madison, and was never intended but for the convenience of the immediate community No postmaster was silly enough to mail a letter because it had my stamp upon it. I, however, sometimes neglected to pull off the stamp before mailing them, and some of them went through without being removed, although they had plainly stamped on them ' Paid,' and so charged against me in the way-bills ; still considerable excitement was caused in the northern cities by their accidental appearance, although no word nor figure was upon the stamp, and after the words ' Paid in Money,' had no more meaning than if I had drawn the figure of a *Jackass* on one corner of the letter. Still the keen perceptions of James Gordon Bennett of the *New York Herald* found an immense and ingenious fraud practiced upon the Government by the postmaster at Madison, and called hastily for justice to be visited upon the moral deformity of the offending postmaster at Madison ; his exquisite sense of purity could not conceive how a sense of duty on the part of the officers of the distributing office could allow the offence of the postmaster at Madison to go unnoticed. He devoted nearly a column of the *Herald* to the subject, and I found myself suddenly famous through the *Herald's* cleverness in discovering villany. Shortly after the *Herald's* attention, an agent of the Government was sent especially to investigate the fraud ; but he was a sensible gentleman, and was immediately convinced that no wrong was intended, and so reported to his Government.

"I had, moreover, many applications from persons in New York, Boston and Philadelphia to purchase stamps; one was collecting the various stamps of the world, and was exceedingly desirous of adding my postal stamp to the list; others felt much curiosity in seeing the postal stamp of which so much had been said; would I not sell a few ?

"You may imagine how much I was astonished at the sudden interest in my stamps, when I never dreamed of their being known beyond the immediate neighborhood of my post office. These last, though, were never gratified, and they had to be content with the *Herald's* discoveries, I was continued, without further complaint, until commissioned by the Confederate States, when I made the proper returns and paid up all dues in money. If the foregoing is of service to you, I shall be pleased.

Very respectfully, &c.,

"S. J. PERRY."

"MR. J. W. SCOTT."

The article from the *Herald* is also reprinted, in conjunction with Mr. Perry's letter, and is a very mild affair to have so aroused his wrath. That article gave a sketch and description of the stamp and said it was "printed in gold on a white ground." The only point of interest to philatelists is the statement that the envelope which the writer had before him had been marked "Due 3" by the New York Post Office, showing that the stamp was not recognized by the postal authorities of that city.

Status of the Label. I think Mr. Perry's letter fully establishes the status of this label. It was not issued as a stamp and no effort was ever made to have it do duty as such. It is on a par with the cards issued by Postmaster Riddell of New Orleans, inscribed with various values and "Receivable in payment of postage, and redeemable at the New Orleans Post Office." In this connection we must not forget the numerous "tokens" marked "Good for one cent" etc., issued by business houses, at the time of the civil war, to supply the want of fractional currency.

Government Issues.

The development of the Post Office Department has been retarded by many causes, more especially in the early and middle parts of our comparatively brief national life. Among the causes may be mentioned : Excessive rates of postage, the competition of express and local delivery companies, abuse of the franking privilege, the fact that prepayment of postage was not compulsory, and the lack of adhesive stamps.

As was shown on page 6, the Act of Congress, approved March 3rd, 1845, greatly reduced the rates of postage and made them uniform throughout the country. Since that time, there have twice been advances in the rates, **Rates of postage.** once for letters to be transported for distances greater than 3,000 miles, and once for drop letters; but, on the whole, there has been a steady and consistent decrease in the postal charges. It should be remembered that the extremely low rates granted to newspapers, magazines and similar publications have, particularly in recent years, vastly increased both labor and expenditure in the Post Office Department. It is probable that this, more than any other cause, is responsible for this branch of the Government not being self-supporting. But these forms of literature have always been regarded as such great and valuable educators, that their encouragement has been held superior to any considerations of economy.

The competition of private carriers was for many years the occasion of great loss to the postal revenue. This competition decreased with the **Private competition.** introduction of lower rates of postage and, in 1861, its entire discontinuance was enforced through the courts.

The franking privilege, which has at times been granted recklessly and used to an excessive degree, is now much restricted, though it still imposes a **Franking.** great burden on the postal service.

The lack of a law compelling the prepayment of postage caused heavy losses to the department. A paragraph in the report of the Postmaster-General, dated December 2nd, 1848, gives us some useful information on this **Prepayment of postage.** subject as follows :

"Whether the suggestions for the modification of the Act of 1845 be adopted or not, all matter sent in the mails should be prepaid. This might indemnify the department for the great loss sustained for the transmission of letters not taken from the office. Nearly two millions of dead letters are annually returned to the department, upon which it not only loses the postage, but pays two cents each for advertising; and this is in addition to the expense incurred in opening and returning those of value to the writers, and destroying those of no value. Newspapers, periodicals, pamphlets, and essays of various kinds, probably not less in number than the dead letters, are sent to the offices and never called for, or if called for refused, and remain as dead matter in them. From a careful examination it has been ascertained that 52,000 annually are received and remain as dead matter in the office at New York; at Boston and Baltimore about 10,000 annually ; and at Philadelphia about 2,600."

A step in the right direction was made in the Act of Congress, approved March 3rd, 1851, by which the ordinary rate of postage was made three cents if prepaid and five cents if not prepaid, but it was not until 1855 that prepayment was made compulsory.

One of the great hindrances to the advancement of the postal service was the want of adhesive stamps. It was well-known that postage stamps **Status of Postmasters' stamps.** had been successfully introduced by the postmasters of New York and other cities. These stamps were appreciated by the public, but, at the same time, they were not regarded with the confidence which would have been evoked by a Government issue. They represented only an implied contract between the postmaster who issued them, and the public. There was a possibility of great abuse in such a condition of affairs. There was nothing to prevent every postmaster in the country making and selling his own stamps. Not only might the stamps be used as a source of individual revenue on the part of a postmaster but, in case of his death, default, or the succession of another to the office, they would probably be repudiated and a heavy loss be sustained by the holders. The necessity for governmental control of postage stamps was as evident as was the imperative demand of the public for their issue.

ISSUE OF 1847.

Although it would seem that the need of improvements in the postal service, especially the introduction of postage stamps, must have long been apparent to the most casual observer, it was not until 1847 that Congress took action to provide them.

The first issue of postage stamps by the Government was authorized by the Act, approved March 3rd, 1847, which provided as follows :

First stamps authorized.

And be it further enacted, that to facilitate the transportation of letters by mail, the Postmaster-General be authorized to prepare postage stamps, which, when attached to any letter or packet, shall be evidence of prepayment of the postage chargeable on such letter, which said stamps the Postmaster-General may deliver to any deputy postmaster who may apply for the same, the deputy postmaster paying or becoming accountable for the amount of the stamps so received by him, and if any of said stamps shall not be used, but be returned to the General Post Office, the amount so returned shall be credited to such deputy postmaster. And such deputy postmaster may sell or dispose of any stamps so received by him to any person who may wish to use the same, but it shall not be lawful for any deputy postmaster to prepare, use, or dispose of any postage stamps not authorized by and received from the Postmaster-General. And any person who shall falsely and fraudulently make, alter or forge any postage stamp with intent to defraud the Post Office Department, shall be deemed guilty of felony and, on conviction. shall be subject to the same punishment as provided in the 21st Section of the Act approved March 3rd, 1825, etc.

This Act was to take effect July 1st, 1847, from which date the use of the postmasters' stamps or any which were not authorized by the Postmaster-General became illegal. It will be observed that the Act made no provision for the compulsory prepayment of postage.

As provided by law, a contract was made by the Postmaster-General with Messrs. Rawdon, Wright, Hatch & Edson of New York, for engraving and printing the stamps for a period of four years.

Contractors.

In order that certain varieties, which will be described in the succeeding issues, may be better understood, it seems desirable to give here a brief description of the manufacture of plates for stamps.

Manufacture of stamp plates.

The first step is making the die. This is usually engraved on a piece of soft steel a little larger than the design. As a rule, only one design is engraved on such a block. But there are exceptions. The dies for the so-called government counterfeits of the 1847 issue are placed side by side on the same block. The die being engraved, it is hardened by heating it in a bath of cyanide of potassium and then dipping it in cold oil.

Die.

The next step is making the transfer roll. Its name indicates its purpose, to transfer the design from the die to the plate. This roll is of soft steel, in shape like a small grindstone. A stamp roll is usually about four

Transfer roll.

inches in diameter, with an edge broad enough to receive the design. The roll is placed in the carrier of a transfer press and forced against the die—which rests on the bed of the press—with a pressure of many tons, produced by compound leverage. With this tremendous pressure resting on it, the bed, carrying with it the die, is moved back and forth under the roll until the soft steel of the latter is forced into every line of the die, even the faintest scratch made by a diamond point. The lines of the die are, of course, reversed on the roll and those which were sunken in the former are in relief in the latter. A number of transfers are often made on the same roll and occasionally transfers of several different stamps. The roll is hardened in the same manner as the die.

Plate. The plate, duly ruled into spaces for the stamps, then takes the place of the die on the press and, by the same methods used to produce the roll, the latter is forced into the plate, reproducing in the minutest details the design on the die. This is repeated as many times as there are to be stamps on the plate. Guide lines, scratches, etc., are burnished out, the plate is hardened and is then ready for the printer.

Double transfers or shifts. In making the plate it sometimes happens that the transfer roll is set down upon it, slightly out of the intended position. The pressure on the roll forces into the soft plate those lines which are most in relief. When the incorrect position of the roll is noticed it is moved to the proper place, and the impression is then "rocked" into the plate. As a result of thus twice placing the design, some of the lines are duplicated. These are called double transfers, shifted transfers and shifts. I shall not attempt to list all the varieties which are known, but shall mention a few of the more prominent.

The stamps of this issue were engraved on steel by Rawdon, Wright, Hatch & Edson. This firm occupied the top floor of the building at the corner of William and Wall streets, New York, now the United States Custom House. The portraits were originally prepared for use on bank bills, stock certificates and other securities and were afterwards adopted for the stamps. The designs are thus officially described :

Designs. FIVE CENTS. Portrait of Franklin, after painting by John B. Longacre, three-quarters face, looking to the left, on an oval disk with dark ground, white neckerchief and fur collar to coat, the whole surrounded with a faintly engraved wreath of leaves, on which, in the two upper corners, are the letters "U" and "S", and in each of the two lower corners a large figure "5". In a curved line around the upper portion of the medallion are the words "POST OFFICE", and around the lower part the words "FIVE CENTS". A border of fine straight lines goes around the entire stamp. Color, light brown.

TEN CENTS. Portrait of Washington, from Stuart's painting, three-quarters face, looking to the right, on an oval disk with dark ground, white neckerchief and black coat, faint wreath of leaves around all, on which, in the upper corners, are the letters "U" and "S", and in each of the lower corners a large Roman numeral "X". In a curved line around the upper and lower parts of the medallion, as in the case of the 5 cent stamp, are the words "POST OFFICE" and "TEN CENTS". Color, black. A border of fine straight lines goes around the whole stamp.

The stamps measure 18½x23¼ mm.

There were one hundred stamps on each plate, arranged in ten rows of ten. Only one plate was made for each value and both were, so far as can be learned, without imprint or plate number.   **Plates.**

The paper varies much in color, the usual range is from gray to dull blue, but it is sometimes quite white. The genuineness of the white paper has been denied by some writers, but copies of the stamps exist with full   **Paper.** original gum and on paper which does not show the faintest trace of blue color, but is a distinctly yellowish white. The paper also varies in quality from thick and opaque to thin and transparent. Both values are known with a species of watermark, a band of short parallel lines, giving the appearance of closely laid paper. These lines are produced in the course of manufacturing the paper. They are caused by the stitches which join the ends of the cloth band on which the paper pulp is led from the vat. Copies also exist on laid paper. They are of a high degree of rarity and have only been seen in unused condition.

The gum is yellow or yellow white, usually thin and inclined to crackle. This gum was applied by hand by two apprentices of the con-   **Gum.** tractors, an apprentice engraver and an apprentice printer. Besides their regular duties these men were employed as watchmen. Three nights in each week they gummed the sheets of stamps (being paid for work overtime), and hung them up about the room to dry.

The following shades and varieties have been seen :   **Reference List.**

Imperforate.

Grayish Blue Wove Paper.

Aug. 5th, 1847.

5 cents pale brown, brown, dark brown, black-brown, purple-brown, olive-brown, red-brown, orange-brown, red-orange

10 cents full black, gray-black, greenish black

Yellowish White Wove Paper.

5 cents dark brown
10 cents full black

Grayish Pelure Paper.

5 cents dark brown
10 cents full black

Lilac-gray Laid Paper.

5 cents deep orange-brown
10 cents gray-black

Varieties :

5 cents brown. Horizontal half and another copy, used as 7½ cents

10 cents black. Vertical half used as 5 cents. Cancelled: "Bradford, Me., Sept. 19, 1849", "New Haven, Conn., June 13, 1851", etc.

10 cents black. Diagonal half used as 5 cents. Cancelled: "Augusta, Ga., Aug. 18, 1847", "Boston, Mass., Sept. 28, 1847", "New Haven, Conn., June 14, 1851", etc.

10 cents black. Double transfer, particularly noticeable in the double outlines of "POST OFFICE" and the letters "U" and "S" in the upper corners.

The finished sheets were forwarded to the Post Office Department at Washington, as was the custom until February, 1855. From February 18th, 1855, until May 18th, of that year, the experiment was tried of having the stamps sent by the contractors direct to the deputy postmasters who applied for them. The first Stamp Agent was Jessey Johnson. He was appointed May 18th, 1855. The office of the Stamp Agent was located with the contractors, at that date Toppan, Carpenter, Casilear & Co., in the Jayne Building, Chestnut Street, Philadelphia. Until 1869, the stamps were delivered to the Stamp Agent at the place of manufacture and by him forwarded to Washington for distribution. After February 1st, 1869, they were forwarded by the Stamp Agent, through the registry division of the New York Post Office, to the various postmasters on their orders, duly approved by the Post Office Department at Washington. Now that the stamps are manufactured by the Bureau of Engraving and Printing the routine is the same but the distributing point is, of course, Washington.

The Act approved March 3rd, 1847, was to take effect on July 1st of that year and it was expected that the stamps would be ready for use on that date. But owing to various delays on the part of contractors none of the stamps were available for sale until August 5th, 1847. In connection with this date we find an interesting anecdote in Tiffany's *History of the Postage Stamps of the United States*, reprinted from the *Hartford Times* of August 5th, 1885:

"Thirty-eight years ago to-day the first postage stamps were used in the United States. * * * On the 25th of March, 1840, John M. Niles of Hartford, became Postmaster-General and signalized his administration by many reforms. * * * It was necessary to cap all by a genuine innovation, and he performed this by suggesting the postage stamp. The suggestion was received with ridicule, and Mr. Niles soon after retired. * * * When Cave Johnson assumed the post office, on the 5th of March, 1845, he found it an Herculean task to re-instate the reform measures of Mr Niles. * * * Among the measures of Mr. Niles that he adopted was the postage stamp idea. * * * The matter took form as a bill. * * * Approved March 3rd, 1847. The date of the issue was appointed as July 1st, but there was a delay in the contractors' work and the time ran over a month.

On the 5th of August, soon after the opening of the Postmaster-General's office for the day, an old gentleman called to see Mr. Johnson on business. The gentleman was the Hon. Henry Shaw, a New Yorker, * * * and the father of the well-known Henry Shaw, Jr. (Josh Billings) * * * Mr. Johnson came into his office accompanied by the printer of the new stamps, a few minutes after Mr. Shaw had arrived, on that August morning. Sheets of the stamps were laid before the Postmaster-General, who, after receipting for them, handed them to his visitor to inspect. Mr. Shaw returned them after a hasty glance, and then drawing out his wallet, he counted out fifteen cents, with which he purchased two of the stamps—the first two ever issued. The five cent stamp he kept as a curiosity, and the ten cent stamp he presented to Governor Briggs, as an appropriate gift."

Methods of distributing stamps to Postmasters.

First stamps sold.

The following orders for stamps were sent to and executed by the contractors :

		5 Cents.	10 Cents.
June	3, 1847.	600,000	200,000
Mch.	15, 1848.	800,000	250,000
Mch.	20, 1849.	1,000,000	300,000
Feb.	5, 1850.	1,000,000	300,000
Dec.	9, 1850.	1,000,000	
	Total,	4,400,000	1,050,000

Of these quantities 3,712,000 five cent and 891,000 ten cent stamps were distributed to postmasters for sale. A small portion were returned to the Department after the appearance of the next issue.

It appears to have been the intention of the Government to prohibit any use of the stamps of the 1847 issue after July 1st, 1851, the date fixed for the issue of that year. In June, 1851, instructions were issued to deputy postmasters that the five and ten cent stamps then current must not be recognized as prepaying letters after the 30th of that month. The public were requested to return any of the stamps which they held and exchange them for the new issue. I have, however, seen a copy of the five cents used as late as January 4th, 1858. *Stamps declared invalid for postage.*

The report of the Postmaster-General, dated November 15th, 1851 (for the fiscal year ending June 30th, 1851), says : "Directions for the destruction of the dies and plates employed in the manufacture of the postage stamps formerly used, have been given, and for counting and burning such of the stamps as have not been issued to postmasters or have been returned." *Destruction of dies, plates and remainders.*

It has been said that the first contract for the manufacture of stamps did not provide, as was done in all subsequent contracts, that the dies and plates should be the property of the Government. Consequently they were claimed by the contractors. This may explain the anxiety of the Post Office Department to secure the return and destruction of the remainders of the 1847 issue and the forbidding of their future use. That this anxiety was groundless is proved by the following affidavit :

NEW YORK, Dec. 12, 1851.

Have this day destroyed dies of 5 and 10 cent stamps, also the plates of same.
1 5c stamp plate, 100 on, 1847 issue.
1 10c   "   "   100 "   "   "

RAWDON, WRIGHT, HATCH & EDSON.

Witness :
    WM. BRADY, P. M., N. Y.
    JOHN MOOR.
    G. W. JOHNSON.

The care taken to destroy the remainders of the 1847 issue doubtless accounts for the scarcity of the stamps in unused condition.

The report of the Postmaster-General, dated December 4th, 1852, says : "Stamps in the hands of postmasters, June 30th, 1851, being such as remained of the old issue, and which were charged to them on that day $8,849.61." *Stamps unsold.*

In the same report under the head of " Expenditures " we find :
 " For postage stamps redeemed,   . $3,809.35."
 " For postage stamps of old issue returned
         to the Department,   .   .   8,229.20."
Mr. Tiffany, in his *History of the Postage Stamps of the United States*, adds these two amounts together and claims a total of $12,038.55 of the 1847 issue were returned by the deputy postmasters. This is manifestly incorrect, both from the wording of the report, and because more stamps could not be returned than were outstanding. The stamps redeemed were probably of the 1851 issue.

In the report dated December 1st, 1853, are also given as items of expenditure :
     "Stamps returned, old issue,   .   . $68.05."
     "Stamps on hand, overcharged, old issue,   85.90."
Presumably the stamps represented by the last item should be deducted from the number reported as delivered to postmasters.

It will be seen from these figures that only a comparatively small number of stamps of the 1847 issue were not returned to the Department by the deputy postmasters. Many of these were probably used because of failure to receive promptly the stamps of the new issue, and some may have been used in succeeding years.

The Act of March 3rd, 1851, established postal rates of ten and twenty cents to foreign countries, but no ten cent stamps were issued until May, 1855. In spite of instructions to the contrary, we may assume that, during this period, the stamps of the 1847 issue were, when obtainable, used to pay the foreign rates.

Issue of 1851-55.

The report of the Postmaster-General, dated November 29th, 1851, says :

"A contract has been made for the supply of the postage stamps authorized by the act of March last. These stamps are believed to be of superior quality, and are furnished at a less price than was formerly paid. Some of those furnished soon after the execution of the contract were found to be deficient in adhesive qualities, but it is believed that there will be no ground for future complaint. * * *

Streets of cities made post routes.

The streets, avenues, roads and public highways of the cities of New York, Boston, Philadelphia, and New Orleans have been established as post routes under the 10th section of the postage act of March 3, 1851, and letter carriers appointed for the service thereon. If it is the intention of Congress to transfer the whole despatch business of the cities to the letter carriers of the department, further legislation for that purpose is desirable "

The Act referred to in the foregoing was approved March 3rd, 1851. It is entitled "An Act to reduce and modify the Rates of Postage in the United States" and provides as follows :

Act reducing rates of postage.

Special rate for prepaid letters.

"Be it enacted, etc., that from and after the 30th day of June, 1851, in lieu of the rates of postage now established by law, there shall be charged the following rates, viz : For every single letter in manuscript, or paper of any kind, upon which information shall be asked for or communicated, in writing, or by marks or signs, conveyed in the mail for any distance, between places in the United States, not exceeding 3,000 miles, when the postage upon said letter shall have been prepaid, three cents, and five cents when the postage thereon shall not have been prepaid; and for any distance exceeding 3,000 miles, double these rates ; for every such single letter or paper when conveyed wholly or in part by sea, and to or from a foreign country, for any distance over 2,500 miles, twenty cents, and for any distance under 2,500 miles, ten cents, excepting however, all cases where such postages have been or shall be adjusted at different rates by postal treaty or convention already concluded or hereafter to be made ; and for a double letter there shall be charged double the rates above specified ; and for a treble letter, treble these rates ; and for a quadruple letter. quadruple these rates ; and every letter or parcel not exceeding half an ounce in weight, shall be deemed a single letter. and every additional weight of half an ounce, or every additional weight of less than half an ounce, shall be charged with an additional single postage. And all drop letters or letters placed in any post office, not for transmission, but for delivery only, shall be charged with postage at the rate of one cent each, and all letters which shall hereafter be advertised as remaining over or uncalled for in any post office shall be charged with one cent in addition to the regular postage, to be accounted for as other postages now are."

The rates for circulars, handbills, pamphlets, engravings and newspapers (excepting those coming from the publishers, on which postage was not to be paid by stamps), were "one cent for each ounce or fraction thereof, for distances under 500 miles, and an additional rate for each additional 1,000 miles or fraction thereof."

The Act further specifies that the Postmaster-General shall provide "suitable postage stamps of the denomination of three cents, and such other denominations as he may think expedient to facilitate prepayment of postages provided for in this Act."

Stamps announced. An official circular, dated June 10th, 1851, announced and described the one, three and twelve cent stamps.

Date of Issue. The stamps were issued July 1st, 1851.

In September of that year the carriers' stamp with the head of Franklin was issued. It was replaced in the following November by the Eagle carriers' **Carriers' stamps.** stamp. These stamps will be referred to more fully in a chapter devoted to the carriers' stamps.

An Act, approved August 30th, 1852, provided as follows:

Reduction of rates for printed matter. "From and after September 30th, 1852, postage on all printed matter passing by mail, instead of the rates now charged, shall be as follows: Each newspaper, periodical, unsealed circular, or other article of printed matter, not exceeding three ounces in weight, to any part of the United States, one cent; and for every additional ounce or fraction thereof one cent additional."

By the Act approved March 30th, 1855, the Act of March 3rd, 1851, was amended as follows:

Rates increased. Be it enacted, etc. That in lieu of the rates of postage now established by law, there shall be charged the following rates to wit: For every single letter in manuscript, or paper of any kind in which information shall be asked or communicated in writing, or by marks or signs, conveyed in the mail, for any distance between places in the United States not exceeding 3,000 miles, three cents; and for any distance exceeding 3,000 miles, ten cents. And for a double letter, there shall be charged double the rates above specified; and for a treble letter, treble these rates; and for a quadruple letter, quadruple these rates; and every letter or paper not exceeding half an ounce in weight shall be deemed a single letter; and every additional weight of half an ounce or every additional weight of less than half an ounce, shall be charged with an additional single postage; and upon all letters passing through or in the mail of the United States, except such as are to or from a foreign country, the postage as above specified, shall be prepaid, except upon letters and papers addressed to officers of the Government on official business, which shall be so marked on the envelope. And from **Prepayment** and after the first day of January, 1856, the Postmaster-General may require postmasters to **required.** place postage stamps upon all prepaid letters, upon which such stamps may not have been placed by the writers. * * *

Registation. And be it further enacted: That for the greater security of valuable letters, posted for transmission in the mails of the United States, the Postmaster-General be, and hereby is authorized to establish a uniform plan for the registration of such letters on application of parties posting the same, and to require the prepayment of the postage, as well as a registration fee of five cents, on every such letter or packet, to be accounted for by postmasters receiving the same, in such manner as the Postmaster-General may direct; Provided, however, that such registration shall not be compulsory, and shall not render the Post Office Department or its revenues liable for the loss of such letter or package, or the contents thereof.

By this Act compulsory prepayment of postage on letters and a system of registration were for the first time provided.

An Act, approved January 2nd, 1857, extended the compulsory prepayment of postage to all transient printed matter, the postage to be "prepaid by stamps or otherwise, as the Postmaster-General may direct."

Designs and colors. The official description of the designs and colors is as follows:

ONE CENT. Profile bust of Franklin, looking to the right, on an oval disk with dark ground, the words "U. S. POSTAGE" in outline capitals on a curved panel above, and the words "ONE CENT" in similar letters on a curved panel below. On the corners, and partly surrounding the two panels, are convolute scroll-work ornaments, nearly meeting in points on the sides. Color, indigo blue.

THREE CENTS. Profile bust of Washington, after Houdon, facing to the left, on an oval disk with very dark ground and a white line border. Around this oval is a beautifully tessellated frame, terminating in each of the four corners with a fine lathe-work rosette.   At the top of the stamp is a straight panel, with a piece at each end cut off, bearing the words " U. S. POSTAGE " in white capitals ; at the bottom of the stamp, in a similar panel and with similar letters, are inscribed the words " THREE CENTS."   A fine line encloses the stamp, forming a rectangle.   Color, brick-red.

FIVE CENTS.   Portrait of Jefferson, after a painting by Stuart, three-quarters face, looking to the right, on an oval disk with dark ground and a distinct white border, on the upper and lower portions of which are four irregular, shaded segmental spaces.   Around the whole is a four-sided oblong frame, with rounded corners terminating in slight incissions, the whole filled in with two rows of geometric lathe-work, and bearing in a waved line at the top the words " U. S. POSTAGE " in white capitals, and at the bottom the words " FIVE CENTS ", similarly displayed.   Color, brown.

TEN CENTS.   Portrait of Washington, after the painting by Stuart, three-quarters face, looking to the left, on an oval disk with very dark ground, and a border which is white below and slightly shaded above.   Around the upper portion of the medallion, on a dark ground, are thirteen white stars, above which again in a white panel are the words, in small solid capitals, " U. S. POSTAGE," connecting two circular spaces on the corners, each containing the Roman numeral " X."   Below the medallion, in a waved panel, are the words " TEN CENTS " in large white capitals.   The whole is surrounded with shaded scroll-work of a highly ornate character.   Color, dark green.

TWELVE CENTS.   Portrait of Washington, after the painting by Stuart, three-quarters face, looking to the left, on an oval disk with dark ground and a fine shaded line border.   Above the medallion and conforming to its curve, on a light background, are the words " U. S. POSTAGE " in white shaded capitals, and below the medallion, similarly inscribed and displayed, are the words " TWELVE CENTS ".   Around the whole, and enclosed in a fine double-lined rectangle, is a beautifully tessellated frame, separated at each of the four corners by a lathe-work rosette.   Color, black."

The stamps of this issue vary slightly in size.   The dimensions are : 1 cent, 20x26mm.; 3 cents, 20x25mm.; 5 cents, 19½x25½mm.; 10 cents, 19x24¼mm.; 12 cents, 20x25mm.   *Sizes.*

There are several types of the one and ten cent stamps.   The three and five cents have each only one type in this issue, but in the perforated issue of 1857 they present other varieties.   It seems best to describe the various types under the issue in which they make their initial appearance.   *Types.*

TYPE I.

TYPE II.

ONE CENT.   Type I.   This is the full and complete form of the stamp as it appears on the die.   In this form there is a curved line outside and

Types of the one
cent stamp. parallel to the labels containing the words "U. S. POSTAGE" and "ONE CENT."
Between the upper label and the curved outer line is a row of minute colored
dots. These are not found between the lower label and the outer line.
Below the lower label and line is a scroll, turned to the right and left, having
the ends carried under and rolled up until they form little balls. In the
center the scroll is only a line, forming, with the outer line, a double curve.
There are graceful arabesques at each corner, spreading along the sides and,
to a less degree, along the top and bottom. The distinguishing marks of
this variety, the rolled up ends of the scroll, may be seen to better advantage
on the reprints and proofs than on the stamps themselves.

Type II. Is much the same as type I but the balls forming the ends
of the scrolls and frequently the extreme tips of the arabesques have been
cut away.

Type III. This is the so-called "broken circle." In this the center
of the curved lines is missing and the scrolls and corner ornaments are less
perfect. This variety may occur at the top or bottom of the stamp or in
both places.

Type IV. This is type III with the broken lines recut. This variety
also may be found at either the top or bottom of the stamp or both. It
closely resembles type II yet may easily be distinguished from it. The
curved lines outside the labels are deeper and harder than the other lines of
the stamp. The recutting often begins and ends abruptly, not joining smoothly
the original line. The central part of the row of minute dots between the
upper label and the curved line has disappeared. The recutting is usually
confined to the outer lines but it can occasionally be seen in other parts of the
stamp, especially the top of the upper label.

Of these four varieties only two are properly called types. The other
two are really sub-varieties, but their frequent occurrence, especially in the
perforated issue of these stamps, seems to demand for them recognition as
types. Types I and II come from two different transfer rolls (Nos. 46 and
47), though both are from the same original die. On the second roll the
ball-like ornaments were cut away. Type III is caused by not "rocking"
the transfer roll sufficiently far. Proof of this is found in a stamp which
combines types I and II, showing the broken circle at the top and full
ornaments at the bottom. Type IV is an attempt to remedy the defects of
type III. The last two are, therefore, plate varieties and sub-varieties of
type II. In the 1857 issue, however, the third variety must be accepted as a
type, as there is abundant evidence to show that, in that issue, it is not due to
defective workmanship but is made from a transfer roll from which the
ornaments and lines have been completely cut away.

In the 1851 issue type IV is the commonest variety, type II is nearly
as frequently met, type III is quite scarce and type I decidedly so, especially
in unused condition. In the 1857 issue type III is the common variety,
while types II, IV and I are much scarcer, in the relative order here given.

THREE CENTS. Type I. There is a thin, straight line of color on each
Types of the three
cent stamp. of the four sides of the stamp. In preparing the earlier plates of this value
the surface of each plate was laid off in little upright rectangles. These were

not formed by continuous horizontal and vertical lines ruled across the plate but each stamp was provided with its rectangular frame, separated by a space of ½ to 1½mm. from the adjacent frames. Into each of these rectangles the design was transferred.   There were similar frame lines on the die and it will be readily understood that they would frequently fail to fall exactly on the lines ruled on the plate, thus causing some portion of them to appear double. Very exhaustive lists of these varieties have been published, but, when we remember that there were twenty-eight plates of this value, each containing two hundred stamps, the hopelessness of finding or correctly placing all the varieties is at once apparent, to say nothing of the lack of interest or value in such a restoration.

FIVE CENTS. Type I. On examining the stamps we observe that, surrounding the central medallion, there is an irregularly shaped mat of colorless lathe-work. The outer line of this lathe-work is formed of a series of loops. Outside these loops are two thin lines of color, separated by a thin colorless line, all following the outline of the lathe-work and forming slight projections in the middle of each of the four sides. This is the form of the original die and of the stamps on the first plate for this value. The complete projections on the four sides are the distinguishing feature of type I. *Types of the five cent stamp.*

TEN CENTS. There is a line of color above and following the outlines of the label inscribed " U. S. POSTAGE " and a similar line below the label with the words " TEN CENTS ". The upper line is curved, like the label, and is usually very faint. The lower one is wavy and follows the double curve of the label. *Types of the ten cent stamp.*

Type I.   Both the lines are complete.

Type II. One or both of the lines are broken in the center. As in the case of the one cent stamp, this is due to insufficient rocking of the transfer roll.

Type III. One or both of the lines have been recut.

Type IV. The outer lines are as in type I, but the arabesque ornaments at the sides have been slightly cut away.

Type V. The same as type II, with the side ornaments cut away.

Type VI. The same as type III, with the side ornaments cut away.

Type II is the variety commonly found. Types I and III are much scarcer. Types IV, V and VI are also quite scarce in the imperforate issue. The plates from which the stamps of the last three types were printed were doubtless prepared with a view to facilitating perforation but some sheets were issued imperforate.

The paper used for this issue was of fine quality, hard and crisp. At first it was quite thick and opaque but, previous to the appearance of the perforated stamps, it became thinner and slightly transparent. It is often stained yellow or brownish by the gum. The one and three cent stamps have been seen on paper watermarked with a band of lines, as described in the 1847 issue. The three cent stamp has also been chronicled on ruled writing paper, but careful examination proved that the ruled lines were merely an offset from the paper to which the stamp had been affixed. *Paper.*

The gum was thick and smooth, varying from almost white to a dark brownish yellow.

Hard White Wove Paper.

Imperforate.

July 1st, 1851.　　1 cent (type I) pale blue, blue, dark blue

1 cent (type II) pale blue, blue, dark blue, pale dull blue, dark dull blue, slate-blue, sky blue, black-blue

1 cent (type III) pale blue, blue, dark blue, bright blue, dark dull blue

1 cent (type IV) pale blue, blue, dark blue, pale dull blue, dark dull blue, sky blue, greenish-blue, bright blue, gray-blue, black-blue, very dark ultramarine

July 1st, 1851.　　3 cents (type I) red, pale orange-red, dark orange-red, brown-red, pale rose-red, rose-red, dark rose-red, lilac-rose, lake, rosy lake, Indian red

January 5th, 1856.　5 cents (type I) brown, red-brown, dark red-brown, carmine brown

May 4th, 1855.　　10 cents (type I) yellow-green, dark green

10 cents (type II) yellow-green, dark green, blue-green

10 cents (type III) yellow-green, dark green, blue-green

10 cents (type IV) yellow-green

10 cents (type V) yellow-green, dark green

July 1st, 1851.　　12 cents gray-black, black, deep smudgy black

Varieties :

1 cent blue.　Numerous double transfers, the most notable of which shows the outlines of "ONE CENT" repeated across the face of the letters

3 cents rose.　Double transfers, the most distinct being that which shows a horizontal line through the words "THREE CENTS"

3 cents.　Diagonal half used as 1 cent.　Cancelled: "San Francisco, Cal., May 30, 1853", and "May 31st, 1853".　Used on circulars

12 cents black.　Diagonal half used as 6 cents.　Cancelled: "San Francisco, Cal., Sept. 9, —— ", "Sonora, Cal., Feb. 13, 1852 ", etc.

12 cents black.　One and diagonal half of another copy used as 18 cents.　Cancelled: "Sacramento, Cal., Apl., 5, —— "

12 cents black.　Impression on the back

　　　It is interesting to note that the majority of the bisected stamps of this issue are on letters from California, indicating a shortage of the lower values in that, at that date, remote section of the country.　Many of the covers bearing these split stamps are hand-stamped " Via Nicaragua.　Ahead of the mails ".　At that time the mails between the Atlantic and Pacific coasts were carried by a steamship company via the isthmus of Panama. A rival company, operating by the Nicaragua route, sought the contract for transporting the mails, basing their claim, in part, upon their quicker service. The hand-stamp was applied in furtherance of this claim.

Halves of the ten cent stamp, supposed to have done duty as five cents, have long been known and accepted by collectors. At the time this work appeared in serial form such a divided stamp was listed among the varieties of this issue. After an extremely careful examination of that particular copy and a number of others, I have reached the conclusion that all the bisected ten cent stamps of the 1851-55 issue which I have seen are fraudulent. Reference to the postal laws of the period shows that the only purpose of a five cent stamp was to pay the registration fee. It is, of course, not impossible that a letter might have been mailed with that fee prepaid and the regular postage unpaid, but it is, highly improbable. From and after January 1st, 1856, all postage was required to be prepaid in stamps. I have never seen a bisected ten cent stamp that was not cancelled later than that date. Until very strong evidence in its favor is forthcoming, I shall doubt the genuineness of any split ten cent stamp of this issue. *Bisected ten cent stamp.*

The most dangerous examples of this would-be variety were made in San Francisco, a number of years ago, by a man who had, in some way, secured a discarded cancelling stamp of the post office of that city. I have seen a number of the counterfeit provisionals made by him. All were on pieces of buff laid paper, apparently portions of government envelopes of the 1864 issue, the higher values of which were extensively used by the express companies of the Pacific coast, and all were cancelled "Dec. 22, 1858".

The design for a stamp of the value of twenty-four cents was approved on April 24th, 1856. Following this approval the plate was made and the stamps printed and gummed. We can, however, find no record that they were issued until June, 1860, when they appeared perforated. But imperforate specimens in pairs and blocks are well-known and the existence of nearly an entire sheet in this condition is reported on excellent authority. I have seen two imperforate copies used on the original envelopes. *Imperforate twenty-four cent stamp.*

The imperforate thirty and ninety cent stamps of this series have been much discussed. One thing, at least, cannot be denied, that is that they exist genuinely imperforate, not trimmed, since they are in pairs and strips. They are on the same paper as the perforated copies and have the same gum. A well-known philatelist makes this statement : "I, myself, bought a thirty cent orange, imperforate, at the New York post office in 1860. And I distinctly remember having used one on a letter containing some photographs." *Imperforate thirty and ninety cent stamps.*

The most important evidence in favor of this stamp is furnished by a copy which was purchased by Messrs. Morgenthau & Co. in the summer of 1899. This copy is on a letter sent from New York to Lyons, France. The cancellation covers a large portion of the stamp and is dated October 2nd, 1860. The stamp has fine margins on three sides and shows a portion of the adjoining stamp at the left. It is printed in the peculiar brown-orange shade in which the imperforate copies are always found. It establishes, beyond doubt, the use of the thirty cent stamp in imperforate condition.

There was a cancelled copy of the imperforate ninety cents in the Hunter collection. Beyond question or contradiction, these three values, twenty-four, thirty and ninety cents, exist imperforate. It is, however, my opinion, that they do not constitute a part of the 1851-55 series but are varieties of the 1857-60 series which have escaped perforating. I shall place them under that heading.

Plates. The plates for the 1851-55 issues each consisted of two panes of one hundred stamps, arranged in ten rows of ten. The panes were placed side by side and separated by a single vertical line. This line marked the place at which the printed sheets were to be cut apart, to make the smaller sheets sold in the post offices. This practice is still continued, the panes being cut apart instead of perforated. This accounts for the imperforate edges found on one or two sides of each sheet of stamps.

Imprints. The imprint of the engravers appears at the middle of each side of the plate, the tops of the letters being toward the stamps. On the earlier plates of the one, three and twelve cents the inscription reads : " Toppan, Carpenter, Casilear & Co., BANK NOTE ENGRAVERS, Phil., New York, Boston & Cincinnati." Below " Note " and " Engravers " the plate number appears thus : " No. 1 P." On a few plates the "P" is omitted.

In 1855 the name "Casilear" was dropped from the imprint. The exact date cannot be given, but the name appears in order No. 95 of the Post Office Department and is missing from No. 96, which is dated July 6th, 1855.

The later plates of the one, three and twelve cents and all plates of the five and ten cents, with the possible exception of plate 1 of the latter value, have the imprint " Toppan, Carpenter & Co.," etc., etc., in the same style and arrangement as on the earlier plates.

Plate numbers. From lack of records and the fact that the same plates were used for both the imperforate and the perforated stamps only an incomplete list of the plate numbers can be given. Those given in the following list are known to exist imperforate. Beyond doubt there were other plates of the one cent stamps in this condition and possibly also of the three, ten and twelve cent values. The various types of the one and ten cent stamps appear to have been used or produced on the various plates quite at the fancy of the workman and without any system. It is, therefore, impossible to assign to them any special plate numbers.

1c blue	No. 1.
3c red (type I)	No. 1, 2, 3, 4, 5, 6.
5c brown (type I)	No. 1.
10c green	No. 1.
12c black	No. 1.

The plates of the one cent stamps of this and the succeeding issue were numbered consecutively from 1 to 12 and probably at least half of them were used for the imperforate stamps. No. 8 is the lowest number known perforated. Likewise the plates of the three cent stamps were numbered from 1 to 28 and number 10 is the lowest perforated number so far found. A plate of the twelve cents, which I suspect to be No. 2, exists both imperforate and perforated.

The name "Casilear" appears on the plates of the two issues, as follows :

1 cent, on No. 1,	not on No. 9 to 12.
3 " " " 1, 2, 3, 4,	" " " 10 to 28.
5 "	" " " 1, 2.
10 "	" " " 2, 3.
12 " " " 1,	" " " 3.
24 "	" " " 1.
30 "	" " " 1.
90 "	" " " 1.

It has not been possible to obtain lists of the stamps supplied by Toppan, Carpenter, Casilear & Co., and Toppan, Carpenter & Co. in each fiscal year for which they held the contract, and the reports of the quantities delivered by the Post Office Department to the deputy postmasters are quite incomplete. The records of the contractors were destroyed on March 4th, 1872, at the burning of the Jayne building in Philadelphia. Such information as is obtainable is here presented.

First delivery.

The first stamps of this issue were delivered by the contractors on June 21st, 1851, and consisted of 100,000 one cent, 300,000 three cents, and 100,000 twelve cents.

Through the valued assistance of an influential friend the following report has been obtained from the Post Office Department :

"Stamps received from Toppan, Carpenter, Casilear & Co., June 21, 1851 to July 6, 1855 :

Statistics of manufacture.

Fiscal year ending	12 cent.	10 cent.	3 cent.	1 cent.	Value.
June 30, 1851	200,000	......	1,710,000	400,000	$ 79,300.00
June 30, 1852	480,000	......	49,410,000	6,860,000	1,608,500.00
June 30, 1853	......	......	51 210,000	4,450,000	1,580,800.00
June 30, 1854	60,000	......	47,820,000	8,450,000	1,526,300.00
June 30, 1855	......	......	20,220,000	3,900,000	645,600.00
July 6, 1855	120,800	747,000	15,001,800	2,767,700	566,927.00
Total,	868,800	747,000	185,371,800	26,827,700	$6,007,427.00

Ten cent stamps appear to have been issued to postmasters on May 4th, 1855, though no invoice is noted from Toppan, Carpenter, Casilear & Co., to include them, until July 6th, 1855. They should doubtless be considered as having been received prior to June 30th, the end of the fiscal year."

The report of the Postmaster General, dated December 1st, 1853, supplies the following :

"Number of stamps issued to postmasters for sale in the fiscal years ending June 30th, 1852 and June 30th, 1853 :

Deliveries to postmasters.

	1 cent.	3 cent.	12 cent.	Amount.
1852	5,489,242	48,410,035	237,042	$1,535,638.51
1853	4,736,311	51,461,040	146,655	1,608,792.91
Total,	10,225,553	99,871,075	383,697	$3,144,431.42

Stamps sold by postmasters, year ending June 30th, 1852, . $1,316,563.59
    "   "   "   "   "   "   June 30th, 1853,   1,629,262.12
Leaving in hands of postmasters,   .   .   198,605.71"

From 1853 to 1859 the reports of the Postmaster General do not unfortunately, supply statistics of the quantities of stamps delivered to postmasters or of those sold to the public.

The different values of this issue were intended, primarily, for the payment of certain specific rates, though any value might be used in making up a rate. The one cent stamps were to pay the postage on newspapers and drop-letters. The three cent stamp represented the rate on ordinary letters and two of them made up the rate for distances over 3,000 miles. The five cent stamps were for the registration fee and two of them were frequently used to pay the rate over 3,000 miles, after it was changed in March, 1855. Ten cents was the rate to California and other points distant more than 3,000 miles. The twelve cent stamps were for quadruple the ordinary rate. The twenty-four cent stamp represented the single rate on letters to Great Britain. Thirty cents was the corresponding rate to Germany. The ninety cent stamp was apparently intended merely to facilitate the payment of large amounts of postage.

Purpose of the
various values.

ISSUE OF 1857-60.

The stamps of this issue differ from those of the 1851-55 issue only in that they are perforated. This change, being merely a detail of manufacture, was effected without legislation. There are, therefore, no official documents to reproduce. But the following bit of inside history may be somewhat interesting. It is extracted from a letter addressed to the Commissioner of Internal Revenue on the subject of plates for revenue stamps :

"Having been requested by Messrs. Butler & Carpenter to state such facts as might be within my knowledge in reference to a fair price to be charged for engraving stamp plates, I beg leave to say that, as the business partner of my firm (Toppan, Carpenter & Co.,) I negotiated all the contracts in reference to Postage Stamps which were made with the Government from 1851 to 1861 (10 years) and, therefore, I have personal knowledge of what I shall state. *(Letter concerning perforating and new plates.)*

In 1857 the Postmaster General determined to introduce the perforation of Postage Stamps. In order to do this it became necessary for us to make 3 new plates of 1 cent, 6 plates of 3c, 1 plate of 5c, 1 plate of 10c, 1 plate of 12c and 1 plate of 24c, in all, 13 plates, besides a large outlay to procure the necessary machinery for perforating the stamps, and, in view of the fact that our first contract with the Government would expire in about 4 months from that time and might not be renewed, we felt it to be necessary to protect ourselves against loss by asking that, in case the contract for furnishing Postage Stamps should not be renewed with us at the end of our term, that in that case the Government should indemnify us from loss by paying us $500 for the engraving of each of the 13 plates, or $6,500 for the whole of the plates, and a further sum of $3,000 for the perforating machine with the necessary machinery. This was promptly agreed to by the Postmaster General and a contract to that effect was made and executed on the 6 Feb. 1857. The plates and perforating machinery were, of course, to become the property of the Government, in the contingency of our losing the contract and the Government paying for the plates and machinery.

I have given the above facts not only from my own recollection of them but from the contract with the P. O. Department, which is before me."

(Signed) S. H. CARPENTER,

PHILADELPHIA, April 2nd, 1863.   of the late firm of Toppan, Carpenter & Co.

The first stamps were perforated and delivered to the Government on February 24th, 1857. *(First delivery.)*

The designs are the same as in the 1851-55 issue with the addition of three new values which are thus officially described :

"TWENTY-FOUR CENTS. Portrait of Washington, after the painting by Stuart, three-quarters face, looking to the right, on an oval disk with very dark ground, surrounded by a solid curved border, bearing above the words *(Designs and colors.)* "U. S. POSTAGE" and below the words "TWENTY FOUR CENTS" in white capitals, the two inscriptions being separated on each side by a small triple rectangle. Around the whole of this is a mass of badly mixed lathe-work, forming a frame of irregular oblong form, with rounded corners and curved incisions, all enclosed by a fine outer line. Color, very dark lilac.

THIRTY CENTS. Profile bust of Franklin, looking to the left, on an oval disk with a very dark ground, and with a slightly shaded border. In an irregular panel at the top are the words " U. S. POSTAGE ", in two lines of white capitals ; at the bottom in a panel, are the Arabic numerals " 30 "; on the two sides are the words "THIRTY" and "CENTS" respectively, in white capitals ; at each of the four corners is a shield, placed obliquely, with fine radiations, and connected with ornate shaded scrolls. The two sides and the top of the stamp are enclosed by a fine double line, ending in six spear points. Color, orange.

NINETY CENTS. Portrait of Washington, in generals' uniform, after the painting by Trumbull, three-quarters face, on a very dark oblong ground with arched top. In a solid panel, conforming to the curve of this arch, are the words " U. S. POSTAGE " in white capitals, while at the bottom of the portrait, in a straight panel, with rounded ends, are the words "NINETY CENTS" Connecting these two panels, and forming an oblong frame for the portrait, are scroll-work ornaments, resting on a sort of pedestal. Color, deep indigo blue."

Sizes. The sizes of these stamps were : Twenty-four cents, 19¼x25mm.; thirty cents, 20x25mm.; ninety cents, 19x24½mm.

The types are the same as in the preceding issue, with the addition of a few caused by alterations to admit of perforating. These additional varieties are :

Types of the three cent stamp. THREE CENTS. Type II. The horizontal frame lines at top and bottom have been removed from both the transfer roll and the plate. On many specimens the side lines appear to be closer to the body of the design than on the imperforate stamps.

Type I is known as the variety "with outer lines" and type II as the variety "without outer lines." This, of course, refers only to the lines at the top and bottom of the stamps.

Types of the five cent stamp. FIVE CENTS. Type II. The outer line of color on the projecting ornaments at top and bottom has been cut away. This is usually spoken of as "ornaments partly removed."

Type III. The cutting has been carried still further and both the outer and inner lines and part of the colorless loops have been cut away. This variety is called "ornaments entirely removed."

These types are from two different transfer rolls, though both occur on the same plate. They are arranged in horizontal rows, the first, third, sixth and tenth rows being of type II and the balance of the plate of type III.

Types of the ten cent stamp. TEN CENTS. Type VI of this stamp has not been noted in the per- forated state, though it may exist. Types IV and V are those commonly found, while types I, II and III are much scarcer.

Paper. The paper used for this issue was thin, hard and brittle, much of it semi-transparent, white but usually tinted by the gum and often colored on the surface from poorly wiped plates. I have recently seen copies of the three cents (type II), on paper which showed faint laid lines. This appears to be much the same paper as was used for some values of the 1861-66 issue.

The gum was thin and smooth and varied in color from yellow-white to almost brown.

White Wove Paper.

Perforated 15, 15½.

Feb. ——, 1857. 1 cent (type I) pale blue, blue, dark blue, bright blue, dull blue

1 cent (type II) pale blue, blue, dark blue, dull blue, bright blue

1 cent (type III) pale blue, blue, dark blue, dull blue, gray-blue, dark ultramarine

1 cent (type IV) blue, dark blue, gray-blue

Feb. 24th, 1857. 3 cents (type I) pale rose-red, rose-red, rosy-lake, lake, dull red, Indian red

3 cents (type II) pale rose-red, rose-red, rosy lake, lake, orange-red, red, brown-red

Feb. ——, 1857. 5 cents (type I) brick red, rose-brown, pale red-brown, red-brown, dark red-brown, carmine-brown, brown, gray-brown

5 cents (type II) brown, dark brown, gray-brown, orange-brown

5 cents (type III) brown, dark brown, gray-brown, bistre-brown, orange-brown

Feb. ——, 1857. 10 cents (type I) dark green

10 cents (type II) yellow-green, dark green, bright blue-green, blue-green, gray-green

10 cents (type III) yellow-green, dark green

10 cents (type IV) yellow-green, dark green, blue-green, dark blue-green, gray-green

10 cents (type V) yellow-green, dark yellow-green, dark green, bright blue-green, blue-green, gray-green

Feb. ——, 1857. 12 cents gray-black, greenish black, full black, deep smudgy black

June 15th, 1860. 24 cents bright lilac, lilac, gray-lilac, gray, slate, blackish violet, dull reddish lilac

Aug. 12th, 1860. 30 cents yellow-orange, orange, red-orange

Aug. 13th, 1860. 90 cents indigo, dark indigo

Varieties :

1 cent blue, dark blue. Double transfers. The most pronounced shows the shadings of " ONE CENT " repeated like links below the panel

3 cents (type I) rose-red. Double transfers, notably that with the horizontal line through " THREE CENTS "

3 cents (type I) rose. Vertical pair, imperforate horizontally

3 cents (type I) rose. Horizontal pair, imperforate vertically

24 cents gray-lilac.   Imperforate
30 cents brown-orange.   Imperforate
90 cents indigo.   Imperforate

White Laid Paper.

Perforated 15, 15½.

3 cents (type II) dull rose-red

It may be well to say here that no imperforate or part-perforate varieties of stamps which are normally perforate, will be listed in this work, except **Imperforate and part-perforate stamps.** such as are known in pairs or blocks. Owing to defects in manufacture, stamps are frequently found which have such widely spaced perforations as to allow trimming by those who enjoy producing such fraudulent novelties. For this reason it seems best to refuse recognition to all varieties except such as are entirely beyond suspicion.

The three cents of this and the preceding issue is frequently found in shades of brown and almost black. The thirty cents is also known in brown. **Shades and change-lings.** These shades are merely the result of chemical changes, natural or artificial. The same discolorations occur in similar shades in other issues. They are largely due to what is commonly called "oxidization." "Sulphuretting" would more correctly express the change. Stamps printed in mineral inks are particularly subject to such darkening of their colors, especially those in red and orange shades.

The greenish shades of the twenty-four cents in this and the succeeding issue are due to the action of acids or strong sunlight. I am not certain that the twenty-four cents in dull reddish-lilac was ever issued as a stamp. I have seen copies, both imperforate and perforated, in old collections of proofs and essays and I am inclined to think it belongs in that category rather than among stamps. I have, however, no positive evidence to confirm this belief.

In addition to the above stamps and varieties the thirty cents is known printed in black. It is imperforate and on the regular paper. This has **The black thirty cent stamp.** usually been regarded as a proof. But Mr. Francis C. Foster states that, at the time he obtained his copy, he was told that it was a stamp and had been in use, and that shortly afterwards he made inquiry at the Washington post office and was informed that it was actually on sale at that office for a few days but, because the cancellation did not show up well, the color was changed. However, it must be remembered that the twenty-four cents also exists in black, identical with this thirty cents in shade and paper. And copies of the five, twenty-four and ninety cents are known in various colors, imperforate and printed on the regular paper. It has never been claimed that these latter varieties are anything but proofs in trial colors.

Many of the plates of the 1851-55 issue were also employed for printing the stamps of the 1857-60 issue. The new plates are of the same dimensions as **Plates and Imprints.** those of the preceding issue and have the imprint in the same position. The imprint is, with a few exceptions, of the second variety. The known exceptions are plates of the one, twelve, thirty and ninety cents, on which the imprint is "TOPPAN, CARPENTER & CO., PHILADELPHIA", in small white-faced capitals, on a tablet of solid color with square ends. There is a thin colored line parallel to the top and sides of the tablet but none at the bottom. Below this there is, on the one cent "No. 12. P.", on the three cents the numeral "3" only, and on the thirty and ninety cents "No. 1 P."

The following plate numbers are known to have been used for the perforated stamps :

Plate numbers.

1c blue		No. 8, 9, 10, 11, 12.
3c red	(type I)	No.
3c red	(type II)	No. 10, 11, 12, 13, 14, 15, 16, 17, 18, 19, 20, 21, 22, 23, 24, 25, 26, 27, 28.
5c brown	(type I)	No. 1.
5c "	(type II)	No. 2.
5c "	(type III)	No. 2.
10c green		No. 2, 3.
12c black		No. 3.
24c lilac		No. 1.
30c orange		No. 1.
90c indigo		No. 1.

On comparing this list with that of the plates of the 1851 issue it will be seen that plates 7, 8 and 9 of the three cents and plate 2 of the twelve cents are not listed. They exist, but it has been impossible to secure information which would correctly locate them. Neither has it been possible to learn which plates of the three cents of type I were used for the perforated issue. It is probable that the name "Casilear" did not appear on any plates used for the perforated stamps, with the possible exception of the three cents of type I.

The statistics of this issue are, unfortunately, very incomplete. The following extracts, taken from the annual reports of the Postmaster General, are all that can be supplied at present :

"Number of postage stamps issued to postmasters during the fiscal years ending as follows :

Deliveries to postmasters.

Year ending June 30th, 1859 :

1 cent.	3 cent.	5 cent.	10 cent.	12 cent.
44,432,300	142,087,800	486,560	3,765,560	1,429,700

Whole number 192,201,920.   Value $5,279,405.00.

Year ending June 30th, 1860 :

1 cent.	3 cent.	5 cent.	10 cent.	12 cent.	24 cent.
50,723,400	159,463,600	579,360	3,898,450	1,653,500	52,350

Whole number 216,370,660.   Value $5,920,939.00."

"Larger denominations of postage stamps have been adopted and introduced, especially for the purpose of affording requisite facilities to prepay the postage on letters to foreign countries, and of removing all excuses heretofore existing of paying such postages in money. The new denominations are twenty-four cents, thirty cents and ninety cents. The two latter have been introduced since July 1st last, and the sales up to November 1st have been as follows :

Thirty cent stamps,   .   140,860 ; amounting to $42,258.00
Ninety cent stamps,   .   15,840 ;   "   "   14,256.00

Previously to July 1st there were issued of the

Twenty-four cent stamps,   .   52,350 ; amounting to $12,564.00
From July 1st to Nov. 1st,   .   287,975 ;   "   "   69,114.00

Total issues of new denominations,   497,025 ; amounting to $138,192.00

Year ending June 30th, 1861 :

Quarter ending	1 cent.	3 cent.	5 cent.	10 cent.
Sept. 30, 1860	12,756,100	36,512,700	146,920	922,150
Dec. 31, 1860	14,778,085	39,171,800	178,640	1,154,910
March 31, 1861	14,174,768	41,922,956	223,000	852,900
June 30, 1861	12,184,839	33,615,600	128,640	995,730
	53,893,762	151,223,036	677,200	3,925,690
	12 cent.	24 cent.	30 cent.	90 cent.
Sept. 30, 1860	384,800	170,000	103,860	11,960
Dec. 31, 1860	243,825	201,150	105,960	6,200
March 31, 1861	232,400	147,325	65,040	4,110
June 30, 1861	192,875	132,125	65,140	2,010
	1,053,900	650,600	340,000	24,280

Whole number 211,788,518.　　Value $5,908,522.60."

There are no available statistics covering the number of stamps issued between June 30th, 1861 and the appearance of the new issue in August of that year. In view of the impending change and the reasons which prompted it, we may assume that the quantity was restricted as far as possible.

ISSUES OF 1861-66.

ISSUE OF 1861.

The breaking out of the civil war, in April, 1861, and the natural desire of the government that its stamps should not be used to the profit of the seceding states were the causes of the issue of 1861.

An article in the *Chicago Times-Herald* in September 1896, says :

Historical.

At the post office department I was told that in May, 1861, Postmaster General Montgomery Blair issued an order requiring all postmasters to return to the department all postage stamps and stamped envelopes in their possession, but I was unable to see the order, as no copy is preserved in the files of the department, and its precise language is unknown.

I sought further information in the files of the *National Intelligencer,* preserved in the library of Congress, which was the organ of the department in 1861. I found in the issue of June 13th, 1861, the following "extract from the department files," introduced by appropriate editorial comment, published for the information of the public :

"There are now no postmasters of the United States, in the seceded States, authorized to sell stamps or collect postage, since the 1st of June, for this government. Postmasters, therefore, must treat all matter since the 1st of June coming from the seceded States, and mailed within these States, as unpaid matter to be held for postage. All such matter is ordered to be sent to the dead letter office at Washington to be disposed of according to law."

In the issue of the following day, June 14, 1861, the following appeared as an editorial paragraph :

"In consequence of the retention and improper use of postage stamps by delinquent postmasters in some of the seceded States, the Postmaster General has ordered a new stamped envelope, which will be ready for use in a few days, and that by the 1st of August there will be a new stamp with devices altogether different from the present."

In August, 1861, the following circular letter was sent to postmasters throughout the country :

POST OFFICE DEPARTMENT.

POSTMASTER............... FINANCE OFFICE........1861.

SIR : You will receive herewith a supply of postage stamps which you will observe are of a new style, differing both in design and color from those hitherto used, and having the letters U. S. in the lower corners of each stamp, and its respective denomination indicated by figures as well as letters. You will immediately give public notice through the newspapers and otherwise, that you are prepared to exchange stamps of the new style for an equivalent amount of the old issue, during a period of six days from the date of the notice, and that the latter will not thereafter be received in payment of postage on letters sent from your office.

Announcement of the 1861 issue.

You will satisfy yourself by personal inspection that stamps offered in exchange have not been used through the mails or otherwise ; and if in any case you have good grounds for suspecting that stamps, presented to you for exchange, were sent from any of the disloyal states, you will not receive them without due investigation.

Redemption of stamps of the 1857-60 issue.

Immediately after the expiration of the above period of six days, you will return to the Third Assistant Postmaster General all stamps of the old style in your possession, including such as you may obtain by exchange, placing them in a secure package, which must be carefully registered in the manner prescribed by Chapter 39, of the Regulations of this Department.

Be careful also to write legibly the name of your office as well as that of your county and state. A strict compliance with the foregoing instructions is absolutely necessary, that you may not fail to obtain credit for the amouut of stamps returned.

Instead of sending stamps to the Department you can, if convenient, exchange them for new ones at some city post office, where large supplies are to be found. It being impossible to supply all offices with new stamps at once, you will deliver letters received from Kentucky, Missouri, Illinois, Ohio, Indiana, Maryland and Pennsylvania, prepaid by stamps of the old issue, until September 10th, those from other loyal states east of the Rocky Mountains until the first of October, and those from the states of California and Oregon and from the Territories of New Mexico, Utah and Washington, until the first of November, 1861.

Your Obedient Servant,
A. N. ZEVELY,
Third Assistant Postmaster General.

Extension of time for redemption. In a subsequent order the dates specified in the last paragraph of the foregoing circular were extended to November 1st, 1861, December 1st, 1861, and January 1st, 1862 for the respective sections.

Authority to declare stamps invalid. The question of the authority of the Postmaster General to declare the stamps of the 1857 issue obsolete and invalid for postal purposes has been much discussed. The action met with public approval at the time and was, presumably, within his province. The acts of Congress did not restrict him to the employment of any particular designs for stamps or require their continuance in use after adoption, thus, constructively, leaving all such details to his discretion. The dicta of the head of a department, on matters placed within his control, have the authority of law, unless they are in conflict with a provision of the Constitution or of the statutes of the United States.

Envelopes not declared invalid. It is curious that the order of the Postmaster General seems to have applied only to the adhesive stamps and not to the stamped envelopes then current. No mention of envelopes is made in the official circular quoted above. A correspondent of the *Stamp Collectors Magazine* says, in the number for August, 1867 :

"We do not think that the 1860 envelopes were outlawed, though they of course soon gave place to the new issue of 1861, but upon this point we are not certain. We know that the one cent envelope and wrapper were never thus treated, however, but when the lowest rate of postage (newspapers and drop letters) was raised from 1c to 2c in 1863, the stock on hand was sold to applicants for two cent wrappers or envelopes, the value being completed by the addition of a 1c adhesive to each 1c wrapper or envelope. When the stock of the old series was thus got rid of, the new 2c value was supplied. No more of the 1c envelopes were printed, but they have always been, and to-day are, recognized at their face value whenever offered."

The report of the Postmaster General, dated December 2nd, 1861, gives additional information concerning the changes in the postage stamps :

Report of Postmaster General. The contract for the manufacture of postage stamps having expired on the 10th of June, 1861, a new one was entered into with the National Bank Note Company of New York, upon terms very advantageous to the Department, from which there will result an annual saving of more than thirty per cent. in the cost of the stamps.

In order to prevent the fraudulent use of the large quantity of stamps remaining unaccounted for, in the hands of postmasters in the disloyal states, it was deemed advisable to change the design and the color of those manufactured under the new contract, and also to modify the design of the stamp upon the stamped envelope, and to substitute as soon as possible the new for the old issues. It was the design of the Department that the distribution of the new stamps and envelopes should commence on the first of August, but, from unavoidable delays, that of the latter did not take place until the 15th of that month.

The number of postage stamps of the new style issued up to the 9th of November was 77,117,520 and the number of new stamped envelopes, 8,039,650. All post offices in the loyal states with the exception of certain offices in Kentucky and Missouri, have been supplied therewith Those of the old issue have been exchanged and superseded. The old stamps on hand, and such as were received by exchange, at the larger offices, have been to

a great extent counted and destroyed, and those of the smaller offices returned to the Department. It is proper to state that, in anticipation of the substitution of the new stamps and
envelopes for the old issue, but limited supplies of the latter were sent to postmasters during
June and July, so that the amount thereof remaining in their hands was comparatively small.

The additional expense incurred by the change is very inconsiderable, in view of the
greatly dimished cost of the new stamps as compared with that of the old, while the
prevention thereby of the use of stamps unaccounted for in the hands of disloyal postmasters
saves the Department from severe loss. Although the enumeration and destruction of the
old stamps and envelopes is not yet completed, there is ample evidence that few received in
exchange were sent from disloyal States.

In this connection an extract from a proclamation of John H. Reagan,
ex-Postmaster General of the Confederate States, dated May 13th, 1861, is
also of interest :

"All postmasters are hereby required to render to the Post-office Department at
Washington, D. C., their final accounts and their vouchers for postal receipts and expenditures, up to the 31st day of this month, taking care to forward with said accounts all postage
stamps and stamped envelopes remaining on hand, belonging to the Post Office Department
of the United States, in order that they may receive the proper credits therefore, in the
adjustment of their accounts."

Confederate
Postmaster General
orders U. S. stamps
returned.

It would be interesting to know the result of this order. It is doubtful
if, in the disturbed state of the country, it was obeyed to any extent. However, at a period long subsequent to 1861, there were in the Post Office   Remainders.
Department a large quantity of the stamps of the 1857-60 issue. It is understood that the majority of these had been found in Southern post offices,
after the war, and returned to Washington. We know that one prominent
dealer acquired 2,000 complete sets by indirect purchase. Another well-
known dealer was presented with 1,800 sets, in return for his assistance in
arranging the government collection of stamps. All these sets were in full
sheets. There is no available record of the number of stamps returned to the
Department by postmasters or of those destroyed.

By act of Congress, approved March 3rd, 1861, the Act of March 3rd,   Act of March 3rd,
1851, was amended to require the rate of ten cents, prepaid, on all letters from   Increase in rate to
points east of the Rocky Mountains to any state or territory on the Pacific   the Pacific Coast.
Coast and vice versa. Postage on all drop letters was required to be pre-paid
by means of stamps.

The same portraits and busts were used on the stamps of the 1861
issue as on the corresponding values of the 1857 issue. They were, however,
newly engraved and the surrounding devices were of entirely new designs.

The official description of the designs is as follows :

"ONE CENT. Profile head of Franklin, looking to the right, in an ellipse
as large as could be placed upon the stamp, viz., 1 by ¾ inch. The entire
ground within the enclosure is formed of lathe-work. The outer three-   Designs.
sixteenths of an inch of this space is more open. The upper corner spaces
contain the Arabic figure '1', and the lower the white capital letters 'U'
and 's' in the left and. right, respectively—all four corners having ornate
surroundings. The words 'U. S. POSTAGE' are placed above and 'ONE
CENT' below the bust, following the curvature of the elliptic lathe-work upon
which they rest. The portrait is probably intended as a copy from Rubricht.

THREE CENTS. A profile of Washington, looking to the left, rests upon
an oblong tablet of lathe-work, which is scarcely separated from the rest of
the stamp by a border of lighter work of the same character. The entire

ground of the stamp, except touches at and near the outer corners, is of this machine design. The large Arabic figure '3' appears in the upper corners, and between them, in two lines, are 'U. S.' and 'POSTAGE', the latter word taking the curve of the head close below. At the bottom, also in two lines of white capitals, are the words 'THREE' and 'CENTS', the ends of the lines tending upward. In the lower corners are the Gothic capitals 'U' and 'S', of the same size as the figures; all four are white, except slight tracery near the middle of each.

FIVE CENTS. A portrait of Jefferson rests upon a cross-hatched elliptical tablet 17-32 by 43-64 of an inch. This is surrounded by a border of lathe-work, principally in a triple line design, reaching the limits of the stamp and giving the general outline of a parallelogram, though the corners are rounded, and midway of each side it swells outward. A large white Arabic figure '5' is placed in each of the upper corners, and resting on each end of the line 'U. S. POSTAGE', which rises in the middle to surmount the upper curve of the tablet. Similar white capitals form the words 'FIVE CENTS', below the tablet, and the Gothic capitals 'U' and 'S', slightly distorted, are placed in the lower corners.

TEN CENTS. The head of Washington is upon a hatched ground whose cross lines are almost imperceptible, and is enclosed by four small white stars on each side, with the words 'U. S. POSTAGE' above and 'TEN CENTS' below. There are five more stars at the top of the stamp. The number '10', in Arabic figures, is placed in each upper corner, in an appropriate inclosure of ornamental design, and the white capitals 'U' and 'S' are seen in the left and right lower corners, respectively.

TWELVE CENTS. The face of Washington is placed upon a cross-hatched elliptical ground ½ by ⅝ inch, which is surrounded to the edge of the stamp by a very fine geometrical design, with a serrated outer white line, edged with a black hair line and the trace of an ornament in the middle of each side, with a larger one at each corner, outside the lines mentioned. The number '12' in Arabic figures, inclined as in the 2-cent stamp, is placed in each upper corner, with 'U. S. POSTAGE' between, bordering the medallion line. Below, in the corners, are the white capitals 'U.' and 'S.' with the words 'TWELVE CENTS' just below the medallion line and rising at each end above the 'U.' and 'S.' The portrait is the same as that on the 10 cent stamp.

TWENTY-FOUR CENTS. The portrait is the smallest in the series, and inclosed by very fine lathe-work ⅛ of an inch wide, the general outline of which is irregularly hexagonal. On each outer side, above the middle line, are four small five-pointed stars, enlarged in size from the lowest one up. At the top are three more stars, the smallest one in the middle. To the right and left of these, in the corners, and within an elliptical space, are the white faced and shaded Arabic numerals '24' inclined slightly to the left and right. In each lower corner is a large five-pointed star, completing the thirteen; upon the left of these is the letter 'U', and upon the right 'S', tending inward at the top. Curled-leaf ornaments above and at the side of these stars complete the principal features of the stamp. The portrait ground is cross lined vertically and horizontally.

THIRTY CENTS. The portrait is inclosed in a circle 21-32 of an inch in diameter. The background of this space is obliquely cross lined at right angles. The inscriptions 'U. S. POSTAGE' above and 'THIRTY CENTS' below the circle, followed it closely; the number '30' leans outward in the upper corners, and the white capital letters 'U' and 'S' in the lower left and right hand corners, respectively, incline inward. Around the sides are scroll-work ornamentations.

NINETY CENTS. The portrait stands upon a background similar to that of the 5, 12 and 15 cent stamps. The border, about 3-32 of an inch wide, is crossed with rays. The outer line of this border rises at the top to a Gothic apex. The denomination numerals '90' appear at each side of the tablet, on its border, one-fourth of an inch from its highest point. Across the top of the stamp, upon an independent pennant tablet, whose ends fall about the border, are the words 'U. S. POSTAGE', in white shaded capitals. The words 'NINETY' and 'CENTS' are upon the left and right lower quarters of the border, which rests upon branches of oak and laurel tied with a small ribbon. The extreme lower corners are filled with the letters 'U' and 'S' in the left and right, respectively."

The dimensions of the stamps are: One cent, 19½x25mm.; three cents, 20x25mm.; five cents, 20½x25¼mm.; ten cents, 20½x24¼mm.; **Sizes.** twelve cents, 19½x24½mm.; twenty-four cents, 19½x24mm.; thirty cents, 20x24½mm.; ninety cents, 19½x24¼mm.

The issue of 1861 may be divided into two sections. They are, however, so intimately related and, with two exceptions, vary so slightly in design that it is difficult to consider them separately. The first section, usually **Premières gravures.** referred to as the *premières gravures*, was issued in the early part of August, 1861. The 14th of that month is usually given as the date of issue, though I have not found the authority for the statement. It may, possibly, have been deduced from a paragraph in the report of the Postmaster General just quoted, which says: "It was the design of the Department that the distribution of the new stamps and envelopes should commence on the first of August, but, from unavoidable delays, that of the latter did not take place until the 15th of that month." The most which can be asserted, on this authority, is that the stamps were issued previous to the 15th of the month but not on the 1st, as originally intended. The three and twelve cents of this series present a decidedly unfinished look, especially at the corners. Philatelists have long been familiar with these two values but, used specimens not being known, they were regarded as essays. The other values differ so slightly from the ordinary types that they escaped notice for thirty-five years. The discovery of the earlier variety of the ten cents lead to the study of the whole series and the eventual discovery of the complete set of the first types.

The first designs did not give full satisfaction and improvements were ordered. These were quite extensive on the three and twelve cents but very slight on most of the other values. So far as known no changes, beyond **Alterations.** those of color, were made in the twenty-four and thirty cents. Altering the designs and making new plates involved a considerable delay. Meantime the need of new stamps was urgent. To meet this demand, it was found necessary

Date of issue of
second series.
to issue the stamps of the first types. The scarcity of these varieties proves that this issue was restricted as much as possible. The first stamp to be issued in the altered design was, naturally, the three cents, that being the ordinary rate of postage and, consequently, the value most in demand. A copy of this stamp is known cancelled August 18th, 1861, four days after the date of issue assigned to the stamps of the first types. Several other values are known cancelled in that month. So far, used copies of the one, thirty and ninety cents have not been reported. When it was first discovered that this issue was composed of two series, it was believed that the stamps of the second types were not ready for use until September, 1861, and the two series were designated as the August and September issues, respectively. But from the information supplied by the cancellations we perceive that these titles are incorrect and must be abandoned.

Types of the first
and second series.
The differences between the first and second types may be described as follows :

ONE CENT. From the numerals in the upper corners arabesque ornaments extend downward and also across the top, resting upon the curved frame-line of the stamp. The extreme tip of the upper left-hand ornament is directly above the " P " of " POSTAGE ". In the first type this tip rests upon the curved line but does not extend below it. In the second type there is a strong dash under the tip and below the line. Other, though lighter, dashes appear further down the curve, above the " s " and opposite the " U " of " U. S." There are also shading lines under the upper ornament on the right. None of these marks appear in the first type. The vertical shadings in the corner spaces which enclose the numerals and the letters " U " and " s " are increased in the second type.

THREE CENTS. The first type of this stamp is probably better known to collectors than any other value in the set. Outside the irregular rectangle of lathe-work there are only some trifling ornaments and the stamp looks bare and unfinished. In the second type this has been remedied by the use of more elaborate ornaments, especially at the corners, which have been built out so that the outline of the design is now approximately rectangular.

FIVE CENTS. The two types of this stamp differ but little. The delicate, leaf-like ornaments at the corners lack, in the first type, the leaflet (if we may so term it), which projects farthest.

TEN CENTS. In the upper part of the stamps are *five* white stars on a background of ruled lines. The background is separated from the label containing " U. S. POSTAGE ", by a curved white line. In the second type a heavy line of color has been cut along the lower ends of the background lines, above and following the curve of the white line. An outer line has also been added to all the ornaments above the stars.

TWELVE CENTS. The first type of this stamp differs so materially from the second, that, at first glance, one scarcely recognizes it as a prototype. There is nothing outside the mat of lathe-work except a thin wavy line following the outline. In appearance it is even more unfinished than the three cents of the first type. To make the second type, small ovals and arabesques were added at each corner and little scrolls at the sides. These additions, as in the case of the three cents, make the outline of the stamp about rectangular.

No variations have been found in the twenty-four and thirty cent stamps. As there was but one plate for each value, it is not probable that any changes were made in the designs. The colors of the first printing differ very decidedly from those of the ordinary stamps. A few slight retouches may be found on some of the twenty-four cent stamps, but they probably indicate a late touching up of the plate, rather than alterations in the die.

NINETY CENTS. Above the ribbon with " U. S. POSTAGE " the lines of the frame meet in an obtuse angle, made by parallel lines of color, separated by a white space about one-half millimetre wide. To form the second type a strong point of color was added at the apex of the lower lines of the angle and a series of little dashes drawn through the center of the white space, making a broken line of color, between and parallel to the other lines. On many of the stamps this broken line is too faint to be seen, but the colored point usually stands out clearly. The leaf beside the " U " in the lower left corner has been recut and now has vertical instead of horizontal lines of shading. If, instead of these trifling marks, something more elaborate had been added to fill out the very bare upper part of the stamp, the improvement in its appearance would have been greater.

Beyond doubt the eye is best pleased by stamps whose outlines fill out a rectangle. The designers of our earlier stamps either failed to appreciate this idea or to carry it out. Thus we find in many of the stamps of the older issues an unsatisfactory bareness and lack of completeness, notably at the corners. On the other hand, many of our later issues appear painfully plain and lacking in variety when compared with the graceful designs and elaborate ornamentation of the earlier issues.

Characteristics of the premières gravures. The paper of the *premières gravures* is very thin, hard and extremely brittle. The stamps are easily cracked, unless handled very carefully. The paper is also quite transparent and much of the designs may be seen from the backs of the stamps. The gum is very dark brown, sometimes staining the paper. The colors are very dark and rich and the ink heavily applied, occasionally giving a blurred appearance, though, as a rule, the impressions are very fine and clear.

Reference List.

First Types.

Very Thin Yellowish-white Wove Paper.

Perforated 12.

Aug. 14th, 1861.   1 cent indigo
                   3 cents brownish lake, lake
                   5 cents orange-brown
                   10 cents dark yellow-green, dark green
                   12 cents gray-black
                   24 cents violet, deep violet
                   30 cents red-orange
                   90 cents slate-blue

Varieties :

3 cents brownish lake.   Imperforate
90 cents slate blue.   Imperforate

Color varieties. The three cents has been seen printed in pink, scarlet and carmine-lake, but it is not probable that it was ever issued in these colors.

It is probable that most of the stamps of the second types made their appearance early in September, 1861. The dates given in the following list are those of the earliest cancellations which I have been able to discover. The alterations in the types were accompanied by pronounced changes in the colors of the stamps.

The paper is still thin but tougher than in the preceding group. The gum is very dark brown as before.

Reference List.

Second Types.

Thin White Wove Paper.

Perforated 12.

June 4th, 1862.   1 cent deep dull blue
Aug. 18th, 1861. 3 cents pink, bright rose

Aug. 30th, 1861.   5 cents pale buff, deep buff, brownish yellow, deep brownish yellow, mustard, olive-yellow

Sept. 20th, 1861.   10 cents dark green

                  12 cents full black

Oct. 8th, 1861   24 cents slate

Sept. 16th, 1861.   30 cents pale orange

                  90 cents marine blue

Variety:

3 cents bright rose. Imperforate

    In the course of time many other changes in the colors took place,
some of them at a comparatively early period. A few dates of early cän-
cellations are given. The paper varies from thin to quite thick and the gum
from brown to yellowish white.

White Wove Paper.   Color varieties.

Perforated 12.

1 cent pale dull blue, dull blue, gray-blue, slate-blue, pale
blue, blue, bright blue, Prussian blue, chalky blue,
ultramarine, deep ultramarine

3 cents pale rose, rose (Feb. 28th, 1862), rose-red, deep
rose-red, brownish rose, pale brown-red, brown-
red, dull red, carmine-lake, orange-red, scarlet

5 cents red-brown (June 23rd, 1862), dark red-brown,
brick red, orange-brown, yellow brown, brown
(April 10th, 1863), bistre-brown, gray-brown, dark
brown, black-brown (July 18th, 1863)

10 cents pale yellow-green, yellow-green (Sept. 4th, 1863),
dark yellow-green, blue-green (Dec. 21st, 1863)

12 cents gray-black, gray

24 cents violet, black-violet, brown-violet, lilac, gray-lilac
(Aug. 11th, 1863), gray, red-lilac, deep red-lilac

30 cents orange, deep orange

90 cents pale blue, blue, dark blue, bright blue, indigo

Varieties:

3 cents rose.	Imperforate
3 cents carmine-lake.	Imperforate
3 cents scarlet.	Imperforate
3 cents rose.	Impression on the reverse
30 cents orange	Imperforate

    The *Stamp Collectors Magazine* for April, 1867, says the color of the
5 cents was changed from yellowish to brown in March, 1862.

    I have seen two copies of the 90 cents in a pale ultramarine shade. I   Ninety cents
am inclined to think that they are changelings.   ultramarine.

    Many philatelists have claimed that the three cents scarlet is only a
finished proof. But the fact remains that it was on sale in at least one post

office. Mr. J. W. Scott kindly supplies the following information concerning this stamp. The first copy which he saw was on a letter coming from New **Three cents scarlet.** Orleans. As the shade was unusual he desired some of the stamps for his stock. Finding they were not on sale at the New York Post Office, he sent a dollar to the Postmaster at New Orleans and received its equivalent in stamps of the desired shade. These he sold to his customers at about twenty-five cents each. Subsequently he sent three dollars to New Orleans and received in return an entire sheet of one hundred of the stamps. On sending the third time his order was filled with the three cents rose. This would certainly appear to be conclusive evidence of the issue of this stamp in the regular way.

ISSUE OF 1863.

The Act of Congress, approved March 3rd, 1863, abolished carriers' fees and established a prepaid rate of two cents for drop letters. This made necessary the issue of a stamp of corresponding value, which took place on July 1st of that year.

The official description of this stamp is as follows :

Design. "Two CENTS. A full face of Andrew Jackson fills the entire tablet, which is as wide as the stamp, three-fourths of an inch, and only one-sixteenth less in its long diameter than the stamp, fifteen-sixteenths of an inch, space being left at the top for the words 'U. S. POSTAGE' above the elliptical ground, which is cros-hatched. The word 'TWO' and the distorted capital 'U' in black fill the left lower corner, the word 'CENTS' and a distorted capital 'S' the right. An Arabic '2' in white is placed in each upper corner, inclined outward towards the left and right, respectively, and resting upon small black disks. Appropriate scroll decorations complete the upper part. The face of Jackson on this stamp is probably after the portrait by Dodge."

The stamp measures 20½x24½mm. The paper varies from thin to quite thick and the gum from brownish to almost white.

Reference List.   White Wove Paper.

Perforated 12.

July 1st, 1863.   2 cents gray-black, greenish black, full black

Varieties :

2 cents gray-black. Imperforate vertically
2 cents gray-black. Horizontal half, used as one cent
2 cents gray-black. Diagonal half and another copy, used as three cents
2 cents gray-black. Vertical half and another copy, used as three cents

Most of the bisected stamps bear the cancellations of small towns in New York and Connecticut with dates from June to October, 1866. I have also heard of a copy cancelled in Butler, Pa., in July, 1864.

At some date between April, 1862, and August, 1867, several values of the 1861-63 series were issued on thin laid paper, similar to that used for the document revenues. The stamps are found on paper with the vergures close together and wide apart and also placed both vertically and horizontally.

Stamps on laid paper.

White Laid Paper.

Reference List.

Perforated 12.

	1 cent deep blue
	2 cents gray-black
April 12th, 1862.	3 cents dull rose, rose
	5 cents brown

The two and three cent stamps of this series are occasionally found on brown paper and are known to collectors as the "Francis patent" stamps. A lengthy account of this patent and the stamps made under it was given in the *Metropolitan Philatelist* for December, 1897. The patent was granted to Dr. S. W. Francis, of New York city, and its principal features were soaking the paper in an alkaline fluid, which turned it brown, and cancellation by means of a small sponge, saturated with some acid and attached to the thumb. A touch of this sponge, when handling the letters, would obliterate the stamp. On all cancelled copies which I have seen the color of the paper has been turned to a deep blue.

"Francis patent" stamps.

By order of the Third Assistant Postmaster General the National Bank Note Co. prepared 10,000 of these stamps. As the Post Office Department wished a report from a postmaster upon the practicability of the invention, some of the stamps were sent to Newport, R. I., for experiment. Under date of March 30th, 1865, the postmaster at Newport wrote to Dr. Francis :

"I have this day personally tested your method of cancelling postage stamps. After thorough and systematic experiments, I feel it due you to certify hereby to the valuableness of your invention. I shall communicate·with the Hon. Third Assistant Postmaster General of my experiments."

This letter is not at all conclusive as to the actual sale to the public or the use of the stamps. Yet it would appear that a thorough test of the merits of the invention could not otherwise have been attained. A mere demonstration of the efficacy of the cancellation could have been made by any one and at any time. I am inclined to believe that the stamps were used for a short time and to a limited extent.

Brown Wove Paper.

Reference List.

Perforated 12.

2 cents deep black
3 cents dull brown-red

ISSUE OF 1866.

The Act of Congress, approved March 3rd, 1863, also conferred on the Postmaster General the power to fix the registration fee at such rate as he should deem best, provided it did not, in any case, exceed twenty cents.

Registration.

In 1866 the rate was fixed at fifteen cents, which made necessary the issue of a stamp of like value. It is officially described as follows :

"FIFTEEN CENTS. The portrait of Lincoln appears upon a cross-hatched elliptical ground 9-16 by ¾ of an inch. On each side of this are fasces, and above are the words 'U. S. POSTAGE' in white capitals upon a tablet curled at each end, and encircling the number '15'; in Arabic figures, in each upper corner; the figures lean outward to the right and left and backward. At the bottom, the words 'FIFTEEN CENTS' in similar letters to those above and on a like ground, except that the latter terminates abruptly at the ends when reaching the fasces. The letters 'U. S.' in the lower corners are in bold-faced white capitals, the letters leaning to correspond with the numerals in the upper corners."

The stamp measures 19¼x24¾mm.

The paper is moderately thick and the gum ranges in color from brownish to white.

White Wove Paper.

Perforated 12.

April 15th, 1866.   15 cents full black, gray-black

The stamps of the issues of 1861-66 were engraved and printed by the National Bank Note Co., New York. The plates each contained two hundred stamps, arranged in two panes—ten rows of ten stamps each—placed side by side and usually separated by a vertical line, which served as a guide when the sheets were cut apart. Most of the plates bore the imprint of the engravers at the center of the top, outside edge (before severing) and bottom of each pane. So far as known the *premières gravures* had the imprint at the bottom only, which was also the case with a few of the later plates. The imprints at the top and sides were "NATIONAL BANK NOTE CO., NEW YORK" in small white capitals, on a small colored panel with rounded ends, surrounded by two thin colored lines. The imprint at the bottom was "NATIONAL BANK NOTE COMPANY" in very small white capitals, framed in a rectangle of pearls, on a panel of solid color. At the left of the panel were the words "ENGRAVED BY THE" and at the right "CITY OF NEW-YORK.", all in large colored capitals. Below the panel were "No.——Plate" in outline letters, with the plate number between the words. The number was separately engraved and appears in at least two styles of type.

The numbers of the plates were as follows :

ISSUE OF 1861.—First Types.

1 cent	No. 1.
3 cents	No. 2.
5 cents	No. 3.
10 cents	No. 4.
12 cents	No. 5.
24 cents	No. 6.
30 cents	No. 7.
90 cents	No. 8.

ISSUE OF 1861.—Second Types.

1 cent	No. 9, 10, 22, 25, 27.
3 cents	No. 11, 12, 13, 14, 19, 20, 21, 23, 24, 32, 33, 34, 35, 36, 37, 42, 43, 44, 45, 46, 47, 48, 49, 52, 54, 55.
5 cents	No. 17.
10 cents	No. 15, 26.
12 cents	No. 16.
24 cents	No. 6.
30 cents	No. 7.
90 cents	No. 18.

ISSUES OF 1863 AND 1866.

2 cents	No. 28, 29, 30, 31, 50, 51, 53.
15 cents	No. 41.

The numbers 38, 39 and 40, which are missing from the sequence, are those of the stamps for newspapers and periodicals, issued in 1865. Numbers 56, 57, 58, 59 and 60, quoted in previous lists of plate numbers, belong to new plates made for the re-issue of 1875 and not to the original series. The three cents pink was printed from plate 12, the three cents scarlet from plate 19, the three cents carmine-lake from plate 34, the imperforate stamps of the last shade from plate 52, and the imperforate three cents rose from plate 11.

On January 23rd, 1867, one hundred sets of the ten denominations of this issue were surcharged "Specimen" in "Old English" type. On February 28th, 1867, the same surcharge was applied to twenty thousand more sets. This was done by order of the Third Assistant Postmaster General. A few copies have been seen with the final letter of the surcharge inverted.

"Specimen" stamps.

The records of the Stamp Agent show that the following quantities of stamps were printed and delivered by the contractors. It will be noted that the earliest date is August 16th, 1861, which is later than the accepted date of issue. It is scarcely probable that any such amount of stamps were printed on the date given, but rather that they were the product of several previous days, placed on record on that date :

Statistics of manufacture.

1861	1 cent.	2 cents.	3 cents.	5 cents	10 cents.
Aug. 16	1,623,000	....	3,281,000	32,600	87,800
" 17	620,500	....	1,726,000	18,100.	50,800
" 20	368,000	....	945,000	16,400	50,200
" 22	14,000	....	81,000	1,500	12,800
" 24	572,000	....	1,451,500	18,540	339,600
" 28	705,000	....	1,430,000	6,900	39,900
" 29	497,000	....	928,000	28,100	26,200
" 31	320,400	....	540,000	4,800	15,500
Sept. 1 to Nov. 29	12,577,900	....	40,752,500	196,340	1,136,590
Nov. 29 to Dec. 31	3,838,500	....	12,596,000	92,500	241,100
1862	47,548,800	....	182,559,820	1,858,220	4,347,040
1863	36,930,400	28,151,500	243,977,700	992,400	3,226,250
1864	1,453,570	50,514,900	314,942,400	963,840	3,672,500

	1 cent.	2 cents.	3 cents.	5 cents.	10 cents.
1865	4,525,700	50,098,500	304,914,550	1,204,820	4,025,200
1866	7,843,800	51,146,500	288,912,000	1 134,260	4,135,660
1867	10,330,000	58,046,700	294,818,700	949,760	4,478,890
Jan. to Mch. 1868	3,774,400	18,607,900	78,802,700	262,300	1,573,810
Apl. to June "				222,920	
July to Sept. "				168,820	

| Total, | 133,542,970 | 256,566,000 | 1,772,658,870 | 8,173,120 | 27,459,840 |

1861	12 cents.	15 cents.	24 cents.	30 cents.	90 cents.
Aug. 16	39,750		28,250	18,260	3,500
" 17	25,200		17,100	10,950	550
" 20	32,700		12,550	8,700	
" 22	1,300		1,200	500	
" 24	51,700		65,500	5,430	50
" 28	12,400		81,000	35,000	100
" 29	900		12,050	15,050	
" 31	8,900		9,600	4,600	700
Sept. 1 to Nov. 29	295,525		219,925	71,240	4,140
Nov. 29 to Dec. 31	57,300		74,050	31,280	55,600
1862	773,800		817,250	338,950	14,830
1863	723,570		1,090,925	320,800	29,970
1864	1,094,325		1,706,825	513,360	41,840
1865	960,275		1,843,340	522,830	64,860
1866	938,850	578,460	1,969,875	579,580	69,320
1867	1,193,775	1,256,900	1,898,850	534,460	72,670
Jan. to Mch. 1868	955,800	303,940	110,425	73,620	8,280
Apl. to June "			43,425	83,910	7,630
July to Sept. "			54,850	55,890	10,880

| Total, | 7,166,070 | 2,139,300 | 10,056,990 | 3,224,410 | 384,920 |

Beyond doubt a part of the stamps printed in the year 1867 were embossed with grills, since stamps so treated were issued in August of that year. The records for the two succeeding years carefully specify the respective quantities of stamps of each value which were and were not embossed. But the records for 1867 are silent on this subject. The statistics just quoted are, therefore, misleading, inasmuch as they would lead us to infer that all stamps printed in 1867 were without embossing, while we have knowledge to the contrary.

The annual reports of the Postmaster General give the following quantities of stamps as having been issued to deputy postmasters from July 1st, 1861, to June 30th, 1867. It must be remembered that a few stamps of the 1857 series may have been issued in July and the early part of August, 1861, and that stamps without embossing were issued later than June 30th, 1867. The figures of these reports are, therefore, only approximate and not exact:

Stamps issued during the fiscal year ending June 30th, 1862 :

QUARTER ENDING:

	Sept. 30, 1861.	Dec. 31, 1861.	Mch. 31, 1862.	June 30, 1862.	Total.
1 cent	14,092,800	16,416,400	15,346,850	14,165,800	*60,021,250
3 cents	32,570,400	51,122,100	51,203,650	48,844,100	183,740,250
5 cents	312,780	288,840	242,040	185,640	1,029,300
10 cents	1,143,140	1,477,690	792,090	645,530	4,058,450
12 cents	374,925	352,825	181,875	137,125	1,046,750
24 cents	314,325	293,975	193,250	182,575	984,125
30 cents	155,260	102,520	68,100	70,160	396,040
90 cents	13,810	9,740	2,370	5,020	30,940

Whole number of stamps 251,307,105. Value $7,078,188.00.

Stamps issued during the fiscal year ending June 30th, 1863 :

QUARTER ENDING:

	Sept. 30, 1862.	Dec. 31, 1862.	Mch. 31, 1863.	June 30, 1863.	Total.
1 cent	19,810,000	13,563,700	18,986,300	16,494,000	68,854,000
3 cents	79,213,100	54,502,900	63,910,000	61,367,400	258,993,400
5 cents	1,255,120	417,460	283,860	262,580	2,219,020
10 cents	2,543,670	1,157,840	1,072,600	922,040	5,676,150
12 cents	436,200	200,475	197,050	160,950	994,675
24 cents	424,375	210,300	242,550	267,125	1,144,350
30 cents	214,500	54,290	75,040	90,220	434,050
90 cents	6,560	3,250	11,370	3,560	24,740

Whole number of stamps 338,340,385. Value $9,683,394.00.

Stamps issued during the fiscal year ending June 30th, 1864 :

QUARTER ENDING:

	Sept. 30, 1863.	Dec. 31, 1863.	Mch. 31, 1864.	June 30, 1864.	Total.
1 cent	959,900	490,700	289,100	356,600	2,096,300
2 cents	16,562,600	11,588,900	13,469,700	12,153,900	53,775,100
3 cents	56,767,600	62,333,200	74,481,000	78,056,100	271,637,900
5 cents	266,660	179,300	263,440	195,600	905,000
10 cents	589,580	662,030	897,160	770,460	2,919,230
12 cents	170,325	195,250	314,200	196,750	876,525
24 cents	257,025	324,225	413,150	419,525	1,413,925
30 cents	69,570	85,970	133,860	106,500	395,900
90 cents	6,400	8,640	10,800	8,890	34,730

Whole number of stamps 334,054,610. Value $10,177,327.00.

Stamps issued during the fiscal year ending June 30th, 1865 :

QUARTER ENDING:

	Sept. 30, 1864.	Dec. 31, 1864.	Mch. 31, 1865.	June 30, 1865.	Total.
1 cent	345,300	462,700	175,200	1,137,600	2,120,800
2 cents	11,930,500	12,960,300	14,477,250	12,381,200	*49,749,250
3 cents	83,151,200	79,388,600	85,933,850	78,039,300	326,512,950
5 cents	303,120	247,180	275,340	381,440	*1,207,180

	Sept. 30, 1864.	Dec. 31, 1864.	Mch. 31, 1865.	June 30, 1865.	Total.
10 cents	1,049,040	955,340	1,100,640	1,061,440	4,166,460
12 cents	307,425	275,450	322,900	310,850	1,216,625
24 cents	454,575	419,075	480,300	454,400	1,808,350
30 cents	140,540	131,960	141,650	156,940	571,090
90 cents	22,800	9,570	19,490	14,890	66,750

Whole number of stamps 387,419,455. Value $12,099,787.50.

Stamps issued during the fiscal year ending June 30th, 1866:

QUARTER ENDING:

	Sept. 30, 1865.	Dec. 31, 1865.	Mch. 31, 1866.	June 30, 1866.	Total.
1 cent	1,944,000	1,268,900	2,264,300	1,973,400	7,450,600
2 cents	11,648,600	11,291,000	13,831,600	10,783,400	47,554,600
3 cents	69,479,900	71,461,300	73,911,100	68,910,000	283,762,300
5 cents	263,600	284,440	400,240	256,200	1,204,480
10 cents	902,000	962,120	1,280,750	911,070	4,055,940
12 cents	196,525	230,000	365,000	202,475	994,000
15 cents	....	....	....	166,000	166,000
24 cents	442,575	466,175	490,800	512,275	1,911,825
30 cents	103,720	120,520	167,990	123,090	515,320
90 cents	15,880	14,460	15,210	8,290	53,840

Whole number of stamps 347,668,905. Value $10,810,355.00.

Stamps issued during the fiscal year ending June 30th, 1867:

QUARTER ENDING:

	Sept. 30, 1866.	Dec. 31, 1866.	Mch. 31, 1867.	June 30, 1867.	Total.
1 cent	1,792,600	1,813,500	2,919,300	2,445,100	8,970,500
2 cents	13,101,500	13,430,000	15,807,800	15,333,100	57,672,400
3 cents	72,915,600	73,375,300	74,088,200	74,642,800	295,021,900
5 cents	240,620	237,200	288,940	198,360	965,120
10 cents	950,610	993,240	1,202,670	986,560	4,133,080
12 cents	197,125	175,250	302,700	273,125	948,200
15 cents	213,240	199,220	318,380	318,260	1,049,100
24 cents	540,300	426,500	550,250	505,675	2,022,725
30 cents	152,510	135,990	161,120	135,450	585,070
90 cents	26,210	19,610	26,270	14,420	86,510

Whole number of stamps 371,454,605. Value $11,565,357.00.

At the places marked * there are evidently accountant's or typographical errors in the amounts given for some of the quarters, since, in each case, the sum of the several quarters does not agree with the total given in the report, yet the latter is apparently correct, as it is essential to the grand total and value of the stamps issued, as stated in the report.

Issue of 1867.

A matter of anxiety to every government is the possible counterfeiting or misuse of its securities. In the case of postage stamps there does not seem to be so much fear of counterfeiting as that cancellations may be removed and the stamps used again. For many years after stamps came into use in this country it was customary, in many of the smaller offices, to cancel them with pen and ink. It is said that, by aid of chemicals, cancellations of this sort are not difficult to remove and it is possible that this was occasionally done, though it is to be doubted that it was practiced to any extent. Yet much study appears to have been devoted to preventatives of such a possibility. Collectors of proofs and essays know how numerous were the efforts in this direction. In the *American Journal of Philately* for 1889 (pages 239 and 485) is given a list of thirty-three patents, designed to prevent the cleaning and re-use of stamps. With one or two exceptions, these patents do not appear to have been considered of sufficient merit or practicability to be brought into use. Strange to say, the only one which received an extended trial, the grill, is omitted from the list.

Precautions against the cleaning of stamps.

The report of the Postmaster General, dated November 26, 1867, says:

"Experiments are in progress with a postage stamp printed on embossed paper, which seems to afford good security against fraud. The fibres of the paper being broken, cancelling marks almost necessarily penetrate, so that they cannot easily be removed without destroying the stamp. The adhesive properties are also promoted and other advantages secured which commend the invention to favorable notice."

This device is covered by patent No. 70,147, granted to Charles F. Steel, Brooklyn, N. Y., October 22nd, 1867.

Patent for grilling stamps.

The recorded description is as follows:

PATENT POSTAGE STAMP.

No. 70,147.

CHARLES F. STEEL, Brooklyn, N. Y.

October 22d, 1867.

The paper is gummed, embossed so as to impair its texture in parts, smoothed, and printed on portions of its face. In cancelling, the paper in its broken portions absorbs the ink, rendering the latter irremovable and preventing the fraudulent second use of the stamp.

CLAIM—*First*, A postage stamp having the paper partly broken, opened, and weakened, the use and for the purposes herein set forth.

Second, In the above, applying the gum or equivalent adhesive material before such treatment of the paper, as and for the purposes herein specified.

Third, In combination with above steps, the flattening of the whole or a portion of the surface of the paper prior to the printing operation, as and for the purposes herein explained.

Fourth, Leaving a space which is embossed and partially broken, as indicated, and not flattened, substantially as and for the purpose herein specified.

From the language of the patent we may infer that at the time the application was filed it was intended that the embossing should precede the printing of the stamps. It is evident that experience soon showed this order of manufacture to be impracticable and the following routine was adopted. The sheets were printed, gummed, pressed, embossed, perforated and lastly pressed under hydraulic pressure of about five hundred tons. This pressure was so great as to reduce the embossed portion nearly to the level of the rest of the stamp but the important part, the breaks in the paper, remained.

In this connection the following letter is of some interest :

New York, Aug. 11, 1868.

Sir :—

Transfer of patentee's rights. At the instance of the National Bank Note Co. of this city, I beg to advise you that I have granted to that company the sole and exclusive right to manufacture embossed postage stamps under my patent for embossed stamps.

I have the honor to be
Very respectfully yours,

Hon. Alex. W. Randall,   Chas. F. Steel.
    Postmaster General,
        Washington, D. C.

The fact that the Government required its postage stamps to be embossed and that the National Bank Note Co. held the exclusive rights to the patent covering this process, had much to do in securing for that company the contract of October 3rd, 1868, for the manufacture of postage stamps for the four succeeding years.

Process of making the grill roller. The grill is produced by a roller and not, as is generally supposed, by a plate. To make this roller, a cylinder of soft steel is placed in a turning lathe and a knurl pressed firmly against it. A knurl, it may be explained, is a small steel wheel which is fitted in a clamp and has its rim covered with small pyramidal bosses. As the cylinder slowly revolves in the lathe the bosses of the knurl are forced into it and produce on its surface similar protruberences and depressions. When finished the entire surface of the roller is covered with tiny pyramids which form a continuous spiral around it. If, while in this shape, it is applied to stamps the variety known as "grilled all over" will result. If, however, it is desired to produce the small rectangular grills it is only necessary to plane off a sufficient number of rows of points, in vertical and horizontal bands.

Manner of use. When in use, the roller rests above a bed of sheet lead into which its points press corresponding depressions. When a sheet of stamps is laid upon this bed and passed beneath the roller the paper is forced into the depressions and embossing is produced.

Effect of the grill. The intention of the grill was to break the fibre of the paper, so that the cancelling ink would penetrate it instead of merely spreading over the surface. This result was accomplished in the stamps with grill covering the entire surface and those with the large grills, 18x15 and 13x16mm. But the later and smaller forms seem to have been less effective. They rarely produced more than a roughening of the surface and, the paper not being sufficiently broken, the cancelling ink failed to penetrate it.

Sizes of grills. In its first form the grill covered the entire stamp. This process so weakened the perforated sheets that they were difficult to handle and when the stamps were torn apart their margins were ragged and unsightly. To remedy this the embossing was reduced to rectangles which covered only a part of the surface of each stamp. The size of these rectangles was gradually reduced and the impressions, which were at first clear, sharp and deep, became fainter and less distinct. The same gradual deterioration is to be noticed in the grills of the 1869 issue. In the 1870 issue the number of grills which are clear and strong is comparatively small. The majority are faint, uncertain in outline, and often show only a single row or a few points. These defects are not to be attributed so much to wear of the roller as to insufficient support by the leaden bed, to the harder paper used for this series and, possibly, to excessive pressure in the hydraulic press.

The grills were embossed with the points both up and down, as viewed from the face of the stamps. The normal position is points up, for the grill which covers the entire stamp and for those grills which range from 18x15mm. to 12x14½mm. These grills are frequently found reversed. The smaller sizes (usually grouped as 11x13mm. and 9x13mm.) have the grill with points down. These smaller grills are occasionally found with the points up. They do not appear to have attracted much attention from philatelists and the only one of which I have a memorandum is a three cents with grill 9x13mm. Points up and points down.

There are numerous oddities in the shape of divided, double and triple grills. These are liable to occur on any value and with any size of grill. They do not seem to be of sufficient interest to warrant an attempt to list them. Oddities of grilling.

It sometimes happened that a part of a stamp was folded over at the time it was being embossed. The result of such an accident is a stamp which appears to have parts of two grills, one with points up and the other with points down. I have in my collection a three cent stamp which has been so folded that it appears to have parts of five or six grills.

There is also known an oddity in the stamps embossed all over   This is a strip of stamps from the top row of a sheet of the three cents, which appears to have the embossing, on the upper half of the stamps and on the margin with the points down while on the remainder of the stamps the points are up. Examination with a strong magnifying glass shows that the embossing with points up was first applied but failed to cover the upper half of the stamps of this row. To remedy this the embossing process was repeated. But in the second operation the sheet was reversed, bringing the points of the grill down. Thus a part of each stamp is really embossed with points both ways but, to the unaided eye, the effect is as at first stated. To a similar accident we owe a horizontal pair of three cent stamps on which the grill covers the whole of one stamp but only half of the other.

There is one variety of grill which has attracted much attention. This variety shows a strip of embossing extending from top to bottom of the stamp and varying in width. This is an impression from a continuous band of bosses which encircled the grill roller at each end. Probably these bands were intended to maintain a firm hold on the sheet of stamps and prevent it from slipping. It was only when a sheet was incorrectly placed, while being embossed, that this variety occurred. So far, it has only been found on the stamps of the 1870 issue, but impressions on the margins of sheets of the Marginal grills.

1867 and 1869 issues show it to have existed on the rollers in use at those dates and its existence on the stamps is, therefore, a possibility.

The date at which the grilled stamps came into use is unsettled. The *American Journal of Philately* for June, 1871 (page 67) gives the date as

Date of issue. August 8th, 1867. Tiffany's *History of the Postage Stamps of the United States* says "adopted May 8th, 1867." The date of the patent is Oct. 22nd, 1867, but that is presumably the date on which it was granted and the process may have been put into use earlier. The first mention of the grilled stamps in a philatelic magazine is in the *Stamp Mercury* for Nov. 25th, 1867, which says : "The three cent stamps, and we suppose the others also, are now embossed in little squares over the face." It is scarcely probable that so important a change could have been effected without attracting prompt attention and it is possible that the date of issue is very near to that of the above notice. On the other hand, if at first issued in small quantities and as an experiment (such a claim is made and has the support of some slight evidence) some time may have elapsed before the stamps met the attention of philatelists, though scarcely so long as from May to November. There is in the collection of Mr. H. E. Deats a pair of the three cents grilled all over, on the original cover and cancelled "Savannah, Ga. Aug. 23, 1867." All things considered, August 8th, 1867, seems a very probable date.

In April, 1868, the *Stamp Mercury* chronicled the two, three and twelve cents with the grill. The *American Journal of Philately* for May, 1868 (page 23), says : "All the values under twelve cents are now submitted to this process as also will the higher denominations be when the present stock on hand is consumed." The same journal, in December of that year (page 82), says : "The 24 and 30 cents of the present issue have at length been issued with the rectangular embossment on the backs and we learn from official quarters that the 90 cents will be subjected to the same treatment this month." But it was not until February, 1869 (page 23), that the editor was able to report the appearance of the latter value.

In the *Philatelic Journal of America* for May, 1889, we find the announcement of the discovery of a copy of the thirty cents with grill cover-

Five and thirty cents grilled all over. ing the entire stamp. The five cents with that variety of grill was first chronicled in the *American Journal of Philately* for July, 1891. Several copies of each of these stamps have since been found.

The one cent also exists with the grill covering the entire stamp. I

One cent grilled all over. have seen an unused block of four in this condition. I have no doubt as to the genuineness of the grill but I am not certain that the stamp was ever issued for use.

The paper varies from moderately thick to very thin. Beginning with the former quality, for the stamps embossed with large grills, it gradually

Paper. decreases in thickness as the grills are reduced in size, until those of the smaller dimensions are, many of them, on an extremely thin and brittle paper. The paper at first in use was slightly soft but it became harder as it lost in thickness and the quality last in use was very hard and crisp.

The gum is white, yellowish and occasionally almost brown.

I have carefully examined and measured all the stamps of the following list. The list has been elaborated from one compiled by Mr. J. B. Leavy and published in the *American Journal of Philately* for April, 1896, some new discoveries and a number of varieties in my own collection being added.

GRILL WITH POINTS UP.

Grill covering the entire stamp.

1 cent blue	12½x12 points to the 10mm.
3 cents rose, rose-red	" " " "
5 cents dark brown	" " " "
30 cents orange	" " " "

Variety :

3 cents rose-red.   Imperforate

Rectangular Grill.

	Rows of Points.	Size in mm.
3 cents rose	22x18	18x15
3 cents rose-red	17x20	13x16
3 cents rose	17x19	13x15½
3 cents rose	17x18	13x14½
3 cents rose	16x21	12½x16½
3 cents rose	16x20	11½x16
3 cents rose, rose-red	16x19	12½x15½
3 cents rose	16x18	12½x14½
3 cents rose	15x18	12x14½

Variety :

3 cents rose-red. Imperforate.	16x19	12½x15½

GRILL WITH POINTS DOWN.

Grill covering the entire stamp.

3 cents rose	12½x12 points to the 10 mm.
5 cents dark brown	" " " "

Rectangular Grill.

3 cents rose	17x19	13x15½
2 cents black	15x19	12x15
3 cents rose	"	"
3 cents rose	15x18	12x14½
2 cents black	"	14½x14
3 cents rose	"	"
3 cents rose	15x17	11½x13½
1 cent bright blue	14x18	11x14
2 cents gray-black	"	"
3 cents rose-red, lake	"	"
12 cents black	"	"
1 cent light blue, dark blue	14x17	11x13½
2 cents gray-black	"	"
3 cents rose, rose-red, brown-rose, lake	"	"

	Rows of points.	Size in mm.
5 cents brown	14x17	11x13½
10 cents dark green, blue-green	"	"
12 cents black, gray-black	"	"
15 cents black	"	"
1 cent pale blue	14x16	11x13
2 cents black	"	"
3 cents pale rose, rose, rose-red, lake	"	"
10 cents dark green	"	"
12 cents black	"	"
15 cents gray-black	"	"
1 cent deep blue	14x15	11x12
3 cents rose	"	"
10 cents blue-green	"	"
1 cent dull blue	13x17	10x13½
3 cents rose-red	"	"
3 cents rose	13x16	10x13
2 cents black	12x18	9x14
3 cents rose	"	'
12 cents gray·black	"	"
15 cents gray-black	"	"
1 cent pale blue, deep blue, dark blue, pale ultramarine	12x17	9x13½
2 cents greenish black, gray-black	"	"
3 cents rose, rose-red, brown-red, lake	"	"
5 cents yellow-brown, red-brown, brown, dark brown, black-brown	"	"
10 cents blue-green, yellow-green	"	"
12 cents black, gray-black	'	"
15 cents black, gray-black, greenish black	"	"
24 cents gray-lilac	"	"
30 cents pale orange, deep orange	"	"
90 cents deep blue	"	"
1 cent bright blue, pale blue, dark blue	12x16	9x13
2 cents gray-black	"	"
3 cents rose, rose-red, brown-red	"	"
5 cents yellow-brown, dark brown	"	"
10 cents blue-green	"	"
12 cents black	"	"
15 cents gray-black	"	"
24 cents gray-lilac, gray	"	"
30 cents orange	"	"
3 cents rose-red	12x15	9x12
3 cents rose	11x17	8½x13½
2 cents gray-black	11x16	8½x13
3 cents rose-red	"	"

Varieties :

| 3 cents rose-red.   Imperforate | 12x17 | 9x13½ |

	Rows of points.	Size in mm.
3 cents rose-red. Imperforate horizontally	12x17	9x13½
2 cents black. Vertical half and another copy, used		
as three cents	14x17	11x13½

I have in my collection an interesting oddity in the shape of a fifteen cents (with grill 12x17 rows of points, measuring 9x13½ mm.) printed in blackish purple. This can scarcely be called an error of color, as no value of the series was printed in that color. It was probably caused by the plate being wiped with a cloth that had been used for the same purpose on a plate inked with purple.

Fifteen cents blackish purple.

The records show the following quantities of stamps to have been printed and delivered to the Stamp Agent :

Statistics of manufacture.

1868	1 cent	2 cents	3 cents	5 cents	10 cents,
Jan. to Mch.	1,489,800	14,400,200	42,864,700	....	671,770
Apl. to June	3,219,800	15,475,900	47,431,400	....	1,281,720
July to Sept.	2,814,600	14,558,400	76,486,200	....	854,150
Oct. to Dec.	3,004,200	16,405,700	80,855,700	174,960	940,200
1869					
Jan. to Mch.	3,351,200	15,718,900	74,266,200	290,520	902,130
Apl. to June	475,300	....	....	149,180	639,410
July to Sept.	....	....	....	67,520	. .....
Total	14,354,900	76,559,100	321,904,200	682,180	5,289,380

1868	12 cents	15 cents	24 cents	30 cents	90 cents,
Jan. to Mch.	639,100	......	......	......	......
Apl. to June	759,175	206,420	......	......	......
July to Sept.	624,800	333,340	......	......	......
Oct. to Dec.	703,600	428,420	68,775	74,210	8,360
1869					
Jan. to Mch.	810,925	706,420	62,275	69,940	11,310
Apl. to June	48,000	489,580	46,050	53,730	4,400
July to Sept.	....	372,180	57,075	84,860	6,750
Total	3,585,600	2,536,360	234,175	282,740	30,820

At the foot of this record is a memorandum of the following quantities of stamps "burned by Stamp Agent :"

Stamps destroyed.

3 cents, 400,000; 5 cents, 424,100; 15 cents, 3,040; 24 cents, 268,450; 30 cents, 73,100; 90 cents, 123,930.

No date is given for this destruction nor any information as to the proportionate quantities of the stamps with and without embossing.

It will be observed that stamps of the 1867 series continued to be printed long after the 1869 issue was in use.

The annual reports of the Postmaster General supply the following statistics of stamps distributed to deputy postmasters:

Deliveries to postmasters.

Stamps issued during the fiscal year ending June 30th, 1868 :

QUARTER ENDING:

	Sept. 30, 1867.	Dec. 31, 1867.	Mch. 31, 1868.	June 30, 1868.	Total.
1 cent	2,163,300	2,805,300	3,774,400	3,219,800	11,962,800
2 cents	12,594,000	14,356,800	18,607,900	15,475,900	60,989,600
3 cents	71,696,900	74,390,800	78,802,700	74,431,400	299,321,800
5 cents	192,860	269,400	262,300	222,920	947,480
10 cents	1,093,730	1,195,930	1,573,810	1,281,720	5,145,190
12 cents	201,075	416,875	995,800	759,175	2,372,925
15 cents	295,900	324,360	303,940	206,420	1,130,620
24 cents	476,225	366,700	110,425	43,425	996,775
30 cents	107,520	130,370	73,620	83,910	395,420
90 cents	18,430	13,550	8,280	7,630	47,890

Whole number of stamps 383,310,500.   Value $11,736,264.00.

Stamps issued during the fiscal year ending June 30th, 1869:

QUARTER ENDING :

	Sept. 30, 1868.	Dec. 31, 1868.	Mch. 31, 1869.	June 30, 1869.	Total.
1 cent	2,814,600	3,004,200	3,736,600	4,043,400	13,598,800
2 cents	14,558,400	16,405,700	18,111,900	18,115,450	67,191,450
3 cents	76,486,200	80,855,700	84,327,500	87,008,000	328,677,400
5 cents	168,820	174,960	290,520	149,180	783,480
6 cents	....	....	60,200	1,085,750	1,145,950
10 cents	854,150	940,200	1,007,560	928,270	3,730,180
12 cents	624,800	703,600	917,050	817,900	3,063,350
15 cents	233,340	428,420	784,160	606,700	2,052,620
24 cents	54,850	68,675	93,225	77,650	294,400
30 cents	55,890	74,210	86,650	89,980	306,730
90 cents	10,880	8,360	16,330	16,610	52,180

Whole number of stamps 420,896,540.   Value $12,706,220.00.

When we remember that there were no six cent stamps in the issue of 1867 nor five cent stamps in that of 1869, we at once perceive that the two issues are hopelessly mixed in the foregoing table and that it is of little value to philatelists.

Plates.

The plates of the 1861-66 issues were used for the stamps of the 1867 issue. The following list is probably incomplete but it contains all the numbers that I have seen or that have been chronicled. It has not been found possible to secure minute measurements of the grills on many of the stamps and we will, therefore, have to be content with the grouping of sizes adopted in the priced catalogues.

Plate numbers.

Grill covering the entire stamp.

1 cent blue	No.
3 cents rose	No. 11, 52
5 cents brown	No. 17
30 cents orange	No. 7

Variety :

3 cents rose.	Imperforate	No. 52
	Grill 18x15 mm.	
3 cents rose		No.
	Grill 13x16 mm.	
3 cents rose		No. 14

Variety :

3 cents rose.	Imperforate	No. 14
	Grill 11½x14 mm.	
2 cents black		No.
3 cents rose		No.
	Grill 11x13 mm.	
1 cent blue		No.
2 cents black		No. 29
3 cents rose		No. 36
5 cents brown		No. 17
10 cents green		No.
12 cents black		No. 16
15 cents black		No. 41
	Grill 9x13 mm.	
1 cent blue		No. 10, 22, 27
2 cents black		No. 28, 30, 50, 51, 53
3 cents rose		No. 11, 32, 34, 55
5 cents brown		No. 17
10 cents green		No. 15, 26
12 cents black		No. 16
15 cents black		No. 41
24 cents lilac		No. 6
30 cents orange		No. 7
90 cents blue		No. 18

Varieties :

3 cents rose.	Imperforate	No. 55
3 cents rose.	Imperforate horizontally	No. 55

The fact that many of the grilled stamps are rarer than the same values without the grill has tempted counterfeiters to imitate the embossment. This has been done with more or less success. Except for imitations of the grill covering the entire stamp the 1867 issue has not suffered greatly from the efforts of the counterfeiters. The stamps of the 1869 issue are rarer without than with the embossing and, consequently, have been but little tampered with. The 1870 issue has been the chosen field for most of the fraudulent operations, both because many of the grilled stamps of that issue are rare while those ungrilled are plentiful and because the generally poor embossing of that period renders the detection of the counterfeits very difficult.

Temptations to counterfeiting grills.

There is no absolute rule by which the genuine grills may be known from the bad. The best guide is experience, gained by careful study of specimens which are undoubtedly genuine. Size is not a guide, as may be inferred from an examination of the list on a preceding page. Neither is position a test. It has been asserted that genuine grills always have their sides parallel with the sides of the stamps. But this is manifestly incorrect. The sheets of stamps, when laid on the bed of the grill machine, might easily be placed askew, as we know was done in the case of the stamps which show a band of embossing. It may be remarked, *en passant*, that the lines of grill points in this band are usually somewhat out of the perpendicular. As was noted in describing the grill roller, the rows of points form a spiral around the roller. While this spiral deviates but little from the perpendicular, it still deviates and the claim of absolute perpendicularity for the grill becomes untenable.

Size and position not a test.

The general characteristics of all grills are the same. The bosses which produced them are pyramidal in shape and their effect is to break tiny crosses (x) in the paper. On a few grills the breaks assume a slightly different shape, thus ✕ .

Characteristics of genuine grills.

The grills with the points up present, on the face of the stamps, the appearance of a series of small squares, defined by depressed vertical and horizontal lines. Within the squares the paper has been pushed up by the bosses and broken. Viewed from the reverse the appearance is the exact opposite, the lines of the squares being raised and those within them depressed. On the reverse also, the breaks produced by the bosses show more distinctly the shape of crosses, which shape becomes more pronounced with the introduction of harder paper and smaller grills. The grills with points down have the same general appearance but, of course, reversed.

The grills of the 1869 and 1870 issues were made by the same process as those of the 1861 issue, but from differences in the paper, wearing of the machinery, and ever lessening care in manufacture, the characteristic marks are much less distinct and often quite invisible. Many of the grills on the 1870 issue are little more than pin pricks.

The counterfeit grills, as a rule, fail to reproduce the markings of the originals, especially the crosses in the squares. Many of them are simply a series of small square depressions in the paper, having the intervening spaces quite out of proportion, as compared with originals. There is, however, a genuine type of the grill covering the entire stamp which presents the appearance of small squares with still smaller depressed squares in their centres, but having otherwise the ordinary characteristics of the grills. This variety is found only on the three cent stamp and is due to a few of the earliest impressions having been made against a backing of cardboard. This was too hard and did not permit the bosses to penetrate the paper. So a backing of lead was adopted and the grills with cross-shaped breaks were obtained. Except in this instance, a square grill, instead of a cross, may without hesitation be pronounced a counterfeit.

Grills which lack the x breaks.

Grills too strongly embossed should be regarded with suspicion. The flattening effect of the hydraulic press must not be overlooked.

Cancellations are also a test in many cases. When the ink was thin it usually penetrated the breaks in the paper and may be distinctly seen on the reverse of the stamp. When, on the contrary, it was thick it covered only the raised parts of the grill and the depressed places were left untouched. In this connection may be mentioned a clever counterfeit, made from a three cent stamp with a genuine grill measuring 9x13 mm., to which has been added a fraudulent embossing covering the entire stamp. Because a portion of the grill shows the genuine markings and the cancellation covering the raised parts the balance is apt to be accepted as genuine. Examination shows the grill in different parts of the stamp to be quite dissimilar in character. When the stamp is viewed in a certain light the rectangle of genuine grilling stands out distinctly from the fraudulent part.

In the case of uncancelled stamps the character of the grill, the gum, and the shades of the printing ink must supply the tests.

The grills of the 1867 issue all measure 12½x12 rows of points to the 10 mm.

Cancellations a test.

Grill fraudulently enlarged.

ISSUE OF 1869.

Historical. The issue of 1869 was preceded by a contest, both in and out of Congress, many details of which may be found in a file of the *Congressional Globe.* Messrs. Butler & Carpenter, of Philadelphia, protested against the awarding of the contract to the National Bank Note Co., of New York, on the ground that their firm had made the lowest bid. A commission was appointed to investigate the claim and the relative merits of the bids of the two companies. The commisssion reported in favor of the National Bank Note Co. and, on October 3d, 1868, the contract was awarded in accordance with this finding. As was mentioned on page 98, the control of the embossing patent had much to do with securing this award.

Date of issue. By the terms of the contract the stamps were to be ready February 1st, 1869. They were not ready, however, until March of that year, and then were only issued to postmasters as the stock of stamps of the 1861-66 types was exhausted. They made their appearance in the latter part of April. Mr. Tiffany gives the date of the issue as March 19th, 1869, but elsewhere says: "About the end of April they began to appear." Possibly some were issued to postmasters on March 19th, but with restrictions as to their use, as set forth in the following circular :

POST OFFICE DEPARTMENT.

FINANCE OFFICE, March 1st, 1869.

SIR :—

Circular auuounc-
ing the issue.

At an early day, in the regular course of business, the Department will issue to Postmasters stamps of new designs. (See description annexed). In the proposed issue the six cent stamp is substituted for the five cents. You are required to exhaust all of the present style on hand, before supplying the public with the new ; and in no case will you be allowed to make exchanges for individuals, or to return stamps to the Department to be exchanged. The stamps now in use are not to be disregarded, but must be recognized in all cases equally with the new ones.

Special attention is called to the fact that sheets of all denominations below 15 cents contain 150 stamps. The 15 cents and all higher denominations contain 100 stamps on each sheet. This must be borne in mind to prevent mistakes in counting, as in the present issue each denomination has but 100 stamps to the sheet. Special requests for the new style of stamps will be disregarded until the stock of the present issue in possession of the Department is exhausted. Due notice will be given of the date of issue of any new design of stamped envelopes, therefore all inquiries respecting them will be disregarded.

A. N ZEVERLY,
Third Assistant Postmaster General.

Changes iu the
designs and colors. Apparently all the values were on sale by about the middle of May, as the *American Journal of Philately* for May 20th, 1869 (pages 57 and 58), gives a brief description and criticism of each value and says : "The

unqualified praise we bestowed on the new issue in our first accounts was due to it having been given from an inspection of the proofs, and those are always worked off with great care; the colors also were much better selected than those adopted by the authorities. Besides the tints being changed, all the designs were more or less altered by enlarging the figures, and in the case of the thirty cents a totally different design was adopted."

The designs, as originally prepared, differed from those finally accepted and issued in having much smaller numerals of value, which were more in harmony with their surroundings and not so obtrusive and disproportionate. *Original designs.* There was a five cent stamp of the design that was afterwards used for the six cents; the ten cents bore a portrait of Lincoln and the ninety cents that of Washington; the thirty cents was of similar style to the fifteen and twenty-four cents, with a copy of the picture of the surrender of Burgoyne. It was not the intention to print any of these stamps in two colors. All the values of this set except the fifteen and ninety cents exist in the shape of fully finished, gummed and perforated stamps.

The official description of the adopted designs and colors is as follows: *Designs and colors.*

"ONE CENT. Head of Franklin, after bust by Cerrachi, looking to the left, surrounded by a circle of pearls; 'U. S. POSTAGE' on a curved tablet at the top; 'ONE CENT' on two similar tablets at bottom, with the numeral '1' in a small panel between the words. Color, Roman ochre.

TWO CENTS. Post horse and rider, facing to left, surrounded by ornamental scroll-work; 'UNITED STATES POSTAGE' on a fringed curtain at top; 'TWO CENTS' on a scroll at bottom, with large numeral '2' between the words. Color, light brown.

THREE CENTS. Locomotive heading to the right, surrounded by ornamental scroll-work; 'UNITED STATES POSTAGE' on a curved and a horizontal tablet at top; 'THREE CENTS' on wide curved tablets at bottom, with large numeral '3' between the words. Color, ultramarine blue.

SIX CENTS. Head of Washington, after Stuart's painting, three-quarter face, looking to right; frame square, tessellated near the corners, with a circular opening, lined with pearls; 'U. S.' in upper left and right corners of frame, respectively; the word 'POSTAGE' in upper bar of frame; 'SIX CENTS' in lower, with the large numeral '6' between the words, and 'UNITED STATES' on each side. Color, ultramarine blue.

TEN CENTS. Shield, on which is resting an eagle with outspread wings, eagle looking to left; 'UNITED STATES POSTAGE' in upper section of shield; the number '10' in lower; the words 'TEN CENTS' in a scroll at bottom; the whole design surmounted by thirteen stars arranged in a semi-circle. Color, orange.

TWELVE CENTS. Ocean steamship, surrounded by ornamental scroll-work; 'UNITED STATES POSTAGE' at top; 'TWELVE CENTS' at bottom, with large numeral '12' between the words. Color, milori green.

FIFTEEN CENTS. Landing of Columbus, after the painting by Van-derlyn, in the Capitol at Washington; ornamental scroll-work at top and bottom; 'U. S. POSTAGE' at top; 'FIFTEEN CENTS' at bottom, with numeral '15' underneath. Colors: Picture, Prussian blue; scroll and ornamental work, light brown.

TWENTY-FOUR CENTS. Declaration of Independence, after the painting by Trumbull, in the Capitol at Washington; ornamental and scroll work at top and bottom; 'U. S.' surrounded by ovals at upper left and right corners, respectively; the word 'POSTAGE' between the two; 'TWENTY-FOUR CENTS' in scroll at bottom, with numeral '24' underneath. Colors: The picture, purple lake; scroll and ornamental work, light milori green.

THIRTY CENTS. Eagle, facing to left with outspread wings, resting on shield, with flags grouped on either side; the words 'U. S. POSTAGE' in upper section of shield; the numeral '30' in lower; the words 'THIRTY CENTS' across the bottom; thirteen stars arranged in a semicircle at top of design. Colors: Eagle and shield, carmine; flags and other parts, blue.

NINETY CENTS. Head of Lincoln, from a photograph, in an oval, three-quarters face, looking to right, surrounded by ornamental and scroll work; numeral '90' at each of the upper corners; 'U. S. POSTAGE' at top of oval; 'NINETY' and 'CENTS' in scroll at lower left and right corners of oval, respectively; 'U. S.' at lower left and right corners of stamp, respectively. Colors: Portrait in black; surrounding ornamental and scroll work, carmine."

Sizes. The sizes of the stamps are: One cent, $20\frac{1}{4} \times 20\frac{1}{4}$ mm.; two cents, $20\frac{1}{4} \times 20$ mm.; three cents, $20\frac{1}{2} \times 20$ mm.; six cents, $20 \times 19\frac{3}{4}$ mm.; ten cents, $20 \times 19\frac{3}{4}$ mm.; twelve cents, $20\frac{1}{4} \times 20$ mm.; fifteen cents, $21\frac{3}{4} \times 21\frac{3}{4}$ mm.; twenty-four cents, 22×22 mm.; thirty cents, $22 \times 22\frac{1}{4}$ mm.; ninety cents, $21\frac{3}{4} \times 22$ mm.

Purport of the designs. The lower values were intended to be emblematic of the postal progress of the country. The one cent stamp fittingly bore the portrait of Franklin, the first colonial Postmaster General, also the first under the federation of states which became the United States. The two, three and twelve cent stamps illustrated the advance from the post boy on horseback to the facilities afforded by the railway and ocean steamship.

Types of the fifteen cents. There are three types of the fifteen cents. In type I the central picture is surrounded by a frame of three parallel lines. Across the top of the picture the middle line of the three is thicker than the other two and at the middle of the top the lines form a diamond-shaped ornament. This type is usually spoken of as "with diamond" or "picture framed." In type I there is also, within the space for the picture, a band about $\frac{3}{4}$ mm. wide, formed of short diagonal lines. This band extends across the bottom and the two ends of the tablet but not across the top. In type II the frame lines and the diamond are omitted. There is a band of lines, as in type I, but it is 1mm. wide, the lines are horizontal and the band extends all around the inside of the tablet. Type III differs from type II in the absence of the band of shading lines, of which only a solitary line remains, crossing the top of the tablet where the outline curves up to a point under the " T " of "POSTAGE." The object of the bands of lines was to form a background for the picture and make less noticeable any slight misplacing of it. Type I was the first issued. Type III is only known in the re-issue of 1875.

The medallions of the fifteen, twenty-four and ninety cents are each surrounded by a thin line of color. These lines were not on the original dies, but were added separately to each subject on the various plates. Also, on the twenty-four cents, the space for the medallion is framed by a border of pearls inside of which are two thin colored lines. These lines were not on the die, but were added in the same manner as those surrounding the medallions. I have seen a proof having three lines inside the border of pearls but I have not found a stamp showing more than two lines.

Additional lines drawn on the plates.

The paper is moderately thick and quite hard.

The gum varies from yellowish-white to brown.

The grill has the same characteristics as in the 1867 issue but it is smaller and nearly square. Complete sets of all values may be found with the grill measuring 9x9½mm., 12x12 rows of points, and 9x9mm., 12x11 rows of points. The ten and twelve cents are also known with a grill measuring 8½x9mm., 11x11 rows of points. The normal position of the grill is with the points down but a few copies have been noticed which have the points up.

Sizes of the grill.

White Wove Paper.

Reference List.

Perforated 12.

Embossed with a Grill.

April, 1869.

1 cent pale brown-orange, brown-orange, dark brown-orange

2 cents yellow-brown, red-brown, pale brown, brown, dark brown

3 cents ultramarine, deep ultramarine, dull blue, gray-blue

6 cents pale ultramarine, deep ultramarine, dull blue

10 cents yellow-orange, orange, deep orange

12 cents yellow-green, green, deep green, blue-green

15 cents (type I), dark blue and dark red-brown, dark blue and red-brown, dark blue and pale red-brown

15 cents (type II), dark blue and dark red-brown, dark blue and red-brown, dark blue and pale red-brown

24 cents dark violet and yellow-green, dark violet and deep yellow-green, dark violet and blue-green

30 cents pale rose and pale ultramarine, rose and ultramarine, rose and dark ultramarine, dark rose and ultramarine, dark carmine and dull ultramarine

90 cents black and carmine, black and rose-carmine

Varieties :

2 cents yellow brown. Diagonal half and another copy, used as three cents

2 cents yellow brown. Vertical half and another copy, used as three cents. Cancelled, December 25th, 1869

3 cents ultramarine. Vertical two-thirds, used as two cents. Cancelled, April 2nd, 1870

15 cents (type I), dark blue and red-brown. Medallion
    inverted

24 cents dark violet and blue-green. Medallion inverted

30 cents rose and ultramarine. Flags inverted

1 cent brown-orange. Without grill

2 cents yellow-brown. Without grill

3 cents pale ultramarine, dull blue. Without grill

15 cents (type II), dark blue and red-brown. Without
    grill

24 cents dark violet and blue-green. Without grill

30 cents carmine-rose and dull ultramarine. Without grill

90 cents deep black and deep carmine. Without grill

Inverted medallions.

The stamps which have a part of the design inverted are both rare and interesting. Tiffany's *History of the Postage Stamps of the United States* says in regard to this variety of the fifteen cents :

Said to be errors in the plate.

" The error is not, as is sometimes supposed, an error in printing, but in the plate. Two plates, one for each color, had to be used. Originally there were 150 stamps, as in the smaller values, but upon the plate for printing the picture, it is said one picture was reversed, and the error once discovered, the plate was cut down to print only 100 stamps, as stated in the circular. It is probable that no copies with the error were ever circulated."

The same work says of the twenty-four cents :

" There is the same error of this stamp, ' reversed picture,' stated to be from the same cause, a defect in the plate, as for the 15 cents, and the same remarks apply."

Also of the thirty cents it is stated :

" There is also an error of this stamp in which the flags are reversed. It is also stated to be an error on the plate, but may be only an error in printing."

Evidence to the contrary.

These statements appear to lack confirmation. The records of the contractors show that the plates for the four values which were printed in two colors, were originally made with only one hundred designs on each. This smaller size was adopted because of the difficulty of securing good " registering" when printing with large plates. The official circular of March 1st, 1869, quoted on a previous page, and which was sent out before the stamps were ready for issue, distinctly states : "The 15 cents and all higher denominations, contain 100 stamps on each sheet."

The claim that none of the errors were circulated would seem to be fully refuted by the fact that the majority of the existing copies are used.

Proof that they are errors in printing.

Of course it is not impossible that, on one of the plates for each value, one of the designs was reversed but it is far more probable that all of the errors are due to misprinting. I have seen sheets of proofs from many of the plates of the bicolored stamps and none of them contain such an error. It is well known that David H. Anthony, of New York, an agent of the Government for the sale of revenue stamps, and who also sold the then current postage stamps, had an entire sheet of the fifteen cents with the medallion inverted. One copy was purchased of him and went into the Rasmus collection. The rest of the sheet was returned to the post office and exchanged for perfect copies. There is also the celebrated block of four of the twenty-four cents in the collection of Mr. William Thorne and the pair of the same stamp in the collection of Mr. F. W. Hunter. Thus at least a part of the errors are proved to be due to misprinting.

On the other hand, there is some testimony in support of the claim that one or more of the designs, on the various plates, were inverted. In the *American Journal of Philately* for December 1870 (page 141), we read :

" We are now enabled to inform our readers, and friends of the press, of a little circumstance that has been kept pretty well concealed ; but perhaps these few lines may open the eyes of the people who pay the taxes.

After a few hundred sheets of the 15 and 24 cent stamps of the 1869 issue had been delivered, it was discovered that a few of the stamps on each sheet had the picture inverted in the frames. The government refused to receive them, and only half sheets of these values were issued. This mistake would have compelled the company to prepare new plates for these values, and of course they would not have been paid for them, so they adopted the bright dodge of setting the papers to run down the new issue, so that they would be required to get new plates by the department, which they would be paid for. We all know how well they succeeded ; however, to philatelists this makes two interesting varieties which are very scarce."

Another claim concerning the errors.

In further confirmation of this Mr. J. W. Scott states that, at the time attention was first called to the fifteen cents with inverted medallion, he examined his stock and found half a dozen used copies. Believing it to be an error in the plate, he tried to buy at the New York post office sheets containing it, but could get only half sheets, which were without it. He then sent money throughout the country, to all offices which he thought might have this value, asking always for full sheets. In some instances his money was returned because the office could only supply half sheets and on other occasions the half sheets were sent. In no case did he secure an entire sheet, and the half sheets supplied to him were always the same half and without the error. Hence his conclusions, as published in the paragraph just quoted from the *American Journal of Philately.*

Only half sheets on sale.

With all due respect to such an authority and with full appreciation of the value of this testimony I cannot unhesitatingly accept these conclusions, since there is much to be said on the other side. Primarily, every plate made by the great bank note companies is subjected to the most searching and microscopical scrutiny by several experts. Plates, which to ordinary eyes would appear perfect, are marked in numerous places for fuller and deeper impressions and other improvements. It is not to be conceived that such a glaring defect as an inverted design would be overlooked or allowed to pass uncorrected. As was explained on page 47, the design could readily be obliterated and a fresh transfer entered in its place. With this simple expedient at command, it is absurd to think that the contractors continued to produce sheets of stamps of each of which, owing to defects, the government would accept only one half. In further contradiction of the half sheet theory it must be remembered that the contractors had for the fifteen cents four plates for the frames and two for the centers, and for both the twenty-four and thirty cents two plates for each part. Even should we grant an error in one plate, the others were still available.

Defective plates improbable.

A ninety cents with inverted medallion was listed in the catalogues for many years. But no copy is known to exist, and philatelists have long

Ninety cent stamp
with inverted
medallion.
ago decided that the variety originated in the imagination of a western dealer-collector. Wishing to give eclat to an auction, he inserted in the catalogue of the sale this and certain similar and equally mythical varieties of the higher values of the State Department stamps. No collector in the United States was able to get a view of them, unlimited bids did not secure them at the sale, and it could never be learned to whom they were sold ; therefore, it has been concluded that they were only a *tour de fantasie.* But I am informed, by a gentleman whose sources of information are entirely reliable, that this variety once existed, though no copy was ever allowed to be circulated. My informant once saw, among a lot of misprints and similar oddities, sheets of the four bi-colored values of this series all with inverted centeres. Of two values there were two sheets each, and of the other two values four sheets each. But he does not remember of which there were two and of which four. Though he was not interested in stamps, he was attracted by the oddity of these varieties and tried hard to obtain copies of them, but without success, and the whole lot was burned.

Bisected three
cent stamp.
　　The split three cents is an interesting variety. All the copies of this provisional with which collectors are acquainted, were used by Frank J. Bramhall (Assistant Assessor of the 6th Division of the 6th District of Virginia) in mailing, to residents of that division, blank forms for statements of the amount of their income and personal property, liable to taxation. These forms were merely folded, endorsed with the name and address of the tax-payer, the date, and the name and office of the official mailing them. Such documents would be carried in the mails as printed matter, at the rate of two cents each. Apparently there was a scarcity of two cent stamps and, to over-come the difficulty, three cents stamps were bisected. On some of the documents two-thirds of one stamp were used and on others a third from two different stamps. It is said that several hundred of these provisionals were used, but the finder destroyed the philatelic value of the greater part of them by removing the stamps from the documents. .The only copy available at this writing is dated April 2nd, 1870.

Varieties without
grill.
　　It is not known whether the varieties without grill are the result of accident or design. Their scarcity makes it certain that but few were issued in this condition, probably one or two small lots. The shades of the higher values seem to be identical in all copies, suggesting only one printing. But the three cents appears in two slight shades, and the two cents has frequently a thicker and darker gum than the other ungrilled varieties ; which would indicate a second printing of these two values. Ungrilled originals of the six, ten and twelve cents are not believed to exist. Copies which have very faint grills are frequently offered, with the claim that they are without grill but, when the stamps are viewed at the proper angle and in a good light, a trained eye will usually detect the grill. The originals without grill may be distin-guished from the re-issue of 1875 by the shades and by having brown gum, while the re-issued stamps have a crackled white gum.

Stamps on double
paper.
　　There is in the collection of Mr. H. G. Mandel a block of three cent stamps of this issue on double paper. The upper paper, which received the impression, is quite thin and is embossed over the entire surface. The under

paper is thicker and serves merely as a backing for the other. The thirty cents is also known on double paper, without any grill. It is printed in colors slightly darker than those of the ungrilled stamp on ordinary paper. These varieties are fully finished, gummed and perforated. Whether they were ever in use or are only essays has not been determined.

Articles have been written about certain lines and dots found on the stamps of this issue, especially on the values which are printed in two colors. These lines are found parallel to the sides of the stamps and also crossing them, either vertically or horizontally, at the center. The dots are usually at or near the middle of some of the four sides. Some writers have published elaborate lists of the various positions and combinations of these lines and dots. As they were merely guide marks on the plates, intended to insure the correct placing of the designs, and should have been erased after the plates were finished, they have no apparent philatelic value or interest. *Plate maker's guide marks.*

The plates of the lower values contained three hundred stamps each and those of the four higher values one hundred stamps each. The impressions from the plates of the lower values were divided vertically, making sheets of one hundred and fifty stamps. There is some evidence that the sheets of the higher values were divided in like manner into sheets of fifty stamps, though, from the official circular of March 1st, 1869, it would appear that the original intention was to issue them in full sheets of one hundred. *Plates.*

The imprint used for this issue is "NATIONAL BANK NOTE CO., NEW YORK," in small white capitals, on a colored panel with rounded ends. Two thin lines of color surround the panel. On the values from one to twelve cents inclusive, the imprint appears four times on each sheet of three hundred stamps, *i. e.*, at the top and bottom of each half sheet of one hundred and fifty. Each imprint is accompanied by "*No.*" and numerals corresponding to the recorded number of the plate. These plate numbers are placed at the top and bottom of the second vertical row of stamps on each side of the central dividing line. On the four higher values the imprints and plate numbers are arranged as on the lower values, so far as is known. On each value, those at the bottom are in the color of and belong to the plate of the vignette or central part of the stamp, and those at the top belong to the plate for the outer part of the stamp and correspond to it in color. Certain plates of the twenty-four and thirty cents appear to have been left without numbers, at least sheets of proofs show them in that condition, but numbers may have subsequently been added to the plates. *Imprints and plate numbers.*

In addition to the imprints and plate numbers there were certain other marks on the margins of the plates. On the values from one to twelve cents inclusive, these marks were placed at the middle of the top and bottom, and indicated the line on which the sheets were to be cut in half. The half sheets of one hundred and fifty stamps, fifteen horizontal rows of ten stamps each, were marked for further division into fifties, if desired. These marks were placed on the sides of the plates, between the fifth and sixth and the tenth and eleventh rows. On the one and two cent values the marginal marks were short straight lines. On the three to twelve cents they were composed of three lines, forming an arrow head. The four higher values had, at the *Marginal marks.*

middle of each of the four sides, a T shaped mark which, on the printed sheets, shows the colors of both the frame and the vignette plates.

Plate numbers.   The numbers of the plates were as follows :

1 cent	No. 1, 2.
2 cents	No. 3, 4, 5, 6, 27, 28.
3 cents	No. 7, 8, 9, 10, 11, 12, 25, 26, 29, 30.
6 cents	No. 13, 14.
10 cents	No. 15, 16.
12 cents	No. 17, 18.
15 cents (type I)	Frame No. 19. Vignette No. 19.
15 cents (type II)	" " 23. " " 23.
15 cents (type I)	" " 31. " " 23.
15 cents (type III)	" " 32. " " 23.
24 cents	" " 20: " " 20.
24 cents	" " 20. " " 24.
24 cents	" " — " " 20.
30 cents	" " 21. " " 21.
30 cents	" " — " " —
90 cents	" " 22. " " 22.

The dashes (—) in the above table indicate plates which have no number.

Plate No. 33, given in previous lists, is a new plate of the one cent value, which was made for the re-issue of 1875. It contains only 150 stamps.

Statistics of   The records show the following quantities of stamps to have been
manufacture.   prepared and delivered to the agent of the Government :

1869	1 cent.	2 cents.	3 cents.	6 cents.	10 cents.
Mch. to Dec. inclusive	11,077,050	57,387,500	268,857,750	2,593,600	1,960,280
1870 Jan. to Apl. inclusive	5,528,100	26,356,100	117,618,150	2,289,150	1,339,420
Total,	16,605,150	83,743,600	386,475,900	4,882,750	3,299,700

1869	12 cents.	15 cents.	24 cents.	30 cents.	90 cents.
Mch. to Dec. inclusive	2,595,400	776,180	139,975	151,520	34,940
1870 Jan. to Apl. inclusive	417,550	662,760	95,375	92,590	12,520
Total,	3,012,950	1,438,940	235,350	244,110	47,460

The report of the Postmaster General, dated November 15th, 1870, gives the following quantities of stamps supplied to deputy postmasters :

Stamps issued during the fiscal year ending June 30th, 1870:

QUARTER ENDING:

	Sept. 30, 1869.	Dec. 31, 1869.	Mch 31, 1870.	June 30, 1870.	Total.
1 cent	3,179,300	3,944,100	5,284,900	4,835,800	17,208,100
2 cents	17,493,600	19,285,300	23,151,250	17,900,500	77,830,650
3 cents	87,559,900	84,567,400	97,434,900	89,449,100	359,011,300
5 cents	67,520	....	....	....	67,520
6 cents	706,500	741,050	2,091,750	1,678,450	5,217,750
10 cents	821,500	744,340	1,282,250	986,210	3,834,300
12 cents	909,500	809,625	399,825	234,975	2,353,925
15 cents	470,620	482,780	576,700	439,780	1,969,880
24 cents	66,675	67,725	78,350	30,700	243,450
30 cents	108,340	84,980	82,570	60,660	336,550
90 cents	12,060	12,300	12,330	8,330	45,020

Whole number of stamps 468,118,445.   Value $13,976,768.00.

We know from other sources of information that, during the period covered by this table, stamps of the 1867, 1869 and 1870 issues were supplied to the deputy postmasters. Thus its value as a guide to philatelists is, unfortunately, greatly reduced.

It is said that forged grills have been placed upon the stamps of the re-issue of 1875. As the ungrilled stamps of the 1875 printing have been, of late years at least, scarcer than those printed in 1869, it is not probable that this fraud has been extensively practiced. In the *Philatelic Journal of America* for March, 1895, is an account of a counterfeit of the ninety cents which was made in Brussels. This was produced by some photo-gelatin process and is said to have been very perfect. Fortunately, before any of the imitations were circulated, the forger was arrested and the plate destroyed.

This beautiful series, so much admired by philatelists, did not please the public. From its first appearance it met with adverse criticism in the public press. Objections were made to the size, shape, colors, designs and gum. Interesting extracts from the newspapers of the period will be found in the, *American Journal of Philately* for 1869 (pages 57, 58, 74, 110, 111, and 146). In the same journal for August, 1869 (page 100), we find a note that a correspondent "wishes we would give engravings of the new U. S. stamps, as the high values are only to be found in a few of the large cities of the North." This indicates one of the reasons for the unpopularity of the issue. The general public did not see the handsome high values of the series. They used only the lower values, especially the three cents which, it must be admitted, was neither an interesting nor a dignified production.

Whether, as was suggested in a paragraph quoted on a preceding page, the National Bank Note Co. were interested in stirring up unfavorable comment, in the hope of bringing about a change in the issue, we have no means of knowing. Probably the stamps printed in two colors were difficult and expensive to produce but, as the terms of their contract required them to supply any new designs and plates without expense to the Government, it is doubtful if they were anxious to make so costly a change.

Whether it was due to the press, the public or the contractors, it was not long before the stamps of the 1861 type were reverted to. The *American Journal of Philately* for September, 1869 (page 107), says : "A new set of adhesives are in preparation for our country, all of the 1869 set having been withdrawn from circulation in the city except the four lowest values, and those of 1861 used in their stead." And in the number for the succeeding month (page 114), we read : "At present the National Bank Note Company are working upon 2 and 3 cents stamps only, as the post office authorities propose to call in the rest of the new issue, owing to manifold objections made by the community at large."

The stamps used instead of the different values of the 1869 series, were of the 1867 issue, rather than that of 1861, since they had the grill.

Stamps of the preceding issue again brought into use.

Issue of 1870.

The stamps of the 1869 series having failed to please either the public or the press, it was decided to replace them by a new issue. The report of the Postmaster General, dated November 15th, 1870, explains the reasons for the change and gives a brief description of the new stamps :

Historical.

" The adhesive stamps adopted by my predecessor in 1869, having failed to give satisfaction to the public, on account of their small size, their unshapely form, the inappropriateness of their designs, the difficulty of cancelling them effectually, and the inferior quality of the gum used in their manufacture, I found it necessary, in April last, to issue new stamps, of larger size, superior quality of gum, and improved designs. As the contract then in force contained a provision that the stamps should be changed, and new designs and plates furnished at the pleasure of the Postmaster General, without additional cost to the department, I decided to substitute an entire new series, one-third larger in size, and to adopt for designs the heads, in profile, of distinguished deceased Americans. This style was deemed the most eligible because it not only afforded the best opportunity for the exercise of the highest grade of artistic skill in composition and execution, but also appeared to be the most difficult to counterfeit. The designs were selected from marble busts of acknowledged excellence, as follows :

One cent, Franklin, after Rubricht ; two cents, Jackson, after Powers ; three cents, Washington, after Houdon ; six cents, Lincoln, after Volk ; ten cents, Jefferson, after Power's statute ; twelve cents, Clay, after Hart ; fifteen cents, Webster after Clevenger ; twenty-four cents, Scott, after Coffee ; thirty cents, Hamilton, after Cerrachi ; ninety cents, Commodore O. H. Perry, profile bust, after Wolcutt's statute.

The stamps were completed and issues of them began in April last. The superior gum with which they are coated is not the least of the advantages derived from the change."

The proposed new issue was announced as early as September, 1869. The *American Journal of Philately* for December of that year (page 143), gave a list of the portrait busts selected for the series. The stamps were not placed on sale, however, until about April 15th, 1870. The issue was announced by the following official circular :

CIRCULAR TO POSTMASTERS.

Circular announcing the issue.

Post Office Department.
Office of Third Assistant Postmaster General.
April 9th, 1870.

New Series of Postage Stamps.

At an early date, in the regular course of business, the Department will issue to Postmasters, postage stamps of a new design. (See description annexed).

You are required to exhaust all of the present style on hand before supplying the public with the new ; and in no case will you be allowed to make exchanges for individuals or to return the stamps to the Department to be exchanged.

The stamps now in use are not to be disregarded, but must be recognized in all cases, equally with the new ones. The stamps known as the series of 1861, of which a few are supposed to be yet outstanding, are also to be recognized. Those issued prior to the commencement of the war of the Rebellion were long since declared to be valueless.

Special attention is called to the fact that each sheet, of all denominations of the new series, contains but 100 stamps. This must be borne in mind to prevent mistakes in counting, as in the present issue some of the denominations have 150 stamps to the sheet.

Special requests for the new style of stamps will be disregarded until the stock of the present issue, in possession of the Department, is exhausted.

WM. H. TERRELL,
Third Assistant Postmaster General.

The date of issue is given by Mr. Tiffany as May, 1870, but this appears to be slightly incorrect. The *American Journal of Philately* for April 20th, 1870, gave a colored illustration of the three cents and announced the series as issued. In describing the stamps it said : "For reference we reprint from the extra of 25th March." A copy of this extra is not available but it is understood to have been merely a single leaf, giving a list of the new stamps, their designs and colors. In view of the date of the circular of the Third Assistant Postmaster General it would seem doubtful if the stamps were actually in issue on March 25th. Possibly they were described from proofs or from a set shown by some official. Probably the actual date of issue was not far from April 15th, 1870.

Date of issue.

The seven cent stamps did not appear with the other values of the series, that rate not being established until April 7th, 1870. Concerning this value the report of the Postmaster General, dated November 15th, 1870, says:

The seven cent stamp.

"Upon the conclusion of the postal treaty with the North German Confederation, fixing the single letter rate by direct steamers at seven cents, to take effect the 1st of July last, a stamp of that denomination was adopted, and the profile bust of the late Edwin M. Stanton selected for the design. This has been completed in a satisfactory manner but, owing to the temporary discontinuance of the direct mail steamship service to North Germany, it has not been issued to postmasters."

The discontinuance referred to was caused by the Franco-Prussian war.

Mr. Tiffany again seems to be in error when he gives the date of issue of this stamp as July, 1870. He was probably misled by the fact that the postal treaty above referred to was to go into effect on the 1st of that month. But it is quite evident that the appearance of the stamp was delayed until a much later date. The *American Journal of Philately* for July 20th, 1870 (page 84), says :

Date of issue.

"The seven cent stamp that we described, but omitted to state its value, has been printed off in a variety of colors and has a very beautiful appearance. They were intended to have been issued last week ; but the war in Europe and consequent stopping of the Bremen steamer, has made them useless for the present. It is very doubtful if they will be issued till peace has been established in Europe."

In the August number of the same journal (page 95), we read :

"We understand that the new seven cent stamp will be adorned with the profile of Stanton, but they will not be issued yet."

On November 15th, 1870, the report of the Postmaster General, previously quoted, distinctly says : "It has not yet been issued to postmasters."

Finally, the records of the contractors show that no seven cent stamps were printed until March, 1871.

First printing of the seven cent stamp.

It was not until April 20, 1871, that the *American Journal of Philately* reported : "The seven cent stamp * * has at length made its appearance."

At that late date it could have been of but little avail for correspondence to Germany, as the letter rate to that country was reduced to six cents by the postal treaty which was signed at Washington on March 3rd, and at Berlin on May 14th, 1871, taking effect "on the date of the dispatch of the first mail." On December 1st, 1871, a treaty was made with Denmark which established a rate of seven cents for letters to that country, beginning January 1st, 1872, and thus renewed the usefulness of the stamp of that value.

The official description of the stamps of the 1870 series is as follows :   **Designs.**

"ONE CENT. A lined rectangular ground is left uncovered near the edges of the stamp on all sides. Inside this a more distinctly outlined border of scroll work and conventionally foliated ornaments fills the space to the medallion, which contains a profile bust of Franklin. The sides of this border are symmetrically curved inward, the corners being ornamentally rounded, and on it, resting upon and following the upper curve of the medallion, is a narrow panel bearing the words 'U. S. POSTAGE'. The words 'ONE' and 'CENT', in white capitals, at the bottom, appear in two curves, drooping at the ends and separated by an ornate, heavy-faced, white figure '1'

TWO CENTS. An oval medallion, containing the profile bust of Jackson, after Powers' statue, rests upon a shield covering almost the entire stamp and placed upon a faint-lined rectangular ground. On this shield, above the medallion, is an ornamented tablet, curving with the ellipse, except at the ends of the line, which tend outward, and bearing the words 'U. S. POSTAGE'. Faint traces of leafy branches curving upward fill the space at the bottom and sides of the shield not covered by the medallion. Across this, upon a ribbon-like double-curved tablet flowing at the ends, are the words, in white capitals, 'TWO' and 'CENTS', divided by the denomination figure '2'.

THREE CENTS. Nearly the whole face of the stamp is taken up by a shield resting upon a dimly lined ground, on which shield the bust of Washington, after Houdon's statue, in an oval frame, is placed, surmounted by a curved ornamented tablet bearing the words 'U. S. POSTAGE'. Under the portrait, on a flowing ribbon with forked ends, are the words 'THREE CENTS', separated by a large Arabic white-faced figure '3'.

SIX CENTS. On a delicately lined ground appears a dark rectangular mass of color, with heavy side projections nearly one-third of the length, on which is the bust of Lincoln in an oval medallion, surmounted by a panel bearing the words 'U. S. POSTAGE'. Below the medallion, on a waved ribbon with forked ends, are the words 'SIX CENTS', in white capitals, separated by a large white Arabic figure '6'.

SEVEN CENTS. A large rectangular tablet, ornamented at the four corners with heavy balls, rests upon a background, the edges of which alone appear. On this tablet is an oval medallion containing the profile bust of Stanton, surmounted by a curved panel bearing the words 'U. S. POSTAGE', while below the medallion is a similar panel bearing the words 'SEVEN CENTS' in white capitals, separated by a white Arabic figure '7'

TEN CENTS. A large faint-lined shield rests upon a darker rectangular ground. On this shield is a profile bust of Jefferson, in an oval medallion, with the words 'U. S. POSTAGE' above and 'TEN CENTS', separated by the number "10', below, displayed in the same way as the legends on the six cent stamp.

TWELVE CENTS. On a lined rectangular frame is a raised panel of the same shape, with beveled edges. On this panel rests an oval medallion, bearing the profile bust of Henry Clay. Above and below, in curved tablets, connected on the sides by triangular joints, are respectively the words, in white capitals, 'U. S. POSTAGE' and 'TWELVE CENTS', the two latter words being separated by the number '12' in Arabic figures. The words of denomination are of block letters.

FIFTEEN CENTS. On a lined rectangular frame, with triangular panels set in near each corner, is an oval medallion bearing the profile bust of Daniel Webster. Above, in a curved tablet, ending on either side in a circular knob, are the words, in shaded white letters, 'U. S. POSTAGE'. Below, in a similar tablet, but without knobs, in small white letters, are the words 'FIFTEEN CENTS', separated by the number '15' in ornamented Arabic figures.

TWENTY-FOUR CENTS. The denomination numerals, '24' in Gothic type, are in each of the upper corners, conforming in their position to the curve of an ornamental tablet, placed immediately above an ellipitical medallion bearing a profile bust of Gen. Winfield Scott. Thirteen five-pointed stars are placed on this tablet; two at each end are blank white, while each of the eleven remaining bears a small Gothic capital letter, constituting the legend 'U. S. POSTAGE', in the color of the stamp. The denomination is given at the bottom in small white Gothic capitals 'TWENTY-FOUR', close up to and following the ellipse line, and 'CENTS' in a straight line, in the middle, below. In the left lower corner appears a flag, loosely gathered around its staff, the muzzle end and part of the wheels of a piece of field artillery, and a pile of shells ; in the right are three muskets stacked.

THIRTY CENTS. On a rectangular-lined ground is placed a heavy beveled tablet, rounded in a half circle at the bottom, and with the upper corners described by bastion-like projections. From this point down to the half circle—a distance of half an inch—the tablet is straight lined on its sides and narrower than the stamp by about one-sixteenth of an inch. On the tablet is an elliptical medallion bearing the profile bust of Alexander Hamilton. The legend, 'U. S. POSTAGE', above the medallion, is curved as on the 6-cent stamp, except that no panel encloses it, and the words 'THIRTY' and 'CENTS' appear in black capitals at the bottom, on a double-curved ribbon, dropping inward, with forked ends.

NINETY CENTS. The upper half of an elliptical medallion bearing the profile bust of Commodore Perry, is bounded by a rope, attached at each end by eye-splices to a swinging panel describing the lower half of the ellipse, and bearing the words 'NINETY' and 'CENTS' in block letters, assigned to the left and right of the number '90'. A plain tablet is the basis of the stamp, and is beveled except within one-eighth of an inch of the corners, where it exhibits sharp edges. In each upper corner is a five-pointed star, raised in the center, and in each lower corner the flukes of an anchor and part of the shank project from under the panel."

The stamps of this issue are of uniform size, measuring 20x25mm.

The paper is white wove, varying from thin to moderately thick. On many of the stamps the surface of the paper is slightly tinted by the ink. This is particularly the case with the thirty cents, which has always a gray surface from this cause.

The gum ranges from yellowish to brown.

I have recently seen the six and twenty-four cent stamps on double paper. The former was on the original cover and cancelled " Providence, R. I., Nov. 1st, 1870." These stamps were doubtless made under patent 86,952, issued February 16th, 1869, to Charles F. Steel of New York. Further reference to this patent will be made in the next chapter. This double paper was composed of a very thin paper, backed by a thicker and firmer one. The impressions were to be made on the thin paper which, it was expected, would be destroyed by any attempt to remove a cancellation. Strange to say, the two copies which I have seen were both printed on the thicker paper, which, of course, completely nullified the intention of the inventor. I think it is quite probable that other denominations of this issue exist on double paper. *Stamps on double paper.*

The stamps of this series were issued both with and without the grill and both styles appear to have been in use at the same time. The *Stamp Collectors' Magazine* for June 1st, 1870 (page 89), announces the appearance of the one, two, three, six and ten cents and says : " The 1 cent and 10 cents are on paper impressed with the quadrilled square ; the others, if we may judge simply from our specimens, are on plain paper." Other journals, when describing the stamps, do not speak of the embossing, either because it was lacking on the specimens in hand or because it was considered too familiar a feature to require comment. The records of the contractors do not make any mention of embossing on this series. *Grills.*

It had long been evident that the grill did not produce the results claimed for it nor add anything to the usefulness of the stamps. A clause in the contract required the stamps to be embossed and some pretense of applying the process was maintained at first. But it was not regularly used and finally was abandoned altogether. At such times as it was used the result was generally insignificant. On the majority of the stamps only a portion of the grill can be seen, on some of them only a few points. There are also strips in which some stamps show the grill while others have absolutely no trace of it. These defects should not be attributed to the wearing of the grill roller. They are due to the deterioration of the leaden bed on which the sheets of stamps rested. This bed had so yielded to pressure that it did not hold the sheets firmly against the roller and, as a consequence, the grill was often imperfect and sometimes lacking entirely. The pressure of the hydraulic press also helped to obliterate the grill. *Defective grills.*

Philatelists have had much cause to regret that this obsolete device was ever impressed on the stamps of this issue. Many values are rare with the grill and, as a consequence, have tempted the forgers. When a grill is *Counterfeit grills.*

strongly impressed it is usually possible to decide as to its merits or demerits. When, however, it is indistinct, it becomes extremely difficult to pronounce upon its character   It is impossible to establish any fixed rules for distinguishing the good from the bad. A thorough understanding of the characteristics of all genuine grills, as well as of the paper, gum and shades of the stamps of this particular issue, are the most reliable guides. With study and experience there comes an instinctive knowledge of the subject, to which one cannot give adequate verbal expression.

It may be of passing interest to know what became of the grill rollers —the only important part of the machinery—after their use was discontinued.

Destruction of the grill rollers. In 1884, the American Bank Note Co., who held the contract for printing the tickets for the New York and Brooklyn Bridge, were called upon to provide a machine to destroy the tickets which had been used. The grill rollers were utilized to make this machine. Around them were cut alternate grooves and knife-like edges and they were placed in such juxtaposition that, when the tickets were passed between them, they were cut into shreds. The machine was afterwards abandoned for some other process, but its interest for philatelists ceased when there was no further possibility of it being used to produce grills.

The grills of the 1870 issue vary somewhat in size, though they have not such an extensive range as those of the 1867 issue. Several values have *Varieties of the grill.* been found with the grill extending from top to bottom of the stamp and varying in width. As was explained on page 99, this variety is caused by a continuous band of bosses on each end of the roller.

As many of the grills show only a few points, it would be impossible to assign every specimen to a particular heading and, therefore, it seems best to give separate lists of the sizes of the grills and shades of the stamps.

The following list has been arranged from one compiled by Mr. J. B. Leavy, and published in the *American Journal of Philately* for April, 1896, to which I have added a number of varieties from personal observation :

Reference List of grills.	Rows of points.	Size in mm.
1 cent ultramarine	10X10	8x8
2 cents red-brown	"	"
1 cent ultramarine	10X12	8x10
2 cents red-brown	"	"
3 cents green	"	"
3 cents green	10X13	8x10½
3 cents green	11X11	8½x9
6 cents carmine-rose	11X12	8½x9½
1 cent ultramarine	11X13	8½x10½
2 cents red-brown	"	"
3 cents green	"	"
7 cents vermilion	"	"
12 cents pale dull violet	"	"
15 cents bright orange	"	"
24 cents dull purple	"	"
90 cents carmine-lake	"	"

	Rows of points.	Size in mm.
90 cents carmine-lake	11x15	8½x12½
3 cents green	12x14	9x11
24 cents dull purple	12x15	9x12
90 cents carmine-lake	"	"
1 cent ultramarine	13x15	10x12
2 cents red-brown	"	"
3 cents green	"	"
6 cents carmine-rose	"	"
7 cents vermilion	"	"
10 cents brown	"	"
15 cents bright orange	"	"
30 cents black	"	"
1 cent ultramarine	13x16	10x12½
3 cents green	"	"
7 cents vermilion	"	"
90 cents carmine-lake	"	"

The stamps are found in the following colors and shades :

Reference List of colors.

White Wove Paper.

Perforated 12.

With grill 8 to 8½x8 to 10½mm.

April 15th, 1870.   1 cent pale ultramarine, ultramarine, deep ultramarine,
      2 cents pale red-brown, red-brown, orange-brown
      3 cents pale green, green
      6 cents carmine-rose
April, 1871.   7 cents scarlet-vermilion
April 15th, 1870.   12 cents pale dull violet
      15 cents bright orange
      30 cents full black
      90 cents carmine-lake

With grill 9 to 10x11 to 12½mm.

1 cent pale ultramarine, ultramarine, dark ultramarine,
  bright ultramarine
2 cents pale red-brown, red-brown, orange-brown
3 cents pale green, green, pale yellow-green, yellow-green,
  deep green
6 cents pale carmine-rose, carmine-rose, carmine
7 cents scarlet-vermilion, vermilion
10 cents yellow-brown, brown, dark brown
15 cents bright orange, orange, deep orange
24 cents pale dull purple
30 cents full black
90 cents carmine-lake

Varieties :

1 cent ultramarine.   Grill extending from top to bottom
2 cents red-brown, pale red-brown   "   "   "
3 cents yellow-green, light green   "   "   "
6 cents carmine-rose, carmine   "   "   "
7 cents scarlet-vermilion   "   "   "
10 cents yellow-brown   "   "   "
12 cents dull violet   "   "   "
30 cents full black   "   "   "

Without grill.

1 cent pale ultramarine, ultramarine, dark ultramarine,
    bright ultramarine, gray-blue, dull blue, chalky
    blue
2 cents pale red-brown, red-brown, deep red-brown,
    orange-brown, brown, dark brown
3 cents gray-green, pale green, green, yellow-green
6 cents pale rose, rose, brown-rose, rose-carmine, carmine,
    brown-carmine, violet-carmine
7 cents scarlet-vermilion, orange-vermilion, vermilion
10 cents yellow-brown, brown, dark brown, gray-brown,
    dark gray-brown
12 cents pale dull violet, dull violet, gray-violet
15 cents pale bright orange, bright orange
24 cents red-purple, purple, deep purple, gray-purple
30 cents full black, gray-black
90 cents carmine-lake, lake

Varieties :

2 cents red-brown. Diagonal half and another copy,
    used as three cents. Cancelled at Hardy, Ala.,
    April 2nd, 1872
3 cents green. Imperforate
3 cents green. Impression on the reverse

Double paper.

6 cents carmine
24 cents purple

Plates.   Each of the plates of the 1870 issue contained two hundred stamps, arranged is two panes, side by side. The impressions from these plates were divided into sheets of one hundred stamps each. The imprint appears at the middle of the top and bottom of each half of the plate. Between each imprint and the central dividing line is the number of the plate, in script numerals, preceded by "*No.*" Two styles of imprint were used. The first was "NATIONAL BANK NOTE CO. NEW YORK", in white capitals, on a small panel with rounded ends, surrounded by two thin colored lines. The second imprint was "ENGRAVED AND PRINTED BY THE—NATIONAL BANK NOTE CO. NEW YORK", in two lines of white capitals, on a tablet with pearled edge and

surrounded by a single thin colored line.   The first variety has been seen on
plates numbered as high as 27 and the second on 32 and higher numbers.

The plate numbers are :   Plate numbers.

1 cent	No. 16, 17, 50, 51, 52, 53.
2 cents	No. 12, 13, 14, 15, 28, 30, 34, 35, 45, 46, 47.
3 cents	No. 1, 2, 3, 4, 5, 6, 7, 8, 9, 10, 11, 25, 29, 31, 32, 36, 37, 38, 39, 40, 41, 42, 43, 44, 54, 55.
6 cents	No. 26, 27.
7 cents	No. 33.
10 cents	No. 18, 19, 48, 49.
12 cents	No. 24.
15 cents	No. 20.
24 cents	No. 21.
30 cents	No. 22.
90 cents	No. 23.

The imperforate three cent stamps were printed from plate 11.

Only a very limited amount of information can be obtained in regard
to the plate numbers of the embossed stamps.   The following numbers are
all that are known but, doubtless, many other plates were used, especially for
the one, two and three cent stamps.   Plate numbers of the grilled stamps.

2 cents	No. 45.
3 cents	No. 11.
7 cents	No. 33.
12 cents	No. 24.
15 cents	No. 20.
24 cents	No. 21.
30 cents	No. 22.
90 cents	No. 23.

The records show the following quantities of stamps to have been
printed and delivered to the Stamp Agent :   Statistics of manufacture.

	1870 Apl. to Dec. inclusive.	1871 Jan. to Dec. inclusive.	1872 Jan. to Dec. inclusive.	1873 Jan. to Apl. inclusive.	Total.
1 cent	13,404,400	21,573,400	64,705,900	38,408,000	138,091,700
2 cents	54,674,800	90,416,500	73,018,200	22,626,400	240,735,900
3 cents	252,804,450	369,632,700	417,952,400	164,570,100	1,204,959,650
6 cents	4,666,450	8,270,250	10,193,050	4,269,100	27,398,850
7 cents	....	1,486,700	1,066,100	394,100	2,946,900
10 cents	2,619,180	3,395,870	3,443,270	1,187,240	10,645,560
12 cents	665,995	1,104,600	1,075,525	484,325	3,330,445
15 cents	1,026,840	1,856,680	1,871,420	826,860	5,581,800
24 cents	122,000	229,450	299,625	135,975	787,050
30 cents	131,580	258,620	366,573	106,770	863,543
90 cents	23,100	119,240	57,580	13,530	213,450

REMAINDERS.

1 cent.	2 cents.	3 cents.	6 cents.	7 cents.	10 cents.
12,227,300	5,826,900	56,092,900	1,155,250	422,600	925,440

12 cents.	15 cents.	24 cents.	30 cents.	90 cents.
363,050	390,700	581,450	509,060	85,570

These remainders doubtless represent an undistributed balance of stamps from several preceding issues and not from the 1870 issue alone.

Deliveries to postmasters. The reports of the Postmaster General supply the following statistics of stamps distributed to deputy postmasters:

Stamps issued during the fiscal year ending June 30th, 1871:

QUARTER ENDING:

	Sept. 30, 1870.	Dec. 31, 1870.	Mch. 31, 1871.	June 30, 1871.	Total.
1 cent	3,684,800	5,163,000	5,699,100	5,605,900	20,152,800
2 cents	17,222,300	22,756,850	24,571,100	21,174,300	85,724,550
3 cents	86,944,500	97,146,100	99,791,100	93,719,500	377,601,200
6 cents	1,414,100	1,723,500	2,109,900	2,038,150	7,285,650
7 cents	....	....	166,400	427,600	594,000
10 cents	803,880	886,260	963,030	926,430	3,579,600
12 cents	231,500	246,350	303,725	232,675	1,014,250
15 cents	326,480	346,640	503,320	463,620	1,640,060
24 cents	30,300	78,075	57,725	71,925	238,025
30 cents	28,920	67,320	69,110	70,150	235,500
90 cents	5,070	9,910	14,770	30,790	60,540

Whole number of stamps 498,126,175.   Value $14,630,715.00.

Stamps issued during the fiscal year ending June 30th, 1872:

QUARTER ENDING:

	Sept. 30, 1871.	Dec. 31, 1871.	Mch. 31, 1872.	June 30, 1872.	Total.
1 cent	4,846,000	5,422,400	6,531,800	10,862,900	27,663,100
2 cents	21,669,200	23,001,900	25,918,800	21,383,600	91,973,500
3 cents	94,873,100	102,041,000	105,623,600	101,963,800	404,501,500
6 cents	2,002,700	2,119,500	2,722,950	2,384,600	9,229,750
7 cents	449,600	361,100	257,300	247,900	1,315,900
10 cents	808,860	677,550	922,970	708,160	3,117,540
12 cents	268,775	299,425	338,675	318,475	1,225,350
15 cents	378,180	411,560	580,900	431,460	1,802,100
24 cents	52,775	47,025	116,500	61,950	278,250
30 cents	58,350	51,010	108,990	57,580	275,930
90 cents	24,380	12,680	13,650	21,440	72,150

Whole number of stamps 541,455,070.   Value $15,840,649.00.

Stamps issued during the fiscal year ending June 30th, 1873:

QUARTER ENDING:

	Sept. 30, 1872.	Dec. 31, 1872.	Mch. 31, 1873.	June 30, 1873.	Total.
1 cent	25,335,200	21,976,000	26,206,100	24,335,400	97,852,700
2 cents	11,398,900	14,316,900	17,518,700	13,158,800	56,393,300
3 cents	100,535,000	109,830,000	109,519,800	108,729,600	428,614,400
6 cents	2,323,250	2,762,250	3,026,250	2,589,600	10,701,350
7 cents	166,300	394,600	270,300	281,100	1,112,300
10 cents	713,210	1,098,930	932,230	673,100	3,417,470
12 cents	270,775	347,600	324,250	322,925	1,265,550
15 cents	399,000	457,060	536,440	502,900	1,895,400
24 cents	35,975	85,200	84,400	75,425	281,000
30 cents	70,220	129,780	73,320	71,990	345,310
90 cents	8,160	24,330	7,500	12,750	52,740

Whole number of stamps 601,931,520.   Value $16,681,189.00.

As the stamps of the 1870 issue appeared in April of that year and the contract of the National Bank Note Co. expired on April 30th, 1873, it is evident that the preceding tables do not accurately report the total issue of the stamps manufactured by that company.

ISSUES OF 1873-75.

Historical. In December, 1872, the Postmaster General, as required by law, advertised for bids for supplying the postage stamps that would be required by the Post Office Department for a period of four years, beginning May 1st, 1873. This contract was awarded to the Continental Bank Note Co. of New York.

By order of the Department, the designs prepared by the National Bank Note Co., in 1870, were continued in use. The new contractors completed their first plate on April 7th, 1873, and began printing stamps at once. It is not possible to say how soon after May 1st, the issue of the stamps to the public was begun. The first notice of them appears in the *American Journal of Philately* for August 15th, 1873 (page 126), where we read :

"The difference is easily noticed without the aid of the Company's imprint, the colors being paler than heretofore, and of a slightly washy appearance."

This, however, was not the only difference, for the manufacturers had provided other means of identifying the stamps made by them. On most of Secret marks on the stamps. the values they placed secret marks. These marks were quite sufficient to distinguish their stamps from those of the preceding contractors but, at the same time, were of so unobtrusive a nature as to escape detection for many years, even by the sharp eyes of philatelists. Much interest was excited by the announcement in March, 1895, of the discovery of the secret mark on the twelve cents. This was followed, in succeeding months, by the finding of similar marks on all the other values of the series expect the thirty cents.

Undoubtedly the object of these marks was to provide a simple and positive proof that the stamps bearing them were the product of the Con- Purpose of the secret marks. tinental Bank Note Co. For several years previous to 1873 there had been much complaint, both by the public and the press, as to the quality of our postage stamps, not only in regard to the designs and colors but also as to poor printing and gumming. It is understood that the Continental Bank Note Co. believed that large quantities of the stamps made by their predecessors were of inferior quality. And they feared, because the designs used by the two contractors were identical, that these inferior stamps might, at some later date, be thrown on their hands by the Government, with the claim that they were produced under their contract and must be replaced by them. To forestall any such possibility the secret marks were added.

The new contractors also made haste to provide themselves with new plates, made from the altered dies, that they might not be required to make any use of the plates of their predecessors. By the date of the commencement of their contract they had an ample supply of plates for all values from one to fifteen cents inclusive. In view of these facts, I have never believed in printings by the Continental Bank Note Co. from plates of the National Bank Note Co., except for the three higher values, though such printings have been listed in various publications. The correctness of this conclusion is confirmed by those whose position enables them to speak with authority.

The following enlarged illustrations will assist the reader in understanding the description of the secret marks :

NATIONAL BANK NOTE CO.

1 cent.   2 cents.   3 cents.   6 cents.   7 cents.   10 cents.

CONTINENTAL BANK NOTE CO.

1 cent.   2 cents.   3 cents.   6 cents.   7 cents.   10 cents.

NATIONAL BANK NOTE CO.

12 cents.   15 cents.   24 cents.   90 cents.

CONTINENTAL BANK NOTE CO.

12 cents.   15 cents.   24 cents.   90 cents.

Briefly described, the secret marks are as follows :

ONE CENT. A small curved dash in the first pearl at the left of the numeral "1."

TWO CENTS. A short diagonal line below the colorless ball at the left of the "s" of "u. s." This line can only be seen on very clearly printed copies. But if, at this point, the space between the ornamental outline of the panel which is inscribed "u. s. POSTAGE" and the first vertical line of the background (counting toward the left) is blurred or partly filled with color, it may be accepted as an indication of the presence of the line. On all the stamps printed by the National Bank Note Co. this space is quite clear and white.

THREE CENTS. A heavy shading below the upper fork of the ribbon which bears the word "THREE."

SIX CENTS. In the curve of the ribbon bearing the word "SIX" the first four lines, counting from the left, are recut and deepened.

SEVEN CENTS. Two small semi-circles drawn around the ends of the lines which outline the ball in the lower right corner.

TEN CENTS. A small colored semi-circle in the white ball which terminates the right hand end of the panel inscribed "U. S. POSTAGE."

TWELVE CENTS. The two white balls of the "2" of "12" have been cut away until they are nearly crescent shape.

FIFTEEN CENTS. In the triangle in the upper left corner, two lines at the lower angle have been deepened and form a sort of "V."

TWENTY-FOUR CENTS. In the star at the extreme right of the semi-circle above the medallion five lines have been much deepened and two others slightly so.

THIRTY CENTS. No secret mark have been discovered on this value, though the engraver who added the marks to the other stamps is positive that the thirty cents was similarly treated.

NINETY CENTS. Five lines of the star in the upper right corner have been deepened.

The Continental Bank Note Co. did not make new plates for the twenty-four, thirty and ninety cent stamps. They did not print any stamps of these **No secret marks on** values before the year 1874 and then felt themselves safe in using the plates **the three higher** of the National Bank Note Co. For these reasons we do not find any secret **values.** marks on the stamps of these three values which were printed by the first named company. They may only be distinguished by differences in the shades, paper and gum. Our knowledge of the secret marks which were intended to appear on these stamps is obtained from proof impressions from the altered dies.

Except for the addition of the secret marks the designs of the stamps of the 1873 series are the same as those of the 1870 issue. The size is, of course, unchanged.

A circular, issued by the Third Assistant Postmaster General, under date of June 21st, 1875, announced the reduction of the rate of postage to **Five cent stamp** five cents, to those countries which had united in the Universal Postal Union, **announced.** and the preparation of a stamp of that value. It may be interesting to know which countries constituted the Postal Union at its inception. The treaty was signed at Berne on Oct. 9th, 1874, by delegates from the following countries :   •

Germany, Austria, Hungary, Belgium, Denmark (including Iceland and the Faroe islands), Egypt, Spain (including the Balaeric isles, the Canary **Countries to the** islands, the Spanish possessions on the northern coast of Africa, and the **Universal Postal** postal establishments of Spain on the western coast of Morocco), Great **Union.** Britain (including the island of Malta), Greece, Italy, Luxemburg, Norway, Netherlands, Portugal (including Madeira and the Azores), Roumania, Russia (including the Grand Duchy of Finland), Servia, Sweden, Switzerland, Turkey and the United States. Subsequently this treaty was duly approved and ratified by the governments of each of these countries and acts of ratification were exchanged at Berne on May 3rd, 1875. At that date France also gave its adhesion to the treaty, with certain reservations, the principal of which was that the treaty should not enter into effect, so far as France was concerned, until January 1st, 1876. For the other countries the treaty took effect on July 1st, 1875.

The above mentioned circular further stated :

"The changes in foreign postages will render unnecessary the further use of the 7, 12 and 24 cent stamps and stamped envelopes, and they will accordingly be discontinued.

In order to avoid the liability to mistake caused by the near similarity in color between the two and ten cent stamp, the former will in future be printed in vermilion, the color of the discontinued seven cent stamp."

Three denominations discontinued.

The stock of the discontinued values was ordered to be used up, so far as possible. These changes were to take effect on July 1st, 1875.

Mr. Tiffany gives the date of issue of the five cent stamp as Oct. 5th, 1875, but this is evidently incorrect. As will be seen, on a subsequent page, in the tables of stamps issued to deputy postmasters, 363,180 of this value were issued in the quarter ending June 30, 1875. And in the *American Journal of Philately* for June 20th, 1875 (page 90) we find the stamp illustrated and described as "come to hand." The report of the Postmaster General, dated Nov. 15th, 1875, says : "To meet the new letter rate of foreign postage under the treaty of Berne, postage stamps of the denomination of five cents began to be issued on the 21st of June last." This statement is apparently based on the circular previously quoted, and may not be absolutely correct. The stamp was probably issued between the 15th and 30th of June, 1875.

Date of issue of the five cent stamp.

The description of the stamp is as follows :

Design.

"FIVE CENTS (Taylor). Tablet, legend, and denomination are of a style very similar to the 10 cent stamp. The portrait of Gen. Zachary Taylor is the only full face in the series. The dress is an open double-breasted military coat within which appear the neck stock and high white collar."

The stamp is of the same size as the other denominations of the series, 20x25mm.

The die for this stamp was supplied to the contractors by the Bureau of Engraving and Printing, by whom the vignette had been used on the six ounce tobacco stamp of the series of 1871. To conform with the rest of the series the vignette was placed in a medallion, surrounded by devices identical with those on the ten cent stamp. The head was too large for the medallion and the result was incongruous.

Origin of the die.

The years covered by the contracts of the Continental Bank Note Co. were prolific in designs and patents intended to prevent the cleaning and re-use of postage stamps. Some of these ideas were given a trial while others apparently did not get beyond the preparatory stage.

The majority of collectors are probably not aware that this company made use of the grill. In spite of the admitted failure of this device, when used by their predecessors, they provided themselves with the necessary machinery and applied the process to a few thousand stamps. The correctness

Grills.

of this statement is vouched for by the Treasurer of the company, the Superintendent of the stamp department, the patentee of the process and the man who made the grill roller. In the collection of a New York amateur is an impression from the roller, on a sheet of white paper the size of a sheet of stamps. There are also in two New York collections, a very few copies of the grilled stamps. The grill is small and very clearly impressed. It measures 7¼x9½mm., or 10x12 rows of points. The grills are placed 14mm. apart horizontally and 18mm. vertically. The bosses, instead of being perfect pyramids, as on previous grills, are not brought to a point but have the top truncated. Thus the impressions have the appearance of a group of tiny rectangles instead of crosses.

What is known as the Fletcher or cog-wheel grill—patent 91,108, issued to C. A. Fletcher, June 8th, 1869—was applied to the one and three **Fletcher or cog-wheel punch.** cent stamps of this series. It was produced by eight punches, shaped like the letter U and placed in a circle with the openings inward. These punches cut through the paper but did not remove anything. The result was suggestive of a wheel with cogs. The expectation was that, the stamp having been attached to an envelope, it would be impossible to remove it without destroying it. Ten thousand copies of these stamps were made and placed on sale in the post office at Washington, D. C., in the year 1877.

The stamps of the 1873-75 series were also printed, by way of experiment, on various papers which had been chemically treated. They are known **Chemical papers.** on yellow-brown and violet paper, the latter both wove and laid. These papers being sensitive to chemicals, any attempt to remove the cancellation would at once become evident. Postmarked copies have been seen, but the stamps are not known to have been issued for postal use, and the best informed collectors regard them as being only essays.

In the preceding chapter reference was made to stamps printed on the **Double paper.** double paper patented by Charles F. Steel. The following extract from the *Coin and Stamp Journal* for January, 1877, indicates a somewhat extensive printing of the stamps of this issue on that paper :

"It is not generally known, and will be news to our collectors, that about a year ago, 20,000,000 stamps were issued to the public, printed on double paper. The upper portion receiving the impression was soft and porous and it was supposed that any attempt to clean off the cancelling mark would render the impressed portion perfectly pulpy and thus effectually destroy it. The stamps did not meet with much favor and the plan was abandoned."

These stamps seem to have been lost sight of until a few years ago when search was made and a number of values discovered. The catalogues present quite an extensive list but it is doubtful if all these values were really printed on the double paper. Many stamps on the soft porous paper used by the American Bank Note Co. are not difficult to split and might be mistaken for those on the double paper. But experienced collectors can usually tell the difference. As a rule, when an attempt is made to split the stamps of the American Bank Note Co., they do not separate smoothly for their entire length but the paper divides unevenly and the attempt results in tearing off a piece of the stamp. On the contrary, those which are really on the double paper will separate easily and evenly throughout. Occasionally these stamps may be separated by soaking them in water. There were apparently only one or two printings and the collector who becomes familiar with the shades of the inks which were used can always tell the stamps by that means.

Another variety of the double paper had the surface paper weakened by numerous short horizontal cuts, the object being, of course, to increase the difficulty of removing a cancellation. I have seen the three cent stamp printed on this paper, gummed and perforated like the regular issue. It is stated that this stamp was sold to the public at the post office at Washington, D. C.

Variety of the double paper.

A somewhat similar patent was issued to the same patentee. In the application for the patent it is described as follows :

169,125. (Filed March 15, 1875).

CHARLES F. STEEL,

New York, New York.

To all whom it may concern :

Be it known that I, Charles F. Steel, Superintendent of the manufacture of postage stamps for the Continental Bank Note Company, in New York City, in the State of New York, have invented certain improvements relating to postage stamps of which the following is a specification :

Starched paper.

Many efforts have been made by myself and others to produce a practically successful postage stamp, from which the cancelling ink cannot be removed to allow of their fraudulent re-use. My present invention is for that purpose.

I take a soft unsized paper, analogous to blotting paper, quite soft and absorbent. Having printed the face from the properly engraved plates, and allowed the ink thereon to dry properly, I treat the back with a solution of starch of just a proper consistency, having the effect both to lay a thin coating or covering on the back surface, and also to fill the interstices between the fibers in the paper, so as to give the back surface of the paper a firmer character than the front. Then, after flattening in a press, I apply British gum or other adhesive layer on the back of the starch layer, and having again pressed the sheet of stamps, they are ready for shipment and used like ordinary stamps. My improved stamp is cheaper to produce than the double thickness stamp described in my patent of 1869 (No. 86,952) while it possesses in a great degree the same desirable qualities. The soft face will readily absorb the cancelling ink, and will be soaked and washed away on any attempt to remove the latter.

This soft body paper should be of such a character, as to be removed and destroyed by a moderate friction after being wetted, care being taken to avoid employing so extremely soft a paper as will become destroyed by ordinary unskillful manipulation in affixing the stamp. What is called in the trade "water leaf" paper will suffice.

The layer of starch should be of such consistency as to strike a little, but only a little, into the thickness of the paper. The qualities of the soft body induce less disposition in the stamp to curl when moistened and applied on a letter, there is also less disposition to curl after the gumming, in the process of manufacture. Less care is required in the subsequent pressing and preparation, in the handling and shipment. A thinner and lighter paper may be employed. I claim as my invention—A Postage or Revenue stamp formed wholly of water-leaf or other soft and absorbent paper, provided on the back with a filling coating of starch or analogous material, and a superposed coating of ordinary gum, substantially as and for the purpose set forth.

In testimony whereof I have hereunto set my hand, on this 13th day of March, 1875, in the presence of two subscribing witnesses.

CHAS. F. STEEL.

Witnesses : WM. C. DEY,

M. A. VAN NAMEE.

Stamps made according to this patent are occasionally seen. Postally cancelled copies have not been reported, but all, so far as we know, are cancelled with pen marks. They are, presumably, only essays.

The paper used by the Continental Bank Note Co. varied greatly. The majority of the stamps are on a stiff, hard paper, varying from quite thin to moderately thick. A few copies have been seen which are on a semi-transparent, almost pelure paper. At some time during the second contract of this company, 1877 to 1881, a paper was introduced which somewhat resembles that used by the American Bank Note Co. in that it is porous, but it is thinner

The papers in regular use.

and not quite as soft. A few months before the consolidation with the American Bank Note Co., which took place February 4th, 1879, the Continental Bank Note Co. began to use a thick, soft, porous paper, very similar to, if not the same as, that used after the consolidation, or from 1879 to 1894. It is practically impossible to distinguish the printings of the two companies on this paper and it seems best to attribute all such to the American Bank Note Co. I have seen authentic specimens of the one and three cents printed by the Continental Co. on this paper. The colors are soft, pale and rather blurred. The one cent is in pale blue and sky blue and the three cents in gray-green and deep green. The former value was printed from plates 307 and 327 and the latter from plates 265 and 290. Beyond this I have no information regarding the printings on this paper.

In addition to these papers and the double paper, previously mentioned, there was a thick hard paper with vertical or horizontal ribbing. It **Ribbed paper.** must be admitted that this is not an extremely interesting variety but, possibly because some values are difficult to find on this paper, it has attracted the attention of philatelists and attained a place in the catalogues. Many of the departmental stamps are quite common on ribbed paper and, on the contrary, some of the regular issue are scarce. Strange to say, most philatelists pay very little attention to the former but seem eager to secure the latter.

Mr. Crawford Capen says in the *Post Office* for February, 1897 (page 151): "The first use of paper of this kind was made in 1873, the largest use in 1874 and the final use late in 1875 or possibly early in 1876." The number of shades of the different values is comparatively limited and would seem to warrant the conclusion that the stamps represent a few printings but an extended period of distribution.

Stamps on this paper are not easy to distinguish, at least not until one has acquired a certain degree of familiarity with their characteristics. A notable point is a richness and fullness of color, combined with clearness of impression and a high finish which often gives them a sort of sheen. By this quality and their characteristic shades an expert is frequently able to select stamps on this paper, without having to look for the ribs. By holding the stamps horizontally between the eye and a good light the ribbing may usually be detected. As a rule, it is vertical on the stamps of the regular issue and horizontal on the departmental stamps, though there are, of course, exceptions. Mr. Capen also recommends wetting the stamps thoroughly and watching them as they dry. The appearance of the ribbing is usually that of fine corrugations, but occasionally it is more like that of closely laid paper. Some of the stamps on the soft porous paper also present an appearance of ribs, but they are too close together and are only an effect of the wire-wove paper. Some of the department stamps, especially those of the Department of Justice, show, in the background of the medallion, distinct vertical lines, very like ribs. These are not the real thing but were caused by the fibres of the cloths, which were used in wiping the plates, and which drew the ink into slight ridges.

The gum is yellowish or brownish; on a very few specimens it is almost white.

The stamps are found in the following shades and varieties :

Perforated 12.

White Wove Paper.

May 1st, 1873. 1 cent pale ultramarine, ultramarine, deep ultramarine, pale dull blue, dull blue, chalky blue, pale gray-blue, gray-blue, sky blue, bright blue

2 cents red-brown, deep red-brown, orange-brown, dark brown, black-brown, gray-brown, bistre-brown, brown

3 cents bright yellow-green, pale yellow-green, yellow-green, deep yellow-green, green, dark green, blue-green, dark blue-green, olive-green, pale dull green, dull green, dark dull green, gray-green

6 cents dull rose, brown-rose

7 cents vermilion, scarlet-vermilion

10 cents pale brown, brown, dark brown, chocolate, pale yellow-brown, yellow-brown, orange-brown, red-brown, pale gray-brown, gray-brown

12 cents dull violet, deep violet, black-violet

15 cents pale orange, orange, red-orange

24 cents bluish purple, deep bluish purple

30 cents gray-black, greenish black

90 cents pale rose-carmine, rose-carmine

June, 1875. 2 cents orange-vermilion, vermilion, scarlet vermilion, deep scarlet-vermilion

5 cents blue, dark blue, greenish blue, deep greenish blue

Varieties :

1 cent pale ultramarine. With grill $7\frac{1}{4}$x$9\frac{1}{2}$mm.
2 cents dark brown " "
3 cents green " "
6 cents dull rose " "
7 cents vermilion " "
12 cents dull violet " "
15 cents pale orange " "
1 cent ultramarine. Paper cut with a cog-wheel punch.
3 cents blue-green " " " "
2 cents scarlet-vermilion. Imperforate.
3 cents dull green "
3 cents gray-green. Horizontal pair, imperforate between.
10 cents brown " " " "

Horizontally or Vertically Ribbed Paper.

1873-76. 1 cent pale ultramarine, ultramarine, gray-blue, dull blue, sky blue

2 cents red-brown, orange-brown, dark orange brown,
    pale brown, brown

3 cents yellow-green dark yellow-green, green, dark
    green, pale blue-green

6 cents dull rose, brown-rose

7 cents vermilion

10 cents pale brown, brown

12 cents black-violet

15 cents deep orange, red-orange

24 cents bluish purple (?)

30 cents gray-black

90 cents rose-carmine (?)

2 cents vermilion

5 cents dark blue

Double Paper.

1876.

1 cent dark ultramarine

2 cents dark brown

3 cents green, dark green, pale blue-green

6 cents dull rose

10 cents brown

30 cents gray-black

2 cents scarlet-vermilion

5 cents dark blue

Variety:

3 cents dark blue-green. Surface paper weakened by
    short horizontal cuts.

Soft Porous White Wove Paper.

1878.

1 cent pale blue, sky blue

3 cents gray-green, deep gray-green

The twenty-four and ninety cents have been reported on ribbed paper, but, until the information is confirmed by acknowledged experts, it seems best not to give full credit to the report.

The plates of the 1873-75 issue contained two hundred stamps each. The impressions were divided vertically through the middle into sheets of one hundred stamps. The imprint appears at the middle of the top and bottom of each half of the plate. It is very much like the second style used by the National Bank Note Co. and reads " PRINTED BY THE—CONTINENTAL BANK-NOTE CO. NEW YORK.", in two lines of white capitals, on a panel with pearled edges and surrounded by a thin colored line. Between each imprint and the central dividing line appear " *No.*" and the plate number. Numbers 2 to 193 inclusive are ordinary numerals, inserted with punches. Numbers 1 and 219 to 310 inclusive (excepting 233) are script numerals, from 5½ to 7½mm. high, engraved on the plates. Of numbers 194 to 218 inclusive and 233 nothing definite is known. These numbers were assigned to the newspaper and periodical stamps of the 1875 issue but there is no evidence that they were ever placed on the plates.

Plates.

The plate numbers are :

1 cent	No. 12, 13, 16, 26, 125, 126, 127, 128, 142, 143, 144, 146, 147, 156, 157, 158, 159, 160, 181, 182, 229, 230, 294, 295, 298, 299, 300, 301, 307, 308.
2 cents brown	No. 2, 3, 4, 6, 161, 162, 163, 164, 165, 166, 167, 168, 169, 234, 241, 242.
2 cents vermilion	No. 161, 162, 163, 164, 165, 166, 167, 168, 169, 234, 241, 242, 245, 246, 296, 297.
3 cents	No. 1, 5, 7, 8, 9, 10, 11, 14, 15, 17, 19, 20, 129, 130, 131, 132, 133, 135, 136, 138, 139, 148, 149, 150, 151, 152, 153, 154, 155, 170, 171, 172, 173, 174, 175, 176, 177, 178, 179, 180, 183, 184, 185, 186, 187, 188, 189, 190, 191, 192, 193, 219, 220, 221, 222, 223, 224, 225, 226, 227, 228, 231, 232, 235, 236, 237, 238, 239, 240, 250, 251, 252, 253, 254, 255, 256, 258, 259, 260, 261, 262, 263, 264, 265, 266, 267, 268, 269, 270, 271, 272, 273, 274, 275, 276, 277, 278, 279, 280, 281, 282, 283, 286, 287, 288, 289, 290, 291, 292, 293, 309, 310.
5 cents	No. 243, 244, 247, 248, 284, 306.
6 cents	No. 18, 21, 304, 305.
7 cents	No. 22.
10 cents	No. 23, 25, 302, 303.
12 cents	No. 24, 137.
15 cents	No. 31.

The only plate numbers which have been found for the stamps on ribbed paper are :

7 cents	No. 22.
15 cents	No. 31.

Much has been written concerning the use of hand and steam presses by the Continental Bank Note Co. It is certain that we find among the work of this company many poorly printed stamps, which some have claimed to be the product of steam presses. Among the stamps of this period we find many copies of what are known as "plain frames," *i. e.* stamps on which the outer part of the design is very faint and occasionally has almost disappeared. This is the only issue in which they are so numerous as to attract attention. It is more probable that they are due to poor workmanship and worn plates than to any fault of the presses, since many of these inferior stamps are of denominations which have always been printed by hand.

The facts, however, are these. During the time of its contracts with the Government, the Continental Bank Note Co. was located in the Ball and Black building, at the corner of Broadway and Prince street, New York. At this place they had nineteen hand presses and here most of the stamps were produced. The company had also an office in Greenwich street, where they had a steam press on which two plates could be used at one time. On this press were printed one, two and three cent stamps of the regular issue and two and three cent stamps of the Post Office Department.

These are the only values which the company printed by steam. The press was used during the years 1873 to 876, though not constantly. At one time it was stopped for a year. For the Post Office Department 578,500 two cent and 480,000 three cent stamps were printed. Of the three values of the regular issue many millions were printed.

Plates used on the steam press.

The following plates were used on the steam press :

1 cent	No. 156, 157, 182.
2 cents	No. 166, 169, 246.
3 cents	No. 129, 130, 131, 132, 133, 170, 171, 172, 173, 174, 175, 176, 180, 187, 193.
2 cents, P. O. Dept.	No. 37, 38.
3 cents " "	No. 36, 40.

The contracts from 1877 to 1885 stipulated that only hand presses should be used. It was not until the contract beginning July 1st, 1885, that printing by steam presses was required and then only for the lower values.

Statistics of manufacture.

The records of the Stamp Agent show the following quantities of stamps to have been printed and delivered to him :

YEAR ENDING DECEMBER 31ST :

	1873.	1874.	1875.	1876.	Total.
1 cent	59,355,000	117,930,000	122,937,500	148,067,500	448,290,000
2 cents	39,013,000	58,206,550	87,372,500	68,505,000	253,097,050
3 cents	248,132,500	436,919,500	481,156,500	495,085,000	1,661,293,500
5 cents	....	....	9,870,000	5,420,000	15,290,000
6 cents	6,177,500	17,659,000	7,845,000	6,630,000	38,311,500
7 cents	588,500	1,370,000	1,120,000	....	3,078,500
10 cents	3,318,500	3,795,000	5,137,500	9,220,000	21,471,000
12 cents	1,000,000	1,175,000	740,000	....	2,915,000
15 cents	1,344,500	....	755,000	952,500	3,052,000
24 cents	....	....	365,000	....	365,000
30 cents	....	590,000	....	192,500	782,500
90 cents	....	197,000	....	....	197,000

This table settles definitely the much discussed question of printings of the twenty-four, thirty and ninety cent stamps by the Continental Bank Note Co.

I regret that I am unable to supply any information regarding the quantities of stamps manufactured after the year 1876. I had hoped to obtain the figures but, thus far, my efforts have been unavailing.

The annual reports of the Postmaster General supply the following statistics of stamps distributed to deputy postmasters :

Stamps issued during the fiscal year ending June 30th, 1874 :

QUARTER ENDING:

	Sept. 30, 1873.	Dec. 31, 1873.	Mch. 31, 1874.	June 30, 1874.	Total.
1 cent	21,545,600	25,641,700	31,548,400	32,338,200	111,073,900
2 cents	11,365,050	17,247,600	14,689,500	16,790,100	60,092,250
3 cents	106,718,300	108,041,600	115,068,100	111,708,600	441,536,600
6 cents	2,953,950	2,636,550	3,394,050	3,014,300	11,998,850
7 cents	229,700	231,100	413,700	351,300	1,225,800
0 cents	832,490	827,010	1,028,360	1,183,570	3,871,430
2 cents	316,475	281,050	330,825	376,375	1,304,725
5 cents	495,140	324,100	85,700	49,100	954,040
4 cents	54,125	86,675	102,500	42,075	285,375
0 cents	55,420	126,130	100,040	44,890	326,480
0 cents	10,680	17,980	17,040	18,270	63,970

Whole number of stamps 632,733,420.   Value $17,275,242.00.

Stamps issued during the fiscal year ending June 30th, 1875 :

QUARTER ENDING :

	Sept. 30, 1874.	Dec. 31, 1874.	Mch. 31, 1875.	June 30, 1875.	Total.
1 cent	28,373,200	34,206,700	38,451,300	29,921,100	130,952,300
2 cents	13,728,800	15,808,500	17,883,100	21,982,800	69,413,200
3 cents	109,835,800	116,605,600	118,961,600	115,932,500	461,325,500
5 cents	....	....	....	363,180	363,180
6 cents	2,801,650	2,756,700	3,197,400	2,892,450	11,648,200
7 cents	349,800	425,700	415,000	381,400	1,571,900
0 cents	899,550	1,043,230	1,081,780	1,435,690	4,460,250
2 cents	257,550	310,000	334,500	418,175	1,320,225
5 cents	113,760	107,960	212,400	199,260	633,380
4 cents	86,525	35,175	44,525	105,550	271,775
0 cents	108,830	74,020	51,170	102,890	336,910
0 cents	20,090	8,710	9,200	7,650	45,650

Whole number of stamps 682,342,470.   Value $18,271,479.00.

Stamps issued during the fiscal year ending June 30th, 1876 :

QUARTER ENDING :

	Sept. 30, 1875.	Dec. 31, 1875.	Mch. 31, 1876.	June 30, 1876.	Total.
1 cent	25,036,600	30,909,700	33,427,300	35,853,200	125,226,800
2 cents	16,647,000	19,696,200	19,934,400	18,280,000	74,557,600
3 cents	112,466,600	120,030,400	120,640,200	121,529,000	474,666,200
5 cents	3,241,620	2,033,420	2,510,860	2,123,400	9,909,300
6 cents	1,394,550	1,950,200	1,830,900	1,949,850	7,125,500
3 cents	1,243,620	1,188,910	1,970,530	1,595,670	5,998,730
5 cents	131,320	263,840	331,860	215,140	942,160
3 cents	40,460	119,260	100,040	89,680	349,440
3 cents	4,100	6,980	9,380	2,900	23,360

Whole number of stamps 698,799,090.   Value $18,773,454.00.

Stamps issued during the fiscal year ending June 30th, 1877 :

QUARTER ENDING :

	Sept. 30, 1876.	Dec. 31, 1876.	Mch. 31, 1877.	June 30, 1877.	Total.
1 cent	25,520,800	34,380,800	41,494,000	40,070,000	141,465,600
2 cents	16,489,500	16,211,300	19,070,900	17,921,150	69,692,850
3 cents	111,583,700	112,827,900	116,530,000	115,192,300	456,133,900
5 cents	1,931,480	1,968,440	2,499,240	2,313,600	8,712,760
6 cents	1,419,400	1,213,800	1,747,700	1,558,150	5,939,050
10 cents	1,351,580	1,397,560	1,912,260	1,793,040	6,454,440
15 cents	171,720	130,000	289,500	229,420	820,640
30 cents	64,620	58,520	114,450	90,180	327,770
90 cents	3,680	19,000	7,320	3,660	33,660

Whole number of stamps 689,580,670.   Value $18,181,676.00.

Stamps issued during the fiscal year ending June 30th, 1878 :

QUARTER ENDING :

	Sept. 30, 1877.	Dec. 31, 1877.	Mch. 31, 1878.	June 30, 1878.	Total.
1 cent	34,402,700	43,103,600	45,931,400	40,296,700	163,734,400
2 cents	15,542,400	16,756,500	20,093,000	17,993,600	70,366,500
3 cents	115,943,700	118,525,600	130,316,300	118,542,900	483,328,500
5 cents	1,968,780	2,247,640	2,961,640	2,656,040	9,834,100
6 cents	1,523,350	1,266,200	1,727,500	1,419,500	5,936,550
10 cents	1,651,880	1,613,860	2,444,470	2,145,270	7,855,480
15 cents	183,240	233,020	360,640	193,700	970,600
30 cents	65,600	105,010	180,850	60,500	411,960
90 cents	12,040	2,960	4,150	4,700	23,850

Whole number of stamps 742,461,940.   Value $19,468,618 00.

Stamps issued during the fiscal year ending June 30th, 1879 :

QUARTER ENDING :

	Sept. 30, 1878.	Dec. 31, 1878.	Mch. 31, 1879.	June 30, 1879.	Total.
1 cent	36,379,400	47,287,000	48,958,600	47,405,400	180,030,400
2 cents	15,820,600	18,654,800	21,576,300	18,309,900	74,383,600
3 cents	115,967,700	122,577,100	129,675,600	125,633,600	493,854,000
5 cents	2,143,860	2,375,320	3,138,800	2,545,640	10,203,620
6 cents	1,382,600	1,430,600	1,686,200	1,254,000	5,753,400
10 cents	1,767,690	2,065,890	2,615,130	2,274,380	8,723,090
15 cents	200,660	239,160	382,040	178,500	1,000,360
30 cents	71,180	97,240	128,170	92,350	388,940
90 cents	4,920	5,600	6,270	4,580	21,370

Whole number of stamps 774,358,780.   Value $20,117,259.00.

After February 4th, 1879, when the Continental Bank Note Co. was consolidated with the American Bank Note Co., the latter assumed and completed the contract held by the former company. Doubtless, many of the stamps distributed in the last two quarters of the fiscal year ending June 30th, 1879, were the product of the American Bank Note Co., but it is not possible to separate the stamps of the two companies in the official statistics and the report of the Postmaster General must be taken as it stands.

By an order of Postmaster General Frank Hatton, dated January 14th, 1885, a committee was appointed to cancel various plates for printing stamps, both ordinary and official. This committee was also to destroy certain stamps which were no longer required, including 545,600 of the seven, 503,750 of the twelve, and 364,950 of the twenty-four cents. The committee reported, on February 24th, 1885, that they had carried out their instructions. The especial object of this order was the destruction of the remainders of the official stamps, and a more extended reference to this event will be made when considering those stamps.

Remainders
destroyed.

ISSUE OF 1879.

On February 4th, 1879, the Continental Bank Note Co. was consolidated with the American Bank Note Co., under the name of the latter. The contracts of the former company were assumed by the new organization. . Subsequent contracts were also secured by the American Bank Note Co., who continued to supply the stamps required by the Post Office Department until January 1st, 1894.

As has been previously stated, the Continental Bank Note Co. began, about the end of 1878 or the beginning of 1879, to use a soft porous paper for their stamps. The American Bank Note Co. continued the use of paper of this quality, as it was found to give the best results, especially when steam presses were employed. The new company used many of the plates of its predecessor, also the plates of the National Bank Note Co. for the thirty and ninety cent and probably for some of the ten cent stamps. It is certain that ten cent stamps without the secret mark, and which are undoubtedly the work of the American Bank Note Co., exist. It is claimed by some writers that these are from the Continental Bank Note Co's plates from which the secret mark has worn away. In support of this statement pairs and blocks are reported, on which the mark shows with varying degrees of indistinctness and is sometimes almost invisible. It is scarcely possible that this claim is correct, as the secret mark is deeply cut and ought to be about the last thing to wear away. And there are certain other points about the stamps which are peculiar to the plates of the National Bank Note Co. and which lead me to believe they are from those plates. The question can only be settled by finding the stamps with marginal imprint or plate number or by examination of the records of the contractors. It is to be regretted that there is no prospect that the privilege of making such an examination will be granted.

The gum used by the American Bank Note Co was generally yellowish but occasionally it was quite brown and, in their later printings, was sometimes almost white.

The stamps are found in the following shades :

Soft Porous White Wove Paper.

Perforated 12.

Plates of other companies used.

Reference List.

1879.   1 cent pale bright blue, bright blue, deep bright blue, sky blue, blue, dark blue, gray-blue, dull blue, dark dull blue, dark ultramarine

2 cents vermilion, scarlet-vermilion, orange-vermilion, orange

3 cents pale bright green, yellow-green, dull green, deep dull green, gray-green, dark green, myrtle green

5 cents blue, dark blue, indigo

6 cents pale dull rose, dull rose, brown-rose

10 cents (National plate) yellow-brown

10 cents pale yellow-brown, yellow-brown, orange-brown, red-brown, gray-brown, brown, dark brown, black-brown

15 cents pale orange-yellow, orange-yellow, orange, red-orange, orange-red, pale red

30 cents (National plate) gray-black, greenish black

30 cents full black, jet black

90 cents (National plate) dull carmine-rose, carmine-rose, rose-carmine

Variety:

90 cents carmine-rose. Imperforate.

Except when otherwise stated, these stamps were printed from the plates of the Continental Bank Note Co. or from plates made from the dies of that company. The following plates of the Continental Co. are known to have been used by the American Co.:

1 cent	No. 301.	**List of Continental plates used.**
2 cents	No. 296, 297.	
3 cents	No. 292, 309, 310.	
6 cents	No. 305.	
15 cents	No. 31.	

The following plates were probably used :

5 cents   No. 306.
6 cents   No. 304.
10 cents   No. 302. 303.

It is reasonable to suppose that many other plates of the lower values were used.

In the course of time, as they were required, new plates were made. They bore the imprint "AMERICAN BANK NOTE COMPANY", in heavy faced, shaded capitals, without frame or other surroundings. The imprints and plate numbers occupied the same positions as on the plates of the previous contractors. The numbers were all in small italic numerals. The plates contained two hundred stamps each, and the impressions were divided vertically into sheets of one hundred stamps, as in the preceding issues.   **Plates of the American Bank Note Co.**

The numbers of these plates were as follows :   **Plate numbers.**

1 cent   No. 319, 320, 327, 328, 336, 337, 344, 353, 354, 355, 356.
2 cents   No. 338, 339, 391, 392, 393, 394, 412, 413.

3 cents   No. 311, 312, 321, 322, 323, 324, 329, 330, 334, 335,
           340, 341, 341A, 342, 343, 345, 346, 347, 348,
           349, 350, 350A, 351, 352, 357, 358.
5 cents   No. 325, 326, 379, 380.
10 cents   No. 377, 378.
30 cents   No. 405.

During the years 1881 to 1888 inclusive there were many changes in
the engraving, designs and colors of the stamps, also stamps of the 1870 types
and colors were in issue concurrently with the new varieties. As official statistics only take notice of values, it is impossible to decide how many stamps of
each particular variety were issued and I can only reprint the tables as they
are given in the reports of the Postmaster General ; they will be found at the
end of the next chapter.

ISSUES OF 1881-88.

ISSUE OF 1881-82.

About 1881 the contractors decided to deepen the lines of certain of the designs, in order that the wiping of the plates might be made easier and heavier impressions produced. Four values were so treated. Philatelists are accustomed to speak of these stamps with deepened lines as being re-engraved but this is not altogether correct. The dies of the one and three cents were retouched and those of the six and ten cents were re-engraved (*i. e.* newly engraved) except the busts. The distinction is somewhat technical. It cannot be claimed that either process improved the appearance of the stamps. Their delicacy and clearness were destroyed and the impressions from the altered designs are heavy, blurred and uneven. The stamps may be distinguished by the following peculiarities :

Retouched and re-engraved dies.

ONE CENT. The vertical lines of the background have been much deepened in the upper part of the stamp, so that, in many impressions, the background appears to be solid Lines of shading have been added inside the arabesques in the upper corners. The fine shadings outside the arabesques and at the ends of the upper label have been nearly obliterated by the recutting. Mr. Tiffany describes three varieties of this stamp, distinguished principally by the condition of the oval below the bust, as showing either a light spot, a shadow, or a background of uniform solidity. These varieties are not in any way due to differences in engraving but to the amount of ink on the plate and perhaps, in some small degree, to the condition of the plate as regards wear.

Description of the alterations.

THREE CENTS. Vertical lines have been added to the background of the medallion, but they can only be seen on proofs or very clearly printed copies. The vertical lines of the shield have been deepened, making the shadows of the medallion appear, by contrast, only about one-half as wide as before. At the bottom the horizontal lines of the background have been deepened, thus obliterating the fine vertical shadings below the ends of the ribbon bearing the value. A short horizontal dash has been cut, about a millimetre below the " TS " of " CENTS ".

SIX CENTS. The horizontal lines of the panel have been re-engraved, obscuring the shadings of the edges and of the oval and giving it a uniformly solid appearance. The vertical lines of the background have also been re-engraved. There are now only three of these lines at each side of the panel, where formerly there were four.

TEN CENTS. The lines of the medallion, the shield and the background have all been re-engraved. In the medallion the diagonal hatching lines have disappeared. At the left side, where there were formerly five vertical lines between the medallion and the edge of the shield, there are now but four. The fine vertical shadings below the ribbon bearing the value are nearly obliterated by the deepened horizonal lines of the background. The re-engraved die was made from a transfer of the old National die and so has not the secret mark.

Mr. Tiffany says the re-engraved stamps began to appear in November, 1882. This date is much too late for at least three values. The *Philatelic*
Record reported the one cent in March, 1882, the ten cents in June and the six cents in November of that year. The change in the three cents was made earlier than in any of the other values but does not appear to have attracted the attention of any of the philatelic journals. I have it on excellent authority that the three cents was recut in June, 1881, the one cent in July, 1881, the ten cents in March, 1882, and the six cents in May of that year, and that stamps from the new plates were issued to the public about one month later than the date named in each instance.

About 1882 or 1883 two stamps of this series, the one and three cents, were printed on double paper, a very thin surface paper, backed by a thicker and harder paper. The surface paper was punctured by many small holes, about 1½mm. in diameter. These holes were arranged in circles—eight holes to a circle—and the circles were placed at such intervals that one would fall on each stamp. The printed stamps did not differ in appearance from the ordinary varieties but, of course, the ink had passed through the holes and portions of the design were printed on the backing paper. Any attempt to erase a cancellation would be almost certain to tear the thin surface paper, while the application of liquids would cause the stamp to separate into two parts, one showing a circle of small holes and the other a white surface with a circle of colored dots. These stamps are known to collectors as the "Douglas patent." It is understood that 10,000 of them were printed. They were placed on sale at the city post office in Washington. After a trial, it was decided not to permanently adopt them and their issue was discontinued.

The paper, gum, size of plates and location of the inscriptions and plate numbers are the same as in the issue of 1879. This remark will apply to subsequent issues by the American Bank Note Co. unless especial mention to the contrary is made.

Dates of issue.

"Douglas patent" stamps.

Reference List.

Soft Porous White Wove Paper.

Perforated 12.

Aug. 1881.   1 cent dull ultramarine, ultramarine, bright ultramarine, gray-blue, slate-blue, dull blue, chalky blue

July 1881.   3 cents yellow-green, gray-green, blue-green

June 1882.   6 cents brown-rose, dull rose, claret, deep claret, Indian red

April 1882.   10 cents pale yellow-brown, yellow-brown, orange-brown, red-brown, olive-brown, brown, violet-brown, black-brown

Double Paper.

Die cut with a circle of small holes.

1 cent gray-blue
3 cents gray-green

The following plates were used for this issue :   **Plate numbers.**

1 cent	No. 359, 360, 361, 362, 363, 364, 387, 388, 389, 390, 401, 402, 406, 407, 422, 423, 424, 425, 475.
3 cents	No. 365, 366, 367, 368, 369, 370, 371, 372, 373, 374, 375, 376, 381, 382, 383, 384, 385, 386, 395, 396, 397, 398, 408, 409, 410, 411, 414, 415, 416, 417, 418, 419, 420, 421.
6 cents	No. 426, 427.
10 cents	No. 403, 403A, 404, 404A, 480, 481.

For the " Douglas patent " stamps the only plate numbers which we know are : One cent, No. 362 and three cents, No. 367.

Beginning in 1885, the plates of the American Bank Note Co. bear a serial letter as well as a number. There are usually five plates to each letter. This change was occasioned by the use of a steam press which accommodated   **Serial letters.** five plates at a time. It is obvious that, in printing with this press, the five plates must all be in the same stage of wear or the printing would be uneven. By means of the letters each group of plates could easily be kept together and, being subjected to an equal amount of work, they would remain in the same relative condition. A letter was usually assigned to the first plate of each denomination, even when only one plate was made, since more might be added later.

Under this system the following plates were provided for the issue of   **Plate numbers.** 1881-82 :

1 cent	No. C. 497, 498, 499, 500, 501.
	D. 502, 503, 504, 505, 506.
	I. 527, 528, 529, 530, 531.
10 cents	No. M. 547, 548, 549, 550, 551.

ISSUE OF APRIL 10TH, 1882.

The five cent stamp with the portrait of General Taylor had never given satisfaction. The full-faced portrait was too large for its surroundings and also not in accord with the profile busts on the other values. After the   **Historical.** death of President Garfield it was decided to place his portrait on the five cent stamp. The original intention was to print the stamp in black, the color of mourning—as was done with the fifteen cents of the 1866 issue, after the ath of President Lincoln—but the color finally adopted was a dark brown.

Design.   The official description of the stamp is as follows :

"FIVE CENTS (Garfield). On a rectangular-lined tablet, the greater portion of which is raised in the shape of a shield, is an elliptical medallion bearing the portrait of President Garfield. The medallion is bordered by a line of small white beads, the legend 'U. S. POSTAGE', being at the bottom of the stamp in small black block letters. The words 'FIVE' and 'CENTS' are above the legend and partly on the lower edge of the tablet, divided by a large five-pointed star, upon which is the white-faced figure '5' upon a black ground. The star is outlined with white, and the denomination words are each on lines curved downward at the ends."

The stamp measure 20x25½mm.

For several years the catalogues have listed two varieties of this stamp, the first having the background of the medallion composed of horizontal **Varieties.** lines crossed by fine diagonal lines, and the second showing the horizontal lines only. Although well aware that there was but one die for this value, I was, at one time, led to accept the two varieties, on the theory that they represented plates made from two transfers, one of which was not sufficiently deep to bring out the finer lines. It is now understood that the plates are all alike and all have the fine lines. The absence of the diagonal lines from a stamp is caused by the ink having been removed from them by too much pressure in wiping the plate and by the operation having been performed lengthwise of the lines instead of across them. It is also probable that wearing of the plate affects the appearance of the lines.

It was intended to issue this stamp to the public on March 1st, 1882. The first delivery to the Post Office Department was made on February 7th, **Date of issue.** 1882. A few of the stamps were obtained by favor and used on the 14th of that month. They were also reported in the European philatelic journals in March of that year but, according to the report of the Postmaster-General and the daily newspapers, they were not put on sale until April 10th, 1882.

The stamps which were distributed in advance of their being placed on sale at the post offices were very probably from the first sheet printed. This **The first sheet.** sheet appears to have been sent to the Post Office Department at Washington and treated somewhat as a curiosity. I am led to this conclusion by a copy of the stamp which has been shown me by Mr. C. F. Rothfuchs. This copy is attached to a printed form which was used by the Department when filling orders from private individuals for stamps. This form was in use during the time the reprints and re-issues were on sale, from 1875 to 1884, and possibly for even a longer period. It is addressed to a gentleman in the Post Office Department and reads as follows :

WASHINGTON, D. C.,
Feb. 10th, 1882.

SIR :—

In response to your personal application of this day you will find herewith inclosed the following specimens of postage stamps, viz :

Issue of 1882, 1—5c Garfield, $0 05.

This stamp is from the first sheet printed and one of the first sold by the Department.

The stamp which is attached to this document is printed in a very dark brown having a tinge of red, instead of the grayish tone of the later printings.

Soft Porous White Wove Paper.

Perforated 12.

April 10th, 1882.   5 cents yellow-brown, bistre-brown, Van Dyke brown, black-brown, gray-brown, gray

The plates for this issue were numbered as follows :

5 cents   No. 399, 400, 488, 489
K. 537, 538, 539, 540, 541

ISSUE OF OCTOBER 1ST, 1883.

An Act of Congress, approved March 3rd, 1883, provided as follows :

"Upon all matter of the first class (as defined by chapter 180 of the Laws of Congress, approved March 3rd, 1879, entitled :   An Act, etc.) postage shall be charged, on and after the first day of October, A. D., 1883, at the rate of two cents for each half ounce or fraction thereof, and all acts, so far as they fix a different rate of postage than herein provided upon said first class matter, are to that extent hereby repealed."

Concerning this change the report of the Postmaster General, dated November 8th, 1883, says :

"Soon after the passage of the Act of March 3rd, 1883, preparations were begun to carry the new law into effect.   The change left the 3-cent denomination of postage stamps of little utility, it no longer representing the single rate of postage on any class of matter, and it was determined to discontinue its issue.   As the public would undoubtly have regarded with disfavor the dropping of Washington from portraits forming the distinguishing feature in the series of postage stamps, it was decided to replace the old 3-cent stamp by a new one bearing the profile of the first President, thus restoring it to its old place on the stamp in most general use.   It was also decided to issue a new stamp of the value of four cents, a denomination not previously in use, and designed to cover two rates of letter postage.   The portrait of Jackson, formerly on the 2-cent stamp, was transferred to this new (4-cent) stamp."

The official description of these two stamps is as follows :

"TWO CENTS.   A plain tablet ; above the oval surrounding the head are the words 'UNITED STATES POSTAGE' and underneath the tablet are the words 'TWO CENTS.'   It may be added that the tablet is shaped like the shield on the 3 cent stamp of this series and that the figure '2' separates the words 'TWO' and 'CENTS,'. which form a straight line, resting partly on the point of the tablet and partly on the darkly shaded ground below.   This is the first stamp of the series with the legend unabbreviated.   The medallion is elliptical, and bears the profile bust of Washington.

FOUR CENTS.   The tablet is rectangular and beveled, covering the entire stamp, the lower half in solid color.   The legend, like that on the 2 cent stamp of even date, is in the unabbreviated form, 'UNITED STATES POSTAGE,' following the upper line of an elliptical medallion, bearing the profile bust of Andrew Jackson, and is in small white capitals.   In each lower corner is a large white figure '4.'   Below these and in an unbroken straight line are the words 'FOUR CENTS,' in small white capitals with a very small star at the right and left and immediately under the figure '4'."

These stamps are both of the same size, 20x25½mm.

It has been claimed that there are two varieties of the two cent stamp,
distinguishable by the presence or absence of a shadow below the shield, but

these differences are entirely due to the amount of ink applied and to the condition of the plates.

Date of Issue. According the report of the Postmaster General the stamps were issued on October 1st, 1883.

Reference List.
Soft Porous White Wove Paper.

Perforated 12.

Oct. 1st, 1883.   2 cents orange-brown, red-brown, copper-brown, metallic red, Indian red

4 cents deep green, blue-green, dark blue-green

Plate numbers. The following plates were made for these stamps :

2 cents   No. 430, 431, 432, 433, 434, 435, 436, 437, 438, 439, 440, 441, 442, 443, 444, 445, 446, 447, 448, 449, 450, 451, 452, 453, 454, 455, 458, 459, 460, 461, 462, 463, 465, 466, 467, 468, 469, 470, 471 472, 473, 474, 476, 477, 478, 479.

A. 483, 484, 485, 486, 487.
B. 490, 491, 492, 493, 494.
E. 507, 508, 509, 510, 511.
F. 512, 513, 514, 515, 516.
G. 517, 518, 519, 520, 521.
H. 522, 523, 524, 525, 526.
J. 532, 533, 534, 535, 536.
N. 553, 554, 555, 556, 557.
O. 558, 559, 560, 561, 562.
P. 563, 564, 565, 566, 567.
Q. 568, 569, 570, 571, 572.
U. 588, 589, 590, 591, 592.
V. 593, 594, 595, 596, 597.

4 cents   No. 456, 457.
L. 542, 543, 544, 545, 546.

The *Philatelic Record* for December, 1888, says : " Mr. F. De Coppet has sent us a specimen of the 2 cents red brown (head of Washington) on
Laid paper. paper laid horizontally." A similar note subsequently appeared in various other journals. When the De Coppet collection was offered at auction this stamp was listed as lot 2002. I have not been able to trace the copy further than this. I am inclined to doubt that the stamp was really on laid paper. Among stamps of the current and recent issues we frequently find copies which show what appear to be laid lines. Experts in printing, however, pro- nounce these lines to be merely an effect produced by a worn blanket on the printing press, the threads being pressed into the damp paper in printing. It is possible that Mr. De Coppet's stamp belonged in this category.

The stamps of this and various earlier issues are found surcharged
"Specimen" stamps. " SPECIMEN ". This overprint was applied to stamps intended for distribution to foreign countries through the Universal Postal Union. The complete set comprises the following varieties :

Ordinary postage stamps.	Issue of 1879 : 15, 30, 90c
	Issue of 1881-82 : 1, 3, 6, 10c
	Issue of Apl. 1882 : 5c
	Issue of Oct. 1883 : 2, 4c
Special Delivery stamps.	Issue of 1885 : 10c
Newspapers and Periodical stamps.	Issue of 1879-85 : 1c to $60
Postage Due stamps.	Issue of 1879 : 1, 2, 3, 5, 10, 30, 50c

The report of the Third Assistant Postmaster General, dated Nov. 5th, 1887, says :

" Upon the change in the rate of postage on first class matter, from 3 to 2 cents a half ounce, on the 1st of October, 1883, large quantities of 3 and 6 cent stamps and stamped envelopes were left in the hands of the postmasters and of the public. As those in the hands of the public could not be used, except at a loss, under the new rate, it was thought to be just that the Department should redeem them by giving the 2 cent denomination of stamps and envelopes for them.   Orders to this effect were accordingly given to postmasters, December 12, 1883 ; but at the same time, they were forbidden to send to the Department the stamps and envelopes thus redeemed.   The result was a large and very general accumulation of unsalable stock in the post offices, over one-third probably of all the post offices in the country having more or less of it.   On January 1, 1886, it was determined to relieve postmasters of this accumulation of valueless material ; but as the volume of it was so great that it could not be conviently handled if called in at once, circulars were sent monthly to a limited number of postmasters, directing them to return to the Department whatever amount they might have on hand.   As fast as the stock was received under these notices it was counted and destroyed, the proper credits for it being given postmasters in their accounts. *(margin note: Redemption of the three and six cent stamps.)*

By February, 1887, this unsalable stock had become so greatly reduced that all postmasters were instructed to return at once such of it as they might still have on hand."

Mr. Tiffany says the face value of the stamps and envelopes destroyed " soon reached the comfortable little sum of $731,503.61."

The contract for the manufacture of postage stamps, for the four years beginning July 1st, 1885, was awarded to the American Bank Note Co. This contract provided that all ordinary postage stamps were to be printed on steam presses.   The custom of specifying that the paper should be equal to the sample attached to the contract was also changed and a standard paper, made according to a formula, was required. *(margin note: Contract requiring printing by steam and standard paper.)*

By Act of Congress, approved March 30th, 1885, the rate of postage on first-class matter was further modified.   The Act provided as follows :

" That upon all matter of the first class, as defined by Chapter 180 of the Laws of Congress, approved March 3rd, 1879, entitled : An Act, etc., and by that Act declared subject to postage at the rate of three cents for each half ounce or fraction thereof, and reduced by Act of March 3rd, 1883, to two cents for each half ounce or fraction thereof, postage shall be charged, on and after the first day of July, 1885, at the rate of two cents for each ounce or fraction thereof ; and drop letters shall be mailed at the rate of two cents per ounce or fraction thereof, including delivery at letter carrier offices, and one cent for each ounce or fraction thereof where free delivery by carriers is not established." *(margin note: Postal rates modified.)*

ISSUE OF JUNE 15TH, 1887.

A one cent stamp of a new design was issued on June 15th, 1887.   It is officially described as follows :

" ONE CENT.   A profile bust of Benjamin Franklin upon a disk with shaded background, the lower portion of the oval disk being bordered with pearls, and the upper portion with a curved panel, containing, in small white letters, the words ' UNITED STATES POSTAGE.'   The whole is engraved in line *(margin note: Design.)*

upon a shield-shaped tablet with a truncated pyramidal base, bearing on it the words 'ONE CENT' on either side of the figure ' 1 '."

The stamp measures 20x25¼ mm.

Soft Porous White Wove Paper.

Perforated 12.

June 15th, 1887   1 cent dull ultramarine, ultramarine, bright ultramarine

Variety .

1 cent dull ultramarine.   Imperforate.

The plates used for this issue were numbered :

1 cent   No. R. 573, 574, 575, 576, 577.

S. 578, 579, 580, 581, 582.

T. 583, 584, 585, 586, 587.

F.F. 644, 645, 646, 647, 648.

G.G. 649, 650, 651, 652, 653.

J.J. 664, 665, 666, 667, 668.

P.P. 694, 695, 696, 697, 698.

U.U. 719, 720, 721, 722, 723.

ISSUES OF 1887-88.

By an official circular, dated August 15th, 1887, the following changes were announced :

"On or about the 12th of September, 1887, the following changes in the series of postage stamps will be made :

The color of the 2-cent stamp will be green, instead of the present color, metallic red. The color of the 3-cent stamp (issues of which are still made to some of the larger post offices) will be vermilion instead of green."

In addition to the above, the circular announced changes in the designs and colors of certain of the stamped envelopes ; the four cents was to be printed in carmine, the five cents in blue, the thirty cents in brown and the ninety cents in purple. The two stamps and the envelopes were duly issued in the new colors and, during the next year, the four, five, thirty and ninety cent adhesives appeared in colors corresponding to those newly adopted for the envelopes of the same values. The philatelic journals chronicled the thirty cents in February, 1888, the five and ninety cents in March and the four cents in December, of that year. On the subject of these last changes the report of the Postmaster General for 1888 and the Postal Guide are both silent. The customary official circular, announcing the contemplated changes, appears also to have been omitted.

Soft Porous White Wove Paper.

Perforated 12.

Sept. 12th, 1887.   2 cents pale bright green, bright green, deep green, yellow-green

3 cents pale red, scarlet

Dec. 1888.   4 cents rose-carmine, carmine

March 1888.   5 cents dark blue, indigo
Feb. 1888.   30 cents brown-orange, orange-brown, deep orange-brown
March 1888.   90 cents purple, bright purple

Varieties :

2 cents deep green.   Imperforate
5 cents dark blue   "
30 cents orange-brown   "
5 cents indigo.   Pale pink paper

The imperforate thirty cent stamps are from plate No. 405.

The only copy of the five cent stamp on colored paper which I have seen was shown me by Mr. F. O. Conant. It had full original gum and presented a generally satisfactory appearance. Concerning it, Mr. Conant wrote : Five cent stamp
on pink paper.

"The five cents blue, Garfield, on pink paper, is one of a lot of ten or fifteen, purchased at the Portland, Me., post office in 1889, by one of the local collectors. The paper appears to be too evenly colored to be the result of accident. Among the lot was a pair with the top margin. The color showed evenly on the margin, as on the stamps."

In printing these stamps the following plates were used : Plate numbers.

2 cents   No. N. 553, 554, 555, 556, 557.
                O. 558, 559, 560, 561, 562.
                P. 563, 564, 565, 566, 567.
                Q. 568, 569, 570, 571, 572.
                U. 588, 589, 590, 591, 592.
                V. 593, 594, 595, 596, 597.
                W. 598, 599, 600, 601, 602.
                X. 603, 604, 605, 606, 607.
                Y. 608, 609, 610, 611, 612, 613.
                Z. 614, 615, 616, 617, 618.
                A. A. 619, 620, 621, 622, 623.
                B. B. 624, 625, 626, 627, 628.
                C. C. 629, 630, 631, 632, 633.
                D. D. 634, 635, 636, 637, 638.
                E. E. 639, 640, 641, 642, 643.
                H. H. 654, 655, 656, 657, 658.
                I. I. 659, 660, 661, 662, 663.
                K. K. 669, 670, 671, 672, 673.
                L. L. 674, 675, 676, 677, 678.
                M. M. 679, 680, 681, 682, 683.
                N. N. 684, 685, 686, 687, 688.
                O. O. 689, 690, 691, 692, 693.
                Q. Q. 699, 700, 701, 702, 703.
                R. R. 704, 705, 706, 707, 708.
                S. S. 709, 710, 711, 712, 713.
                T. T. 714, 715, 716, 717, 718.

3 cents	No. 421.
4 cents	No. L. 542, 543, 544, 545, 546.
5 cents	No. K. 537, 538, 539, 540, 541.
30 cents	No. 405.
90 cents	No. 23 (National Bank Note Co.)

It is possible that a few other and earlier plates may have been used for the two, four and five cent stamps.

Plate 613 of the two cents was added to serial letter Y to replace plate 611 which was broken.

————————

As has been said before, the reports of the Postmaster General make no distinction between stamps of the same value but of different issues. The following statistics of stamps delivered to deputy postmasters between July 1st, 1879, and June 30th, 1890, are, therefore, presented with the regret that they are not in more satisfactory shape for the purposes of philatelists.

Deliveries to postmasters.

Stamps issued during the fiscal year ending June 30th, 1880:

QUARTER ENDING:

	Sept. 30, 1879.	Dec. 31, 1879.	Mch. 31, 1880.	June 30, 1880.	Total.
1 cent	42,968,000	54,511,200	66,025,900	62,944,700	226,449,800
2 cents	16,289,750	18,865,550	23,080,900	18,349,500	76,585,700
3 cents	128,951,300	129,452,900	148,615,700	134,583,700	541,603,600
5 cents	2,606,180	3,021,100	3,847,340	3,297,160	12,771,780
6 cents	1,496,150	1,329,200	1,850,000	1,689,350	6,364,700
10 cents	2,209,580	2,266,220	3,194,350	2,679,780	10,349,930
15 cents	266,120	243,140	307,440	298,420	1,115,120
30 cents	84,640	95,280	134,010	101,620	415,550
90 cents	7,700	7,080	5,620	5,390	25,790

Whole number of stamps 875,681,970. Value $22,414,928.00.

Stamps issued during the fiscal year ending June 30th, 1881 :

QUARTER ENDING:

	Sept. 30, 1880.	Dec. 31, 1880.	Mch. 31, 1881.	June 30, 1881.	Total.
1 cent	57,783,200	68,475,600	77,951,000	61,097,300	265,307,100
2 cents	17,166,450	20,455,250	25,918,400	23,111,950	86,652,050
3 cents	132,174,800	142,142,100	151,953,500	141,143,400	567,413,800
5 cents	3,182,800	3,799,220	3,944,540	3,923,120	14,849,680
6 cents	1,226,200	1,768,950	1,698,250	1,711,600	6,405,000
10 cents	2,514,310	2,932,810	3,553,620	2,988,740	11,989,480
15 cents	213,140	235,240	424,020	214,180	1,086,580
30 cents	62,090	118,440	121,840	95,800	398,170
90 cents	3,900	6,050	6,050	10,590	26,590

Whole number of stamps 954,128,450. Value $24,040,627.00.

Stamps issued during the fiscal year ending June 30th, 1882 :

QUARTER ENDING :

	Sept. 30, 1881.	Dec. 31, 1881.	Mch. 31, 1882.	June 30, 1882.	Total.
1 cent	58,349,000	69,592,200	78,612,900	77,380,600	283,934,700
2 cents	23,499,400	26,407,400	28,861,200	27,578,800	106,346,800
3 cents	161,825,800	166,676,000	183,352,000	168,609,900	680,463,700
5 cents	4,030,440	4,522,120	5,193,520	5,531,200	19,277,280
6 cents	1,923,700	1,922,750	2,108,300	2,013,700	7,968,450
10 cents	2,955,210	3,554,290	4,362,110	3,670,080	14,541,690
15 cents	324,600	326,560	536,720	299,460	1,487,340
30 cents	90,280	142,290	153,910	123,920	510,400
90 cents	7,790	10,050	6,170	5,960	29,970

Whole number of stamps 1,114,560,330.   Value $28,679,528.00.

Stamps issued during the fiscal year ending June 30th, 1883 :

QUARTER ENDING :

	Sept. 30, 1882.	Dec. 31, 1882.	Mch. 31, 1883.	June 30, 1883.	Total.
1 cent	69,662,500	84,371,300	94,134,200	86,031,000	334,199,000
2 cents	24,177,300	32,501,100	32,435,000	30,777,650	119,891,050
3 cents	167,930,400	174,138,800	182,868,500	174,862,100	699,799,800
5 cents	5,226,760	5,733,460	6,233,340	5,838,560	23,032,120
6 cents	1,941,300	2,519,050	2,404,700	1,885,450	8,750,500
10 cents	3,276,840	3,668,370	4,538,500	3,596,450	15,080,160
15 cents	401,280	329,160	479,400	289,260	1,449,100
30 cents	112,770	116,340	138,280	97,620	465,010
90 cents	9,180	8,130	6,260	3,490	27,060

Whole number of stamps 1,202,743,800.   Value $30,307,179.00.

Stamps issued during the fiscal year ending June 30th, 1884 :

QUARTER ENDING :

	Sept. 30, 1883.	Dec. 31, 1883.	Mch. 31, 1884.	June 30, 1884.	Total.
1 cent	84,582,100	96,221,900	102,338,100	93,814,700	376,956,800
2 cents	157,598,100	238,918,900	278,928,200	251,623,900	927,069,100
3 cents	95,461,000	5,000	25,200	34,900	95,526,100
4 cents	1,541,200	5,244,200	4,800,500	4,558,050	16,143,950
5 cents	5,197,080	6,111,000	7,570,580	6,635,740	25,514,400
6 cents	898,050	....	40,000	53,750	991,800
10 cents	3,498,540	3,712,420	4,885,750	3,916,370	16,013,080
15 cents	282,340	265,260	377,860	166,740	1,092,200
30 cents	75,600	110,910	150,930	96,460	433,900
90 cents	7,250	6,220	7,740	5,920	27,130

Whole number of stamps 1,459,768,460.   Value $29,077,444.00.

Stamps issued during the fiscal year ending June 30th, 1885 :

QUARTER ENDING :

	Sept. 30, 1884.	Dec. 31, 1884	Mch. 31, 1885.	June 30, 1885.	Total.
1 cent	80,576,800	90,425,900	97,158,000	96,403,200	364,563,900
2 cents	244,084,350	247,443,400	279,510,900	266,120,800	1,037,159,450
3 cents	. . . . . .	200,000	66,000	153,000	419,000
4 cents	3,913,100	4,282,750	4,718,525	4,289,900	17,204,275
5 cents	6,391,360	6,716,700	7,756,340	6,958,940	27,823,340
6 cents	. . . .	. . . .	40,000	14,000	54,000
10 cents	3,388,460	4,090,170	4,761,940	4,057,520	16,297,790
15 cents	255,540	344,480	302,900	273,940	, 1,176,860
30 cents	89,160	71,860	150,010	93,210	404,240
90 cents	5,870	3,860	4,910	5,440	20,080

Whole number of stamps 1,465,122,935. Value $28,429,628.00.

Stamps issued during the fiscal year ending June 30th, 1886 :

QUARTER ENDING:

	Sept. 30, 1885.	Dec. 31, 1885.	Mch. 31, 1886.	June 30, 1886.	Total.
1 cent	78,335,600	100,412,900	117,394,800	114,386,800	410,530,100
2 cents	247,262,600	285,245,400	303,255,800	312,142,600	1,147,906,400
3 cents	200,000	155,500	319,600	201,200	876,300
4 cents	2,257,300	3,563,850	3,008,150	3,248,550	12,077,850
5 cents	5,999,860	7,259,800	8,652,680	7,875,080	29,787,420
6 cents	55,000	50,700	2,100	50,500	158,300
10 cents	3,594,110	4,662,610	5,012,440	4,558,010	17,827,170
15 cents	258,600	348,500	323,940	267,520	1,198,560
30 cents	64,950	135,450	126,400	75,930	402,730
90 cents	3,410	7,770	3,500	4,590	19,270

Whole number of stamps 1,620,784,100. Value $31,172,364.00.

Stamps issued during the fiscal year ending June 30th, 1887 :

QUARTER ENDING :

	Sept. 30, 1886.	Dec. 31, 1886.	Mch. 31, 1887.	June 30, 1887.	Total.
1 cent	80,669,900	117,101,800	124,744,900	109,769,700	432,286,300
2 cents	249,142,600	351,213,400	326,290,200	319,516,150	1,246,162,350
3 cents	61,100	312,000	791,500	100,000	1,264,600
4 cents	2,141,500	4,158,700	3,795,350	3,343,300	13,438,950
5 cents	6,258,400	9,073,660	9,553,400	7,614,280	32,499,740
6 cents	1,700	1,000	54,000	1,000	57,700
10 cents	3,582,310	5,243,850	5,933,240	4,417,120	19,176,520
15 cents	256,040	540,780	414,520	419,520	1,630,860
30 cents	89,710	115,030	130,900	97,410	433,050
90 cents	5,710	12,480	8,450	8,810	35,450

Whole number of stamps 1,746,985,520. Value $33,774,156.00.

Stamps issued during the fiscal year ending June 30th, 1888 :

QUARTER ENDING :

	Sept. 30, 1887.	Dec. 31, 1887.	Mch. 31, 1888.	June 30, 1888.	Total.
1 cent	89,936,700	113,015,900	125,318,700	121,718,200	443,989,500
2 cents	296,217,000	348,012,100	368,931,300	334,520,200	1,347,680,600
3 cents	101,500	604,100	1,884,700	1,441,100	4,031,400
4 cents	2,976,250	3,750,700	3,924,675	3,592,125	14,243,750
5 cents	7,704,880	8,718,160	10,740,620	9,045,560	36,209,220
6 cents	61,000	. . . . . .	100,000	5,600	166,600
10 cents	4,320,780	5,239,780	5,699,870	4,671,230	19,931,660
15 cents	277,020	451,560	357,640	336,940	1,423,160
30 cents	67,370	181,120	98,480	95,760	442,730
90 cents	5,920	11,490	18,990	18,120	54,520

Whole number of stamps 1,868,173,140.   Value $36,293,183.00.

Stamps issued during the fiscal year ending June 30th, 1889 :

QUARTER ENDING :

	Sept. 30, 1888.	Dec. 31, 1888.	Mch. 31, 1889.	June 30, 1889.	Total.
1 cent	97,022,600	127,794,600	130,074,600	118,141,500	473,033,300
2 cents	325,272,100	356,527,900	387,213,000	339,427,900	1,408,440,900
3 cents	825,300	1,715,400	2,005,200	1,545,700	6,091,600
4 cents	3,055,700	3,553,650	4,018,900	3,744,100	14,372,350
5 cents	8,492,220	9,224,540	10,202,080	9,116,680	37,035,520
6 cents	110,000	9,200	50,500	16,600	186,300
10 cents	4,558,150	5,359,320	5,711,450	5,355,020	20,983,940
15 cents	278,700	519,900	262,560	291,500	1,352,660
30 cents	75,290	116,840	158,300	84,330	434,760
90 cents	6,400	8,410	11,800	22,900	49,510

Whole number of stamps 1,961,980,840.   Value $37,996,027.00.

Stamps issued during the fiscal year ending June 30th, 1890 :

QUARTER ENDING :

	Sept. 30, 1889.	Dec. 31, 1889.	Mch. 31, 1890.	June 30, 1890.	Total.
1 cent	164,097,000	88,688,400	154,806,500	143,659,400	551,251,300
2 cents	455,168,500	305,910,500	424,057,300	390,981,500	1,576,117,800
3 cents	3,588,900	1,085,500	2,805,400	2,666,500	10,146,300
4 cents	5,872,150	2,184,050	5,050,800	3,782,200	16,889,200
5 cents	12,815,920	6,501,240	10,411,180	9,851,580	39,579,920
6 cents	228,500	17,100	612,650	465,950	1,324,200
10 cents	6,439,050	4,427,610	6,671,150	4,961,210	22,499,020
15 cents	603,560	218,680	334,860	235,700	1,392,800
30 cents	156,090	66,860	154,300	90,840	468,090
90 cents	15,470	2,150	34,960	15,850	68,430

Whole number of stamps 2,219,737,060.   Value $42,734,108.00.

ISSUE OF 1890.

From the report of the Third Assistant Postmaster General, dated Oct. 30th, 1890, we obtain the following information:

Historical. "The old contract for adhesive postage stamps expired on the 30th of June, 1889. To afford time in which to make needful preparations for the new contract, the old contract was extended for a period of three months, until the 30th of September, under a right reserved to the Department by the terms of the contract.

After a full examination of the subject an advertisement was issued, under date of June 17, 1889, calling for sealed proposals, to be received until the 17th day of July, for furnishing all the stamps which should be called for during the four years commencing October 1, 1889. The specifications furnished to bidders set forth the requirements of the contract with the utmost minuteness. They will be found in full in a copy of the contract in the appendix to this report.

The call was made for bids for ordinary stamps of two different sizes, to wit, those then in use, measuring 1 by 25-32 inch, and a smaller size, measuring ¾ by ⅞ inch. The sizes and styles of newspaper and periodical, postage-due, and special-delivery stamps were left unchanged.

An important change was that the color of each of the several denominations of stamps was prescribed by the specifications, with the purpose of preventing arbitrary and unnecessary changes during the existence of the contract. Samples of the stamps in the selected colors, appropriately cancelled, were attached to the specifications and blank forms of proposal furnished to bidders. Proposals were called for separately for stamps to be printed, first by hand-presses; second, by steam-power presses in which a portion of the work is to be done by steam and a portion by hand; and third by steam power presses on which all the work is done by steam; with the right reserved to the Department to make the award upon any one of the three classes of bids. The classification of the bids will appear fully in the copy of the specifications referred to. * * *

In response to the advertisement two bids were submitted, one by Mr. Charles F. Steel, of Philadelphia, and the other by the American Bank Note Company, of New York, the old contractors for furnishing stamps. The bid of Mr. Steel amounted, upon the basis referred to, to $155,017.39 for stamps of the larger size, and to $151,489.06 for stamps of the smaller size printed on hand-roller presses; to $124,642.36 for stamps of the larger size, and to $122,094 77 for stamps of the smaller size printed on steam-power presses on which a part of the work is done by steam and a part by hand; and to $120,723 for stamps of the larger size, and to $117,587.51 for stamps of the smaller size printed on all steam-power presses. The bid of the American Bank Note Company was for printing the ordinary stamps on steam-power presses only, and for the remaining kinds of stamps on hand-roller presses only, and the totals were $158,033.87, comprehending ordinary stamps of the larger size, and $148,235.47 embracing ordinary stamps of the smaller size. The difference between the amount of this bid and that of Mr. Steel for stamps printed on all steam-power presses was $37,310.87 for stamps of the larger size, and $30,647.96 for stamps of the smaller size.

At the opening in public of the bids, a protest was made by the American Bank Note Company against the award to Mr. Steel, on the ground that he was not eligible as a bidder under the terms of the advertisement restricting the bids to steel-plate engravers and plate-printers. This protest was shortly afterwards withdrawn, and, preliminary to an award, Mr. Steel was, upon the 1st of August, called upon to demonstrate his facilities for carrying out the contract. Though not engaged in the business, and being unprovided with a plant for printing and engraving, he promised to procure all the necessary equipment and material in time to manufacture and begin the delivery of the stamps on the 1st of October, or shortly thereafter. The specifications called for a fire-proof building in which to manufacture and store the stamps, but though called upon repeatedly to do so, Mr. Steel failed to submit for inspection suitable premises for the purpose. He offered only one building, though promising a choice of several different ones, and that building utterly failed to meet the requirement. The award was consequently witheld, and it becoming evident that Mr. Steel was either unwilling or unable to comply with his proposal, the Postmaster-General, under date of September 11, 1889, issued an advertisement calling for new proposals for a contract for the four years commencing December 1, 1889. At the same time provision was made for a temporary supply of stamps for the interval between October 1 and December 1 by calling on the American Bank Note Company to furnish a specified number of stamps, under the provisions of the contract giving the right to order an extra quanity not exceeding a three months' supply.

At the time appointed for closing the receipt of the new proposals, on the 26th of September, two bids were submitted. One was from the Franklin Bank Note Company and the other was from the American Bank Note Company, both of New York. The bid of the Franklin Bank Note Company amounted, on the basis of the quantities specified in the previous advertisement, to $163,904.82 for stamps of the larger size, and to $163,904 82 for stamps of the smaller size, printed on all steam-power presses, and the bid of the American Bank Note Company amounted, on the same basis and for the same class of work, to $157,641.93 for stamps of the larger size and to $149,215.31 for stamps of the smaller size. The bid of the American Bank Note Company was $391.94 less than its bid under the former advertisement for the larger stamps and $979.84 more for the smaller stamps.

Subsequent to the receipt of these proposals another call was made by letter of the Postmaster-General, dated October 8, upon Mr. Steel to comply with the requirements of his bid submitted in July, and he responded on the 12th of October by declining to proceed further in the matter. There appeared to be no alternative but to make a selection from the other bids already received, especially in view of the fact that, through the time lost in the endeavor to induce Mr. Steel to comply with his proposal, the Department had exhausted its resources for obtaining temporary supplies of stamps. The contract was therefore, on the 23d of October, awarded to the American Bank Note Company under its bid received on the 17th of July (it being the lowest of all the bids, except that of Mr. Steel, received under both advertisements) the award being made for ordinary stamps of the smaller size. No hesitation was felt in awarding the contract for stamps printed on all steam-power presses, the work having been satisfactorily done by that process during the preceding four years. As already shown, the successful bid amounted, upon the basis of the number of stamps issued during the year ending March 31, 1889, to $148,235.47. This amount was $9,406.46 more than the cost of corresponding kinds and numbers of stamps under the previous contract. It is to be observed, however, that under the terms of the new contract, the cost of preparing dies, rolls, and plates for new designs of stamps, or for additional denominations, is to be borne by the Department, while under the previous contract, the contractor was required to make these changes at the discretion of the Department and at his own expense; and, moreover, that by the new contract the two-cent stamps, constituting by far the greater portion of all the issues, are printed in much more expensive color than formerly.

The contract was duly executed, and it being found impracticable to prepare stamps of the new designs prior to December 1, arrangements were made with the American Bank Note Company by which stamps of the old style were to be furnished at the old contract rates until such time as the new stamps should be ready for issue. The issue of the new stamps was begun in time to place them on sale at the leading post-offices on February 22, last."

When the contract was signed, on Nov. 7th, 1889, the date at which it was to become operative was advanced to Jan. 1st, 1890.

The specifications furnished to intending bidders on this stamp contract provided in regard to colors as follows :

" The colors selected for the several denominations of the two sizes of ordinary stamps for which proposals are invited are respectively as follows : **"Sample" stamps in the proposed colors.**

The ordinary stamps of the larger size (A):

1 cent, ultramarine blue	6 cent, dark red
2 cent, metallic red	10 cent, light brown
3 cent, vermilion	15 cent, orange
4 cent, milori green	30 cent, black
5 cent, chocolate	90 cent, carmine

The colors adopted for this size of stamps are show on the specimens herewith, each being surcharged with the word ' Sample.'

For ordinary stamps of the smaller size (B):

1 cent, ultramarine blue	6 cent, vermilion
2 cent, carmine	10 cent, milori green

3 cent, royal purple	15 cent, steel blue
4 cent, chocolate	30 cent, black
5 cent, light brown	90 cent, orange

The colors adopted for this size are shown on the specimens herewith, each designated as ' Sample A.'

The inks to be used in printing the stamps must be of the colors shown on the samples for the corresponding kinds and denominations, and be fully equal in quality thereto. The use of aniline inks will not be allowed "

These sample stamps were prepared and overprinted by the American Bank Note Co., on a special order from the Post Office Department. In **Additional varieties.** addition to the varieties enumerated in the specifications, several others are known to collectors. They are: the two cents printed in dull lake, carmine-lake and scarlet-vermilion, and surcharged "SAMPLE"; the four cents green, ten cents brown and ninety cents carmine, overprinted "SAMPLE" and having the letter "A" added in manuscript, in black ink; and the five cents blue (Garfield) surcharged " SAMPLE A " in manuscript, in red ink.

The one, two, three, six, ten, fifteen, thirty and ninety cent stamps were placed on sale at one hundred and ten of the larger post-offices on February **Dates of issue.** 22nd, 1890. The four and five cent stamps were not issued until June 2nd of that year. The eight cent stamp did not form a part of the series as originally prepared and was not issued until about three years later, March .21st, 1893. Its introduction was due to the reduction of the registration fee from ten to eight cents, on January 1st, 1893.

The official description of the designs and colors is as follows:

"ONE CENT. Profile bust, after Rubricht, of Benjamin Franklin looking to the left, on an oval disk, with dark background and narrow white **Designs and colors.** border, immediately above which, set in a panel conforming to the curve of the disk, are the words 'UNITED STATES POSTAGE' in white capitals, and below which, in slightly larger and shaded letters, arranged in a waved line running nearly the whole width of the stamp, are the words 'ONE CENT'. Just above these latter words, on either sides, is a white numeral of denomination —the arabic figure ' 1 '—in a small oval space, surrounded by an ornate scroll, the upper portion of which is connected with and serves as a support to the panel around the medallion. The whole is placed upon a distinctly lined oblong tablet, seven-eighths of an inch high by three-fourths of an inch wide, with beveled sides and bottom. The color is ultramarine blue.

TWO CENTS. Profile bust, after Houdon, of George Washington, looking to the left, on an oval disk. The surroundings of the medallion are the same as in the 1-cent stamp, with the necessary change of figures and letters representing the denomination. Color, carmine. An improved quality of color for the 2-cent stamp was adopted May 12, 1890.

THREE CENTS. Profile bust, after Powers, of Andrew Jackson, looking to the left, on an oval disk. The surroundings of the medallion are the same as in the 1-cent stamp, with the necessary change of figures and letters representing the denomination. Color, purple.

FOUR CENTS. Portrait of Abraham Lincoln, after a photograph from life, three-quarters face, looking to the right, on an oval disk. The surroundings of the medallion are the same as in the 1-cent stamp, with the necessary change of figures and letters representing the denomination. Color, velvet brown.

FIVE CENTS. Portrait of U. S. Grant, after a photograph from life, three-quarters face, looking to the right, on an oval disk. The surroundings of the medallion are the same as in the 1-cent stamp, with the necessary change of figures and letters representing the denomination. Color, light brown.

SIX CENTS. Portrait of James A. Garfield, after a photograph from life, three-quarters face, looking to the left, on an oval disk. The surroundings of the medallion are the same as on the 1-cent stamp, with the necessary change of figures and letters representing the denomination. Color, light maroon.

EIGHT CENTS. Portrait of Gen. William T. Sherman, after a photograph from life, full face. The surroundings of the picture are the same as those on the stamps below the 10-cent denomination with the necessary change of figures and letters representing the value. Color, lilac.

TEN CENTS. Portrait of Daniel Webster, after a daguerreotype from life, three-quarters face, looking to the left, on an oval disk, with dark background and narrow white border, around the upper half of which, set in a panel conforming to its curve, are the words 'UNITED STATES POSTAGE', in small white capitals, the words 'TEN CENTS' in somewhat similar letters being placed in a like panel below the medallion. Below this again, in the two lower corners of the stamp, are plain Arabic numerals of denomination, ' 10 ', set in circular spaces surrounded with ornate scrolls not unlike those in the 1-cent stamp. The whole is placed upon an oblong tablet, seven-eighths of an inch high by three-fourths of an inch wide, with beveled sides and bottom. The color is milori green.

FIFTEEN CENTS. Portrait of Henry Clay, after a daguerreotype from life, three-quarters face, looking to the left, on an oval disk. The surroundings of the medallion are substantially the same as in the 10-cent stamp, with appropriate changes of figures and letters representing the denomination. Color, deep blue.

THIRTY CENTS. Profile bust of Thomas Jefferson, after Ceracchi, looking to the left, on an oval disk. The surroundings of the medallion are the same as in the 10-cent stamp, with necessary change of the letters and figures of denomination, the latter, however, being of block form. Color, black.

NINETY CENTS. Profile bust of Commodore O. H. Perry, after Wolcott's statue, looking to the left, on an oval disk. The surroundings of the medallion are substantially the same as in the 30-cent stamp, with the necessary changes of the letters and figures of denomination. Color, orange."

The stamps are of uniform size, 19x22mm.

The paper, gum and perforation are the same as in previous issues made by the American Bank Note Co. **Paper, etc.**

There are some minor varieties of the two cent stamps which are of trifling interest. These are colorless marks, commonly called " caps ", above

Capped numerals. one or both of the numerals of value. They are caused by damaged transfer rolls. By some means, probably over hardening, a bit of the roll was chipped off. In one instance the break occurred above the right-hand numeral, in another above the left, and in the third above both numerals. These three transfers and others which were not damaged were used in conjunction and the resulting combinations are interesting to specialists. There is in the collection of Mr. H. E. Deats a strip of ten stamps, from the upper right quarter of plate VV246, of which the first three stamps (counting from the left) have caps on the left-hand numeral, and the other stamps of the row have caps on both numerals. In the same collection are similar strips from plates TT235, VV247 and VV248, all the stamps of which have caps on the numeral at the left, and a strip from plate VV245 with caps on both numerals. Mr. Deats' strips from plates SS232, TT236, 238 and 239 do not show any caps. Nos. UU240, 241, 242, 243 and 244 are on plates of the one cent stamp. The other adjacent numbers I have not seen. It is possible that some of them are of the capped varieties.

In view of the rigid and almost microscopical examination to which stamp plates are understood to be subjected it is surprising that these defective plates were not discovered, or, if discovered, were allowed to be used.

The following shades and varieties are found in this issue :

Reference List.

Soft Porous White Wove Paper.

Perforated 12.

Feb. 22nd, 1890.	1 cent pale ultramarine, ultramarine, dark ultramarine, gray-blue, dull blue
	2 cents lake, violet-lake, lilac-rose, carmine-lake, pale carmine, carmine, deep carmine, carmine-rose, bright aniline rose, deep aniline rose, rose, crimson
	3 cents bright purple, deep purple
June 2nd, 1890.	4 cents dark yellow-brown, black-brown
	5 cents orange-brown, deep orange-brown, bistre-brown, dark brown
Feb. 22nd, 1890.	6 cents claret, claret-brown, rose-brown
March 21st, 1893.	8 cents gray-lilac, gray-violet
Feb. 22nd, 1890.	10 cents deep blue-green, dark gray-green
	15 cents indigo, deep indigo
	30 cents gray-black, full black
	90 cents yellow-orange, orange, red-orange

Varieties:

2 cents carmine. Cap on right numeral

2 cents carmine-lake, carmine, carmine-rose, rose. Cap on left numeral

2 cents carmine-lake, carmine-rose. Caps on both numerals

8 cents magenta. Error. Color of the eight cents of the Columbian issue

1 cent deep ultramarine,   Imperforate

2 cents carmine-rose, carmine	Imperforate
3 cents purple	"
4 cents dark yellow-brown	"
5 cents orange-brown	"
6 cents claret	"
8 cents gray-lilac	"
10 cents deep blue-green	"
15 cents indigo	"
30 cents black	"
90 cents orange	"

Bisected stamps. Bisected stamps of this and subsequent issues are not at all uncommon. By the present rules of the Post Office Department such varieties are not receivable for postage and, even should one be accepted at the office where a letter is mailed, the postmaster at the office of delivery is instructed to treat the letter as unpaid. On occasions, the exhaustion of the lower values in a post office has appeared to warrant the use of bisected stamps and such varieties have even been endorsed by the postmaster, despite the rule of the department. But, on the other hand, many such oddities have been passed through the post by favor or carelessness and collectors will probably do well to entirely eschew such varieties in the later issues.

Proofs. While this issue was being prepared, proofs were made, from plates of the two, four and five cents, in a variety of shades which closely approach those of the issued stamps. There were five shades of the two cents, eleven of the four cents and thirteen of the five cents. These proofs are on the regular paper gummed and finished except that they are not perforated. There would be no occasion for mentioning them, were it not that they are occasionally offered for sale as imperforate varieties of the issued stamps and collectors should be informed of their true character.

Plates. In this issue many plates of the one and two cent values contained four hundred stamps each. All the other plates contained two hundred stamps each. The impressions were, as usual, cut into sheets of one hundred stamps. The imprints and plate numbers were in the same style and occupied the same positions as on previous plates of the same contractors. In addition some, if not all, of the plates had the inscription "AMERICAN BANK NOTE COMPANY" at the outer side of each pane of one hundred stamps.

In the following list the figures enclosed in parenthesis indicate the number of the stamps on each plate.

The numbers of the plates were as follows: **Plate numbers.**

1 cent	(400)	C.	11, 12, 13, 14, 15.
	(400)	G.	36, 37, 38, 39, 40.
	(400)	Q.	89, 90, 91, 92, 93.
	(400)	BB.	145, 146, 147, 148, 149.
	(400)	FF.	165, 166, 167, 168, 169.
	(400)	UU.	240, 241, 242, 243, 244.
	(400)	C1.	280, 281, 282, 283, 284.
	(400)	D1.	285, 286, 287, 288, 289.
	(400)	F1.	295, 296, 297, 298, 299.

2 cents

(400)	A.	1,	2,	3,	4,	5.	
(400)	B.	6,	7,	8,	9,	10,	71
(400)	D.	16,	17,	18,	19,	20.	
(400)	F.	31,	32,	33,	34,	35.	
(400)	H.	41,	42,	43,	44,	45.	
(200)	K.	56,	57,	58,	59,	60.	
(200)	L.	61,	62,	63,	64.	65.	
(200)	M.	66,	67,	68,	69,	70.	99.
(200)	N.	74,	75,	76,	77,	78.	
(200)	O.	79,	80,	81,	82,	83.	
(400)	P.	84,	85,	86,	87,	88.	
(400)	R.	94,	95,	96,	97,	98.	
(200)	S.	100,	101,	102,	103,	104.	
(200)	T.	105,	106,	107,	108,	109.	
(200)	U.	110,	111,	112,	113,	114.	
(200)	V.	115,	116,	117,	118,	119.	
(400)	W.	120,	121,	122,	123,	124.	
(200)	X.	125,	126,	127,	128,	129.	
(400)	Y.	130,	131,	132,	133,	134.	
(400)	Z.	135,	136,	137,	138,	'39.	
(200)	AA.	140,	141,	142,	143,	144.	
(400)	CC.	150.	151,	152,	153,	154.	
(400)	DD.	155,	156,	157,	158,	159.	
(400)	EE.	160,	161,	162,	163,	164.	
(400)	GG.	170,	171,	172,	173,	174.	
(400)	HH.	175,	176,	177,	178,	179.	
(200)	II.	180,	181,	182,	183,	184.	
(200)	JJ.	185,	186,	187,	188,	189.	
(200)	KK.	190,	191,	192,	193,	194.	
(200)	LL.	195,	196,	197,	198,	199.	
(400)	NN.	205,	206,	207,	208,	209.	
(200)	OO.	210,	211,	212,	213,	214.	
(200)	PP.	215,	216,	217,	218,	219.	
(400)	QQ.	220,	221,	222,	223,	224.	
(200)	RR.	225,	226,	227,	228,	229.	
(400)	SS.	230,	231,	232,	233,	234.	
(400)	TT.	235,	236,	237,	238,	239.	
(200)	VV.	245,	246,	247,	248,	249.	
(200)	WW.	250,	251,	252,	253,	254.	
(200)	XX.	255,	256,	257,	258,	259.	
(200)	YY	260,	261,	262,	263,	264.	
(400)	A1.	270,	271,	272,	273,	274.	
(400)	B1.	275,	276,	277,	278,	279.	
(400)	E1.	290,	291,	292,	293,	294.	
(400)	G1.	300,	301,	302,	303,	304.	
(400)	H1.	305,	306,	307,	308,	309.	
(400)	I1.	310,	311,	312,	313,	314.	

	(400) J1.	315, 316, 317, 318, 319.
	( ) K1.	320, 321, 322, 323, 324.
	( ) L1.	325, 326, 327, 328, 329.
	( ) M1.	330, 331, 332, 333, 334.
	( ) N1.	335, 336, 337, 338, 339.
	( ) O1.	340, 341, 342, 343, 344.
	( ) P1.	345, 346, 347, 348, 349.
3 cents	(200)	21, 72.
4 cents	(200) J.	51, 52, 53, 54, 55.
	(200) MM.	200, 201, 202, 203, 204.
5 cents	(200) I.	46, 47, 48, 49, 50.
6 cents	(200)	23.
8 cents	(200) ZZ.	265, 266, 267, 268, 269.
10 cents	(200) E.	26, 27, 28, 29, 30.
15 cents	(200)	22.
30 cents	(200)	24.
90 cents	(200)	25.

Plates 71 and 99 were added to the groups lettered B and M to replace damaged plates.

Stamps from the following plates are known in imperforate condition :

2 cents	D. 18, F. 34.
3 cents	21.
5 cents	I. 46.
6 cents	23.
15 cents	22.
30 cents	24.
90 cents	25.

The annual reports of the Postmaster General and of the Bureau of Engraving and Printing supply the following statistics of stamps issued to deputy postmasters :

Stamps issued during the fiscal year ending June 30th, 1891 :

QUARTER ENDING :

	Sept. 30, 1890.	Dec. 31, 1890.	Mch. 31, 1891.	June 30, 1891.	Total.
1 cent	121,144,100	146,001,900	160,068,400	151,494,100	578,708,500
2 cents	394,563,400	435,499,000	464,456,200	425,781,700	1,720,300,300
3 cents	2,053,700	2,596,300	3,334,400	2,900,700	10,885,100
4 cents	3,471,350	5,248,100	4,878,250	3,764,100	17,361,800
5 cents	9,227,460	11,054,240	12,197,780	10,433,200	42,912,680
6 cents	531,550	720,050	391,650	348,550	1,991,800
10 cents	4,915,680	5,783,260	6,939,180	5,447,650	23,085,770
15 cents	362,560	475,000	580,960	267,080	1,685,600
30 cents	91,790	186,330	160,530	88,410	527,060
90 cents	13,430	11,230	7,790	12,280	44,730

Whole number of stamps 2,397,503,340. Value $46,239,050.00.

Stamps issued during the fiscal year ending June 30th, 1892 :

QUARTER ENDING :

	Sept. 30, 1891.	Dec. 31, 1891.	Mch. 31, 1892.	June 30, 1892	Total.
1 cent	123,667,200	172,387,600	170,077,700	159,108,400	625,240,900
2 cents	402,173,600	474,486,800	489,161,800	447,493,500	1,813,315,700
3 cents	2,085,800	3,619,000	4,228,200	2,749,600	12,682,600
4 cents	3,810,000	5,281,900	5,164,200	4,559,100	18,815,200
5 cents	9,329,180	12,404,380	12,515,540	10,705,520	44,954,620
6 cents	570,750	780,900	626,650	295,650	2,273,950
10 cents	4,808,690	6,448,900	6,770,290	5,758,880	23,786,760
15 cents	404,720	543,840	443,420	258,360	1,650,340
30 cents	129,290	135,410	129,910	116,670	511,280
90 cents	12,990	8,000	7,480	10,390	38,860

Whole number of stamps 2,543,270,210.　Value $48,850,562.00.

Stamps issued during the fiscal year ending June 30th, 1893 :

QUARTER ENDING :

	Sept. 30, 1892.	Dec. 31, 1892.	Mch. 31, 1893.	June 30, 1893.	Total.
1 cent	133,659,850	160,812,800	51,128,400	90,341,300	435,942,350
2 cents	439,410,000	470,560,800	72,173,600	217,612,200	1,199,756,600
3 cents	2,357,550	3,834,000	1,117,100	1,671,300	8,979,950
4 cents	4,270,600	5,639,875	1,031,300	2,559,300	13,501,075
5 cents	10,487,330	11,838,540	1,197,460	4,997,260	28,520,590
6 cents	632,950	1,074,550	164,450	365,800	2,237,750
8 cents	....	....	139,250	1,403,250	1,542,500
10 cents	5,241,000	6,151,400	735,350	1,697,130	13,824,880
15 cents	310,470	679,600	46,640	113,720	1,150,430
30 cents	123,650	119,180	12,910	34,870	290,610
90 cents	15,820	23,380	170	1,990	41,360

Whole number of stamps 1,705,788,095.　Value $32,527,151.00.

Stamps issued during the fiscal year ending June 30th, 1894 :

QUARTER ENDING :

	Sept. 30, 1893.	Dec. 31, 1893.	Mch. 31, 1894.	June 30, 1894.	Total.
1 cent	78,059,300	71,907,600	116,841,900	138,586,300	405,395,100
2 cents	275,632,700	200,240,200	275,930,000	403,934,600	1,155,737,500
3 cents	1,221,900	2,096,500	4,719,900	3,774,200	11,812,500
4 cents	2,161,900	1,871,450	5,598,000	4,574,650	14,206,000
5 cents	3,948,140	3,434,380	9,857,560	9,582,440	26,822,520
6 cents	402,400	303,400	959,800	1,043,800	2,709,400
8 cents	1,013,750	781,200	1,609,000	1,727,450	5,131,400
10 cents	1,722,600	1,719,670	3,137,300	3,050,150	9,629,720
15 cents	118,740	79,380	231,200	368,440	797,760
30 cents	81,190	13,830	49,450	148,610	293,080
90 cents	530	660	5,050	9,030	15,270

Whole number of stamps 1,632,550,250.　Value $31,189,821.00.

Stamps issued during the fiscal year ending June 30th, 1895 :

QUARTER ENDING :

	Sept. 30, 1894.	Dec. 31, 1894.	Mch. 31, 1895.	June 30, 1895.	Total.
1 cent	131,620,000	29,186,600	....	....	160,806,600
2 cents	432,205,100	23,404,300	.. ..	....	455,609,400
3 cents	2,517,100	....	.. ..	... ...	2,517,100
4 cents	2,875,400	....	....	....	2,875,400
5 cents	9,026,120	....	... ...	....	9,026,120
6 cents	40,500	... .	....	.. ..	40,500
8 cents	1,228,550	2,138,450	2,046,900	.. ..	5,413,900
10 cents	2,419,030	....	....	.... ..	2,419,030
15 cents	217,020	47,560	....	....	264,580
30 cents	75,550	37,438	... .	....	112,988
90 cents	9,120	70,381	....	....	79,501

Whole number of stamps 639,165,119. Value $12,184,668.30.

ISSUE OF 1893.

COLUMBIAN SERIES.

The reasons for the issue and other particulars concerning it are given in the report of the Third Assistant Postmaster General, dated November 20th, 1892, as follows :

Historical. "During the past summer the determination was reached by the Department to issue, during the progress of the Columbian Exposition at Chicago, a special series of adhesive postage stamps of such a character as would help to signalize the four hundredth anniversary of the discovery of America by Columbus. This course was in accordance with the practice of other great postal administrations on occasions of national rejoicing, and it was consistent with the idea of a display at the Exposition of such articles as would illustrate the history, progress and administrative functions of the Post-Office Department, which Congress, by statute, has directed to be made part of a general governmental exhibit. The same idea had been carried out in a limited way during the Centennial Exposition at Philadelphia, in 1876, by the issue, concurrently with that event, of a specal design of stamped envelopes appropriate to the celebration. The measure was not only calculated to prove a popular one, but to be the means, through the sale of the stamps to the collectors, and by specially stimulating the use of the stamps by the public, of adding largely to the revenue of the Department.

The collecting of stamps is deserving of encouragement, for it tends to the cultivation of artistic tastes and the study of history and geography, especially on the part of the young, by the examination and comparison of stamps of different nations of the world, and to a more accurate knowledge of their postal systems. The new stamps will be purchased in large quantities simply for the use of collections, without ever being presented in payment of postage; and the stamps sold in this way will of course, prove a clear gain to the Department.

The benefits to accrue to the Exposition from the issue of such a series of stamps, by constantly drawing to it public attention, both at home and abroad, are too patent to need elaboration.

The necessary arrangements for manufacturing the new stamps were made with the present contractors for furnishing all the other stamps in use. The work was begun late in September last, and it has progressed with such rapidity that a supply of upwards of 100,-000,000 of the leading denominations has already been accumulated. It is expected that the full series will be completed in time to place the stamps on sale on Monday the 2d of January, the period fixed for their issue being the whole of the calendar year 1893, and the estimated quantity to be required during that time being 3,000,000,000. The new stamps are, however, not intended to displace the current series of stamps, but will be in addition thereto; so that anyone needing postage stamps will be able to procure either or both kinds, as he may prefer.

The principal feature of the Columbian stamps, with two exceptions, is the delineation of some scene in the life of Columbus associated with the discovery of America, one of the exceptions being a stamp bearing a profile portrait of Columbus, similar to that on the souvenir 50 cent coin issued by the Treasury Department, and the other a stamp bearing portraits of Queen Isabella and Columbus in three-quarters face. There is a general resemblance in the two portraits of Columbus, both being taken from the same original picture. To properly illustrate the subjects selected it was found necessary to adopt a larger size than that in present use, the new stamps being of the same height and of nearly double the length of the regular stamps, the engraved space measuring seven-eights of an inch by 1 11-32 inches.

The denominations are the same as those in the present series, except that the 50-cent stamp is substituted for the 90-cent, and additions are made of 1, 2, 3, 4 and 5 dollars, such high denominations having been heretofore called for by some of the principal post-offices.

The subjects on some of the stamps—1-cent, 2-cent, 5-cent, 6-cent, 50-cent and 2-dollar stamps—are copied from the works of American artists."

The report of the Postmaster General for 1892 covers much the same ground and says, among other things:

" In addition, the ' mania,' as it is called, for collecting postage stamps, as specimens, is universal throughout the world. It affects every class and condition of people, and is not confined by age or sex. It is shared, perhaps, by millions of people, from the school boy and girl to the monarch and the millionaire, and the value of stamps in private collections which will never be drawn upon to pay postage may safely be placed at many millions of dollars. The beauty and unique character of the new Columbian stamps will cause their sale in large quantities, simply for use in collections; and not only will they be purchased in single or partial sets by collectors, but in view of the limited time in which they will be issued, they will be accumulated in great quantities by dealers and others to meet future demands. * * *

An official view of stamp collecting.

The introduction of the new stamps, though not designed primarily for that object, will prove to be a revenue measure of the highest importance to the public service. The net profit to be derived from their issue, that is the extra amount beyond the ordinary revenue that would have resulted from the sale and use only of ordinary stamps, may be fairly placed at $2,500,000."

Appendix L. of the report of the Postmaster General for 1892, supplies some interesting information about the contract for this issue:

" The following statement, reference to which has been made in the foregoing report of the Postmaster-General, is presented to show the particulars of the arrangement entered into by the Department for the issue of the new series of postage stamps intended to commemorate the discovery of America by Columbus.

Negotiations with the contractors.

The contract now in force for furnishing the current series of adhesive postage stamps is with the American Bank Note Company of New York, and was entered into nearly three years ago; and as this contract does not expire until the 31st of December, 1893, and specifically calls for ordinary stamps of entirely different sizes and designs from those contemplated as proper for the new series, its provisions could not be availed of by the Department to carry out its intentions.

The Department, moreover, had no right to call for proposals for procuring the proposed stamps under a new contract, since to have the work done by other parties would interfere with the rights of the contractors which obligated the Department to procure from them all the stamps that should be needed during the contract term. Besides, as work of this character involves much machinery not in general use, it was hardly to be expected that other parties would go to the expense of a special equipment in view of the limited quantity of stamps to be issued, and of the duration of time in which they were to be furnished.

The number of new stamps to be required, as stated in the report, was estimated at 3,000,000,000, and negotiations were entered into with the contractors for supplying the stamps under a special arrangement. It was at first thought by the Department that, inasmuch as the new stamps were to be about double the size of the present stamps, a fair compensation would be about double the present contract price, or, say 15 cents a thousand. Upon a full consideration of the subject, however, this price was objected to by the contractors as not affording a remuneration proportioned to the increased labor and cost of the work. It was contended by them that the making of the new stamps involved a large increase of their machinery for printing, gumming, and pressing the stamps, as well as a great enlargement of their floor space, power, appliances, and force of operatives; and that, when the work was at an end, they would be left in possession of a great deal of special material and equipment which, from a business point of view, would be worthless. They urged for example, that it would double the number of machines used in printing the stamps, they being now printed in sheets of 400, while the new stamps would contain only 200 impressions to the sheet.

A special point was made that the requirement to double their capacity came during the last year of the contract, and that the extra facilities to be provided would be unnecessary to meet the demands for the ordinary stamps, in the event they should be successful in the competition for the next contract. The result of the deliberations was the submission of a proposition to furnish the desired Columbian stamps, 3,000,000,000 in number, at 18¾ cents per thousand, upon the condition that the present contract should be extended for a period of six months beyond the time fixed for its expiration. The price named was adjudged to be somewhat extravagant; and upon carefully considering the subject in all its aspects, it was decided to offer 17 cents per thousand for the stamps with, the desired extension of the contract. After much hesitation on the part of the contractors, and as the result of several personal conferences with them during the past summer, they accepted this offer.

The necessary orders were accordingly made to carry the arrangement into effect, the

six months' extension being covered by one clause of the contract giving the right of extension direct for three months, and under another clause giving the Department the right to
call at any time during the contract term for an extra quantity of stamps, not to exceed a
supply for three months. It may be stated that the price paid, under the regular contract, for
the special-delivery, and newspaper and periodical stamps, which correspond closely in size
with the proposed Columbian stamps, is 18 cents per thousand, or 1 cent per thousand more
than the price agreed upon for the new stamps.

The course followed by the Department in this matter is the same that has been pur-
sued in all cases heretofore where it has been found necessary to introduce new kinds or
sizes of postage stamps or stamped envelopes differing from those covered specifically by
contracts in force, a course, indeed, which seems to be the only one practicable in such a
contingency."

The eight cent stamp. As was noted in the preceding chapter, the fee for registered letters
was reduced from ten to eight cents, on January 1st, 1893. In conformity
with this change, eight-cent stamps were added to both the regular and the
Columbian series.

A circular of the Post Office Department, dated February 28th, 1893,
says :

"On the 1st of March, 1893, the Department will begin the issue of the following
articles of stamped paper:

1. An 8-cent postage stamp of the Columbian series, intended for use in the payment of the reduced fee on registered matter. This stamp is of the same general style as the
other denominations of Columbian stamps, and bears a reproduction of the picture painted
by Francisco Jover, the original of which is now in Spain, entitled "Columbus Restored to
Favor.' The color of the stamp is magenta-red."

The other sections of the circular refer to the eight-cent stamp of the
regular issue, the Columbian envelopes and the foreign reply postal card.

The designs are officially described as follows :

"The stamps are executed from line engravings on steel, the general
design of the upper portion of all of them being substantially the same. The
Designs and colors. details of this design are, first, a white-faced imprint of the years '1492' and
'1892', in the upper left and right hand corners, respectively ; then, in white
shaded capitals beneath, in a waved line, the words 'UNITED STATES OF
AMERICA', below which, in a narrow tablet conforming to the curved frame
of the picture under it, are the words of denomination : for example, 'POSTAGE
TWO CENTS', 'POSTAGE TWO DOLLARS', etc. These words end on either side
of the stamp in a space of circular form with ornamental surroundings, within
which are Arabic numerals of value—standing alone in the case of denominations under $1, but accompanied by the dollar mark in denominations of $1
and upwards, as '2' (meaning cents), '$2', etc. Underneath all this is the
scene represented inclosed in a plain white frame with arched top, extending
nearly the entire length of the stamp, and taking up, in every case, probably
three-fourths of its whole face, the appropriate designation of the picture
being given in small white capitals at the bottom. The scenes represented
are these :

ONE CENT. 'Columbus in Sight of Land', after the painting by
William H. Powell. This reproduction is enclosed in a circle. On the left
of it is represented an Indian woman with her child, and on the right an
Indian chief with headdress of feathers—each figure in a sitting posture.
Color, Antwerp blue.

TWO CENTS. 'Landing of Columbus', after the painting by Vanderlyn,
in the rotunda of the Capitol at Washington. Color, purple maroon.

THREE CENTS. 'Flagship of Columbus', the Santa Maria in mid-ocean, from a Spanish engraving. Color, medium shade of green.

FOUR CENTS. 'Fleet of Columbus', the three caravels, Santa Maria, Nina and Pinta, from a Spanish engraving. Color, ultramarine blue.

FIVE CENTS. 'Columbus Soliciting Aid of Isabella', after the painting by Brozik, in the Metropolitan Museum of Art in New York City. Color, chocolate brown.

SIX CENTS. 'Columbus Welcomed at Barcelona', scene from one of the panels of the bronze doors by Randolph Rogers in the Capitol at Washington. On each side of the scene represented is a niche, in one of which is a statue of Ferdinand and in the other a statue of Balboa. Color, royal purple.

EIGHT CENTS. 'Columbus Restored to Favor', after a painting by Jover. Color, magenta red. Issued March 1, 1893.

TEN CENTS. 'Columbus Presenting Natives', after the painting by Luigi Gregori, at the University of Notre Dame, South Bend, Indiana. Color, Vandyke brown.

FIFTEEN CENTS. 'Columbus Announcing His Discovery', after the painting by R. Baloca, now in Madrid. Color, dark green.

THIRTY CENTS. 'Columbus at La Rabida', after the painting by R. Maso. Color, sienna brown.

FIFTY CENTS. 'Recall of Columbus', after the painting by A. G. Heaton, now in the Capitol at Washington. Color, carbon blue.

ONE DOLLAR. 'Isabella Pledging Her Jewels', after the painting by Munoz Degrain, now in Madrid. Color, rose salmon.

TWO DOLLARS. 'Columbus in Chains', after the painting by Leutze, now in Providence, R. I. Color, toned mineral red.

THREE DOLLARS. 'Columbus Describing Third Voyage', after a painting by Francisco Jover. Color, light yellow green.

FOUR DOLLARS. Portraits in circles, separated by an ornate device, of Isabella and Columbus, the portrait of Isabella after the well known painting in Madrid and that of Columbus after the Lotto painting. Color, carmine.

FIVE DOLLARS. Profile of head of Columbus, after a cast provided by the Treasury Department for the souvenir 50-cent silver piece authorized by act of Congress. The profile is in a circle, on the right of which is the figure of America, represented by an Indian woman with a crown of feathers, and on the left a figure of Liberty, both figures being in a sitting posture. Color, black."

The stamps measure 34x22mm.

The paper, gum and perforation are the same as in other issues by the American Bank Note Company.

Soft Porous White Wove Paper.

Reference List.

Perforated 12.

Jan. 1st. 1893.   1 cent pale blue, deep blue

2 cents red-lilac, red-violet, gray-violet
3 cents green, deep green
4 cents ultramarine, deep ultramarine
5 cents chocolate, red-brown, yellow-brown, brown
6 cents purple, red-purple
Mch. 1st, 1893.   8 cents pale magenta, magenta, lilac-rose
Jan. 1st, 1893.   10 cents deep yellow-brown, black-brown, gray-black, gray
30 cents orange, pale brown-orange, deep brown-orange
50 cents slate
1 dollar scarlet, salmon-red
2 dollars rose-brown, deep rose-brown
3 dollars pale yellow-green, gray-green, olive-green
4 dollars pale aniline rose, carmine-rose, carmine-lake
5 dollars gray-black, full black

Varieties:

2 cents red-lilac.   Imperforate.
4 cents deep blue.   Error.   Color of the one cent.

It has been said that several values of this series exist in imperforate condition but, with the exception of the two cents, I have not been able to
Varieties.   see them nor even to learn of an actual holder of any such varieties.   We occasionally see the six cents in a dull blue, this is is not an error of color but the results from exposure to light.

In September, 1893, Mr. J. V. Painter obtained from the post office
Error of color.   at Cleveland, Ohio, a sheet of four cent stamps printed in blue instead of ultramarine.   So far as I am aware, no other copies of this error have ever been found.

The plates of this issue contained two hundred stamps each, arranged in twenty rows of ten stamps.   The impressions were divided horizontally
Plates.   into sheets of one hundred stamps.   On each plate the imprint, plate number and serial letter appear twice at both top and bottom and the imprint also appears twice at each side.

Plate numbers.   The plate numbers are as follows:

1 cent	No. J.	46,	47,	48,	49,	50.
	K.	51,	52,	53,	54,	55.
	P.	65,	66,	67,	68,	69.
	MM.	149,	150,	151,	152,	153.
	OO.	159,	160,	161,	162,	163
	VV.	194,	195,	196,	197,	198.
2 cents	No. A.	1,	2,	3,	4,	5.
	C.	11,	12,	13,	14,	15.
	E.	21,	22,	23,	24,	25.
	F.	26,	27,	28,	29,	30.
	G.	31,	32,	33,	34,	35.
	H.	36,	37,	38,	39,	40.
	I.	41,	42,	43,	44,	45.
	O.	60,	61,	62,	63,	64.

	Q.	70, 71, 72, 73, 74.
	T.	78, 79, 80, 81, 82.
	U.	83, 84, 85, 86, 87.
	V.	88, 89, 90, 91, 92.
	X.	94, 95, 96, 97, 98.
	EE.	109, 110, 111, 112, 113.
	FF.	114, 115, 116, 117, 118.
	GG.	119, 120, 121, 122, 123.
	HH.	124, 125, 126, 127, 128.
	JJ.	134, 135, 136, 137, 138.
	KK.	139, 140, 141, 142, 143.
	LL.	144, 145, 146, 147, 148.
	NN.	154, 155, 156, 157, 158.
	PP.	164, 165, 166, 167, 168.
	QQ.	169, 170, 171, 172, 173.
	RR.	174, 175, 176, 177, 178.
	SS.	179, 180, 181, 182, 183.
	TT.	184, 185, 186, 187, 188.
	UU.	189, 190, 191, 192, 193.
3 cents	No. L.	56, 57.
	R.	75, 76.
4 cents	No. D.	16, 17, 18, 19, 20.
5 cents	No. B.	6, 7, 8, 9, 10.
6 cents	No. Z.	104.
8 cents	No. II.	129, 130, 131, 132, 133.
10 cents	No. Y.	99, 100, 101, 102, 103.
15 cents	No. M.	58.
30 cents	No. N.	59.
50 cents	No. S.	77.
1 dollar	No. W.	93.
2 dollars	No. AA.	105.
3 dollars	No. BB.	106.
4 dollars	No CC.	107.
5 dollars	No. DD.	108.

The four cents in the wrong color was printed from plate D. 17.

From the annual reports of the Postmaster General we learn that the following quantities of Columbian stamps were delivered to deputy postmasters:

Stamps issued during the fiscal year ending June 30th, 1893 :

QUARTER ENDING :

Deliveries to postmasters.

	Sept. 30, 1892.	Dec. 31, 1892.	Mch. 31, 1893.	June 30, 1893.	Total.
1 cent	....	43,296,000	130,941,550	72,410,800	246,648,350
2 cents	....	116,290,000	361,904,350	259,207,700	737,402,050
3 cents	....	1,011,400	4,360,150	2,188,600	7,560,150
4 cents	....	1,976,300	9,258,600	3,442,350	14,677,250
5 cents	....	3,289,500	9,917,750	6,801,160	20,008,410

	Sept. 30, 1892.	Dec. 31, 1892.	Mch. 31, 1893.	June 30, 1893.	Total.
6 cents	....	289,700	1,556,550	878,650	2,724,900
8 cents	....	....	877,950	3,905,150	4,783,100
10 cents	....	1,318,900	5,169,710	2,450,590	8,939,200
15 cents	....	170,600	580,630	323,820	1,075,050
30 cents	....	85,500	197,420	156,950	439,870
50 cents	....	46,400	83,748	22,608	152,756
1 dollar	....	5,800	18,161	9,866	33,827
2 dollars	....	5,800	8,488	3,238	17,526
3 dollars	....	5,800	6,425	2,763	14,988
4 dollars	....	5,800	5,222	2,764	13,786
5 dollars	....	5,800	5,228	2,754	13,782

Whole number of stamps 1,044,504,995.   Value $21,076,395.00.

Stamps issued during the fiscal year ending June 30th, 1894 :

QUARTER ENDING :

	Sept. 30, 1893.	Dec. 31, 1893.	Mch. 31, 1894.	June 30, 1894.	Total.
1 cent	35,540,300	157,064,700	....	9,943,250	202,548,250
2 cents	151,971,500	571,917,200	....	3,299,050	727,187,750
3 cents	1,746,100	1,922,600	....	273,450	3,942,150
4 cents	1,581,700	2,768,650	....	155,000	4,505,350
5 cents	4,538,380	10,701,260	....	1,250	15,240,890
6 cents	504,300	1,101,050	....	378,350	1,983,700
8 cents	765,750	5,101,800	....	6,950	5,874,500
10 cents	1,862,690	5,683,370	....	32,740	7,578,800
15 cents	169,800	302,940	....	30,210	502,950
30 cents	43,990	116,440	....	18,000	178,430
50 cents	10,916	37,044	....	44,084	92,044
1 dollar	9,238	12,455	....	580	22,273
2 dollars	1,258	5,395	....	22,421	29,074
3 dollars	538	3,805	....	9,369	13,712
4 dollars	608	4,075	....	8,931	13,614
5 dollars	2,613	2,540	....	9,465	14,618

Whole number of stamps 969,728,105.   Value $19,399,719.00.

From the foregoing table we may infer that the delivery of Columbian stamps by the Post Office Department was stopped on December 31st, 1893, when exactly two billion stamps had been issued, and was resumed at some date subsequent to March 31st, 1894, presumably to relieve the department of a surplus.   Many, if not all, of the stamps distributed in the quarter ending June 30th, 1894, were delivered to the post office of the city of Washington.

From the report of the Postmaster General for 1894, we learn that the table of distributions in the fiscal year ending June 30, 1893, includes 16,800 "proof specimens" (1,050 sets of sixteen denominations), which were supplied to the Post Office Department.   These 1,050 sets are understood to have consisted of 50 sets of die proofs on India paper and 1,000 sets of plate proofs on cardboard.

It will also be noticed that the grand total of this issue is only slightly

Proofs.

more than two billion stamps instead of three billion, as called for by the contract. Concerning this reduction the report of the Postmaster General, dated November 25th, 1893, says:

"In 1889, the usual contract for the manufacture of adhesive postage stamps was made with the American Bank Note Company at the price of 7.47 cents per thousand. In 1892 Postmaster General Wanamaker entered into an arrangement with the same company for an issue of stamps commemorative of the discovery of America by Columbus, known as 'Columbian stamps,' for use during the year 1893 It was agreed that the issue of these stamps to be taken and paid for by the Government should not be less than three thousand millions (3,000,000,000) in number; that the price should be 17 cents per thousand, and further, that the existing contract for the ordinary stamps should be extended three months and that an additional three months' supply should be taken and paid for by the Government.

Modification of the contract.

It was supposed that these stamps would be in great demand by the stamp collectors of the world, and that the contract would result in a large profit to the government; indeed, a profit in all of \$2,500,000 was estimated.

Experience did not establish the correctness of this estimate. In fact as early as June last I became satisfied that the extra sales of stamps induced by this issue would not be likely to yield enough profit to make good the extra cost of their manufacture.

As this arrangement was made without advertisement or competition, and was no part of the original contract of November 7, 1889, I had serious doubts as to its validity and binding force upon the Government, and the question arose: What ought to be done in the interest of the Government?

First, I called the attention of the contracting company to this subject. They met this with an opinion from eminent counsel that the contract was a valid obligation, that it was duly executed and was within the power of the Postmaster General to make emergency contracts without advertising or competition.

Negotiations ensued, with the result that the contracting company waived its claim of right and agreed to the proposition of the Department that the issue of these stamps should be limited to 2,000,000,000, also waiving claim for profits on the other 1,000,000,000 of these stamps. The other parts of the agreement to remain in force.

The result is a saving, in cost of manufacture of 1,000,000,000 stamps, of the difference between the existing contract price for ordinary stamps, 7.47 cents per thousand, and the contract price for the Columbian issue, 17 cents per thousand, being 9.53 cents per thousand, or \$95,300 in all.

The present indications are that the amount of these stamps as limited by this last arrangement will be sufficient to meet all demands during the year.

The action of the American Bank Note Company in this matter is highly commended, since it must result in a considerable loss of profits."

The report of the Third Assistant Postmaster General for 1893 also voices the disappointment of the Department at the comparatively small sales of the Columbian stamps to dealers and collectors and estimates the probable *Purchases by stamp* sales to them during 1893 at not more than \$100,000. It is, of course, not *dealers and collectors.* possible to say how large were the investments of collectors and dealers. It has been reported that one speculator invested \$125,000 and it is well known that another bought to the amount of \$30,000 and one firm to the amount of \$20,000. It is believed that the bulk of these purchases were subsequently sold to business houses and used for postal purposes. The extent of smaller purchases and the ultimate disposition of the stamps cannot be ascertained. But there is little doubt that, as a speculation, the issue was a failure, both for the Government and for individuals.

In June, 1899, such of the Columbian stamps as were still in the city post office at Washington were withdrawn and destroyed. The denominations *Unsold stamps with-* and quantities were: *drawn and destroyed.*

| 6 cents | 48,400 | 4 dollars | 3,357 |
| 3 dollars | 2,937 | 5 dollars | 5,506 |

In March, 1900, the Department learned that a few stamps of this issue were still in the post office at Philadelphia and they were at once recalled and destroyed. There is no available record of the denominations and quantities included in this lot.

ISSUE OF 1894-95.

Though the government had long manufactured its own fiscal stamps at the Bureau of Engraving and Printing in Washington, the postal issues had prior to July 1st, 1894, always, been supplied by private firms, under contracts with the Post Office Department. But, at the date mentioned, a departure was made from this long-established method. On this subject I quote from the report of the Third Assistant Postmaster General, dated October 31st, 1894 :

"I think it proper to give here a detailed account of the matters connected with the termination of the old contract with the American Bank Note Company for furnishing postage stamps, and the making of a new arrangement therefor with the Bureau of Engraving and Printing of the Treasury Department.

By advertisement, dated the 16th of October, 1893, published in number of prominent newspapers for four weeks, the Department invited proposals up to the 15th of November, 1893, ' from parties carrying on the business of steel-plate engraving and plate printing,' or from those who had ' had experience in conducting that business,' for furnishing adhesive postage stamps of the several classes in use during the period of four years, beginning on the 1st of July, 1894, it having been formally arranged by the late Postmaster-General that the existing stamp contract with the American Bank Note Company should, by an extention of three months from the date fixed in it for its termination, and by the purchase of an extra supply of stamps sufficient for the wants of post-offices for three months thereafter, be carried up to June 30, 1894, the end of the fiscal year.

History of the contract.

Under the call thus made three proposals were received, the amount of each, based upon the process of printing them in vogue and upon the number of stamps issued during the fiscal year 1893, being as follows:

Hamilton Bank Note Company, of New York	$179,294 40
American Bank Note Company, of New York	162,401.61
Charles F. Steel, of Philadelphia	146,454.93

As soon as these bids were made known, the American Bank Note Company, for various reasons, strenuously protested against an award of the contract to Mr. Steel, the lowest bidder, and he, in a similar way, entered a protest against the giving of the contract to the American Bank Note Company. Subsequently these protests were formally presented in writing, and oral and written arguments were thereafter made, from time to time, up to the 21st of February, 1894.

In the meantime, on the 29th of November, 1893, the Chief of the Bureau of Engraving and Printing of the Treasury Department, with the approval of the Secretary of the Treasury, claiming the right to compete for the work under a clause in the official specifications issued to bidders, submitted a formal estimate, amounting, upon the basis above stated, to $139,487.74, and thereupon urged—his estimate being lower than any of the bids submitted—that the Bureau be awarded the contract.

For various reasons—the two prominent being the convenience of having the work done at Washington, where nearly all the other securities of the Government are printed and the saving to be secured in the cost of manufacture—the claim of the Bureau of Engraving and Printing was recognized on the 21st of February, 1894, by Departmental Order No. 18 of that date, awarding it the work, and by a formal agreement, entered into June 9, 1894, between the Post-Office and Treasury Departments, prescribing rules for the transaction of all business relating to the matter, Copies of these papers will be found appended to this report, marked No. 18.

Under the agreement thus entered into, the Bureau of Engraving and Printing is now regularly engaged in manufacturing all the postage stamps needed by the Post-Office Department, and is daily issuing them for the use of postmasters throughout the country, the same as was formerly done when the contract with the American Bank Note Company was in force.

Early difficulties. In entering upon the work under this new arrangement, a great many difficulties were necessarily encountered. A large number of printing machines had to be fitted up by the Bureau, perforating and gumming machines had to be secured, a considerable force of employes had to be trained to do the work promptly, large numbers of new plates for printing were needed, arrangements for storing and shipping the enormous number of stamps constantly required had to be made, to say nothing of many details entering into the intercourse between the two Departments in the transaction of their respective shares of this business. But I am happy to say that everything has been satisfactorily arranged, and the work is now proceeding without serious interruptions.

Transfer of stamps from New York. Some weeks prior to the 1st of July, 1894, when the arrangement above described went into effect, it became necessary to transfer from the custody of the American Bank Note Company in New York to that of the Bureau of Engraving and Printing in this city the entire stock of stamps not required for issue up to the date mentioned, the object being to avoid any break in the continuity of supplies to postmasters, and to that end to furnish the Bureau with a working stock while its own preparations for manufacture were still in a more or less incomplete state.

Accordingly, under detailed directions given by this office, enough stamps to fill all orders up to the 1st of July were segregated from the general stock, and the remainder were shipped here by registered mail and placed in the vault of the Bureau.

The transfer was affected expeditiously, without loss and without expense (the stamps being transported as free mail matter), except the cost of cartage from the railroad station in this city to the Bureau of Engraving and Printing, amounting to not over $50; so that on the 30th of June everything at New York was cleared up and the business of making and issuing stamps ended, and on the following day the work was going on here, with but little change of methods and with no material impediments.

The number of stamps of all kinds thus transferred amounted to nearly six hundred and forty-five million, of the face value of over $17,000,000.

Transfer of dies, rolls and plates. All the dies, rolls, and working plates of postage stamps, of present and past series, were transferred at the same time, and are now in the custody of the Bureau of Engraving and Printing.

Dates of issue of the new series. The stock of ordinary stamps of the manufacture of the American Bank Note Company thus transferred have been issued by the Bureau of Engraving and Printing, according to denominations, up to the following dates, since which issues have been made from the Bureau's own manufacture:

1 cent	Oct 10, 1894
2 cents .	Oct. 5, 1894
3 cents	Sept. 24, 1894
4 cents .	Sept. 11, 1894
5 cents	Sept 28, 1894
6 cents	July 18, 1894
10 cents	Sept. 17, 1894
15 cents .	Oct. 15, 1894
30 cents (discontinued)	Oct. 31, 1894
90 cents (discontinued) .	Oct. 31, 1894

A large quantity of 8 cent stamps of the manufacture of the American Bank Note Company is still on hand.

Additions to the designs. After the awarding of the contract to the Bureau of Engraving and Printing it was decided not to alter the general designs of the stamps then in use but to add to them a mark by which they might be distinguished from those made by the previous contractors. The mark adopted was a small double-lined triangle, placed in each upper corner. Each triangle has the top and outer side parallel to the adjacent top and side of the stamp, and the inner side slightly curved to correspond to the curve of the medallion. Within the inner triangle there is a small colored dot at the middle of each of the three sides.

Varieties of the triangle. There are three varieties of the triangle :

Type I. The horizontal lines of the background are of equal thickness within and without the triangle.

Type II. The lines are thinner within the triangle than without.

Type III. The space between the double lines of the triangle is blank and the lines in the inner triangle are thin.

At first all values had the triangle of type I, afterwards types II and III were used on the two cent stamps. A die of the three cents with triangle III was also made but it has not yet been put into use. The other values remain as at first. Plate 170 of the two cents presents an interesting variety. In the upper left quarter, the first three vertical rows at the left side are of type II, the balance of the plate is of type III.

Concurrently with the placing of the new contract it was decided to abandon the denominations of thirty and ninety cents, substituting for them stamps of fifty cents and one dollar, and to add stamps of two and five dollars **New denominations.** to the series, for which denominations there was some demand at the larger post offices. These four new values are officially described as follows :

"FIFTY CENTS. Head of Thomas Jefferson, same as the head on the **Designs and colors.** old 30-cent stamp. Color, orange.

ONE DOLLAR. Head of Commodore O. H. Perry, same as the head on the old 90-cent stamp. Color, black.

TWO DOLLARS. Head of James Madison, after the portrait by Gilbert Stuart. Color, sapphire blue.

FIVE DOLLARS. Head of John Marshall, after the portrait by Inman. Color, gray green."

The stamps are of the same size as those of the issue of 1890, *i. e.*, 19x22mm.

At first a soft, porous, wove paper was used, similar in quality to that employed by the American Bank Note Co., though not showing as coarse a **Paper.** "weave." Afterwards other varieties appeared. In 1895 an attempt was made to counterfeit the two cent stamp and, as a check upon such frauds, a watermark was introduced into the paper. When the watermark was first **Watermark.** used it was so faint that it was often difficult to discover any trace of it and, as a preventive of forgeries, it was of little or no value. But, in the course of time, it was improved and is now more distinct, though it is still inferior to most of the watermarks used in the other countries. A smaller device and harder paper would probably give a much better result.

The watermark consists of the letters " U S P S " (United States Postal Service), in double-lined Roman capitals, 16mm. high.

On each quarter sheet of one hundred stamps there are ten horizontal rows of nine letters each, so arranged as to read in regular order either upward, downward, to right or to left, from any starting point ; thus :

```
U   S   P   S   U   S   P   S   U
S   P   S   U   S   P   S   U   S
P   S   U   S   P   S   U   S   P
S   U   S   P   S   U   S   P   S
U   S   P   S   U   S   P   S   U
S   P   S   U   S   P   S   U   S
P   S   U   S   P   S   U   S   P
S   U   S   P   S   U   S   P   S
U   S   P   S   U   S   P   S   U
S   P   S   U   S   P   S   U   S
```

Many of the stamps of this issue and also those of the corresponding series of postage-due stamps appear to have laid lines in the paper, in addition **Laid, double and ribbed paper.** to the watermark. The probable cause of this variation was explained on page 152. The one and two cent stamps are also known on double paper, similar to that used by the Continental Bank Note Co. This paper is watermarked and the variety is probably due to some accident or variation in manufacture rather than to any intentional change in the paper. A copy of the five cents without watermark has been seen on paper ribbed with fine horizontal and vertical lines (the latter being slightly more pronounced) and having the effect of coarsely woven linen cloth. These lines are sufficiently raised to produce distinct vertical ridges in the printing ink on the face and to have taken up, on the back, some ink from the sheet which lay below it after printing. It has been suggested that in the course of manufacture the paper pulp was left standing on the cloth carrier until the impression of the fibres was transferred to it.

The eight cent stamp has been found on paper watermarked with a large double-lined capital "R", apparently a portion of the watermark **Paper watermarked "U S I R"** "U S I R" (United States Internal Revenue). This would indicate that a sheet of the paper designed for revenue stamps had been used for printing postage stamps.

Several values of this series have also been reported on bluish chemical **Chemical paper.** paper but, on all copies which I have seen, it was very evident that the discoloration was due either to accident or an attempt to deceive.

The gum varies from white to yellow. The perforation is the regulation 12.

The following shades and varieties exist :

Reference List.
                              Perforated 12.

                         Porous White Wove Paper.

                            Without Watermark.

Oct. 10th, 1894.   1 cent pale ultramarine, ultramarine, deep ultramarine, gray-blue, pale dull blue, dull blue, deep dull blue, dark blue

Oct. 5th, 1894.   2 cents (type I) pale pink, pink, aniline rose, rose, deep rose, carmine-rose, dull lilac-rose, lilac-rose, salmon-red, red, scarlet, brown-red, rose-carmine, carmine violet-carmine, carmine-lake, lake, crimson

2 cents (type II) rose-red, rose, aniline rose, rose-ver-
    milion

2 cents (type III) rose, rose-vermilion

Sept. 24th, 1894.   3 cents dull purple, purple, deep purple

Sept. 11th, 1894.   4 cents dark yellow-brown, gray-brown, black-brown

Sept. 28th, 1894.   5 cents yellow-brown, orange-brown, dark orange-brown,
        red-brown

July 18th, 1894.   6 cents claret, claret-brown

Mch. 25th, 1895.   8 cents violet-brown, plum

Sept. 17th, 1894.   10 cents dark green, blue-green, dark blue-green

Oct. 15th, 1894.   15 cents indigo, dark indigo

Nov. 1st, 1894.   50 cents yellow-orange, orange, red-orange

Nov. 15th, 1894.   1 dollar black

Dec. 10th, 1894.   2 dollars sapphire blue, deep sapphire blue

Dec. 10th, 1894.   5 dollars deep yellow-green

Varieties :

2 cents (type III) bright rose. Imperforate vertically

2 cents (type I) bright rose. Imperforate horizontally

5 cents yellow-brown   "   "

6 cents claret-brown   "   "

50 cents orange   "   "

3 cents purple   Imperforate

4 cents dark yellow-brown   "

5 cents orange-brown   "

10 cents dark blue-green   "

Watermarked U. S. P. S.

April 29th, 1895.   1 cent pale ultramarine, ultramarine, pale blue, blue, dark
        blue, navy blue, deep dull blue

May 2nd, 1895.   2 cents (type I) rose, carmine-rose, carmine, pale aniline
        rose

2 cents (type II) bright aniline rose, rose, rose-carmine

2 cents (type III) bright aniline rose, rose, rose-carmine,
        carmine, lilac-rose, scarlet, rose-vermilion, pink,
        crimson, carmine-lake

Oct. 31st, 1895.   3 cents purple, deep purple

June 5th, 1895.   4 cents dark yellow-brown, gray-brown, black-brown

June 11th, 1895.   5 cents orange-brown, dark orange-brown, deep brown

Aug. 31st, 1895.   6 cents claret, deep claret, claret-brown

July 22nd, 1895.   8 cents brown-violet, plum

June 7th, 1895.   10 cents bright blue-green, blue-green

Sept. 10th, 1895.   15 cents indigo, dark indigo

Nov. 9th, 1895.   50 cents yellow-orange, orange, red-orange

Aug. 12th, 1895.   1 dollar black

Aug. 13th, 1895.   2 dollars sapphire blue, deep sapphire blue

Aug. 16th, 1895.   5 dollars dark yellow-green, dark green

Varieties :

1 cent deep dull blue.	Imperforate
2 cents (type III) carmine-rose	"
3 cents purple	"
4 cents dark yellow-brown	"
5 cents deep orange-brown	"
6 cents claret-brown	"
8 cents plum	"
10 cents blue-green	"
15 cents indigo	"
50 cents red-orange	"
1 dollar black	"
2 dollars sapphire blue	"
5 dollars dark yellow-green	"

Watermarked U. S. I. R.

8 cents brown-violet

Plates. All the plates of the one, two and ten cents and a few of the three, four and five cents values contain four hundred stamps each. All the other plates contain two hundred stamps each. The impressions are, as usual, divided into sheets of one hundred stamps. The lines of division are indicated by arrow heads in the margins and on some of the plates by ruled lines. On the plates with two hundred stamps the imprint appears at the middle of the top and bottom of each half of the plate, on those having four hundred stamps, it is placed at the top—or bottom—and outer side of each quarter of the plate. The plate number is always placed at the right of the imprint.

Imprints and numbers. Three varieties of imprint and three styles of numerals have been used for this issue. For numbers 1 to 154 inclusive shaded numerals 3¼ mm. high were used. From number 155 to 327 inclusive the numerals were more ornate and only 2¾ mm. high. Above number 327 a third style was introduced and still remains in use. In this the numerals are thin and without shading and 2¾ mm. in height.

The first style of imprint used was a plain rectangle with a thin frame line. This was applied to the postage and postage due stamps from plate 1 to 75 inclusive and also to number 159. The second style of imprint was made by cutting the frame line more firmly and clearly and adding at each end a rosette and an arrow-head ornament. This imprint has been used on all postage and postage due stamps above plate 75 with the exception of number 159. In the third type the letters are all capitals, the panel is much longer, the ends are octagonal and finished by a three branched ornament. This imprint appears only on the Special Delivery and the Newspapers and Periodicals stamps.

Plate numbers. The list of plate numbers, up to March 1st, 1901, is as follows :

1894. Without Watermark.

1 cent   (400) No. 2, 6, 15, 17, 18, 21, 24, 27,
                       29, 31, 33, 35, 98, 99, 101, 102,
                       119, 120, 121, 122.

2 cents (type I)   (400) No.   1,   3,   4,   5,   7,   8,   9, 10,
                              11, 12, 13, 16, 19, 20, 22, 23,
                              25, 26, 30, 32, 78, 79, 80, 82,
                              88, 89, 96, 97, 110, 111, 112, 113,
                             114, 115, 116, 117, 124, 125, 144.
2 cents (type II) (400) No. 126, 131, 132, 133.
2 cents (type III) (400) No. 141, 142, 143, 145, 146, 148, 149, 150,
                             151, 152, 153, 154, 155, 156, 157, 158.
3 cents   (400) No. 44, 46, 47, 48.
                   (200) No. 91, 95, 103, 107.
4 cents   (400) No. 45, 50, 51, 59.
                   (200) No. 92, 94, 104, 106.
5 cents   (400) No. 49, 53, 54, 56.
                   (200) No. 128, 129, 130, 134, 161, 162, 163, 164.
6 cents   (200) No. 28.
8 cents   (200) No. 58.
10 cents   (400) No. 55, 62, 63, 64.
15 cents   (200) No. 52.
50 cents   (200) No. 75.
1 dollar   (200) No. 76.
2 dollars   (200) No. 84.
5 dollars   (200) No. 85.

Varieties :

2 cents Imperforate vertically   No. 153.
2 cents   "   horizontally No.
5 cents   "   "   No. 130.
6 cents   "   "   No. 28.
50 cents   "   "   No. 75.
3 cents   "   No. 47.
4 cents   "   No. 50.
5 cents   "   No. 53.
10 cents   "   No. 63.

1895.   Watermarked U. S. P. S.

1 cent   (400) No. 24, 29, 33, 35, 98, 99, 101, 102,
                             119, 120, 121, 122, 165, 166, 167, 168,
                             177, 178, 179, 180, 234, 237, 240, 245,
                             276, 277, 278, 280, 294, 295, 296, 297,
                             298, 299, 300, 301, 304, 308, 310, 313,
                             314, 333, 334, 335, 336, 344, 345, 346,
                             347, 348, 350, 352, 355, 360, 362, 365,
                             366, 367, 369, 370, 371, 439, 440, 441,
                             442, 443, 444, 445, 446, 452, 453, 454,
                             455, 493, 494, 495, 496.
2 cents (type I)   (400) No. 78, 79, 80, 82, 88, 96, 97, 111,
                             112, 113, 114, 115, 116, 117, 124, 125,
                             144.

2 cents (type II) (400) No. 126, 131, 132, 133, 169, 170.
2 cents (type III) (400) No. 141, 142, 143, 145, 146, 148, 149, 150,
151, 152, 153, 154, 155, 156, 157, 158,
160, 170, 171, 172, 173, 174, 175, 176,
181, 182, 183, 185, 186, 187, 188, 191,
198, 199, 201, 202, 203, 204, 205, 206,
207, 209, 210, 211, 212, 213, 214, 215,
216, 217, 218, 219, 220, 221, 222, 223,
224, 225, 226, 227, 228, 229, 230, 231,
232, 233, 235, 236, 238, 239, 241, 242,
243, 244, 274, 275, 279, 281, 282, 283,
290, 291, 292, 293, 307, 311, 312, 315,
316, 317, 318, 319, 320, 321, 322, 323,
324, 325, 326, 327, 328, 329, 330, 331,
332, 337, 338, 339, 340, 341, 342, 343,
349, 354, 356, 358, 361, 363, 364, 368,
372, 374, 376, 379, 382, 383, 384, 385,
387, 388, 393, 394, 395, 396, 397, 398,
399, 400, 401, 402, 403, 404, 405, 406,
411, 412, 413, 414, 415, 416, 417, 418,
419, 420, 421, 422, 423, 424, 425, 426,
427, 428, 429, 430, 431, 432, 433, 434,
435, 436, 437, 438, 464, 465, 466, 467,
468, 469, 470, 471, 472, 473, 474, 475,
476, 477, 478, 479, 480, 481, 482, 483,
484, 485, 486, 487, 488, 489, 490, 491,
497, 498, 499, 500, 501, 502, 503, 505,
506, 507, 508, 509, 510, 511, 512, 513,
514, 515, 516, 517, 522, 523, 524, 525,
550, 551, 552, 553, 556, 557, 558, 559,
560, 561, 562, 563, 593, 594, 595, 596,
745, 746, 747, 748, 753, 754, 755, 756,
758, 759, 760, 761, 762, 763, 764, 765,
774, 775, 776, 777, 778, 779, 780, 781,
782, 783, 784, 785, 786, 787, 788, 789,
798, 799, 800, 801, 802, 803, 804, 805,
806, 807, 808, 809, 814, 815, 816, 817,
838, 839, 840, 841, 842, 843, 844, 845,
850, 851, 852, 853, 854, 855, 856, 857,
858, 859, 860, 861, 866, 867, 869, 870,
875, 876, 877, 878, 885, 886, 887, 888,
895, 896, 897, 898, 904, 905, 906, 907,
910, 911, 912, 913, 914, 915, 916, 917,
918, 919, 920, 921, 926, 927, 1008, 1009,
1010, 1011, 1024, 1025, 1026, 1027, 1032,
1033, 1034, 1035, 1038, 1039, 1040, 1041,
1046, 1047, 1048, 1049, 1054, 1055, 1056,

<pre>
                                1057, 1066, 1067, 1068, 1069, 1070, 1071,
                                1072, 1073, 1074, 1075, 1076, 1077, 1080.
2 cents (type III) (360) No. 988, 989, 990, 991.
3 cents   (200) No. 91, 95, 103, 107, 447, 448, 449, 450.
4 cents   (200) No. 92, 94, 104, 106, 194, 195, 196, 197,
                                456, 457, 458, 459, 460, 461, 462, 463.
5 cents   (200) No. 128, 129, 130, 134, 161, 162, 163, 164,
                                189, 190, 192, 193, 250, 251, 252, 253,
                                351, 353, 357, 359, 389, 390, 391, 392.
6 cents   (200) No. 28, 184, 248, 373, 386, 451.
8 cents   (200) No. 58, 249, 555, 928, 929, 930, 931.
10 cents   (400) No. 55, 62, 63, 64, 302, 303, 305, 306.
15 cents   (200) No. 52, 264.
50 cents   (200) No. 75, *286.
1 dollar   (200) No. 76, *287.
2 dollars   (200) No. 84, *289.
5 dollars   (200) No. 85, *288.
</pre>

The plates marked with an asterisk (*) have not yet been put in use.

Varieties :

<pre>
1 cent   Imperforate   No. 314, 334, 336.
2 cents   "   No. 319, 340.
3 cents   "   No. 103, 107.
4 cents   "   No. 94, 106.
5 cents   "   No. 251, 351.
6 cents   "   No. 373.
8 cents   "   No. 249.
10 cents   "   No. 305.
15 cents   "   No. 52.
50 cents   "   No. 75.
1 dollar   "   No. 76.
2 dollars   "   No. 84.
5 dollars   "   No. 85.
</pre>

The following plates were prepared but, because of defects, were never put to press :

<pre>
1 cent   No. 14, 309.
2 cents   No. 86, 87, 200, 208, 268, 504, 868, 909.
5 cents   No. 375, 377, 378, 380.
10 cents   No. 61.
</pre>

On the 16th of April, 1900, small books of two-cent stamps were placed on sale at the post offices. In these books the stamps are arranged in blocks of six, separated by paraffined paper (to prevent adhesion), and protected by covers of thin cardboard. On the covers is printed brief information concerning the rates of domestic and foreign postage, money orders and registration. The purpose of these books is to enable one to carry stamps in his pocket without risk of damaging them. The books are of three sizes, containing either twelve, twenty-four or forty-eight stamps. They are sold at twenty-five, forty-nine and ninety-seven cents, respectively ; an advance, in

Books of stamps.

each instance, of one cent over the face value of the stamps. Each block of
six stamps is composed of two vertical rows of three and has a stub at the top.
There are perforations between the stamps and above the top pair, but none
at the sides or bottom of the block. Hence, each stamp has one or more
blank edges. It was not possible to produce these blocks with plates of the
ordinary form and, therefore, special plates were made for the purpose. These
plates contain 360 stamps each. Thus far, only four of them have been made,
as will be observed on referring to the list of plate numbers. The report of
the Third Assistant Postmaster General for 1900, states that, between April
16th and June 30th of that year, there were sent to post offices 2,263,040
books, of which 945,281 were sold to the public.

The annual reports of the Postmaster General supply the following
statistics of stamps issued to deputy postmasters :

Deliveries to postmasters.

Stamps issued during the fiscal year ending June 30th, 1895 :

QUARTER ENDING :

	Sept. 30, 1894.	Dec. 31, 1894.	Mch. 31, 1895.	June 30, 1895.	Total.
1 cent	....	152,440,100	177,613,700	182,294,850	512,348,650
2 cents	....	499,920,600	535,462,800	522,322,850	1,557,706,250
3 cents	94,800	4,871,200	5,737,300	4,030,350	14,733,650
4 cents	816,150	5,934,300	6,121,600	4,940,400	17,812,450
5 cents	25,660	9,487,880	12,170,760	10,782,430	32,466,730
6 cents	796,300	1,351,950	1,179,650	1,113,650	4,441,550
8 cents	... .	....	70,450	1,897,800	1,968,250
10 cents	460,350	4,042,680	5,044,470	3,614,290	13,191,790
15 cents	....	436,480	450,880	500,830	1,388,190
50 cents	... ...	99,540	36,440	15,880	151,860
1 dollar	... ...	11,620	10,751	11,850	34,221
2 dollars	. ...	3,355	4,967	1,790	10,112
5 dollars	....	1,570	2,737	1,679	5,986

Whole number of stamps 2,156,259,689. Value $41,167,121.00.

Stamps issued during the fiscal year ending June 30th, 1896 :

QUARTER ENDING :

	Sept. 30, 1895.	Dec. 31, 1895.	Mch. 31, 1896.	June 30, 1896.	Total.
1 cent	150,408,800	195,385,600	191,537,200	192,496,600	729,828,200
2 cents	507,871,400	547,252,400	574,552,500	544,997,500	2,174,673,800
3 cents	3,839,500	5,464,500	5,988,400	4,218,800	19,511,200
4 cents	4,355,850	7,643,400	6,381,300	4,850,600	23,231,150
5 cents	9,550,200	11,398,440	12,139,680	10,905,720	43,994,040
6 cents	1,067,100	1,651,850	1,513,450	1,404,850	5,637,250
8 cents	1,997,400	2,345,850	2,757,750	2,084,000	9,185,000
10 cents	3,725,360	4,612,550	4,898,550	4,027,560	17,264,020
15 cents	331,820	652,380	603,740	4'0,940	1,998,880
50 cents	15,620	27,820	28,270	17,510	89,220
1 dollar	12,470	13,852	9,645	6,610	42,577
2 dollars	8,345	5,415	2,075	335	16,170
5 dollars	3,175	3,180	2,465	1,140	9,960

Whole number of stamps 3,025,481,467. Value $57,774,638.00.

Stamps issued during the fiscal year ending June 30th, 1897 :

QUARTER ENDING :

	Sept. 30, 1896.	Dec. 31, 1896.	Mch. 31, 1897.	June 30, 1897.	Total.
1 cent	145,068,800	189,247,500	194,221,800	196,113,400	724,651,500
2 cents	507,131,600	553,723,400	582,508,700	575,663,300	2,219,027,000
3 cents	3,883,400	5,486,500	5,956,700	4,459,700	19,786,300
4 cents	4,473,900	6,139,600	5,909,250	5,232,900	21,755,650
5 cents	9,612,140	12,200,960	12,250,880	10,310,040	44,374,020
6 cents	1,125,250	1,512,450	1,516,750	1,429,450	5,583,900
8 cents	1,771,550	2,587,000	2,473,900	2,472,900	9,305,350
10 cents	3,712,880	4,621,050	4,665,050	4,120,410	17,119,390
15 cents	360,280	596,740	491,860	443,940	1,892,820
50 cents	20,480	37,180	14,170	37,970	109,800
1 dollar	2,040	10,600	3,880	6,815	23,335
2 dollars	190	880	1,060	20	2,150
5 dollars	60	50	1,560	1,000	2,670

Whole number of stamps 3,063,633,885.   Value $58,480,780.00.

In the *Postal Guide* for 1898 the number of stamps of the several denominations which were issued without watermark is reported as follows : **Quantities of stamps without watermark.**

1 cent	404,168,300
2 cents	1,271,048,700
3 cents	20,214,300
4 cents	16,718,150
5 cents	30,688,840
6 cents	5,120,800
8 cents	2,426,100
10 cents	12,263,180
15 cents	1,583,920
50 cents	175,330
1 dollar	35,046
2 dollars	10,027
5 dollars	6,251

Whole number of stamps 1,764,458,944.   Value $34,411,516.00.

The table of deliveries during the year ending June 30th, 1895, includes 750 copies of each value which were sent to the Universal Postal Union.

In 1897 the current series, as well as the special delivery, postage due and newspaper stamps were surcharged "UNIVERSAL—POSTAL—CONGRESS," in three lines, and presented to the delegates to the Congress of the Universal **Stamps with various imprints.** Postal Union, then in session at Washington.   One hundred and twenty-five sets were surcharged.   In 1898, 300 each of the one and five cents and 200 of each of the other values were "delivered for the Post Office album." Most, if not all, of these stamps were surcharged "Specimen", in small type, in either black or magenta.

Concerning the counterfeit of the two cent stamp, which was mentioned on a preceding page, the annual report of the Fourth Assistant Postmaster **Counterfeit two cent stamp.** General for 1895, furnishes the following information :

"Counterfeiters have plied their vocation for ages and in many forms, but never until the last year have they directed their attention to the manufacture of spurious postage stamps. A bold scheme to defraud the Government by means of counterfeit stamps was developed through our inspectors last spring. This scheme was operated from Chicago and the adjacent Canadian territory. The counterfeiters having produced a supply of bogus stamps, established their headquarters in Hamilton, Ontario, under the title of 'The Canadian Novelty and Supply Company.' Advertisements were then inserted in various newspapers, alleging that this company had received large quantities of stamps in payment for their novelties, which they desired to dispose of at a great discount, in order to convert the stamps into money. The stamps were declared to be in good condition and were offered at the rate of $115 worth for $100   Under the direction of an inspector, a party in Chicago ordered $100 worth of these stamps, which upon examination were found to be cleverly executed counterfeits. Several packages of them, then in a Chicago express office, were seized, and the inspectors at once undertook the work of discovering the criminals. Developments proved that this scheme had been nipped in its incipiency, and it is believed that less than 100,000 of these counterfeit stamps were produced, the greater portion of which have been confiscated. The investigation resulted in the discovery of the perforating machine and other paraphernalia used by the counterfeiters and the arrest of Charles O. Jones, Tinsa McMillan, alias Mrs. Mack, and Warren T. Thompson."

At the time this counterfeit was first reported it was generally understood that the credit of the discovery was due to a stamp collector who, having been sent to examine a package of the stamps which his employers had ordered by C. O. D. express, at once detected the fraud and notified the authorities. It is also certain that the counterfeits were promptly detected by the watchful eyes of philatelists in many parts of the country. The postmarks on the envelopes to which they were affixed showed an extensive distribution throughout the middle west.

In official eyes the counterfeits were probably dangerous and many of them might have escaped detection in large post offices where the clerks are very busy and cancelling machines are largely employed. But their poor appearance ought to have attracted the attention of anyone at all observing and they certainly would have been at once detected by the average stamp collector.

They were made by some process of photo-lithography and apparently were copied from a block of stamps of type I. The general appearance Description of the is much blurred, especially around the triangles, while the shading at the counterfeit. sides and bottom, indicating the beveled edge of the panel, is almost solid, instead of showing fine ruled lines. The original stamps measure 19x22mm. while the counterfeits vary from 19 to 19¼x22½ to 23mm. The perforating was done with a machine of the correct gauge, 12, which perforated only one row at a time, thus often producing irregular spacing between the rows. The color is a very good reproduction of the rose-carmine shade of the genuine stamps and the coarse wove paper is sufficiently like that of the originals not to attract attention. It is said that there were three printings of the counterfeits. The first was in blocks of twenty-five, five rows of five stamps each ; the second was in blocks of fifteen, three rows of five stamps each ; and the third in strips of five. Some of the last printing were yet imperforate when the malefactors were arrested.

ISSUE OF 1898.

TRANS-MISSISSIPPI SERIES.

In the latter part of the year 1897, the daily papers announced the intention of the Postmaster General to issue a series of celebration stamps in commemoration of the Trans-Mississippi exposition, to be held at Omaha in the summer of 1898. This exposition was, doubtless, an event of considerable local interest and worth, but scarcely of that degree of national or historical importance which we except in events that are honored by commemorative issues of stamps.

Collectors, dealers and philatelic societies protested against this issue, as being unnecessary and undignified. But their protests were unheeded and the stamps duly made their appearance, to be greeted with little praise and much unfavorable criticism. When the issue was first announced it was promised that the vignettes would be printed in black and the borders in colors. But this idea was subsequently abandoned, on the plea that the Bureau of Engraving and Printing had "found it impossible to furnish satisfactorily or in the time desired supplies of the several denominations in two colors." The promise that the issue would surpass the beautiful Columbian issue was also honored in the breach. The stamps are poorly conceived and executed, overloaded with ornaments, heavy in color and blurred in printing.

The stamps are officially described as follows :

"The Trans–Mississippi stamps differ materially in size from the ordinary series, the engraved space being about seven-eighths of an inch wide by about one and three-eighths long. The designs are also radically unlike Designs and colors. those of the ordinary stamps—consisting of a border (substantially the same in all the denominations, except that the figures and letters representing values are different), and a central scene indicative in some way of the development of the great region beyond the Mississippi River. The scenes and the borders are all printed from line engravings on steel, executed by the Bureau of Engraving and Printing of the Treasury Department.

The border, which forms in its inner line an irregular oval framework to each of the scenes represented, consists of a fluted figure on either side, with interior cross-bars, beginning in a single line near the bottom of the stamp, and enlarging until it reaches a shield in each of the upper corners, wherein is engraved in white the Arabic numeral of denomination—the dollar mark being also included in the case of the one and two dollar stamps.   At the top, connecting the two shields, and united to the fluted framework on the two sides, is a curved tablet, on which are engraved in small white capitals the words ' UNITED STATES OF AMERICA '.   Above this, on either side, are heads of wheat, and between these a small scroll.   Immediately below the central scene is the title of the picture in diminutive white Gothic letters on a curved tablet, and below this on either side, in scrolls, are the words of value, ' ONE ', ' TWO ', and so on, in white capitals, except in the case of the two highest denominations, when ' $1.00 ' and ' $2.00 ' are substituted for letters. Above each of these is a projecting ear of corn, and at the bottom of all, on a straight black tablet, are the words ' POSTAGE ONE CENT ', ' POSTAGE TWO CENTS ', and so on.

The scenes represented on the stamps, together with the colors of the several denominations, are these :

ONE CENT.   'Marquette on the Mississippi', from a painting by Lamp-recht, now in possession of the Marquette College of Milwaukee, Wis., repre-senting Father Marquette in a boat on the Upper Mississippi, preaching to the Indians.   Color, dark green.

TWO CENTS.   ' Farming in the West ', from a photograph, representing a western grainfield with a long row of plows at work.   Color, copper red.

FOUR CENTS.   ' Indian Hunting Buffalo ,' reproduction of an engraving in Schoolcraft's History of the Indian Tribes.   Color, orange.

FIVE CENTS.   ' Fremont on Rocky Mountains ', modified from a wood engraving, representing the Pathfinder planting the U. S. flag on the highest peak of the Rocky Mountains.   Color, dark blue.

EIGHT CENTS.   ' Troops Guarding Train ', representing a detachment of U. S. soldiers convoying an emigrant train across the prairies ; from a drawing by Frederic Remington, permission to use which was kindly given by the publisher, R. H. Russell of New York.   Color, dark lilac.

TEN CENTS.   ' Hardships of Emigration ', from a painting kindly loaned by the artist A. G. Heaton, representing an emigrant and his family on the plains in a ' prairie schooner', one of the horses having fallen from exhaustion. Color, slate.

FIFTY CENTS.   'Western Mining Prospector', from a drawing by Frederic Remington (permission to use which has been kindly given by the publisher, R. H. Russell of New York), representing a prospector with his pack-mules in the mountains, searching for gold.   Color, olive.

ONE DOLLAR.   'Western Cattle in Storm', representing a herd of cattle preceded by the leader, seeking safety from a gathering storm ; reproduced from a large steel engraving after a picture by J. MacWhirter—the engraving having been kindly loaned by Mrs. C. B. Johnson.   Color, ~~light brown~~ *black*

TWO DOLLARS.   'Mississippi River Bridge', from an engraving—a representation of the great bridge over the Mississippi, at St. Louis.   Color, sapphire blue."

It will be noticed that the colors officially assigned to the highest two denominations are not those in which the stamps were actually issued.

The stamps are of uniform size and measure 34x22mm.

The paper, gum, perforation and watermark remain the same as in the previous issue by the Bureau of Engraving and Printing, but the watermark is placed sideways.

Perforated 12. Reference List.

Porous White Wove Paper.

Watermarked U. S. P. S.

June 17th, 1898.   1 cent gray-green, yellow-green, dark yellow-green, dark green

2 cents bright. rose-red, rose-red, copper-red, brown-red, dark brown-red

4 cents yellow-orange, orange, red-orange

5 cents deep blue, dark blue

8 cents lilac-brown, violet-brown

10 cents gray-violet, slate-violet, lilac-gray

50 cents sage green, deep sage green

1 dollar black

2 dollars orange-brown, deep orange-brown

Variety :

8 cents violet-brown. Imperforate horizontally

The plates of this series each contained one hundred stamps. The impressions were divided vertically into sheets of fifty stamps, ten rows of five stamps each. The imprint was "BUREAU, ENGRAVING & PRINTING", in Plates. white capitals on a small rectangular panel, surrounded by a thin colored line and having a trident shaped ornament at each end. The plate number and imprint appeared at the top and bottom of each sheet of fifty stamps, above or below the third and fourth stamps, counting from the central line of the plate. The plate number was always placed at the right of the imprint.

The plates used for this issue were numbered : Plate numbers.

1 cent   No. 590, 591, 592, 598, 600, 601, 605, 607, 612, 635, 709, 710, 711, 712.

2 cents   No. 597, 608, 610, 611, 616, 619, 621, 622, 623, 624, 625, 626, 627, 628, 629, 630, 631, 632, 633, 638, 639, 640, 641, 642, 644, 645, 647, 648, 649, 650, 651, 652, 653, 654, 655, 656, 657, 658, 659, 660, 661, 662, 663, 664, 665, 666, 667, 668, 669, 670, 671, 672, 673, 674, 675, 676, 677, 678, 679, 680, 681, 683, 684, 685, 686, 687, 688, 689, 690, 691, 692, 693, 694, 695, 696, 697, 698, 699, 700, 701, 702, 703, 704, 705, 706, 707, 708, 713, 714, 715, 716, 717, 718, 719, 720, 721, 722, 724, 725, 726, 727, 728, 729, 732, 733, 734, 735, 737, 738, 739, 740, 741, 742, 743, 744, 749, 750, 751, 752.

4 cents   No. 599, 634, 636.

5 cents   No. 602, 614, 618.

8 cents   No. 609, 643.

10 cents   No. 604, 617, 620.
50 cents   No. 603.
1 dollar   No. 606.
2 dollars   No. 613.

The eight cent stamps, imperforate horizontally, are from plate 609.

Plates 589, 723, 730, 731 and 736 for two cent stamps, plate 637 for **Plates prepared** five cent stamps and plate 757 for eight cent stamps were prepared but, being **but not used.** defective, were never put to press.

The following plates were prepared with a view to printing the stamps in two colors but they were never used :

No. 576	1 cent, border (defective).
No. 577	1 cent, border.
No. 578	1 cent, vignette.
No. 579	1 cent, border.
No. 580	1 cent, vignette.
No. 581	4 cents, border.
No. 582	2 cents, border.
No. 583	2 cents, vignette.
No. 584	4 cents, vignette.
No. 585	8 cents, border.
No. 586	5 cents, border.
No. 587	5 cents, vignette.
No. 588	10 cents, border.

About a year after the discontinuance of this issue, two plates of the four cent denomination were made. These plates were numbered 1036 and **Plates for** 1037. The former bore only the border of the stamp, the latter, only the **experimental work.** vignette. These plates were prepared solely for experimental work in connection with the bicolored series to be issued in commemoration of the Pan-American exposition at Buffalo, in 1901.

The following tabulation of the number of stamps that was issued of each denomination, is compiled from the annual reports of the Postmaster General :

QUARTER ENDING :

	Mch. 31, 1898.	June 30, 1898.	Sept. 30, 1898.	Dec. 31, 1898.	Total.
1 cent	17,635,500	28,796,900	24,561,000	70,993,400
2 cents	26,268,000	76,163,900	57,288,900	159,720,800
4 cents	1,271,750	1,591,650	2,061,100	4,924,500
5 cents	1,622,900	2,339,680	3,731,600	7,694,180
8 cents	897,800	896,100	1,133,300	2,927,200
10 cents	998,230	1,236,530	2,395,000	4,629,760
50 cents	50,410	33,790	446,200	530,400
1 dollar	20,695	15,860	20,345	56,900
2 dollars	14,120	11,555	30,525	56,200

Whole number of stamps 251,553,340.   Value $5,617,691.00.

There are included in this table 900 stamps (100 of each denomination) which were delivered to the Third Assistant Postmaster General to be used for exchanging and similar purposes. These stamps were surcharged "Specimen" in very small type. The surcharge is hand-stamped in black or magenta. I have not found any record of the customary deliveries to the Universal Postal Union.

"Specimen" stamps.

The stamps of this series were not issued after December 31st, 1898, but they will continue to be available for postage at any future time.

ISSUE OF 1898.

In January, 1898, the color of the one cent stamp was changed to green and in March of the same year that of the five cents to dark blue. These are **Changes in colors.** the colors assigned to these two values by the Universal Postal Union. The change was made in accordance with the agreement of the Post Office Department of the United States to adopt the colors recognized by the Union, on or before January 1st, 1899. At subsequent dates the colors of the four, six, ten and fifteen cents were changed. This was done to avoid possible confusion, which might arise from stamps of different denominations being printed in nearly the same colors.

The size, paper, watermark, gum and perforation remain the same as in the series of 1894-95.

Reference List.

Perforated 12.

Porous White Wove Paper.

Watermarked U. S. P. S.

Jan. 17th, 1898.	1 cent pale yellow-green, yellow-green, dark yellow-green, dark gray-green, green, dark green
Oct. 7th, 1898.	4 cents rose-brown, claret-brown, dark claret-brown, lilac-brown, red-brown
Mch. 8th, 1898.	5 cents blue, deep blue, dark blue
Dec. 31st, 1898.	6 cents magenta, lake, brownish lake, brown-carmine
Nov. 11th, 1898.	10 cents yellow-brown, dark yellow-brown, orange-brown, brown, gray-brown
Nov. 30th, 1898.	15 cents olive-green, deep olive-green

The number of stamps on the plates and the arrangement of the imprints and plate numbers are the same as for the corresponding values of the issues of 1894-95. Up to March 1st, 1901, the following plates are reported to have been used for the stamps in the new colors:

Plate numbers.

1 cent (400) No. 439, 440, 441, 442, 446, 452, 493, 494, 495, 496, 526, 527, 528, 529, 534, 535, 536, 537, 538, 539, 540, 541, 542, 543, 544, 545, 546, 547, 548, 549, 564, 565, 566, 567, 572, 573, 574, 575, 766, 767, 768, 769, 770, 771, 772, 773, 794, 795, 796, 797, 810, 811, 812, 813, 818, 819, 820, 821, 822, 823, 824, 825, 826, 827, 828, 829, 830, 831, 832, 833,

846, 847, 848, 849, 862, 863, 864, 865, 936, 937,
938, 939, 940, 941, 942, 943, 944, 945, 946, 947,
952, 953, 954, 955, 956, 957, 958, 959, 960, 961,
962, 963, 964, 965, 966, 967, 968, 969, 970, 971,
972, 973, 974, 975, 976, 977, 978, 979, 984, 985,
986, 987, 992, 993, 994, 995, 1000 1001, 1002,
1003, 1004, 1005, 1006, 1007, 1012, 1013, 1014,
1015, 1016, 1017, 1018, 1019, 1020, 1021, 1022,
1023, 1028, 1029, 1030, 1031, 1042, 1043, 1044,
1045, 1050, 1051, 1052, 1053, 1058, 1059, 1060,
1061, 1062, 1063, 1064, 1065.

4 cents   (200) No. 460, 461, 462, 463, 530, 531, 532, 533, 790, 791,
792, 793.

5 cents   (200) No. 389, 390, 391, 392, 407, 408, 409, 410, 834, 835,
836, 837, 948, 949, 950, 951, 980, 981, 982, 983.

6 cents   (200) No. 451, 922, 923, 924, 925.

10 cents (400) No. 302, 303, 305, 306, 518, 519, 520, 521, 932, 933,
934, 935, 996, 997, 998, 999.

15 cents (200) No. 264.

Plate 442 of the one cent stamp is said to have been used for one printing in green, but philatelists have been unable to verify the statement.

In the summer of 1898, 63,300,000 one cent and 62,000,000 two cent stamps were surcharged "I. R.", to be used as revenue stamps. As these stamps were taken from the reserve stock of the Bureau of Engraving and Printing and not from the Post Office Department, the accounts of that department were not in any way affected.

In the fiscal years 1899 and 1900 large quantities of stamps were overprinted for Cuba, Guam, Puerto Rico and the Philippine Islands. As in the preceding instance, the stamps had not been transferred to the Post Office Department and, therefore, the statistics of the regular postal issues remain unchanged.

From the annual reports of the Postmaster General we obtain the following tables of stamps issued to deputy postmasters:

Stamps issued during the fiscal year ending June 30th, 1898:

QUARTER ENDING:

	Sept 30, 1897.	Dec. 31, 1897.	Mch. 31, 1898.	June 30, 1898.	Total.
1 cent	157,455,100	232,761,200	240,260,800	196,354,700	826,831,800
2 cents	537,752,000	626,453,400	687,151,300	556,126,500	2,407,483,200
3 cents	3,843,500	6,969,000	7,972,500	4,872,000	23,657,000
4 cents	4,850,100	7,061,200	7,237,000	5,634,850	24,783,150
5 cents	10,185,920	12,760,360	13,890,700	10,396,880	47,233,860
6 cents	1,279,200	2,506,100	1,608,650	1,694,500	7,088,450
8 cents	2,198,350	3,363,150	3,391,100	2,479,950	11,432,550
10 cents	3,860,740	5,446,540	5,508,160	3,782,880	18,598,320
15 cents	364,640	818,020	846,260	355,240	2,384,160
50 cents	12,350	48,040	84,840	7,720	152,950

Marginal notes:
Stamps surcharged "I. R."

Stamps surcharged for Cuba, etc.

Deliveries to postmasters.

	Sept. 30, 1897.	Dec. 31, 1897.	Mch. 31, 1898.	June 30, 1898.	Total.
1 dollar	6,775	11,177	7,463	4,135	29,550
2 dollars	75	65 ·	800	165	1,105
5 dollars	70	620	2,055	115	2,860

Whole number of stamps 3,369,678,955.   Value $64,160,613.00.

Stamps issued during the fiscal year ending June 30th, 1899:

QUARTER ENDING:

	Sept. 30, 1898.	Dec. 31, 1898.	Mch. 31, 1899.	June 30, 1899.	Total.
1 cent	146,382,500	228,217,500	239,954,600	236,461,150	851,015,750
2 cents	511,569,400	645,124,600	676,813,200	669,610,100	2,503,117,300
3 cents	4,435,800	8,080,100	8,033,200	6,806,800	27,355,900
4 cents	3,551,750	7,664,500	7,178,200	6,495,550	24,890,000
5 cents	8,221,560	11,900,260	12,115,800	11,931,950	44,169,570
6 cents	1,098,350	1,982,450	2,202,300	1,645,050	6,928,150
8 cents	1,850,500	3,552,900	3,338,100	2,778,800	11,520,300
10 cents	3,749,460	5,037,590	4,972,100	4,887,050	18,646,200
15 cents	311,760	900,680	632,220	438,150	2,282,810
50 cents	16,680	26,730	17,620	16,850	77,880
1 dollar	755	2,975	6,195	4,615	14,540
2 dollars	20	950	155	75	1,200
5 dollars	15	245	1,015	1,005	2,280

Whole number of stamps 3,490,021,880.   Value $66,208,893.50.

Stamps issued during the fiscal year ending June 30th, 1900:

QUARTER ENDING:

	Sept. 30, 1899.	Dec. 31, 1899	Mch. 31, 1900.	June 30, 1900.	Total.
1 cent	207,987,600	237,771,250	274,354,100	245,519,650	965,632,600
2 cents	662,801,300	702,439,500	755,100,600	705,386,600	2,825,728,000
2 cents, in stamp books	....	....		40,400,904	40,400,904
3 cents	5,730,500	7,999,700	10,149,000	5,745,450	29,624,650
4 cents	6,661,200	8,374,750	9,037,700	7,589,550	31,663,200
5 cents	13,138,400	13,248,050	15,893,300	13,860,300	56,140,050
6 cents	2,368,700	2,742,550	2,275,400	1,839,850	9,226,500
8 cents	3,364,650	4,036,950	4,043,400	2,848,700	14,293,700
10 cents	4,978,320	6,088,780	6,718,700	5,032,850	22,818,650
15 cents	788,800	856,700	701,020	565,560	2,912,080
50 cents	8,710	17,420	20,780	26,360	73,270
1 dollar	8,020	7,685	8,505	1,860	26,070
2 dollars	110	175	1,495	665	2,445
5 dollars	1,220	75	1,075	75	2,445

Whole number of stamps 3,998.544,564.   Value $76,436,757.08.

The table for 1899 includes 750 copies each of the one, four, six, ten and fifteen cents and 850 copies of the five cents, which are reported as being **Deliveries to the Universal Postal Union.** delivered to the Third Assistant Postmaster General.   As it is customary to send 750 copies of each new issue to the Universal Postal Union, it is probably safe to assume that such was the destination of this lot.

In the table for 1900 are included 1,300 stamps (100 copies of each denomination of the series), which were also delivered to the Third Assistant Postmaster General. These were intended for the Government display at the Paris exposition, for exchanging, etc. The majority of the stamps were surcharged "Specimen" in small type, in black.

"Specimen" stamps.

Finally, the Post Office Department received, as specimens, 240 copies of the new stamp books, valued at $101.28. These are also included in the table for 1900.

ISSUE OF 1901.

PAN-AMERICAN SERIES.

In the annual report of the Third Assistant Postmaster General for 1900, we find the following announcement :

PROPOSED ISSUE OF PAN-AMERICAN POSTAGE STAMPS.

Official description of the stamps. "At the instance of the authorities of the Pan-American Exposition, to be held at Buffalo, N. Y., from May 1 to October 31, 1901, the Postmaster General has authorized the issue of a special series of postage stamps to commemorate the exposition, which, owing to its magnitude and international character, is fairly entitled to this mark of recognition by the Post Office Department. The new stamps will be furnished to all postmasters upon their requisitions, and the first issue will be made at the time the exposition is inaugurated, May 1, 1901, the stamps being withdrawn from sale at the close of the exposition, October 31.

It has been decided to issue these stamps in six denominations, 1, 2, 4, 5, 8, and 10 cents, and to make them the most artistic series ever issued by the Department. The Bureau of Engraving and Printing has co-operated to this end and has consented to print the issue in two colors, an undertaking which involves considerable difficulty, particularly in view of the enormous amount of other work required of it. The Bureau of Engraving and Printing took control of the manufacture of postage stamps in July, 1894, and has steadily improved the character of this work up to date. In executing the wishes of the Department as to the Pan-American series, it has thus far equaled all expectations. The result is a stamp that will, I believe, at once delight the eye and otherwise gratify the Department and the public. The designs selected represent the latest and most improved modes of transportation and auxiliaries thereto, as appears from the following descriptions :

Denomination.	Subject.	Color.	Legend.
1 cent	Lake steamer	Green	Fast lake navigation.
2 cents	Railway train	Red	Fast express.
4 cents	Automobile	Red-brown	Automobile.
5 cents	Steel-arch bridge	Blue	Bridge at Niagara Falls.
8 cents	Ship-canal locks	Lilac	Canal locks at Sault Sainte Marie.
10 cents	Ocean steamship	Light brown	Fast ocean navigation.

ONE CENT.—The lake steamer presents the port bow, the pilot house is well forward, and it is propelled by side wheels.

TWO CENTS.—The train of four cars is drawn by a locomotive with four drivers ; four parallel tracks are shown.

FOUR CENTS —The automobile is of the closed-coach order, with two men on the box and a part of the United States Capitol at Washington as a background.

FIVE CENTS.—This presents the largest single span steel bridge in the world ; two trolley cars are seen upon it, and a full view of Niagara Falls is shown under, beyond, and up the river, with the graceful springing arch as a frame.

EIGHT CENTS.—The great ship-canal locks at Sault Sainte Marie, Mich., are given in a view from a higher point, including the immediate surroundings.

TEN CENTS —An ocean steamship of the American line, with two smokestacks and masts, presents its starboard bow, lapped by a rising wave.

These stamps are of uniform dimensions—0.76 by 1.06 of an inch—the longer side being horizontal. The borders take the colors of the regular series on the same denominations at this date The words "Commemorative series, 1901" and "United States of America" next below, appear above the vignette; and the legend, in a line next below the central opening, with the denomination in a line at the bottom, appears in the same order on all stamps of the series All the lettering is in white Roman capitals. The numerals are all white-faced Arabic in the Roman type, except the 10 cents, which is the block-letter type of figure, condensed to secure space for the two figures The openings for the central illustrations are so varied as to prevent a minute description here ; but their borders are well separated from the central pictures. All the central illustrations are from photographs, as the objects represented appear to-day, and are to be printed in black."

The Post Office Department began forwarding the stamps to postmasters on April 25th, and they were placed on sale throughout the country on May 1st. Although the issue will be discontinued on October 31st, the stamps will remain valid for postage.

The engraving is carefully executed but there is nothing especially interesting in either the pictures or their borders. The colors are similar to, though not the same as, those of the corresponding values of the regular series.

The stamps measure 26½x19½mm. The paper is the same as is used for the regular issue of postage stamps and has the watermark "U S P S". The perforation has the regular gauge and the gum is yellowish white.

Perforated 12.

Porous White Wove Paper.

Watermarked U. S. P. S.

Reference List.

May 1st, 1901.   1 cent deep blue-green and black
2 cents carmine and black, rose-carmine and black
4 cents chocolate and black, dark red-brown and black
5 cents ultramarine and black
8 cents brown-violet and black
10 cents yellow-brown and black, orange-brown and black

As the stamps are printed in two colors it is necessary to use two plates for each value, one for the border and one for the vignette. The plates each contain two hundred stamps, arranged in twenty horizontal rows of ten stamps each. The impressions are divided horizontally into sheets of one hundred stamps. The imprint is the same as that used on the plates of the regular issue. It appears only on the plates for the borders and is placed above the third and eighth stamps of the top row and below the corresponding stamps of the bottom row. The number of the border plate is placed at the right of each imprint. The number of the vignette plate appears only once. It is placed below the fifth stamp of the bottom row. There appear also, in the borders, registry marks, platemen's initials, figures indicating the face value of the stamps, etc.

Plates and imprints.

As this chapter is written on the day on which the stamps appear, it is, of course, impossible to give a list of the plate numbers.

CARRIERS' STAMPS.

The subject of the stamps used in payment of the fees for delivering and collecting letters presents many difficulties and complications. The period at which they were used is now remote and, with a few exceptions, records concerning the stamps are entirely lacking. So far as we can learn, they were issued under a variety of circumstances and with varying degrees of authority, from the highest in the land to that of individuals who possessed but the shadow of authority, due to their being employees of the Government.

The power to issue stamps is vested in Congress alone. For reasons to be given later, it seems best to separate the special delivery stamps from the general classification of carriers' stamps and to give them a chapter by themselves. After this segregation there remain but two stamps which were issued as carriers' stamps under an Act of Congress. These are the "Franklin" and "eagle" carriers The stamps of the United States City Despatch Post were issued by the authority of the Postmaster General. Others, such as the "horseman" and "eye" stamps of Baltimore, appear to have been issued by postmasters. And still others were created by letter carriers, on their own responsibility. Some of the letter carriers were, at the time they issued their stamps, in receipt of a fixed salary from the Government, while others were paid only the fees received for the delivery and collection of the letters carried by them. It will readily be understood that the latter class were anxious to increase their receipts as much as possible. Stamps would appear to be a likely means to this end. Their use would obviate the trouble of collecting the carriers' fee upon the delivery of letters and insure its prepayment on drop letters. They could also be used on letters sent from other places, to hasten their delivery in the city in which the stamps were current.

The history of the carriers' stamps is so involved with that of the local posts that it is difficult to consider them separately. Indeed, one was often the outcome of the other or was established because of the success or failure of the other. In some cases the Government was the successor of the local post and retained in its service the employees of the latter. It cannot be denied that the private posts were usually the more enterprising, the first in the field and the first to adopt improvements. In years gone by, the majority of the stamps which are now recognized as carriers' stamps and of semi-official origin, were believed to be issues of the local posts. Within a few years a considerable number have been transferred from the latter to the

Origin of the various stamps.

Local Posts and the carrier service.

former class, through the researches of philatelists. While the local posts were competitors of the Government, the carriers were its employees and assistants. Their stamps, therefore, had the consent, either actual or implied, of those in authority. These stamps are commonly found in company with stamps of the regular Government issues and cancelled by official cancellations. It is largely by means of these cancellations that the status of the carriers' stamps has been established. The local stamps, on the contrary, bear the cancellations of the local posts, thus indicating their private nature. The carriers' stamps undoubtedly performed an auxiliary service of the Post Office Department and for this reason, if for no other, their right to a place in a collection of United States postage stamps would appear to be established.

The rates charged for delivering letters varied at different times and even in different localities at the same time. At one period, also, there was no charge for letters carried to the post office but only for those delivered **Rates.** from it. The report of the Postmaster General for 1855 gives a table showing the deliveries by carriers in several cities and the amounts received for the service. A foot note to this table says: "The rates charged for carrying letters, papers, etc., in the several cities vary; which accounts for the apparent discrepancies in the amounts received." On the subjects of changes in rates and competition of the local posts we find many interesting things in the older philatelic magazines and in Government publications. The reader will find it interesting, at this point, to turn to the historical notes at the beginning of this work, and read the quotation from the *Stamp Collector's Magazine* on pages 6 to 8.

Before the year 1845, New York was the only city in which carriers' stamps were used. The stamps in use there were those of the United States City Despatch Post and a few of Greig's City Despatch Post which were issued provisionally. Each had a face value of three cents. Whether the same rate prevailed in other cities I am unable to say. By Act of Congress, approved March 3rd, 1845, the rate for drop letters was fixed at two cents and carriers were allowed an additional charge of a like amount for delivery. At that date carriers did not receive a fixed salary. Their remuneration was derived entirely from the fees for delivering letters. The Act of March 3rd, 1851, reduced the rate for the delivery of letters to one cent each and, for the first time, provided for collecting letters and conveying them to the post office. This latter work had previously been performed by the private posts. In this change in methods we find an explanation of the large number of one cent carriers' stamps which came into use about that date. Though the Government provided a one cent stamp in the issue of 1851, the carriers preferred to sell their own stamps, whenever they were permitted to do so.

In the report of the Postmaster General, dated December 3rd, 1859, we find the following remarks concerning the local posts and delivery by carriers:

PENNY POST.

"The system of delivering letters by carriers at the domicil of the citizen was first recognized by the Act of 3rd March, 1825, and has within a few years been successfully introduced into several of our principal cities. Though constant endeavors have been made to **Review of the** improve it, it is still imperfect in its details, and unsatisfactory, alike to the public and to the **carrier service.** department, in its operations. The system cannot be regarded as having accomplished the object of its establishment, so long as it does not command and deliver the local correspondence of the different cities in which it exists, which, thus far, it has wholly failed to do. This correspondence is now almost entirely in the hands of private expresses, whose rates are so low as to make a successful competition with them, on the part of the government, impossible Their charge for the delivery of a letter is generally one cent, while this amount is necessarily exacted by the department for the carriers, and one cent in addition is collected on the local correspondence. as the postage fixed by the Act of 1825, on 'drop letters.' Hence the aggregate postage on the city correspondence, under existing laws, which require that the system shall be self-sustaining, is at least two cents, which precludes the possibility **Suggested legislation.** of any successful competition with the private expresses. I therefore recommend the repeal of this provision of the Act of 1825, so far as it can be construed as applying to 'drop letters' delivered by carriers. This would not result in any perceptible diminution of the postal revenues, inasmuch as the correspondence which would be thus secured by the department, does not now pass through its offices. It is true that the Postmaster General might, in his discretion, arrest the operation of these private expresses by declaring the streets and avenues of the cities to which they belong to be post roads ; but until the department is prepared to deliver city letters as cheaply and promptly as such companies can possibly do, I should regard the exercise of this power as unwise, if not harsh and oppressive."

In 1860, Congress acted on these recommendations, and rather more fully than was desired, if we may judge from the report of the Postmaster General for that year. In it he says :

"In the last annual report it was recommended that the provision of the Act of 1825, levying a postage of one cent on 'drop letters,' should be repealed, in order that the department by a reduction of its rates might be enabled more successfully to compete with **Legislation too sweeping.** private expresses in the delivery of the local correspondence of the cities. This repeal was made, but Congress went further and declared that thereafter the charge on each letter delivered by a carrier should be not exceeding one cent. The effect of this was to take from the department the discretion in regulating the charge which had been conferred upon it by the acts of July 2, 1836, and March 3, 1851 It has been satisfactorily ascertained that, in the smaller and sparsely populated cities and towns, the compensation fixed by the recent act is wholly insufficient to support the carrier system. Yet in this class of cities and towns the public demand the delivery of their letters by carriers, and are entirely willing to pay for the service a rate of compensation which would render it remunerative As the discretion previously existing upon the subject has never been abused, and as there is no probability that the rate would ever be raised beyond what would be cheerfully submitted to by the public, I recommend that the provision of the Act of last session be repealed, and that the department shall have authority to collect such postage on all letters delivered by carriers, as shall be deemed necessary to compensate them for the service, provided that it shall not exceed two cents per letter.

The Acts of July 2, 1836, and March 3, 1851, contemplated that the same charge should be made for the delivery of letters into the post office as for their delivery at the domicil of **Charge for convey-** the citizen. From some unexplained cause, this provision of the law was not executed, and **ing letters to the** the service of delivering letters into the post office for transmission has been gratuitously **post office.** performed. No reason could be urged in support of this usage, since this service, thus rendered without any return, has always, to the extent of its performance, cost the department as much as that for which compensation has been exacted. Orders have accordingly been given for the enforcement of this view of the law. and the revenue derived from this source, added to the other receipts of the carrier system, will give it adequate support in the large cities at the low rate of one cent established by the existing law, provided it can command the entire local correspondence for delivery. This can be accomplished only by placing the postal system on the same footing in the cities that it occupies in the rural dis-**Suppression of the** tricts. That same necessity would arise was clearly foreseen by Congress, and in the tenth **local posts.** section of the Act of March 3, 1851, the Postmaster General was authorized to establish post routes within all cities and towns. where the postmasters are appointed by the President of the United States. By virtue of this Act I have by a formal order declared all the streets, lanes, avenues, etc., within the corporate limits of the cities of Boston, New York and Philadelphia, to be post roads, and have notified all engaged in the transportation and delivery of letters, for compensation, in said cities, that they would thereby expose themselves to the penalties imposed by the third section of the Act of March 2, 1827. The private expresses in the cities named have acquiesced in the legality of this step, with the exception of one in Philadelphia, known as 'Blood's Express,' which has continued the regular delivery of letters in defiance of the order of the department.

A bill in equity was filed with a view of restraining the company from this habitual and persistent violation of the postal laws, but upon full argument and consideration had on **Exposition of the** the questions involved, the injunction was denied. The ground assumed by the learned **laws relating to** judges in their decision—a copy of which accompanies this report - is that the statute of **post roads.** March 3, 1851, did not intend to confer upon the government the same monopoly as carriers of letters, packets, etc., over the post routes thereby authorized to be established, as was conferred upon it by the Act of March 2, 1827, in reference to the general post roads of the country. While entertaining the most profound respect for the tribunal pronouncing this opinion, it is but proper to say that its reasoning has not impressed me, nor have I been able to adopt the conclusions at which it has arrived. The streets, alleys, etc., of Philadelphia are now, by virtue of the Act of March 3, 1851, 'post routes'; this is not denied. The statute of March 2, 1827, declares that ' no person other than the Postmaster General, or his authorized agents, shall set up any foot or horse post for the conveyance of letters and packets upon *any post road, which is or may be established* as such by law ; and that every person who shall offend, shall incur a penalty,' etc. If the words ' *any* post road which is or *may* be established,' do not embrace those declared to be such by law in the city of Philadelphia, it is not easy to conceive what terms could be employed sufficiently comprehensive for the purpose. The *quo animo* imputed to Congress in the enactment of the Act of March 3, 1851, is by no means made apparent in the course of the argument The monopoly created by the Act of March 2, 1827, would seem to extend alike to every post road then existing or thereafter to exist, whether pervading the country or the city, or connecting different post offices with each other or with the domicil of the citizen. There is no restriction in the language, and to impose one by construction is to impair, if not to defeat, the carrier system which Congress has recognized as a necessary integral part of the postal service. It seems that every consideration which can be urged in support of the monopoly, conceded to exist on the general post roads of the country, will equally apply to that claimed for those of the city. As the constitutional power for the purpose is not seriously controverted, with a view of relieving the department from future litigation upon the question, I recommend that, in terms so precise and emphatic as not to be mistaken by the courts, Congress shall apply the provisions of the Act of March 2, 1827, to all post routes established in the cities under the authority of the statute of March 3, 1851.

No objection, on the score either of policy or principle, can be successfully urged against the suppression of the private expresses occupied in the conveyance of letters and packets in our cities. The growth of these cities, and the wants of our civilization, render the ministrations of the postal service, in the delivery of letters and packets at the residence of the citizen, as indispensable as they are in the transportation and delivery of the mails at the various post offices in the country districts. But the service can only be maintained as a unit by clothing it with the rights and privileges of a complete government monopoly in all the fields of its operation. Some of its branches are well known to be heavy burdens upon the department ; and they would be insupportably oppressive, were it not for the relief afforded by other branches which are remunerative, but which will continue to be so only so long as the competition of private enterprise is effectually excluded.

Government monoply essential to success.

There are now four daily deliveries of letters and packets by carriers in the city of New York, four in Philadelphia, and three in Boston ; and the number will be increased from time to time, as the increase of population and correspondence will justify it. The high price of labor, however, and the low rates of our postages, forbid the hope that, without some change in the existing laws, the system can ever attain the perfection which distinguishes it in some of the European capitals. While this is admitted, it should also be stated that its operations thus far have been more successful than could have been anticipated, in view of the obstacles it has had to encounter."

This report includes a copy of a letter from Hon. John A. Dix, Postmaster at New York, from which the following is quoted :

" The carriers and collectors are paid from the carriers' fund, which is composed of the postage on city letters, one cent each, one-quarter of the fees on letters received by the mails and delivered by the carriers. Also one cent each, and the fees (one cent each), on letters collected from the lamp-post boxes and carried to the post office to be transmitted by the mails Three quarters of the fees on letters received by the mails and delivered by the carriers are paid to the respective carriers by whom the deliveries are made, and constitute a part of their compensation. They have also an equal share each of the carriers' fund, the collectors being first paid from it.

Letter from the postmaster at New York.

I deem it proper to say that the reduction of the fee for delivering letters received by the mails from two cents to one, would have rendered it impossible to keep up the carrier system with proper efficiency, had not the Postmaster General carried into effect the provisions of law authorizing a fee to be charged for letters collected from the street boxes and carried to the post office to be transmitted by the mails. This order, though the fee was limited to one cent while the law authorized two, produced some dissatisfaction at the time it was issued, but it was so manifestly necessary, and the charge for carrying a letter to the post office for the mail was so reasonable that there was a general acquiescence in the propriety as soon as the matter was fully understood. In the discussions to which it gave rise, no satisfactory reason was shown why the same fee should not be charged for delivering a letter received by the mails, and for carrying a letter to the post office to be transmitted by mail. It is presumed that Congress, by which the charge for both was authorized, saw no propriety in making compensation to the carrier in one case and requiring him to perform the service gratuitously in the other."

By the Act above referred to, that of June 15th, 1860, carriers were, for the first time, given a fixed salary.

Prepayment of carriers' fees, as such, was never made compulsory. By the Act of March 3rd, 1863, the rate on drop letters was increased to two cents (which may be understood to include the carriers' fee), and prepayment compelled. At the same time the delivery tax on letters not of local origin was abolished.

Prepayment of carriers' fees.

The report of the Postmaster General for 1854, gives statistics of letters, circulars, newspapers, etc. delivered by carriers and the amounts received for carriage in the cities of New York, Philadelphia, Boston, Baltimore and New Orleans. The report for 1856 adds to the list Harrisburg, Pa., Lowell, Mass., Syracuse, N. Y. and Manchester, N. H. In the three succeeding years the following additions were made : 1857 : Rochester, N. Y.; 1858 : Troy, N. Y., Providence, R. I. and Roxbury, Mass.; 1859 : Washington, St. Louis and San Francisco. After 1859 these statistics ceased, probably for the reason that, after that year, the carriers were paid a fixed salary and there was no further occasion for keeping the accounts from which the statistics were collected. It is not clear whether the cities mentioned in the reports of the Postmaster General were the only ones in which deliveries by carriers were made, at the several dates given, or if they were merely selected for statistical purposes.

Cities which had carriers' service.

The carriers' stamps must be divided into two classes, official and semi-official. To the first class belong only the Franklin and eagle carriers. The second class is more extensive and covers all stamps issued by officials or employees of the government for the purpose of securing or indicating payment of the carriers' fees. It seems best to describe the semi-official stamps first, because many of them were issued prior to the official carriers' stamps and because they were of a somewhat experimental nature.

Official and semi-official stamps.

We know that the first of the semi-official carriers' stamps, and in fact the first postage stamp used in the United States, was issued in the city of New York in 1842. But records concerning most of the stamps of this class are absolutely lacking and, for the majority of them, even the dates of issue are not well established. It is not possible, therefore, to arrange them in chronological order and it seems most suitable to consider them under an alphabetical arrangement of the cities in which they were issued.

Arrangement.

A variety of dates are given for the different carriers' stamps in philatelic magazines, handbooks and catalogues. As some of them are manifestly incorrect and nearly all are given without any statement of the authority or reason for so fixing the date, I have decided to give only dates which are confirmed by records or which have been obtained from cancelled specimens, either by personal examination or by reports from reliable philatelists. When two dates are given for a stamp they are the earliest and latest known dates of use. When no other dates can be obtained, those which are assigned to the stamps in the older philatelic publications will be given, but such dates will be enclosed in parentheses, as an indication that they lack confirmation.

Dates of use.

THE BALTIMORE CARRIERS' STAMPS.

Of the history of the carriers' stamps used in Baltimore we know very little. The several varieties, known as the "Horseman", "Post Office Despatch" and "Carrier's Dispatch" (or "eye type") have long been classed among the carriers' stamps. But nothing appears to be known of the dates at which they were issued or by whom and upon what authority the issues were made.

A few years ago, at my request, Mr. F. G. Sweet of Baltimore, kindly tried to secure some information about the various carriers' stamps used there. In an interview with one of the old residents, who had been in a position to acquire information on the subject, he was told as follows:

"The fees derived from the collection and distribution of mail by carriers were, in Baltimore at least, a perquisite of the postmaster. For the central portion of the city, where the mail was naturally the heaviest, the postmaster employed full salaried carriers and supplied them with regular stamps of his own, such as the 'horseman', 'eye stamps', etc. Grafflin, it seems, was employed by the postmaster on a kind of commission basis, to collect and distribute mail in the less populous sections of the city and, for this purpose, had his own stamps whose franking powers were, of course, recognized by the Baltimore postmaster." *Stamps said to have been supplied by the postmaster.*

These statements would be very interesting if we could be positive of their correctness. Unfortunately, the gentleman went far astray in his assertions concerning the Grafflin post, and this makes us doubtful of the accuracy of his other statements.

As it has been suggested on several occasions that the Grafflin was a carriers' stamp, it may be well to say here that it was a local, pure and simple. The post was originally a branch of Blood's post of Philadelphia. In 1853 or '54 Joseph Grafflin bought it from Blood and ran it for a few years under his own name. He issued his stamps about the beginning of 1856, but had no connection with the post office beyond that, as many local posts did, he collected letters and deposited them in the post office, to be forwarded to other places. These statements are made upon the authority of the widow and brother of Mr. Grafflin. *Grafflin's local post.*

From carefully noting the dates on a large number of original covers bearing the stamps of the Baltimore carriers, it becomes evident that the three varieties were in use coincidently, probably by carriers in different parts of the city. The earliest dates are found on the "Post Office Despatch" stamps, the next earliest on the "Eye" stamps, and the "Horseman" stamps occupy the third place. *Several designs in concurrent use.*

POST OFFICE DESPATCH.

Description. Typographed in blocks of ten, two vertical rows of five, each stamp differing from the others. Probably these blocks were repeated to make up a plate, but this is not certain. A reproduction of a reconstructed block of the ten types will be found among the illustrations and will make further description unnecessary. The stamps measure 20x11½mm.

Reference List.

Imperforate.

Thin Bluish Wove Paper.

Jan. 1, 1853.—Oct. 11, 1855.   1 cent scarlet, dull vermilion.   10 varieties
Feb. 16, 1854.   1 cent blue.   10 varieties

Bluish Laid Paper.

1 cent blue.   10 varieties

White Wove Paper.

Sept. 18, 1852.   1 cent red.   10 varieties
Sept. 2, 1854.—April, 1855.   1 cent blue, light blue, bright blue, dark blue,
                                              dull blue, dull dark blue.   10 varieties
Jan. 29, 1859.—June, 1861.   1 cent gray-green.   10 varieties

White Laid Paper.

Jan. 9, 1858.—Mch. 23, 1858. 1 cent dark blue, deep dull blue.   10 varieties

Dates of use. Mr. C. H. Coster, says in his monograph on the "*Private Posts of the United States*": "These stamps were in use in 1852. Although we have been unable to obtain the proof, we believe that they have a semi-official character, like the *U. S. P. O.* of Philadelphia, and that they were issued by the government for use in Baltimore, or by the postmaster of that city for the same purpose."

In the *American Journal of Philately* for February, 1889. Mr. J. W. Scott gives the dates : "Oct. 4, 1852, 1 cent red on bluish paper ; Nov. 24, 1852, 1 cent blue on bluish paper." But he says nothing regarding the source from which these dates were derived.

Counterfeits. These stamps, like most of the carriers' and locals, have been extensively counterfeited. The counterfeits, however, may be readily detected by comparison with the illustration of the genuine types. The easiest test is found in the relative positions of the "T" of "CENT" and the "H" of "DESPATCH". The commonest counterfeit has a small oval "O" in "ONE", while all the genuine stamps have a large round "O". There is a counterfeit which closely resembles type VI of the originals, but comparison will show many small differences.

CARRIER'S DISPATCH.

These are also known as the " Eye " stamps. Typographed on ordinary white paper. There are no varieties, all the stamps being reproductions of one original type. Size : 22x16½mm. The number of stamps in a sheet is not known.

Description.

Imperforate.

Reference List.

White Wove Paper.

Jan. 1, 1856.—Feb. 19, 1859. 1 cent blue, dull blue, dark blue
Oct. 21, 1858.—May 10, 1861. 1 cent pale rose, rose, deep rose, rose-red, red,
        brown-red, pale vermilion, vermilion

The *American Journal of Philately* for December 20th, 1874, suggests that these stamps were issued by the postmaster of Baltimore. There is nothing to be learned from references in other philatelic publications.

There are numerous counterfeits of these stamps, both in the proper and in fancy colors. They are usually less blurred in appearance than the genuine stamps. The counterfeit most frequently met has the "N"s in "ONE" and "CENT" too narrow. Another counterfeit is readily distinguished by the narrow "R"s in "CARRIER'S", and a third by having all the letters of "CARRIER'S DISPATCH", as well as the pigeons in the corners, too large.

––––––––––

GOVERNMENT CITY DISPATCH (HORSEMAN).

Typographed in a pane of ten varieties, two vertical rows of five stamps, each differing slightly from the others. Two of the varieties are quite prominent; the second stamp in the pane has the three rays below the letters, "VER" of "GOVERNMENT"; only about half the usual length ; on the seventh stamp the inscription on the streamer is " ONE SENT ". The pane is repeated several times on each sheet. Mr. F. W. Hunter had at one time an irregular block which showed portions of three panes in one row and a part of a pane in the row below. Furthermore, one of the three panes was placed tête bêche to the other two. From this it was thought probable that the plate contained one hundred stamps, in ten panes, arranged in two rows of five. But there is evidence which contradicts this theory. I have recently seen several of these stamps, each of which showed, at one end, an overlapping impression of a small portion of another stamp. From these double impressions I conclude that the plate contained only one group of ten stamps, that several

*Description,
varieties and
plate.*

impressions were taken on one sheet of paper, and that, through carelessness, one impression slightly overlapped another.   Size : 23¼x17mm.

Reference List.   Imperforate.

White Wove Paper.

Aug. 19, 1857.—Sept. 20, 1860. 1 cent rose, lilac-rose, rose-red, red, vermilion, brown-red, deep brown-red. 10 varieties
Sept. 19, 1857.—Mch. 18, 1861. 1 cent black, gray-black. 10 varieties

Principal varieties .

1 cent rose, red, etc.	Short rays
1 cent " " "	"SENT"
1 cent black, gray-black.	Short rays
1 cent " "	"SENT"

The *American Journal of Philately* for 1888, says: " 1851, 1 cent rose, 1 cent red ; 1860, Sept. 1, 1 cent black." The first date is probably

Dates of use.   copied from the same journal for 1877, and is doubtless as incorrect as is the last.   In the number dated December 20th, 1874, we read concerning this stamp : " This was used in Baltimore in 1861, but was, I am inclined to think, issued by the U. S. P. O. in that city for carriers use."

Coster says (1882) : " All efforts to obtain information about this post have been unavailing. However, I have learned from private sources that the stamps of the *Government City Dispatch* were issued by the postmaster of Baltimore."

While August 19th, 1857, is the earliest cancellation that I have seen, it is my opinion that the red stamps were in use for some time previous to that date. The red stamps are usually more clearly printed than those in black, and indicate an earlier and unworn state of the plate.

There are a number of counterfeits of the " Horseman " stamps but

Counterfeits.   none of them are very good and all may be distinguished by the fact that they lack the small white ornaments which are found in the upper corners of the originals.

The Boston Carriers' Stamps.

Records of the Boston carriers' stamps are yet to be discovered ; consequently, there is little to be said concerning them, beyond what may be learned from examination of the stamps and the covers to which they are affixed.

U. S. Penny Post.

Description.
Plate.

The stamps are engraved in *taille douce* and printed on yellowish white wove paper. Owing to their rarity and the limited number of copies available for examination, it has not been possible to form any conclusion as to the number of stamps on the plate. As each was separately engraved it is probable that the plate was not large. A specimen, formerly in the collection of Mr. F. W. Hunter, shows portions of several adjacent stamps, sufficient to prove there were at least three rows of three stamps each. Probably the plate contained twelve or fifteen stamps, possibly as many as twenty-five. The ornaments in the corners appear to have been inserted by means of punches, the remainder of the design is hand-engraved. Size : 18x22mm.

Imperforate.

Reference List.

Yellowish White Wove Paper.

1849.   2 cents black

I have never seen a cancelled copy of this stamp. The *American Journal of Philately* for December, 1874, mentions the stamp but says nothing concerning any date of issue or use. Coster says : " Issue of ——?" The *Philatelic Journal of America* for January, 1889, says : " The earliest dates of letters bearing the stamps of this post that are now recorded are 1849."

Date of use.

The counterfeits are too poor to require description. They are roughly made by lithography or typography, while the originals are finely engraved.

Counterfeits.

PENNY POST.

Description. Typographed on pelure paper. Size : 21½x9½mm. All the stamps appear to be reproductions of a type-set original and there are no varieties. Occasionally some of the rays of the corner ornaments are broken or missing but this is probably due to poor printing or defective electrotypes.

Reference List.   Imperforate.

Pelure Paper.

Nov. 8, 1849.—Apl. 26, 1851. (1 cent) dull blue, deep dull blue

Date of issue. The *American Journal of Philately* for February, 1889, gives the date of issue of this stamp as April 3rd, 1845. This is possibly founded on a remark in Coster's book : "We possess, on a letter dated 1845, a hand-stamp of this post, which gives us reason to suppose it commenced business about that period." Perhaps this hand-stamp was confused with the adhesive stamps.

Counterfeits. Counterfeits are numerous but not dangerous. The lines of the diamonds which form the frame are continuous, while in the originals they are broken, each diamond being a separate piece of type. The stars in the corners are two small and usually have five points instead of eight rays. There is no period after "POST". Finally, most of the counterfeits have a single-lined outer frame which does not appear on the originals.

PENNY POST PAID.

Description. Typographed on ordinary wove paper, varying from grayish to blue-gray in color. Size : 20½x12½mm. Like the preceding issue, these stamps appear to have been reproduced from a type-set original and show no varieties.

Reference List.   Imperforate.

Grayish Wove Paper.

July 20, 1850.—July 26, 1854. (1 cent) blue, dull blue

Bluish Gray Wove Paper.

(1 cent) deep blue, dull blue

Counterfeits. Counterfeits of this stamp are plentiful but are not difficult to detect. The frame is extremely well imitated as is also the word "PENNY", though the letters of the latter are a little too much spaced. In "POST" the letters are not enough shaded and are too narrow, especially the " o " which, in the originals, is nearly round. The greatest difference is in the word " PAID " In the original stamps this word is in Roman capitals, set close together. In the counterfeits the letters are in block type and widely spaced. In some of the counterfeits, in the bottom row of the type-set border, the block nearest the right corner is turned sideways. This is not known to occur in the genuine stamps. The *American Journal of Philately* for June, 1872, mentions a counterfeit of this stamp which has only twenty-six pieces of type in the frame, instead of twenty-eight.

Hand-stamped in color on colored wove paper. Diameter : 14mm.	Description.
Imperforate.	Reference List.
Bluish Wove Paper.	

(1853). (1 cent) red

Outside of catalogues I have been unable to find any reference to this stamp. I have, however, seen it in black, used as a cancellation for the stamp last described. It is possible, of course, that the hand-stamp was used both as a cancellation mark and for the production of adhesive stamps, as is known to have been done on other occasions. But, pending confirmation by specimens on the original cover, the stamp is listed with much reserve.

Cancellation or hand-stamp.

HILL'S POST.

Before leaving the subject of the Boston carriers' stamps a few words must be said about another stamp which may possibly belong to this category. This is Hill's post, now classed among the locals (Standard catalogue, 60th edition, L147). Very little is known about this post. Oliver B. Hill was probably its proprietor. From the Boston city directory we obtain the following extracts :

1843	Hill, Oliver B., grocer; 172 Hanover St.; House, etc.				
1844	"	"	"	"	"	"
1845	"	"	———	———	"
1846	"	"	Clerk	———	"
1846-47	"	"	Post Office	———	"
1847-48	"	"	Penny Post	———	"
1848-49	"	"	" "	———	"
1849-50	"	"	———	———	"
1850-51	"	"	Oysters, 52 Kneeland St.	"

When two years are given together the period covered is from July 1st to July 1st. In the two years left blank there is no record of his occupation, merely his name and residence. We do not know whether the words " Post office " imply a connection with the Government post office or merely the office of a private post   But it is well known that the term "penny post " was applied both to local posts and to letter carriers.   The name Oliver B Hill does not appear in the official register which contains the names of all postmasters, clerks, contractors, etc.   Copies of the stamps are known with cancellations dated in 1849 and early in 1850.   The limited information which we now possess does not appear to warrant the inclusion of this stamp among the carriers.

THE CHARLESTON CARRIERS' STAMPS.

After the uncertainty which surrounds most of the carriers' stamps, it is a pleasure to turn to those used in this city. We have very full and complete information concerning them, the circumstances under which they were issued, by whom and at what dates. Much of this information was obtained by the efforts of Mr. W. H. Faber, a resident of the city and personally acquainted with the carriers by whom the stamps were issued. Their history may be briefly summarized as follows :

In 1849, John H. Honour received from Washington an appointment as letter carrier for the city of Charleston. He engaged his brother-in-law, E. J. Kingman, to assist him, the service being conducted in the name of Mr. Honour. About two years later they separated and divided the carrier business of the city between them, one taking the eastern half and the other the western. At the same time Mr. Kingman was appointed a carrier by the Postmaster of Charleston. Each carrier was under bonds to the Government in the sum of $2,000.

Historical.

In March, 1858, Mr. Kingman retired and his place was taken by Joseph G. Martin. In the summer of the same year, John F. Steinmeyer, Jr. was added to the carrier force. In 1860, Mr. Honour retired and John C. Beckman was appointed in his place. Mr. Martin retired early in 1861, but the service was continued by the other two carriers until about 1865.

Each of these carriers issued stamps. At first the stamps were made from engraved dies, but there is nothing to show whether they were printed from plates or from groups of electrotypes. It has been suggested that they were hand-stamped but the few copies which I have been able to examine have every appearance of having been printed on a press. Afterwards the stamps were set up from type and some of those issued by Mr. Steinmeyer appear to have been printed from electrotypes. The stamps were the product of local printing offices. Most of them were gummed with gum arabic which was applied, not by the printer, but by the owner himself. A few of the stamps were printed on rose or yellow paper but the majority of them were on the ordinary bluish writing paper of that period. For many years the catalogues listed several of the stamps on white paper. Prominent philatelists claim to have seen them and others, equally prominent, deny their existence on this paper. I have not been able to locate any copies in the hands of philatelists and, as there is a possibility that this paper may be merely the ordinary bluish or grayish paper from which the color has been discharged, I have decided not to list them.

STAMPS OF JOHN H. HONOUR.

Typographed from an engraved die. Printed in black on thin, colored wove paper. Size : 15½x19½mm.

Imperforate.

Colored Wove Paper.

July 14, 1849.　　　2 cents black on rose, brown-rose
　　　　　　　　　　　2 cents black on yellow

Only a very few copies of this stamp are known.

Typographed from an engraved die on thin, colored wove paper. Size : 22x26mm.

Imperforate.

Colored Wove Paper.

Aug. 16, 1849.　　　2 cents black on rose

The *American Journal of Philately* for December, 1888, describes this stamp as on yellow surfaced paper and not on rose paper, colored through, as we now know it. Probably the writer was misinformed. Coster calls the color " bistre-rouge."

Printed from a type-set plate, in black, on glazed paper, colored on the surface. I have only seen three varieties but, doubtless, more exist. The plate probably contained from ten to twenty-five stamps. Size : 15x11mm.

Imperforate.

Wove Paper, Glazed and Surface-Colored.

Oct. 20, 1849.—Mch. 5, 1850.   2 cents black on yellow, lemon-yellow, orange-
yellow

Principal variety :

2 cents black on yellow.   Error, " ccnts " instead of " cents "

The *American Journal of Philately* for December, 1888, lists this stamp
on yellow surfaced paper, blue writing paper and white paper. As the second
paper has been dropped from the catalogues for some years, it was probably
found to have been listed by error.   The reason for omitting the third paper
has already been explained.

Similar to the preceding but with six pearls at each side, instead of
five. Type-set and printed on colored wove paper.   The number of varieties
is not known. Size : 15x13mm.

Imperforate.

Colored Wove Paper.

May 8, 1850.   2 cents black on gray-blue

Some philatelists claim that this stamp is merely a variety in the plate
of the preceding issue.   When we consider the similarity of the two stamps,
the conclusion does not appear unreasonable.

Similar to the two preceding stamps but with the word " Paid " added
at the top of the inscription. Type-set and printed, in black, on colored wove
paper, varying in thickness.   Mr. C. T. Harbeck has in his collection sixteen
varieties of this stamp.   It is probable that the plate contained twenty-five
varieties arranged in five rows of five stamps each.   It is also possible that,
as this stamp was in use for several years, there was more than one setting
and printing of it.   It is supposed that there were the same number of varieties
of the stamps on pink pelure paper as on the other papers but, owing to the
rarity of the pink stamps, it has not been possible to confirm this theory.
Size : 14½x12½mm.

Imperforate.

Colored Wove Paper.

Apl. 25, 1851.—July 7, 1853.   2 cents black on gray-blue, blue-gray, gray,
greenish gray

Principal variety :

Apl. 12, 1852.   2 cents black on gray-blue. Error, "CENS"
                             instead of 'CENTS"

                        Pelure Paper.

                        2 cents black on pink

| | Type-set and printed, in black, on colored wove paper. There are |
| probably varieties of this stamp, as always occurs when stamps are type-set, |
| Description. | but, owing to the uniform shape and size of the ornaments which compose |

the border, the differences are so minute that they have not attracted the
attention of philatelists. The *American Journal of Philately* for December, 1888, says : "Typographed in sheet showing minor varieties." Size :
16½x17mm.

Reference List.   <center>Imperforate.</center>

Colored. Wove Paper.

Dec. 4, 1854.—July 6, 1855. 2 (cents) black on gray-blue

Strange to say, Mr. J. G. Martin, one of the Charleston carriers, says :
"There was never a Honour issued of the description of the above," (see
Stamp repudiated *American Journal of Philately* for March, 1898). None the less, I have seen
by J. G. Martin. four copies, all on the original covers, and all cancelled in Charleston at or
between the dates here given. As the carrier service was at that time practically a monopoly of Messrs. Honour and Kingman it is not probable that they
would tolerate an attempt to establish a similar service and it is also doubtful
whether the field was sufficiently large to attract the enterprise of others. As
Mr. Martin was not connected with the carrier service until some four years
after this stamp was in use, it is possible that he was not familiar with it or
that his memory was at fault. Prominent philatelists have long considered
this stamp to be one of the Honour issues and, apparently, with good reason.

Type-set and printed on colored wove paper. Minor varieties doubt-
Description. less exist, as in the preceding stamp, but the differences are so trifling that
they have escaped notice. Size : 17½x13mm.

Reference List.   <center>Imperforate.</center>

Colored Wove Paper.

(1856).   (2 cents) black on gray-blue, gray

The date is taken from Coster's book. In the *American Journal of Philately* for December, 1888, we find the date given as February 24th, 1852, but the correctness of this has been doubted.

Printed from a type-set plate on colored wove paper. Several varieties have been seen but the differences are minute. Size : 17x12½mm.

Imperforate.

Colored Wove Paper.

Feb. 21, 1858. (2 cents) black on gray-blue

This date is taken from the only copy on the original cover which I have seen. The year is not very legible but I believe it to be as here given. Coster gives the date "1859 or '60." The *American Journal of Philately* for December, 1888, says "May 9th, 1852." This also appears to be questioned.

STAMPS OF E. J. KINGMAN.

Printed on colored wove paper from a type-set plate. The number of varieties is not known. I have seen only three. Mr. Kingman thinks the sheets contained two rows of five stamps each. Size : 17x12½mm.

Imperforate.

Colored Wove Paper.

Jan. 19, 1851.—Jan. 20, 1858. 2 cents black on gray-blue
2 cents black on green

Coster and the *American Journal of Philately* both give 1850 as the date of this stamp. It is quite possible that they are correct.

Type-set and printed on colored wove paper. Several varieties, probably not less than ten. Size : 14½x12½mm.

Imperforate.

Colored Wove Paper.

1851 (?) 2 cents black on gray-blue

I have copied the date from a memorandum but cannot recall my authority for it. The Honour stamp of similar design was issued in the same year.

STAMP OF JOSEPH G. MARTIN.

Description.

Type-set and printed on colored wove paper. Several varieties have been seen. Mr. Martin says, in the *American Journal of Philately* for March, 1898 : "I think there were twenty-five on a sheet, square, face value fifty cents." From the word "square" we may infer that the stamps were arranged in five rows of five stamps each. Size : 17x13mm.

Reference List.

Imperforate.

Colored Wove Paper.

1858.   2 cents black on gray-blue

Date of use.

Cancelled copies have not been seen but the date, 1858, is probably correct. Much earlier dates have been assigned to the stamp but they must be wrong, as Mr. Martin did not become a carrier until 1858.

STAMPS OF JOHN F. STEINMEYER.

Description.

Impression from a type-set plate on colored wove paper. There are, doubtless, varieties of this stamp but they have not been chronicled. Size : 17x13mm.

Reference List.

Imperforate.

Colored Wove Paper.

1858 or 1859.   2 cents black on gray-blue

Date of use.

The *American Journal of Philately* for February, 1889, gives the date of this stamp as 1850, but that is as manifestly incorrect as the locating of the post in Philadelphia, which is done by the same journal and by Coster.

Description.

Typographed on various papers. The sheets contain ten stamps, arranged in two vertical rows of five. There do not appear to be any varieties other than trifling differences in the impression. Size : 17x11½mm.

Imperforate.

Thin Colored Wove Paper.

1858 or 1859.   2 cents black on gray-blue, gray

Thick Colored Wove Paper.

2 cents black on yellow

2 cents black on rose, dull rose

STAMP OF JOHN C. BECKMAN.

Type-set and printed in black on colored wove paper. The stamp is of the same design as that issued by Mr. Martin and those issued in 1850-58 by Messrs. Honour and Kingman. Only one copy is known but, doubtless, there were originally several varieties. Size : 17x13mm.   Description.

Imperforate.   Reference List.

Colored Wove Paper.

1860.   2 cents black on gray-blue

Counterfeits of the stamps of the Charleston carriers are plentiful. Apparently they all emanate from one source, probably that which supplied many of the reprints and counterfeits of the United States local stamps. The   Counterfeits. distinguishing marks of the counterfeits are not easy to describe, though they are unmistakable when compared with genuine stamps or good photographs. There is a clearness and carefulness in the printing which is not found in the originals. The letters of the inscriptions have a general resemblance, but comparison at once shows them to be from different fonts. The ornaments which form the borders are very sharp and are carefully set, while those of the original stamps are worn and carelessly arranged. In the second type of the Steinmeyer stamps, the ornaments which form the border at top and bottom have a shading on the inner side, while those at the sides have it on the outer side. In the commonest of the counterfeits the ornaments and, consequently, the shadings are reversed. There is another counterfeit which has all the ornaments correctly placed except the one on the right side, but a small oval has been added at the centre of the top and bottom borders, which is not found on the genuine stamps. Finally, the colors are not correct. The rose, yellow and green are too bright and the gray-blue, which varies a great deal in the originals, is nearly always a light " French gray " in the counterfeits. In the last color the paper is hard and highly finished and a little too thick. Comparison with the accompanying photogravure reproductions will enable the collector to readily detect the counterfeits.

THE LOUISVILLE CARRIERS' STAMPS.

Historical. Thanks to the researches of Mr. F. W. H. Hahn of Louisville, we have quite full and satisfactory information concerning the carriers' stamps of that city. The carrier service was first established by the Louisville post office about 1854, one carrier being employed for the purpose. Charles P. Smith was first appointed. He delivered letters to houses and offices for a fee of two cents each but did not collect them for delivery to the post office. On January 1st, 1856, David B. Wharton succeeded Smith as carrier. Late in the year 1857 he decided to use stamps for collecting his fees and had them prepared. But before many of the stamps were used—certainly not over fifty, and some claim none at all—he was succeeded by Wilson Gough. This took place about the end of 1857 or possibly on January 1st, 1858. Soon after this Joseph G. Brown was appointed to assist Gough. Gough did not issue stamps and only retained the office a few months. On April 1st, 1858, S. B. McGill was appointed carrier, and he and Brown continued to act in this capacity until September 30th, 1860. Brown and McGill decided to improve the service by issuing stamps. They bought from D. B. Wharton the outfit of letter boxes which he had had prepared and also the remainder of his stamps. There is a possibility that a few of the Wharton stamps were used while the Brown & McGill stamps were being prepared. These stamps were used only on letters bearing the regular United States postage stamps, not on circulars or private mail which did not pass through the post office. They paid the fee for delivering letters from or to the post office. The stamps were on sale in the post office, though not usually at the window at which the Government's stamps were sold. These carriers were under bonds of $2,000 each to the Government.

STAMPS OF DAVID B. WHARTON.

Lithographed by Robyn & Co. in sheets of fifty stamps, arranged in two panes of twenty-five, five rows of five stamps each. The panes were separated by a space of 4mm. Each stamp was surrounded by a thin frame line, forming a rectangle about 24½x18½mm. The rectangles were separated by a space of 1mm. vertically and ½mm. horizontally. The words "ROBYN & CO. LITH." appear at the bottom of each stamp, extending from the left corner to about the middle of the stamp.

Description.

Imperforate.

Reference List.

White Wove Paper.

1857.   (2 cents) blue-green

I have not seen any good counterfeits of this stamp.

STAMPS OF BROWN & McGILL.

Lithographed by Hart & Maypother, successors to Robyn & Co. The stamps are made in imitation of the Wharton stamp, from which they differ only in the lettering of the upper label and the omission of the name of the makers. They are enclosed in a single-lined frame, measuring about 24½x19¼mm. Having seen only single copies, I am unable to give the distance between the stamps and their arrangement. The size of the sheets is not known but it was probably the same as for the Wharton stamp.

Description.

Imperforate.

Reference List.

White Wove Paper.

June 12, 1858.—June 29, 1860. (2 cents) dull blue, dark blue
April 13, ——   (2 cents) black

Mr. Hahn claims that none of the Brown & McGill stamps were printed in black and that, if such exist, they must be either discolored stamps or proofs. There is in the collection of Mr. C. T. Harbeck a fine copy, printed in black, which has every appearance of being genuine and in its original condition. It is on a letter, postmarked "April 13th" but with the year omitted. Apparently it is an early impression. It is my opinion that this is the color in which the stamp was first printed.

The black stamp.

In a communication which was printed in the *American Journal of Philately* for April, 1898, Mr. Hahn says :

"About the year 1865 or 1866, Hussey, of New York, asked Mr. McGill for some remainders of the Brown & McGill stamps. He may have had some on hand but certainly wanted more and ordered Hart & Maypother to print 200 from the original stone. But, the original not existing, a poor imitation or forgery was made and the stamps sent to Hussey as originals or reprints. The fact is, McGill, at the time, believed the forged stamps to be reprints."

Counterfeits.

These so-called reprints are not very successful imitations of the originals. The eagle is quite incorrect in size and pose, the foliage is too abundant, the letters are too large, and there is an eight-pointed ornament at each side, instead of a small oval of crossed lines. There must have been more than one printing of these imitations, for I possess copies which differ widely in shade and paper.

In addition to the foregoing—which may be called the official counterfeit—there are a number of others. The poorest of them should not deceive any one but it may be said that, instead of the small ovals which should separate the upper and lower labels, they show only two or three faint scratches. There is one counterfeit which quite closely resembles the original, but the work is too well done, the letters are slightly too large and the wings of the eagle do not touch the oval.

Coster says that these stamps were issued in New York and the *American Journal of Philately* for 1888 assigns them to Baltimore. All of which proves nothing, except that it is easy to be mistaken.

THE NEW YORK CARRIERS' STAMPS.

To the city of New York belongs the distinction of placing in use the first stamp in the United States and the second in the world. This was a stamp of the City Despatch Post, issued in 1842. This post was a private Historical. enterprise and belongs to the large and interesting group of local posts. At the same time, its history is so involved with that of the government carrier service in this city—which was modelled upon and succeeded the private post —that one cannot thoroughly consider the one without the other. In addition to this, a few stamps of the City Despatch Post were used provisionally by its official successor, the United States City Despatch Post.

GREIG'S CITY DESPATCH POST.

In the *American Journal of Philately* for June, 1894 (page 284), we find an article on the subject of this post, written by Charles Windsor, the son of its originator. At the commencement he says: "The founder, sole proprietor, manager and director was Henry Thomas Windsor, a London merchant, then on a visit to the United States, and residing temporarily in the suburb of Hoboken." In traveling through the country Mr. Windsor, who was familiar with the English postal system, was struck with the inefficiency of our postal arrangements and the excessive charges. He decided, as a business venture, to establish a private post in New York city. He associated with him his friend Alexander M. Greig, in whose name the post was established, with the idea that it would be more successful under the name of a well-known resident than under that of a stranger and alien.

The *American Journal of Philately* for May, 1872, reproduces the following circular:

NEW YORK CITY DESPATCH POST.

Principal Office, 46 William Street.

The necessity of a medium of communication by letter from one part of the City to another, being universally admitted, and the Penny Post, lately existing, having been relinquished, the opportunity has been embraced to re-organize it under an entirely new proprietary and management, and upon a much more comprehensive basis, by which Despatch, Circular announcing
the City Despatch
Post. Punctuality and Security,—those essential elements of success,—may at once be attained, and the inconvenience now experienced be entirely removed.

The Proprietors of the "City Despatch Post" enter upon the undertaking with an earnest impression of its responsibilities, and with a full determination so to perform the required duties as to merit the confidence and support of their fellow-citizens. They have engaged the most efficient and trustworthy Assistants and Letter Carriers, and no expense will be spared to bring the whole advantage of a well-considered system into active operation.

The following is a brief outline of the plan :

BRANCH OFFICES.—Letter Boxes are placed throughout every part of the City in conspicuous places ; and all letters deposited therein, not exceeding two ounces in weight, will be punctually delivered three times a day, at 9, 1, and 4 o'clock, at three cents each ; option being given, either to free the letter, in the manner shown in the following regulations, or leave the postage to be collected of the party to whom the letter is addressed

POST-PAID LETTERS —Letters which the writers desire to send free, must have a free stamp affixed to them. An ornamental stamp has been prepared for this purpose, and may be procured at the Principal Office as above, or at those stores which will be advertised in the daily papers as having authority to sell them. The charge will be 36 cents per dozen, or 2 dols. 50 cents per hundred ; the reduction of price for the larger quantity being made with a view to the accommodation of those parties sending a considerable number of circulars, accounts, &c. Parcels not exceeding 1 lb. in weight will be charged a proportionate rate.

NO MONEY MUST BE PUT INTO THE BOXES.

All letters intended to be sent forward to the General Post-Office for the inland mails must have a free stamp affixed to them.

Letters and Newspapers addressed to the Editors of the Public Press, will be delivered free.

UNPAID LETTERS —Letters not having a free stamp will be charged three cents, payable by the party to whom they are addressed, on delivery.

REGISTRY AND DESPATCH.—A Registry will be kept for Letters which it may be wished to place under special charge. Free stamps must be affixed to such letters for the ordinary postage, and three cents additional be paid, (or an additional free stamp be affixed,) for the Registration ; but all such Letters must be specially deposited at the Principal Office.

A special "Despatch" will be expedited with any Letter or Packet, not exceeding one pound in weight, (to an address within the limits,) at 12½ cents a mile, upon application at the Principal Office.

The advantages offered by this undertaking are :—

FIRST.—The secure and prompt transmission of all Registered Letters containing any special notice or matter, by which means legal evidence may be obtained of the due delivery of the same ; and the immediate despatch of any letter or small package requiring instant delivery.

SECONDLY.—The certain and expeditious delivery of Mercantile Letters and Circulars, of Invitations and Replies (either under free stamp or unpaid), and every description of Commercial, Professional, and Social Correspondence ; thus bringing the most distant parts of the City in effect near to each other, and providing the means of constant intercourse at a very moderate charge.

ALEXANDER M. GREIG, Agent.

The Limits of the Despatch Post will extend to Twenty-First Street.

It is interesting to note, in connection with this enterprise, the features of registration and special delivery, which are evidently not as modern ideas as we are accustomed to think.

The post began its operations on January 1st, 1842. It appears to have been very successful and to have provided an efficient and satisfactory

Success of the post.

service. It soon attracted the notice of the Post Office Department as, owing to its superior service, it secured the handling of much of the local mail and thus reduced the revenue of the post office. The removal of such a rival was felt to be imperative. We do not know exactly what means were employed to accomplish this end. In the article previously referred to, Mr. Windsor

Discontinuance of the post.

says : "The Government soon proscribed the continuance of the Post, asserting it to be an infringement of governmental rights." And in another place : "The Government compelled him to discontinue it." But it is possible that other means than force were employed to bring about the result. In the *American Journal of Philately* for April, 1877, we find the following letter :

POST OFFICE DEPARTMENT.

CONTRACT OFFICE.

August 1, 1842.

SIR :—By an order made on Saturday, but journalized to-day, the Postmaster General has established a letter carrier arrangement for the City of New York, to be called the

Letter concerning
carrier service for
New York City.

"United States City Despatch Post," for the conveyance of letters from one part of the city to another, subject to a charge on each letter of three cents, under the 20th section of the Act of 1836, and authorizes you to employ Alex. M. Greig, nominated by you, as letter carrier. Other carriers are to be appointed from time to time, as may be required, and you are requested to nominate for that purpose. And you are also authorized to obtain the necessary fixtures, pouches, boxes, labels, stamps, etc., at not exceeding $1,200 for the whole, and to appoint a clerk to superintend said establishment at not exceeding $1,000 per annum. You will be pleased to report the date of the commencement of this arrangement.

Very respectfully, your obedient servant,

S. R. HOBBIE,
First Asst. P. M. General.

JOHN LORIMER GRAHAM, ESQ.,
  Postmaster, New York.

From this letter we may conclude that the Post Office Department, having seen the success of a local delivery service, had determined to establish such for itself, as authorized by the Act of July 2nd, 1836. By taking Mr. Greig into its service it removed a rival and, at the same time, secured an efficient and experienced employee. The City Despatch Post was probably abandoned temporarily, although this is not positive. We know that it was in business in 1848 and continued until 1859. But our interest in it is only as the predecessor of the Government post.

Engraving.
Size of sheets.

The stamps of the City Despatch Post were engraved on steel by Rawdon, Wright & Hatch, 48 Merchants Exchange. They were printed on grayish white paper, in sheets of forty-two stamps, seven rows of six stamps each.

Stamps used
provisionally.

It is well-known that these stamps were used provisionally for the service of the United States City Despatch Post, presumably during the preparation of stamps for the latter. The stamps thus used bear the cancellations employed in the New York post office, usually the letters "u s" in an octagon, occasionally a circle with date and the words "NEW YORK" or "U. S. CITY DESPATCH POST." The only dated copy of which I have a memorandum is not on the original cover. It is cancelled "Feb. 15," presumably 1843, but, as usual, the year is not given. This, of course, does not prove that the stamp was not in use at an earlier date.

The stamps measure 18½x22mm.

Imperforate.

Grayish White Wove Paper.

Reference List.

Feb. 15 (1843?)   3 cents black

Manuscript
surcharge.

In the collection of Mr. H. E. Deats there is a copy of this stamp which has the words "*United States*" written across the top in red-violet ink. Nothing is known of the history of this surcharge but its intention is apparent. The letter to which this is attached is dated August 14th, 1842. The cancellation is apparently "Aug. 19th," but examination shows the "9" to be an inverted "6."

Imperforate.

                              Grayish White Wove Paper.

Aug. 16, 1842.   3 cents black.   Surcharge in red-violet

UNITED STATES CITY DESPATCH POST.

Turning to the letter quoted on the preceding page, we cannot fail to observe that the Postmaster General exceeded his authority when he ordered the preparation of stamps, since that is the exclusive prerogative of Congress. It is possible that the "stamps" to which he referred were the hand stamps used to cancel letters and indicate postage paid; in which case it was the Postmaster of New York who overstepped the limits of authority. A careful examination of certain facts leads me to the conclusion that the matter had been thoroughly considered and discussed previous to the writing of this letter, that the accessories therein ordered had already been purchased, and that, so far as they were concerned, the letter was a mere formality. The principal confirmation of this statement is found in dated cancellations. It is generally understood that the service was put in operation on August 1st, 1842, and I have seen a copy of the stamp cancelled "August 5th, 1842." It will be evident, at a glance, that this order, made in Washington on the 1st, could not have been carried into effect in New York by the 5th, unless the stamps had been previously prepared.

Authority exceeded. (margin note)

Preparations made in advance of formal orders. (margin note)

The following circular was first reproduced in the *American Journal of Philately* for February, 1872 :

UNITED STATES CITY DESPATCH POST.

Hours of delivery every day (Sunday excepted) at the principal office, upper P. O., Park, and lower P. O., Merchant's Exchange.

Letters deposited before 8, 12, 3, and at the stations before 7, 11 and 2, will be sent out for delivery at 9, 1 and 4.

Letters to be sent free must have a free stamp attached to them, which can be purchased at the upper and lower post offices and at all the stations. The charge will be 36 cents per dozen. 2 dols 50 cents per hundred. All letters intended to be sent forward to the General Post-office for the inland mails must have a free stamp attached to them. Letters not having a free stamp will be charged 3 cents on delivery.

JOHN LORIMER GRAHAM, P. M.

NEW YORK, June, 1843.

Official circular. (margin note)

This circular is again printed in an article in the *American Journal of Philately* for April, 1877. The writer calls attention to its previous publication and the date and adds : "We afterwards obtained a very large card bearing precisely the same matter, but dated sometime in 1842, this was evidently issued simultaneously with the stamps."

The circular was also printed in the Manual of the Common Council of the City of New York for 1842-43, with the addition of an almost verbatim reproduction of the paragraphs in Greig's circular which related to registration and the advantages claimed for the undertaking (see *Philatelic Journal of America*, Vol. V, page 127), and with this further addition :

Additions to the circular. (margin note)

" Limits, U. S. City Despatch Post will extend to Twenty-second Street.

An additional number of sworn carriers have been employed to carry city letters wholly independent of letters received by the mails."

The stamps were engraved on steel by Rawdon, Wright & Hatch, and are said to have been in sheets of one hundred. The paper varies in color and quality. At first it was of moderate thickness and colored through. **Engraving.** This was soon changed for a thick paper, slightly glazed on the surface and **Size of sheets.** **Paper.** usually not colored through or only lightly tinted. This paper sometimes appears to be ribbed. The paper longest in use was highly glazed and colored on the surface only. The shades are numerous, especially on the paper last described. Size: 18½x22mm.

Wove Paper, Colored Through.   **Reference List.**

3 cents black on rosy-buff

Aug. 5, 1842.—Sept. 1, 1842. 3 cents black on gray-blue, dull gray-blue
3 cents black on pale green

Thick Wove Paper, Glazed and Surface-Colored.

Feb. 22, 1842.—Oct. 24, 1846. 3 cents black on light blue, blue, bright blue, deep blue, dark blue, pale greenish blue, greenish blue

July 4, 1843.—July 23, 1845. 3 cents black on bluish green, green, dark green, olive-green

Variety :

3 cents black on greenish blue, green. Double impression

Several of the older writers mention copies of this stamp printed in violet. As the color was dropped from the catalogues many years ago, it was probably found not to exist.

On at least two occasions the stamps of the United States City Des- **Stamps used to pay** patch Post were used to pay regular postage to other cities. This is proved by **regular postage.** original covers bearing the stamps. The first of these is addressed to Phila- delphia and bears five of the stamps. On holding the cover to a strong light there can be seen, written on the paper underneath the stamps :

"Paid 3 cents for City Despatch
12½ for Philadelphia. Paid "

The stamps are cancelled " U. S." in an octagon, as usual. On the cover are the circular date stamp " New York, May 30 " and the word "PAID", both in red. There are also the figures " 12 " in dark blue ink, apparently written by the mailing clerk. The second cover is similar to the first. It is addressed to Ridgefield, Conn., and bears three stamps, underneath which is written "Paid 10c." The cancellations are like those just described, the date being June 13th, and the written figures " 10." It is unfortunate that neither cover bears anything to show the year in which it was used.

It will be noticed that the written figures and the amount of the postage stamps do not exactly agree but such discrepancies appear to have been lightly regarded at that period Even the official circular offers 3 cent stamps at 2½ cents each, when purchased by the hundred.

Change in rates. By Act of Congress, approved March 3rd, 1845, the rate for drop letters was reduced to two cents. Carriers were allowed to charge a like amount. We do not know what steps, if any, were taken in the city of New York to meet this reduction. Indeed, to judge by the numerous three cent stamps of the United States City Despatch Post to be found on letters dated in 1845 and 1846, it would appear that the old rates were maintained. Possibly an effort in the direction of a reduction may be indicated by a stamp, formerly in the collection of Mr. F. W. Hunter, which is here illustrated.

The stamp is on the original letter, which is dated February 14th, 1846. The surcharged numeral and the bar over the word " THREE " are in A provisional surcharge. red, of the same shade as the cancellations. There are two cancellations : first, the usual circle with the name of the post, date and hour ; second, another circle with the words " NEW YORK—FEB. 14—2 cts.," the numeral " 2 " being identical with that used for the surcharge.

Reference List. Imperforate.
Thick Glazed Paper, Surface-Colored.

Feb. 14, 1846.   2 cents on 3 cents green. Surcharge in red

It is to be regretted that we have been unable to learn anything of the history of this surcharge.

Counterfeits. There are counterfeits of the stamps of this post but they are not dangerous. They are poorly made by lithography, while the originals are finely engraved on steel. None of the portraits on the counterfeits at all resemble that on the original stamp.

CITY DESPATCH.

Nothing is known of the history of this stamp. The older philatelic

publications assign it to Boston and give 1845 as the year of issue. We now know it to belong among the New York carriers' stamps and to have been Historical. the successor of the United States City Despatch Post. The stamps are roughly typographed, probably from metal clichés reproduced from a wood Description. cut. Size: 19x24½mm. There are no varieties. The number of stamps in a sheet is not known.

Imperforate.
Reference List.

White Wove Paper.

March 13, 1846.   2 cents brown-red

The above date is taken from a cancelled copy of the stamp. Another copy has been seen bearing the date " Dec. 9," but not that of the year.

The counterfeits are lithographed and differ from the originals in many points. They measure 20x26mm., the letters of the inscriptions are too tall, Counterfeits. and the outer line of the oval is equally distant from the frame line at each side, while in the originals it approaches nearer to the line at the left than to that at the right.

U. S. MAIL.

Coster, in 1882, and the *American Journal of Philately*, in 1888, say that the stamps of this type were issued by the Postmaster of New York. By the Act of March 3rd, 1851, the rate for delivery of letters from or to the Reduction of the post office was reduced to one cent each. As we find copies of these stamps carriers' fee. cancelled early in 1849, we must conclude that, in this city, the reduction was made fully two years earlier than the date of the Act referred to. Probably this was brought about by the competition of the local posts.

The stamps are typographed on thick wove paper, colored through, and on thick glazed paper, colored on the surface only   Diameter : 16mm. The stamps are all of one type. The number in a sheet is not known but a Description. block of twenty (four rows of five) has been seen. There exists also a pair of the stamps, one of which is placed semi tête-bêche to the other, *i. e.* sideways. This pair is on buff glazed paper. The same variety may occur on the other papers but it has not been reported.

Imperforate.
Reference List.

Thick Wove Paper, Colored Through.

Feb. 13, 1849.—Sept. 12, 1849. 1 cent black on pale dull rose, dull rose, rose

Thick Wove Paper, Glazed and Surface-Colored.

Dec. 8, 1849.—June 1, 1853. 1 cent black on buff, brownish buff
Sept. 16, 1850 —Aug. 13, 1851. 1 cent black on yellow, bright yellow

.

Variety :

1 cent black on buff.   Semi tête-bêche

I have seen a cover bearing three of the yellow stamps, which apparently paid the regular postage.   The letter was mailed in New York city on July 24th, 1851, and was addressed to Newburgh, N. Y.

There are two counterfeits of these stamps which are quite well made. The first is hand-stamped, is 17mm. in diameter and many of the letters are too broad, especially those in "ONE CENT".   The second counterfeit is typographed.   The circles and the letters are too thick, the diameter is 17mm., there is no period after the "U" and the letters are too broad, especially those of the word "ONE".   The yellow glazed paper is very like that of the original stamps.   The other two colors are not well imitated.

THE PHILADELPHIA CARRIERS' STAMPS.

Of the history of the carriers' stamps used in the city of Philadelphia we know nothing. For many years the stamps have been accepted by philatelists as belonging among the semi-official carriers' stamps and the manner in which they were used appears to confirm this conclusion. But, beyond what may be learned from examination of the stamps, we have little information. All the stamps bear the letters "U. S. P. O." and were at one time believed to be issues of the *Union Square Post Office*, a local post of New York city. After it was discovered that the stamps emanated from Philadelphia and belonged among the carriers' stamps, it was decided that the letters were the initials of the words "UNITED STATES POST OFFICE", which is probably correct.

```
U. S.P.O.
PAID.
L1 CenLP
```

Type-set stamps with the value and certain letters in the lower part. The letters are: "H", "S", "L P" and "L S". In the *American Journal of Philately* for February, 1889 (page 57), there is listed a variety with the letters "L H" but this was probably intended for the variety with the letter "H" only. There are a number of varieties of setting for each letter or pair of letters. I have seen five varieties with the letter "H", one with "S", two with "L P", and five with "L S". It is believed that all these varieties, and probably others, occurred in one setting. But we have not seen any fragments of sheets, or even a pair, to assist in confirming this theory. The number of stamps in a sheet and the manner in which the varieties were arranged are, therefore, yet to be ascertained.

Letters on the stamps.

The purpose of these letters has never been satisfactorily explained. I venture to suggest that they are the initials of the carriers on whose routes they were employed. It is evident from the dates of the cancellations that the different varieties were in use at the same time. As the carriers were not paid a fixed salary but only for the letters they handled, it would be necesssry that the stamps used by them should be marked in some way, in order that each might receive proper credit and compensation. Hence the initials. In subsequent issues the same end was attained by using stamps printed on paper of different colors or in inks of various colors. Reference to the preceding chapters will show that, in other cities, carriers' stamps of

Meaning of the letters.

different designs or printed on different papers were used concurrently. In all these instances the object was, doubtless, to secure a division of the carriers' fees, in accordance with the work performed by each.

Earliest cancellation. In the collection of a New York philatelist there is a copy of this stamp, bearing the letters " L S " and cancelled " M—18, 1849 ". Beyond the initial letter, the month is illegible. It must be March or May. Accepting the latter, this is the earliest known cancellation on any of the lettered stamps.

These stamps are printed on thick, soft, rose-colored paper and measure about 15½x11½mm.

Reference List.

Imperforate.

Colored Wove Paper.

May 18, 1849—May 25	1 cent black on rose.	" L S "
	1 cent black on rose.	" L P "
June 16, 1849.	1 cent black on rose.	" S "
July 16, 1850—Aug. 10	1 cent black on rose.	" H "

Counterfeits. There are two counterfeits of these stamps. The first is in imitation of the variety with the letters " L P ". It measures 14½x11½mm The frame lines are much too thin and there is no period after " CENT ". The letters of " PAID " are only 1¾mm. high, instead of 2¼mm. They are also narrower and set a little closer together than on the genuine stamps. The color of the paper is usually too pale. The second counterfeit is not nearly so dangerous. It is in imitation of the varieties lettered " L P " and " L S " and is printed on thin lilac-rose paper. It is 16½mm. long and varies in height from 9¼ to 10mm. The letters of the inscriptions are all too short and too heavy faced.

Description. Type-set stamps, of similar design to those just described but without the letters in the lower corners. It is not known whether or not these stamps formed part of the setting of those with the letters but, from the fact that the stamps on blue, vermilion and yellow paper are only known without the letters, it is inferred that they are from another setting. From the postmarks we conclude that the stamps from the two settings were in use coincidently. The stamps measure 15½x11½mm. and are printed on a variety of papers. The rose-colored paper is thick and soft and is colored through. The other papers are glazed and colored on the surface only. Seven varieties of this setting are known. The sheets probably contain from ten to twenty-five stamps.

Reference List.

Imperforate.

Thick Wove Paper, Colored Through.

May 14, 1849.	1 cent black on rose, dull rose

Thick Wove Paper, Glazed and Surface-Colored.

May 11, 185c—Dec. 19, 1850.	1 cent black on blue, dark blue
	1 cent black on vermilion
	1 cent black on yellow

The *American Journal of Philately* for 1889 (pages 56 and 57), gives a reference list of the Philadelphia carriers' stamps, which includes this stamp in black on white paper. As no such variety appears in subsequent lists we may infer that it was found not to exist. It was probably confounded with one of the varieties of the stamp next to be described.

So far as I am aware, there are no counterfeits which sufficiently **Counterfeits.** resemble the genuine stamps to merit description.

Lithographed in color on a variety of papers. Apparently each stamp in the sheet differs from the others. I have recognized sixteen varieties. It is possible that some of them may be due to defective printing but, on the **Description.** other hand, I have seen a number of copies of most of them, which would indicate that the varieties are constant. It has been said that the sheet contained twenty or twenty-five stamps but I have not been able to confirm the statement. A vertical strip of three and a horizontal pair—the latter with margin from the right of the sheet—are all that I have seen, otherwise than singly.

The *American Journal of Philately* for 1889, says the stamps were engraved on wood and others have called them type-set and typographed. It is probable that the writers were led to these conclusions by the variations in **Method of** the relative positions of the inscriptions and ornaments to each other and to **production.** the surrounding frame. But a careful examination of the stamps shows them to be lithographed. The differences in position of the component parts were caused by transferring each part separately, instead of the design as a whole. None of these stamps are common, but those most often seen are printed in gold bronze on black, surface-colored paper. This paper is highly glazed and has a purple sheen when held to the light. Size: 19½x15½mm.

Imperforate.   **Reference List.**

White Wove Paper.

Mch. 18, 1850.—Oct. 8, 1852.   1 cent dull blue, dark dull blue
Aug. 5, 1852.—Dec. 15, 1852.   1 cent black

Thick Wove Paper, Glazed and Surface-Colored.

Mch. 31, 1851.—Dec. 13, 1851.   1 cent gold on black

The older philatelic publications list this stamp in black on blue paper. I have not been able to locate a copy and have reached the conclusion that the stamp which they intended to describe was that printed in blue on white paper, which latter they do not mention.

There are at least four counterfeits of these stamps. One may be easily recognized by having a period after the "o" in the upper label and the serif of the "1" pointing to the left. In all the genuine stamps the serif is **Counterfeits.** turned toward the right. On each of the other counterfeits there are two

short and nearly vertical dashes below the "o" of "u. s. p. o." As some of
the genuine stamps have two dots in nearly the same position, this cannot be
regarded as a positive test and any doubtful specimens should be compared
with photographic reproductions of the original varieties.

TYPE I.   TYPE II.

We have now to consider two hand-stamps which are certainly very
puzzling. In addition to the fact that they are of some considerable degree of
rarity, they appear to have been used, at different times, as adhesive stamps,
envelope stamps and postmarks. It is not always possible to decide for
which of the last two purposes they were used. This confusion is largely
due to the irregular manner in which they were hand-stamped on the envelopes. Type I is usually applied at the left side, sometimes in the upper corner but more often in a position about equally distant from the upper and
lower edges. Type II is commonly placed near the middle of the upper
side and occasionally in the upper right corner. Collectors in Philadelphia
have advanced the theory that people, when intending to use these envelopes,
took them to the post office and had them stamped, paying one cent each
for the impressions. The work was probably done hastily, which would account for the irregular positions of the hand-stamps.

Various uses of the designs.

There is in the Tapling collection an unused, unaddressed envelope,
stamped with type I, which may be accepted as corroborative evidence that
stamped envelopes were prepared from this design.

It is said that when type II was used to make adhesive stamps, it was
always impressed on the margins of the one cent stamps of the regular issue
of 1851. I have never seen the adhesives of this type on any other paper
but am not prepared to assert that they were never made otherwise. I have
also seen a letter, dated July 18th, 1856, bearing a one cent stamp of the
1851 issue, which was cancelled with type II, the cancellation being partly
on the stamp and partly on the envelope.

Adhesive stamps of type II.

The stamps of type I measure 21x17mm., those of type II, 27x18½
mm. They are hand-stamped on various papers, in blue, red and black ink.
Blue was commonly used for type I, black for the adhesive stamps of type
II, and red for the envelopes. Coster says the red color was used for
letters on which the fee was paid at the time they were deposited in the post
office. The limited number of copies, especially those with dated cancellations, and the absence of information concerning these stamps, does not
permit us even to venture a theory regarding the colors. They may have
been employed for different carriers, they may mark different periods of use,
or they may have been used at convenience and indicate nothing.

Colors.

The paper is usually wove. Most of the buff envelopes have a strong
tinge of orange and some might call them by the latter name. A copy of

type II has been seen on gray paper, so thick as to be almost cardboard. **Paper.** The catalogues have long listed an envelope of this type, stamped in blue on buff paper. I have not been able to confirm the existence of this envelope but, as I am equally unable to disprove it, I do not feel warranted in refusing to list it.

Information about the dates of use of these stamps is sadly lacking. The cancellations usually have only the month and day. The *American Journal of Philately* for March, 1891 (page 132) gives the date of type I as **Dates of use.** 1851. The *Philatelic Monthly and World* for March, 1892 (page 23) places type II at 1852-53, which date is also given by Coster. The only two dates which I have been able to secure are included in the following list:

ADHESIVE STAMPS.   **Reference List.**

Imperforate.

Various Papers.

1 cent blue on buff.	Type I
1 cent blue on blue	"
1 cent red on white	"
1 cent black on white.	Type II
1 cent black on gray	"

ENVELOPES.

Various Papers.

	1 cent blue on buff.	Type I
	1 cent blue on blue	"
	1 cent red on buff	"
	1 cent blue on buff	Type II
Mch. 31, 1856.	1 cent black on buff	"
	1 cent black on blue	"
	1 cent black on white	"
	1 cent red on buff	"
	1 cent red on blue	"
July 5, 1852.	1 cent red on white	"

Type I is often cancelled with the small red star which was extensively used as a cancellation for the Philadelphia carriers' stamps and also for the Government carrier (Eagle) issued November 17th, 1851, and to be described **Cancellations.** in a subsequent chapter. Another cancellation closely resembles the stamps of type II. It may be known by the inscription "U. S. P. O. DESPATCH" which is in Roman capitals, while on the stamps it is in sans-serif capitals. Envelopes bearing this cancellation mark are sometimes offered for sale as carriers' envelopes and unscrupulous people have even gone so far as to cut these marks from envelopes and affix them to others, that they might appear to have been used as adhesives.

The *Philatelic Monthly and World* for September, 1898, chronicles an envelope which has, at the left side, a stamp of type I printed in blue and cancelled with the red star, and, in the upper right corner, a stamp of type II impressed in red. The description does not specify whether the latter is the cancellation mark or the device used to indicate postage prepaid.

WELLS, FARGO & CO.'S PONY EXPRESS STAMPS.

The pony express has always been a subject of interest, both to the student of history and the ordinary reader. Its conception and management were bold, daring, spectacular—thoroughly in keeping with the men, the life and the phenomenal development of the great west. It existed in a history-making epoch and itself helped to make history. As an exhibition of American pluck and nerve, it appeals to all admirers of large ideas and bold deeds.

In *Filatelic Facts and Fallacies*, volumes II and III, we find a number of interesting articles on the origin and management of the pony express. These articles are from the pen of Mr. H. B. Phillips—widely known as a writer and authority on western franks—and from them the following extracts have been selected :

The original pony express. "It is popularly supposed that Wells, Fargo & Co. started the original Pony Express, but such is not the case. Wells, Fargo & Co. operated the Pony express in 1861, but with that of 1860 they had nothing to do.

John S. Jones, a government freighter, and William H. Russell (of the firm of Russell, Majors & Waddell, also government freighters to Salt Lake in 1857-58), started a stage and express line between Leavenworth and Denver, via the Smoky Hill route, in the spring of 1859, which they operated during that summer. The following winter the firm was re-organized, absorbing the John Hockaday line, operating between St. Joseph and Salt Lake City, and was styled 'The Central Overland California and Pike's Peak Express Company,' with William H. Russell as President. This is the company that organized and operated the original Pony Express of 1860. * * *

After months of preparation in establishing stations, procuring riders and relays of horses, at last, on April 3rd, 1860, at four o'clock P. M., the first express was simultaneously dispatched from both ends of the run—San Francisco and St. Joseph, Mo.

The following advertisement, from the *Evening Bulletin* of April 1st, is an official record of the established rates of postage, it being understood that they carried nothing whatever but letters :

'The Central Overland Pony Express Company will start their letter express f om San Francisco to New York and ii.termediate points on Tuesday, April 3rd.

Letters will be charged, between San Francisco and Salt Lake City, $3.00 for each half ounce and under, and at that rate according to weight. To all points beyond Salt Lake City, $5.co for each half ounce and under, and at that rate according to weight. All letters must be enclosed in stamped envelopes.

Wm. W. Finney, Agent, San Francisco.

In this connection the term 'stamped envelopes' does not mean, as at the present time, the envelopes made by the Government, but that all letters offered for transmission should be prepaid with the Government rate of postage, an adhesive stamp on the envelope being included in the term 'stamped envelopes.'

No adhesive stamps were prepared or used by this company, either for sale to the public or for the purpose of collecting postage. Hand stamps were placed in use at both ends of the line, following the usual custom of Western expresses at that time.   *   *   *

The Pony made the time promised for it and carried the letters and news, but the projectors were never compensated in money for their outlay.   As an undertaking it was a success, but financially it was a failure.

The cost of establishing and maintaining the Pony Express was enormous.   Relays of horses were kept at each station and riders employed at every third station and, as the country produced nothing at that time, all supplies had to be hauled by wagon from the Missouri river, Utah or California.

The newspapers were its principal patrons.   The California press depended entirely upon the Pony Express for news, until the completion of the overland telegraph line in the fall of 1861.   *   *   *

The letters were wrapped in oil silk for protection against wet, but that did not avail when swimming swollen streams.   Occasionally hostile Indians chased the pony.   On one occasion the rider was shot and scalped, the horse escaping with the 'machillas,' and months afterwards they were found and the inclosed letters forwarded to their destinations.

The express carrying the news of Abraham Lincoln's election went through from St. Joseph to Denver, 665 miles, in two days and twenty-one hours.   The riders usually rode about seventy-five miles, but an instance is remembered where one rode nearly 300 miles, those who should have relieved him being, for some reason or another, disabled.   He made it in schedule time, too, but at the end had to be lifted from the saddle, almost dead.   The distance from St. Joseph to S·cramento was about 1,900 miles and was covered in eight days. Think of that, for horse and human flesh and blood to do !

The pony rider was usually a little bit of a man, brim full of spirit and endurance. *   *   *   Both horse and rider went flying light, the rider carried no arms but a revolver, and nothing that was not absolutely necessary.   He rode a splendid horse that was born for a racer, with a skeleton saddle, lightly shod or not at all.   There were about eighty riders in the saddle all the time, night and day, stretching in a long, scattering, fleeting procession from Missouri to California—forty flying eastward and forty to the west—using some four hundred horses continuously."

The breaking out of the war of the rebellion necessitated some changes in transporting the mails between the eastern states and the Pacific coast. These changes are briefly described in the report of the Postmaster General, dated December 2nd, 1861 :

OVERLAND CALIFORNIA MAIL.

"By the 9th section of an Act of Congress approved March 2, 1861, entitled ' An Act making appropriations for the service of the Post Office Department during the fiscal year ending June 30, 1862', authority is given to the Postmaster General to discontinue the mail service on the southern overland route (known as the Butterfield route) between St. Louis and Memphis and San Francisco, and to provide for the conveyance, by the same parties, of a six-times-a-week mail by the 'central route'; that is, 'from some point on the Missouri River, connecting with the east, to Placerville, California.' *(margin: Changes in mail routes and contracts.)*

In pursuance of this Act, and the acceptance of its terms by the mail company, an order was made on the 12th of March, 1861, to modify the present contract, so as to discontinue service on the southern route, and to provide for the transportation of the entire letter mail six times a week on the central route, to be carried through in twenty days eight months in the year, and in twenty-three days four months in the year, from St. Joseph, Missouri (or Atchison, Kansas) to Placerville, and also to convey the entire mail three times a week to Denver City and Salt Lake ; the entire letter mail to California to be carried, whatever may be its weight, and in case it should not amount to 600 pounds, then sufficient of other mail to be carried each trip to make up that weight, and the residue of all mail matter to be conveyed in thirty-five days, with the privilege of sending it from New York to San Francisco in twenty-five days by sea, and the public documents in thirty-five days ; a pony express to be run twice a week until the completion of the overland telegraph, through in ten days eight months and twelve days four months, in the year, conveying for the Government, free of charge, five pounds of mail matter; the compensation for the whole service to be one million of dollars per annum, payable from the general treasury, as provided by the act ; the service to commence July 1, 1861, and terminate July 1, 1864. *(margin: Pony express.)*

The transfer of stock from the southern to the central route was commenced about the 1st of April, and was completed so that the first mail was started from St. Joseph on the day prescribed by the order, July 1, 1861."

The portion of the above mentioned act which refers to the pony express is especially interesting to philatelists.   It reads :

"They shall also be required, during the continuance of their contract, or until the

Tariff on private correspondence. completion of the Overland Telegraph, to run a Pony Express ; semi-weekly, at a schedula-tion of ten days eight months, and twelve days four months, carrying for the Government, free of charge, five pounds of mail matter, with the liberty of charging the public for trans-portation of letters by said Express not exceeding one dollar per half ounce. '

Stamps. Our interest lies in the last clause, since, by reason of it, the pony express stamps were issued and through it they claim a place among the semi-official carriers. Though the act does not, in so many words, authorize the contractors to issue stamps, it most distinctly authorizes the carrying of letters and fixes the rate of postage that may be charged. The manner in which payment of this charge should be indicated was a matter of detail to be left to the managers of the express. It may also be remarked that no objection was ever made to the employment of the stamps.

The following advertisement appeared in the San Francisco daily papers of July 1st, 1861 :

Advertisement.

> " Wells, Fargo's Pony Express service will commence July 1st, 1861, between Placerville and San Francisco, connecting at Placerville with the Overland Mail Co's Pony Express.
> Letters must be enclosed in our 20c Govt. Franked Envelopes and charges beyond Placer-ville prepaid at the rate of $1 00 per ½oz. or fraction. All letters not enclosed in Govt. Franked Envelopes will be charged 25c each.
> WELLS, FARGO & Co.''

The Overland Mail Co. held the contract for the "central route." I have not been able to learn the exact relations, at that date, between that company and Wells, Fargo & Co., but I believe that the latter were sub-con-tractors to the former.

Whether the pony express stamps were used from both ends of the route or only from the California end, is another point on which definite information is lacking.

Description. The stamps were lithographed by Britton & Rey, of San Francisco. There were two designs, the so-called garter type and the well-known pony express stamps. The former are 15½mm. in diameter and the latter measure 21x24¼mm. I cannot say which variety was first in use but I believe the garter type to have been.

Reference List. Imperforate.

Thin White Wove Paper.

July 1, 1861.   1 dollar deep blue, dark dull blue

Imperforate.

White Wove Paper.

1 dollar deep rose, carmine-rose
2 dollars deep gray-green
4 dollars black, gray-black

The first printing of the pony stamps was on quite thick paper. The paper of the later printings varies from ordinary to thin. It is said that only **Paper and gum.** the stamps of the first printing were gummed and that subsequent printings were issued ungummed.

On the completion of the overland telegraph line, in October, 1861, the contract for pony express service terminated. By a circular, dated October 26th, 1861, the company announced to its agents the discontinuance **Stamps withdrawn** of the service and called in all the stamps remaining unsold. At a subsequent **and subsequently** date the stamps were re-issued and used for the business of the express com- **re-issued.** pany but they were, of course, no longer government carriers' stamps. The ten and twenty-five cent stamps were then added to the series, but with them we have no concern.

The leading collectors of the United States locals and franks have been consulted but they are unable to say whether or not the two dollars rose and four dollars green stamps were issued between July 1st and October 26th, **Change in colors.** 1861. As such a change of colors would appear to be unnecessary and con- fusing, the consensus of opinion is that they probably were not issued until a subsequent date. Pending more definite information they are not listed here.

The garter stamps were printed in sheets (or panes) of sixteen, four rows of four stamps each. Copies are frequently found with a pen mark in red ink. This is not believed to be a cancellation but to have been applied **Counterfeits of the** to some unused remainders to destroy their franking power. So far as known, **garter stamps.** these stamps have not been reprinted but they have been quite extensively counterfeited. The counterfeits differ from the genuine stamps in a number of minor details, such as a period instead of a comma between "WELLS" and "FARGO". The mark by which they may be readily distinguished is a hori- zontal dash between "½ oz." and "$1.00" This dash is not found on the original stamps. We occasionally see genuine copies on which such a dash has been drawn with pen and ink. Probably this was done to make them conform to the illustrations in the catalogues, which, for many years, were modeled after the counterfeits.

The pony stamps were printed in panes of twenty, five rows of four stamps each. Two panes constituted a sheet.

There was a considerable quantity of remainders of most of the values, but, rumors to the contrary notwithstanding, there is no evidence that any reprints were made until about the first of April, 1897. A son of Mr. Joseph **Reprints of the pony** Britton (a member of the firm of Britton & Rey, makers of the pony express **express stamps.** stamps and many California locals), became interested in stamp collecting. His father wished to aid him with his collection and made search for samples of the firm's work in that line, but found none. He then sought for the stones from which the different stamps had been printed and eventually found

.

the original dies of the pony express stamps. These dies consisted of the complete design for the one dollar stamp, the frame for the ten cents and the numerals for the other values, including a " 3 " which was never used. The design for the one dollar stamp had the value in the plural. In making up the stone for the originals of this value the final " s " was removed, with the exception of a small piece which makes a sort of period after the word. On many copies of the stamp traces of the outlines of the letter may be seen.

These die designs were on a stone with a number of other small designs, some of which had been in frequent use. As a consequence, the designs for the pony express stamps had become much worn and some of the finer lines were nearly obliterated. In an effort to remedy this, the dies were retouched Because of to this wearing and retouching, the reprints may be easily distinguished from the originals. Some of the principal points by which the former may be recognized are : The crown of the hat is almost white, instead of being shaded. There is no shading at the left of the nose of the horse. The hoof is separated from the right forefoot. The mouth of the horse is open nearly half way up to the eye, while in the originals the lips are only slightly apart. Diagonal lines have been added to the shading between the forelegs and under the body of the horse. At the right of the scroll containing the word "DOLLARS" there are fourteen lines of shading instead of eleven. On the ten and twenty-five cent stamps the faint white arabesques in the upper corners are missing. On the two and four dollars the word of value is followed by a period, which does not occur on the originals.

By transfers from the retouched dies a new stone was made up, containing twenty stamps, in five vertical rows of four. All the stamps in each vertical row were the same. Beginning at the right they were : 10, 25 cents, 1, 2 and 4 dollars. From this stone impressions were taken in colors approximating those of the original stamps. As a result, we have not only reprints but various combinations of colors and values of which there were no originals and which, therefore, are merely fancy articles.

The paper of the reprints is moderately thin, soft and very white. They are clearly printed and look very fresh and new. The inks are apparently aniline. It is said that when Mr. Britton applied to Wells, Fargo & Co. for the loan of a set of the pony express stamps, to be used as a guide to colors, he was given a set of counterfeits, as they were in a more available shape and in approximately, the same colors as the originals. Whatever may have been the cause, the colors are not very well imitated. While we are only interested in the reprints of the three varieties which were used as carriers' stamps, it may be well, for the sake of completeness, to describe all of them. The numbers in parenthesis indicate the number of reprints made of each stamp.

Imperforate.

White Wove Paper.

April 1897.

10 cents brownish bistre (92)

25 cents pale vermilion (112), brown-carmine (132)

25 cents dull blue (116)

1 dollar pale vermilion (112), brown-carmine (132)

2 dollars gray-green (108)

2 dollars pale vermilion (112,) brown-carmine (132)

4 dollars full black (116)

4 dollars gray-green (108)

In the prints in blue and black we find that the one dollar stamp has the word of value in the plural. Presumably, these printings were made before the error in the die was noticed but, it being observed, the stone was corrected before the impressions in the other colors were made.

On the whole the reprints are not very deceptive. A curious point is that they are very evidently lithographs, while the originals have more the appearance of steel engravings.

It is satisfactory to know that the stone from which the reprints were made has been cleaned off and the original die has been deposited in the historical museum of Wells, Fargo & Co. So we need have no apprehension of further reprintings.

There are a number of counterfeits of these stamps. The majority of them are too poor to need description. The better counterfeits differ in many points from the genuine stamps. The letters of "WELLS, FARGO & Co." are too thin ; the tail of the horse is too straight and stiff ; the foot of the rider is too small and stands out from instead of touching the body of the horse. Perhaps the most notable difference is found in the edges of the escutcheon which contains the vignette. These edges are turned over and form points at the corners ; in the counterfeits the points meet at the upper left corner, and at the upper right corner they nearly touch, whereas, in the genuine stamps there is quite a space between the points at both corners.

Counterfeits of the pony express stamps.

THE FRANKLIN CARRIERS' STAMP.

By referring to page 65 it will be seen that, by Act of Congress, approved March 3rd, 1851, the Postmaster General was authorized to prepare

Legislation affecting the carrier service. postage stamps of such denominations as he considered expedient; the carrier's fee was fixed at one cent per letter; and the streets, avenues, roads and public highways of the cities of New York, Boston, Philadelphia and New Orleans were established as post routes and letter carriers appointed for service thereon.

This would appear to constitute the first determined effort on the part of the Post Office Department to take the carrier service into its own hands. In pursuance of this intention, and by the authority conveyed in the act mentioned above, a carriers' stamp was issued on September 29th, 1851. This stamp is officially described as follows:

"ONE CENT CARRIER STAMP.—Profile bust of Franklin, looking to the left, on an oval disk, with very dark ground and a distinct white border.

Design and color. Around this disk is a tesselated frame, separated at the four corners by lathe-work rosettes, similar to those in the 12-cent stamp. In straight panels, at the top and bottom of this frame, are the words 'CARRIERS' and 'STAMP', respectively, a white star on a dark circle being at the beginning and end of each word. The whole is enclosed in a fine single-line rectangle. Color, indigo-blue, on rose-colored paper. The denomination is not shown."

Paper. The stamps were printed on a soft paper, of moderate thickness and colored a dull rose.

I have never seen an unused copy with original gum but I presume

Gum. the stamps had the thick, smooth, brown gum which was used on the other stamps of the issues of 1851 and 1857.

The stamps are imperforate and measure 19½x24½mm.

Imperforate.

Rose Wove Paper.

Sept. 29th, 1851.   (1 cent) bright blue, dull blue, dark dull blue

The date of issue is taken from official records. From the same source we learn that the Franklin stamp was replaced by the "Eagle" car-

Period of use. riers' stamp on November 17th, 1851. It does not appear, however, to have been declared obsolete, but remained available for postage. Copies on the original cover are scarce and the postmarks seldom have the year, but only the month and day. The only complete date which I have seen is April 1st, 1854.

It is said that in the records of the Post Office department it is stated: "First carriers' stamps received from contractors Oct. 21, 1851, 300,000" Here is, obviously, a mistake. Probably the date should be Sept. 21, 1851.

The reports of the Postmaster General do not supply any statistics of the quantities of this stamp distributed to postmasters but there appears to have been only the one delivery of 300,000 copies to the Post Office depart- *Number of stamps issued.* ment. If this entire quantity was distributed to postmasters it is to be doubted that all of the stamps were issued to the public. The scarcity of copies would lead us to conclude that only a limited number were used. Probably, on the appearance of the "Eagle" stamp, the remainders were returned to Washington and destroyed.

There was only one plate for this stamp. It contained two panes of one hundred stamps (ten rows of ten stamps each), placed side by side and separated by a single vertical line. The imprint of the contractors appeared *Plate and Imprint.* at each side, about 3mm from the stamps. It read: "Toppan, Carpenter, Casilear & Co. BANK NOTE ENGRAVERS. Phila. New York. Boston & Cincinnati". The plate was not numbered.

The sheets of reprints show the plate to have been damaged at some time. In the second horizontal row there is a large crack extending across eight stamps, four on each side of the line which divides the two panes. This *Plate damaged.* crack was probably made in heating the plate for printing. Had it occurred in the course of manufacture it is safe to conclude that the plate would have been abandoned and another made to replace it.

It is understood that this stamp was used only in the cities of Boston, New Orleans, New York and Philadelphia.

A strip of three cancelled copies has been seen. This is supposed to have been used instead of a three cent stamp to pay the regular postage.

We occasionally see copies of the Franklin and "Eagle" carriers' stamps which are printed in brown-orange on a hard white paper, known as "bond" paper. In the case of the latter design these have always been con- *Impressions in brown-orange.* sidered to be proofs. But for the former a much more pretentious position has been claimed. I am certainly at a loss to understand why one should be held in any more esteem than the other, or than proofs of the two stamps in this same color on India paper. Nor do I see any reason for regarding it with more favor than proofs of other stamps of the same date on bond paper, for instance the five cents of the 1851 issue, in various trial colors.

The favor in which the brown-orange Franklin stamp has been held can probably be ascribed to the following circumstance. In 1869, Dr. H. C. Yarrow, a well-known philatelist of that period, addressed some inquiries to the Post Office Department at Washington. In reply he received the following letter from W. M. Ireland, chief-clerk to the Third Assistant Postmaster General, (See *American Journal of Philately*, August 20th, 1869, page 93):

POST OFFICE DEPARTMENT.

WASHINGTON, August 10, 1869.
MY DEAR SIR :—Yours referring to "carriers' stamp" has come to hand. The following is as near a description of it as can be made: Head of Franklin, looking to left;

Official letter in
reference to the
brown-orange
stamp. frame oval geometrical lathe work ; ornamental multirayed stars at corners.   The word
" Carriers " in straight line at top of stamp ; the word " Stamp " in straight line at lower
margin.   A five-pointed star at each end of the words, in brackets. Color " *Orange 'Brown.*"
Typographed in color on white paper.   Shape upright rectangular.   Proofs were issued
printed in blue on pink paper ; also in green and yellow.   It was issued about Sept. 29,
1851, but was suppressed almost immediately, owing to its great similarity to the then three
cent stamp. . Only about 300,000 were ever issued   There is but one specimen, a cancelled
one, now in possession of the Department. I regret there are none, else you should be
supplied. The plate was, according to our best information, destroyed after the stamps
were suppressed.

Truly yours,
W. M. IRELAND.

Upon this mass of misstatements has been based the claim that the
original color of this stamp was brown-orange and that the copies in blue on
rose-colored paper represent a second printing.

Who has ever seen a *proof* of this stamp in blue on pink paper ?

The statement as to the number that were issued is doubtless derived
from the record of 300,000 copies delivered by the contractors. The impro-
bability of so many stamps having been issued has already been mentioned.

There may have been a cancelled copy of the brown-orange stamp in
the possession of the Post Office Department at the time this letter was
written but to-day the official collection contains nothing better than a reprint
in blue on rose paper.

As the plate was in existence until August, 1897, the value of the
writer's " best information " on that point is small.

The statement that the stamp was withdrawn on account of its resemblance to the three cent stamp then in current use has been, for many years,
accepted and repeated without question. There is certainly very little resemblance between the two stamps. Had Mr. Ireland said the one cent stamp,
the resemblance in color and design would have been more apparent.

All of which is merely additional proof of the too frequent carelessness
and inaccuracy of official statements.

From the comments of the editor of the *American Journal of Philately*
on the foregoing letter it is evident that he considered the impressions in
brown-orange to be proofs in a trial color. He says :

Editorial comment
on the Franklin
stamp. " We have only been able to see four of these stamps, two of which were blue on pink
paper, and *both were cancelled,* we think by a number of square dots similar to the stamps of
the French Republic. We took both of these from letters ourselves. Another was printed
in orange on India paper, and was obtained by the owner direct from the P. O. Department
at Washington.   The remaining one now lies before us, and is printed in brown of the shade
described in the letter, on similar paper to the 1851 issue U. S. stamps ; it is uncancelled.
The plate from which this one is printed appears to be cracked, the imperfection extending
across the stamp on a line with the chin of Franklin."

The copy on India paper was, of course, a proof. In a previous paragraph I have called attention to the crack in the plate and expressed the
opinion that it marked a late, rather than an early, state of the plate. If my
conclusion is correct it would prove that the impressions in brown-orange were
not the first taken from the plate.

In the *Stamp Collector's Magazine* for May, 1870, the well-known
English collector, Mr. E. L. Pemberton, writes :

" Recently some half dozen of the rare carrier's stamp, head of Franklin, unused, have
appeared ; they are in dark, rather brown yellow, are ungummed, on tough thinnish paper;
whether these are stamps as issued I do not know, but I have received them some time back

as proofs. * * * Did the issue consist of orange-brown (or more properly brown-yellow) on plain paper, and of blue on pink paper, or of the latter only. all others being proofs or specimens? I think the latter, because the unused brown-yellow has been known for years, as existing in the Ph. collection, and by hearsay as described by Levrault (p. 111), heading Baltimore, *brun rouge sur blanc.* As American proof-stamps, or, more correctly speaking, the great majority, have been obtainable at various times, and as the blue on pink, which undoubtedly exists as a *bona-fide* emission, has remained unknown until lately, it is more than probable that the only one issued for postage was the blue on pink, others being proofs or specimens."

Opinion of Mr. E. L. Pemberton.

In addition to all the foregoing we might ask why, if brown-orange was the original color, were not the reprints made in that color?

The only evidence in favor of the brown-orange specimens to which any apparent value attaches is found in the *Illustriertes Briefmarken Journal* for February 2nd, 1895, (page 44) in which a cancelled copy in this color is described. On communicating with the author of the article, Mr. Theodore Haas, he very kindly forwarded the stamp for examination. By a careful scrutiny of the postmark it is possible to discern the letters " EW-ORK ", following a circular line, and below them "FEB 12 ". The cancellation is in red and is evidently part of the familiar postmark which was in use in the city of New York in 1851 and proximate years.

A cancelled copy of the brown-orange stamp.

Beyond doubt, the cancellation is genuine. More than this I am not willing to admit. One swallow does not make a summer and one cancelled copy does not prove a postal issue. I have seen too many cancelled proofs, envelope stamps used as adhesives, fiscals used postally, unauthorized bi-sected stamps, and similar novelties which have passed through the mails by accident or favor, to place much faith in a single example of anything out of the usual.

It may also be remarked that the date of the cancellation, February 12th—it must be 1852 or later—is not sufficiently near to the date of issue to serve as an argument in favor of priority of the brown-orange color.

I am not unwilling to be convinced that the brown-orange stamp is a postage stamp, but the arguments to that effect must be stronger than those which have, thus far, been advanced. Until they are forthcoming, my conclusion must be that the stamp in this color is merely a proof.

The reprints of the Franklin carriers' stamp have been described elsewhere. It does not appear to have tempted the counterfeiters.

THE EAGLE CARRIERS' STAMP.

As has been previously stated, the Franklin carriers' stamp was replaced by one of a new design, after it had been in issue only a few weeks. This change was probably due to the resemblance between the carriers' stamp, and the one cent of the then current series. In the *American Journal of Philately* for August 20th, 1869, we find the following letter concerning the new stamp:

POST OFFICE DEPARTMENT.

FINANCE OFFICE.

July 30th, 1869.

SIR :—Your communication of the 20th instant is received. The blue stamp, '' Eagle,'' was used for prepaying city lettters delivered by carriers. It was issued about Nov. 17, 1851, and was withdrawn January 27th, 1852. It was very little used except in Philadelphia, Pa., and Cincinnati, Ohio.

Very respectfully,

W. H. H. TERRELL*

H. C. YARROW,   Third Asst. P. M. General.

New York.

It is possible that by the date mentioned in this letter (January 27th, 1852), it had been discovered that the one cent stamp of the regular issue could be used for the carriers' fee as well as a special stamp, and that the latter was superfluous. But from the evidence of postmarks we know that the " Eagle " stamps continued in use for many years. Perhaps, however, none were issued to postmasters after the date given.

Mr. Tiffany, in his *History of the Postage Stamps of the United States*, says:

" As a matter of fact, however, the published reports of the Postmaster General, show that there were issued :

4,777,552 from Nov., 1851 up to June, 1852
4,370,383 " June, 1852 " " " 1853
7,103,416 " " 1853 " " " 1854 "

I must confess that I cannot find these figures in my file of reports of the Postmaster General. I do find, however, in the report dated December 1st, 1853, a note of the number of one cent stamps issued in two of these years as follows:

" Fiscal year ending June 30th, 1852, 5,489,242
" " " " 1852, 4,736,311 "

There is nothing to assist us to explain the disagreement in these figures. We might reasonably expect the use of one cent stamps of the regular

---

*By a typographical error the *American Journal of Philately* gives the name of the Third Assistant Postmaster General as " W. H. H. Correll."

issue to greatly exceed that of the carriers' stamps; in which case it is not impossible that Mr. Tiffany's figures are those for the current one cent stamps and that the second table covers both those stamps and the carriers '.

The stamp is thus officially described:

"ONE CENT CARRIER STAMP.—Picture of an eagle on the branch of a tree, poised for flight, looking to the left, on an oval disk, partly filled with clouds and sunrays. Around this disk is a solid band, separated on the right and left sides by a lined panel, and bearing above the words "U. S. P. O. DESPATCH ", and below the words "PRE-PAID ONE CENT ", all in white capitals. Above and below the band, and forming corners to the stamp, are laurel and oak leaves, oak to the left and laurel to the right. Color, indigo blue. This stamp, unlike all other stamps in the series, is of less height than width." *Design and color.*

The stamps were printed on hard white wove paper. The gum varied from yellowish to brown. The sheets were divided by vertical and horizontal lines into rectangles about 23½x19mm.

The stamps were issued imperforate. In the Hunter collection there was a copy, on the original cover, which had a sort of rough pin perforation, probably made with a sewing machine. This perforation is interesting though, of course, unofficial.

Imperforate.

White Wove Paper.

April 13, 1852—Oct. 21, 1859.   1 cent greenish blue, blue, dull blue, dark dull blue, indigo

Variety:

Nov. 9, 1851.   1 cent dark dull blue.   Pin perforated

The plate contained two panes of one hundred stamps (ten rows of ten stamps each), placed one above the other and separated by a space of 11 mm. Through the middle of this space was drawn a thin horizontal line. *Plate and imprint.* The imprint was the same as that on the Franklin carriers' stamp and was placed at the bottom of each pane, about 3mm from the stamps. Most of the impressions do not show any plate number but a few are known which have "No. 1 " below the letters "EN " of "ENGRAVERS", in the imprint of the upper pane. Until very recently it was believed that this number appeared only on the reprints but we now know that it exists on some of the original stamps.

The reprints are described in the chapter devoted to that subject.

There is only one counterfeit that is at all dangerous. It is lithographed, while the originals are finely engraved. It differs from the genuine in *Counterfeits.* many minor details, especially the foliage around the oval. There is also a period instead of a hyphen, between "PRE " and " PAID ". This counterfeit is found both imperforate and perforated.

SPECIAL DELIVERY STAMPS.

While the special delivery stamps are, in a sense, carriers' stamps, it seems best to consider them under a separate heading, for the reason that the ordinary rates of postage now include delivery by carrier, in all places where such a service is in operation, and for the additional reason that the special delivery stamps are intended to prepay an extra and specific service, for which a relatively high fee is charged.

An Act of Congress, approved March 3rd, 1885, provided in part as follows:

Act authorizing the special delivery stamps.

" Sec. 3. That a special stamp of the face valuation of ten cents may be provided and issued, whenever deemed advisable or expedient, in such form and bearing such device as may meet the approval of the Postmaster General, which, when attached to a letter, in addition to the lawful postage thereon, the delivery of which is to be at any free-delivery office, or at any city, town, or village containing a population of four thousand and over, according to the Federal census, shall be regarded as entitling such letter to immediate delivery within the carrier limit of any free-delivery office which may be designated by the Postmaster General as a special-delivery office, or within one mile of the post-office at any other office coming within the provisions of this section which may in like manner be designated as a special-delivery office.

"Sec. 4. That such specially stamped letters shall be delivered from seven o'clock ante meridian up to twelve o'clock midnight at offices designated by the Postmaster General under section three of this Act.

Under the authority of this Act a stamp of a special design was prepared and supplied to 555 post offices. It was issued to the public on October 1st, 1885. The design is thus officially described :

Design.

"TEN CENT SPECIAL DELIVERY. A line engraving on steel, oblong in form; dimensions, 13-16 by 1 7-16 inches; color, dark blue. Design : On the left an arched panel, bearing the figure of a mail messenger boy on a run, and surmounted by the words 'UNITED STATES '; on the right an oblong tablet, ornamented with a wreath of oak and laurel surrounding the words 'SECURES IMMEDIATE DELIVERY AT A SPECIAL DELIVERY OFFICE '. Across the top of the tablet is the legend 'SPECIAL POSTAL DELIVERY ', and at the bottom the words 'TEN CENTS ', separated by a small shield bearing the numeral ' 10 '."

A circular of the Post Office Department, dated August 11th, 1885, included the following instructions to postmasters concerning the special delivery stamps :

" They are to be sold by postmasters in any required amount, and to any person who may apply for them, but they can be used only for the purpose of securing the immediate delivery of letters addressed to and received in the mails at any of the offices designated as special-delivery offices. Under no circumstances are they to be used in the payment of postages of any description or of the registry fee, nor can any other stamps be employed to secure special delivery except the special-delivery stamp. The special-delivery stamp must be in addition to the lawful postage, and letters not prepaid with at least one full rate of postage, in accordance with the law and regulations, must be treated as held for postage, even though bearing a special-delivery stamp.

Registered letters will be entitled to immediate delivery, the same as ordinary letters, when bearing a special-delivery stamp in addition to the full postage and registry fee required by the law and the regulations." *Instructions to postmasters.*

If, for any reason, the addressee of a special delivery letter cannot be found, the messenger returns the letter to the post office, endorses on the back the reason for non-delivery, and attaches a label bearing the following : *Procedure in case of non-delivery.*

NOTICE.

A Special Delivery Stamp affixed to any article of mail matter is intended only to secure an immediate delivery—or one offer of immediate delivery. If the article cannot for any cause be delivered when FIRST offered, it then becomes ordinary mail matter and is thereafter treated and delivered accordingly.

The special delivery service was popular and successful from the first. But a demand soon arose for its extension to all post offices. If it was desired to send a letter to a place other than one of the large cities, the sender found it necessary to consult a list of the special delivery offices. Such a list was not always at hand. Hence arose uncertainty and inconvenience, which tended to curtail the use of the stamp. It was felt that the service would only become thoroughly efficient when the privilege was extended to all post offices.

There was also found to be some uncertainty as to the meaning of the word "letter," as used in the Act, and also as to whether it was the intention of Congress that "immediate delivery" should include delivery on Sunday. The first question was temporarily settled by holding the word to mean only first-class matter chargeable at letter rates of postage. The second was left to the further action of Congress.

Finally, the requirement of delivery until midnight was found to be a hardship, since it compelled the post offices in many small towns to remain open long after all mails had arrived and all collections for the day had been made.

The action that was taken on these various points is set forth in the following extract from an official circular :

SPECIAL DELIVERY SYSTEM.
Circular of information and instruction.
POST OFFICE DEPARTMENT,
OFFICE OF THE POSTMASTER GENERAL,
WASHINGTON, D. C., August 10, 1886.

To all postmasters except at free delivery offices :

By the act of August 4, 1886, the Congress has authorized the extension of this system to all post offices and to all mailable matter. That act is as follows, viz : *Official circular and regulations.*

"That *every article of mailable matter* upon which the special stamp provided for by section three of the act of Congress approved March third, eighteen hundred and eighty-five entitled 'An act making appropriations for the service of the Post-Office Department for the fiscal year ending June thirtieth, eighteen hundred and eighty-six, and for other purposes, shall be duly affixed, *shall be entitled to immediate delivery*, according to said act, within the carrier-delivery limit of any free-delivery office, and *within one mile of any other post office* which the Postmaster-General shall at any time designate as a special-delivery post office. *The postmaster shall be responsible for such immediate delivery of every such article*, and shall cause delivery to be made of all such articles received at his office bearing such stamp and entitled to delivery thereat, and *may employ any persons, including clerks and assistants at third and fourth class offices, as messengers*, on such terms as he shall fix as compensation for such delivery ; and to defray the expense thereof, *such postmaster shall be entitled*, upon the adjustment of his quarterly account, *to eighty per centum of the face value of all such special-delivery stamps* received at his office and recorded, according to said act and the regulations of the Post-Office Department, during the quarter ; *and such allowance shall be in full of all the expenses of such delivery : Provided*, That the Postmaster General may, in his discretion, direct any free-delivery office to be excepted from the foregoing provision, and require the delivery to be made entirely by special messengers, according to the provisions of the act to which this is amendatory : *And provided further*, That he may contract for the immediate delivery of all articles from any post office, at any price less than eight cents per piece, when he shall deem it expedient.   * * *

The following orders and regulations are prescribed under the foregoing acts :
    1   Every post office in the United States and Territories and the District of Columbia now established, and which shall be established while the foregoing acts remain, is hereby designated as a special-delivery office, and will be governed by said acts and the orders and regulations thereunder.
    2. These regulations shall take effect and be in force on and after October 1, 1886.
    3   On and after said last-named date every postmaster will be held responsible for the immediate delivery, according to said acts and these regulations, of every article of mailable matter which may be received addressed to his office, properly stamped with a special-delivery stamp.
    4. Such immediate delivery *must* be made when the article is directed to an addressee residing or having a place of business within one mile of the post office. *The obligation* to so deliver does not extend to an addressee beyond that distance, but the postmaster will be at liberty to make such delivery beyond such limits, and to receive the compensation therefor as in any other case. It is commended to him as a proper and considerate thing to be done, in accomodation of the sender, whenever it is reasonably convenient.
    5. The hours within which immediate delivery shall be made shall be at least from 7 a. m. to 7 p. m., and further until the arrival of the last mail, provided that such arrival be not later than 9 p. m. This requirement as to the hours of delivery does not necessarily extend to the transaction of any other postal business after the usual office hours. Special orders for later delivery may be made for first-class offices.
    Postmasters are not required to make delivery of special-delivery matter on Sunday, nor to keep their offices open in any different manner on that day from what is now provided by regulation. Postmasters will be at liberty, however, to deliver special-delivery letters and parcels arriving on Sundays. * *
    No change will be made in the general style of the special delivery stamp now in use.
    The words "Secures immediate delivery at a special-delivery office" will, however, be changed to read, "Secures immediate delivery at any post-office" But, as stamps with the former words are now in the hands of postmasters and the public, their use will be continued until the present supply shall be exhausted

    Similar instructions to postmasters at free-delivery offices fixed the hours for the delivery of letters bearing the special delivery stamps at from 7 A. M. to 11 P. M., unless otherwise ordered by the Postmaster General.

    The stock of stamps of the first design was sufficient to last until September 6th, 1888, when those with the new wording were issued to postmasters. In philatelic publications their appearance is first noted in the *Philatelic Record* for December, 1888.

    In 1893 the Columbian stamps were issued. These stamps were of about the same dimensions as the special delivery stamp, and one denomina-

Change of color.

tion, the one cent, was of the same color. This caused some confusion and gave rise to mistakes in the payment of postage and the treatment of letters bearing the stamps. It was accordingly decided to change the color of the special delivery stamp.

The report of the Third Assistant Postmaster General for 1894, says :

"Its color was changed from blue to orange, January 24, 1893, and so continued to January 5, 1894, when printing in blue was resumed. The *issue* of the orange-colored stamp was not discontinued until the 19th of May, 1894, when the stock on hand at the manufactory was exhausted.

In all there were 5,099,500 stamps of the orange color sent to postmasters."

The stamp of the new color was reported in use as early as January 28th, 1893.

In 1894 the contract for the manufacture of postage stamps passed from the American Bank Note Company to the Bureau of Engraving and Printing at Washington. The new contractors placed marks on all the ordinary postage stamps, in order that their work might be distinguished from that of their predecessors. The changes made in the special delivery stamp were the addition of small ornamental dashes under the words " TEN " and "CENTS ", the drawing of lines of shading across the face of the numeral " 10 ", and a deepening of the lines defining the edge of the bevel of the background panel. *{Changes in the design.}*

The stamps of this type were issued on ordinary paper on October 10th, 1894. On August 16th, 1895, they appeared on paper watermarked with the letters "U S P S"

On the sheets of special delivery stamps printed by the Bureau of Engraving and Printing we find groups of letters in the margin at the upper left corner. An explanation of these letters is given in the following extract from the *American Philatelist* for 1886, (page 10): *{Platemen's initials.}*

"A rule of the Bureau of Engraving and Printing requires that, each time a plate of stamps is printed from, the plateman must cut his initials on the margin of the plate, so that, should any irregularity occur, the responsibility may be more easily traced."

This note refers to revenue stamps. Why the rule has been applied to special delivery stamps and not to other varieties of postage stamps I am unable to explain.

The stamps measure 36½x21 mm.

The papers used for the various issues were : first, the thick, soft, porous paper employed by the American Bank Note Company ; next, a similar paper used by the Bureau of Engraving and Printing ; and lastly, the watermarked paper mentioned just above. *{Paper.}*

The gum used by the first contractors varied from pure white to brown. That employed by the present manufacturers is either white or yellowish. *{Gum.}*

The following shades and varieties are to be found :

PRINTED BY THE AMERICAN BANK NOTE CO.

Perforated 12. *{Reference List.}*

Thick Soft Porous Wove Paper.

Oct. 1st 1885. 10 cents (" Special Delivery Office ") light blue, blue, deep blue

Sept. 6th, 1888. 10 cents (" Any Post Office ") light blue, blue, deep blue

Jan. 24th, 1893. 10 cents (" Any Post Office ") yellow-orange, orange, deep orange

PRINTED BY THE BUREAU OF ENGRAVING & PRINTING.

Perforated 12.

Thick Soft Porous Wove Paper.

Oct. 10th, 1894. 10 cents ("Any Post Office") blue, dark blue, marine blue

Watermarked "U. S. P. S."

Aug. 16th, 1895. 10 cents ("Any Post Office") blue, dark blue, marine blue

Variety :

10 cents dark blue.   Imperforate

Plates.   The plates each contain one hundred stamps, arranged in ten rows of ten.   Usually the sheets are divided vertically into half sheets of fifty stamps This seems to have been the rule with all of the blue stamps but those printed in orange were often, if not always, issued in full sheets of one hundred The imprint is placed at the middle of the top and bottom of each half sheet The plate number appears between each imprint and the central dividing line.   The imprint of the American Bank Note Co. is as usual, merely the name of the company in small, heavy-faced, shaded capitals.   The imprint of the other contractors is "BUREAU, ENGRAVING & PRINTING", in white Roman capitals, on a colored panel having truncated corners and surrounded by a thin colored line.   At each end of the panel is a large three branched ornament.

The following numbers are found on the plates of the special delivery stamps :

AMERICAN BANK NOTE CO.

Plates of 1885-88.

10 cents blue ("Special Delivery Office") (100) No. 495, 496.
10 cents blue ("Any Post Office") (100) No. 552.
10 cents orange ("Any Post Office") (100) No. 552.

Plates of 1890-93.

10 cents blue ("Any Post Office") (100) No 73.
10 cents orange ("Any Post Office") (100) No. 73.

BUREAU, ENGRAVING & PRINTING.

Plate numbers.   Plates of 1894-95.

Unwatermarked

10 cents blue ("Any Post Office") (100) No. 77.

Watermarked "U. S. P. S."

10 cents blue ("Any Post Office") (100) No. 77, 257, 381, 492,
880, 881, 882, 883

A plate, numbered 682, was made but, being defective, it has never been put to press.   The imperforate stamps are from plate No. 257.

The annual reports of the Postmaster General supply the following statistics of the quantities of stamps delivered to deputy postmasters :

Fiscal year	Sept. 30.	Dec. 31.	Mch. 31.	June 30.	Total.
		QUARTER ENDING :			
1885-86	2,074,320	1,265,750	241,990	117,500	3,699,560
1886-87	215,880	492,050	254,980	283,030	1,245,940
1887-88	329,970	393,810	311,670	296,340	1,331,790
1888-89	347,360	*521,940	302,440	†403,910	1,575,650
1889-90	719,130	359,610	526,810	515,340	2,120,890
1890-91	596,510	680,750	641,550	650,540	2,569,350
1891-92	660,100	764,530	783,790	908,800	3,117,220
1892-93	720,670	886,090	1,032,090	889,220	3,528,070
1893-94	1,020,610	862,990	806,560	983,860	3,674,020
1894-95	905,300	1,053,380	954,820	995,280	3,908,780
1895-96	1,059,630	1,187,490	1,104,420	1,114,730	4,466,270
1896-97	1,025,720	1,095,630	1,046,610	1,178,370	4,346,330
1897-98	1,277,880	1,349,660	1,354,910	1,182,280	5,164,730
1898-99	1,425,710	1,570,100	1,447,810	1,491,350	5,934,970
1899-1900	1,828,070	1,646,880	1,846,440	1,619,260	6,940,650

Deliveries to postmasters.

Whole number of stamps 53,624,220. Value $5,362,422.00.

*600 of these are " specimens."

†111,900 of these are " specimens."

It is understood that the 600 stamps were surcharged with the word " SPECIMEN " in red and sent to the Universal Postal Union. The second and larger lot of " specimens " were probably proofs. — "Specimen" stamps and proofs.

The deliveries in the fiscal year ending June 30th, 1895, are made up of 1,004,980 stamps printed by the American Bank Note Co. and 2,903,800 stamps printed by the Bureau of Engraving and Printing. In the latter number are included 750 copies which were sent to the Universal Postal Union.

In 1898 the tri-ennial congress of the Universal Postal Union convened in Washington and, at that time, 125 sets of all the stamps in current use, including the special delivery stamp, were surcharged " UNIVERSAL— POSTAL—CONGRESS " and presented to the attending delegates. In the same year 150 copies of the special delivery stamp were supplied " for the Post-office album." — Stamps surcharged "Universal Postal Congress".

The deliveries for 1900 include 50 copies which were furnished to the Third Assistant Postmaster General for exchanging and similar purposes. These and the 150 copies mentioned in the preceding paragraph were hand-stamped " Specimen " in black or magenta.

During the last three years 126,850 special delivery stamps have been overprinted for use in Guam and the Philippine Islands but, as they were taken from the reserve stock of the Bureau of Engraving and Printing and not from the supplies of the Post Office Department, the statistics are not affected. — Stamps surcharged for Guam and the Philippine Islands.

The *Postal Guide* for 1898 says that 3,596,500 of the stamps supplied by the Bureau of Engraving and Printing were on unwatermarked paper.

OFFICIAL STAMPS.

ISSUE OF 1873.

Historical.

The use of stamps by the different departments of the Government was decreed by Act of Congress, approved March 3rd, 1873. The stamps were prepared by order of the Postmaster General, and their issue, on requisitions of the various departments, was commenced on May 24th, 1873. The stamps went into use on July 1st of that year. Their purpose was to abolish the much-abused franking privilege, to show exactly the amount of work performed for the other branches of the Government by the Post Office department and reduce the large annual deficit of that department.

The following extract, on the subject of the franking privilege, is taken from the *American Journal of Philately* for 1873 (page 109):

Franking.

" The second Congress of the United States met in Philadelphia on the 24th of October, 1791. George Washington was President, John Adams was Vice-President and Jonathan Trumbull was Speaker of the House of Representatives. The first act passed by this body related to ' certain fisheries of the United States,' and the second was an act to establish the post office and post roads within the United States This act contained thirty sections and was approved February 20th, 1792. Among other things it provided :
' That the following letters and packets, and no other, shall be received and conveyed by post free of postage, under such restrictions as are hereinafter provided ; that is to say : All letters and packets to or from the President or Vice-President of the United States, and all letters and packets, not exceeding two ounces in weight, to or from any member of the Senate or House of Representatives, the Secretary of the Senate, or Clerk of the House of Representatives, during their actual attendance in any session of Congress, and twenty days after such session. All letters to and from the Secretary of the Treasury and his assistant, Comptroller, Register, and Auditor of the Treasury, the Treasurer, the Secretary of State, the Secretary of War, the commissioners for settling the accounts between the United States and individual states, the Postmaster General and his assistant ; Provided, That no person shall frank or enclose any letter or packet, other than his own ; but any public letter from the department of the Treasury may be franked by the Secretary of the Treasury, or the Assistant Secretary, or by the Comptroller, Register, Auditor, or Treasurer ; and that each person before named shall deliver to the post office every letter or packet enclosed to him, which may be directed to any other person, noting the place from whence it came by post, and the usual postage shall be charged thereon.'
This law was altered every few years, and each time large numbers of public officials were added to the free list, till at last the loads of unpaid mail matter so embarrassed the post office revenue that strenuous exertions were made to do away with the whole system, which were happily crowned with success last winter."

The report of the Postmaster General for 1869 stated that no less than 31,933 persons were authorized to employ the franking privilege and estimated the annual expense to the Post Office Department for transporting free mail matter to be $5,000,000

There appeared to be but one remedy for this abuse, to abolish the franking privilege and to provide, by means of appropriations, for the payment of postage on all matter sent through the mails by the various departments.

An Act of Congress, intended to effect this reform, was approved January 27th, 1873, and provided :

" That the franking privilege be hereby abolished from and after the first day of July, Ano Domini 1873, and that henceforth all official correspondence of whatever nature, and other mailable matter sent from or addressed to any officer of the Government or person now authorized to frank such matter, shall be chargeable with the same rates of postage as may be lawfully imposed upon like matter sent by or addressed to other persons Provided, that no compensation or allowance shall be now or hereafter made to Senators or Members and Delegates of the House of Representatives on account of postages." *The franking privilege abolished.*

An Act of Congress, approved March 3rd, 1873, appropriated a sum of money, which was estimated to be sufficient for the purchase of postage stamps for the use of the various departments. Section 4 of this Act also provided :

" That the Postmaster General shall cause to be prepared a special stamp or stamped envelope, to be used only for official mail matter for each of the executive departments, and said stamps and stamped envelopes shall be supplied by a proper officer of said departments to all persons under its direction requiring the same for official use, and all appropriations for postage heretofore made shall no longer be available for said purpose, and all said stamps and stamped envelopes shall be sold or furnished to said several departments or clerks only at the price for which stamps and stamped envelopes of like value are sold at the several post offices." *Official stamps and envelopes authorized.*

The report of the Postmaster General, dated November 14th, 1873, expresses satisfaction with the results of the new law, as far as they were then apparent, *i.e.*, for the first quarter of the fiscal year beginning July 1st, 1873 The report supplies a memorandum of the quantities of stamps issued in that quarter, saying :

" Section 4 of the Act of March 3, 1873, making it the duty of the Postmaster General to provide official stamps and stamped envelopes for the several Executive Departments, has been strictly complied with. The stamps and envelopes furnished have been executed in the highest style of art, and will compare favorably with those of any other country. From July 1st to September 30th of the current year, the following varieties, numbers, and values were issued : *Deliveries during the first quarter year.*

To whom issued.	Number of Denominations.	Number of stamps.	Value.
The Executive	5	5,150	$200.00
The State Department	14	60,495	20,749.70
The Treasury Department	11	7,842,500	407.000.00
The War Department	11	446 500	17,689 00
The Navy Department	11	247,230	12,239 00
The Post Office Department	10	10,054,660	354,535.00
The Interior Department	10	1,058,475	59,171.00
The Department of Justice	10	65,400	3,900 00
The Department of Agriculture	9	275,000	20,730 00
Making a total	91	20,055,410	896,213.70

It cannot be expected that the sales of official stamps will average throughout the year the extraordinary sums above given for the first quarter. A general supply having been obtained, subsequent orders will be made only for the actual consumption "

From the report of the Third Assistant Postmaster General, dated November 1st, 1878, we learn that a large portion of the stamps mentioned in the foregoing table were issued in advance of the date on which the law became operative, though they were not debited to the various departments until the first quarter of the fiscal year beginning July 1st, 1873, since, previous to that date, the appropriations for the purchase of the stamps were not *Stamps issued before July 1st, 1873.*

available.   The following quantities were issued between May 24th and
July 1st, 1873 :

The Executive	4,650
State Department	60,495
Treasury Department	6,317,500
War Department	440,500
Navy Department	160,830
Post Office Department	5,510,610
Interior Department	970,475
Department of Justice	65,400
Department of Agriculture	135,000
Total stamps	13,665,460
Total value	$494,974.70

The report of the Postmaster General for 1873 also gives the following
brief description of the designs and colors of the official stamps :

Official description.
" The stamps for the Departments, other than the Post Office, do not differ materially
from those for sale to the public, except that each Department has its own distinctive color
and legend.   The colors are : For the Executive, carmine ; State Department, green ;
Treasury, velvet brown ; War, cochineal-red ; Navy, blue ; Post Office, black ; Interior,
vermilion ; Department of Justice, purple ; and Department of Agriculture, straw color.
In the stamps for the Post Office Department the medallion head gives place to a
numeral representing the value, with the words ' POST OFFICE DEPARTMENT ' above and the
denomination expressed in words below.   All the official stamps correspond in denominations
with those issued for the public, except in the case of the State Department, for which four
of higher value were made for dispatch bags.   These four are of the denominations of $2
$5, $10 and $20, respectively, are of larger size and printed in two colors, and bear a pro-
file bust of the late Secretary Seward."

Official circular.
A circular of the Post Office Department, dated May 15th, 1873, calls
the attention of postmasters to the repeal of the franking privilege and to the
fact that special stamps and envelopes have been provided for the use of
the several departments.   The designs and colors are described in language
similar to that just quoted from the report of the Postmaster General.   The
circular concludes :

" Postmasters at all offices will be furnished with the official stamps of this Department,
in suitable denominations and amounts, as far as they can be supplied.   The Department
will exercise its own discretion in filling requisitions, and will send only in such denominations and amounts as the needs of an office may seem to require.   The less important offices,
say those at which the money order system has not been established, will need only three
cent stamps, but comparatively few offices will require stamps above the denomination of
six cents.   The higher denominations will be supplied to a few of the larger offices only.
Postmasters will combine stamps of the most convenient denominations at hand to meet
emergencies for which they may have no single stamp exactly filling the rate required."

Designs.
As was said in a previous paragraph, the stamps for the various departments were, with the exception of those for the Post Office Department, not
unlike the same values of the general issue which was then current.   The
series of finely engraved profile busts, which distinguishes the issues of 1870-
73, was retained.   The numerals and words of value in the lower part of the
stamps were arranged in much the same way as on the corresponding stamps
of the regular issue.   The features which, aside from the color, distinguish
the set for each particular department are most prominent in the upper part
of the stamps, replacing the words " U. S. POSTAGE ".   The additions to the
lower part are usually of less importance.   The devices used may be briefly
described as follows :

DEPARTMENT OF AGRICULTURE. A panel, curved above the central oval, bears the word "AGRICULTURE". In the upper left corner are "DEPT. OF" and in the upper right corner the letters "U. S." entwined.

THE EXECUTIVE. A panel, curved above the oval, bears the word "EXECUTIVE" In the upper corners are respectively "U" and "S", in small circles, surrounded by arabesques. The background is filled with vertical stripes, alternately light and dark, representing the bars on the national shield.

DEPARTMENT OF THE INTERIOR. A broad ribbon, arched above the portrait, is inscribed "DEPT. OF THE INTERIOR". In the upper corners are six-pointed stars and, at right and left in the lower part of the stamps, small shields bearing the letters "U" and "S". On the 1, 2, 3, 6, 10 and 30 cent stamps these shields are placed above the ends of the ribbons bearing the value, and on the other four denominations they are in the lower corners.

DEPARTMENT OF JUSTICE. The word "JUSTICE" is curved above the central oval, with "DEPT." in the upper left and "OF" in the upper right corner. Six-pointed stars, bearing the letters "U" and "S", occupy the same positions as the small shields on the stamps of the Department of the Interior

NAVY DEPARTMENT. The words "NAVY" and "DEPT." are inscribed diagonally across the upper corners. There is a large star in each upper corner and a smaller one at the middle of each side. The top and sides of the stamps are bordered by a cable. The letters "U" and "S", in small hexagons, are placed as were the same letters on the stamps of the Departments of the Interior and Justice.

DEPARTMENT OF STATE. Above the medallion is arched, "DEPT. OF STATE" with foliated ornaments below each end. Large letters "U" and "S", somewhat distorted, occupy the same positions as on the stamps of the three departments just described. To this set are added four new values, 2, 5, 10 and 20 dollars. These stamps are about twice the size of the lower values and are alike in design. A large portrait of Wm. H. Seward, printed in black, occupies the central oval, at each side of which are fasces. Above the oval appears, in two lines of large shaded captials, "DEPARTMENT OF STATE." Small arabesques fill the upper corners. The value, in large white captials, occupies a straight tablet across the bottom, above each end of which are the letters "U. S. OF A." In the case of the 20 dollars the word "DOLLARS" is abbreviated to "DOLLS."

TREASURY DEPARTMENT. The word "TREASURY", in a wavy line, crosses the top of the stamps Below it, at left and right respectively, are "U. S." and "DEPT." Drapery with fringes and cords ornaments the sides.

WAR DEPARTMENT. The letters "U" and "S" occupy the upper corners and the words "WAR" and "DEPT." are curved beneath them. Elongated national shields appear in the lower part of the stamps and shadings to represent the folds of the flag at the sides.

POST OFFICE DEPARTMENT. For this department a special design was adopted. Large numerals, with "OFFICIAL" above and "STAMP" below, occupy a colorless central oval, above which is curved "POST OFFICE DEPT."

The upper spandrels are blank except for a small round boss. The words and numerals of value are arranged as on the sets for the other departments. The letters "u" and "s", in small circles, appear above the ends of the ribbons bearing the value on the 1, 2, 3, 6, 10 and 30 cents, at each side of the value on the 24 cents, and in the lower corners on the 12, 15 and 90 cents.

The stamps are of two sizes, viz : 1 to 90 cents, 20x25 mm.; 2 to 20 dollars, 25½x39½ mm.

Mr. E. D. Bacon has called my attention to an interesting feature of the four higher denominations of the Department of State, which has, hitherto, been overlooked by philatelists. On comparing several copies of any of these stamps, it will be found that they differ slightly one from another. This difference lies in the spacing between the tablet bearing the value and the ornaments adjacent to its upper corners. The variations in position are slight but distinct. The explanation of these variations is simple. There was only one die for the borders of the four stamps and it did not include the tablet at the bottom. In making a plate for any of these four denominations, the border was transferred first and then the label of value was added to each transfer. Slight differences would naturally result from this process. Some of the ornaments also show traces of retouching. By means of these variations it would be possible to "plate" these stamps, should one be inclined to attempt it.

Varieties of the higher values of the Department of State.

At the time the official stamps came into use the contract for the manufacture of postage stamps was held by the Continental Bank Note Co. Subsequently, through consolidation and new contracts, the work passed into the hands of the American Bank Note Co. We may, therefore, expect to find the official stamps on the characteristic papers of the two companies, *i.e.* thin hard, ribbed and double papers for the former and soft porous paper for the latter. When we examine the stamps we find these anticipations are confirmed. The gum is the same as that used for the regular issues at corresponding dates.

Paper.

Reference List.

Perforated 12.

Hard White Wove Paper.

DEPARTMENT OF AGRICULTURE.

May 24th, 1873.

1 cent golden yellow, deep golden yellow, olive-yellow, pale orange-yellow

2 cents golden yellow, deep golden yellow, olive-yellow

3 cents golden yellow, deep golden yellow, olive-yellow, pale orange-yellow

6 cents golden yellow, deep golden yellow, olive-yellow, pale orange-yellow

10 cents golden yellow, deep golden yellow, olive-yellow

12 cents golden yellow, deep golden yellow, olive-yellow, pale orange-yellow

15 cents golden yellow, deep golden yellow, olive-yellow, pale bright yellow

24 cents golden yellow, deep golden yellow, olive-yellow, pale orange-yellow

30 cents golden yellow, deep golden yellow, olive-yellow

Variety:

3 cents golden yellow. Imperforate.

THE EXECUTIVE.

May 24th, 1873.

1 cent carmine, deep carmine

2 cents carmine, deep carmine

3 cents carmine, deep carmine, violet-rose

6 cents pale carmine, carmine, deep carmine

10 cents pale carmine, carmine, deep carmine

DEPARTMENT OF THE INTERIOR.

May 24th, 1873.

1 cent rose-vermilion, scarlet vermilion

2 cents rose-vermilion, scarlet-vermilion

3 cents rose-vermilion, scarlet-vermilion

6 cents rose vermilion, scarlet-vermilion

10 cents rose vermilion, scarlet-vermilion

12 cents rose-vermilion, scarlet-vermilion

15 cents rose-vermilion, scarlet-vermilion

24 cents rose-vermilion, scarlet-vermilion

30 cents rose-vermilion, scarlet-vermilion

90 cents rose vermilion, scarlet-vermilion

DEPARTMENT OF JUSTICE.

May 24th, 1873.

1 cent purple, red-purple

2 cents purple, light purple

3 cents purple, red-purple, bluish purple

6 cents purple, red purple, bluish purple, light purple

10 cents purple, bluish purple

12 cents purple

15 cents purple

24 cents purple

30 cents purple

90 cents purple

NAVY DEPARTMENT.

May 24th, 1873.

1 cent dull blue, dark blue, gray-blue, ultramarine, dark ultramarine, bright ultramarine

2 cents dull blue, dark blue, gray-blue, ultramarine, bright ultramarine

3 cents dull blue, dark blue, gray-blue, pale ultramarine, ultramarine, bright ultramarine

6 cents dull blue, dark blue, gray-blue, pale ultramarine, ultramarine, bright ultramarine

7 cents dull blue, dark blue, gray-blue, ultramarine,
   bright ultramarine

10 cents dull blue, dark blue, gray-blue, dark ultramarine, bright ultramarine

12 cents dull blue, dark blue, ultramarine, bright ultramarine

15 cents dull blue, dark blue, gray-blue, pale ultramarine, ultramarine, bright ultramarine

24 cents dull blue, dark blue, gray-blue, ultramarine,
   bright ultramarine

30 cents dull blue, dark blue, dark ultramarine, bright
   ultramarine

90 cents dull blue, dark blue, ultramarine, dark ultramarine, bright ultramarine

Variety:

2 cents deep green, deep yellow-green.   Error of
   color

POST OFFICE DEPARTMENT.

May 24th, 1873.   1 cent black, gray black
2 cents black, gray-black
3 cents black, gray-black
6 cents black, gray-black
10 cents black, gray-black
12 cents black, gray-black
15 cents black, gray-black
24 cents black, gray-black
30 cents black, gray-black
90 cents black, gray-black

Varieties:

1 cent gray-black.   Paper with gray surface
2 cents gray-black   "   "   "   "
3 cents gray-black   "   "   "   "
6 cents gray-black   "   "   "   "
10 cents gray-black   "   "   "   "
12 cents gray-black   "   "   "   "
15 cents gray-black   "   "   "   "
24 cents gray-black   "   "   "   "
30 cents gray-black   "   '   "   "
90 cents gray-black   "   "   "   "
6 cents gray-black.   Diagonal half used as three
   cents

DEPARTMENT OF STATE.

May 24th, 1873.   1 cent dark yellow-green, dark blue-green, dark gray-
   green

2 cents dark yellow-green, dark blue-green, dark gray-green

3 cents dark yellow-green, dark blue-green, bright blue-green, deep grass green

6 cents dark yellow-green, dark blue-green, bright blue-green

7 cents dark yellow-green, dark blue-green, bright blue-green

10 cents dark yellow-green, dark blue-green, bright blue-green

12 cents dark yellow-green, dark blue-green, bright blue-green

15 cents dark yellow-green, dark blue-green, bright blue-green

24 cents dark yellow-green, dark blue-green

30 cents dark yellow-green, dark blue-green

90 cents dark yellow-green, dark blue-green

2 dollars green and black, bluish green and black

5 dollars green and black, bluish green and black

10 dollars green and black, bluish green and black

20 dollars green and black, bluish green and black

TREASURY DEPARTMENT.

May 24th, 1873.

1 cent pale yellow-brown, yellow-brown, brown, dark brown

2 cents pale yellow-brown, yellow-brown, brown, dark brown

3 cents pale yellow-brown, yellow-brown, brown, dark brown, red-brown

6 cents pale yellow-brown, yellow-brown, brown, dark brown, gray-brown

7 cents pale yellow-brown, yellow-brown, brown, dark brown

10 cents pale yellow-brown, yellow-brown, brown, dark brown

12 cents pale yellow-brown, yellow-brown, brown, dark brown, red-brown

15 cents pale yellow-brown, yellow-brown, brown, dark brown

24 cents pale yellow-brown, yellow-brown, brown, dark brown

30 cents pale yellow-brown, yellow-brown, brown, dark brown, red-brown

90 cents pale yellow-brown, yellow-brown, brown, dark brown

WAR DEPARTMENT.

May 24th, 1873.   1 cent pale rose red, rose-red, dull rose-red, pale
                         brown-rose, brown-rose, dull lake

                         2 cents pale rose red, dull rose-red, pale brown-rose,
                         brown-rose, deep brown-rose

                         3 cents pale rose-red, rose-red, dull rose-red, pale
                         brown-rose, brown-rose, lilac-rose

                         6 cents pale rose-red, rose-red, dull rose-red, pale
                         brown-rose, brown-rose

                         7 cents pale rose-red, rose-red, dull rose-red, pale
                         brown-rose, brown-rose, deep brown-rose

                         10 cents pale rose-red, rose-red, dull rose-red, pale
                         brown-rose, brown-rose

                         12 cents pale rose-red, dull rose-red, pale brown-rose,
                         brown-rose

                         15 cents pale rose-red, rose-red, dull rose-red, pale
                         brown-rose, brown-rose, deep brown-rose

                         24 cents pale rose-red, dull rose-red, pale brown-rose,
                         brown-rose

                         30 cents pale rose-red, rose-red, dull rose-red, pale
                         brown-rose, brown-rose, deep brown-rose

                         90 cents pale rose-red, rose-red, dull rose-red, pale
                         brown-rose, brown-rose

Horizontally or Vertically Ribbed Paper.

DEPARTMENT OF AGRICULTURE.

1873-76.   1 cent deep golden yellow
                  2 cents deep golden yellow
                  3 cents deep golden yellow
                  6 cents deep golden yellow
                  10 cents deep golden yellow, olive-yellow
                  12 cents deep golden yellow
                  15 cents deep golden yellow
                  24 cents deep golden yellow, olive-yellow
                  30 cents deep golden yellow, olive-yellow

THE EXECUTIVE.

1873-76.   1 cent carmine
                  2 cents carmine
                  3 cents carmine
                  6 cents carmine
                  10 cents carmine

DEPARTMENT OF THE INTERIOR.

1873-76.   1 cent scarlet-vermilion

DEPARTMENT OF JUSTICE.

1873-76.   1 cent purple

NAVY DEPARTMENT.

1873-76.   1 cent dull blue, dark blue
                  2 cents dull blue
                  3 cents dull blue
                  6 cents dull blue
                  7 cents dull blue
                  10 cents dull blue
                  12 cents dull blue
                  15 cents dull blue, dark blue
                  24 cents ultramarine
                  30 cents dull blue
                  90 cents dull blue, ultramarine

POST OFFICE DEPARTMENT.

1873-76.   1 cent gray-black
                  2 cents gray-black
                  3 cents gray-black
                  6 cents gray-black
                  10 cents gray-black
                  12 cents gray-black
                  15 cents gray-black
                  24 cents gray-black
                  30 cents gray-black
                  90 cents gray-black

Varieties:

3 cents gray-black. Paper with gray surface
6 cents gray-black   "   "   "   "
10 cents gray-black   "   "   "   "
12 cents gray-black   "   "   "
24 cents gray-black   "   "   "   "
30 cents gray-black   "   "   "   "
90 cents gray-black   "   "   "   "

DEPARTMENT OF STATE.

1873-76.   1 cent dark yellow-green
                  2 cents dark yellow-green, dark blue-green, dark gray-
                      green
                  3 cents dark yellow-green
                  6 cents dark yellow-green
                  7 cents dark yellow-green
                  10 cents dark yellow-green
                  12 cents dark yellow-green
                  15 cents dark yellow-green

24 cents dark yellow-green
30 cents dark yellow-green, dark blue-green
90 cents dark yellow-green, dark blue-green

TREASURY DEPARTMENT.

1873-76.   1 cent dark brown
2 cents dark brown, yellow-brown
3 cents dark brown
6 cents dark brown, brown
7 cents dark brown
10 cents dark brown
12 cents dark brown
15 cents dark brown
30 cents dark brown
90 cents dark brown

WAR DEPARTMENT.

1873-76.   1 cent pale rose-red, pale brown-rose, deep brown-rose
2 cents pale rose-red, dark rose-red
3 cents brown-rose, deep brown-rose
6 cents pale rose-red
7 cents pale brown-rose
10 cents bright rose-red, brown-rose
12 cents dark rose-red, brown-rose
15 cents pale rose-red, dark rose-red
24 cents pale rose-red
30 cents bright rose-red
90 cents dark rose-red

Double Paper.

POST OFFICE DEPARTMENT.

1876.   3 cents gray-black
24 cents gray-black
90 cents gray-black

DEPARTMENT OF STATE.

1876.   3 cents blue-green

TREASURY DEPARTMENT.

1876.   3 cents dark yellow-brown
10 cents dark yellow-brown
90 cents dark yellow-brown

The two cent stamp of the Navy Department printed in green, the color of the stamps of the Department of State, has been the subject of much **Navy Department, two cents green.** discussion among philatelists. Opinions have differed as to it being a genuine error or only a proof for color. The firm who first discovered it and placed it on the market purchased their copies, together with a quantity of other United States stamps, from a man who was evidently not a philatelist, and was therefore free from any suspicion of wishing to bring forward new varieties, and who stated that he found the stamps in an old trunk. The purchasers of this lot have always believed the stamp to be a genuine error. I copy the following from a letter of Mr. C. F. Rothfuchs:

> "I would now like to say a few words about the two cents Navy in green. Some years ago I received five copies, a strip of three and a pair. They had the original gum on the back They were kept by gentleman (not a collector) who was a clerk in the State Department when they were received at that department. This gentleman has a nephew, a bright boy about 14 years of age, who is a stamp collector and who received the stamps from his uncle and traded them with me for a lot of foreign stamps which he wanted to fill up vacant spaces in his album.
>
> In view of this information, it is my opinion that, by mistake, the plate of the two cents Navy was used instead of the two cents State. I have never heard of a two cents Navy in green being found in the Navy Department."

Finally, under date of April 7th, 1899, Mr. R. A. Tarr writes me that he has recently seen a copy of the Navy department error, cancelled and on the original cover.

The bi-sected six cents of the Post Office Department, which is mentioned in the reference list, was shown me by Mr. S. M. Castle. It is used, in connection with a three cent stamp, on a six cent envelope of the 1874 issue for the Post Office Department. The cancellation is "Niagara Falls, June 18th," the year not being given. *Post Office Dept., bi-sected six cents.*

In the collection of Mr. F. O. Conant is an interesting oddity, in the shape of a three cent stamp of the Post Office Department used as a postage due stamp. On the envelope is a duly cancelled copy of the three cents green of the 1879 issue. But the letter was evidently overweight, since it bears the handstamp "DUE 3". In payment of this shortage a three cent Post Office Department stamp has been affixed, partly over the original cancellation, and cancelled in turn. This was done at Berlin Falls, N. H., April 30th, 1880. It may be added that this does not represent an attempt to create a curiosity, since neither writer, receiver nor postmaster were in the least interested in philately. *Post Office Dept. stamp used as a "due" stamp.*

The catalogues, following the lead of collectors, have listed the stamps of the Post Office Department on white and gray-surfaced paper. This distinction is scarcely warranted by any actual merit in the two varieties. The paper is the same, the difference being merely a matter of appearance. When the plates were thoroughly wiped the paper came from the press clear and white. When the wiping was imperfectly done the ink which remained on the surface of the plate discolored the paper and made it appear of a gray tint. The contrast between the two varieties is often very marked and leading philatelists have seen fit to place the two sets in their collections, thus giving them a standing. *Post Office Dept., gray-surfaced paper.*

Some of the bi-colored values of the Department of State were at one time reported with the medallion inverted but, as was explained on page 114, they were purely imaginary articles. *State Department, inverted medallions.*

In the *Philatelical Journal* for February 20th, 1875, we find the following letter concerning the use of the higher values of the State Department stamps.

"SIR :—The following explanation of the use of the 10 and 20 dollars stamps may be useful. These two values are no longer used on packages ; the heavy mails of the State Department are now sent to the City Post-office, and charged against the Department. The account is settled monthly by payments in the high value stamps. These are turned over by the city postmaster to the General Post-office as vouchers for the account, and are destroyed. Thus you will see that neither used nor unused copies are to be had.

Yours truly,
C. E. D.

Washington, January 1st, 1875."

State Department, alleged use of the higher values.

This communication is given for what it is worth and in the hope that quoting it may possibly elicit further information on the subject. Unless it can be confirmed I am not inclined to accept the statement, in view of the fact that the law required that postage on all letters and packages should be prepaid by means of stamps.

Plates.

The plates for the official stamps varied in size. The majority contained one hundred stamps each, a few had two hundred, while those for the four higher values of the Department of State had only ten, arranged in two rows of five stamps each. The latter stamps being printed in two colors, two plates were required for each value. However, the same vignette plate (No. 123) was used in connection with the frame plates of all four values. The impressions from the plates of two hundred stamps were divided vertically into sheets of one hundred stamps each.

Imprints and plate numbers.

The imprint was the same as that on the plates of the ordinary stamps at the same date, *i. e.*, "PRINTED BY THE—CONTINENTAL BANK NOTE CO. NEW YORK ", in two lines of white capitals, on a panel with pearled edges and surrounded by a thin colored line. On the plates having one hundred stamps the imprint was placed at the top and bottom, over or under the second, third and fourth stamps from the left. The plate number, preceded by "*No.*" was placed over or under the sixth stamp from the left. On the plates having two hundred stamps the imprint appeared at the middle of the top and bottom of each half of the plate. The plate number was placed between each imprint and the vertical dividing line. On the impressions from the plates of the four higher values of the Department of State we find the imprint, in green, below the second, third and fourth stamps of the lower row, while at the top it is printed in black and, beginning at the left of the first stamp, extends over that and the second stamp. "*No.*" and the plate number, in green, are placed over the third stamp and "*No.*" and a number, in black, over the fourth and fifth stamps. The imprint and number in green belong to the frame plate and those in black to the vignette plate.

In the following list of numbers of the plates for the official stamps, the figures enclosed in parenthesis indicate the number of stamps on the plate.

Plate numbers.

DEPARTMENT OF AGRICULTURE.

1 cent	(100)	No. 65.
2 cents	(100)	No. 64.
3 cents	(100)	No. 57.
6 cents	(100)	No. 72.
10 cents	(100)	No. 114.
12 cents	(100)	No. 73.

15 cents (100) No. 105.
24 cents (100) No. 145.
30 cents (100) No. 100.

THE EXECUTIVE.

1 cent   (100) No. 82.
2 cents (100) No. 75.
3 cents (100) No. 63.
6 cents (100) No. 76.
10 cents (100) No. 111.

DEPARTMENT OF THE INTERIOR.

1 cent   (100) No. 52.
2 cents (100) No. 45.
3 cents (100) No. 27.
6 cents (100) No. 56.
10 cents (100) No. 109.
12 cents (100) No. 49.
15 cents (100) No. 93.
24 cents (100) No. 104.
30 cents (100) No. 95.
90 cents (100) No. 108.

DEPARTMENT OF JUSTICE.

1 cent   (100) No. 85.
2 cents (100) No. 90.
3 cents (100) No. 28.
6 cents (100) No. 77.
10 cents (100) No. 97.
12 cents (100) No. 91.
15 cents (100) No. 99.
24 cents (100) No. 115.
30 cents (100) No. 110.
90 cents (100) No. 113.

NAVY DEPARTMENT.

1 cent   (100) No. 80.
2 cents (100) No. 50.
3 cents (100) No. 34.
6 cents (100) No. 53.
7 cents (100) No. 119.
10 cents (100) No. 101.
12 cents (100) No. 92.
15 cents (100) No. 94.
24 cents (100) No. 107.
30 cents (100) No. 96.
90 cents (100) No. 106.

POST OFFICE DEPARTMENT.

1 cent	(200)	No. 43.
2 cents	(100)	No. 37, 38, 285.
3 cents	(100)	No. 36, 40.
	(200)	No. 30, 41, 140, 141.
6 cents	(200)	No. 39, 47, 249.
10 cents	(100)	No. 62.
12 cents	(100)	No. 71.
15 cents	(100)	No. 66.
24 cents	(100)	No. 74.
30 cents	(100)	No. 68.
90 cents	(100)	No. 88.

DEPARTMENT OF STATE.

1 cent	(100)	No. 55.
2 cents	(100)	No. 59.
3 cents	(100)	No. 70.
6 cents	(100)	No. 83.
7 cents	(100)	No. 112.
10 cents	(100)	No. 98.
12 cents	(100)	No. 78.
15 cents	(100)	No. 118.
24 cents	(100)	No. 117.
30 cents	(100)	No. 116.
90 cents	(100)	No. 67.
2 dollars	(10)	No. frame 121, vignette 123.
5 dollars	(10)	No. " 120, " 123.
10 dollars	(10)	No. " 122, " 123.
20 dollars	(10)	No. " 124, " 123.

TREASURY DEPARTMENT.

1 cent	(200)	No. 44.
2 cents	(200)	No. 42.
3 cents	(200)	No. 29, 33.
6 cents	(100)	No. 51.
7 cents	(100)	No. 103.
10 cents	(100)	No. 58.
12 cents	(100)	No. 46.
15 cents	(100)	No. 84.
24 cents	(100)	No. 134.
30 cents	(100)	No. 69.
90 cents	(100)	No. 61.

WAR DEPARTMENT.

1 cent	(100)	No. 48.
2 cents	(200)	No. 35.
3 cents	(100)	No. 32.
6 cents	(100)	No. 60.
7 cents	(100)	No. 102.

10 cents	(100)	No. 79.
12 cents	(100)	No. 54.
15 cents	(100)	No. 87.
24 cents	(100)	No. 86.
30 cents	(100)	No. 81.
90 cents	(100)	No. 89.

The number 81, which had been assigned to the thirty cents of the War Department, was, by mistake, engraved on the plate of the one cent Executive. As soon as the error was noticed the number was defaced by chisel marks and the correct number, 82, inserted beside it. The two cents of the Navy Department printed in green is, of course, from plate 50, the only plate for that value.

The following quantities of official stamps were printed and delivered to the Stamp Agent during the first four years they were in use :

Statistics of manufacture.

Year ending December 31st, 1873 :

DEPARTMENT :

	Agriculture.	Executive.	Interior.	Justice.	Navy.
1 cent	93,500	10,800	144,500	30,800	58,500
2 cents	131,300	11,500	427,500	30,400	135,500
3 cents	321,000	12,100	1,214,500	85,500	206,000
6 cents	126,500	10,700	894,800	66,000	125,600
7 cents	....	....	....	....	13,400
10 cents	46,500	10,600	66,300	21,400	38,000
12 cents	48,500	....	169,500	44,800	28,000
15 cents	46,900	....	97,300	33,500	26,500
24 cents	39,500	....	49,400	20,500	13,800
30 cents	43,300	....	53,500	22,200	12,400
90 cents	....	....	37,900	10,000	10,600
Total	897,000	55,700	3,155,200	365,100	668,300

	Post Office.	State.	Treasury.	War.	Total.
1 cent	1,336,000	45,800	3,223,400	487,500	5,430,800
2 cents	714,500	46,300	3,446,500	285,500	5,229,000
3 cents	15,434,000	45,600	7,027,000	552,500	24,898,200
6 cents	1,587,000	42,700	1,437,000	156,000	4,446,300
7 cents	....	45,800	329,200	38,000	426,400
10 cents	242,200	45,200	520,300	28,700	1,019,200
12 cents	528,000	45,600	1,142,500	37,200	2,044,100
15 cents	171,500	45,600	1,178,900	25,000	1,625,200
24 cents	65,500	45,800	290,000	27,600	552,100
30 cents	67,800	45,300	184,100	23,300	451,900
90 cents	37,800	42,400	137,500	23,900	300,100
2 dollars	....	700	....	....	700
5 dollars	....	700	....	....	700
10 dollars	....	700	....	....	700
20 dollars	....	700	....	....	700
Total	20,184,300	498,900	18,916,400	1,685,200	46,426,100

Year ending December 31st, 1874:

DEPARTMENT:

	Agriculture.	Executive.	Interior.	Justice.	Navy.
1 cent	152,000	....	190,000	....	95,000
2 cents	154,500	....	....	....	95,000
3 cents	95,000	....	....	....	95,000
6 cents	95,000	....	....	....	95,000
7 cents	....	....	....	....	95,000
10 cents	134,200	....	97,500	....	95,000
12 cents	95,000	....	....	....	95,000
15 cents	95,000	....	....	....	47,500
24 cents	133,900	....	39,500	....	47,500
30 cents	130,000	....	39,000	....	47,500
90 cents	......	....	....	....	47,500
Total	1,084,600	....	366,000	....	855,000

	Post Office.	State.	Treasury.	War.	Total.
1 cent	2,667500	....	....	192,500	3,297,000
2 cents	....	....	....	192,500	442,000
3 cents	13,567,500	38,500	....	192,500	13,988,500
6 cents	....	....	684,000	195,000	1,069,000
7 cents	....	....	....	....	95,000
10 cents	....	....	....	192,500	519,200
12 cents	....	....	....	192,500	382,500
15 cents	....	....	....	192,500	335,000
24 cents	192,500	....	....	95,000	508,400
30 cents	192,500	....	....	95,000	504,000
90 cents	195,000	....	....	....	242,500
2 dollars	....	1,800	....	....	1,800
Total	16,815,000	40,300	684,000	1,540,000	21,384,900

Year ending December 31st, 1875:

DEPARTMENT:

	Agriculture.	Executive.	Interior.	Justice.	Navy.
1 cent	....	....	97,500	....	375,000
2 cents	....	....	95,000	....	352,500
3 cents	....	9,500	1,010,000	37,500	735,000
6 cents	....	....	372,500	....	370,000
7 cents	....	....	....	....	185,000
10 cents	....	....	....	....	190,000
12 cents	....	....	141,500	....	175,000
15 cents	....	....	47,000	....	180,000
24 cents	....	....	46,500	....	185,000
30 cents	....	....	95,000	....	187,500
90 cents	....	....	....	....	187,500
Total	....	9,500	1,905,000	37,500	3,122,500

	Post Office.	State.	Treasury.	War.	Total.
1 cent	....	... .	970,000	190,000	1,632,500
2 cents	....	....	960,000	195,000	1,602,500
3 cents	9,997,500	37,500	1,935,000	485,000	14,247,000
6 cents	1,280,000	32,500	895,000	185,000	3,135,000
7 cents	....	....	92,500	180,000	457,500
10 cents	85,000	....	80,000	185,000	540,000
12 cents	92,500	....	85,000	175,000	669,000
15 cents	85,000	....	95,000	177,500	584,500
24 cents	90,000	....	90,000	182,500	594,000
30 cents	82,500	....	116,000	180,000	661,000
90 cents	87,500	... .	80,000	192,500	547,500
2 dollars	....	1,980	....	....	1,980
5 dollars	....	1,870	....	....	1,870
10 dollars	....	1,930	....	....	1,930
20 dollars	......	1,940	....	....	1,940
Total	11,800,000	77,720	5,398,500	2,327,500	24,678,220

Year ending December 31st, 1876 :

DEPARTMENT :

	Interior.	Post Office.	Total.
1 cent	....	....	....
2 cents	220,000	185,000	405,000
3 cents	190,000	6,175,000	6,365,000
6 cents	....	....	....
7 cents	....	....	... .
10 cents	90,000	....	90,000
12 cents	....	....	....
15 cents	... .	....	....
24 cents	....	....	....
30 cents	... ...	......	.. ....
90 cents	47,500	....	47,500
Total	547,500	6,360,000	6,907,500

I greatly regret that I have not been able to obtain further statistics of deliveries to the Stamp Agent. The foregoing tables are not sufficiently extensive to enable us to make comparisons and deductions of much value. It is particularly to be regretted that we have no statistics of the quantities delivered in 1879 and subsequent years, as there are a number of questions connected with the official stamps printed by the American Bank Note Co. which might be settled if we had at command the records of the quantities supplied under the contracts of that company.

From the fact that, in 1876, stamps were prepared for only two departments, and for a limited number of values at that, we must infer either a great decrease in their use or considerable overproduction in previous years.

It may be well to remark that these tables do not include the special printing of official stamps made in 1875, which stamps were surcharged "SPECIMEN" and sold as companion sets to the reprints and re-issues of the several series of ordinary postage stamps.

OFFICIAL STAMPS.

ISSUE OF 1879.

After the consolidation of the Continental Bank Note Co. with the American Bank Note Co., in February, 1879, the latter company printed such official stamps as were required, using the soft porous paper which distinguishes all stamps produced by them. As it has not been possible to obtain access to the records of the printings, the list of official stamps on this paper is compiled from discoveries reported by philatelists. Some of the stamps are very common on this paper—for example many values of the Interior and War departments—while others are quite scarce.

Perforated 12.

Soft Porous White Wove Paper.

DEPARTMENT OF AGRICULTURE.

1879.

1 cent bright orange-yellow
2 cents bright orange-yellow
3 cents bright orange-yellow
6 cents bright orange-yellow

DEPARTMENT OF THE INTERIOR.

1879.

1 cent pale vermilion, vermilion
2 cents scarlet-vermilion
3 cents pale vermilion, vermilion, scarlet-vermilion
6 cents pale vermilion, vermilion, scarlet-vermilion
    rose-vermilion
10 cents pale vermilion, vermilion
12 cents vermilion
15 cents vermilion
24 cents vermilion

DEPARTMENT OF JUSTICE.

1879.

3 cents bluish purple, deep bluish purple
6 cents bluish purple

NAVY DEPARTMENT.

1879.

1 cent dull blue
2 cents dull blue
3 cents dull blue
6 cents dull blue

POST OFFICE DEPARTMENT.

1879.

1 cent gray-black
2 cents gray-black
3 cents gray-black
6 cents gray-black
12 cents gray-black
15 cents gray-black

DEPARTMENT OF STATE.

1879.

15 cents green
30 cents green

TREASURY DEPARTMENT.

1879.

1 cent dark brown
3 cents dark brown, dark yellow-brown
6 cents dark brown, dark yellow-brown
10 cents dark brown, dark yellow-brown
12 cents dark brown
15 cents dark brown
30 cents dark brown, dark yellow-brown
90 cents dark brown, dark yellow-brown

WAR DEPARTMENT.

1879.

1 cent pale dull rose, pale brown-rose, brown-rose, dull lake
2 cents pale dull rose, deep brown-rose, pale dull vermilion, dull vermilion
3 cents pale dull rose, brown-rose
6 cents pale dull rose, dull rose, pale brown rose, brown rose
10 cents pale dull rose, deep rose, dull brown-rose
12 cents pale dull rose, dull brown-lake
24 cents pale dull rose
30 cents pale dull rose

Variety:

3 cents deep rose. Imperforate

In addition to these varieties, the one cent Executive and the one and seven cents Department of State, all surcharged "SPECIMEN", are found on soft porous paper, but copies of these values without the surcharge have not been discovered.

"Specimen" stamps.

I have in my collection a three cents green, of the regular issue of 1882, which is overprinted, in black, in two lines, "P. O. DEPT.—24C." with a bar across the original value. This stamp was presented to me by Mr. C. A. Townsend, who writes me that he knows nothing about the stamp except that he found five or six copies (including one pair) in a large quantity of stamps which he purchased some years ago. The stamps had been accumulated by a young lady who was not a philatelist but had made the oft repeated attempt to collect a million stamps. My copy is uncancelled.

A possible provisional issue.

The American Bank Note Co. made only one plate for official stamps. This was for the one cent stamp of the Post Office Department. This plate was numbered 428 and contained two hundred stamps. For printing any other official stamps the plates of the Continental Bank Note Co. were used. On consulting the list given in the preceding chapter, it will be seen that there was only one plate for each of the official stamps, except for the two, three and six cents Post Office Department and the three cents Treasury Department. For printing the latter stamp plate 29 was used by the American Bank Note Co. and probably the plates with the highest numbers were employed for the three stamps of the Post Office Department. To give a list of the numbers of the other plates which were used would be an unnecessary repetition.

Plates.

It was scarcely to be expected that the official stamps would be received with favor, either by individuals who were deprived of the franking privilege coincidently with the advent of the stamps, or by the various branches of the government, which were required to expend large sums for the purchase of these stamps from the Post Office Department. As early as February, 1874, we read in the *American Journal of Philately*

"The sales of postage stamps at the post office of the House of Representatives frequently exceed $50 a day The members begin to feel the inconvenience and loss to themselves from the abolition of the franking privilege, now that they are daily called upon to send public documents to their constituents at their own expense. They say they do not mind putting stamps on their letters, but when it comes to paying postage on heavy books, the burden is too heavy to be long endured. There is a good deal ot talk of a revival of franking as applied to public documents only. Another plan is to authorize, by law, the Public Printer to mail the documents, free of postage, to such persons as the members shall direct ; and still another is to have a stamping machine with an engraved steel die kept in the Clerk's office to stamp documents for free transmission through the mails."

Abolition of franking causes dissatisfaction.

However, no immediate legislative action was taken in the direction of repeal or modification of the law, and Congress continued to make annual appropriations of such sums as it was estimated would be required, by the various departments, for the purchase of stamps.

By an Act which was approved August 15th, 1876, a slight change was effected in the law, with respect to the manner of crediting the Post Office Department for the work of carrying the correspondence of the other departments. This Act provided :

" That the Secretaries respectively of the Departments of State, Treasury, War, Navy and Interior and the Attorney General, are authorized to make requisitions upon the Postmaster General for the necessary amount of postage stamps for the use of their Departments, not exceeding the amount stated in the estimates submitted to Congress, and upon presentation of proper vouchers therefore at the Treasury, the amount thereof shall 'be credited to the appropriation for the Post Office Department for the same fiscal year."

Change in method of obtaining stamps.

The first important change in the law was contained in the Act, approved March 3rd, 1877, which provided in part as follows :

" That it shall be lawful to transmit through the mail, free of postage, any letters, packages or other matter relating exclusively to the business of the Government of the United States :   Provided, that every such letter or package to entitle it to pass free shall bear over the words ' Official Business' an endorsement, showing also the name of the Department, and if from a bureau or office, the names of the Department and bureau or office, as the case may be, whence transmitted   And if any person shall make use of any such official envelope to avoid the payment of postage on his private letter, package or other matter in the mail, the person so offending shall be deemed guilty of a misdemeanor and subject to a fine of three hundred dollars, to be prosecuted in any court of competent jurisdiction.

" Penalty " envelopes authorized.

That, for the purpose of carrying this Act into effect, it shall be the duty of each of the Executive Departments of the United States, to provide for itself and its subordinate officers the necessary envelopes, and in addition to the endorsement designating the Department in which they are to be used, the penalty for the unlawful use shall be stated thereon.

That Senators, Representatives and Delegates in Congress, the Secretary of the Senate and the Clerk of the House of Representatives, may send and receive through the mail all public documents printed by order of Congress, and the name of each Senator, Representative, Delegate, Secretary of the Senate, and Clerk of the House, shall be written thereon, with the proper designation of the office he holds, and the provisions of this section shall apply to each of the persons mentioned therein until the first day of December following the expiration of their terms of office."

It will be observed that by this Act the franking privilege was to a certain extent, restored. The so-called " penalty " envelopes were created and, by their use, the official stamps were almost entirely superseded for franking correspondence *from* the departments. But subordinate officers, especially postmasters, continued to use the stamps on correspondence *to* the departments and elsewhere, as required.

Use of official stamps much reduced.

The effect of these changes appears to have been felt very soon by the Post Office Department. The Third Assistant Postmaster General, in his report for the fiscal year ending June 30th, 1877, says : " The total receipts for the year were $1,112,612.24 less than those of the preceding year. The decrease is due largely to the reduction in receipts for official postage stamps, the amount derived from that source during the last fiscal year being only $370,730.47 against $1,281,389.43 for the previous year." It should be remembered that these figures do not include the stamps used by the Post Office Department but only those purchased from it by the other departments.

Decreased receipts of the Post Office Department.

The Postmaster General, in his annual report for 1878, complains of the added burden without compensation, saying that, in addition to the official correspondence of the various departments which must be transmitted free, members of Congress might now send almost anything except letters through the mails and were availing themselves of the privilege and sending vast quantities of books, documents, seeds, shrubs, etc., etc.

By a subsequent amendment of the law the use of official stamps was almost entirely done away with. On this subject the report of the Postmaster General for 1885, says :

Use of official stamps further decreased. " The use of official stamps and stamped envelopes was wholly discontinued by this Department, and substantially so by the other Departments on the 30th of June, 1879, under the Act authorizing the use of official penalty envelopes."

The Act here referred to was approved March 3rd, 1879, and provided as follows :

Franking privilege extended. . " That the provisions of the fifth and sixth sections of the Act entitled ' An Act establishing post routes and for other purposes ', approved March 3d, 1877, for the transmission of official mail matter be, and they are hereby, extended to all officers of the United States Government, and made applicable to all official mail matter transmitted between any of the officers of the United States, or between any such officer and either of the Executive Departments or officers of the Government *   * . And the provisions of said fifth and sixth sections are hereby likewise extended and made applicable to all official mail matter sent from the Smithsonian Institution."

In conformity with this Act the Third Assistant Postmaster General issued the following :

CIRCULAR TO POSTMASTERS.

POST OFFICE DEPARTMENT,
OFFICE OF THE THIRD ASSISTANT POSTMASTER GENERAL,
Division of Postage Stamps, Stamped
Envelopes, and Postal Cards,
Washington, D. C., April 22, 1879.

USE OF FREE ENVELOPES—DISCONTINUANCE OF OFFICIAL POSTAGE STAMPS.

Circular of the Post Office Department. Under the provisions of Sections 5 and 6 of the Act of Congress " establishing post-routes, and for other purposes," approved March 3, 1877, and Section 29 of the " Act making appropriations for the Post Office Department," &c., approved March 3, 1879, the Department will begin the issue, on May 1st next, of envelopes for official business, which will secure the free transmission through the mails of all official matter, and which are intended to supersede the post office envelopes now in use, as well as official postage stamps and official stamped envelopes. Accordingly, the issue of official stamps and official stamped envelopes will be discontinued on and after the date named.

These free envelopes will be of the same sizes as the present post office envelopes, will be of the same color, (canary,) and will contain the same general forms of printing. Each envelope, however, will bear, in addition, the words " *Post Office Department, Post Office at* ———, *Official Business,*" and the penalty imposed by law for its misuse, as follows : " *A penalty of $300 is fixed by law for using this envelope for other than official business.*' When 500 of these free envelopes are ordered at one time, of either the Nos. 1, 2, or 3 sizes, the name of the post office will be printed in; also when 250 of the No. 4 size. In all other cases, a blank will be left for the name of the post office, which must be written in by the postmaster before using the envelope.

☞*The name of the office, it must be understood, is required by law to appear on the envelopes, and, when not in print, must be in writing.*

POST OFFICE ENVELOPES, AND OFFICIAL STAMPS AND STAMPED ENVELOPES
NOW ON HAND.

The stock of post office envelopes now in the hands of postmasters will, until exhausted, continue to be used, as heretofore, by the attachment of official postage stamps ; so, also, official stamped envelopes now in the hands of postmasters at Presidential offices will be used, as heretofore, until exhausted.

As soon, however, as such envelopes or the official stamps on hand are about to become exhausted, requisition must be made for a supply of the free envelopes, and the official postage stamps remaining on hand must be returned, registered, to the Department. If the official postage stamps now on hand should become exhausted before the post office envelopes, then the remaining envelopes should be returned to the Department and a supply of free envelopes ordered.

It is expected that postmasters will use these envelopes without waste, and never permit them to be used on other than strictly official business. Any violation of this instruction will be regarded as good ground for dismissal from office, besides subjecting the offender to the penalty of the law.

A. D. HAZEN,

Third Ass't Postmaster Gen'l.

It must be remembered that this circular applied only to the stamps and envelopes of the Post Office Department. With the exception of the Executive, which had discontinued the use of stamps in 1877, the other departments continued to use them to some extent.

The complete and final abolishment of the official stamps was effected by an Act of the Forty-eighth Congress, Session 1, Chapter 234, from which the following is quoted :

"SECTION 3. That section twenty-nine of the Act of March 3d, 1879, be, and it is hereby amended so as to read as follows :

The provisions of the fifth and sixth sections of the Act entitled ' An act establishing post-routes and for other purposes,' approved March 3d, 1877 for the transmission of official mail matter be, and they are hereby, extended to all officers of the United States Government not including members of Congress, the envelopes of such matter in all cases to bear appropriate endorsements containing the proper designation of the office from which or officer from whom the same is transmitted, with a statement of the penalty for their misuse. And the provisions of said fifth and sixth sections are hereby likewise extended and made applicable to all official mail matter of the Smithsonian Institution : *[Official stamps entirely abolished.]*

Provided, That any department or officer authorized to use the penalty envelopes may enclose them with return address to any person or persons from or through whom official information is desired, the same to be used only to cover such official information and endorsements relating thereto :

Provided further, That any letter or packet to be registered by either of the Executive Departments or Bureaus thereof, or by the Agricultural Department, or by the Public Printer, may be registered without the payment of any registry fee ; and any postpaid letter or packet addressed to either of said Departments or Bureaus may be delivered free ; but where there is good reason to believe the omission to prepay the full postage thereon was intentional, such letter or packet shall be returned to the sender :

Provided further, That this act shall not extend or apply to pension agents or other officers who receive a fixed allowance as compensation for their services, including expenses of postage.

And Section 3915 of the Revised Statutes of the United States, so far as the same relates to stamps and stamped envelopes for official purposes, is hereby repealed.

Approved July 5th, 1884."

Thus the use of the official stamps was brought to an end.

From the annual reports of the Postmaster General we obtain the following statistics of official stamps delivered to the different departments during the years they were in use. The reader will kindly bear in mind that the year is always the fiscal year ending June 30th:

DEPARTMENT OF AGRICULTURE.

	1 cent.	2 cents.	3 cents.	6 cents.	7 cents.	10 cents.	12 cents.	15 cents.	24 cents.	30 cents.	90 cents.
1874	60,000	95,000	80,000	60,000		50,000	19,000	14,000	30,000	32,000	
1875	30,000	80,000	15,000	25,000		45,000	32,000	40,000	30,000	50,000	
1876		25,000	30,000								
1877	5,000	15,000	20,000	5,000							
1878			50,000								
1879		5,000	40,000	10,000							
1880			40,000	5,000							
1881	200		60,000	5,000							
1882	65	10,000	59,000			50	50		50	50	
1883	150	150	50,000	10,000		65	65	50	65	65	
1884			50			150	150		150	150	
Total	95,415	230,150	435,050	120,000		95,265	51,265	54,050	60,265	82,265	

THE EXECUTIVE.

	1 cent.	2 cents.	3 cents.	6 cents.	7 cents.	10 cents.	12 cents.	15 cents.	24 cents.	30 cents.	90 cents.
1874	1,600	2,100	9,100	1,900		1,550					
1875											
1876	2,200	3,000	5,400	2,100		2,300					
1877	3,000	4,000	9,000	1,500		1,300					
1878											
1879											
1880											
1881											
1882											
1883											
1884											
Total	6,800	9,100	23,500	5,500		5,150					

DEPARTMENT OF THE INTERIOR

	1 cent.	2 cents.	3 cents.	6 cents.	7 cents.	10 cents.	12 cents.	15 cents.	24 cents.	30 cents.	90 cents.
1874	108,600	227,900	854,000	425,700	.....	71,750	122,850	71,500	49,275	46,150	16,525
1875	45,000	164,000	700,000	294,300	.....	50,600	63,200	32,100	34,000	26,150	10,020
1876	14,000	253,000	615,000	336,000	.....	105,200	77,500	18,500	18,250	52,250	15,000
1877	16,500	92,500	833,000	263,000	.....	7,600	21,000	8,000	5,500	4,000	12,100
1878	31,300	11,200	171,300	30,000	.....	1,000	20,000	.....	4,200	3,200	4,700
1879	25,400	31,000	337,000	60,000	.....	2,700	27,000	75,000	8,800	3,800	3,782
1880	12,000	10,000	268,000	59,000	.....	.....	2,000	26,000	.....	500	1,000
1881	.....	.....	180,000	.....	.....	.....	.....	.....	.....	.....	.....
1882	8,000	30,800	341,200	65,500	.....	35,500	5,800	3,500	3,600	2,000	1,000
1883	14,000	23,000	699,000	59,000	.....	.....	10,000	2,000	.....	.....	.....
1884	20,000	570,000	260,000	130,000	.....	10,000	10,500	10,500	10,500	250	250
Total	394,800	1,413,400	5,258,500	1,722,500	.....	284,350	359,850	247,100	134,125	138,300	64,377

DEPARTMENT OF JUSTICE.

	1 cent.	2 cents.	3 cents.	6 cents.	7 cents.	10 cents.	12 cents.	15 cents.	24 cents.	30 cents.	90 cents.
1874	9,000	7,400	39,000	27,000	.....	3,000	7,500	4,000	800	2,000	300
1875	6,000	4,000	29,000	7,000	.....	4,000	6,000	4,000	2,600	3,000	500
1876	.....	4,500	33,000	12,000	.....	3,500	3,300	1,800	500	600	400
1877	10,000	10,000	34,000	14,000	.....	4,000	2,000	.....	1,000	1,500	1,500
1878	.....	.....	23,000	10,000	.....	4,000	4,000	2,000	.....	.....	.....
1879	.....	.....	23,000	14,000	.....	2,000	4,000	1,000	1,500	1,500	500
1880	.....	.....	.....	.....	.....	.....	.....	.....	.....	.....	.....
1881	.....	.....	.....	.....	.....	.....	.....	.....	.....	.....	.....
1882	.....	.....	.....	.....	.....	.....	.....	.....	.....	.....	.....
1883	.....	.....	.....	.....	.....	.....	.....	.....	.....	.....	.....
1884	.....	1,000	1,000	.....	.....	.....	.....	.....	.....	.....	.....
Total	25,000	26,900	183,000	84,000	.....	20,500	26,800	12,800	6,400	8,600	3,200

NAVY DEPARTMENT.

Year	1 cent.	2 cents.	3 cents.	6 cents.	7 cents.	10 cents.	12 cents.	15 cents.	24 cents.	30 cents.	90 cents.
1874	22,800	48,350	110,700	58,800	6,000	13,210	22,300	12,500	10,000	8,600	2,070
1875	25,000	37,000	80,000	35,000	7,000	20,000	15,000	13,000	4,000	5,000	2,700
1876	15,000	25,000	95,000	40,000	......	10,000	10,000	8,000	4,000	8,000	2,000
1877	15,000	20,000	95,000	43,000	2,000	8,000	10,000	......	6,000	4,000	4,000
1878	10,000	20,000	65,000	30,000	......	......	......	......	......	1,000	......
1879	4,000	13,000	15,000	22,000	1,000	4,000	4,000	4,000	2,000	3,000	500
1880	......	7,000	15,000	5,000	......	......	......	......	......	......	......
1881	5,000	......	......	......	......	......	......	......	......	......	......
1882	10,000	6,000	15,000	1,000	......	......	......	......	......	......	......
1883	......	25,000	40,000	......	......	......	......	......	......	......	......
1884	......	......	......	......	......	......	......	......	......	......	......
Total	106,800	201,350	580,700	234,800	16,000	55,210	61,300	37,500	26,000	29,600	12,270

POST OFFICE DEPARTMENT.

Year	1 cent.	2 cents.	3 cents.	6 cents.	7 cents.	10 cents.	12 cents.	15 cents.	24 cents.	30 cents.	90 cents.
1874	632,300	399,250	16,906,000	787,950	......	79,500	218,600	67,860	47,900	37,600	30,150
1875	98,900	126,500	11,873,200	1,089,600	......	......	25,250	12,120	11,550	13,920	9,250
1876	232,300	247,300	10,435,200	745,900	......	101,200	13,975	9,280	9,500	60,400	4,950
1877	56,600	29,900	8,057,600	191,450	......	300	12,900	8,760	9,600	9,300	8,900
1878	67,500	78,100	9,701,400	310,850	......	1,250	18,055	6,500	5,700	5,680	9,700
1879	26,650	13,550	8,324,300	181,050	......	200	10,000	4,765	3,375	6,375	2,250
1880	......	......	......	......	......	......	......	......	......	......	......
1881	......	......	......	......	......	......	......	......	......	......	......
1882	......	......	......	......	......	......	......	......	......	......	......
1883	......	......	......	......	......	......	......	......	......	......	......
1884	......	......	......	......	......	......	......	......	......	......	......
Total	1,114,250	894,600	65,297,700	3,306,800	......	182,450	298,780	109,285	87,625	133,255	65,200

DEPARTMENT OF STATE.

	1 cent.	2 cents.	3 cents.	6 cents.	7 cents.	10 cents.	12 cents.	15 cents.	24 cents.	30 cents.	90 cents.
1874	9,800	9,800	25,800	13,800	7,800	7,800	5,800	5,800	5,800	5,800	2,043
1875	.....	10,000	10,000	25,000	10,000	20,000	7,000	7,000	2,000	7,000	1,500
1876	5,000	5,000	5,000	10,000	5,000	.....	1,000	1,000	1,000	1,000	.....
1877	15,000	15,000	68,400	33,300	15,000	30,000	1,000	1,000	1,000	1,000	.....
1878	.....	.....	.....	.....	.....	.....	.....	.....	.....	.....	.....
1879	.....	.....	.....	.....	.....	.....	.....	.....	.....	.....	500
1880	.....	.....	.....	.....	.....	.....	.....	.....	.....	.....	.....
1881	.....	.....	.....	.....	.....	.....	2,000	1,000	1,000	1,400	600
1882	.....	.....	.....	.....	.....	.....	.....	3,000	2,000	1,400	700
1883	2,000	2,000	.....	.....	.....	3,100	2,000	4,000	1,000	1,000	800
1884	.....	.....	.....	.....	.....	4,000	2,000	.....	.....	1,500	500
Total	31,800	41,800	109,200	82,100	37,800	64,900	20,800	22,800	13,800	20,100	6,643

	2 dollars.	5 dollars.	10 dollars.	20 dollars.
1874	463	363	363	363
1875	1,000	.....	.....	.....
1876	500	.....	.....	.....
1877	1,245	.....	.....	.....
1878	.....	.....	.....	.....
1879	.....	.....	.....	.....
1880	.....	.....	.....	.....
1881	.....	.....	.....	.....
1882	300	.....	.....	.....
1883	.....	.....	.....	.....
1884	.....	.....	.....	.....
Total	3,508	363	363	363

TREASURY DEPARTMENT.

	1 cent.	2 cents.	3 cents.	6 cents.	7 cents.	10 cents.	12 cents.	15 cents.	24 cents.	30 cents.	90 cents.
1874	1,000,000	1,244,500	4,350,000	1,315,000	120,000	250,000	483,000	433,000	100,000	96,500	50,500
1875	250,000	......	1,150,000	600,500	75,000	150,000	......	......	......	100,000	75,000
1876	550,000	300,000	1,800,000	540,000	......	100,000	100,000	50,000	......	110,000	......
1877	300,000	240,000	1,050,000	550,000	25,000	100,000	100,000	100,000	......	110,000	67,000
1878	600,000	450,000	1,500,000	600,000	......	100,000	100,000	80,000	......	70,000	59,000
1879	200,000	250,000	1,400,000	500,000	......	391,500	100,000	80,000	......	80,000	70,000
1880	...	...	...	...	...	...	...	...	...	...	...
1881	...	...	...	...	...	...	...	...	...	...	...
1882	...	...	...	...	...	200,000	...	...	...	...	...
1883	...	...	...	...	...	...	...	...	...	...	...
1884	...	...	...	...	...	...	...	...	...	...	...
Total	2,900,000	2,484,500	11,250,000	4,105,000	220,000	1,291,500	783,000	663,000	100,000	456,500	312,500

WAR DEPARTMENT.

	1 cent.	2 cents.	3 cents.	6 cents.	7 cents.	10 cents.	12 cents.	15 cents.	24 cents.	30 cents.	90 cents.
1874	187,300	70,300	225,300	116,950	6,600	20,600	18,000	17,700	19,900	15,750	4,650
1875	173,660	64,550	186,600	113,600	10,700	13,550	20,750	23,025	18,600	31,875	2,200
1876	83,750	51,800	231,000	144,050	13,110	50,725	29,830	14,430	12,080	12,840	3,245
1877	83,580	102,850	519,200	281,450	6,770	26,170	31,830	14,510	7,610	21,150	270
1878	128,100	102,300	575,500	325,000	125	30,425	57,975	17,025	21,325	18,825	4,425
1879	249,500	133,300	829,300	574,050	8,600	26,018	127,710	37,100	17,115	44,120	3,112
1880	1,527,550	61,000	442,933	270,433	53	41,075	89,755	25,250	12,025	36,541	3,380
1881	121,150	125,580	774,524	518,540	3,020	19,495	113,095	27,520	15,870	38,230	6,520
1882	109,500	113,980	680,425	518,440	2,950	30,445	133,375	53,550	33,220	58,240	6,800
1883	102,500	84,200	747,455	445,000	2,800	43,600	102,050	30,400	11,300	35,600	6,650
1884	534,700	957,300	181,000	277,300	1,000	40,700	67,700	25,500	31,900	23,470	6,920
Total	3,301,230	1,867,160	5,393,137	3,584,813	55,728	342,753	792,070	285,960	200,925	336,641	48,172

The official stamps having become obsolete, it is said that the various departments were requested to return to the Post Office department any unused stamps which they had on hand, and that some of the departments complied with this request while others declined, on the ground that they had paid for the stamps and should not be expected to give them up unless properly compensated. Concerning such official stamps as had been manufactured but not distributed to the departments, the Third Assistant Postmaster General made the following recommendations :

POST OFFICE DEPARTMENT,
OFFICE OF THE THIRD ASSISTANT POSTMASTER GENERAL,
WASHINGTON, D C., January 14, 1885.

SIR :—The issue and use of official stamps was discontinued under the third section of the Act of July 5, 1884 (General Statutes, 1st Session, 48th Congress), extending the use of penalty envelopes to all classes of official correspondence. At that time the contractors for furnishing stamps, the American Bank Note Co., of New York, had and now have in their vaults at the manufactory, as shown by the weekly reports made to this office, the following numbers and denominations of official stamps, viz :

Denomination.	Executive	State.	Treasury.	War.	Navy.	
1 cent	3,500	13,500	1,292,950	37,170	421,200	Schedule of unissued official stamps.
2 cents	1,900	4,000	1,921,500	75,340	381,150	
3 cents	1,100	11,900	534,000	104,463	454,800	
6 cents	4,700	10,600	169,000	2,787	355,300	
7 cents	. . . . . .	7,500	201,200	161,772	276,900	
10 cents	4,950	8,000	13,300	231,947	267,290	
12 cents	. . . . . .	24,300	444,000	25,130	236,199	
15 cents	. . . . . .	22,300	610,400	108,540	216,000	
24 cents	. . . . . .	31,500	279,500	103,675	219,800	
30 cents	. . . . . .	24,700	20,600	6,159	217,300	
90 cents	. . . . . .	35,257	37,000	167,728	233,830	
2 dollars	. . . . . .	472	. . . . . .	. . . . . .	. . . . . .	
5 dollars	. . . . . .	1,707	. . . . . .	. . . . . .	. . . . . .	
10 dollars	. . . . . .	1,767	. . . . . .	. . . . . .	. . . . . .	
20 dollars	. . . . . .	1,777	. . . . . .	. . . . . .	. . . . . .	
	16,150	199,280	5,523,450	1,024,711	3,279,769	

Denomination.	Interior.	Post Office.	Justice.	Agriculture.
1 cent	56,000	2,888,750	24,300	149,585
2 cents	13,700	449,400	21,000	55,150
3 cents	40,500	263,100	79,700	37,950
6 cents	37,800	559,700	47,500	101,000
7 cents	. . . . .	. . . . . .	. . . . . .	. . . . . .
10 cents	32,050	144,250	19,400	84,935
12 cents	99,450	321,220	17,500	91,735
15 cents	52,200	146,715	20,200	87,350
24 cents	10,175	259,875	13,600	112,635
30 cents	48,700	209,045	13,100	99,535
90 cents	20,523	254,600	6,300	. . . . . .
	411,098	5,496,655	262,600	810,875

Grand Total, 17,024,588.

As it is not likely that these stamps will be needed for use by the government, to avoid any risks that may attend their custody, I would respectfully recommend that they be counted and destroyed under the supervision of a committee to be appointed by the Postmaster General, and the facts certified under affidavit by the committee.

Destruction recommended.

There are also in the vaults of the contractors certain other stamps of the regular series that have been rendered unserviceable by reason of changes at various times in the rates of postage, and as it is improbable that these stamps will ever be required for issue, I would recommend that they also be counted and destroyed in like manner, and by the same committee suggested with regard to the official stamps.

Other unissued stamps.

These stamps are in number and denomination as follows :

Denomination.	Ordinary.	Newspaper and Periodical.	Total.
3 cents	.	223,750	223,750
7 cents	545,600	. . . . .	545,600
9 cents	. . . . . .	101,240	101,240
12 cents	503,750	. . . . . .	503,750
24 cents	364,950	. . . . .	364,950
Total	1,414,300	324,990	1,739,290

I have excepted from this recommendation the three-cent stamps of the ordinary series, of which there are 135,800 in the vault, for the reason that, though their general issue has been discontinued, occasional calls are made for them by some of the larger offices.

Three-cent stamps excepted.

The total number of stamps in the foregoing lists, recommended to be destroyed, is 18,763,878, which at the contract price of 9.19c per thousand, would amount to $204.52.

In the event that this recommendation should meet with your approval, permit me to suggest that the work of counting and destruction be performed by the committee selected to supervise the cancellation of the dies, etc., at the several places of manufacture.

Very respectfully, your obedient servant,

A. D. HAZEN,

Hon. FRANK HATTON,   *Third Assistant Postmaster General.*
        Postmaster General.

These suggestions appear to have met with the approval of the Postmaster General and they were accordingly embodied in the following order :

POST OFFICE DEPARTMENT,
OFFICE OF THE POSTMASTER GENERAL,
WASHINGTON, D. C., January 14, 1885.

Ordered (No. 75), that A. G. Sharp, Chief Post Office Inspector, Geo. W. Wells, Chief of the Finance Division of the Office of the Third Assistant Postmaster General, and C. M. Walker, Chief Clerk of the Post Office Department, be designated as a committee to visit the postage stamp manufactory at New York, the stamped envelope manufactory at Hartford, Conn., and the postal card manufactory at Castleton, N. Y., and in connection with the Government agent at each of these places, to dispose of, as hereinafter indicated, the dies, rolls and plates of the several series of postage stamps, stamped envelopes and postal cards heretofore and now in use.

POSTAGE STAMPS.

At New York, the Committee will effectually cancel all plates of the following series and denominations of postage stamps, except one working plate of each : Plates ordered to be cancelled.

Issue of 1847 : Denominations, 5 and 10 cents.

Issue of 1851 : Denominations, 1, 3, 5, 10, 12, 24, 30 and 90 cents, also two separate designs of 1-cent carrier stamps.

Issue of 1861 : Denominations, 1, 2, 3, 5, 10, 12, 15, 24, 30 and 90 cents.

Issue of 1865 (newspaper and periodical) : Denominations, 5, 10 and 25 cents.

Issue of 1869 : Denominations, 1, 2, 3, 6, 10, 12, 15, 24, 30 and 90 cents.

Issue of 1870 (current series) : Denominations, 3, 5 (Taylor), 7, 12 and 24 cents.

Issue of 1874 (newspaper and periodical) : Denominations, 3 and 9 cents.

Executive (official) : Denominations, 1, 2, 3, 6 and 10 cents

Department of State (official) : Denominations, 1, 2, 3, 6, 7, 10, 12, 15, 24, 30 and 90 cents, and $2, $5, $10 and $20.

Treasury Department (official) : Denominations, 1, 2, 3, 6, 7, 10, 12, 15, 24, 30 and 90 cents.

War Department (official) : Denominations, 1, 2, 3, 6, 7, 10, 12, 15, 24, 30 and 90 cents.

Navy Department (official) : Denominations, 1, 2, 3, 6, 7, 10, 12, 15, 24, 30 and 90 cents.

Post Office Department (official) : Denominations, 1, 2, 3, 6, 10 12, 15, 24, 30 and 90 cents.

Department of the Interior (official) : Denominations, 1, 2, 3, 6, 10, 12, 15, 24, 30 and 90 cents.

Department of Justice (official) : Denominations, 1, 2, 3, 6, 10, 12, 15, 24, 30 and 90 cents.

Department of Agriculture (official) : Denominations, 1, 2, 3, 6, 10, 12, 15, 24 and 30 cents.

The one plate of each kind and denomination of postage stamp reserved as above, and the dies and rolls from which they have been produced, together with all the cancelled plates, to be inventoried, waxed, and carefully boxed and sealed, and placed in the vault of the stamp manufactory in the custody and under the control of the agent, one copy of such inventory to be given to the agent, and one to be sent by the committee to the Department.

The committee will also superintend the cancellation of any worn out and unserviceable plates of the current series of postage stamps that may be in the possession of the contractors.   *   *   *   *   *   *   *

The committee will also supervise the counting and destruction of

Stamps ordered to be destroyed. certain discontinued issues of postage stamps, at the postage stamp manufactory at New York, in accordance with the accompanying recommendation of the Third Assistant Postmaster General.

Upon completing the work for which they are appointed, the committee will make a written report.

FRANK HATTON,
Postmaster General.

On February 24th, 1885, the committee reported: "We have counted and destroyed by burning, in accordance with instructions, the official and **Committee report** uncurrent stamps, numbering 18,438,888. The schedule of denominations is **the destruction.** herewith transmitted." (*House Executive Documents*, 1884-85, 48*th Congress, Session II, No.* 264.)

The schedule was the same as that given in the letter of the Third Assistant Postmaster General, except that it did not include the newspaper **Newspaper stamps** and periodical stamps. The decision to destroy was evidently reconsidered **not destroyed.** in the case of those stamps, and it is understood that at least a part of them were subsequently used.

As has been previously remarked, the tables of quantities of stamps delivered to the Stamp Agent are not sufficiently extensive or complete to be **High values of the** of much value for comparison, yet we can make some limited deductions **Dept. of State.** from them. Let us consider the four higher values of the Department of State. Comparing the number received by the Stamp Agent with the deliveries to the Department and the quantity burned, we find a difference of exactly five hundred of each value. We cannot, with present information, explain this discrepancy. It is possible that the stamps not accounted for were proofs, though I am advised, by those who are well informed about such matters, that this is not probable. For the present we will have to leave the question for the consideration of those who are interested in such matters.

NEWSPAPER AND PERIODICAL STAMPS.

ISSUE OF 1865.

It has been remarked in previous chapters that, in its earlier years, the postal service suffered much annoyance and loss through the competition of local delivery and express companies. Through legislation the Government finally secured exclusive control of the business of transporting letters but in the matter of handling newspapers the express companies continued to be active and successful rivals of the Post Office Department. They carried papers quickly and cheaply from publishers to distributing agents. On the other hand, the routine of the postal service, which required the papers to be carried to the post office, assorted, forwarded and again assorted before delivery, caused vexatious delays. An attempt to overcome this difficulty was made in an Act of Congress, approved March 3rd, 1863, which provided as follows :

"The Postmaster General may, from time to time, provide by order the rates and terms upon which route agents may receive and deliver, at the mail car or steamer, packages of newspapers and periodicals, delivered to them for that purpose by the publishers or any news agent in charge thereof, and not received from nor designed for delivery at any post office." *Act concerning transportation of newspapers.*

As the Post Office Department was anxious to secure the carrying of newspapers it is probable that the privileges granted by this Act were promptly made available. It is to be presumed that the postage was paid to the route agents to whom the packages of papers were delivered. Such a return to the old-fashioned method of collecting postage in money, without the use of stamps or other vouchers for the Government, could not fail to be unsatisfactory. As a remedy, postage stamps were brought into use, at some time during the summer of 1865. Concerning them the report of the Postmaster General, dated November 15th, 1865, says briefly :

"New stamps have been adopted of the denominations of 5, 10 and 25 cents for prepaying postage on packages of newspapers forwarded by publishers or newsdealers under the authority of law, whereby a revenue will be secured hitherto lost to the Department." *Announcement of first newspaper stamps.*

The stamps are thus officially described :

"The 5, 10 and 25 cent newspaper and periodical stamps are alike in general style, 2 by 3¾ inches in dimensions, the denominations being repeated in Arabic and Roman numerals, in the upper corners Arabic and midway of the sides Roman. The numbers ' 10 ' and ' 5 ', five-eighths of an inch high, are white-faced, while those at the sides are the color of the stamp. On the *Designs.*

25-cent stamp the side figures are also Arabic. The numerals in the upper corners of the 10 and 25 cent stamps are inclined outward; those on the 5-cent are perpendicular.

The letters 'U' and 'S' appear near the top in a horizontal line and, immediately beneath, the word 'POSTAGE', in a line curved downward at each end. Next below this, in the middle of the stamp and surrounded by a border of lathe-work, are the several profile medallion portraits in a misty style of engraving. The Washington medallion is circular, 1 1-8 inches in diameter. The Franklin is an ellipse, 1 1-16 by 1 5-16 inches; while the Lincoln is a parallelogram with clipped corners, 7-8 by 1 3-8 inches. Below the tablets are the words representing the denominations, and 'NEWSPAPERS AND PERIODICALS', in three lines. After this, reference is made as follows: 'SEC. 38. ACT OF CONGRESS APPROVED MARCH 3D 1863.' Below the border line proper – the heavy white line—at the bottom, in very small type, are the words 'NATIONAL BANK NOTE COMPANY, NEW YORK'."

The profile busts are intended to suggest coins or medals. The stamps measure 51x94½ to 95½mm.

The stamps differ from other issues of United States postage stamps in that they are typographed instead of being engraved in *taille douce*. On the

plates, as originally made, the surface of the plate between the stamps was not cut away, consequently it received the ink like those parts of the design which were not incised. The result was that the stamps had a border of color. Subsequently the plate of the five cents was altered by removing the surface between the stamps, thus producing what is known as the "white border". Mr. Tiffany says that 20,140 of the five cents with colored border were issued, and "In 1868-69 there were issued 33,420 more of the five cent value, but these were improved by having the broad colored border removed." I do not know upon what authority he bases these statements, but I am not inclined to accept them without question. By referring to the tables of statistics which accompany this chapter it will be seen that he quotes the quantities of the first and last years of issue but ignores the 80,000 copies issued in the two intervening years. The relative quantities to be found of the two varieties of the stamp suggest that those with the colored border were in use for only a limited period and were replaced by the second type at an early date.

The stamps were perforated 12 and were issued ungummed.

At first they were printed on a paper which was moderately thick, hard,

opaque and very white, unless discolored by age. Afterwards a very thin, tough, almost pelure paper was used. The latest printings were on a thin, crisp, semi-transparent paper.

They are found in the following shades :

Perforated 12.

COLORED BORDER.

White Wove Paper.

5 cents pale dull blue, dull blue, dark dull blue, deep bright blue

> 10 cents pale gray-green, gray-green, deep gray-green, green, deep green, bluish green
>
> 25 cents pale orange-red, orange-red, vermilion, scarlet, carmine-red, brown-carmine; brown-red
>
> Pelure Paper.
>
> 10 cents pale gray-green, gray-green, deep gray-green
>
> 25 cents orange-red, scarlet
>
> WHITE BORDER.
>
> White Wove Paper.
>
> 5 cents pale blue, blue, pale bright blue, bright blue, deep bright blue, gray-blue, deep gray-blue
>
> Pelure Paper.
>
> 5 cents blue, bright blue, deep bright blue

The plates each contained twenty stamps, arranged in four rows of five stamps. The impressions were divided horizontally into sheets of ten stamps each. The imprint was "NATIONAL BANK NOTE CO. NEW YORK," in colored Roman capitals, on a small white panel having rounded ends and surrounded by two fine white lines. The imprint was placed above the middle stamp of the upper row and below the corresponding stamp of the lower row. On the sheets of stamps with the colored borders the plate numbers were in large ornamental figures and were placed about 11mm. to the right of the imprint, thus coming above or below the corner of the adjacent stamp. In removing the colored border from the five cent stamp both plate numbers were erased. To replace them the same number was engraved close to the end of the imprint —at the right of the upper and at the left of the lower imprint—in small white figures, 1½mm. high. The plate numbers were : — Plates. Imprint. Plate numbers.

5 cents	No. 38.
10 cents	No. 39.
25 cents	No. 40.

The *Stamp Collector's Magazine* for May, 1867, says :

"For some reason these labels are only regularly sold at the post office in Chicago, Illinois, where they have always been procurable since the time of issue, but other offices have occasionally kept them in stock" Other writers say, "only at Chicago, Ill. and Milwaukee, Wis." It is difficult to understand this restricted use, but probably, in other cities, the publishers continued to favor the express companies. — Restricted use.

The stamps were usually cancelled with a brush dipped in black or blue ink. Specimens with postmarks are nearly always bogus. Genuinely used copies are scarce, as the wrappers to which they were attached were usually thrown away as waste paper. Furthermore, the cancelled stamps are seldom in good condition. This is probably due to the large size of the stamps and to their having been hurriedly and carelessly affixed to the packages. — Cancellation.

On January 21st, 1867, there was made, by order of A. N. Zevely, Third Assistant Postmaster General, a special printing of 1,000 copies of each — "Specimens," denomination of this issue. These stamps were overprinted "SPECIMEN" in large gothic type.

A few years ago there were in the hands of collectors and dealers in Boston, a number of the ten cent stamps which differed in perforation from the regular issue. The gauge ranged from 11 to 14½ and there were often three different perforations on a stamp. The copies were all on pelure paper and all had the perforations much closer to the design than usual, often cutting the outer white line. They were said to have been purchased from "a reliable person who stated that he bought them from the Post Office Department." Personally, I believe these perforations to be of a private nature, but I give the information of their existence for what it is worth.

The report of the Postmaster General, dated November 15th, 1869, says :

Use of stamps discontinued. "The issue of periodical stamps was discontinued by my predecessor about 1869."

No reason is given for this action nor any further information on the subject. We do not know whether such of the stamps as were in the hands of postmasters were used up or returned to Washington.

Statistics of manufacture. During the time the stamps were in use the following quantities were received by the Post Office Department from the contractors :

	5 cents	10 cents.	25 cents.
1865	10,040	20,040	5,040
1866	38,230	120,230	10,230
1867	30,000	95,000	......
1868	55,220	140,020	31,080
1869	10,200	25,200	100
Total	143,690	400,490	46,450

Deliveries to postmasters. The annual reports of the Postmaster General furnish the following statistics of deliveries to deputy postmasters :

Stamps issued during the fiscal year ending June 30th, 1866 :

QUARTER ENDING :

	Sept. 30, 1865.	Dec. 31, 1865.	Mch. 31, 1866.	June 30, 1866.	Total.
5 cents	10,000	10	......	10,130	20,140
10 cents	10,000	10,010	......	20,130	40,140
25 cents	5,000	10	......	130	5,140

Whole number of stamps 65,420. Value $6,306.00.

Stamps issued during the fiscal year ending June 30th, 1867 :

QUARTER ENDING :

	Sept. 30, 1866.	Dec. 31, 1866.	Mch. 31, 1867.	June 30, 1867.	Total.
5 cents	10,000	10,000	20,000	......	40,000
10 cents	30,000	20,000	50,000	......	100,000
25 cents	5,000	......	..	.....	5,000

Whole number of stamps 145,000. Value $13,250.00.

Stamps issued during the fiscal year ending June 30th, 1868 :

QUARTER ENDING :

	Sept. 30, 1867.	Dec. 31, 1867.	Mch. 31, 1868.	June 30, 1868.	Total.
5 cents	10,000	. . . . .	10,000	20,000	40,000
10 cents	20,000	25,000	20,000	50,000	115,000
25 cents	. . . . . .	. . . . . .	5,000	. . . . . .	5,000

Whole number of stamps 160,000.　Value $14,750.00.

Stamps issued during the fiscal year ending June 30th, 1869 :

QUARTER ENDING :

	Sept. 30, 1868.	Dec. 31, 1868.	Mch. 31, 1869.	June 30, 1869.	Total.
5 cents	15,200	10,020	10,200	. . . . . .	35,420
10 cents	45,100	25,020	25,200	. . . . . .	95,320
25 cents	15,060	5,020	100	. . . . . .	20,180

Whole number of stamps 150,920.　Value $16,348.00.

The reprints of this and succeeding issues of newspaper stamps will be described in a chapter devoted to that subject. **Reprints.**

Counterfeits of these stamps are occasionally seen and some of them are rather dangerous. They are made by photo-lithography. They usually appear blurred, especially in the white lathe-work surrounding the medallions. They are too small, measuring 48¾ to 50½mm. by 92¼ to 94½mm. The perforation is nearly always incorrect, 11, 11½ or 12½. **Counterfeits.**

NEWSPAPER AND PERIODICAL STAMPS.

ISSUE OF 1875.

From 1869 to 1874 inclusive the postage on newspapers and periodicals was again collected in money. From the report of the Postmaster General, dated November 14th, 1873, it is apparent that this system was both unsatisfactory and unprofitable. He says :

System suggested by the Postmaster General.

"In my report for 1869 I had the honor to suggest a plan for the prepayment of postage on newspapers and other matter of the second class by we ght of packages, rather than by the present system, which requires the manipulation of each particular paper and allows the payment of postage at either the mailing office or the office of delivery. A careful revision of the subject confirms me in the opinion that the postage on all such matters should be collected in advance at the mailing office. Collections are now made with great difficulty, and there is no provision whatever by which dishonesty or negligence can be detected. No stamps are used for the payment of such postage, and the Department is compelled to accept in full satisfaction whatever sums of money postmasters choose to charge against themselves. So execrably bad is this system that postal officers of high standing have estimated that not more than one-third of the postage properly chargeable on newspapers is accounted for and paid over."

The suggestions of the Postmaster General were duly considered by Congress and resulted in an Act, approved June 23rd, 1874, which provided :

Plan authorized by Congress.

"SECTION 5. That on and after the first day of January, 1875, all newspapers and periodical publications, mailed from a known office of publication or news agency and addressed to regular subscribers or news agents, shall be charged the following rates :
On newspapers and periodical publications issued weekly and more frequently than once a week, two cents for each pound or fraction thereof, and on those issued less frequently than once a week three cents for each pound or fraction thereof ; Provided that nothing in this Act shall be held to change or amend Section 99 of the Act entitled : 'An Act to revise, consolidate and amend the statutes relating to the Post Office Department,' approved June 8th, 1872.
SECTION 6. That on and after the first day of January, 1875, upon the receipt of such newspapers and periodical publications at the office of mailing, they shall be weighed in bulk, and the postage paid thereon by a special adhesive stamp, to be devised and furnished by the Postmaster General ; which shall be affixed to such matter or to the sack containing the same, or upon a memorandum of such mailing, or otherwise as the Postmaster General may from time to time provide by regulation."

The stamps were first sent out to postmasters on December 11th, 1874, and went into use on January 1st, 1875.

In the report of the Third Assistant Postmaster General, dated November 15th, 1875, we find further interesting details concerning the stamps, the manner of using them and the success of the system :

System found satisfactory.

"On the first day of January, 1875, the new law requiring prepayment of postage by stamps on all newspapers and periodicals, sent from a known office of publication to regular subscribers through the mails, went into operation. The system inaugurated to carry the law into effect was approved by you in October, 1874, and has been found by experience to be admirably adapted to the purpose for which it was devised. No complaints of abuses on the part of publishers or postmasters have been received at this office during the nine months that have elapsed since the law went into effect. Indeed, it has worked so well in all its details, and has given such general satisfaction, that the idea of returning to the old system, or materially modifying the new one, ought not to be entertained.

Previous to the time when this law began to operate, no stamps were required for the payment of postage on newspapers sent to regular subscribers, as the postage was collected in money quarterly at the office of delivery. Last year there were 35,000 post offices at which newspaper postage was collected, while under the present true system of the absolute prepayment of all postages, the whole amount is collected at about 3,400 offices. the latter representing the number of places in the United States at which newspapers and periodicals are mailed.

The papers for subscribers living outside of the county in which they are published are made up in bulk at the publication office, carried to the post office, and there weighed. The postage is computed on the whole issue, the proper amount in stamps handed to the postmaster, who gives the publisher a receipt as evidence of payment, and on the stubs of the receipt book he affixes and cancels the stamps, which correspond in value with the sum mentioned in the receipt. Thus, one transaction is all that is required in paying the postage upon a single issue of any regular publication The stubs with their cancelled stamps are kept in the post office, as vouchers for the postage paid. In no case are the stamps affixed to the papers or packages that pass through the mails. Manner of using the stamps.

These stamps are twenty-four in number, and were prepared by the Continental Bank Note Company, of New York, from designs selected in October, 1874. The denominations are as follows, viz.: 2 cents, 3 cents, 4 cents, 6 cents, 8 cents, 9 cents, 10 cents, 12 cents, 24 cents, 36 cents, 48 cents, 60 cents, 72 cents, 84 cents, 96 cents, $1.92, $3, $6, $9, $12, $24, $36, $48 and $60. These denominations were found to be necessary, in order that payment might be made on any given quantity from one pound to one ton, at both the two and three cent rate, with the use of not to exceed five stamps in any transaction." Reason for the various denominations.

At first it was required to cancel the stamps with a punch but afterwards various forms of post office "killers " and even pen cancellations were allowed to be used. The stubs with the cancelled stamps attached were sent, at regular intervals, to the Post Office Department at Washington and, after comparison with the accounts, were destroyed. Cancellation.

The following is the official description of the designs:

1, 2, 3, 4, 6, 8, 9 and 10 CENTS. Emblematical figure of America, looking to the right and modeled after Crawford's statue upon the dome of the Capitol. The left hand rests on a shield and holds a wreath; the right grasps a sword. The head is adorned with a coronet of stars, surmounted by an eagle's head. The vignette stands in an arched frame, and at the sides and top are slabs containing the inscriptions: " NEWSPAPERS " on the left, "PERIODICALS" on the right, and "U. S. POSTAGE " at the top. At the bottom are shaded capitals representing the value, which is also indicated by large figures in the upper corners. The lower corners are ornamented by shields. The color of these stamps is black. Designs and colors.

12, 24, 36, 48, 60, 72, 84 and 96 CENTS. Vignette of Astraea, or Justice, in niche, curved at, the top, holding in her right hand the balance, and resting with her left on a shield bearing the United States coat of arms. The figure is full-robed, mailed and girdled as to the upper part, and helmeted. Surmounting the helmet is an eagle with outstretched wings. Figures representing values on shields in upper corners, values also in sunken letters below, richly ornamented. Inscriptions on sides and at top in shaded capitals on lined ground. Color, pink.

ONE DOLLAR AND NINETY-TWO CENTS. Vignette of Ceres, Goddess of Agriculture, in curved niche. She holds in her left hand an ear of corn; her right, holding a wreath, rests against the hip. The figure faces to the front, and is clad in full, flowing robes. "u. s. POSTAGE" at the top; other inscriptions in italic letters on obelisks at either side, resting on the lower slab, containing value in white capitals. Value also in figures in upper corners. Color, deep brown.

THREE DOLLARS Goddess of Victory, in curved niche, full robed, girded, with sword to the left, and mantel thrown over shoulders. The right hand is stretched forward, holding a wreath; the left rests on a shield. Figures of value in upper corners; value below in letters, on either side of a large figure " 3 ". Inscriptions in solid labels, on either side, and on lined ground above. Color, vermilion.

SIX DOLLARS. Clio, the Muse of History, in curved niche, full-robed, the toga thrown over the left shoulder. In her right hand she holds a stylus; in the left, a tablet. Figures of value in upper corners, surrounded by curved ornaments. Inscriptions in white shaded letters on sides, and above in dark letters, on lined ground. Color, light blue.

NINE DOLLARS. Minerva, the Goddess of Wisdom, full-robed, in curved niche. The left hand is placed across her breast, holding a portion of her toga ; the right is grasping a spear. Figures of value in upper corners. Inscriptions on sides in shaded italics, and above in small letters on lined ground. Value also in letters below on scroll. Beneath is a large " 9 ", in curved ornaments. Color, orange.

TWELVE DOLLARS. Vesta, the Goddess of the Fireside, full-robed, in curved niche. The left hand lifts her drapery ; the right holds a burning lamp. Figures of value in upper corners on tablets ; value also in letters on beaded frame beneath. Inscriptions in solid italic letters on sides, and in small white letters above. Color, rich green.

TWENTY-FOUR DOLLARS. Goddess of Peace, in curved niche—a half-naked figure, leaning against a broken column. She holds in her left hand an olive branch, while the right grasps three arrows. The value is in words beneath, on a solid tablet ; also in figures, in ornamented curves, in upper corners. Inscriptions in white shaded letters above and on sides, between which latter and each upper corner is a large, six-pointed star. Color, purplish slate.

THIRTY-SIX DOLLARS. Figure representing Commerce, in full garments, in curved niche. She holds in her left hand the caduceus, the winged rod of Mercury ; in her right, a miniature ship. Figures of value in upper corners and in ornamented capitals below. Inscriptions, also in ornamented capitals, on sides and above. Color, dull red

FORTY-EIGHT DOLLARS. Hebe, the Goddess of Youth, partly draped, in curved niche. The right hand holds a cup, which she is offering to the eagle, around whose neck is thrown her left hand. Figures of value on shields in upper corners, the word " POSTAGE " between ; value also in letters below, in curved ornaments. The letters " u. s.", in circles, between upper corners and side inscriptions, the latter being in curved labels. Color, light brown.

SIXTY DOLLARS. Vignette of an Indian maiden, standing in a rectangular frame. She is robed from her waist downward. Her right arm is extended while her left hangs by her side. The background is a landscape, trees and vines to the left, and wigwams to the right in the distance. Figures of value on shields in upper corners ; value also in white letters on solid tablet below. Inscriptions in white, on solid labels, above and on sides. Color, rich purple.

The stamps measure 24½x35mm.

The paper is thin, hard and slightly transparent. A few values are occasionally seen on a paper which is thicker and more opaque. The two **Paper.** and three cents are also found on ribbed paper. The gum is thin and smooth, usually yellowish but sometimes almost white. The perforation has the normal guage, 12.

The stamps are found in the following shades and varieties :

Perforated 12.   **Reference List.**

White Wove Paper.

2 cents black, gray-black, greenish black
3 cents black, gray-black
4 cents black, gray-black, greenish black
6 cents black, gray-black
8 cents black, gray-black, greenish black
9 cents black, gray-black, greenish black
10 cents black, gray-black, greenish black
12 cents pale rose, rose, lilac-rose, deep lilac-rose, violet-rose
24 cents pale rose, rose, lilac-rose, deep lilac-rose, violet-rose
36 cents pale rose, rose, lilac-rose, deep lilac-rose
48 cents rose, lilac-rose, deep lilac-rose
60 cents rose, lilac-rose, deep lilac-rose
72 cents rose, lilac-rose, deep lilac-rose
84 cents rose, lilac-rose
96 cents rose, lilac-rose, deep lilac-rose
1.92 cents bistre-brown, dark brown
3 dollars vermilion, orange-vermilion
6 dollars ultramarine, dull ultramarine
9 dollars yellow
12 dollars blue-green
24 dollars dark gray-violet
36 dollars rose-brown
48 dollars vermilion-brown
60 dollars red-violet

Varieties :

2 cents black,   Imperforate
3 cents black   "
4 cents black   "
6 cents black   "
8 cents black   "

9 cents black	Imperforate
10 cents black	"
12 cents bright rose	"
24 cents bright rose	"
36 cents bright rose	"
48 cents bright rose	'
60 cents bright rose	"
72 cents bright rose	·'
84 cents bright rose	"
96 cents bright rose	''
192 cents dark brown	"
3 dollars vermilion	"
6 dollars ultramarine	"
9 dollars yellow	"
12 dollars blue-green	"
24 dollars dark gray-violet	''
36 dollars rose-brown	"
48 dollars vermilion-brown	"
60 dollars red-violet	"

Horizontally Ribbed Paper.

2 cents black
3 cents black

Plates. — The plates each contained one hundred stamps, arranged in ten rows of ten. Before delivery the sheets were divided horizontally into half sheets of fifty stamps. The imprint was "ENGRAVED AND PRINTED BY THE—CONTINENTAL BANK NOTE CO., NEW YORK", in two lines of white Roman capitals, on a panel with beaded edge and surrounded by a thin colored line. The imprint was placed above the two stamps in the middle of the top row and below the corresponding stamps of the bottom row. There were no imprints at the sides, merely three lines forming an arrow head and marking the line at which the sheet should be divided. Numbers were assigned to all the plates but they do not appear on sheets of the lower values (I have not been able to see sheets of the higher values) and probably were not engraved on any of the plates, at least not on the face. Sheets from one of the plates of the two cents show a script figure "2" above the eighth stamp of the top row; and certain sheets of the three cents bear, above the seventh stamp of the same row, a large Roman capital "B", white faced and heavily shaded. The numbers assigned to the plates were:

Plate numbers.

2 cents	No. 200, 218B.
3 cents	No. 206, 233, 233B.
4 cents	No. 215.
6 cents	No. 216.
8 cents	No. 213.
9 cents	No. 211.
10 cents	No. 217.
12 cents	No. 195.
24 cents	No. 198.

36 cents	No. 196.
48 cents	No. 203.
60 cents	No. 202.
72 cents	No. 201.
84 cents	No. 205.
96 cents	No. 204.
192 cents	No. 207.
3 dollars	No. 199.
6 dollars	No. 197.
9 dollars	No. 194.
12 dollars	No. 214.
24 dollars	No. 209.
36 dollars	No. 212.
48 dollars	No. 210.
60 dollars	No. 208.

These stamps are found surcharged with the word "Specimen" in gothic type. This surcharge is of two sizes; one is similar to the well-known surcharge on the stamps of the 1861 issue, while the other is smaller.   "Specimens."

I have only been able to secure incomplete statistics of the quantities of these stamps received by the Stamp Agent from the contractors. During the first three years of manufacture the quantities were :   Statistics of manufacture.

YEAR ENDING DECEMBER 31ST :

	1874.	1875.	1876.	Total.
2 cents	975,000	....	175,000	1,150,000
3 cents	975,000	....	....	975,000
4 cents	792,000	....	....	792,000
6 cents	775,000	... .	....	775,000
8 cents	198,000	....	180,000	378,000
9 cents	200,000	....	35,000	235,000
10 cents	188,000	90,000	125,000	403,000
12 cents	200,000	....	175,000	375,000
24 cents	197,000	....	175,000	372,000
36 cents	100,000	....	45,000	145,000
48 cents	100,000	....	40,000	140,000
60 cents	100,000	....	40,000	140,000
72 cents	100,000	....	40,000	140,000
84 cents	100,000	....	40,000	140,000
96 cents	100,000	....	40,000	140,000
192 cents	20,000	19,500	90,000	129,500
3 dollars	40,000	....	88,000	128,000
6 dollars	20,000	....	62,500	82,500
9 dollars	20,000	....	9,500	29,500
12 dollars	20,000	....	8,500	28,500
24 dollars	5,000	5,000	9,500	19,500
36 dollars	5,000	....	18,500	23,500
48 dollars	5,000	....	9,500	14,500
60 dollars	5,000	....	13,500	18,500
Total,	5,240,000	114,500	1,419,500	6,774,000

The annual reports of the Postmaster General furnish the following statistics of quantities supplied to deputy postmasters:

Deliveries to postmasters.

Stamps issued during the fiscal year ending June 30, 1875:

QUARTER ENDING:

	Sept. 30, 1874.	Dec. 31, 1874.	Mch. 31, 1875.	June 30, 1875.	Total.
2 cents	....	470,700	69,795	49,060	589,555
3 cents	....	260,800	33,930	23,365	318,095
4 cents	....	272,900	26,600	25,665	325,165
6 cents	.. ....	173,250	27,345	25,380	225,975
8 cents	....	51,250	14,000	14,405	79,655
9 cents	....	29,000	7,520	5,210	41,730
10 cents	.....:..	89,150	28,610	32,410	150,170
12 cents	....	84,400	22,340	19,785	126,525
24 cents	....	53,750	20,845	17,820	92,415
36 cents	....	18,300	12,280	8,585	39,165
48 cents	....	17,700	10,940	8,190	36,830
60 cents	....	21,750	10,675	11,381	43,806
72 cents	....	5,700	7,025	6,725	19,450
84 cents	....	4,950	6,850	5,957	17,757
96 cents	....	12,750	10,505	9,910	33,165
192 cents	....	4,225	9,500	6,337	20,062
3 dollars	....	6,969	6,768	7,222	20,959
6 dollars	....	2,585	3,544	3,173	9,302
9 dollars	....	1,151	2,611	1,606	5,368
12 dollars	....	1,350	2,548	2,184	6,082
24 dollars	....	554	1,590	1,046	3,190
36 dollars	....	319	1,009	343	1,671
48 dollars	....	191	831	305	1,327
60 dollars	....	376	640	780	1,796

Whole number of stamps 2,209,215.   Value $815,902.47.

Stamps issued during the fiscal year ending June 30th, 1876:

QUARTER ENDING:

	Sept. 30, 1875.	Dec. 31, 1875.	Mch. 31, 1876.	June 30, 1876.	Total.
2 cents	60,955	59,675	78,265	64,770	263,665
3 cents	23,085	21,470	27,600	23,780	95,935
4 cents	30,495	28,030	35,750	31,850	126,125
6 cents	32,325	25,905	34,570	32,785	125,585
8 cents	14,920	12,515	20,940	16,440	64,815
9 cents	5,920	3,630	6,680	6,420	22,650
10 cents	31,520	32,500	44,320	38,070	146,410
12 cents	20,770	22,555	25,995	24,580	93,900
24 cents	16,830	18,335	22,925	22,960	81,050
36 cents	8,025	9,250	11,875	11,105	40,255
48 cents	6,975	8,065	10,260	9,565	34,865
60 cents	6,025	6,475	10,530	9,280	32,310
72 cents	2,430	2,550	5,825	4,915	15,720
84 cents	2,790	3,185	5,045	4,570	15,595

	Sept. 30, 1875.	Dec. 31, 1875.	Mch. 31, 1876.	June 30, 1876.	Total.
96 cents	11,460	9,940	11,300	10,695	43,390
192 cents	6,290	5,215	7,050	6,415	24,970
3 dollars	6,719	6,319	7,204	5,874	26,116
6 dollars	3,799	1,673	3,682	2,921	12,075
9 dollars	2,571	1,424	1,781	1,576	7,352
12 dollars	2,219	1,672	2,078	1,884	7,853
24 dollars	1,636	404	588	762	3,390
36 dollars	529	515	439	618	2,101
48 dollars	333	96	232	513	1,174
60 dollars	691	648	807	900	3,049

Whole number of stamps 1,290,347.   Value $945,254.75.

Stamps issued during the fiscal year ending June 30th, 1877 :

QUARTER ENDING :

	Sept. 30, 1876.	Dec. 31, 1876.	Mch. 31, 1877.	June 30, 1877.	Total.
2 cents	73,655	66,510	72,180	71,570	283,915
3 cents	26,980	23,600	27,360	27,170	105,110
4 cents	35,480	32,680	33,095	38,040	139,295
6 cents	31,345	28,210	29,560	32,265	121,380
8 cents	19,210	16,095	16,865	20,675	72,845
9 cents	6,210	4,330	5,530	6,240	22,310
10 cents	42,145	37,955	42,170	46,410	168,680
12 cents	26,640	22,495	25,630	24,165	98,930
24 cents	23,005	19,780	23,160	20,815	86,760
36 cents	11,385	10,510	11,080	12,470	45,445
48 cents	9,695	9,435	10,365	10,315	39,810
60 cents	9,119	8,950	11,446	9,705	39,220
72 cents	4,510	4,460	5,205	5,250	19,452
84 cents	3,645	4,285	5,555	4,195	17,680
96 cents	9,190	9,740	10,570	9,605	39,105
192 cents	7,005	5,275	7,575	5,715	25,570
3 dollars	6,746	6,059	6,333	6,215	25,353
6 dollars	3,207	2,926	2,867	3,432	12,432
9 dollars	1,544	1,923	1,384	2,234	7,085
12 dollars	1,978	2,160	1,551	2,260	7,949
24 dollars	926	986	735	738	3,385
36 dollars	409	557	668	499	2,133
48 dollars	289	289	423	191	1,192
60 dollars	853	949	998	900	3,700

Whole number of stamps 1,388,709.   Value $1,000,605.10.

Stamps issued during the fiscal year ending June 30th, 1878 :

QUARTER ENDING :

	Sept 30, 1877	Dec 31, 1877.	Mch. 31, 1878.	June 30, 1878.	Total.
2 cents	84,575	63,740	104,210	75,265	327,790
3 cents	32,100	24,260	43,510	29,050	128,920
4 cents	45,335	31,600	52,810	35,990	165,735
6 cents	40,475	27,120	44,230	33,055	144,880
8 cents	25,090	18,565	25,650	20,115	89,420

	Sept. 30, 1877.	Dec. 31, 1877.	Mch. 31, 1878.	June 30, 1878.	Total
9 cents	7,730	5,190	7,450	4,620	24,990
10 cents	54,285	42,005	64,775	47,705	208,770
12 cents	32,580	20,720	35,035	23,220	111,555
24 cents	26,855	17,490	30,330	20,455	95,130
36 cents	12,350	9,995	15,450	10,690	48,485
48 cents	9,985	7,295	14,045	7,640	38,965
60 cents	11,490	9,335	12,820	8,615	42,260
72 cents	4,945	4,955	8,070	3,945	21,915
84 cents	6,210	4,910	6,345	4,520	21,985
96 cents	12,210	7,870	14,040	8,815	42,935
192 cents	8,250	5,980	9,575	5,475	29,280
3 dollars	7,220	6,219	8,317	5,499	27,255
6 dollars	3,686	2,741	3,165	3,763	12,355
9 dollars	2,336	1,269	1,449	1,530	6,584
12 dollars	2,783	1,802	1,882	2,033	8,500
24 dollars	973	1,232	648	1,177	4,029
36 dollars	825	599	377	470	2,271
48 dollars	660	325	253	540	1,778
60 dollars	`961	960	872	998	3,791

Whole number of stamps, 1,609,578.   Value, $1,093,845.30.

Stamps issued during the fiscal year ending June 30th, 1879:

QUARTER ENDING:

	Sept. 30, 1878.	Dec. 31, 1878.	Mch. 31, 1879.	June 30, 1879.	Total.
2 cents	75,335	75,450	84,980	87,600	323,365
3 cents	29,190	30,240	29,530	13,730	102,690
4 cents	40,380	39,115	43,385	46,900	169,780
6 cents	36,185	30,905	34,455	33,810	135,355
8 cents	21,545	23,295	22,990	24,020	91,850
9 cents	6,750	6,260	6,230	2,340	21,580
10 cents	50,615	49,565	52,390	52,135	204,705
12 cents	25,310	25,095	26,190	26,240	102,835
24 cents	22,210	22,195	23,815	24,600	92,820
36 cents	11,710	12,180	12,730	11,985	48,605
48 cents	9,165	9,660	9,770	9,895	38,490
60 cents	10,065	10,950	11,015	10,180	42,210
72 cents	5,105	5,655	6,365	4,995	22,120
84 cents	4,545	3,825	5,105	5,465	18,490
96 cents	12,820	8,835	11,350	11,240	44,245
192 cents	6,775	6,055	7,115	6,408	26,353
3 dollars	6,566	5,931	7,583	6,662	26,742
6 dollars	3,142	2,558	3,634	2,583	11,917
9 dollars	1,962	2,756	2,416	1,680	7,814
12 dollars	2,131	1,570	2,819	1,752	8,272
24 dollars	836	665	1,231	849	3,581
36 dollars	663	320	781	346	2,113
48 dollars	455	274	528	198	1,450
60 dollars	1,148	927	1,167	1,098	4,340

Whole number of stamps, 1,552,172.   Value, $1,088,412.16.

Newspaper and Periodical Stamps.

Issue of 1879.

In February, 1879, when the leading bank note companies of New York City were consolidated under the name of the American Bank Note Co., the new corporation assumed the contract of the Continental Bank Note Co. for the manufacture of postage stamps. In printing the stamps for newspapers and periodicals the American Bank Note Co. used the plates of its predecessor and did not make any new plates, with the exception of a plate for the one cent value which will be described hereafter. For the two and three cent stamps plates 218B and 233B, respectively, were employed, the other plates of those values having been previously retired from use.

By an Act of Congress, approved March 3rd, 1879, the postage on newspapers and periodicals was fixed at the uniform rate of two cents per pound.

In connection with this change the following official circular was sent to postmasters:

Post Office Department.

Office of the Third Assistant Postmaster General.

Division of Postage Stamps, Stamped Envelopes & Post Cards.

Washington, D. C., April 25, 1879.

The attention of Postmasters is hereby called to the fact that, on and after the first of May proximo, under the act of March 3d, 1879, matter of the second class, commonly known as newspaper and periodical matter, will be entitled to pass through the mail at a uniform rate of 2 cents per pound. Care will be taken not to collect payment on such matter at more than that rate. The same general regulations concerning the collection of newspaper postage, as have been heretofore promulgated, will remain in force and the same books and blanks, together with the newspaper and periodical stamps that are now outstanding, will continue to be used. In future, however, the issue of the three and nine cents denominations of newspaper and periodical stamps will be discontinued.

A. D. Hazen,

Third Assistant Postmaster General.

The rate of postage on printed matter of the second class, when sent through the mails by publishers and news agents, was reduced to one cent per pound by Act of Congress, approved March 3rd, 1885. This rate went into effect on July 1st, 1885, and necessitated the issue of a one cent stamp. On this subject the report of the Third Assistant Postmaster General, dated November 18th, 1885, says:

" To provide for wants that were certain to arise from the change in the rate of postage on newspapers and periodicals sent by publishers and news agents to actual subscribers, authorized by the act of Congress of March 3, 1885, the Department began issuing, on the

[margin notes:]
Change of contractors.

Rate of postage reduced.

Circular to postmasters.

Rate of postage again reduced.

One cent stamp.

3d of June, 1885, newspaper and periodical postage stamps of the denomination of 1 cent, for use after July 1, 1885. This new denomination is of the same design and color as the stamps of the denominations from 2 to 10 cents in the same series ; the only difference is in the numeral and the word indicating the value."

Plate.

For this new value only one plate was made. Like the plates of the series made by the Continental Bank Note Co., it contained one hundred stamps, arranged in ten rows of ten stamps each. At the time of perforating, the printed sheets were divided horizontally into half sheets of fifty stamps. The imprint appears four times on each sheet, that is to say, at the middle of the top. bottom and each side. It is " AMERICAN BANK NOTE COMPANY. NEW YORK." in very small colored Roman capitals, ¾ mm high. The inscription is but 33½ mm. long, thus extending only partly over two stamps. It is not on a panel, as is customary, and is entirely without ornamental surroundings.

Plate number.

Above the imprint at the top of the plate is " No. 482 ", in slanting letters and numerals, 2 mm high.

The paper is the thick, soft, porous paper that was used for all issues made by this company. The gum varies from brownish yellow to white. The perforation is, as usual, 12.

In the course of time the shades of the lower values changed to a considerable extent. The colors and shades are:

Reference List.

Perforated 12.

Thick Soft Porous Wove Paper.

1 cent black, deep black, gray-black

2 cents black, deep black, gray black, greenish black

3 cents black, deep black, gray-black

4 cents black, deep black, gray-black, greenish black

6 cents black, deep black, gray-black

8 cents black, deep black, gray-black

10 cents black, deep black, gray-black, greenish black

12 cents pale brown-red, brown-red, pale carmine, rose-carmine, carmine, dark carmine, brown-carmine. lake

24 cents pale brown-red, brown-red, pale carmine, rose-carmine, carmine dark carmine, brown-carmine, lake, violet-rose

36 cents brown-red, rose-carmine, dark carmine, violet-rose

48 cents pale brown-red, brown-red, dark carmine, lake, violet-rose

60 cents pale brown red, brown-red, rose-carmine, dark carmine, violet-rose

72 cents brown-red, dark carmine, lake

84 cents brown-red, rose-carmine, dark carmine, violet-rose

96 cents brown-red, rose-carmine, dark carmine

192 cents yellow-brown, brown, dark brown

3 dollars carmine-vermilion, deep carmine-vermilion

6 dollars blue, dark blue, chalky blue
9 dollars yellow-orange, orange
12 dollars deep green, deep yellow-green, blue-green
24 dollars dark violet
36 dollars dull rose, brown-rose, Indian red
48 dollars orange-brown, deep orange-brown
60 dollars pale purple, purple, deep purple

Variety:

60 cents dull brown-red.   Imperforate.

On page 285 will be found a letter of the Third Assistant Postmaster General, recommending the destruction of certain obsolete postage stamps, of which a tabular statement is given.   This table includes some newspaper and periodical stamps, viz.:

3 cents	223,750
9 cents	101,240

Suggested destruction of unissued stamps.

A committee was appointed to carry out the suggested destruction. On referring to page 288 it will be seen that, in due course, the committee reported the destruction of the official stamps and the uncurrent stamps of the regular issue but made no mention of any others. We may, therefore, conclude that, at that time, the newspaper and periodical stamps escaped, though it is probable that, at a later date, those of the nine cent denomination were destroyed.

The three cent stamp was again brought into use in the last quarter of the fiscal year ending June 30th, 1885, but the nine cents was not again revived, as will be seen by referring to the accompanying tables.

Three cent stamp again in use.

On pages 152 and 153 reference was made to a series of stamps overprinted "SPECIMEN" in block capitals, which were intended for distribution to foreign countries through the Universal Postal Union. The stamps thus surcharged included the newspaper and periodical stamps, from one cent to sixty dollars. The nine cent stamp was of the Continental printing. The other values were the product of the American Bank Note Co. The denominations from twelve to ninety-six cents inclusive were printed in brown-red.

"Specimen" stamps.

The following statistics of issues of the newspaper and periodical stamps have been compiled from the annual reports of the Postmaster General and certain other sources of information.

Stamps issued during the fiscal year ending June 30th, 1880:

Deliveries to postmasters.

QUARTER ENDING:

	Sept. 30, 1879,	Dec. 31, 1879.	Mch. 31, 1880.	June 30, 1880.	Total.
2 cents	100,620	99,705	97,640	124,220	422,185
4 cents	57,325	58,555	55,655	68,260	240,795
6 cents	38,335	37,320	37,470	44,025	157,150
8 cents	27,750	26,930	28.410	34,240	117,330
10 cents	62,965	61,835	61,707	73,019	259,526
12 cents	28,035	26,965	27,090	31,290	113,380

	Sept. 30, 1879.	Dec. 31, 1879.	Mch. 31, 1880.	June 30, 1880.	Total.
24 cents	26,900	22,475	26,170	30,405	105,950
36 cents	15,890	12,135	13,580	15,670	57,275
48 cents	11,040	9,620	9,965	10,995	41,620
60 cents	14,250	10,820	13,040	13,435	51,545
72 cents	7,640	4,370	6,630	7,005	25,645
84 cents	6,405	3,805	6,485	6,515	23,210
96 cents	12,725	11,910	11,745	14,010	50,390
192 cents	7,940	6,810	7,295	7,675	29,720
3 dollars	8,075	5,964	7,498	7,582	29,119
6 dollars	3,441	3,679	3,606	3,270	13,996
9 dollars	2,138	2,205	1,595	2,206	8,144
12 dollars	2,161	2,657	1,851	2,935	9,604
24 dollars	1,035	939	1,043	1,291	4,308
36 dollars	540	452	779	550	2,321
48 dollars	350	421	381	753	1,905
60 dollars	1,093	1,153	1,153	1,565	4,964

Whole number of stamps, 1,770,082.   Value $1,252,903.30.

Stamps issued during the fiscal year ending June 30th, 1881:

QUARTER ENDING:

	Sept. 30, 1880.	Dec. 31, 1880.	Mch. 31, 1881.	June 30, 1881.	Total.
2 cents	103,675	114,295	108,715	111,615	438,300
4 cents	63,980	69,185	72,430	70,330	275,925
6 cents	39,790	44,410	48,480	44,865	177,545
8 cents	30,845	34,270	36,300	33,780	135,195
10 cents	69,945	80,297	81,411	80,190	311,843
12 cents	28,715	34,230	39,630	34,550	137,125
24 cents	27,050	31,835	35,390	33,370	127,645
36 cents	14,840	17,540	17,225	15,670	65,275
48 cents	12,070	12,050	12,840	12,350	49,310
60 cents	12,585	13,855	16,250	15,780	58,470
72 cents	6,110	7,635	6,285	8,410	28,440
84 cents	4,975	6,890	7,090	6,300	25,255
96 cents	11,385	14,285	14,610	13,570	53,850
192 cents	6,855	9,055	8,725	7,880	32,515
3 dollars	6,472	7,949	8,626	7,813	30,860
6 dollars	2,989	4,454	4,009	3,642	15,094
9 dollars	2,043	1,622	2,875	1,783	8,323
12 dollars	2,428	2,385	2,894	2,504	10,211
24 dollars	932	885	938	960	3,715
36 dollars	340	752	755	653	2,500
48 dollars	275	601	518	456	1,850
60 dollars	1,339	2,082	1,723	1,398	6,542

Whole number of stamps 1,995,788.   Value $1,398,674.00.

Stamps issued during the fiscal year ending June 30th, 1882 :

QUARTER ENDING :

	Sept. 30, 1881.	Dec. 31, 1881.	Mch. 31, 1882.	June 30, 1882.	Total.
2 cents	128,300	131,770	111,145	120,195	491,410
4 cents	79,495	80,320	73,505	79,745	313,065
6 cents	47,170	52,330	48,160	47,580	195,240
8 cents	36,540	37,595	34,940	37,955	147,030
10 cents	89,620	94,675	84,665	84,835	353,795
12 cents	34,595	37,470	39,145	37,430	148,640
24 cents	34,135	37,425	37,680	37,270	146,510
36 cents	18,790	18,580	18,535	19,220	75,125
48 cents	12,795	12,340	14,755	12,445	52,335
60 cents	16,070	16,320	17,765	15,145	65,300
72 cents	6,180	5,735	7,430	7,135	26,480
84 cents	5,925	4,840	7,610	6,445	24,820
96 cents	11,930	14,485	13,905	13,070	53,390
192 cents	8,730	8,640	8,200	10,245	35,815
3 dollars	7,917	6,938	9,292	8,152	32,299
6 dollars	4,186	2,932	4,387	4,425	15,930
9 dollars	1,858	1,484	3,517	1,716	8,575
12 dollars	2,700	2,206	3,555	2,915	11,376
24 dollars	1,100	787	1,461	1,297	4,645
36 dollars	754	483	819	627	2,683
48 dollars	631	370	395	558	1,954
60 dollars	1,824	2,306	2,340	2,006	8,476

Whole number of stamps 2,214,893.   Value $1,602,069.70.   ·)

Stamps issued during the fiscal year ending June 30th, 1883 :

QUARTER ENDING :

	Sept. 30, 1882.	Dec 31, 1882.	Mch. 31, 1883.	June 30, 1883.	Total.
2 cents	106,220	103,940	102,475	101,025	413,660
4 cents	74,245	77,495	77,210	78,925	307,875
6 cents	49,755	50,700	52,345	51,510	204,310
8 cents	36,995	35,700	37,350	36,385	146,430
10 cents	84,820	81,725	85,410	80,020	331,975
12 cents	39,550	41,605	37,995	38,320	157,470
24 cents	41,765	41,695	43,630	40,750	167,840
36 cents	21,335	20,945	22,245	21,515	86,040
48 cents	14,035	16,700	15,975	15,885	62,595
60 cents	16,570	17,725	18,465	19,138	71,898
72 cents	8,070	9,210	8,650	9,525	35,455
84 cents	7,140	7,145	7,385	7,290	28,960
96 cents	12,630	17,405	15,525	16,405	61,965
192 cents	7,645	11,890	8,990	9,405	37,930
3 dollars	7,418	8,882	9,701	9,142	35,143
6 dollars	3,740	4,755	4,087	4,560	17,142
9 dollars	1,901	3,039	2,422	2,632	9,994

	Sept. 30, 1882.	Dec. 31, 1882.	Mch. 31, 1883.	June 30, 1883.	Total.
12 dollars	2,531	2,963	2,958	2,855	11,307
24 dollars	1,417	1,079	1,306	1,803	5,605
36 dollars	807	666	666	946	3,085
48 dollars	563	435	503	648	2,149
60 dollars	2,317	2,072	2,266	2,456	9,111

Whole number of stamps 2,207,939.   Value $1,752,564.50.

Stamps issued during the fiscal year ending June 30th, 1884 :

QUARTER ENDING :

	Sept. 30, 1883.	Dec. 31, 1883.	Mch. 31, 1884.	June 30, 1884.	Total.
2 cents	112,480	118,620	119,420	118,660	469,180
4 cents	85,595	86,830	94,825	88,525	355,775
6 cents	59,795	49,885	64,420	53,035	227,135
8 cents	45,810	39,225	48,865	39,620	173,520
10 cents	90,290	78,795	95,365	94,685	359,135
12 cents	43,310	41,110	41,845	39,585	165,850
24 cents	42,700	40,165	47,545	42,325	172,735
36 cents	24,885	20,605	26,130	22,515	94,135
48 cents	15,555	16,105	17,685	15,625	65,970
60 cents	18,250	18,235	22,195	19,880	78,560
72 cents	7,795	8,855	11,965	8,815	37,430
84 cents	5,800	9,430	7,950	8,330	31,510
96 cents	15,980	17,370	17,295	15,965	66,610
192 cents	8,370	11,245	11,070	9,380	40,065
3 dollars	7,696	10,978	8,708	8,559	35,941
6 dollars	3,958	5,514	4,706	5,227	19,405
9 dollars	2,425	3,459	2,979	3,111	11,974
12 dollars	2,520	3,797	3,374	3,507	13,198
24 dollars	1,260	1,775	1,730	1,025	5,790
36 dollars	614	1,081	1,053	857	3,605
48 dollars	475	965	826	550	2,816
60 dollars	1,711	2,926	2,687	2,235	9,559

Whole number of stamps 2,439,898.   Value $1,923,217.80.

Stamps issued during the fiscal year ending June 30th, 1885 ·

QUARTER ENDING :

	Sept. 30, 1884.	Dec. 31, 1884.	Mch. 31, 1885.	June 30, 1885.	Total.
1 cent	......	......	.....	178,180	178,180
2 cents	118,240	114,135	119,010	134,490	485,875
3 cents	......	......	......	22,730	22,730
4 cents	86,335	86,555	91,200	104,480	368,570
6 cents	56,015	53,560	57,080	64,295	230,950
8 cents	41,010	38,975	44,760	47,680	172,425
10 cents	91,675	92,690	98,860	104,320	387,545
12 cents	40,425	41,635	42,530	55,915	108,505
24 cents	44,850	45,905	44,190	44,445	179,390

	Sept. 30, 1884.	Dec. 31, 1884.	Mch. 31, 1885.	June 30, 1885.	Total.
36 cents	22,705	22,315	25,195	18,040	88,255
48 cents	17,870	16,620	18,760	13,545	66,795
60 cents	18,670	20,080	21,405	15,260	75,415
72 cents	9,745	9,165	9,305	7,330	35,545
84 cents	7,190	6,830	9,515	6,570	30,105
96 cents	17,800	16,770	19,795	14,370	68,735
192 cents	11,010	8,570	13,455	8,250	41,285
3 dollars	10,871	7,967	9,829	9,612	38,279
6 dollars	4,492	4,094	4,983	4,479	18,048
9 dollars	2,852	2,658	2,782	3,084	11,376
12 dollars	3,147	3,307	3,441	3,409	13,304
24 dollars	1,735	1,528	1,539	1,747	6,549
36 dollars	668	790	815	820	3,093
48 dollars	432	820	724	630	2,606
60 dollars	3,106	2,919	3,200	2,529	11,754

Whole number of stamps 2,717,314.   Value $2,047,268.50.

Stamps issued during the fiscal year ending June 30th, 1886 :

QUARTER ENDING :

	Sept. 30, 1885.	Dec. 31, 1885.	Mch. 31, 1886.	June 30, 1886.	Total.
1 cent	225,320	146,160	138,740	144,790	655,010
2 cents	90,930	94,950	113,465	120,180	419,525
3 cents	62,590	36,520	46,040	49,490	194,640
4 cents	49,955	63,205	76,160	82,895	272,215
6 cents	45,655	41,385	53,420	51,095	191,555
8 cents	29,125	29,410	38,890	37,535	134,960
10 cents	67,280	64,705	86,525	87,355	305,865
12 cents	29,045	29,870	37,795	36,345	133,055
24 cents	24,670	23,560	33,905	32,820	114,955
36 cents	13,260	10,935	14,820	16,355	55,370
48 cents	8,445	7,830	11,905	11,210	39,390
60 cents	10,545	10,285	11,860	11,190	43,880
72 cents	5,815	6,840	5,320	7,475	24,450
84 cents	6,225	5,850	5,520	7,245	24,840
96 cents	12,520	10,635	12,480	13,065	48,700
192 cents	10,105	7,025	7,155	7,850	32,135
3 dollars	6,487	5,875	5,066	6,292	23,720
6 dollars	3,255	3,465	3,473	4,200	14,393
9 dollars	2,694	2,515	1,343	2,138	8,690
12 dollars	2,625	2,142	1,662	2,198	8,627
24 dollars	1,185	732	315	746	2,978
36 dollars	506	400	145	310	1,361
48 dollars	390	310	160	85	945
60 dollars	1,356	595	860	1,391	4,202

Whole number of stamps 2,755,461.   Value $1,097,390.00.

Stamps issued during the fiscal year ending June 30th, 1887 :

QUARTER ENDING :

	Sept. 30, 1886.	Dec. 31, 1886.	Mch 31, 1887.	June 30, 1887.	Total.
1 cent	134,625	155,290	164,870	149,760	604,545
2 cents	116,380	126,945	129,440	117,640	490,405
3 cents	40,845	47,740	57,140	56,570	202,295
4 cents	74,165	84,315	92,095	77,700	328,275
6 cents	48,685	50,585	57,495	50,035	206,800
8 cents	35,160	37,565	40,910	42,335	155,970
10 cents	85,795	95,145	96,250	92,738	369,928
12 cents	34,490	35,355	37,590	39,110	146,545
24 cents	31,050	34,845	36,095	32,455	134,445
36 cents	13,625	15,485	18,390	17,465	64,965
48 cents	11,795	8,695	13,460	11,525	45,475
60 cents	12,090	11,050	13,940	13,135	50,215
72 cents	6,835	5,160	8,590	8,755	29,340
84 cents	5,355	5,165	8,835	6,870	26,225
96 cents	13,340	16,295	14,775	14,435	58,845
192 cents	8,620	10,225	9,575	9,075	37,495
3 dollars	6,139	7,794	7,434	8,389	29,756
6 dollars	3,235	4,502	4,747	4,068	16,552
9 dollars	2,103	2,449	3,092	2,842	10,486
12 dollars	2,043	2,258	2,635	3,135	10,071
24 dollars	772	889	975	1,582	4,218
36 dollars	285	342	580	526	1,733
48 dollars	310	253	370	520	1,453
60 dollars	1,035	1,268	1,640	1,615	5,558

Whole number of stamps 3,031,595.   Value $1,364,413.80.

Stamps issued during the fiscal year ending June 30th, 1888 :

QUARTER ENDING :

	Sept. 30, 1887.	Dec. 31, 1887.	Mch. 31, 1888.	June 30, 1888.	Total.
1 cent	261,580	162,960	169,090	180,840	674,470
2 cents	137,130	136,645	132,365	134,430	540,570
3 cents	68,780	64,910	59,570	60,650	253,910
4 cents	98,960	94,615	99,610	97,025	390,210
6 cents	57,815	56,830	59,825	60,240	234,710
8 cents	44,140	41,260	41,690	49,780	176,870
10 cents	107,735	102,470	101,920	109,325	421,450
12 cents	37,115	41,640	37,670	48,125	164,550
24 cents	39,120	37,155	34,530	40,655	151,460
36 cents	17,275	17,935	18,650	19,935	73,795
48 cents	13,785	13,880	12,440	17,050	57,155
60 cents	12,855	12,170	14,530	15,800	55,355
72 cents	7,385	7,630	8,890	11,225	35,130
84 cents	7,830	7,880	8,250	8,350	32,310
96 cents	14,565	16,610	16,875	20,845	68,895

	Sept. 30, 1887.	Dec. 31, 1887.	Mch. 31, 1888.	June 30, 1888.	Total.
192 cents	10,150	11,005	10,775	12,810	44,740
3 dollars	7,436	7,460	8,756	8,488	32,140
6 dollars	4,572	3,477	4,715	4,698	17,462
9 dollars	3,010	2,217	3,113	3,486	11,826
12 dollars	2,777	2,466	3,742	3,573	12,558
24 dollars	752	446	1,313	1,712	4,223
36 dollars	616	173	481	735	2,005
48 dollars	420	100	505	626	1,651
60 dollars	790	1,720	2,103	2,360	6,973

Whole number of stamps 3,464,418. Value $1,588,425.00.

Stamps issued during the fiscal year ending June 30th, 1889 :

QUARTER ENDING :

	Sept. 30, 1888.	Dec. 31, 1888.	Mch. 31, 1889.	June 30, 1889.	Total.
1 cent	136,560	146,360	176,990	236,050	695,960
2 cents	118,300	113,080	130,790	187,155	549,329
3 cents	49,630	49,590	63,660	66,210	229,090
4 cents	88,075	82,290	96,195	103,110	369,670
6 cents	56,695	53,200	64,605	66,940	241,440
8 cents	48,275	42,300	52,440	57,060	200,075
10 cents	96,790	97,455	115,330	112,725	422,300
12 cents	44,405	35,515	40,620	54,880	181,420
24 cents	43,060	31,780	41,750	40,490	157,080
36 cents	27,755	15,560	22,115	20,525	85,955
48 cents	18,055	11,485	15,455	15,915	60,910
60 cents	15,395	12,300	15,605	15,525	58,825
72 cents	9,530	6,710	10,525	8,500	35,265
84 cents	10,560	7,100	8,885	9,595	36,140
96 cents	16,785	16,650	16,055	18,365	67,855
192 cents	11,100	11,345	10,865	10,820	44,130
3 dollars	9,255	6,814	9,656	9,370	35,095
6 dollars	4,902	3,813	5,092	4,476	18,283
9 dollars	2,301	2,135	3,210	3,130	10,776
12 dollars	3,111	2,607	3,506	2,534	11,758
24 dollars	1,252	938	1,176	1,133	4,499
36 dollars	931	598	616	620	2,765
48 dollars	555	360	750	370	2,035
60 dollars	1,830	1,750	2,060	1,570	7,210

Whole number of stamps 3,527,861. Value $1,663,751.00.

Stamps issued during the fiscal year ending June 30th, 1890 :

QUARTER ENDING :

	Sept. 30, 1889.	Dec. 31, 1889.	Mch. 31, 1890.	June 30, 1890.	Total.
1 cent	202,610	168,330	188,200	196,750	755,890
2 cents	153,340	141,730	150,150	160,600	605,820
3 cents	67,070	63,980	56,600	62,300	249,950
4 cents	102,555	86,615	88,000	91,700	368,870

	Sept. 30, 1889.	Dec. 31, 1889.	Mch. 31, 1890.	June 30, 1890.	Total.
6 cents	61,445	59,020	64,300	67,975	252,740
8 cents	48,395	45,275	48,125	55,625	197,420
10 cents	118,245	101,975	105,180	109,770	435,170
12 cents	50,620	49,935	57,850	59,120	217,525
24 cents	40,660	38,225	43,525	41,125	163,535
36 cents	20,490	17,865	21,710	20,575	80,600
48 cents	14,620	12,415	16,450	16,350	59,835
60 cents	15,750	13,235	16,645	18,020	63,650
72 cents	10,165	8,470	11,250	11,100	40,985
84 cents	8,665	6,585	11,435	9,100	35,785
96 cents	22,050	18,130	18,300	22,135	80,615
192 cents	14,215	12,150	12,950	11,375	50,690
3 dollars	10,902	8,128	10,375	12,368	41,773
6 dollars	5,179	5,075	5,025	5,325	20,604
9 dollars	3,354	2,544	3,695	2,656	12 249
12 dollars	3,978	2,347	3,565	3,010	12,900
24 dollars	1,327	1,056	1,530	1,140	5,053
36 dollars	635	442	665	695	2,437
48 dollars	310	480	456	356	1,602
60 dollars	1,065	1,095	1,985	2,515	6,660

Whole number of stamps 3,762,398.   Value $1,711,464.00.

Stamps issued during the fiscal year ending June 30th, 1891 :

QUARTER ENDING :

	Sept. 30, 1890.	Dec. 31, 1890.	Mch. 31, 1891.	June 30, 1891.	Total.
1 cent	216,900	204,100	180,200	215,920	817,120
2 cents	178,300	160,050	147,150	170,660	656,160
3 cents	57,400	56,100	41,600	52,050	207,150
4 cents	106,550	97,875	89,375	102,755	396,555
6 cents	73,850	72,450	63,525	71,005	280,830
8 cents	59,375	57,375	51,325	61,990	230,065
10 cents	129,050	121,400	105,765	121,700	477,915
12 cents	64,375	61,725	61,850	64,335	252,285
24 cents	47,500	44,900	40,275	44,425	177,100
36 cents	25,425	23,325	19 950	22,645	91,345
48 cents	21,200	18,735	14,375	18,355	72,665
60 cents	22,605	18,410	16,540	19,065	76,620
72 cents	12,325	12,450	10,450	11,740	46,965
84 cents	10,975	10,600	9,675	11,435	42,685
96 cents	24,500	23,400	21,500	23,685	93,085
192 cents	15,650	15,585	13,650	12,040	56,925
3 dollars	13,090	11,975	12,235	12,223	49,523
6 dollars	6,729	5,565	5,870	5,930	24,094
9 dollars	3,766	3,990	3,395	3,227	14,378
12 dollars	3,940	2,960	3,900	3,659	14,459

	Sept. 30, 1890.	Dec. 31, 1890.	Mch. 31, 1891.	June 30, 1891.	Total.
24 dollars	1,570	1,520	1,485	1,935	6,510
36 dollars	835	915	655	1,025	3,440
48 dollars	602	525	515	435	2,077
60 dollars	1,792	2,290	1,920	2,310	8,312

Whole number of stamps 4,098,263.   Value $2,055,798.00.

Stamps issued during the fiscal year ending June 30th, 1892 :

QUARTER ENDING :

	Sept. 30, 1891.	Dec. 31, 1891.	Mch. 31, 1892.	June 30, 1892.	Total.
1 cent	194,940	207,250	186,100	219,300	807,590
2 cents	158,325	160,800	159,850	168,775	647,750
3 cents	53,830	44,650	50,250	57,400	206,130
4 cents	91,505	97,025	94,400	107,175	390,105
6 cents	67,735	67,425	69,475	74,075	278,710
8 cents	52,945	62,175	55,250	58,950	229,320
10 cents	118,119	122,215	118,640	134,920	493,894
12 cents	64,265	61,900	63,275	66,800	256,240
24 cents	47,000	44,900	45,600	51,575	189,075
36 cents	22,545	21,975	23,400	25,950	93 870
48 cents	20,620	16,450	17,975	19,425	74,470
60 cents	20,890	16,460	17,700	20,830	75,880
72 cents	12,035	12,025	10,825	11,675	46,560
84 cents	10,560	10,150	10,400	10,850	41,960
96 cents	23,945	23,875	21,775	25,500	95,095
192 cents	14,925	15,700	14,375	17,600	62,600
3 dollars	10,104	12,095	11,050	14,240	47,489
6 dollars	6,024	5,705	5,790	6,263	23,782
9 dollars	3,417	4,057	3,370	3,926	14,770
12 dollars	4,338	3,977	3,550	4,544	16,409
24 dollars	1,400	1,333	1,550	1,649	5,932
36 dollars	465	690	735	772	2,662
48 dollars	185	345	595	737	1,862
60 dollars	2,359	2,375	2,713	3,690	11,137

Whole number of stamps 4,113,292.   Value $2,209,516.00.

Stamps issued during the fiscal year ending June 30th, 1893 :

QUARTER ENDING :

	Sept. 30, 1892.	Dec. 31, 1892.	Mch. 31, 1893.	June 30, 1893.	Total.
1 cent	200,650	203,030	199,850	201,050	804,580
2 cents	148,900	168,220	169,800	166,500	653,420
3 cents	47,150	50,620	55,000	50,100	202,870
4 cents	101,325	99,340	107,650	97,000	405,315
6 cents	63,875	66,380	75,275	63,500	269,030
8 cents	55,150	57,380	64,575	58,825	235,930
10 cents	123,435	128,195	132,840	124,035	508,505
12 cents	64,350	70,380	72,900	64,650	272,280

	Sept. 30, 1892.	Dec. 31, 1892.	Mch. 31, 1893.	June 30, 1893.	Total.
24 cents	46,875	48,920	49,250	44,325	189,370
36 cents	24,900	26,085	23,475	21,575	96,035
48 cents	20,175	19,080	20,400	18,500	78,155
60 cents	19,690	22,410	21,375	18,045	81,520
72 cents	12,125	12,225	12,675	13,025	50,050
84 cents	11,800	11,150	10,475	11,575	45,000
96 cents	24,500	23,200	23,200	20,600	91,500
192 cents	14,200	12,050	13,175	12,150	51,575
3 dollars	13,777	10,667	12,912	9,980	47,336
6 dollars	7,165	5,455	6,655	5,605	24,880
9 dollars	4,395	3,105	3,330	3,585	14,415
12 dollars	4,670	4,625	3,520	3,360	16,175
24 dollars	1,980	1,315	1,395	1,400	6,090
36 dollars	1,575	605	540	810	3,530
48 dollars	1,560	555	520	610	3,245
60 dollars	4,618	5,297	5,685	4,685	20,285

Whole number of stamps 4,171,091.   Value $2,850,324.00.

Stamps issued during the fiscal year ending June 30th, 1894 :

QUARTER ENDING :

	Sept. 30, 1893.	Dec. 31, 1893.	Mch. 31, 1894.	June 30, 1894.	Total.
1 cent	214,850	195,200	201,100	224,200	835,350
2 cents	171,200	151,425	154,650	175,700	652,975
3 cents	60,550	52,400	52,300	59,600	224,850
4 cents	104,525	92,100	94,350	111,050	402,025
6 cents	72,000	64,775	65,675	73,600	276,050
8 cents	66,450	56,550	59,175	64,725	246,900
10 cents	128,710	114,450	118,885	132,240	494,285
12 cents	66,975	63,500	63,650	70,300	264,425
24 cents	47,875	44,500	44,125	49,625	186,125
36 cents	26,625	23,175	25,300	27,375	102,475
48 cents	18,925	17,400	18,925	19,000	74,250
60 cents	19,485	18,545	20,155	19,595	77,780
72 cents	11,500	12,800	12,475	13,250	50,025
84 cents	10,675	11,725	10,550	12,350	45,300
96 cents	26,275	19,450	24,900	22,575	93,200
192 cents	14,800	12,650	15,000	14,975	57,425
3 dollars	12,691	10,045	11,845	11,285	45,866
6 dollars	6,020	4,865	6,050	6,230	23,165
9 dollars	3,747	3,175	4,282	3,975	15,179
12 dollars	4,225	3,030	4,435	3,905	15,595
24 dollars	1,775	1,270	1,475	1,655	6,175
36 dollars	775	665	605	670	2,715
48 dollars	550	580	435	540	2,105
60 dollars	3,630	3,715	5,482	4,960	17,787

Whole number of stamps 4,212,027.   Value $2,613,920.00.

Stamps issued during the fiscal year ending June 30th, 1895 :

QUARTER ENDING :

	Sept. 30, 1894	Dec. 31, 1894.	Mch 31, 1895.	June 30, 1895.	Total.
1 cent	45,936	......	......	......	45,936
2 cents	111,618	......	......	......	111,618
3 cents	48,150	......	......	......	48,150
4 cents	63,829	......	......	......	63,829
6 cents	40,545	......	......	......	40,545
8 cents	70,400	......	......	......	70,400
10 cents	90,888	......	......	......	90,888
12 cents	44,521	......	......	......	44,521
24 cents	29,486	......	......	......	29,486
36 cents	4,390	......	......	......	4,390
48 cents	19,625	......	......	......	19,625
60 cents	25,835	2,663	......	......	28,498
72 cents	10,350	......	......	......	10,350
84 cents	39,700	......	......	......	39,700
96 cents	27,300	32,325	4,898	......	64,523
192 cents	13,650	......	......	......	13,650
3 dollars	12,331	11,425	......	......	23,756
6 dollars	5,695	7,050	......	......	12,745
9 dollars	3,640	......	......	......	3,640
12 dollars	10,215	......	......	......	10,215
24 dollars	2,077	1,698	1,310	......	5,085
36 dollars	595	......	......	......	595
48 dollars	352	435	300	......	1,087
60 dollars	1,795	4,985	1,335	......	8,115

Whole number of stamps 791,347.   Value $1,178,923.32.

On March 7th, 1894, the Third Assistant Postmaster General sent to the contractors an order, in the customary form, to deliver to the Post Office Department at Washington the following supplies :

Order to the contractors for a special printing.

" 25 sheets of blank paper of each three sizes in use, 75 sheets.
And a sample sheet of each denomination and kind of stamps now used, thus:
    1st.   Printed only
    2nd.   Printed and gummed
    3rd.   Printed, gummed and perforated.

Newspaper and Periodical stamps: 25 plates, 3 sheets of each as above, 75 sheets, 100 stamps per sheet	7,500 stamps
Postage Due stamps: 7 plates, 3 sheets of each as above, 21 sheets, 200 stamps per sheet	4,200 stamps
Regular postage stamps: 11 plates, 3 sheets of each as above, 33 sheets :	
1 and 2 cents: 3 sheets each, 6 sheets, 400 stamps per sheet	2,400 stamps
3, 4, 5, 6, 8, 10, 15, 30 and 90 cents: 3 sheets each, 27 sheets, 200 stamps per sheet	5,400 stamps
Making a total of regular issue of 1890 of	7,800 stamps
Special delivery stamp: 1 plate, 3 sheets as above, 100 stamps per sheet	300 stamps
Total number of stamps	19,800 stamps

And 1 sheet from plate (full size) on card board from each of the 44 plates as above."

It will be remembered that, on February 21st, 1894, the Postmaster

General had awarded the contract for the manufacture of postage stamps, for the term of four years, beginning July 1st, 1894, to the Bureau of Engraving and Printing at Washington.   The sheets which were printed by the American Bank Note Co., on the above order, were turned over to the new contractors, to serve as guides for color, paper, etc.   The blank sheets were subsequently used for printing stamps.   It is probable that these stamps could not be distinguished from other early printings of the same stamps by the Bureau of Engraving and Printing.   The three varieties of printed sheets were, in due time, returned to the Post Office Department.   The fully finished sheets were eventually turned into stock and issued to postmasters.   The sheets that were merely printed, without being gummed or perforated, were destroyed.   What became of the sheets of the second class—*i. e.* those which were left imperforate—I am unable to say, except in the case of a half sheet, fifty stamps, of each value of the newspaper and periodical stamps.   These latter passed from official into private hands.   The new owner retained five sets in imperforate condition and had the others perforated—a very unwise act, in my opinion—and offered them for sale.

Following the appearance of these privately perforated stamps in the market there was trouble in official circles.   By whom it was started and just what form it took are only known to those behind the curtain.   It led to seizure of the stamps, arrest of the holder, action at law, scandal, loss of official position and other disagreeable details, much of which was set forth at length in the philatelic journals at the time.   But the true inwardness of the affair was never made public.   Eventually the stamps were restored to their owner, as being rightfully his property, and are once more in the market.   Knowing the circumstances connected with them, the reader must determine for himself their status and collectability.   At the least, they are extremely interesting.

While these stamps are not exactly like any others of the same series, they very closely resemble some of the latest printings by the American Bank Note Co.   It will be observed that the set comprises all values from one cent to sixty dollars, including the nine cents, which thus appears for the first and only time in a printing of the American Bank Note Co.

The paper is very white, fine, close, without sign of weave or grain. The gum is yellowish white and usually crackled.   The perforation gauges 12 and is very clear cut.   It was apparently made by a guillotine machine, one row at a time.   Evidence of this is found in the fact that the rows of perforations are not always parallel nor the holes in line on opposite sides of a stamp. The inks are glossy and apparently aniline.   The impressions are very clear and fine, carefully made and suggestive of proofs.   They have not the softness of the ordinary prints of either the American Bank Note Co. or the Bureau of Engraving and Printing.   The denominations one to ten cents are printed in a pure black, not a greenish, grayish or bluish black.   The color of the twelve to ninety six cents has a suggestion of lilac.   The color is rich but hard and lacks warmth.   The ink of the nine dollars contains more red than usual, that of the twelve dollars more blue, while the thirty-six dollars has more brown.   The other values are lighter and colder in tone.   As nearly as they can be described the colors are as follows:

Marginal notes:
Purpose of this special printing.

Ultimate disposition of the sheets.

Trouble about the newspaper and periodical stamps.

Nine cent stamp printed by the American Bank Note Co.

Paper. Perforation. Colors.

Imperforate and Perforated 12.

White Wove Paper.

1 cent clear deep black
2 cents clear deep black
3 cents clear deep black
4 cents clear deep black
6 cents clear deep black
8 cents clear deep black
9 cents clear deep black
10 cents clear deep black
12 cents rose-carmine
24 cents rose-carmine
36 cents rose-carmine
48 cents rose-carmine
60 cents rose-carmine
72 cents rose-carmine
84 cents rose-carmine
96 cents rose-carmine
192 cents light yellow-brown
3 dollars scarlet-vermilion
6 dollars light ultramarine
9 dollars deep orange
12 dollars blue-green
24 dollars deep dull violet
36 dollars rose-brown
48 dollars pale orange-brown
60 dollars bright purple

NEWSPAPER AND PERIODICAL STAMPS.

ISSUE OF 1894.

Printings from the plates of previous contractors. When, in 1894, the Bureau of Engraving and Printing entered upon the contract to supply the stamps required by the Post Office Department, many difficulties were encounted at the beginning of the undertaking, as was to be expected. It was necessary to provide an increased force of skilled employees, additional machinery, new plates and, in the case of the newspaper and periodical stamps, new designs. The plates for these latter stamps were not ready until the beginning of the year 1895. In the mean time the necessary supplies were obtained by printings from the old plates of the Continental and American Bank Note Companies. These printings have marked peculiarities by which they may, without difficulty, be distinguished from the work of the former contractors. The plates were re-entered before they were put to press and consequently the impressions appear sharp and unworn. The shades of the inks, even that of the black, differ from any previously used. Many of the impressions have the surface of the paper tinted from imperfect wiping of the plates. The paper is white, semi-transparent and with very little grain. The gum is white or yellowish white. At first it was quite rough and crackled but afterwards it became thin and smooth. The perforation of the early printings was blind and the disks of paper, which should have been punched out, usually remained in the holes. Improved machines were used for the sheets of the later printings and the perforation was then clear cut and fine.

The colors are:

Reference List.

Perforated 12.

White Wove Paper.

1 cent clear full black
2 cents clear full black
4 cents clear full black
6 cents clear full black
10 cents clear full black
12 cents dull pink
24 cents dull pink
36 cents dull pink
60 cents dull pink

96 cents dull pink
3 dollars pale scarlet-vermilion
6 dollars very pale ultramarine

New numbers were assigned to the plates but were not engraved on them, at least they do not appear on the printed sheets. Among the old plates used by the Bureau the 72 cents and $1.92 have been reported. Mr. **Plate numbers.** J. M. Bartels, to whom I am indebted for valued information, assures me that neither plate was ever used, though a new number, 65, was assigned to the plate of the 72 cent stamp. The following table may be of interest:

	Old Number.	New Number.		
1 cent	482	37	3	printings.
2 cents	218	38	3	"
4 cents	215	39	5	"
6 cents	216	40	1	"
10 cents	217	41	5	"
12 cents	195	42	5	"
24 cents	198	81	4	"
36 cents	196	43	2	"
60 cents	202	83	4	"
96 cents	204	127	1	"
3 dollars	199	108	2	"
6 dollars	197	118	1	"

Of these stamps the following quantities were issued:

Fiscal year ending June 30th, 1895:   **Deliveries to postmasters.**

QUARTER ENDING:

	Sept. 30, 1894.	Dec. 31, 1894.	Mch. 31, 1895.	June 30, 1895.	Total.
1 cent	198,164	266,100	105,650	....	569,914
2 cents	88,682	215,100	89,400	....	393,182
4 cents	73,321	193,875	77,175	....	344,371
6 cents	9,705	....	.... ..	....	9,705
10 cents	52,257	157,360	65,815	....	275,432
12 cents	31,004	93,625	32,775	....	157,404
24 cents	29,339	78,475	34,950	....	142,764
36 cents	9.935	....	....	....	9,935
60 cents	....	31,272	14,460	....	45,732
96 cents	... ...	....	7,827	....	7,827
3 dollars	....	3,190	6,025	....	9,215
6 dollars	....	1,075	4,175	... .	5,250

Whole number of stamps 1,970,731.   Value $206,289.680.00.

NEWSPAPER AND PERIODICAL STAMPS.

ISSUE OF 1895.

In the report of the Third Assistant Postmaster General for 1894 we read:

Official announcement.

The reader will observe that the series, as announced, contained a denomination, the three cents, which was not included among the issued stamps.

The stamps of this new series were issued on February 1st, 1895. They are thus officially described :

"The denominations of these stamps from 1 to 10 cents, inclusive, are of the same design. The numerals in the upper corners are of equal size in the 1, 2 and 5 cent stamps, while those in the 10 cent stamp are condensed so as to fill the same space that is given to the others, besides being slightly different in style. Those in the 1 and 5 cent denominations are shaded dark on the lower half ; those of the 2 and 10 cent stamps are white faced. All these stamps bear an engraving of the statue of America, by Crawford, which surmounts the dome of the Capitol at Washington, the same subject as that on the lower denominations of the old series, except that the presentation is in full face instead of three-quarters. The words ' U. S. POSTAGE ' at the top of the stamps are in white block letters upon an arched line, and the words ' NEWSPAPERS ' on the left and ' PERIODICALS ' on the right are in vertical lines. The denominations at the bottom are in white Roman letters, and there is a foliate ornamentation in the lower corners.

Designs.

The upper border line of the 25 and 50 cent stamps is broken by two indentations, separating that border into three equal parts, and the side inscriptions follow a curved line upon a scroll. The dimensions of the stamps below the $2 denomination are 27-32 by 1 3-8 inch.

The remaining denominations from $2 to $100, are of the same size as the stamps of the retired series, that is to say, 15-16 by 1 3-8 inch."

The foregoing description may be supplemented by saying: The central figure on the 25 and 50 cent stamps is the same as that on the denominations 12 to 96 cents of the preceding issues. Besides slight alterations in the arrangement of the inscriptions, foliage and other ornaments are added in the lower part of the stamps. The numerals in the upper corners are in small squares instead of shields. The designs of the $2, $5, $10, $20, $50 and $100 denominations are adapted, respectively, from those of the $3, $6, $12, $24, $36 and $60 stamps of the previous series. In each case the arrangement of the surrounding inscriptions is slightly modified.

The sizes in millimetres are : One to fifty cents, 21¼ x 34½ mm ; two to one hundred dollars, 24¼ x 35¼ mm.

These stamps were at first printed on a thick soft paper, much like that used by the American Bank Note Co, but closer grained and less porous. Subsequently they were issued on paper watermarked with the letters " U S P S ". This paper was fully described in the chapter upon the regular postage stamps of the same period.

Paper.

The gum is thin, smooth and yellowish or yellowish white in color. The perforation is the standard 12.

The stamps have been seen in the following colors and shades:

Perforated 12.

Reference List.

Thick Soft White Wove Paper.

Feb. 1st, 1895	1 cent deep black
	2 cents deep black, black
	5 cents deep black
	10 cents deep black
	25 cents, rose, rose-carmine, carmine, lake
	50 cents rose rose-carmine, carmine, lake
	2 dollars scarlet-vermilion, scarlet
	5 dollars dull ultramarine
	10 dollars deep green
	20 dollars black-violet
	50 dollars brown-rose
	100 dollars bluish purple

Watermarked U S P S

Jan. 11th, 1896.	1 cent black, deep black
Nov. 21st, 1895.	2 cents black, deep black
Feb. 12th, 1896.	5 cents black, deep black
Sept. 13th, 1895.	10 cents black, deep black
Oct. 11th, 1895.	25 cents deep rose, lilac-rose, violet-rose, lake
Sept. 19th, 1895.	50 cents deep rose, lilac-rose, violet-rose, lake
Jan. 23rd, 1897.	2 dollars vermilion, scarlet vermilion, scarlet
Jan. 16th, 1896.	5 dollars dark blue
Mch. 5th, 1896.	10 dollars dark yellow-green, dark green
Jan. 27th, 1896.	20 dollars black-violet, violet black
July 31st, 1897.	50 dollars brown-rose, deep brown-rose
Jan. 23rd, 1896.	100 dollars purple, deep purple

The plates each contained one hundred stamps, arranged in ten rows of ten. At the time of perforation the impressions were divided horizontally into

Plates.   half sheets of fifty stamps. The line of division is, as usual, marked by an imperforate edge. The imprint is "BUREAU, ENGRAVING AND PRINTING." in white Roman capitals, on a tablet with octagonal ends. A thin line of color surrounds the tablet and at each end are pointed ornaments. The imprint is placed at the middle of the top, bottom and sides. Three colored lines, meeting in a point above the " v " of " ENGRAVING ", mark the middle point of each side. The plate number is placed at the right of each imprint. The plate numbers are :

Plate numbers.

Without Watermark.

1 cent	No. 90.
2 cents	No. 100.
5 cents	No. 93.
10 cents	No. 105.
25 cents	No. 123.
50 cents	No. 109.
2 dollars	No. 136.
5 dollars	No. 137.
10 dollars	No. 138.
20 dollars	No. 139.
50 dollars	No. 135.
100 dollars	No. 140.

Watermarked U S P S

1 cent	No. 90, 262.
2 cents	No. 100, 265.
5 cents	No. 93, 266.
10 cents	No. 105, 269.
25 cents	No. 123.
50 cents	No. 109, 259.
2 dollars	No. 136.
5 dollars	No. 137.
10 dollars	No. 138.
20 dollars	No. 139.
50 dollars	No. 135.
100 dollars	No 140.

Plates not used.   Certain other plates were prepared for these stamps but they were not put to press. The numbers assigned to them were:

1 cent	No. 36.
25 cents	No. 258.
2 dollars	No. 270.
5 dollars	No. 273.
10 dollars	No. 271.
20 dollars	No. 272.
50 dollars	No. 284.
100 dollars	No. 285.

From the annual reports of the Postmaster General and other sources we obtain the following statistics of stamps issued to deputy postmasters :

Stamps issued during the fiscal year ending June 30th, 1895:

QUARTER ENDING:

	Sept. 30, 1894.	Dec. 31, 1894.	Mch. 31, 1895.	June 30, 1895.	Total.
1 cent	......	......	157,880	312,350	470,230
2 cents	......	......	147,410	329,500	476,910
5 cents	......	......	158,750	294,990	453,740
10 cents	......	......	124,940	270,240	395,180
25 cents	......	......	70,630	133,030	203,660
50 cents	......	......	50,575	99,430	150,005
2 dollars	......	......	16,973	37,756	54,729
5 dollars	......	......	6,140	17,775	23,915
10 dollars	......	......	2,528	9,545	12,073
20 dollars	......	......	885	6,250	7,135
50 dollars	......	......	15	1,949	1,964
100 dollars	......	......	1,515	3,745	5,260

Whole number of stamps 2,254,801. Value $1,319,026.00.

Stamps issued during the fiscal year ending June 30th, 1896:

QUARTER ENDING:

	Sept. 30, 1895.	Dec. 31, 1895.	Mch. 31, 1896.	June 30, 1896.	Total.
1 cent	270,650	273,100	293,150	248,650	1,085,550
2 cents	303,650	314,600	349,750	312,100	1,280,100
5 cents	252,070	236,720	250,160	228,600	967,550
10 cents	257,880	269,290	273,840	270,585	1,071,395
25 cents	99,540	106,820	106,400	121,680	434,430
50 cents	99,010	116,900	110,965	113,700	440,575
2 dollars	23,630	32,485	34,610	32,570	123,295
5 dollars	8,910	11,782	12,380	11,525	44,597
10 dollars	5,583	7,082	8,705	6,510	27,882
20 dollars	2,583	4,430	4,585	4,255	15,853
50 dollars	908	1,355	1,035	915	4,213
100 dollars	932	3,250	3,090	2,950	10,222

Whole number of stamps 5,505,672. Value $2,819,177.00.

Stamps issued during the fiscal year ending June 30th, 1897:

QUARTER ENDING:

	Sept. 30, 1896.	Dec. 31, 1896.	Mch. 31, 1897.	June 30, 1897.	Total.
1 cent	275,200	287,000	249,900	233,050	1,045,150
2 cents	340,925	347,050	320,650	312,400	1,321,025
5 cents	235,640	259,150	242,000	212,570	949,360
10 cents	259,025	285,245	282,825	248,850	1,075,935
25 cents	114,610	118,060	109,594	111,800	454,064
50 cents	117,851	117,020	112,346	118,710	465,927
2 dollars	29,158	31,875	33,692	29,185	123,910
5 dollars	11,259	13,120	10,440	10,780	45,599
10 dollars	6,964	8,130	6,565	5,855	27,514
20 dollars	5,000	4,990	4,280	4,190	18,460
50 dollars	1,255	1,115	930	1,120	4,420
100 dollars	3,265	3,495	3,065	3,090	12,915

Whole number of stamps 5,544,279. Value $3,171,068.00.

Stamps issued during the fiscal year ending June 30th, 1898

QUARTER ENDING :

	Sept. 30, 1897.	Dec. 31, 1897.	Mch. 31, 1898.	June 30, 1898.
1 cent	279,750	264,700	256,100	176,950
2 cents	360,950	338,400	335,150	223,650
5 cents	257,420	244,400	242,130	144,300
10 cents	278,695	280,800	281,905	168,935
25 cents	111,040	106,000	115,860	70,420
50 cents	117,500	115,580	124,290	76,940
2 dollars	35,460	30,940	34,880	21,980
5 dollars	13,085	11,755	13,090	9,635
10 dollars	7,175	7,505	8,450	5,325
20 dollars	4,695	4,430	5,680	3,925
50 dollars	1,000	1,165	1,240	1,525
100 dollars	3,040	3,380	3,285	2,610

Whole number of stamps 5,207,120.   Value $3,119,864.00.

In the foregoing tables no distinction is made between the unwatermarked and those on watermarked paper and, so far as I statistics covering the exact quantities of the two varieties have published.

Other deliveries.   In addition to the issues to postmasters certain other deliver: stamps have been made at various times :

In 1895 there were sent to the headquarters of the Unive Union at Berne 750 copies of each value from 1 cent to $100.

In 1898, 125 sets were surcharged "UNIVERSAL—POSTAL—(and distributed to the delegates attending the meeting of that (Washington.

In the report of the Bureau of Engraving and Printing for year we find a table headed : "Statement showing the Specimer age Stamps for Post-Office Album, Delivered in the Fiscal Year 18, table includes 50 sets of the newspaper and periodical stamps   In report is another table headed :   "Statement showing the Specim(Stamps Delivered to the Third Assistant Postmaster General (Fiscal Year 1898."   This delivery consisted of 500 sets of the new: periodical stamps.

I am unable to say whether or not any of the stamps com last two items were overprinted with the word "SPECIMEN."

The report of the Postmaster General for 1898 says that 18, five dollar stamps were overprinted for use as internal revenue sta report of the Bureau for the same year does not quite agree with th the quantity being given as " 355 sheets, 17,750 stamps."

Finally, in the report of the Bureau for 1899, we find that i 55,000 sets of these stamps were placed on sale to the public and 1,2
Sets sold to the general public.   men " sets delivered to the Third Assistant Postmaster General. contained a quanity of reprints as will be seen on referring to th devoted to that subject.   It has been stated that the sets delive

Third Assistant Postmaster General were all originals except the five dollar stamps. At least a part of them were handstamped " SPECIMEN " in small type. As I have seen original five dollar stamps and reprints of some of the other values with this surcharge. I conclude that the statement regarding the stamps delivered to the Third Assistant Postmaster General is not absolutely correct. It will be shown, on a subsequent page, that all of the 55,000 sets were not sold.

The use of the newspaper and periodical stamps was discontinued on July 1st, 1898. The causes leading up to this are especially interesting to philatelists. The original purpose and manner of use of these stamps are set forth in the report of the Third Assistant Postmaster General, dated November 15th, 1875, as quoted on page 294. A part of this report is clearly a transcription of the postal regulations, which were, in turn, founded on the laws of Congress. Here we read : " The proper amount in stamps handed to the postmaster, etc." From this wording it is evident that, at first, the stamps were sold to publishers and news agents, otherwise they could not have them to hand in. It is quite probable that they were sold to any one who applied for them. At a later date regulations were promulgated by the Post Office Department which forbade the sale of the stamps and required the postage on second-class matter. when mailed in bulk, to be paid in money, and an equivalent amount of stamps to be taken from stock, by the clerk having them in charge, and affixed to the receipt. *Regulations concerning the newspaper and periodical stamps.*

In various official publications we find evidence that the regulations concerning the sale of these stamps were not always observed. For instance, in the *Postal Guide* for 1898, we read : *Regulations not heeded.*

" Postmasters throughout the country are being solicited to sell postage-due stamps and newspaper and periodical stamps and are in some cases complying with such requests, in spite of the law and the rules of the Department Newspaper and periodical stamps are never to be sold to any person nor loaned to other postmasters. Their only proper use is to be affixed to and immediately cancelled on the stub of every receipt given for second-class matter accepted for mailing."

Officials even went so far as to assert that collectors and dealers who held these stamps did so in defiance of the law ; that the stamps *must* have been stolen and were liable to seizure and their holders to punishment. This in spite of the fact that the stamps had been, at one time, freely sold to publishers and news agents, had been given in quantities to the Universal Postal Union and had been sold with the sets of reprints and re-issues from 1875 to 1884. The question appears to have been revived by the trouble over the privately perforated stamps, which were referred to in a preceding chapter, and the Department decided to test the merits of its claims. In May, 1897, certain lots of these stamps, advertised for sale at public auction by a New York dealer, were seized and an action at law instituted to recover the stamps and nominal damages, on the ground that "said stamps were stolen, embezzled and purloined from the Government, that they were prepared and printed for the Government and were and have ever since the time they were printed continued to be the property of the Government, and it has never lawfully *Official opinions.* *Seizure of stamps.* *Legal action taken.*

and voluntarily parted with the possession thereof, nor have any of its officers, employees or agents had lawful authority to part with title and possession thereto."

Collectors and dealers joined together and subscribed liberally to defend this action. Even before the case came to trial the postal officials must have recognized the weakness of their position and—which should have been apparent long before—that the stamps were not necessary for the proper transaction of business between the Post Office Department and publishers. Corroboration of this is found in the following extract from the report of the Third Assistant Postmaster General, dated October 7th, 1897 :

DISCONTINUANCE OF THE USE OF NEWSPAPER AND PERIODICAL STAMPS.

" Under the present law and the Postal Regulations postage on newspapers and periodicals mailed in bulk by publishers and news agents, commonly called second-class matter, is collected by postmasters in money, for which they are required to give receipts to the senders of the matter, and to attach to the stubs of such receipts, retained in books kept in the post office, the equivalent of the money received in newspaper and periodical stamps, or stamps provided solely for that purpose, which are not good for postage on any other class of mail matter, and which are not to be sold, loaned or given away. Every postmaster at whose office this class of matter is mailed is further required to cancel the stamps used therefor, and to transmit them every quarter to the office of the Third Assistant Postmaster General, with the stubs to which they are attached, and with an itemized report showing the names of the mailing parties and of their publications, and the amount of the postage paid thereon ; and these canceled stamps, after being carefully counted and the amounts found to agree with the accompanying reports, are destroyed.

Upon a very slight consideration of this system it will be seen that, as the stamps used are never bought by the senders of second-class matter, are never in their hands, but are always, both before and after use, in the custody of postmasters or their subordinates, who can apply them or not to the stubs of their receipt-books, as they may elect, and in any amounts the use of them in the manner described is unnecessary. A receipt to be given in every case to the sender of such matter, with a manifolded copy of it to be sent by the postmaster to the Department, would present precisely the same evidence of the collection of the postage as is now sought to be secured by the use of the stamps. The only difference would be in the manner of showing the postmaster's collections : under the present plan he simply reports to this office the amount of postage received and sends to the Department the stamps used, while to the Auditor he reports these stamps as sold ; under the other, he would still report the amount of postage received, accompanied by manifolded copies of the receipts given therefor, which could be examined and verified, if necessary, both by the Third Assistant Postmaster General and by the Auditor.

These newspaper and periodical stamps are not only unnecessary, but they involve labor and expense, which could be saved by their abandonment. The cost of their manufacture is not very great, it is true—not over a thousand dollars a year ; but the transmission of them in the mails, the custody of them in post offices, the application of them to the receipt books of postmasters, the canceling and forwarding of them to the Department, and their examination and destruction here, amount to very much more, all of which could be saved.

Not being willing, however, to rely entirely on my own judgment as to the matter, I have had special inquiry made of the postmasters at three very large cities as to whether the present system is a proper one and they have all agreed that so far as concerns the use of newspaper and periodical stamps the system should be modified, and could be without any inconvenient derangement of their office methods.

On the whole, I am thoroughly convinced that the use of the stamps in question affords no protection whatever to the Government or to postmasters, but is expensive and unnecessary, and I accordingly recommend that Congress be asked to authorize their discontinuance, and the substitution of such a system of accountability on the part of postmasters and their subordinates as may be deemed best by the Postmaster General."

The case was tried in April, 1898 and a decision was rendered in favor of the defendant, in which decision the Government ultimately acquiesced. In the meantime, Congress, in compliance with the recommendation of the Postmaster General, ordered the use of the newspaper and periodical stamps to be discontinued on and after July 1st, 1898. This act was approved on June 13th, 1898, and on the next day the following official order was issued :

Discontinuance of the stamps recommended.

ORDER OF THE POST MASTER GENERAL

POST OFFICE DEPARTMENT,

ORDER No. 232.   WASHINGTON, D. C., June 14th, 1898.

Under authority of the act of Congress approved on the 13th instant, making appropriations for the postal service for the next fiscal year, it is hereby ordered that the use of newspaper and periodical postage stamps shall cease on and after the 1st of July, 1898. From that date postmasters will collect in money the postage on second-class matter mailed in bulk by publishers and news agents, and will give receipts therefor, as they have heretofore done; but instead of including this money in the amount covered by the sale of stamps, as is now the practice, they must charge themselves with it in their quarterly returns to the Auditor, by a special entry to be inserted between items 1 and 2 of the official form. *Order discontinuing the use of the stamps.*

Carrying out this change, Sections 103 and 130 of the Postal Regulations are hereby modified so as to read as follows:

SEC 103. POSTAGE-STAMPS: KINDS AND DENOMINATIONS—Of postage stamps two kinds, each consisting of various denominations, are provided, viz: Ordinary stamps which are used to prepay postage on ordinary mail matter of the first, third and fourth classes, as well as on second-class matter mailed by others than publishers and news agents, and the fees on registered matter; and postage due stamps, which are used for the collection of postage due on mail matter that has not been fully prepaid at mailing offices."

"SEC. 130. Second class matter, elsewhere defined, must be brought to the post office and there weighed in bulk, and the postage collected in money, for which receipts, made out on forms taken from books furnished by the Department, are to be given. No credit is ever to be allowed for newspaper and periodical postage; but, for convenience, the postmaster may receive from a publisher or news agent the deposit of sufficient money in advance to pay for more than a single mailing. In every case where advance deposits of postage are thus made, the postmaster must charge against it every mailing, and must see to it that the amount on hand shall never fall below what is necessary to cover any matter that is offered for dispatch. Postmasters must transmit punctually at the end of each quarter, to the Third Assistant Postmaster General, by ordinary mail, in special envelopes provided for the purpose, the stubs of all receipts given for newspaper and periodical postage collected during the quarter, together with the statement required by Section 208."

"Before returning the stubs, the calculations and footings should be reviewed and made correct. The stubs should then be detached from the book, arranged in numerical order, fastened together at the upper left-hand corner, and the name of the post office, county and state written thereon. The postmaster will continue to use what is left of the stub book."

Section 194 will be also modified so as to require postmasters to report specially on their quarterly returns to the Auditor the amount of money collected during the quarter as postage on newspapers and periodicals; and Section 208 will be changed so as to require the quarterly statement of postage sent to the Third Assistant Postmaster General to be made in duplicate.

CH. EMORY SMITH, Postmaster General.

The use of the newspaper and periodical stamps having been discontinued, postmasters were instructed to return to the Post Office Department, for redemption, any stocks of them remaining in their hands. An official circular, dated February 2d, 1899, limited the period of this redemption to the 15th of that month, at which latter date the 55,0co sets of reprints and remainders were offered for sale to the public In compliance with these orders a quantity of the stamps were returned to Washington. The stocks returned consisted of stamps of the various printings of the Bureau of Engraving and Printing and a number printed by the American Bank Note Co. It is even possible that a very few of the Continental Bank Note Co's product may have been included among them. I am not aware that any report of the amount of stamps redeemed has been made public. If published, it would doubtless be confined to a statement of the total value, without giving quantities of the several denominations or separating the issues *Stamps returned to the Post Office Department.*

The stamps returned by postmasters were usually in broken sheets and often stuck together. None of them were used toward making up the 55,coo sets for collectors. Such stamps of those sets as were originals were obtained from undistributed stock in the vaults of the Stamp Agent at the Bureau of Engraving and Printing. The balance of this stock was subsequently destroyed, as were also the stamps returned by postmasters

Only about one half of the 55,000 sets were sold, as is shown in the following extract from the annual report of the Third Assistant Postmaster General for 1900 :

In my report for the fiscal year ending June 30, 1899, it was stated that the Department had realized $117,175 from the sale of obsolete newspaper and periodical stamps at $5 per set. This sum represented the value of the sets reported sold by first-class postmasters to whom they were furnished, but upon final settlement it developed that many postmasters had reported as " sold ", in addition to their actual sales, a number of sets which had simply been placed in the hands of their stamp clerks for sale. Many of these stamps were afterward returned to the Department, and this reduced the value of the sets sold by postmasters from the time they were issued in February, 1899, until their withdrawal from sale December 31, 1899, to $109,945. To this amount should be added the value of 5,000 sets sold by the Department direct, $25,000, making the total income derived from this source $134,945. The newspaper and periodical stamps remaining in the hands of postmasters December 31, 1899, were returned to the Department for destruction. The following statement shows in detail the disposition made of the entire issue :

	Number of sets.	Value at $5 per set.
Placed on sale—At first-class post offices,	50,000	$250,000
At Post Office Department,	5,000	25,000
Total,	55,000	$275,000
Returned to Department unsold,	28,011	140,055
Sold,	26,989	$134,945

The sale of these stamps was discontinued after December 31st, 1899, at all post offices except that of the city of Washington, where the stamps remained on sale until February 10th, 1900.

POSTAGE DUE STAMPS.

ISSUE OF 1879.

Previous to July, 1879, whenever a letter was sent unpaid or insufficiently prepaid, the amount of postage due was written or stamped on the envelope and collected from the addressee. No vouchers were given for money thus collected and there was nothing, beyond the honesty of the postmaster, to insure its delivery to the Government.

As a remedy for this unsatisfactory system an Act of Congress, approved March 3rd, 1879, provided :

"Sec 26. All mail matter of the first-class, upon which one full rate of postage has been prepaid, shall be forwarded to its destination, charged with the unpaid rate, to be collected on delivery ; but postmasters, before delivering the same, or any article of mail matter upon which prepayment in full has not been made, shall affix, or caused to be affixed, and canceled, as ordinary stamps are canceled, one or more stamps, equivalent in value to the amount of postage due on such article of mail matter, which stamps shall be of such special design and denomination as the Postmaster General may prescribe. and which shall in no case be sold by any postmaster nor received by him in prepayment of postage. That, in lieu of the commission now allowed to postmasters at offices of the fourth class upon the amount of unpaid letter postage collected, such postmasters shall receive a commission upon the amount of such special stamps so canceled, the same as now allowed upon postage stamps, stamped envelopes, postal cards, and newspaper and periodical stamps canceled as postages on matter actually mailed at their offices : *Provided,* The Postmaster General may, in his discretion, prescribe instead such regulations therefor at the offices where free delivery is established as, in his judgment, the good of the service may require. *[margin: Act authorizing postage due stamps.]*

Sec. 27. Any postmaster or other person engaged in the postal service who shall collect, and fail to account for, the postage due upon any article of mail matter which he may deliver. without having previously affixed and canceled such special stamps as hereinbefore provided, or who shall fail to affix such stamps, shall be deemed guilty of a misdemeanor, and, on conviction thereof, shall be punished by a fine of fifty dollars."

In accordance with this Act the following official circular was issued :

SPECIAL STAMPS FOR POSTAGE DUE.

POST OFFICE DEPARTMENT,

OFFICE OF THE THIRD ASSISTANT POSTMASTER GENERAL,

DIVISION OF POSTAGE STAMPS, STAMPED ENVELOPES, AND POSTAL CARDS,

WASHINGTON, D. C., May 5, 1879.

By Sections 26 and 27 of the act of Congress " making appropriations for the service of the Post Office Department for the fiscal year ending June 30, 1880, and for other purposes," approved March 3, 1879, it is made the duty of postmasters to affix to all mail matter that has arrived at destination without full payment of postage, and before delivery of the same, an amount of stamps equal to the postage due—the stamps to be of such special design as the Postmaster General may direct. *[margin: Circular announcing the issue of postage due stamps.]*

To avoid any confusion in the accounts of postmasters with the Auditor, and on account of the length of time necessary to prepare for the change contemplated by the above section

in the mode of collecting and accounting for short paid postage, it has been decided *to have the same go into practical operation on the 1st of July next.* The Department, however, *will begin issuing, some time during the present month,* in anticipation of the wants of postmasters special stamps for the collection of postage due, of the denominations of 1, 2, 3 and 5 cents. * * * * *The color of all is the same—a reddish brown*
These stamps are intended exclusively for the collection of postage due on matter arriving at destination through the mails, and are to be used in combination wherever required to cover unusual amounts of postage. They are to be canceled in the customary way, after being attached to mail matter, and are never to be sold or received by postmasters for prepayment of postage.
Postmasters must distinctly understand that these stamps are not to be used until the 1st of July, 1879
A supply of them will be sent at first to all post offices, in advance of requisitions from postmasters, and charged to their account ; but afterwards they must be ordered on blank forms (No. 3285) to be furnished by the First Assistant Postmaster General. With the first supply of stamps, however, blank requisitions for future use will be inclosed.
The stamps will be accounted for to the Auditor the same as other stamps, and will enter into the monthly report of stamps &c., received. sold, and on hand, required by the Regulations to be made by postmasters at Presidential offices to the Third Assistant Postmaster General.
On the next page of this circular will be found the sections of the new Postal law and Regulations relating to the above described stamps, which are published in advance for the information and guidance of postmasters. The distinguishing numbers of the sections cannot now be given ; but the instructions are here printed in the same order in which they will appear in the forthcoming volume of the new Postal Regulations.

A. D. HAZEN,

Third Assistant Postmaster General.

Among other provisions of the regulations were the following:

" At all post offices where the free delivery service has not been established, postmasters will not affix the postage due stamps until the delivery of the matter has been requested. At all free delivery post offices. matters which has not been sufficiently prepaid will be rated up, and postage due stamps of the necessary denominations will be affixed as soon as the matter is received at the post office, unless an order is on file for a letter to be forwarded, in which case it will be forwarded without affixing the postage due stamp."

The stamps of the denominations 1, 2, 3 and 5 cents were first issued **Dates of issue.** to postmasters on May 9th, 1879; those of the other three values, 10, 30 and 50 cents, were issued on September 19th of the same year.

The stamps are thus officially described:

" These stamps are alike, except as to the denominations, which are expressed by Arabic numerals, in the middle, upon an elliptic ground of **Design and color.** delicate lathe work. Upon the upper line of this ground are the words ' POSTAGE DUE ' in white capitals; on the lower border is the denomination, in letters of the same kind. On the left and right side, respectively, and separating these inscriptions, are the letters ' U ' and ' s ' upon white shields. There is a complex angular ornamentation of light line work surrounding this, and the whole rests upon a darker colored beveled tablet, of which but little can be seen, though it covers the entire stamp, which is a parallelogram 1 by 25-32 of an inch in dimensions. The color of all the stamps is a dull red or reddish brown."

The paper is the thick, soft, porous, white wove paper, which was always used by the American Bank Note Company.

The gum varies from pure white to brownish.

The perforation is 12 and the stamps measure 20x25½mm.

The stamps were at first printed in a brown ink having a yellow tone. This was followed by various shades of red-brown and eventually by lake or, as it is usually termed, claret.

The following colors and varieties have been noted:

Perforated 12.

Thick Soft Porous Wove Paper.

May 9th, 1879.   1 cent yellow-brown, pale brown, brown, deep brown, light red-brown, red-brown, lake-brown, carmine-brown, rose-brown, dull-rose, claret, light claret

2 cents yellow-brown, deep yellow-brown, pale brown, brown, deep brown, light red-brown, red-brown, lake-brown, carmine-brown, rose-brown, dull rose, claret, dark claret

3 cents yellow-brown, pale brown, brown, deep brown, red-brown, lake-brown, carmine-brown, claret, light claret, dark claret

5 cents yellow-brown, deep yellow-brown, pale brown, brown, deep brown, red-brown, carmine-brown, rose-brown, claret, light claret, dark claret

Sept. 19th, 1879.   10 cents yellow-brown, deep yellow-brown, pale brown, brown, deep brown, red-brown, lake-brown, carmine brown, rose-brown, dull rose, claret, light claret

30 cents bistre-brown, pale brown, brown, deep brown, red-brown, lake-brown, claret, dark claret

50 cents bistre-brown, pale brown, brown, deep brown, red-brown, claret, dark claret.

Variety:

10 cents yellow-brown   Imperforate

The plates each contained two hundred stamps, arranged in two panes of one hundred (ten rows of ten) placed side by side. Each impression was divided between the panes, making half sheets of one hundred stamps. As usual, this division left one side of each sheet imperforate. The line of separation was marked by arrow heads in the upper and lower margins. The imprint was "AMERICAN BANK NOTE COMPANY," in colored capitals. It was placed above the two stamps in the middle of the top row of each pane and below the corresponding stamps in the bottom row. Between each imprint and the central line of the plate was "*No.*", followed by the plate number in slanting Arabic numerals:

The plate numbers were:

1 cent	No. 313, 314.
2 cents	No. 315, 464.
3 cents	No. 316, 317.
5 cents	No. 318.
10 cents	No. 331.
30 cents	No. 332.
50 cents	No. 333.

Although the law expressly forbade postmasters to receive postage due stamps in prepayment of postage, instances are known in which this was done,

Postage due stamps used to pay regular postage.

and in at least one of them the postmaster himself was responsible for the infraction. In the *American Philatelist*, volume III, page 100, is an article on this subject, a portion of which (the extract here quoted) is reprinted from the *Independent Philatelist* for March, 1885:

" On the afternoon of February 14, 1885, the post office at Bergen Point, N. J., ran short of the one cent stamps on account of the increased local mail of drop letters, and in order to meet the demand the postmaster was obliged to utilize the *one cent unpaid*.

This we learned late on Monday afternoon, and on arrival at the post office found a new supply of one cent stamps ready for customers. The postmaster informs us that about fifty were in use on the afternoon of February 14, and the morning of the 16th, 1885."

The reader is reminded that February 14th is St. Valentine's day which, in the year 1885, fell on Saturday. This will explain the sudden increase in the number of drop letters and the reason that no stamps were used on the 15th.

I have seen an envelope, mailed at Losley, Va., on August 10th, 1893, on which the regular postage was paid by means of a two cent due stamp of the 1879 type, printed in deep claret. The letter was delivered to the addressee in Richmond, Va., without any claim for unpaid postage.

Special printing.

A special printing of the postage due stamps was made in 1879 to supply the wants of collectors and dealers. This will be further described in the chapter on reprints and re-issues. All values of these stamps, printed

" Specimen " stamps.

in red brown, exist with the surcharge " SPECIMEN " in red. These were probably prepared for exchanging through the Universal Postal Union.

Deliveries to postmasters.

From the annual reports of the Postmaster General and other sources we obtain the following statistics of stamps issued to deputy postmasters:

Stamps issued during the fiscal year ending June 30th, 1879:

QUARTER ENDING:

	Sept. 30, 1878.	Dec. 31, 1878.	Mch. 31, 1879.	June 30, 1879.	Total.
1 cent	......	......	......	5,755,400	5,755,400
2 cents	......	......	......	642,900	642,900
3 cents	......	......	.....	8,396,000	8,396,000
5 cents	......	......	......	873,300	873,300
10 cents	......	......	......	......	......
30 cents	......	......	......	......	......
50 cents	......	......	......	......	......

Whole number of stamps 15,667,600. Value $365,957.00.

Stamps issued during the fiscal year ending June 30th, 1880 :

QUARTER ENDING :

	Sept. 30, 1879.	Dec. 31, 1879.	Mch. 31, 1880.	June 30, 1880.	Total.
1 cent	196,900	258,000	349,900	394,200	1,199,000
2 cents	200,800	146,200	167,700	180,300	695,000
3 cents	390,700	640,400	1,013,000	955,800	2,999,900
5 cents	377,700	78,000	152,400	159,400	767,500
10 cents	194,200	65,800	123,400	119,400	502,800
30 cents	47,480	5,000	700	11,100	64,280
50 cents	35,870	10,000	100	10,050	56,020

Whole number of stamps 6,284,500. Value $251,836.00.

Stamps issued during the fiscal year ending June 30th, 1881 :

QUARTER ENDING :

	Sept. 30, 1880.	Dec. 31, 1880.	Mch. 31, 1881.	June 30, 1881.	Total.
1 cent	279,100	465,600	400,500	450,500	1,595,700
2 cents	129,700	227,900	142,500	231,950	732,050
3 cents	967,600	1,231,200	1,147,900	1,287,500	4,634,200
5 cents	91,060	124,980	170,900	133,840	520,780
10 cents	130,740	113,510	137,500	170,500	552,250
30 cents	50	1,400	200	7,650	9,300
50 cents	......	200	400	830	1,430

Whole number of stamps 8,045,710. Value $254,393.00.

Stamps issued during the fiscal year ending June 30th, 1882 :

QUARTER ENDING :

	Sept. 30, 1881.	Dec. 31, 1881.	Mch. 31, 1882.	June 30, 1882.	Total.
1 cent	440,100	525,100	551,200	811,950	2,328,350
2 cents	137,250	203,750	228,950	388,350	958,300
3 cents	1,389,900	1,763,200	1,784,000	1,864,550	6,801,650
5 cents	86,560	127,460	137,940	180,600	532,560
10 cents	128,550	137,270	197,230	276,880	739,930
30 cents	620	1,620	760	8,050	11,050
50 cents	300	400	570	2,200	3,470

Whole number of stamps 11,375,310. Value $352,170.00.

Stamps issued during the fiscal year ending June 30th, 1883 :

QUARTER ENDING :

	Sept. 30, 1882.	Dec. 31, 1882.	Mch. 31, 1883.	June 30, 1883.	Total.
1 cent	580,850	546,525	769,550	578,450	2,475,375
2 cents	190,600	250,725	366,500	436,650	1,244,475
3 cents	1,718,250	2,859,580	2,123,750	1,681,950	7,383,530
5 cents	117,540	94,245	198,760	114,600	525,145
10 cents	205,070	233,365	280,310	230,220	948,965
30 cents	10,730	3,110	1,310	2,810	17,960
50 cents	10,300	650	3,100	400	14,450

Whole number of stamps 12,609,900. Value $404,915.90.

Stamps issued during the fiscal year ending June 30th, 1884 :

QUARTER ENDING :

	Sept. 30, 1883.	Dec. 31, 1883.	Mch 31, 1884.	June 30, 1884.	Total.
1 cent	853,300	863,900	912,600	837,700	3,467,500
2 cents	1,679,100	2,032,100	2,204,000	1,990,400	7,905,600
3 cents	662,050	50,500	11,700	......	724,250
5 cents	100,190	76,500	158,060	119,800	454,550
10 cents	220,300	147,370	402,380	251,220	1,021,270
30 cents	6,930	2,210	16,050	1,170	26,360
50 cents	5,810	1,848	5,010	......	12,668

Whole number of stamps 13,612,198. Value $353,611.00.

Stamps issued during the fiscal year ending June 30th, 1885 :

QUARTER ENDING :

	Sept. 30, 1884.	Dec. 31, 1884.	Mch. 31, 1885.	June 30, 1885.	Total.
1 cent	604,600	758,300	811,200	880,250	3,054,350
2 cents	1,843,550	2,281,800	2,246,250	1,880,900	8,252,500
3 cents	......	10,500	55,500	6,700	72,700
5 cents	71,220	86,920	194,540	130,480	483,160
10 cents	195,240	175,300	211,570	202,315	784,425
30 cents	5,350	1,400	6,540	5,140	18,430
50 cents	5,000	......	70	106	5,176

Whole number of stamps 12,670,741.   Value $308,492.00.

Stamps issued during the fiscal year ending June 30th, 1886 :

QUARTER ENDING :

	Sept. 30, 1885.	Dec. 31, 1885.	Mch. 31, 1886.	June 30, 1886.	Total.
1 cent	473,800	614,100	712,800	591,800	2,392,500
2 cents	534,250	411,400	400,100	545,350	1,881,100
3 cents	700	50,000	5,600	5,000	61,300
5 cents	54,120	73,780	134,780	96,600	359,280
10 cents	124,900	261,200	234,340	150,670	771,110
30 cents	300	310	2,130	520	3,260
50 cents	......	100	1,000	......	1,100

Whole number of stamps 5,469,650.   Value $159,989.00.

Stamps issued during the fiscal year ending June 30th, 1887 :

QUARTER ENDING :

	Sept. 30, 1886.	Dec. 31, 1886.	Mch. 31, 1887.	June 30, 1887.	Total.
1 cent	817,200	952,800	843,000	823,200	3,436,200
2 cents	652,300	907,350	909,250	725,700	3,194,600
3 cents	50,000	5,000	12,700	200	67,900
5 cents	182,160	101,460	135,000	97,580	516,200
10 cents	188,850	273,440	328,210	219,840	1,010,340
30 cents	1,020	5,000	5,150	2,060	13,230
50 cents	1,000	5,020	1,000	1,044	8,064

Whole number of stamps 8,246,534.   Value $235,136.00.

Stamps issued during the fiscal year ending June 30th, 1888 :

QUARTER ENDING :

	Sept. 30, 1887.	Dec. 31, 1887.	Mch. 31, 1888.	June 30, 1888.	Total.
1 cent	936,600	1,403,900	1,868,600	1,312,500	5,521,600
2 cents	705,950	992,500	970,800	661,650	3,330,900
3 cents	60,000	12,500	60,200	4,400	137,100
5 cents	83,800	160,440	215,440	120,780	580,460
10 cents	212,300	320,740	435,160	246,340	1,214,540
30 cents	......	3,300	10,900	580	14,780
50 cents	.....	24	5,350	818	6,192

Whole number of stamps 10,805,572.   Value $283,954.00.

Stamps issued during the fiscal year ending June 30th, 1889 :

QUARTER ENDING :

	Sept. 30, 1888.	Dec. 31, 1888.	Mch. 31, 1889.	June 30, 1889.	Total.
1 cent	1,513,500	1,774,700	1,515,200	1,517,200	6,320,600
2 cents	1,035,850	851,350	88c,850	792,150	3,560,200
3 cents	55,200	11,100	70,200	12,400	148,900
5 cents	183,360	102,260	130,260	103,340	519,220
10 cents	297,020	380,120	328,960	334,100	1,340,200
30 cents	50	220	640	......	910
50 cents	30	100	10	......	140

Whole number of stamps 11,890,170. Value $299,201.00.

Stamps issued during the fiscal year ending June 30th, 1890 :

QUARTER ENDING :

	Sept. 30, 1889.	Dec. 31, 1889.	Mch. 31, 1890.	June 30, 1890.	Total.
1 cent	1,980,200	1,540,900	1,711,800	1,839,300	7,072,200
2 cents	1,261,200	1,059,100	1,051,100	1,253,000	4,624,400
3 cents	23,200	77,500	25,250	13,000	138,950
5 cents	133,160	100,060	140,370	131,300	504,890
10 cents	300,390	282,260	383,020	320,840	1,286,510
30 cents	5,450	1,050	1,310	3,100	10,910
50 cents	100	......	130	100	330

Whole number of stamps 13,638,190. Value $324,712.00.

Stamps issued during the fiscal year ending June 30th, 1891 :

QUARTER ENDING :

	Sept. 30, 1890.	Dec. 31, 1890.	Mch. 31, 1891.	June 30, 1891.	Total.
1 cent	1,915,600	1,887,700	1,99',500	1,877,500	7,673,300
2 cents	1,286,700	1,146,600	1,263,900	1,359,650	5,056,850
3 cents	73,300	24,700	25,600	70,200	193,800
5 cents	116,060	137,640	157,800	143,860	555,400
10 cents	340,060	340,820	420,940	391,340	1,493,160
30 cents	320	40	310	1,000	1,670
50 cents	100	100	300	100	600

Whole number of stamps 14,974,820. Value $361,573.00.

Stamps issued during the fiscal year ending June 30th, 1892 :

QUARTER ENDING :

	Sept. 30, 1891.	Dec. 31, 1891.	Mch. 31, 1892.	June 30, 1892.	Total.
1 cent	2,012,000	2,048,100	2,458,900	2,270,800	8,789,800
2 cents	1,293,300	1,482,600	1,748,400	1,613,100	6,137,400
3 cents	26,500	38,700	80,300	31,800	177,300
5 cents	189,100	132,500	251,800	167,600	741,000
10 cents	301,990	456,600	507,400	431,200	1,697,190
30 cents	2,420	1,700	1,200	300	5,620
50 cents	200	1,300	1,500	100	3,100

Whole number of stamps 17,551,410. Value $425,970.00.

Stamps issued during the fiscal year ending June 30th, 1893:

QUARTER ENDING :

	Sept. 30, 1892.	Dec. 31, 1892.	Mch. 31, 1893.	June 30, 1893.	Total.
1 cent	2,048,950	2,050,000	2,211,500	2,657,000	8,967,450
2 cents	1,619,550	1,435,600	1,698,000	1,845,350	6,598,500
3 cents	74,350	26,900	50,400	41,300	192,950
5 cents	173,750	168,700	213,200	252,860	808,510
10 cents	364,550	418,500	352,700	389,800	1,525,550
30 cents	1,050	2,200	1,400	2,000	6,650
50 cents	850	1,200	200	100	2,350

Whole number of stamps 18,101,960.   Value $423,583.50.

Stamps issued during the fiscal year ending June 30th, 1894 :

QUARTER ENDING :

	Sept. 30, 1893.	Dec. 31, 1893.	Mch. 31, 1894.	June 30, 1894.	Total.
1 cent	1,866,200	2,286,300	3,068,000	2,221,400	8,441,900
2 cents	1,391,750	1,889,900	1,646,750	2,203,300	7,131,700
3 cents	69,000	18,800	125,500	29,600	242,900
5 cents	167,840	121,380	180,460	134,100	603,780
10 cents	366,330	394,940	485,920	361,280	1,608,470
30 cents	1,180	2,880	1,160	1,070	6,290
50 cents	300	1,132	574	1,100	3,106

Whole number of stamps 18,038,146.   Value $428,816.00.

Stamps issued during the fiscal year ending June 30th, 1895 :

QUARTER ENDING :

	Sept. 30, 1894.	Dec. 31, 1894.	Mch. 31, 1895.	June 30, 1895.	Total.
1 cent	1,350,369	......	......	......	1,350,369
2 cents	50,164	......	......	......	50,164
3 cents	29,500	92,600	54,200	14,000	190,300
5 cents	147,160	197,980	211,240	47,940	604,320
10 cents	277,780	......	......	......	277,780
30 cents	2,370	14,470	6,100	490	23,430
50 cents	1,156	10,800	2,604	470	15,030

Whole number of stamps 2,511,393.   Value $92,753.97.

ISSUES OF 1894-95.

On July 1st, 1894 the contract of the American Bank Note Company for the manufacture of postage stamps expired. Such reserve stock of stamps as was in the vaults of the Company was transferred to Washington and issued as required. Concerning this stock the annual report of the Third Assistant Postmaster General, dated October 31st, 1894, says : " Of the postage-due stamps, the transferred stock of the 1 cent denomination was exhausted August 14th, 1894 ; the 2-cent, July 20th, 1894 ; and the 10-cent, September 24th, 1894." The other values were not exhausted until April, 1895."

It has been reported, on supposedly good authority, that the Bureau of Engraving and Printing made printings of the postage-due stamps from the plates of the American Bank Note Co. This statement has, until recently, been generally accepted. But it is now officially denied that any such printings were made and the records of the Bureau confirm this denial. The stamps which have, heretofore, been assigned to these supposed printings were distinguished by the transparency of the paper and the whiteness of the gum. We must now conclude that they were merely a late product of the American Bank Note Co.

In the report of the Third Assistant Postmaster General for 1894 (page 476), we read :

CHANGE OF POSTAGE-DUE STAMPS.

It was also decided, upon the suggestion of the Bureau of Engraving and Printing, to make a change in the designs of the postage-due stamps—the change consisting of a reduction in the size of the stamps and some immaterial changes in the general design. The denominations of the stamps are those of the old series, and the color was intended to be the same but, owing to some difference in the character of the engraved plates, the former color has not been exactly preserved. The new color is somewhat deeper than the old, and some of the earlier issues of the stamps have even been printed a bright red.

The following is a description of the new stamps :

The shape of the whole engraving is oblong, the size being seven-eighths by very nearly three fourths of an inch. In the center is the indication of denomination—large white Arabic numerals being used—surrounded by fine lathework, forming an equilateral device with thin white edges, rounded corners, and curving sides—the four corners of the outline pointing to the top and bottom and two sides of the stamp. Above this is a semi-circular panel bearing in white capitals the words "POSTAGE DUE", with a small cross at each end, and above this still, in the two upper corners, are the letters "u" and "s", over which, and descending some distance on the two sides, is a line of ribbed ruling. At the bottom of the stamp, in a curved panel, are the words of the denomination in white capitals, above which, coming from each of the lower corners, is a large original scroll ornament somewhat resembling a cornucopia.

The stamps measure 18½x22 mm.

They were at first printed on a thin white wove paper, usually semi-transparent. Afterwards, in common with other issues of the same period, they appeared on paper watermarked with the letters " U. S. P. S." They have been reported, as have the stamps of the regular issue, on paper which, in addition to the watermark, showed laid lines, and also on paper which was apparently double. It is claimed, by those who should speak with authority on the subject, that neither of these varieties of paper was intentionally made or used and that they must be due to some accident of manufacture. Such varieties appear to be of only trifling interest.

The gum varies from smooth to rough and from white to brownish. The perforation is as usual.

The colors are :

Perforated 12.

White Wove Paper.

Aug. 14, 1894.   1 cent pale vermilion, vermilion, violet-rose, pale claret, claret, deep claret, lake

July 20th, 1894.   2 cents vermilion, dark vermilion, claret, bright claret, deep claret, lake

Apl. 27th, 1895.   3 cents deep claret, lake
                    5 cents claret, bright claret, deep claret, lake

Marginal notes:
Supposed printings from plates of the American Bank Note Co.
Announcement of the issue.
Color.
Design.
Paper.
Reference List.

Sept. 24th, 1894.   10 cents lake, brownish lake
Apl. 27th, 1895.   30 cents lilac-rose, violet-rose, rose, claret, lake
                     50 cents lilac-rose, violet-rose, brownish claret, lake

Watermarked U S P S

Aug. 1st, 1895.   1 cent dark carmine, violet-rose, claret, bright claret, deep
                     claret, brownish claret, lake
Sept. 14th, 1895.   2 cents violet-rose, claret, bright claret, brownish claret,
                     deep claret, lake
Oct. 30th, 1895.   3 cents crimson, deep claret, lake
Oct. 15th, 1895.   5 cents claret, bright claret, deep claret, brownish claret,
                     lake
Sept. 14th, 1895.   10 cents claret, deep claret, lake
Aug. 21st, 1897.   30 cents lake
Mch. 17th, 1896.   50 cents brownish claret, lake

Plates.
The plates for these stamps are made up of two panes, placed side by side Each pane contains one hundred stamps, arranged in ten rows of ten. The impressions are divided vertically, between the panes, at the time of perforating, thus leaving one edge of each sheet blank.

Imprints.
A line is drawn across the plate between the fifth and sixth horizontal rows. This line terminates in arrow heads in each side margin. There are two varieties of the imprint. The first is "Bureau, Engraving & Printing," in small lower-case letters and initial capitals, on a small rectangular panel, surrounded by a thin colored line. The second variety is made by adding a rosette and a three-pointed ornament at each end of the panel. The imprint is placed above the two stamps in the middle of the top row of each pane and below the corresponding stamps of the bottom row. The plate number is placed at the inner side of each imprint. The plate numbers are:

Plate numbers.

Without Watermark.

1 cent	No. 57, 147.
2 cents	No. 34, 60, 159.
3 cents	No. 70.
5 cents	No. 71.
10 cents	No. 72.
30 cents	No. 73.
50 cents	No. 74.

With Watermark.

1 cent	No. 57, 147, 246, 267.
2 cents	No. 60, 159, 247, 268.
3 cents	No. 70, 254.
5 cents	No. 71, 255.
10 cents	No. 72, 256.
30 cents	No. 73, 260.
50 cents	No. 74, 261.

Four plates for one cent stamps, numbered 66, 67, 68 and 69, were also prepared, but they were never put to press.

From the annual reports of the Postmaster General and other sources we obtain the following statistics of quantities of these stamps issued to deputy postmasters :

Stamps issued during the fiscal year ending June 30th, 1895 :

Deliveries to postmasters.

QUARTER ENDING :

	Sept. 30, 1894.	Dec. 31, 1894.	Mch. 31, 1895.	June 30, 1895.	Total.
1 cent	883,531	2,233,600	2,391,100	1,939,850	7,448,081
2 cents	1,825,036	2,016,250	2,436,400	1,864,450	8,142,136
3 cents	....	....	....	39,100	39,100
5 cents	....	....	....	88,200	88,200
10 cents	62,600	337,790	351,870	339,110	1,091,370
30 cents	......	......	......	700	700
50 cents	.....	......	......	890	890

Whole number of stamps 16,810,477. Value $352,698.53.

Stamps issued during the fiscal year ending June 30th, 1896 :

QUARTER ENDING :

	Sept. 30, 1895.	Dec. 31, 1895.	Mch. 31, 1896.	June 30, 1896.	Total.
1 cent	1,822,900	2,366,800	2,439,400	1,953,700	8,582,800
2 cents	1,578,400	2,405,550	2,236,450	2,029,450	8,249,850
3 cents	95,550	98,100	92,500	96,900	383,050
5 cents	128,550	127,960	180,860	175,540	612,910
10 cents	325,950	400,320	419,150	359,190	1,504,610
30 cents	2,220	2,040	4,040	1,760	10,060
50 cents	1,390	2,634	3,350	1,060	8,434

Whole number of stamps 19,351,714. Value $450,658.00.

Stamps issued during the fiscal year ending June 30th, 1897 :

QUARTER ENDING :

	Sept. 30, 1896.	Dec. 31, 1896.	Mch. 31, 1897.	June 30, 1897.	Total.
1 cent	2,259,600	2,106,000	2,062,900	2,285,000	8,713,500
2 cents	1,937,900	2,130,650	2,072,800	2,315,400	8,456,750
3 cents	39,400	108,500	49,600	103,100	300,600
5 cents	133,880	237,440	181,600	153,740	706,660
10 cents	277,590	344,790	394,410	366,450	1,383,240
30 cents	2,790	2,060	1,180	1,120	7,150
50 cents	2,160	1,520	1,010	570	5,260

Whole number of stamps 19,573,160. Value $443,720.00.

Stamps issued during the fiscal year ending June 30th, 1898 :

QUARTER ENDING :

	Sept. 30, 1897.	Dec. 31, 1897.	Mch. 31, 1898.	June 30, 1898.	Total.
1 cent	2,186,800	2,506,400	2,637,600	2,487,600	9,818,400
2 cents	2,339,350	2,511,800	2,666,250	2,771,500	10,288,900
3 cents	58,000	119,200	114,100	186,000	477,300
5 cents	123,820	149,400	262,360	246,740	782,320
10 cents	245,650	338,730	408,060	492,990	1,485,430
30 cents	740	1,420	1,650	1,310	5,120
50 cents	1,610	1,650	6,470	1,030	10,760

Whole number of stamps 22,868,230. Value $512,856.00.

Stamps issued during the fiscal year ending June 30th, 1899 :

QUARTER ENDING :

	Sept. 30, 1898.	Dec. 31, 1898.	Mch. 31, 1899.	June 30, 1899.
1 cent	2,020,300	1,113,400	949,000	918,700
2 cents	2,405,500	2,147,400	2,450,400	2,151,350
3 cents	96,300	85,500	97,600	39,550
5 cents	119,500	184,200	232,600	135,750
10 cents	243,120	374,600	414,950	276,500
30 cents	2,310	550	330	7,210
50 cents	160	200	20	1,070

Whole number of stamps *16,468,090.   Value *$411,050.00.

*4,500 " specimens ", value $750, included.

Stamps issued during the fiscal year ending June 30th, 1900 :

QUARTER ENDING :

	Sept. 30, 1899.	Dec. 31, 1899.	Mch. 31, 1900.	June 30, 1900.	
1 cent	1,172,300	1,500,000	1,722,200	1,084,000	
2 cents	2,888,900	3,137,200	3,561,600	2,949,500	1
3 cents	111,600	73,100	121,500	104,200	
5 cents	159,500	261,800	270,600	161,800	
10 cents	396,950	371,100	561,850	352,550	
30 cents	460	540	1,690	2,740	
50 cents	390	570	60	710	

Whole number of stamps 20,969,410.   Value $531,265.00.

In the fiscal year ending June 30th, 1895, there were delivei
Universal Postal Union at Berne 750 copies each of the 1, 2 and
stamps.   In the succeeding year a like quantity of the other valu
series were supplied to the Union.   In the reports of the Postmaste:
for those years, these stamps are included in the tables of deliverie
masters.

In the year 1898, 200 stamps of each denomination of this se
delivered "for the Post Office album", and 125 sets were overprinte
" UNIVERSAL—POSTAL—CONGRESS " and presented to the delegates :
that congress.   These two lots are not included in the statistics quo
the reports of the Postmaster General.

The 4,500 " specimens " referred to at the foot of the table of
to postmasters in the fiscal year 1899, consisted of 750 copies of e:
of the series except the one cent.   It is understood that these we1
charged " Specimen " in small Gothic type, in black or magenta ink,
of a hand-stamp.

The table of deliveries for the fiscal year 1900 includes 7(
(100 of each denomination), valued at $101.00, which were deliver
Third Assistant Postmaster General as " specimens ".

During the last three years large quantities of postage due sta
been overprinted for Cuba, Porto Rico and the Philippines.   As t
taken from stock in the Bureau of Engraving and Printing which
been transferred to the Post Office department, the statistics of deli
not affected.

PROVISIONAL ISSUES.

From time to time, and in different parts of the country, postmasters have resorted to a variety of makeshifts to supply temporary shortages of certain values of the postage due stamps. Such provisional issues have usually emenated from small post offices and the majority of them seem to be of entirely honest intent and free from any suspicion of having been made for philatelic purposes. While these issues were not authorized by the Post Office Department, the fact that they were made by postmasters gives them some standing. They are certainly interesting to a specialist.

The following varieties have come under my notice :

In the collection of Mr. F. O. Conant is a cover which was received in Berlin Falls, N. H., on April 30th, 1880. The cover is stamped "Due 3" and a three cent stamp of the Post Office Department has been affixed, to represent the short postage, and has been duly cancelled. A more detailed description of this cover was given on page 267.

Post Office Dept.
stamp used to pay
postage due.

In the *American Journal of Philately* for August, 1895, I find a communication wherein it is stated that provisional postage due stamps were in use in Detroit, Michigan, from June 21st to 27th of that year. I have not seen these stamps but infer from the description that they were made by surcharging (probably with a hand-stamp), the one and two cent stamps of the regular issue "Due 1" and "Due 2" and also by a similar surcharge in manuscript.

Ordinary postage
stamps surcharged
as postage due
stamps.

In the same year in Winside, Nebraska, one cent stamps of the 1890 issue were surcharged "DUE 1" in a circle and used as postage due stamps. The circle is 19mm. in diameter. The word "DUE" is in large capitals, 6mm. high, and is placed above the "1". The surcharge is in magenta ink and appears to have been made with a rubber hand-stamp. I have seen copies used on parts of the wrappers of newspapers and cancelled July 20th and August 6th, 1895.

In North Branch, N. J., two cent postage due stamps were bisected diagonally and used as one cent stamps. The only copy at hand is on a piece of the cover of a magazine which is dated June, 1895.

Bisected stamps.

Mr. W. F. Goerner has shown me a similar provisional which was used in Warwick, R. I., in 1897. In this case two cents stamps were divided vertically. Mr. Goerner writes me:

"In September, 1897, while in Bayside one evening I called upon Mr. O., who stopped there during the summer. Looking over some of the periodicals of the day I was quite surprised to find one or two of them bearing the enclosed provisionals Further search, then and some days later, revealed eight copies. Bayside at that time, had no post office— the mail coming through Warwick. Not knowing whether the stamp was affixed at Providence (whence the mail was originally sent) or Warwick, I went to the latter office to inquire. I found a young woman, the assistant, in charge and asked her if the split stamps had been used at that office. She said : Yes, that they were out of one cent ones and that the postmaster had cut them before and so she supposed it all right to do so and she hoped they had done nothing wrong and that no harm would come from it.

I did not understand what she meant but she soon told me that she thought I might be a post office inspector and that she meant to tell the truth.

If I asked her how long they had been using the stamps in this way, I have forgotten what she told me. But it is my impression that she said it was not very long and that not many were so used. The earliest copy that I saw was on the *Literary Digest* of August 7th, and the latest on the same paper of September 11th."

A more ambitious provisional was issued in Jefferson, Iowa, in October 1895. On this occasion two cent postage due stamps were overprinted on each side "Due 1 cent" and subsequently divided vertically and each half used as a one cent stamp. The surcharge is in black and on my copy reads upward. The following brief history of this provisional is taken from the *Philatelic Era* for May 7th, 1898 :

Stamps bisected and surcharged.

UNITED STATES POST OFFICE.

JEFFERSON, IOWA, February 12, 1898.

To WHOM IT MAY CONCERN :

This is to certify that about the 6th day of October, 1895, my supply of one cent postage due stamps was exhausted. I had made requisition for a new supply and expected them daily, and pending their arrival had a local printer print "Postage Due 1 Cent" on a few half two cent due stamps and these half stamps I used on matter requiring one cent stamps, until arrival of one cent due stamps   Not more than twenty of these one half stamps were used, as I only had thirty printed and had about a dozen left when the new supply arrived, after which the half stamps were not used. I am not a stamp dealer or collector ; know nothing about it and am not in any way interested in it.

Yours,

(Signed) F. R. McCARTHY,

Postmaster, Jefferson, Ia.

I have two covers, used in Jersey City, N. J., in 1897. One is a large envelope, cancelled November 20th, and marked "Due 6". In payment of this shortage three 2 cent stamps of the regular issue were affixed and hand-stamped in purple "Due 2 cts." The surcharge was applied after the stamps were placed on the cover. The other envelope bears a one cent stamp, similarly surcharged in magenta ink. The date of use of the latter is not legible.

Postage due paid by ordinary postage stamps.

I have seen several envelopes which were received in Richmond, Va., between September 20th and 23rd, 1897. Each was marked as being insufficiently prepaid, and the deficient postage was supplied by two cent stamps of the regular issue instead of due stamps.

I have also seen a cover, received in Beaver Dam, Wis., on October 10th, 1894, on which a shortage of one cent was paid by a stamp of the Columbian series.

Reprints, Re-Issues and Special Printings.

In this chapter will be considered not only those printings of obsolete issues which may rightly be called reprints (happily a limited number) but also all re-issues and special printings which, while available for postal purposes, were issued with a view to their sale to stamp collectors rather than for the franking of letters. It is probably superfluous to specify that I am referring only to Government issues, any reprintings of Postmasters' stamps or the semi-official carriers' stamps having been described in the chapters devoted to those subjects.

The first issue of this nature took place early in 1875. The intention of the Government was known in advance, though possibly its full extent was not realized. Strange to say, the proposition to make reprints does not appear to have evoked any protest from philatelists or comment in the stamp journals. A careful search of the leading journals for 1874 and the early months of 1875 is not rewarded by finding any announcement of the impending reprinting or remarks on the subject. Even the appearance of the reprints in the market occasioned only slight comment, at least compared with the storm of protest that such a reprinting would evoke to day.

No protest against the proposed reprinting.

In the *Philatelical Journal* for April 20th, 1875, we find an article entitled "Official Jobbery and Sanctioned Forgery" which appears to be from the pen of the editor, Mr. E. L. Pemberton, and in which the action of the Post Office department is roundly condemned. Speaking of the official stamps—which the authorities had, hitherto, refused to sell to philatelists—he says:

> "Such specimens will be obliterated by the surcharge of the word '*specimen*'; and such specimens likewise will be ungummed! Not very bad, is it? Very neat to offer 5, 10 and 20 dollar stamps of the most puissant department of State, obliterated and ungummed, at their facial values! The G. P. O. evidently thinks that if philatelists are really timbromaniacs, they may as well be humored as have to remain without copies of the things they will not sell in an unobliterated state; *i. e.*, for your 5, 10 or 20 dollars you may purchase a thing which has no facial value, and which the Department would never discount again at any percentage, supposing you ever got tired of the lovely features and god-like nose of Mr. Secretary Seward at four shillings and two pence to the dollar."

Journalistic criticism.

After reading this, it is rather amusing to turn to the official record of the sales of the reprints and re-issues and note that there were only two purchasers of complete sets of the four higher values of the Department of State, one of whom was Mr. E. L. Pemberton.

"A Protest by the National Philatelical Society, New York" was published in *The Philatelist* for July, 1875.

The *American Journal of Philately* was the only journal that took the trouble to describe the stamps.

I have not been able to find any official statement of the reason for making the reprints and re-issues of 1875, but it is generally understood that **Reasons for making** the prime cause was the desire of the Post Office Department to display a full **the reprints.** set of our postal issues, as part of its exhibit at the International Exposition of 1876. The collection of the Department being incomplete and the missing stamps not being obtainable, except by purchase at a considerable advance over their face value, the simplest way to secure them appeared to be by making impressions from the old plates. In addition to this, the Department had received frequent applications from stamp collectors for specimens of its obsolete issues and this seemed a favorable opportunity to provide material to satisfy such requests.

This action of the Post Office Department—as well as similar acts of other governments—gives rise to the thought that, in official eyes, one printing of a stamp is as good as another. The possibility that it may be less satisfactory to others does not appear to be considered, any more than the difficulty of making a successful reproduction, after a lapse of years.

When the stamps were ready for distribution the following circular was issued :

Official circular.   SPECIMEN POSTAGE STAMPS.
——

POST OFFICE DEPARTMENT,
OFFICE OF THIRD ASSISTANT POSTMASTER GENERAL,
Division of Postage Stamps, Stamped Envelopes, and Postal Cards,
Washington, D. C., March 27, 1875.

The Department is prepared to furnish, upon application, *at face value,* specimens of adhesive postage stamps issued under its auspices, as follows :

ORDINARY STAMPS FOR USE OF THE PUBLIC.

1. *Issue of 1847.*—Denominations, 5 and 10 cents. Value of set, 15 cents.
2. *Issue of 1851.*—Denominations, 1, 3, 5, 10, 12, 24, 30, and 90 cents ; also two separate designs of 1-cent carrier stamps. Value of set, $1.77.
3. *Issue of 1861.*—Denominations, 1, 2, 3, 5, 10, 12, 15, 24, 30, and 90 cents. Value of set, $1.92.
4. *Issue of 1869.*—Denominations, 1, 2, 3, 6, 10, 12, 15, 24, 30, and 90 cents. Value of set, $1.93.
5. *Issue of 1870, (current series).*—Denominations, 1, 2 (brown), 2 (vermilion), 3, 5, 6, 7, 10, 12, 15, 24, 30, and 90 cents. Value of set, $2.07.

OFFICIAL STAMPS.

1. *Executive.*—Denominations, 1, 2, 3, 6, and 10 cents. Value of set, 22 cents.
2. *Department of State.*—Denominations, 1, 2, 3, 6, 7, 10, 12, 15, 24, 30, and 90 cents, and $2, $5, $10, $20. Value of set, $39.
3. *Treasury Department.*—Denominations, 1, 2, 3, 6, 7, 10, 12, 15, 24, 30 and 90 cents. Value of set, $2.
4. *War Department.*—Denominations, 1, 2, 3, 6, 7, 10, 12, 15, 24, 30, and 90 cents. Value of set, $2.
5. *Navy Department.*—Denominations, 1, 2, 3, 6, 7, 10, 12, 15, 24, 30, and 90 cents. Value of set, $2.
6. *Post Office Department.*—Denominations, 1, 2, 3, 6, 10, 12, 15, 24, 30, and 90 cents. Value of set, $1.93.
7. *Department of the Interior.*—Denominations, 1, 2, 3, 6, 10, 12, 15, 24, 30, and 90 cents. Value of set, $1.93.
8. *Department of Justice.*—Denominations, 1, 2, 3, 6, 10, 12, 15, 24, and 90 cents. Value of set, $1.93.
9. *Department of Agriculture.*—Denominations, 1, 2, 3, 6, 10, 12, 15, 24, and 30 cents. Value of set, $1.03.

NEWSPAPER AND PERIODICAL STAMPS.

1. *Issue of 1865.*—Denominations, 5, 10, and 25 cents. Value of set, 40 cents.
2. *Issue of 1874.*—Denominations, 2, 3, 4, 6, 8, 9, 10, 12, 24, 36, 48, 60, 72, 84, 96, cents, $1.92, $3, $6, $9, $12, $24, $36, $48, and $60. Value of set, $204.66.

The 1847 and 1851 stamps are obsolete and no longer receivable for postage. The subsequent issues of ordinary stamps are still valid. The newspaper and periodical stamps of 1865 are also uncurrent ; those of the issue of 1874 can be used only by publishers and news agents for matter mailed in bulk, under the Act of June 23, 1874. The official stamps cannot be used except for the official business of the particular Department for which provided.

All the specimens furnished will be *ungummed ;* and the official stamps will have printed across the face the word "Specimen", in small type. It will be useless to apply for *gummed* stamps, or for official stamps with the word "Specimen" omitted.

The stamps will be sold by sets, and application must not be made for less than one full set of any issue, except the State Department official stamps and the newspaper and periodical stamps of the issue of 1874. The regular set of the former will embrace all the denominations from 1 cent to 90 cents, inclusive, valued at $2 ; and any or all of the other denominations ($2, $5, $10, and $20) will be added or sold separately from the regular set, as desired.

The newspaper and periodical stamps of 1874 will be sold in quantities of not less than two dollars' worth in each case, of any denomination or denominations that may be ordered.

Stamps of any one denomination of any issue will be sold in quantities of two dollars' worth and upward.

Under no circumstances will stamps be sold for less than their face value.

Payment must invariably be made in advance, in current funds of the United States. Mutilated currency, internal revenue and postage stamps, bank checks and drafts, will not be accepted, but will in all cases be returned to the sender.

To insure greater certainty of transmission, it is strongly urged that remittances be made either by money order or registered letter. *Applicants will also include a sufficient amount for return postage and registry fee,* it being desirable to send the stamps by registered letter. Losses in the mails or by any mode of transmission must be at the risk of the purchaser.

☞Applications should be addressed to "THE THIRD ASSISTANT POSTMASTER GENERAL, WASHINGTON, D. C."

No other stamps will be sold than are included in the above list ; and specimens of stamped envelopes, (either official or ordinary), or of envelope stamps, postal cards, or *used* stamps, will not be furnished in any case.

A. D HAZEN,
Third Ass't Postmaster Gen'l.

It is probable that there was an issue of this circular bearing an earlier date than that here given.

The circular was re-issued at various subsequent dates. In a copy, dated October 16th, 1882, we find the following changes in the section headed "ORDINARY STAMPS FOR USE OF THE PUBLIC."

5. *Issue of 1870, (current series):*—Denominations, 1, 2 (brown), 2 (vermilion), 3, 5 (Taylor), 5 (Garfield), 6, 7, 10, 12, 15, 24, 30 and 90 cents. Value of set, $2.12. *[margin: Additions to the circular.]*

6. *Issue of 1879, (postage due stamps).*—Denominations, 1, 2, 3, 5, 10, 30 and 50 cents. Value of set, $1.01.

In December, 1883, the 2 cents red-brown (Washington) and 4 cents green (Jackson), issued on October 1st of that year, were added to the so-called 1870 issue. It has not been learned whether or not a circular was ever issued in which these two stamps were mentioned.

Before proceeding to describe the various stamps listed in the circular, it may be well to say a few words regarding their status and also to briefly define the words "reprint" and "re-issue." Reprints are printings of stamps *[margin: Reprints and re-issues diferentiated.]* which are not available for postage, either because the original stamps have been declared obsolete or because the reprints themselves are not allowed to do postal duty. Re-issues are printings of stamps which are available for postage, though the originals may have been replaced by a later issue. In 1851, at the breaking out of the Civil War, the stamps of the issues of 1847, 1851 (including the stamps for delivery by carriers) and 1857 were declared obsolete and invalid for postage. At a later period the stamps for newspapers and periodicals, of the 1865 issue, suffered a similar fate. As a consequence, subsequent printings of any of these stamps must be called reprints. The stamps of the issues of 1861 and 1869 have never been deprived of their franking power and the same privilege extends to any printing of them, without regard to the date at which it was made. The stamps made and sold in 1875 are, therefore re-issues. The other series enumerated in the circular, i.e , the 1870 issue, the department stamps and the newspapers and periodicals stamps of 1874, were then in use and the specimens prepared for sale under the terms of the circular were neither reprints nor re-issues but special printings.

Special treatment for the reprints.

These stamps were not in any way a part of the regular issues of the Post Office Department and were always kept carefully and entirely separate from the regular stock. They were manufactured upon special orders and, when possible, by the makers of the original issues. They were not sold at post offices but from the office of the Third Assistant Postmaster General. A special set of accounts was kept for them, in which every purchase was carefully detailed and the name of the purchaser recorded. From these accounts we learn that the first of the stamps was sold on February 23rd, 1875, and the last on July 15th, 1884. The sale was discontinued and the stock on hand counted on July 16th, 1884, and on the 23rd of the same month the remainders were destroyed, by order of the Postmaster General.

Dates of first and last sales.

Quantities.

It was originally intended to make 10,000 of each denomination of each series, except the four higher values of the State Department and the newspapers and periodicals stamps. But this quantity was supplemented in a few instances, as dealers took advantage of the privilege of buying two dollars worth of any value and bought largely of the lower values of some series.

The records do not give the dates at which the first consignments were received from the various contractors, but it is probable that the deliveries were made late in 1874 and early in 1875. We must content ourselves with saying 1875.

ISSUE OF 1847.

Dies and plates.

The originals of this issue were made by Rawdon, Wright, Hatch & Edson of New York. The reprints were made by the Bureau of Engraving and Printing at Washington. The dies and plates were not the property of the government, but of the contractors, and were destroyed after the termination of the contract. Consequently they were not available when it was decided to reprint. To supply the deficiency new dies were engraved, in imitation of the originals, and new plates made from them. These plates were without imprint or plate number and each contained fifty stamps, arranged in five rows of ten. The original plates contained one hundred stamps each.

The report of G. B. McCartee, Chief of the Bureau of Engraving and Printing, for the fiscal year ending June 30th, 1875, says :

"Engraved two dies for the Post Office Department, Special Agent Commission, die No. 2,088 with one 5 cent and one 10 cent stamp on the same die. Engraved two plates, 5 and 10 cents, postage, 1847. **Official record.**

Printed 11,450—5 cent stamps.
Printed 10,000—10 cent stamps."

These stamps are, strictly speaking, not even reprints but official counterfeits. They differ from the originals in many points, the following being the most notable.

The reprints are slightly shorter and wider than the originals. The initials "R. W. H. & E." at the bottom of each stamp are quite indistinct in the reprints and it is usually difficult to tell what some of the letters are intended **Differences between** to be. They may be further distinguished by the following points : Five **the reprints and** **originals.** cents : In the originals the background of the medallion is formed of vertical and horizontal lines. In the reprints the vertical lines are either very indistinct or entirely wanting. In the originals the left side of the white shirt frill touches the frame of the oval on a level with the top of the "F" of "FIVE", while in the reprints it touches the oval opposite the top of the figure "5". Ten cents : In the reprints the line of the mouth is two straight and there is a sleepy look about the eyes. The white collar is so heavily shaded as to be barely distinguishable from the collar of the coat. In the hair, near the left cheek, there is a lock which appears like a very small white circle with a black dot in the centre ; this is not found on the originals. On the originals there are four horizontal lines between the "CE" of "CENTS" and the lower line of the central oval. On the reprints there are five lines in the same space, the upper line touching the oval and the lower line the tops of the letters "CE".

The stamps of the 1847 issue are usually on a thin crisp bluish wove paper of fine quality. They exist also on laid paper and on thin yellowish-white wove paper. The reprints are on a thicker wove paper, of coarser **Paper.** quality and deeper color (gray or gray-blue) than that of the originals. The five cents is also known on horizontally laid paper. The reprints are usually without gum but a few copies have been seen which have a white gum, very much crackled ; this is apparently simple gum arabic.

The reprints are found in the following colors : **Reference List.**

Imperforate.

Gray-blue Wove Paper.

5 cents bistre-brown, yellow-brown, red-brown, brown,
dark brown, lilac-brown

10 cents black, gray-black

Deep Blue Wove Paper.

5 cents yellow-brown

Gray-blue Laid Paper.

5 cents bistre-brown

From the records we are enabled to compile the following table:

Quantities sold.

	5 cents.	10 cents.
1875, Received	11,450	10,000
July 16, 1884, On hand	6,671	6,117
Sold	4,779	3,883

ISSUE OF 1857.

The only difference between the issues of 1851 and 1857 is that the stamps of the former are imperforate and those of the latter are perforated. As the reprints of this series were all perforated they can only be considered as reprints of the 1857 issue.

The original stamps of this issue were made by Toppan, Carpenter, Casilear & Co. of Philadelphia. The reprints were the work of the Continental Bank Note Co. of New York. In 1874, probably about August, there were sent to the latter Company the original plates of the 5, 24, 30 and 90 cent stamps and the transfer rolls of the 1, 3, 10 and 12 cents. By means of the latter, new plates were made for those four values. These plates had neither imprint nor plate number and contained one hundred stamps each. The original plates contained two hundred stamps each. On the new plates the stamps were set far apart, so that the sheets might be perforated by the machines then in use without damage to the designs, as would have happened had the original plates of these values been used.

The 1 cent stamps are all of type I, with full ornamental scrolls at the bottom. The 3 cent stamps are also of type I, having the outer lines at top and bottom. The 5 cent stamps are from plate No. 2 and, consequently, show the same varieties as the original stamps from that plate, i.e., alternate rows of types II and III. The 10 cent stamps are all of type I, showing full side ornaments and complete lines outside the top and bottom labels. Of each of the other values there was never more than one type, therefore, in the matter of design, the originals and reprints agree. The plates of the 24, 30 and 90 cents each bore the number " 1."

The paper is very white, crisp and hard; the stamps are without gum; the perforation gauges 12 instead of 15, which, of course, affords a very simple test by which to distinguish the reprints.

The colors are as follows:

1 cent (type I) bright blue
3 cents (type I) scarlet
5 cents (type II and III) orange-brown
10 cents (type I) blue-green
12 cents greenish black
24 cents dull violet
30 cents yellow-orange
90 cents indigo

The color of the three cents does not at all resemble any of the shades

[Marginal notes: Plates. / Types. / Paper and perforation. / Reference List.]

of the original and no attempt was made to imitate the scarcer shades of the
five cents.

The records supply the following statistics :

	1 cent.	3 cents.	5 cents	10 cents.
1875, Received	10,000	10,000	10,000	10,000
July 16, 1884, On hand	6,154	9,521	9,122	9,484
Sold	3,846	479	878	516

	12 cents.	24 cents.	30 cents.	90 cents.
1875, Received	10,000	10,000	10,000	10,000
July 16, 1884, On hand	9,511	9,521	9,520	9,546
Sold	489	479	480	454

On August 26th, 1874, the Post Office Department sent an order to
the National Bank Note Co. directing the printing of 10,000 stamps of each
denomination of the issues of 1861 and 1869. This order was filled in due
time and the stamps forwarded to Washington.

ISSUE OF 1861.

The re-issued stamps are of the types known as the "September issue."
The rarer "August issue" was either unknown or unheeded by the postal
officials. For some reason new plates were made for the 1, 2, 5, 10 and 12   **Plates.**
cents. These plates were numbered respectively 56, 57, 58, 59 and 60.
They contained one hundred stamps each while the original plates had two
hundred stamps each. The 3 cent stamps were probably printed from plates
54 or 55. The 15, 24, 30 and 90 cents were from the only plates made for
those values, which were numbered 41, 6, 7 and 18, respectively.

The paper is very white and hard and is almost identical with that   **Paper.**
used by the Continental Bank Note Co. for the same purpose.

The stamps are perforated 12 and have a yellowish-white gum, very
much crackled. They are frequently found without gum but there are usually   **Perforation and gum.**
indications of its presence at some former time. The very positive assertion
of the official circular that "all specimens furnished will be *ungummed*" is
set at naught by the re-issues of this and the 1869 issue.

The stamps were very carefully printed and have a highly finished
appearance, suggestive of proofs. The colors are :

1 cent ultramarine   **Reference List.**
2 cents deep black
3 cents brown-red
5 cents pale brown
10 cents blue-green
12 cents deep black

15 cents deep black
24 cents dark brown-violet
30 cents brown-orange
90 cents dark blue

No attempt was made to reproduce the pink and scarlet three cents or the yellow and red-brown five cents. The grill was not applied to the re-issues of the 1861, 1869 or 1870 series. Re-issued stamps with forged grills are mentioned by Mr. Tiffany but, though I have made extensive search for them, I have never succeeded in finding any copies. The stamps are sufficiently scarce to make it improbable that this sort of fraud would often be attempted.

The following quantities were prepared, sold or destroyed :

Quantities sold.

	1 cent.	2 cents.	3 cents.	5 cents.	10 cents.
1875, Received	10,000	10,000	10,000	10,000	10,000
July 16, 1884, On hand	6,805	9,021	9,535	9,328	9,549
Sold	3,195	979	465	672	451

	12 cents.	15 cents.	24 cents.	30 cents.	90 cents.
1875, Received	10,000	10,000	10,000	10,000	10,000
July 16, 1884, On hand	9,611	9,603	9,654	9,654	9,683
Sold	389	397	346	346	317

ISSUE OF 1869.

The re-impressions of this issue, being made at the same time and by the same firm as those of the 1861 issue, naturally show the same character-
Characteristics. istics of paper, gum, perforation, bright colors and careful printing. The re-issues are without the grill. Most of the original stamps were grilled and the very rare ungrilled varieties may be easily distinguished by their smooth brown gum and duller colors.

For the one cent stamps a new plate, numbered 33, was made. This plate had only one hundred and fifty stamps. All the original plates of this
Plates. denomination had three hundred stamps each. A new plate was also made for the frame of the fifteen cents. This is of a type which was not used for the originals. It is called type III. In types I and II a band of ruled lines, about 1mm. wide, extends around the inner edge of the space for the picture. In type III this band is omitted, with the exception of a solitary line which crosses the top of the tablet below the letters "STA" of "POSTAGE". This new plate bore the number 32.

The following plates are believed to have been used for printing the re-issues, though a few of them lack confirmation :

Plate numbers.

1 cent   No. 33.
2 cents   No. 4.
3 cents   No. 30.

6 cents	No. 13.		
10 cents	No. 15.		
12 cents	No. 17.		
15 cents	Frame No. 32.	Vignette No. 23.	
24 cents	" 20.	" 24.	
30 cents	" 21.	" 21.	
90 cents	" 22.	" 22.	

The colors do not differ greatly from those of the originals but appear brighter and fresher. They are :

Reference List.

> 1 cent dark brown-orange
> 2 cents brown
> 3 cents ultramarine
> 6 cents ultramarine
> 10 cents pale orange
> 12 cents dark blue-green
> 15 cents dark blue and dark brown
> 24 cents dark violet and blue-green
> 30 cents rose-carmine and dark ultramarine
> 90 cents deep black and deep carmine

The one cent stamp is more frequently found on the soft porous paper used by the American Bank Note Co. than on the stiff hard paper of the National Bank Note Co. This would indicate a reprinting by the former company. But the records are silent concerning it and we must content ourselves with the knowledge that the stamp exists. One cent stamp on soft paper.

The statistics of this re-issue are as follows:

	1 cent.	2 cents.	3 cents.	6 cents.	10 cents.	Quantities sold.
1875, Received	10,000	10,000	10,000	10,000	10,000	
July 16, 1884, On hand	1,748	5,245	8,594	7,774	8,053	
Sold	8,252	4,755	1,406	2,226	1,947	

	12 cents.	15 cents.	24 cents.	30 cents.	90 cents'.	
1875, Received	10,000	10,000	10,000	10,000	10,000	
July 16, 1884, On hand	8,416	8,019	7,909	8,465	8,644	
Sold	1,584	1,981	2,091	1,535	1,356	

ISSUE OF 1870.

To speak correctly, this was not a re-issue of the stamps of the 1870 series but a special printing of the 1873 and 1875 issues, which were then current. The work was not done by the National Bank Note Co., makers Dates of delivery. of the 1870 issue, but by the Continental Bank Note Co. and from the plates they were then using. The 1873 set, from one to ninety cents, was probably delivered in Washington not far from May 1st, 1875. The first sale of the stamps was made on May 5th, 1875. The two cents vermilion and five cents (Taylor) were added to the set early in 1876.

It is not easy to understand why a special printing should be made of stamps that were in use at the time. As it was announced that the stamps
would be without gum—and, therefore, unfinished—collectors could scarcely be expected to be eager purchasers, when perfect specimens might be obtained at post offices. Perhaps they were designed to meet orders from abroad. But, in all probability, the intention was to make complete the series of postal issues placed on sale. As has been said in an earlier paragraph, the transactions in these stamps were kept entirely apart from the regular business of the Department and this may account for this series being printed upon a special order instead of being taken from the regular stock.

It is extremely difficult to distinguish the stamps of this printing from those of the regular issue. It requires a keen eye for color and great fami-
liarity with the stamps of the period. The stamps of the special printing have the freshness and appearance of careful workmanship which have been noticed in companion sets. Many of them, however, were printed from worn plates. They are on the peculiarly white, crisp paper which was used for the reprints and reissues. Occasionally one has the crackled white gum, but most of them have none A notable feature of this set is that the perforations are seldom perfect. The stamps were not separated in the usual way, by tearing them apart, but were cut apart with scissors and very carelessly. As a result the perforations were usually much mutilated and the design is frequently dam-aged.

The colors, as nearly as they can be described, are :

1 cent bright ultramarine

2 cents dark brown

2 cents carmine-vermilion

3 cents blue-green

5 cents bright blue

6 cents dull rose

7 cents scarlet-vermilion

10 cents brown

12 cents dull black-violet

15 cents bright orange

24 cents dull purple

30 cents greenish black

90 cents violet-carmine

The highest three values were printed from the plates of the National Bank Note Co., Nos. 21, 22 and 23. The 7 and 15 cent stamps were printed
from the only plates made for those values, viz., Nos. 22 and 31. The 2 cents vermilion were from plates 241 and 242 and the 5 cents (Taylor) was from plate 248. It has not been possible to learn what plates were used for the other values.

The records of the Third Assistant Postmaster General shows that, on
July 16th, 1880, there were received from the Stamp Agent 500 copies of each value of this series. These are, of course, the work of the American Bank Note Co. We have yet to learn the reason for thus adding to a stock which was already too abundant.

A careful examination of a set of these stamps shows them to be a special printing also. So far as we are aware, nothing was ever done to bring this set to the attention of the public. They were unknown to philatelists until discovered and reported by the author (see *American Journal of Philately* for May, 1896).

The paper and the perforation are the same as were then in regular use. The stamps were not gummed. The 2 cents (brown), 7, 12 and 24 cents were obsolete and are, therefore, re-issues. These four values may be readily distinguished by the soft porous paper. All the originals were on the hard paper used by the National and Continental companies. It is very difficult to tell the other values of this set from the stamps of the regular issue. The colors are slightly deeper and richer than usual but the differences are not easily expressed. Very careful comparison with a set known to have been purchased at the period is the only certain way to identify specimens. The stamps are of extreme rarity. Only five complete sets and a few odd copies are known to exist. The colors are : *Characteristics.*

> 1 cent dark ultramarine *Reference List.*
> 2 cents black-brown
> 2 cents scarlet-vermilion
> 3 cents blue-green
> 5 cents deep blue
> 6 cents dull rose
> 7 cents scarlet-vermilion
> 10 cents deep brown
> 12 cents black-violet
> 15 cents deep orange
> 24 cents dull purple
> 30 cents greenish black
> 90 cents dull carmine

It has not been possible to learn the numbers of the plates used for this printing. The 7, 15, 24, 30 and 90 cents must, of course, be from the only plates that were made for those values. *Plates.*

The two special printings of the 1873 series are treated in the records as being one issue and we are, therefore, unable to say how many of each were sold. The total of the two is small and it is probable that the sale of the later printing was extremely limited. The figures are as follows :

	1 cent.	2 cents (brown).	2 cents (vermilion).	3 cents.	5 cents (Taylor).	
1875, Received	10,000	10,000	10,000	10,000	10,000	*Quantities sold.*
July 16, 1880, Received	500	500	500	500	500	
Total	10,500	10,500	10,500	10,500	10,500	
July 16. 1884, On hand	10,112	10,084	9,583	10,233	10,183	
Sold	388	416	917	267	317	

	6 cents.	7 cents.	10 cents.	12 cents.	15 cents.
1875, Received	10,000	10,000	10,000	10,000	10,000
July 16, 1880, Received	500	500	500	500	500
Total	10,500	10,500	10,500	10,500	10,500
July 16, 1884, On hand	10,315	10,027	10,320	10,218	10,331
Sold	185	473	180	282	169

	24 cents.	30 cents.	90 cents.
1875, Received	10,000	10,000	10,000
July 16, 1880, Received	500	500	500
Total	10,500	10,500	10,500
July 16, 1884, On hand	10,214	10,321	10,330
Sold	286	179	170

ISSUE OF 1882.

From the records we learn that there were on hand, at the time of the
Incomplete records. final counting of the stock before its destruction, 7,537 copies of the 5 cent
stamp with the portrait of James A. Garfield, but we do not find any memor-
andum of the quantity originally received. We are probably correct in
Quantity sold. placing the number at the customary 10,000. This would give a total of
2,463 sold to the public.

The stamp was issued on April 10th, 1882, and the special printing
Characteristics. was doubtless made soon after that date. The soft porous paper, on which
the ordinary stamps of the period were printed, was also used for the special
printing. The color is a light brownish gray and the impression is very clear
and sharp, while that of the regular stamps is usually soft and slightly blur-
Plates. red. The special stamps were not gummed. Plates 399 and 400 were probably used for this printing.

ISSUE OF 1883.

Still another printing was received from the Stamp Agency, on Decem-
Date of delivery. ber 5th, 1883. This consisted of 2,000 copies each of the 2 cents red-brown
(Washington), and 4 cents blue-green (Jackson), which were originally issued
October 1st, 1883.

It is scarcely possible to describe the shades so accurately that the
stamps may be distinguished, without fail, from originals. The two cents is
Characteristics. printed in a light red-brown, while the majority of the originals are in shades
of orange-brown and dark red-brown bordering on chocolate. The four
cents is in a dark blue-green, not unlike the shade known as Prussian green.
The impressions are fine and clear, especially that of the two cents, on which
the shadow below the shield is sharp and distinct.

The four cent stamp is without gum but the two cents is an exception
among special printings in that it is gummed. We do not know the numbers

of the plates which were used for the two cent stamps. For the four cents, plates 456 or 457 must have been used.

The records show an extremely limited number of these two stamps to have been sold :

	2 cents.	4 cents.	
Dec. 5, 1883, Received	2,000	2,000	Quantities sold.
July 16, 1884, On hand	1,945	1,974	
Sold	55	26	

CARRIERS' STAMPS.

At the same time that the plates and rolls of the 1851-57 issue were delivered to the Continental Bank Note Co. the plates of the Franklin and "Eagle" carriers' stamps were also placed in their charge, with instructions to make reprintings from them. This was done on two occasions, April 22nd, 1875 and December 17th, 1875, on both of which dates 10,000 copies of each stamp were printed.

The first printing of the Franklin stamps was made on remainders of the original rose-colored paper. The second printing was on a slightly thicker and softer paper of a paler tint. It is very difficult to distinguish the reprints on the first paper from the originals. The latter are found in bright blue, dull blue and dark dull blue. The reprints shade from a marine blue to indigo. But the best test is to be found in the printing. The impression of the originals is clear and fine while the reprints are too heavily inked and often blurred. In the original stamps the background of the medallion shows a hatching of diagonal lines. Traces of these lines can occasionally be seen in the reprints but, as a rule, the background appears to be solid. Around the medallion extends a tessellated band with rosettes at each corner. This band is composed of alternate light and dark diamonds, crossed by groups of colorless lines. On the original stamps these lines are clear and sharp, while on the reprints they are indistinct and often filled with color, especially where they cross the dark diamonds.

Paper.
Color.
Impression.

The reprints of the Franklin stamp are imperforate and without gum.

The reprints of the "Eagle" carriers' stamps are on the hard white paper which was used for other reprints and special printings. They are also found on a coarsely woven paper which some have thought might be the paper of the American Bank Note Co., but it lacks the thickness and softness which characterize that paper. It is probable that this is the paper which was used for the second printing. The paper of the original stamps has usually a yellowish tinge and the gum is smooth, varying in color from brown to yellow-white. The reprints are not gummed.

Paper.

The reprints of the "Eagle" stamp were at first perforated 12 but they were afterwards issued imperforate. There is nothing in the records to show the number prepared and distributed of each variety.

Perforation.

The originals are found in greenish blue, dark dull blue and indigo. The reprints are in bright deep blue and dark blue.

Color.

As was said on page 249, the majority of the original stamps appear to have been printed from the plate before it was numbered. I have never

Plate number. seen or heard of an original sheet which bore a number. I have, however, recently obtained a used stamp which has attached a portion of the marginal imprint and the number " 1." All the sheets of the reprints have this number below the imprint of the upper pane.

The records supply the following figures for the two carriers' stamps:

Quantities sold.

	Franklin.	Eagle.
1875, Received	10,000	10,000
Jan 3, 1876, Received	10,000	10,000
Total	20,000	20,000
July 16, 1884, On hand	2,890	10,320
Sold	17,110	9,680

OFFICIAL STAMPS.

The special printings of the stamps for the various Departments were made by the Continental Bank Note Co. from the plates then in use. With

Plates. the exception of the two, three and six cents of the Post Office Department, there was only one plate for each denomination of each series. The special printings of these three stamps were made from plates 37, 36 and 47, respectively. An enumeration of the numbers of the other plates would be superfluous.

The paper and perforation are the same as were employed for similar printings by the Continental Bank Note Co. Many of the stamps show the mutilation by scissors that was noticed in the special printing of the regular issue of 1873.

The colors do not differ materially from those of the stamps issued to the several departments. They usually appear to be a trifle paler and

Colors. brighter but this may be due to the absence of gum and the whiteness of the paper. The two, three, six and twelve cents of the War Department have a brownish tint, which is not found in the other values of this set.

The stamps are ungummed and each is surcharged "SPECIMEN" in small block letters. The surcharge is in carmine on the stamps of the Agri-

Error in the culture, Navy, Post Office and State Departments. On the stamps of the
surcharge. other Departments it is in blue. On a few of the stamps the word is spelled "SEPCIMEN" in error. This variety occurs on the first stamp of the third horizontal row. It does not, so far as we know, exist on all the denominations that were surcharged. Furthermore it is known on certain stamps and yet is not found in entire sheets of the same stamps, thus proving that it did not exist at all times in the surcharging form. Either there was a mistake in setting up the form, which was afterwards corrected, or, while it was in use, some of the letters were dropped and replaced in wrong order. The error has been found on the following stamps :

Department of Agriculture 2, 15c
Department of the Interior 2c
Department of Justice 1, 2c
Navy Department 2, 7, 12c
Post Office Department 1, 2c
Department of State 1, 2, 3, 7, 24c
War Department 1, 2, 3, 7, 24, 30, 90c

The records say: Aug 21, 1881. Received from Agency, New York, 5,000—1 cent State Department." These stamps are, of course, on the paper of the American Bank Note Co. We also find copies of the 1 cent Executive, 1 cent Navy and 7 cents State Department on this paper, though they are not mentioned in the records. We await further information about them.

Printings by the American Bank Note Co.

The following tables are arranged from the records:

DEPARTMENT OF AGRICULTURE.

Quantities sold.

	1 cent.	2 cents.	3 cents.	6 cents.	10 cents.
1875, Received	10,000	10,000	10,000	10,000	10,000
Jan. 3, 1876, Received	10,000				
Total	20,000	10,000	10,000	10,000	10,000
July 16, 1884, On hand	4,766	5,808	9,611	9,627	9,610
Sold	15,234	4,192	389	373	390

	12 cents.	15 cents.	24 cents.	30 cents.
1875, Received	10,000	10,000	10,000	10,000
July 16, 1884, On hand	9,621	9,630	9,648	9,646
Sold	379	370	352	354

THE EXECUTIVE.

	1 cent.	2 cents.	3 cents.	6 cents.	10 cents.
1875, Received	10,000	10,000	10,000	10,000	10,000
Jan. 3, 1876, Received	10,000				
Total	20,000	10,000	10,000	10,000	10,000
July 16, 1884, On hand	5,348	2,570	6,265	6,515	6,539
Sold	14 652	7,430	3,735	3,485	3,461

DEPARTMENT OF THE INTERIOR.

	1 cent.	2 cents.	3 cents.	6 cents.	10 cents.
1875, Received	10,000	10,000	10,000	10,000	10,000
July 16, 1884, On hand	2,806	8,737	9,912	9,917	9,918
Sold	7,194	1,263	88	83	82

	12 cents.	15 cents.	24 cents.	30 cents.	90 cents.
1875, Received	10,000	10,000	10,000	10,000	10,000
July 16, 1884, On hand	9,925	9,922	9,923	9,925	9,923
Sold	75	78	77	75	77

DEPARTMENT OF JUSTICE.

	1 cent.	2 cents.	3 cents.	6 cents.	10 cents.
1875, Received	10,000	10,000	10,000	10,000	10,000
Jan. 3, 1876, Received	10,000	......	......	......	......
Total	20,000	10,000	10,000	10,000	10,000
July 16, 1884, On hand	271	6,605	9,822	9,837	9,837
Sold	19,729	3,395	178	163	163

	12 cents.	15 cents.	24 cents.	30 cents.	90 cents.
1875, Received	10,000	10,000	10,000	10,000	10,000
July 16, 1884, On hand	9,846	9,843	9,850	9,850	9,848
Sold	154	157	150	150	152

NAVY DEPARTMENT.

	1 cent.	2 cents.	3 cents.	6 cents.	7 cents.
1875, Received	10,000	10,000	10,000	10,000	10,000
July 16, 1884, On hand	818	8,252	9,874	9,884	9,499
Sold	9,182	1,748	126	116	501

	10 cents.	12 cents.	15 cents.	24 cents.	30 cents.	90 cents.
1875, Received	10,000	10,000	10,000	10,000	10,000	10,000
July 16, 1884, On hand	9,888	9,893	9,893	9,894	9,896	9,898
Sold	112	107	107	106	104	102

POST OFFICE DEPARTMENT.

	1 cent.	2 cents.	3 cents.	6 cents.	10 cents.
1875, Received	10,000	10,000	10,000	10,000	10,000
July 16, 1884, On hand	3,985	9,410	9,909	9,913	9,823
Sold	6,015	590	91	87	177

	12 cents.	15 cents.	24 cents.	30 cents.	90 cents.
1875, Received	10,000	10,000	10,000	10,000	10,000
July 16, 1884, On hand	9,907	9,918	9,916	9,919	9,918
Sold	93	82	84	81	82

DEPARTMENT OF STATE.

	1 cent.	2 cents.	3 cents.	6 cents.	7 cents.
1875, Received	10,000	10,000	10,000	10,000	10,000
Jan. 3, 1876, Received	10,000	......	......	......	......
Aug. 12, 1881 "	5,000	.....	......	......	......
Total	25,000	10,000	10,000	10,000	10,000
July 16, 1884, On hand	3,328	4,855	9,207	9,533	9,209
Sold	21,672	5,145	793	467	791

	10 cents.	12 cents.	15 cents.	24 cents.	30 cents.
1875, Received	10,000	10,000	10,000	10,000	10,000
July 16, 1884, On hand	9,654	9,720	9,743	9,747	9,751
Sold	346	280	257	253	249

	90 cents.	2 dollars.	5 dollars.	10 dollars.	20 dollars.
1875, Received	10,000	1,000	1,000	1,000	1,000
July 16, 1884, On hand	9,755	968	988	992	993
Sold	245	32	12	8	7

TREASURY DEPARTMENT.

	1 cent.	2 cents.	3 cents.	6 cents.	7 cents.
1875, Received	10,000	10,000	10,000	10,000	10,000
July 16, 1884, On hand	7,815	9,691	9,916	9,915	9,802
Sold	2,185	309	84	85	198

	10 cents.	12 cents.	15 cents.	24 cents.	30 cents.	90 cents.
1875, Received	10,000	10,000	10,000	10,000	10,000	10,000
July 16, 1884, On hand	9,918	9,925	9,925	9,901	9,926	9,928
Sold	82	75	75	99	74	72

WAR DEPARTMENT.

	1 cent.	2 cents.	3 cents.	6 cents.	7 cents.
1875, Received	10,000	10,000	10,000	10,000	10,000
July 16, 1884, On hand	5,390	8,382	9,882	9,889	9,461
Sold	4,610	1,618	118	111	539

	10 cents.	12 cents.	15 cents.	24 cents.	30 cents.	90 cents.
1875, Received	10,000	10,000	10,000	10,000	10,000	10,000
July 16, 1884, On hand	9,881	9,895	9,895	9,894	9,896	9,894
Sold	119	105	105	106	104	106

NEWSPAPER AND PERIODICAL STAMPS.

ISSUE OF 1865.

The original stamps of this issue were made by the National Bank Note Co., who doubtless printed the reprints also. We do not learn of any special order covering the reprinting of this series but it is possible that the order to make re-impressions of the stamps of the issues of 1861 and 1869 was intended to cover any intermediate issues.

The reprints are from the original plates, numbered 38, 39 and 40.   Plates.

The paper is the same as was used for the re-issues of the 1861 and 1869 series. Some of the original stamps were printed on pelure paper but   Paper. the majority of them were on a crisp white paper, very like that used for the reprints. The perforation is identical and neither originals nor reprints were

Colors.   gummed. There remains, therefore, only color by which to distinguish the
stamps. The shades of the reprints are darker and heavier than those of
the originals. They also have the appearance of having been printed with
thicker inks. The colors are :

5 cents deep dull blue, dark blue, purplish blue
10 cents deep green, dark blue-green
25 cents dark carmine-red

The five cents with colored border was not reprinted.

We do not find in the records any mention of reprintings of these
stamps by the American Bank Note Co., but we occasionally see copies of
Printing by the   the five cents on the soft porous paper peculiar to the issues of that Company.
American Bank   These are undoubtedly reprints, made at some date subsequent to February,
Note Co.   1879, but we have no information beyond the bare fact of their existence.
The shades of these stamps are dull blue, deep dull blue and purplish blue.

There was some delay in delivering the reprints of this issue. To meet
orders for them, 750 copies of each value were obtained from remainders of
Remainders of the   the original issue, which were in the possession of the Post Office Department.
original issue used.   The early orders were, therefore, filled with original stamps. We have no
means of knowing whether or not all these originals were distributed.

The first sale of these stamps was made on April 1st, 1875.

The statistics are :

Quantities sold.	5 cents.	10 cents.	25 cents.
1875, Received (originals)	750	750	750
July 21, 1875, Received (reprints)	10,000	10,000	10,000
Total	10,750	10,750	10,750
July 16, 1884, On hand	4,355	2,235	3,316
Sold	6,395	8,515	7,434

About the time the reprints and re-issues were being prepared, the
Continental Bank Note Co. made new plates for the three values of this series.
Plates made by the   Why these plates were made and put to press, while the original plates were in
Continental Bank   existence and in good order, has never been explained. These new plates
Note Co.   were without imprint or plate number and contained ten stamps each, arranged
in two horizontal rows of five. The stamps printed from these plates are
known in both imperforate and perforated condition. All three values are
Characteristics.   without the colored border. By this change we may readily distinguish the
two higher values. The five cents, when perforated, may be known by the
outer colored line, which has a uniform width of about ¾mm., while on the
originals it is of irregular thickness, in places not more than a hair's breadth.
These stamps are printed on a paper which is thin, hard and very white, such
as was used for the reprints and re-issues. The impression is entirely flat,
lacking the embossing usually seen in the numerals and larger letters of both
Colors.   the originals and reprints. The colors do not agree with those of any other
printing. The inks were evidently thin and did not cover the paper with the
customary strong body of color. The colors are :

5 cents soft dull blue
10 cents dark gray-green
25 cents rose-red

These stamps were, doubtless, intended to form part of the 1875 series of reprints and re-issues, but it is not certain that any of them were ever sold as such. Only a very limited number were acquired by collectors before the destruction of the remainders of obsolete issues.

ISSUE OF 1875.

The special printing of this issue was made by the Continental Bank Note Co. The only values for which there was more than one plate were the two and three cents. There can be very little doubt that the first plates made, Plates. which were numbered respectively 200 and 206, were used for the first special printing. It is reasonable to assume that the two cent stamps which were received in 1883 and 1884 were printed from plate 218B.

The paper is the crisp white paper that was employed for this work, but in these stamps it seems to be more transparent than usual and has a Paper. waxen tone. The stamps are perforated 12 and ungummed.

The impressions were very carefully made. The values two to ten cents, inclusive, are printed in a clear gray-black and the twelve to ninety-six cents, inclusive, in a soft pale rose. The other values I have not seen, nor are they known to the leading specialists in United States stamps, but there is no reason to expect the colors to differ from those of the same values of the regular issue.

On referring to the table compiled from the records, it will be seen that there were deliveries of certain of the lower values in 1883 and 1884. As the last of these deliveries was made about six weeks before the stamps were withdrawn from sale, and as the quantity of the remainders exceeds the number in this delivery, it is quite possible that none of the stamps of that printing were sold. I have a copy of the two cents which is known to have been purchased from the office of the Third Assistant Postmaster-General. It probably belongs to the lot delivered in 1883. The stamp is printed in a rich deep black, on very white, soft paper, like thin blotting paper.

The official figures for this series are :

	2 cents.	3 cents.	4 cents.	6 cents	8 cents'	Quantities sold.
1875, Received	5,000	5,000	5,000	5,000	5,000	
Jan. 3, 1876, Received	10,000	10,000	......	......	......	
Apl. 30, 1883 "	5,000	......	......	......	......	
May 31, 1884 "	5,000	......	5 000	......	......	
Total	25,000	15,000	10,000	5,000	5,0 0	
June 16, 1884, On hand	5,486	8.048	5,549	2,652	3,070	
Sold	19,514	6.952	4,451	2,348	1,930	
	9 cents.	10 cents.	12 cents.	24 cents.	36 cents.	
1875, Received	5,000	5,000	5,000	5,000	5,000	
July 16, 1884, On hand	3,205	3,501	3 687	4,589	4,670	
Sold	1,795	1,499	1,313	411	330	

	48 cents.	60 cents.	72 cents.	84 cents.	96 cents.
1875, Received	5,000	5,000	5,000	5,000	5,000
July 16, 1884, On hand	4 732	4,778	4,826	4,836	4,859
Sold	268	222	174	164	141

	192 cents.	3 dollars.	6 dollars.	9 dollars.	12 dollars.
1875, Received	500	500	500	500	500
July 16, 1884, On hand	459	480	486	496	495
Sold	41	20	14	4	5

	24 dollars.	36 dollars.	48 dollars.	60 dollars.
1875, Received	100	100	100	100
July 16, 1884, On hand	98	98	99	99
Sold	2	2	1	1

ISSUE OF 1895.

In February, 1899, the series of newspaper and periodical stamps which had became obsolete on the first of the preceding July, were placed on sale to the public at the nominal price of five dollars per set. In many of these sets the five higher values were reprints. There was at least a poor excuse for the reprints of 1875, but for those of 1899 there is, in the opinion of good philatelists, absolutely none. For this reprinting we must, to a large extent, blame one or two short-sighted dealers who, valuing a present small profit more than the future good of philately, persuaded our postal authorities to undertake this sale as a source of revenue. We cannot regard stamp peddling as commendable in any government, least of all in a great and wealthy one, and we are glad to know that, in this instance, the resulting sales were so unsatisfactory as to make it improbable that a similar expedient will soon be attempted. It is also quite apparent that this issue was an injury to philately and lessened the interest of collectors in the newspaper and periodical stamps, instead of increasing it.

After the Post Office Department had decided to confer this un-appreciated boon on philatelists, the following circular was issued :

Circular announcing the sale of the newspaper stamps.

SALE OF NEWSPAPER AND PERIODICAL STAMPS.

POST OFFICE DEPARTMENT,
OFFICE OF THE THIRD ASSISTANT POSTMASTER GENERAL,
WASHINGTON, D. C., Feb. 4, 1899.

Announcement is hereby made that, in compliance with numerous requests made to the Postmaster General by collectors and others, enough of the newspaper and periodical stamps lately in use by postmasters to make up 50,000 complete sets have been reserved by the Department for sale, and that on and after the 15th instant, they may be had of post-masters at first-class post offices, or upon application to the Third Assistant Postmaster General, at the rate of five dollars a set—the set consisting of one each of the following twelve denominations : One, two, five, ten, twenty-five, and fifty cents, and two, five, ten, twenty, fifty, and one hundred dollars. When applications are made by mail, the money to pay for the stamps must accompany the order, with ten cents additional to pay for postage and registry fee on the returned packet.

Not less than a full set will in any case be sold ; but as many more whole sets as may be wanted can be bought. When two sets or more are desired, any or all of the several denominations may be had in an unsevered condition, that is to say, in strips not exceeding ten stamps each, or in blocks of four or more.   The Department, however, cannot require postmasters to segregate, for the accommodation of purchasers, marginal strips of stamps bearing plate numbers ; nor can any guarantee be given that the stamps shall be perfectly "centered".   It must also be understood that the stamps are not good for postage, and that after their purchase they cannot be redeemed or exchanged for others by the Government.

The sale of these stamps will continue up to the 31st of December next, unless the stock is sooner disposed of ; but no more than the 50,000 sets will be sold, and no more will hereafter be printed.   In fact, the working plates from which the stamps were printed will shortly be destroyed.

The newspaper and periodical stamps of a former issue—of which fragramentary lots have been returned to the Department by postmasters—will not be sold, but together with the stock of the last issue returned in excess of the 50,000 reserved sets, will all be destroyed,

JOHN A. MERRITT,
Third Ass't P. M. Gen'l.

Although this circular contained the promise that only 50,000 sets would be sold, we now know that that number were distributed to post offices, and, in addition, 5,000 sets were placed on sale at the Post Office Department in Washington, and 1,250 sets supplied to the Third Assistant Postmaster General.   It will be observed that nothing was said about some of the stamps having been especially printed to make up these sets.   On the contrary, the circular was so worded as to convey the impression that all the stamps were remainders. *(Additional sets placed on sale.)*

On attempting to make up the 50,000 sets it was found that there was not on hand a sufficient quantity of five of the values, so reprints were made to supply the deficiency.   The five values were the 5, 10, 20, 50 and 100 dollars.   The reprinting was done in February, 1899, from plates 137, 138, 139, 135 and 140.   The quantities were: *(Plates.)*

	Remainders.	Reprints.
5 dollars	155	49,845
10 dollars	11,640	38,360
20 dollars	8,780	41,220
50 dollars	16,245	33,755
100 dollars	7,685	42,315

(Quantities reprinted.)

It is said that eventually 5,000 originals of each of the four higher values were used and 45,000 reprints.   It has not been ascertained whether or not any originals of the stamps above 2 dollars were included in the 5000 and 1250 sets mentioned in a preceding paragraph.

The reprints are on the regular paper, watermarked U. S. P. S.   They have a smooth white gum while the gum of the originals is yellowish.   The colors lack depth and richness and look cold and thin.   They are: *(Characteristics.)*

5 dollars slate-blue
10 dollars gray-green
20 dollars lilac-gray
50 dollars brownish rose
100 dollars bluish purple

On referring to page 328 it will be seen that 26,989 of the sets were sold; we do not know how many reprints were included in them. *(Quantities sold.)*

POSTAGE DUE STAMPS.

Characteristics. In 1879 there was added to the reproductions of our postal issues a special printing of the stamps for postage due. The stamps of this printing are on the paper of the American Bank Note Co., perforated 12 and without gum. They are printed in dark red brown.

For each of the four higher values there was only one plate, probably the two cent stamps were printed from plate 315, but, in the absence of
Plates. copies with plate numbers attached, we have no means of knowing which plates were used for the one and three cents.

There were prepared, sold and destroyed as follows :

Quantities sold.

	1 cent.	2 cents.	3 cents.	5 cents.
Oct. 25, 1879, Received	5,500	5,500	5,500	3,500
July 16, 1884, On hand	1,080	4,139	5,064	3,251
Sold	4,420	1,361	436	249

	10 cents.	30 cents.	50 cents.
Oct. 25, 1879, Received	3,500	1,500	1,500
July 16, 1884, On hand	3,326	1,321	1,321
Sold	174	179	179

Plates destroyed. From the report of the Postmaster General, dated October 25th, 1897, we learn that, in the preceding summer, the plates of all obsolete issues of stamps were destroyed. The unpleasant possibility of future reprintings of these issues is thus removed.

OFFICIAL SEALS.

Beginning in the year 1872, there have been used in the postal service various adhesive labels, commonly termed official seals. They do not bear any expression of value, have no franking power, and are in no sense postage stamps. Consequently they have no claim to a place in a work devoted to that subject. But—probably because they are in the form of stamps and are affixed to letters—many collectors have thought them to be of interest and have admitted them to their albums. In deference to these collectors I shall briefly describe the several varieties of the seals.

SEALS FOR REGISTERED LETTERS AND PACKAGES.

The first seal issued was designed to secure registered letters from being tampered with while in transit. It was intended to be affixed over the juncture of the flaps of the large envelopes in which registered letters are enclosed. Its issue was announced in a circular of the Third Assistant Postmaster General, dated February 14th, 1872, but it does not appear to have attracted the attention of philatelists until some months latter. It was first described in the *American Journal of Philately* for June, 1872. [margin: Date of issue.]

A communication to the *American Philatelist* for December 10th, 1889, claims that these seals were intended to be used for a variety of purposes. But Mr. Duncan S. Walker refutes this, in the number dated January 10th, 1890. He says:

"Now a word as to the green registered seals. They were never 'issued', as stated by your correspondent in the article mentioned, 'to postmasters, to seal letters opened by mistake, to be returned to the Dead-letter Office and to prevent their contents from falling out.' They were never used for any other purpose than to seal the registered packages in which were carried registered letters. The Post Office Department especially prohibited their use for any other purpose. When the registered package envelope of the design of February, 1872, was adopted for use, these green seals were adopted currently with it. They were issued to postmasters in like quantities with the registered packages, *i. e.* where 1,000 registered packages were sent to a postmaster, he was supplied at the same time with 1,000 registered seals. Although these registered packages were gummed and fastened securely at the top and flap, it was thought the seal, heavily gummed and *intended* to be made, according to the intention of the designer, of brittle paper, would be an additional security. Their use was discontinued when a later style of registered package was adopted." [margin: Purpose of the seal.]

This seal is engraved on steel and printed typographically In the middle is a circle, 31½mm. in diameter, filled with ruled lines which diverge like rays from a central point. Around the circle is a broad white band, [margin: Design.]

inscribed in colored sans-serif capitals, "STAMP HERE—DATE AND PLACE OF MAILING." The two parts of the inscription are separated by small Maltese crosses. At the left, in three curved lines of large white Roman capitals, is "POST—OFFICE—DEPARTMENT", and at the right, similarly arranged, "UNITED —STATES—OF AMERICA". The background is filled with horizontally ruled lines. The word "REGISTERED", in very large shaded capitals, extends entirely across the circle and inscriptions. In the corners are small tablets, surrounded by a triangular device of involved lines. The tablets in the upper corners bear the letters "U. S." in monogram. Those in the lower corners have the letters "P. O. D." interlaced. The entire design is surrounded by a single thin colored line and forms a rectangle 72x40mm.

Gum and perforation. This seal is found on a variety of papers. The gum is yellowish or brownish and the perforation is of the same guage as that of the postage stamps of that date. Copies which are imperforate at either top or bottom are very common. From these and from fragments of sheets which I have seen, I conclude that many of the sheets were not perforated along those two edges. I have never seen any evidence that they were imperforate at the sides.

Reference List.

Perforated 12.

White Wove Paper.

Feb. 14th, 1872.   No value, pale yellow-green, yellow-green, pale gray-green, gray-green, light green, green, dark green

Varieties :

No value, deep green.   Imperforate
No value, gray-green.   Impression on the reverse

Pelure Paper.

No value, light yellow-green

Horizontally Laid Paper.

No value, green, deep green

Plates. The plates for this issue were made by the National Bank Note Co. At least two are known to have existed. The first had thirty seals, arranged in six rows of five; the second had only nine seals, in three rows of three. The smaller plate had neither imprint nor plate number. I have never seen a full sheet from the larger plate and so cannot say whether it had an imprint or not, but the records show that it had no number. The stamps with imperforate margins, mentioned in a previous paragraph, came from the larger plate.

Reprint. The use of this seal was abandoned at some time in the year 1875. It was reprinted about 1880. The reprint was probably sent to the Post Office Department in company with the special printing of the postage stamps of the 1870-79 issue which was placed on sale July 16th, 1880. It was made by the American Bank Note Co. and is on the soft porous paper which they always used for postage stamps. The gum is yellowish-white and rather streaked. The reprint has a very fresh and new appearance and may be readily distinguished by the whiteness of the paper and the bluish tint of the ink.

Soft Porous Wove Paper.

Perforated 12.

July 16th, 1880 (?)   No value, bluish green, deep bluish green

---

SEALS FOR PACKAGES OF STAMPS SENT TO POSTMASTERS.

Two forms of seal have been employed upon packages of stamps sent to postmasters from the United States Postage Stamp Agency or the Post Office Department.   Mr. Tiffany says they were first used about the end of the year 1875.   I have not found any other mention of them. Date of issue.

The first design forms a large rectangle, 102x52mm.   In the centre is the monogram " U. S.", in large white ornamental capitals.   The letters are displayed on a mat of geometric lathework of irregular outline.   A broad band of ruled lines frames the design.   This band is broken at the bottom by a tablet of lathework, at each side by an ornamental device, and at the top by a tablet of solid color, inscribed " U. S. POSTAGE STAMP AGENCY ", in white block capitals, 5mm. high.   At each corner is a trefoil of geometric lathework and the background is filled with a network of interlaced loops. First design.

This seal is lithographed on white wove paper, of poor quality and varying slightly in thickness.   The design is nearly covered by a large type-set inscription reading :

POSTMASTERS RECEIVING THIS PACKAGE Overprint.

WILL PLEASE

NOTE ITS CONDITION.

If showing signs of having been tampered with, report the same and return this package to 3rd Asst. P. M. General, at Washington, D. C.   This package should be opened at the end.   *E. W. Barber,*

3rd Asst. P. M. G.

The first line is in a double curve.   The signature reproduces the autograph of the Third Assistant Postmaster General.   The name of E. W. Barber was subsequently replaced by that of A. D. Hazen.   In the years 1887 and 1888 H. R. Harris filled the position of Third Assistant Postmaster General.   It is reasonable to suppose that there was a seal bearing his name, though I have never seen a copy. Changes in the signature.

At first the seals were printed in brown and the overprint in black. At a later date the colors were changed to rose (often very pale and indistinct) for the lithographed portion, and red for the overprint. Colors.

These seals are imperforate and usually have a margin of about 4mm. all around.   There is nothing to indicate by whom they were made and we have no printed information on this subject or in regard to the number in a sheet.   I list such varieties as I have seen.

White Wove Paper.

Imperforate.

Black surcharge. Signature of E. W. Barber.

1875. No value, yellow-brown

Black surcharge. Signature of A. D. Hazen.

1877? No value, yellow-brown, pale yellow-brown, bistre-brown

Red surcharge. Signature of A. D. Hazen.

1889? No value, rose, pink, pale pink, salmon-pink

Second design. The second design is slightly larger than the first and forms a rectangle 120½x66½mm. The rectangle is almost filled by a mat of geometrical lathe-work. The outline is broken by semi-circular ornaments at each corner.

The design is printed by lithography, on coarse white wove paper. It is nearly covered by a type-set overprint, in black, which reads :

OPEN AT END.

——

THE POSTMASTER TO WHOM THIS PACKAGE IS SENT MUST NOTE
ITS CONDITION AND CAREFULLY COUNT ITS CONTENTS.

If it shows signs of having been tampered with, the fact should be reported to the THIRD ASSISTANT POSTMASTER-GENERAL.

If the count shows a deficiency in the contents of the package, or an excess, the case must be treated as indicated in Sec. 120 P L. & R. The Postmaster should not correspond with the Stamp Agent, but with the Third Assistant Postmaster-General. See also Sec. 1088 as to misdirected packages.

KERR CRAIGE,

Third Assistant Postmaster-General.

Varieties. A second variety has the name of Kerr Craige obliterated by two horizontal bars and that of John A. Merritt printed at the left, in sans-serif capitals. It is probable that this seal was made either to meet an urgent demand or to use up a large quantity which had been prepared with Mr. Craige's name. We may expect that there was a later printing on which only Mr. Merritt's name appeared.

In 1899, Edwin C. Madden became Third Assistant Postmaster General and still retains the office. The current seal bears his name. The design and color are the same as those of the seal just described but the overprint has been reset, different fonts of type being used, and the arrangement of the last three lines slightly changed.

These seals are imperforate and have a margin of about 4mm. on each side. I am unable to say by whom they are made or how many there are in a sheet.

White Wove Paper.

Imperforate.

Black surcharge. Signature of Kerr Craige.

1893? No value, dull rose

Black surcharge. Signature of John A. Merritt.

1897?   No value, dull rose

Black surcharge. Signature of Edwin C. Madden.

1899?   No value, dull rose

SEALS FOR LETTERS OPENED IN THE DEAD LETTER OFFICE, OR THROUGH
MISTAKE, OR DAMAGED IN TRANSIT.

In the early part of 1877—the *American Journal of Philately* for 1888,
gives the date as January, 1877—a seal was issued which was designed to be
used in re-sealing letters opened in the Dead Letter Office. It is said to have
also been used to seal letters opened by mistake and those damaged in transit.
I have not been able to confirm these statements in regard to this particular
seal.

It is engraved in *taille douce* on steel. In a small oval medallion in
the center is a head of Liberty, full-faced. On solid tablets, at left and right
respectively, are "OFFICIALLY" and "SEALED", in white sans-serif capitals. **Design.**
Above these is curved "POST OFFICE DEPARTMENT", in shaded block letters,
and in a double curve below is "UNITED STATES OF AMERICA", in "Old
English" type. In each corner are the letters "U. S." in monogram. The
background is filled with the words "POST OBITUM" in minute Roman capitals,
many times repeated. The entire design is surrounded by a broad rectangular
frame with rounded corners. This frame is composed of closely ruled vertical
lines and is so shaded as to appear to be raised above the rest of the design.
The lower side of the frame bears the inscription, "NATIONAL BANK NOTE
COMPANY, NEW YORK."

There were one hundred stamps on the plate, arranged in ten rows of
ten. There was no plate number. I do not know whether there was an **Plate.**
imprint or not. The work was done by the National Bank Note Co., though
the contract for the manufacture of postage stamps was, at that time, held by
the Continental Bank Note Co.

This seal measures 44x27½mm. It is printed on thin hard paper,
perforated and has brownish gum.

White Wove Paper,   **Reference List.**

Perforated 12.

Jan. 1877.   No value, dark brown, dark red-brown.

It is said that the words "post obitum" were placed on the foregoing
seal as a joke. Either the joke ceased to be amusing or it was decided to be
in poor taste. Consequently a new design was prepared, differing from that **Changes in the**
of the first seal only in the background, the small letters being replaced by a **design.**
pattern of loops in cycloidal ruling. At the same time the vertical lines on
the face of the frame and many of its outlines were recut and strengthened.
The size remained the same as before.

The *American Journal of Philately* for July, 1888, gives the date of **Date of issue.**
issue of this second seal as May, 1879.

There were at least two plates made for this seal. The first contained one hundred impressions, arranged in ten rows of ten. It had no plate number,

at least none was assigned to it at the time it was made. I do not know if it had an imprint or not but I suspect that it bore that of the American Bank Note Co. The second plate contained fifty seals, arranged in ten rows of five. At the middle of each of the four sides was placed the imprint "AMERICAN BANK NOTE COMPANY, NEW YORK," in very small Roman capitals, ¾mm. high and 33½mm. long. This is an exact duplicate of the imprint placed on the plate of the one cent newspaper stamp, issued June 3rd, 1885. This style of imprint is not known to have been used on any other plates, which would tend to confirm the theory that they were both prepared at about the same date. On this second plate, at the right of the imprint in the upper margin, is a figure " 2 ", reversed and apparently inserted with a punch.

These seals are usually printed on a thin hard semi-transparent paper, not at all like that generally used by the American Bank Note Co. Copies
on soft porous paper are scarce. The gum varies from yellowish to pure white.

White Wove Paper.

Perforated 12.

May, 1879.   No value, brown, dark brown, yellow-brown, red-brown, dark red-brown

Mr. M. C. Berlepsch has a sheet of these seals from plate 2 which he claims was printed by the Bureau of Engraving and Printing. I think he is mistaken in this conclusion, which is largely based upon the date at which he obtained the sheet. As will be shown shortly, this work is done by the Government Printing Office and not by the Bureau of Engraving and Printing. The character of the work and the paper are not those of the former establishment. My opinion is that the sheet belongs to one of the older printings by the American Bank Note Co.

In 1888 a further change took place in the official seal. This was first announced in the *American Philatelist*, dated July 10th, 1888. But
copies had been obtained by dealers in the early part of June of that year. This new seal differed from its predecessor in the absence of the inscription on the lower side of the frame and in its generally rough and blurred appearance. It was at first announced as being lithographed. Subsequently it was said to be "printed from relief plates taken from a wood cut."

A lithographed seal certainly exists, though it is quite scarce. I have
not been able to find anything in support of the wood cut theory. An expert in engraving and printing informs me that the rough looking seals which are so common are phot-engraved and typographically printed.

The lithographed seal is evidently the result of an attempt to get rid of the imprint of the National Bank Note Co., which appeared in the lower
border of the engraved seals. On a careful examination of the seal, it becomes apparent that the change was effected by first making a lithographic transfer of the entire design and then covering the inscription with a piece of

the upper border, taken from another transfer. This piece frequently extends a trifle below the bottom line of the lower border and the vertical shading lines usually fail to join. There is another point by which this seal may be distinguished from the photo-engraved seals. In the left border there are eight vertical lines of shading, not counting the line which marks the edge of the outer bevel. The ninth line is interrupted by the edge of the inner bevel. However, this line is unbroken from about the level of the bottom of the " U " of " UNITED " to the edge of the lower bevel. On the photo-engraved stamps this line is broken about 1mm. below the level of the " U ".

This seal is printed on very porous white wove paper and perforated 12. The gum is white. The size remains unchanged.

Porous White Wove Paper.   Reference List.

Perforated 12.

June, 1888.   No value, yellow-brown

The stone bore one hundred and forty-three transfers, arranged in   Stone. thirteen rows of eleven stamps each. It had neither imprint nor number.

Concerning the photo-engraved seals, we find in the *American Philatelist* for January 1cth, 1890, the following :

" The two previous issues were finely engraved and comparatively costly. Being without an appropriation sufficient for their manufacture, the department had the present wretched transfers made and printed at the Government printing office. They were first issued imperforate and were sent in that condition to the Dead-Letter Office and to a few postmasters, but the bulk of them were sent to the Bureau of Engraving and Printing to be perforated."   Historical.

The first lot of these seals could not have been a source of pride to their makers. They were coarsely engraved, over inked and illegibly printed. The central medallion was often little better than a blot. The first printings   Characteristics. were in a chocolate colored ink and the perforation was rough and blind, as much of the paper that should have been punched out remained in the holes. The color will serve to distinguish the stamps of the first printing which were *issued* imperforate from those of later printings which were left in the same condition, either by accident or favor. Subsequently, much clearer impressions were produced in lighter shades of brown. The perforation was also improved. Many, if not all, of the sheets were not perforated around the outside rows, thus leaving certain of the seals imperforate on one or two sides. About 1891, the seals were rouletted, for a time, but perforating was soon resumed. The paper is always thick, usually soft and porous, but sometimes hard and with little or no grain. The gum ranges from brown to pure white. These seals do not differ in size from those previously issued.

White Wove Paper.   Reference List.

Imperforate.

1888.   No value, chocolate, dark chocolate.

Perforated 12.

No value, chocolate, dark chocolate, brown, dark brown, pale brown, rose-brown, bistre-brown, gray-brown.

Varieties :

No value, bistre-brown. Imperforate vertically.
No value, pale brown, gray-brown. Imperforate.
No value, dark chocolate. Double impression.

Rouletted 5½.

1891.   No value, gray-brown.

Sheets. From 1888 until the present time the Government Printing Office has made all the official seals, with the exception of certain type-set varieties. I have not been able to learn much about the plates that have been used. Such sheets and parts of sheets as I have seen did not bear any imprint or plate number. Of the first printing I have seen a sheet of nine rows of eight stamps each, with margins at the sides and bottom but cut close at the top, apparently indicating that part of the sheet had been cut off. In the later gray-brown shade I have seen a sheet with full margins all around, but having only six rows of seven stamps each.

TYPE-SET SEALS.

Origin. The type-set seals have always been something of a puzzle to philatelists. Nothing very definite appears to be known about them. So far as can be learned, they are the result of an attempt at governmental economy. The Post Office Department appears, at one time, to have compelled postmasters to provide stationery and many office fixtures at their own expense. This was probably due to insufficient appropriations by Congress. In many volumes of the *Postal Guide* will be found 'the advertisements of firms who dealt in cancelling stamps, pads, inks, blank-books, etc , etc. I am told that, in at least one number of this publication, official seals, such as I am about to describe, were offered for sale. Most of them are said to have been made by a firm of printers " up in New York State," and the advertisement referred to was probably theirs. This should have appeared about 1889 or 1890, for which years I have not been able to obtain the *Postal Guide*.

The first of the type-set seals was announced in the *American Philatelist,* dated February 11th, 1889. It was described as being on flesh-colored paper; this was probably the color which has since been termed pink or rose.

Design. This seal may be briefly described as follows: A rectangle, 47x29 mm., formed of border type, in a pattern of small scallops. Across the seal, slightly above the middle, are two heavy rules, between which is " OFFICIALLY SEALED ", in large sans-serif capitals, followed by a square period. Above this is " U. S. POST OFFICE DEPARTMENT ", in block type; and below "*Opened through mistake by.*" At the bottom is a dotted line for the signature.

The seal is imperforate, but I have not been able to learn whether it was printed singly or in sheets. The few copies which I have examined did not show any varieties. The paper is soft and of medium thickness.

Reference List.   Colored Wove Paper.

Imperforate.

Feb., 1889.   No value, black on rose

A second variety of this seal differs only in the border, which is of the style known as Greek or "key pattern," and in having a round period after "SEALED". I have seen only four or five copies of this seal, all of which were alike in every detail. I think it is possible that there was only one variety and that the seals were printed one at a time, but the limited amount of material at command does not permit a positive conclusion. This variety is also imperforate. The size is 50½x29mm. The paper is white and the gum yellowish. I do not know at what date it appeared.

Changes in the design and paper.

White Wove Paper.

Imperforate.

No value, black

Reference List.

The variety which, I believe, was next issued has also a Greek border but it is less open than that on the preceding seal. Across the center is "OFFICIALLY SEALED", in fancy capitals, followed by a period and placed between two heavy rules. Above this is "U. S. POST OFFICE DEPARTMENT" in "Old English" letters, set in a curve, with an ornamental dash below "OFFICE". In the lower part are "*Opened through mistake by*" and a dotted line, as on the preceding seal. Size : 50½x29mm.

The only copy of this seal which I have seen was rouletted, in color, across the bottom, from which I infer that it was printed in pairs, like the seals next to be described.

White Wove Paper.

Rouletted 16½ on one side.

No value, black

Reference List.

The foregoing seal appears to have been the predecessor of a group, the members of which differ only slightly from it and from each other. The setting is the same as that just described except that there are dotted lines, instead of solid rules, above and below "OFFICIALLY SEALED", and a large round period between these words but none after the latter one. The size remains unchanged.

Design.

The earliest mention of these seals is in the *American Journal of Philately* for August 15th, 1890, and the color is there given as blue. I was at first inclined to regard this as a misprint but I have since learned that the seal exists in blue, though it is much more common in black.

Colors.

These seals are printed in vertical pairs, separated by a line of rouletting, gauging 11½ or 16½. This rouletting, like all the rouletting of the type-set seals, was made by setting, between the seals, printer's rule which had a serrated edge. The rule received ink at the same time as the designs and, consequently, appears in color. The seals are imperforate except for the rouletting between them.

Rouletting.

The paper varies from thin to medium and the gum is yellowish.

White Wove Paper.

Rouletted 11½ on one side.

Reference List.

Aug. 1890.   No value, dark dull blue

No value, black

Rouletted 16½ on one side.

No value, black

The type-set seals were subsequently printed in blocks of four, probably with a view to increased rapidity of production. In these blocks two of the seals are placed tête bêche to the other two. There are two of these groups : in the first, one of the seals has a period between "OFFICIALLY" and "SEALED"; in the second, all the seals are without the period. Except for the removal of the period the setting remains the same as for the seals which were printed in pairs. These blocks are rouletted horizontally and vertically between the seals but are otherwise imperforate. The rouletting gauges 11½ or 12½.

Rouletted 12½ on two sides.

No value, black.   With period
No value, black.   Without period

Varieties, tête bêche :

No value, black.   Without period
No value, black.   With and without period

Rouletted 11½ on two sides.

No value, black.   Without period

Variety, tête bêche :

No value, black.   Without period

Rouletted 12½ on two sides.

No value, black.   Without period

Variety, tête bêche :

No value, black.   Without period

APPENDIX.

From the Report of the Postmaster General for 1888.

COLONIAL PERIOD.

Massachusetts.—Order of the general court, 1639.—" It is ordered that notice be given that Richard Fairbanks his house in Boston is the place appointed for all letters which are brought from beyond the seas, or are to be sent thither, to be left with him, and he is to take care that they are to be delivered or sent according to the direction. And he is allowed for every letter a penny, and must answer all miscarriages through his own neglect in this kind." *(First colonial postmaster appointed.)*

' *Massachusetts,—May,* 1677.—Mr. John Hayward appointed by the court "to take in and convey letters according to their direction."

Virginia.—Act of assembly, March 13, 1657.—" That all letters superscribed for the public service shall be immediately conveyed from plantation to plantation to the place and person directed, under a penalty of 1 hogshead of tobacco for each default ; and if any extraordinary charge arise thereby, the commissioners of each country are hereby authorized to judge thereof and levy payment of the same. These superscriptions are to be signed by the governor, council, or secretary, or any commission of the quorum, or any of the committee appointed for the militia." *(Conveyance of official letters in Virginia.)*

Virginia.—Act of assembly, March 23, 1661.—Provides that all letters superscribed for the service of his majesty or the public service shall be immediately conveyed from planation to planation to the place and person directed, under a penalty of 350 pounds of tobacco for each default. "If there is any person in the family where the said letters come as can write, such person is required to indorse the day and hour he received them, that the neglect or contempt of any person stopping them may be better known and punished accordingly."

Virginia.—Act of assembly, March 16, 1692.—For encouraging the erection of a post-office under letters patent granted to Thomas Neale, dated February 17, 1692. (This act was conditional, and was never carried into effect.)

New York.—1672 —Establishment of a " post to go monthly from New York to Boston ;" postage to be prepaid. *(Post between New York and Boston.)*

New York.—December 6, 1702.—The Postmaster General ordered that the post between Boston and New York should set out once a fortnight during the months of December, January, and February.

Pennsylvania.—Act of provincial assembly, March, 1683.—"Every justice of the peace, sheriff, or constable within the respective countries of this province and territories thereof, to whose hands or knowledge any letter or letters shall come directed to or from the governor, shall dispatch them within three hours at the furthest after the receipt or knowledge thereof, to the next sheriff or constable, and so forwards as the letters direct, upon the penalty of 20 shillings for every hour's delay. And in such cases, all justices of the peace, sheriffs, or constables are herewith empowered to press either man or horse for that purpose, allowing for a horse or man 2 pence a mile, to be paid out of the public stock."

Pennsylvania.—Act of general assembly, May, 1693.—" To the end that mutual correspondences may be maintained, and that letters may speedily and safely be dispatched from place to place : Be it enacted by the authority aforesaid, that a general post office may be erected by Andrew Hamilton, at Philadelphia, from whence all letters and packets may be with all expedition sent into any of the parts of New England and other the adjacent colonies in these parts of America, at which said office all return and answers may be received. *(First general post office in Pennsylvania.)*

"And be it further enacted by the authority aforesaid, that it shall be lawful for the said Andrew Hamilton, or some other as shall be appointed by the King, to be Postmaster General in these parts, and his deputy or deputies in that office, to demand, receive, and take for the postage of all such letters so by him conveyed or sent by post, as follows :

"All foreign letters from Europe, the West Indies, or any part beyond the seas, 2 pence each single letter which is to be accounted such, although it contain bills of lading, invoices, gazettes, etc., and for each packet of letters, 4 pence. And if packets of letters lie at the office unclaimed for the space of forty-eight hours, the postmasters then sending them forthwith to the respective houses of the persons to whom they are directed. 1 penny more for every such letter or packet. And for all foreign letters outward bound there shall be delivered into the post-office 2 pence each letter or packet The port or inland letters to or from New York to Philadelphia, 4 pence half penny ; to or from Philadelphia to Connecticut, 9 pence ; to or from Philadelphia to Rhode Island, 12 pence ; to or from Philadelphia to Boston, 15 pence ; to or from Philadelphia to the eastern parts of New England beyond Boston, 19 pence ; to or from Philadelphia to Lewis, Maryland, and Virginia, 9 pence ; to and from every place within 80 miles of Philadelphia, 4½ pence. All letters belonging to the public to be received and dispatched free of all charges, and the post to pass ferriage free at all ferries within this province, town of New Castle, and country depending. Pro-vided always, that the said Andrew Hamilton shall within three months next ensuing prefix certain days of his setting forth and return, and shall continue constant posts to pass from Philadelphia to New York, and from Philadelphia to New Castle."

Pennsylvania.—Act of assembly, May, 1697.—Increasing the rates of postage, and paying the postmaster £20 a year for three years.

South Carolina.—Ordinance ratified September 10, 1702.—Whereas several foreign letters are imported into this part of the province, therefore, for the maintainance of mutual correspondence and prevention of many inconveniences that may happen from miscarriages of the same, and that an office may be managed so that safe dispatch may be had, which is most likely to be effected by erecting one general post office for that purpose :

Be it therefore enacted by his Excellency John Granvill, esq , palatine, etc., that every master of a ship shall deliver all letters in his custody to Mr. Edward Bourne, and to no **First postmaster in** other person, and he is required to make an exact list of such letters which shall be fixed in **South Carolina.** some public place in the house of the said Bourne, there to remain thirty days ; and on delivery of each letter he shall write opposite the name of the person addressed the name of person·to whom the letter is delivered ; and the said Bourne shall receive for each and every packet or letter received and delivered one-half royal and no more. If he refuses to perform all or every of these particulars, he shall forfeit for each offense the sum of 40 shillings. And the said Bourne is hereby appointed postmaster to receive all such letters as aforesaid, and no other person whatsoever, anything in the act for raising a public store of powder for the defense of this province, ratified October 8, 1698, contained to the contrary notwithstanding. (Repealed by act of September 17, 1703.)

South Carolina.—Ordinance ratified March 28, 1778.—An act for the erecting of a post-office within the State of South Carolina.

Regulations for the post-offices within the State, in addition to such as are already made by the honorable Continental Congress :

As soon as public offices are established within this State commanders of vessels must deposit all letters addressed to persons within this State, or to any of the United States of America, in the nearest post-office. The master of a vessel delivering such letters shall be entitled to receive from the deputy postmaster of such office 1 shilling and 3 pence currency for every letter so delivered, and the person addressed shall pay to the deputy postmaster 2 shillings and 6 pence for each letter. If letters are not called for within twenty-four hours, the postmaster of the town shall send the letter to the person addressed, and may demand 1 shilling and 3 pence for his trouble more than if the letter were delivered at the post-office. If the addressee cannot be found, the postmaster shall advertise it if not called for within twenty days, and shall be allowed the expense of advertising. The postmaster shall keep his office open from 9 until 1, and from 5 to 7, excepting Sundays in the morning. Post-masters are exempt from militia duty. Post riders shall have preference in crossing ferries. As soon as post-offices are established in this State by the Continental Congress, or the laws of the State, it shall not be lawful for any person to ride post on any public post-road for the carriage of more than ten letters on any private occount, under a penalty of £20.

Act of Parliament, *Act of Parliament, 9th, Queen Anne* (1710), *chapter x.* - Provides that a postmaster-general shall be appointed for North America from and after June 11, 1711 ; that a chief **1710.** letter office be erected at New York ; and establishes rates of postage as follows :

All letters and packets from London to New York, in North America, and thence to London:
    Single, 1 shilling ; double, 2 shillings ; treble, 3 shillings ; ounce, 4 shillings.

All letters, etc., from any part of the West Indies to New York : Single, 4 pence ; double,
    8 pence ; treble, 1 shilling ; ounce, 1 shilling and 4 pence.

All letters from New York to Charleston, the chief office in North and South Carolina, and
    from Charleston to New York : Single, 1 shilling 6 pence ; double, 3 shillings ; treble,
    4 shillings 6 pence ; ounce, 6 shillings.

All letters, etc., from Charleston aforesaid, to any place not exceeding 60 English miles : Single, 4 pence ; double, 8 pence ; treble, 1 shilling ; ounce, 1 shilling 4 pence.

All letters, etc., from Charleston aforesaid, to any place not exceeding 100 English miles : Single, 6 pence ; double, 1 shilling ; treble, 1 shilling 6 pence ; ounce, 2 shillings.

Places where posts are not yet settled to pay according to these rates.

The charge for every person riding post to be 3 pence for every horse-hire or postage for every English mile, and 4 pence for the person riding as guide for every stage ; each person being entitled to carry a bundle of goods weighing less than 80 pounds free, the same "to be laid on the horse rid by the guide."

Only the postmaster-general and his deputies to provide horses or furniture for persons riding post.

If the postmaster fail to furnish horses, etc., to any person riding post within half an hour after demand, conveyance may be obtained elsewhere, and the postmaster shall forfeit the sum of £5.

Debts for postage not exceeding £5 are to be recovered as small tithes are.

Act of Parliament, 4th George III (1763) *chapter xxiv.*—Allows letters on the public service sent to and from the public officials of the higher ranks to pass through the mails free of postage ; and empowers the postmaster-general to authorize certain persons to indorse upon such letters and packets the fact that they are on public business ; printed votes, proceedings in Parliament, and newspapers sent without covers, or in covers open at the side, to go free.

Act of Parliament, 5th George III (1765) *chapter xxv.*—Repeals the act of 1710, fixing the rates of postage of letters between London and the British dominions in America and places within the said dominions, and establishes the following rates to take effect October 10, 1765 : Act of Parliament, 1765.

For all letters and packets passing from London to any port within the British dominions in America, and from any such port unto London : For every single letter, 1 shilling ; double, 2 shillings ; treble, 3 shillings ; ounce, 4 shillings.

For all letters and packets conveyed by sea from any port in the British dominions in America, to any other port within the said dominions : Single, 4 pence ; double, 8 pence ; treble, 1 shilling ; ounce, 1 shilling 4 pence ; and so in proportion for every package of deeds, writs, and other things.

For the inland conveyance of all letters and packets to or from any chief post-office within the British dominions in America from or to any other part of the said dominions, not exceeding 60 British miles : Single, 4 pence ; double, 8 pence ; treble, 1 shilling ; ounce, 1 shilling and 4 pence.

And being upwards of 60 such miles, and not exceeding 100 miles : single, 6 pence ; double, 1 shilling ; treble, 1 shilling 6 pence ; ounce, 2 shillings.

All letters, etc., from New York to any place within 60 English miles thereof, thence back to New York : Single, 4 pence ; double, 8 pence ; treble, 1 shilling ; ounce, 1 shilling 4 pence.

All letters, etc., from New York to Perth Amboy, the chief town in West New Jersey, and from each of those places back to New York, to any place not exceeding 100 English miles, and from each of those places to New York : Single, 6 pence ; double 1 shilling ; treble, 1 shilling 6 pence ; ounce, 2 shillings.

All letters and packets from Perth Amboy and Bridlington to any place not exceeding 60 English miles, and thence back again : Single, 4 pence ; double, 8 pence ; treble, 1 shilling ; ounce, 1 shilling 4 pence.

All letters and packets from Perth Amboy and Bridlington to any place not exceeding 100 English miles, and thence back again : Single, 6 pence ; double, 1 shilling ; treble, 1 shilling 6 pence ; ounce, 2 shillings.

All letters, etc., from New York to New London, the chief town in Connecticut, in New England, and to Philadelphia, the chief town in Pennsylvania, and from those places back to New York : Single, 9 pence ; double, 1 shilling 6 pence ; treble, 2 shillings 3 pence ; ounce, 3 shillings.

All letters and packets from New London and Philadelphia to any place not exceeding 60 English miles, and thence back again : Single, 4 pence ; double, 8 pence ; treble, 1 shilling ; ounce, 1 shilling 4 pence.

All letters, etc., from New London and Philadelphia to any place not exceeding 100 English miles, and so back again : Single, 6 pence ; double, 1 shilling ; treble, 1 shilling 6 pence ; ounce, 2 shillings.

All letters and packets from New York to Newport, the chief town in Rhode Island and Providence Plantation in New England and to Boston, the chief town in Massachusetts Bay in New England, and to Portsmouth, the chief town in New Hampshire, New England, and to Annapolis, the chief town in Maryland, and from every of those places to New York : Single, 1 shilling ; double, 2 shillings ; treble, 3 shillings ; ounce, 4 shillings.

All letters and packets from Newport, Boston, Portsmouth, and Annapolis, to any place not exceeding 60 English miles, and thence back again : Single, 4 pence ; double, 8 pence ; treble, 1 shilling ; ounce, 1 shilling 4 pence.

All letters, etc., from Newport, Boston, Portsmouth and Annapolis, to any place not exceeding 100 English miles : Single, 6 pence ; double, 1 shilling ; treble, 1 shilling 6 pence ; ounce, 2 shillings.

All letters and packets from New York to the chief offices in Salem and Ipswich, and to the chief office in Piscataway, and to Williamsburgh, the chief office in Virginia, and from every of those offices to New York : Single, 1 shilling 3 pence ; double, 2 shillings 6 pence ; treble, 3 shillings 9 pence ; ounce, 5 shillings.

All letters, etc., from the chief offices in Salem, Ipswich, Piscataway, and Williamsburgh, to any place not exceeding 60 English miles : Single, 4 pence ; double, 8 pence ; treble, 1 shilling ; ounce, 1 shilling 4 pence.

All letters, etc., from the chief offices in Salem, Ipswich, Piscataway, and Williamsburgh, to any place not exceeding 100 English miles : Single, 6 pence ; double, 8 pence ; treble, 1 shilling ; ounce, 2 shillings.

And being upwards of 100 miles and not over 200 miles : Single, 8 pence ; double, 1 shilling 4 pence ; treble, 2 shillings ; ounce, 2 shillings 8 pence.

And for every distance not exceeding 100 miles beyond such 200 miles, and for every such further distance : Single, 2 pence ; double, 6 pence ; treble, 8 pence ; and so in proportion for every packet of deeds, writs, etc.

Authorizes the appointment of surveyors in the chief post-offices in America.

Penny post authorized. Empowers the Postmaster-General to establish penny-post offices in America.

Limits the weight of packets sent by penny-post to 4 ounces.

Authorizes the Postmaster-General to demand prepayment of postage on all letters sent out of Great Britian.

Fixes penalties for embezzling any letter, etc.; for robbing the mails ; for misappling postage money ; and for advancing rates and not accounting for same.

PERIOD OF THE CONFEDERATION.

Resolution of Congress, May 29, 1775.—Naming a committee to consider the best means of establishing posts throughout the continent.

Act of July 26, 1775.—Provides for the appointment of a Postmaster-General for the United Colonies, whose office shall be at Philadelphia, his salary to be $1,000 per annum, and that of secretary and comptroller $340 ; that a line of posts be established from Falmouth, New England, to Savannah, Ga.; that deputies shall receive as compensation 20 per cent. on amount collected when said amount does not exceed $1,000, and 10 per cent. for all sums above $1,000 a year ; that deputy postmasters account quarterly with the General Post-Office, and the Postmaster-General annually with the continental treasurers, paying to said treasurers the profits of the post-office ; if the expense should exceed the profits, the deficiency to be made good by the United Colonies and paid to the Postmaster-General by the continental treasurers.

Resolution of July 26, 1775.—Recommending that the Postmaster-General establish a weekly post to South Carolina ; that it be left to the Postmaster-General to appoint a secretary and comptroller.

Benjamin Franklin appointed Postmaster General. *July 26, 1775.*—Benjamin Franklin unanimously chosen Postmaster-General for one year, and until another is appointed.

Resolution of Congress, November 8, 1775.—That all letters to and from delegates of the United Colonies, during the sessions of Congress, be carried free of postage.

Resolution of Congress, January 9, 1776.—That letters to and from private soldiers in actual service be carried free of postage.

Resolution of Congress, April 9, 1776 —That letters directed to any general in the Continental service be carried free of postage.

Resolution of Congress, April 16, 1776.—That only the committee of safety in each colony shall stop the post, open the mail, or detain letters therefrom.

Resolution of Congress, July 8, 1776.—That postmasters be excused from military duty.

Resolution of Congress, August 8, 1776 —That post-riders be exempt from military duty.

Resolution of Congress, August 30, 1776.—That there be employed on the public posts-roads a rider for every 25 or 30 miles, who shall set out three times a week, on receipt of mail, and travel night and day, until it is delivered to the next rider.

Resolution of Congress, September 7, 1776.—That lettters to and from the Board of War and Ordnance, or secretary of the same, be carried free of postage.

Resolution of Congress, November 5, 1776.—That the Postmaster-General be authorized to employ additional riders between Philadelphia and headquarters of armies ; that ferrykeepers shall expedite travel of such riders ; and that the deputy postmaster at the headquarters of the army be allowed four rations per day for subsistence of himself, his riders, and servant.

Resolution of Congress, November 7, 1776.—That Richard Bache be appointed Postmaster-General in place of Dr. Franklin, who is absent.

Act of Congress, January 11, 1777.—That the Postmaster-General be directed to furnish a list of names of disaffected deputy postmasters, and that he assign reasons why the late resolves of Congress for regulating the post-office are not carried into execution.

Act of Congress, February 17, 1777.—Committee appointed to revise regulations of post-office.

Act of Congress, April 12, 1777.—That the Postmaster-General be authorized to increase compensation of postmasters to any sum not exceeding $200, when necessary ; that $2,000 be advanced to the Postmaster-General, he to be accountable.

Resolution of Congress, May 12, 1777.—That postmasters, post-riders, and persons connected with the post-office ought to be exempted from military duty

Resolution of Congress, August 1, 1777.—That the commanding officer in the State of Georgia be directed to establish a post in the southern part of said State.

Resolution of Congress, August 6, 1777.—That $2,000 be advanced to Richard Bache, Postmaster General, he to be accountable.

Resolution of Congress, October 17, 1777.—That the Postmaster-General be authorized to appoint two additional surveyors of the post-office ; and that all surveyors be allowed $6 a day each for all expenses, and in place of all other allowance. That the tour be as follows: One from Casco Bay to Philadelphia, or while that city is in possession of the enemy, to Lancaster ; one from Philadelphia or Lancaster to Edentown, N. C.; and the third from Edentown to Savannah, Ga.

That an inspector of dead letters be appointed, with a salary of $100 a year, to examine dead letters, to communicate to Congress such as contain inimical schemes or intelligence, to preserve letters containing valuable articles, and not to divulge the contents of letters to any but Congress.

That the rate of postage be increased 50 per cent.

That an allowance be made to the present surveyor of the post-office for past extraordinary service.

Resolution of Congress, November 4, 1777.—That $3,000 be advanced to Richard Bache, Postmaster-General.

Articles of Confederation, Article IX.—Ratified July 9, 1778.—Gives to Congress the sole and exclusive right and power of establishing and regulating post-offices in the United States, and exacting " such postage as may be necessary to defray the expenses of the said office." Control of post offices vested in Congress.

Resolution of Congress, April 16, 1779.—That $11,967⅓ be advanced to the Postmaster-General to pay debts

That the present rate of postage shall be doubled.

That the annual salary of the Postmaster-General for the future shall be $2,000.

That the pay of surveyors and comptroller shall be doubled.

Resolution of Congress, December 1, 1779.—That accounts of the Postmaster General be referred to board of the treasury for adjustment and liquidation.

That the salary of the Postmaster-General be increased to $3,500 per annum, from September 1, 1778.

That the comptroller's salary be increased to $2,500 per annum, from September 1, 1778.

Resolution of Congress, December 27, 1779.—That the post shall set out and arrive at the places where Congress shall be sitting twice each week, to go as far as Boston, State of Massachusetts Bay, and to Charleston, S. C.

That no express riders shall be maintained at public expense.

That the three surveyors of the post-office shall be allowed the sum of $40 a day.

That the pay of the Postmaster-General be increased to $5,000. and that of the comptroller to $4,000.

Resolution of Congress, December 28, 1779 —That the rate of postage, until further order of Congress, be 20 prices upon the sums paid in the year 1775.

That single letters directed to any officer of the line, and all letters directed to general officers, or to officers commanding in a separate department, and all letters to and from the ministers, commissioners, and secretaries of the United States at foreign courts, be free.

Resolution of May 5, 1780.—That the present rates of postage be doubled.

That masters of vessels be required to put in the post-office all letters brought by them from abroad

Resolution of June 30, 1780.— Ordering the committee on the post-office to direct the Postmaster-General to make arrangements by which the southern post-riders shall arrive at the place where Congress is sitting only once a week, while the express line established by Governor Jefferson between the southern and northern armies is kept up.

Resolution of September 13, 1780.—Allows the Postmaster-General $1,000 a year salary, to be paid quarterly.

Resolution of December 12, 1780.—Fixes the rate of postage on letters at half the rates paid at the commencement of the present war.

Resolution of August 1, 1781.—Appoints a committee to report the state of the present expenses of the post-office, and a system for regulating the same in future.

Resolution of October 19, 1781.—Changes postage to what it was at the commencement of the war ; authorizes the Postmaster-General to allow such commissions as he shall think proper, not exceeding 20 per cent. (to take effect December 1, 1781). Salary of the Postmaster-General to be $1,250 ; that of Assistant Postmaster-General, $850.

Resolution of January 28, 1782 —Ebenezer Hazard, inspector of dead letters, elected Postmaster-General ; James Bryson, Assistant Postmaster-General

Act of Congress, Oct. 18, 1782.

Act of Congress, October 18, 1782.—1. Continued communication by post shall exist from New Hampshire to Georgia.

2. The Postmaster-General shall superintend the appointment of assistants, etc.

3. The Postmaster-General and his assistants shall not open, detain, delay, secrete, embezzle, or destroy, any letter, packet, or dispatch, except by consent of the person to whom the same may be addressed, or by an express warrant under the hand of the President of Congress of the United States, or, in time of war, of the commanding officer of a separate army, or of the chief executive officer of one of the said States. No franked letter shall be opened by any military officer.

4. The Postmaster-General shall take the oath of office. and forfeit $1,000 for violating it.

5 and 6. Only the Postmaster-General and his deputies shall carry mail-matter.

7. Mail shall be carried at least once a week.

8. List of undelivered letters to be published quarterly by postmasters, and at the expiration of the succeeding quarter to be sent to the Dead-Letter Office.

9. Extra post-riders may be employed when necessary.

10. Postage rates shall be as follows, in pennyweights and grains of silver, estimating each pennyweight as five-ninetieths of a dollar :   Any distance not exceeding 60 miles, 1 pennyweight, 8 grains; upwards of 60 miles and not exceeding 100, 2 pennyweights; upwards of 100 miles and not exceeding 200, 2 pennyweights 16 grains; and so on, 16 grains advance for every 100 miles; and for single letters to or from Europe, 4 pennyweights; double, treble, etc., for increased sizes.   And all letters except dead letters shall remain in the office until postage is paid.

11. Post-riders may be licensed to carry newspapers at such rates as the Postmaster-General may establish.

12. Surplus of income over expenditures to be applied to payment of advances heretofore made to the Postmaster-General; after payment of which, surplus to be devoted to establishment of new offices and routes; if expenses exceed income, the deficiency to be supplied by the superintendent of finance on warrants of the Postmaster-General.

13. Salary of the Postmaster-General to be $1,500; salary of Assistant Postmaster-General to be $1,000.

14. The franking privilege granted to members of Congress and chief officers of the government.

Act of December 24, 1782.—Modification of post-office law; no important changes.

Act of February 28, 1783 —Official letters to be sent free.

Act of November 1, 1783.—The Postmaster-General directed to cause an extra post to be furnished whenever required by the President.

Resolution of April 6, 1784.—Directing the Postmaster-General to discharge account of Jonathan Deare and Joseph Olden, amounting to £4 16s , for disbursements and services in case of robbery of mail at Princeton.

Resolution of April 28, 1784.—That letters and packets to and from the Commander-in Chief of the United States armies shall be carried postage free, and the Postmaster-General is directed to refund to the late commander-in-chief all money paid by him for postage since the time of his resignation.

Resolution of May 11, 1784.—The postmaster at Princeton exonerated from blame in case of the robbery at his office.

Resolution of February 7, 1785.—The Postmaster-General to remove the department to New York on or before the 1st of March next.

Resolution of June 30, 1785 —The Postmaster-General to inquire and report as to best terms for carrying the mails.

Resolution of September 7, 1785.—The Postmaster-General authorized to make contracts for carrying mail.

Resolution of October 5, 1785.—The Postmaster-General authorized to establish cross-posts.

State money refused for postage.

Resolution of June 21, 1786.—That the Postmaster-General be informed that Congress approves his conduct in directing deputy postmasters not to receive the paper money of any State for postage on letters.

Resolution of September 4, 1786 —The Postmaster-General authorized to contract for transportation of the mail, and for establishing cross-posts.

Only specie receivable for postage.

Resolution of September —, 1786.—Directing the Postmaster-General to instruct postmasters to receive no other money than specie in payment of postage.

Authorizing the Postmaster-General to demand postage at the time letters are put into the office.

Resolution of October 23, 1786.—Authorizing the Secretary of the United States of

America for the Department of Foreign Affairs to inspect any letters in any of the post-offices when, in his judgment, the safety or interest of the government requires it, except letters franked by or addressed to members of Congress.

Resolution of February 17, 1787.—Authorizing the Postmaster-General to grant, for a term not exceeding seven years, the privilege of carrying letters and packages upon the cross-roads in Virginia, from Richmond to Staunton, and from Winchester to Staunton

Resolution of October 20, 1787.—Postage rates reduced 25 per cent. The Postmaster-General authorized to fix rates of postage for carriage of large packets in the mails.

Resolution of January 2, 1788.—Post-office continued on old establishment until February next.

Resolution of May 20, 1788.—That mail be regularly transported once a fortnight between Philadelphia and Pittsburgh, Pa , via Lancaster, York, Carlisle, Jamestown, and Bedford.

Resolution of June 11, 1788.—Instructing the Postmaster-General to deliver any letters or packets that may be found in examining dead letters, directed to any officer of the United States on public business, to such officer free of postage charge.

Resolution of August 29, 1788.—Authorizing the Postmaster-General to establish a weekly post from Wilmington to Dover, Del.

PERIOD OF THE CONSTITUTION.

Act September 22, 1789.—For the temporary establishment of the post-office, to continue in force until the end of the next session of Congress, and no longer.

Act August 4, 1790.—Continues in force the act of September 22, 1789, until the end of the next Congress, and no longer.

Act March 3, 1791.—Continues in force the act of September 22, 1789, until the end of the next Congress, and no longer.

This act (March 3, 1791) provides that all letters to and from the Treasurer, Comptroller, and Auditor of the Treasury, and the Assistant to the Secretary of the Treasury, on public service, shall be received and conveyed by the post free of postage.

Act February 20, 1792.—Continues in force the act of March 3, 1791, until the 1st of June, 1792, and no longer, and provides that this act (February 20, 1792) shall continue in force for the term of two years from June 1, 1792, and no longer.

By this act the Postmaster-General authorized to appoint one Assistant Postmaster-General.

This act (February 20, 1792) was the first act, subsequent to the adoption of the Constitution, fixing rates of postage on domestic letters. It established the following rates, to take effect June 1, 1792 :

First postal rates under the Constitution.

For every single letter not exceeding 30 miles, 6 cents.
For every single letter over 30 miles, and not exceeding 60 miles, 8 cents.
For every single letter over 60 miles, and not exceeding 100 miles, 10 cents.
For every single letter over 100 miles, and not exceeding 150 miles, 12½ cents.
For every single letter over 150 miles, and not exceeding 200 miles, 15 cents.
For every single letter over 200 miles, and not exceeding 250 miles, 17 cents.
For every single letter over 250 miles, and not exceeding 350 miles, 20 cents.
For every single letter over 350 miles, and not exceeding 450 miles, 22 cents.
For every single letter over 450 miles, 25 cents.
For every double letter, double the said rates.
For every triple letter, triple the said rates.
For every packet weighing 1 ounce avoirdupois, to pay at the rate of four single letters for each ounce, and in that proportion for any greater weight.

Act February 20, 1792, *section* 10.—Letters and packets passing by sea to and from the United States, or from one port to another therein, in packet-boats or vessels, the property of or provided by the United States, shall be rated and charged as follows :

For every single letter, 8 cents.
For every double letter, 16 cents.
For every triple letter or packet, 24 cents.
For every letter or packet brought into the United States, or carried from one port therein to another by sea, in any private ship or vessel, 4 cents, if delivered at the place where the same shall arrive ; and if directed to be delivered at any other place, with the addition of the like postage as on domestic letters.

Act February 20, 1792, *section* 13.—The postmasters to whom such letters may be delivered shall pay to the master, commander, or other person delivering the same, except the commanders of foreign packets, 2 cents for every such letter or packet.

Act February 20, 1792, *section* 19.—Letters and packets to be received and conveyed by post, free of postage, under certain restrictions :

All letters or packets to or from the President of the United States and the Vice-President of the United States.

All letters or packets, not exceeding 2 ounces in weight, to or from Senators, Representatives,

Secretary of the Senate, and Clerk of the House of Representatives, during their actual
attendance in any session of Congress and twenty days after such session.

All letters to or from the Secretary of the Treasury, Assistant Secretary of the Treasury,
Comptroller, Register, Auditor, Treasurer, Secretary of State, Secretary of War,
commissioners for settling accounts between the United States and individual States,
Postmaster-General, and Assistant Postmaster-General.

Provided, No person shall frank or enclose any letter or packet not his own ; but
public letters or packets, from the Treasury Department, may be franked by the Secretary,
Assistant Secretary, Comptroller, Register, Auditor, or Treasurer.

Each person shall deliver to post-office every letter or packet inclosed to him for other
persons, that postage may be charged.

Act February 20, 1792, *section* 21.—Printers of newspapers authorized to send one
paper to every other printer of newspaper in the United States, free of postage, under
regulations of the Postmaster-General.

All newspapers conveyed by mail for any distanne not more than 100 miles, 1 cent ;
and over 100 miles, 1½ cents ; if any other matter or thing be inclosed, it is subject to letter
rates of postage.

Act February 20, 1792, *section* 26.—Postmaster-General to make provision for receipt
of letters and packets, to be conveyed beyond the sea, or from one port to another in the
United States ; and for every letter so received, a postage of 1 cent shall be paid.

Act May 8, 1794.—To take effect June 1, 1794, without limit as to time. Establishes
General post office a General Post Office. Sections 9, 10, and 13 of this act re-enact sections 9, 10, and 13 of
established. act of February 20, 1792.

Section 19 of this act re-enacts section 19 of act of February 20, 1792, except that it
omits the Assistant Secretary of the Treasury and commissioners for settling accounts between
the United States and individual States, and adds the Commissioner of the Revenue and postmasters ; the letters and packets of post masters not to exceed one half ounce in weight.

Section 26 of this act re-enacts section 26 of act of February 20, 1792.

Act December 3, 1794.—Confers franking privilege on James White, delegate to Congress from the territory of the United States south of the river Ohio.

Act February 25, 1795.—Confers franking privilege on purveyor of public supplies, as
to letters to or from.

Act March 3, 1797.—That all letters or packets to George Washington, now Presi-
Franking privilege dent of the United States, after the expiration of his term of office, and during his life, shall
conferred on be received and conveyed by post free of postage.
George Washington. *Act June* 22, 1798.—Extends the privilege of franking letters and packets to the
Secretary of the Navy, under like restrictions and limitation as are provided in the act May 8,
1794, section 19.

Act March 2 1799, *section* 7.—Establishes a General Post-Office at the seat of government of the United States.

For every letter composed of a single sheet of paper conveyed not exceeding 40 miles,
8 cents ; over 40 miles and not exceeding 90 miles, 10 cents ; over 90 miles and not exceeding 150 miles, 12½ cents ; over 150 miles and not exceeding 300 miles, 17 cents ; over 300
miles and not exceeding 500 miles, 20 cents ; over 500 miles, 25 cents.

Double letters or two pieces of paper, double rates.

Triple letter or three pieces of paper, triple rates ; and for every packet composed of
four or more pieces of paper, or other thing, and weighing 1 ounce avoirdupois, quadruple
rate, and in same proportion for greater weights : *Provided,* No packet of letters conveyed
by the water-mails shall be charged more than quadruple postage, unless containing more
than four distinct letters ; no package to be received weighing more than 3 pounds.

Act March 2, 1799, *section* 8.—Every packet or letter brought in the United States, or
carried from one part to another in private ship or vessel, 6 cents, if delivered in office where
received ; if to be conveyed by post, 2 cents added to ordinary postage.

Act March 2, 1799, *section* 11.--Authorizes postmasters to whom letters may be delivered by masters or commanders of any ship or vessel arriving at any port within the United
States, where a post-office is established, except foreign packets, to pay 2 cents for each letter
or packet.

Act March 2, 1799, *section* 13.—Postmasters authorized to pay mail-carriers 1 cent for
Carriers' fees. each way-letter delivered to them, also mail-carriers authorized to demand and receive 2
cents in addition to the ordinary postage, for every letter delivered by them to persons living
between post-offices on their route.

Act March 2, 1799, *section* 17.—Letters and packets to be conveyed free to and from
the following :

Postmasters—not exceeding one-half ounce in weight.

Senators, Representatives, Secretary of the Senate, Clerk of the House—not exceeding 2
ounces in weight, during actual attendance in any session of Congress, and twenty
days after such session.

All letters and packets to and from the President of the United States, Vice-President of the
United States, Secretary of the Treasury, Comptroller of the Treasury, Auditor of the

Treasury, Register of the Treasury, Treasurer of the United States, Commissioner of the Revenue, supervisors of the revenue, inspectors of the revenue, Commissioners, Purveyor, Secretary of War, accountant of War Office, Secretary of State, Secretary of Navy, accountant of Navy, Postmaster-General, and Assistant Postmaster-General. All may receive their newspapers free of postage. *Provided*, Senators, Representatives, Secretary of Senate, and Clerk of the House shall receive newspapers free during session of Congress and twenty days after.

Letters or packets from any public officer to be franked by person sending.

All letters and packets to and from George Washington, late President, to be received and conveyed free.

Act March 2, 1799, *section* 19.—Re-enacts section 21 of act February 20, 1792.

Act March 2, 1799, *section* 20.—Fixes postage on newspapers at 1 cent each for not more than 100 m les, and 1½ cents for any greater distance Single newspapers from one place to another in the same State shall not exceed 1 cent.

Concealing a letter, or other thing, or any memorandum in writing in a newspaper, subjects each article in packet to a single-letter postage.

Magazines and pamphlets, 1 cent a sheet, for not exceeding 50 miles; 1½ cents for over 50 miles, and not exceeding 100 miles; and 2 cents for any greater distance.

Act March 2, 1799, *section* 25.—Postmaster-General authorized to provide for receipt of letters or packets, to be conveyed by sea to any foreign port or home port. Every letter or packet so received, subject to a postage of 1 cent

Act January 2, 1800, *section* 1.—Confers franking privilege on William Henry Harrison, delegate to Congress from-territory northwest of the Ohio River, to send and receive letters free of postage.

Act April 3, 1800.—Confers franking privilege upon Martha Washington, to send and receive letters and packages free of postage during her life.

Act December 15, 1800, *section* 1.—Confers franking privilege on delegate from territory northwest of the Ohio River, to send and receive letters free of postage.

Act February 25, 1801.—Confers franking privilege on John Adams, President of the United States, after the expiration of his term of office, and during his life, on all letters and packets to him.

Act February 18, 1802.—Confers privilege of franking and receiving letters free of postage to any person admitted, or to be admitted, to take a seat in Congress as a delegate.

Act May 3, 1802, *section* 4, *vol.* 2, *page* 191.—None but free white persons shall be employed in carrying the mails.

Act May 3, 1802, *section* 5.—Franking privilege extended to the Attorney-General, to send and receive all letters, packets, and newspapers free of postage.

Act March 26, 1804, *section* 3.—Letters, returns, and other papers on public service, sent by mail to or from offices of inspector and paymaster of the army, to be received and conveyed free of postage.

Act June 28, 1809.—Letters and packets from Thomas Jefferson, late President of the United States, to be received and conveyed by post free of postage during his life.

Act April 30, 1810, *section* 1, *vol.* 2 *page* 592.—Establishes a General Post-Office at the seat of Government. Postmaster-General shall appoint two Assistant Postmasters-General.

Act April 30, 1810, *section* 11.—Rates of postage on letters and packets :

Single sheet of paper—

	Cents.
Less than 40 miles	8
40 to 90 miles	10
90 to 150 miles	12½
150 to 300 miles	17
300 to 500 miles	20
Over 500 miles	25

Double letters or two pieces of paper, double rates; triple letters or three pieces of paper, triple rates; every packet composed of four or more pieces of paper or other thing, and weighing 1 ounce avoirdupois, quadruple rate; and in same proportion for greater weight: *Provided*, No packet of letters conveyed by the water-mails shall be charged more than quadruple postage, unless containing more than four distinct letters. Weight of packet limited to 3 pounds.

Act April 30, 1810, *section* 12.—Letters or packets brought into the United States, or carried from one port therein to another, shall be charged 6 cents, if delivered at the post-office where the same shall arrive; and if to be conveyed by post to any other place, with 2 cents added to the ordinary rates of p stage.

Act April 30, 1810, *section* 15.—Postmasters authorized, on the receipt of letters from any ship or vessel arriving at any port within the United States where a post-office is established, to pay to the master, commander, or other person delivering the same, except the commanders of foreign packets, 2 cents for every letter or packet.

Act April 30, 1810, *section* 17.—Postmasters authorized to pay mail-carrier 1 cent for every letter brought into their offices; also mail-carrier authorized to demand and receive 2 cents in addition to the ordinary postage, for every letter delivered by him to persons living between post-offices on his route.

Death penalty for robbing the mail. *Act April 30, 1810, section 19.*—Provides that any person convicted of robbing the mail shall be sentenced to ten years' imprisonment, and upon conviction a second time for such offense, shall be punished with death.

Act April 30, 1810, section 24.—Letters and packets to and from the following officers of the United States to be received and conveyed through the mails free of postage :

Postmasters, not exceeding one-half ounce in weight.

Senators, Members, Delegates, Secretary of the Senate, and Clerk of the House, limited to 2 ounces in weight, and during their actual attendance in any session of Congress and twenty days thereafter; excess of weight to be paid for

All letters and packets to and from the President of the United States, Vice-President of the United States, Secretary of State, Secretary of Treasury, Secretary of War, Secretary of the Navy, Attorney-General, Comptroller, Treasurer, Auditor, Register, supervisor of direct tax of district of South Carolina, superintendent of Indian trade, purveyor, inspector and paymaster of the army, accountants of War and Navy Departments, Postmasters-General, Assistant Postmasters-General, John Adams, and Thomas Jefferson.

All may receive their newspapers free of postage

Senators, Representatives, Secretary of the Senate. and Clerk of the House of Repre-. sentatives shall receive their newspapers free of postage only during any session of Congress and twenty days thereafter.

Act April 30, 1810, section 25.—Secretaries of the Treasury, State, War, Navy, and Postmaster-General authorized to frank letters or packets on official business, prepared in any other public office, in the absence of the principal therof.

Act April 30, 1810, section 26.—Printers of newspapers authorized to exchange one copy free of newspapers, under regulations of the Postmaster-General.

Act April 30, 1810, section 27.—Newspapers by mail, 1 cent each for not more than 100 miles; 1½ cents for any greater distance. Single newspapers, from one place to another in the same State, not to exceed 1 cent.

Act April 30, 1810, section 32.—Postmaster-General authorized to provide for the receipt and transmission of leters and packets beyond sea, or from any port in the United States to any other port therein; every letter or packet so received subject to a postage of 1 cent.

Act April 30, 1810, section 34.—Drop or local letters, 1 cent each.

Act April 30, 1810, section 39.—Adjutant-general of the militia of each State and Territory has the right to receive by mail, free of postage, from any major or brigadier-general thereof, and to transmit to said generals, any letter or packet relating solely to the militia of such State or Territory, under certain restrictions.

Act April 18, 1814, section 4.—Secretary of State authorized to transmit by mail, free of postage, one copy of documents ordered to be printed by either House of Congress—namely,

Public documents to be carried free. of communications, with accompanying documents, made by the President to Congress or either House thereof ; of reports made by the Secretary of State, Treasury, War, Navy, Postmaster-General, or commissioners of the sinking-fund, to Congress, or either House thereof, in pursuance of any law or resolution of either House; affirmative reports on subjects of a general nature made to Congress, or either House thereof, by any committee, respectively —for each of the judges of the Supreme Court, of the district courts, and of the Territories of the United States, to any post-office within the United States they may respectively designate

Act December 23, 1814, section 2 —From and after February 1, 1815, there shall be added to the rates of postage established by law 50 per centum on the amount of such rates respectively.

Act February 1, 1816.—Repeals so much of act of December 23, 1814, as imposes 50 per centum additional postage.

Act April 9, 1816, section 1.—Rates of postage after May 1, 1816 :

Every letter composed of a single sheet of paper—   Cents.
    Less than 30 miles.. 6
    Over 30 miles and not exceeding 80 miles................................ 10
    Over 80 miles and not exceeding 150 miles 12½
    Over 150 miles and not exceeding 400 miles................ .... 18½
    Over 400 miles 25

Every double letter or two pieces of paper, double rates.
Every triple letter or three pieces of paper, triple rates.
Every packet containing four or more pieces of paper or one or more other articles, and weighing one ounce avoirdupois, quadruple these rates, and in that proportion for all greater rates. No packet of letters conveyed by water-mails to be charged with more than quadruple postage, unless the same shall contain more than four distinct letters.

Any memorandum written on a newspaper or other printed paper, and transmitted by mail, to be charged with letter postage.

Act April 9, 1816, *section* 3.—Letters and packets to and from Senators, Members, and Delegates of the House, Secretary of the Senate, and Clerk of the House, to be conveyed free of postage for thirty days previous to each session of Congress and for thirty days after the termination thereof; limited to 2 ounces in weight; excess to be paid for.

Act March 1, 1817.—Letters and packets to and from James Madison, President of the United States, after the expiration of his term of office and during his life, to be carried by mail free of postage.

Act March 13, 1820.—Letters and packets to and from the President of the Senate *pro tempore*, and Speaker of the House for the time being, to be received and conveyed by mail, free of postage, during the session of Congress, under certain restrictions.

Act March 3, 1825.—An act to reduce into one the several acts establishing and regulating the Post-Office Department.

Section 1 establishes at the seat of government a general post-office, under the direction of the Postmaster-General. Various Acts of Congress reduced into one.

Act March 3, 1825, *section* 5.—Authorizes the Postmaster General to have mail carried by any steamboat or other vessel which shall be used as a packet in any waters of the United States, on such terms and conditions as shall be considered expedient : *Provided*, That he does not pay more than 3 cents for each letter, nor more than one-half a cent for each newspaper.

Act March 3, 1825, *section* 6 —Master or manager of any steamboat passing from one port or place to another port or place in the United States, where a post-office is established, to deliver all letters or packets addressed to such port or place to the postmaster there, for which he shall receive of such postmaster 2 cents for every letter or packet so delivered, unless the same shall be conveyed under contract with the Postmaster-General.

Act March 3, 1825, *section* 7.—No other than a free white person shall be employed in conveying the mail ; and any contractor who shall employ or permit any other than a free white person to convey the mail shall for every such offense incur a penalty of $20.

Act March 3, 1825, *section* 13.—Rates of postage on letters and packets conyed in the mail of the United States :

For every letter of a single sheet of paper conveyed— Cents

Not exceeding 30 miles	6
Over 30 miles and not exceeding 80 miles	10
Over 80 miles and not exceeding 150 miles	12½
Over 150 miles and not exceeding 400 miles	18¾
Over 400 miles	25

Every double letter or two pieces of paper, double these rates ; every triple letter or three pieces of paper, triple these rates ; every packet of four or more pieces of paper, or one or more other articles, and weighing 1 ounce avoirdupois, quadruple these rates ; and in that proportion for all greater weights : *Provided*, That no packet of letters conveyed by the water-mails sha'l be charged more than quadruple postage, unless the same shall contain more than four distinct letters ; weight of packet limited to 3 pounds.

Unbound journals of legislatures of the several States liable to same postage as pamphlets.

Memorandum written on a newspaper or other printed paper, pamphlet, or magazine, and transmitted by mail, to be charged with letter postage.

Act March 3, 1825, *section* 15.—Every letter or package brought into the United States, or carried from one point therein to another, in any private ship or vessel, to be charged 6 cents, if delivered at the post-office where the same shall arrive ; and if destined to be conveyed by post to any other place, with 2 cents added to the ordinary rates of postage.

Act March 3, 1825, *section* 18.—Postmasters authorized to pay to the master or commander of any vessel, except the commanders of foreign packets, arriving at any port in the United States where a post-office is established, 2 cents for every letter or packet delivered by him to the postmaster.

Act March 3, 1825, *section* 27.—Letters and packets to be conveyed by post free of postage to and from the following :

Postmasters—limited to one-half ounce in weight.

Members, Senators, Delegates, Secretary of the Senate and Clerk of the House—limited to 2 ounces in weight (except documents printed by order of either House of Congress), and during their actual attendance in any session of Congress and sixty days before and after ; excess of weight to be paid for.

All letters and packets to and from the President of the United States, Vice-President of the United States, Secretary of State, Secretary of War, Secretary of Treasury, Secretary of Navy, Attorney-General, Postmaster-General, Assistant Postmasters-General, Comptrollers of Treasury, Auditors of Treasury, Register, Treasurer, Commissioner General Land Offics, ex-Presidents and President of the United States

All of the above to receive newspapers free of postage : *Provided*, That postmasters shall not receive free of postage more than one daily newspaper each, or what is equivalent thereto ; nor shall members of the Senate or House, Clerk of the House, or Secretary of the Senate receive newspapers free of postage after their franking privilege shall cease.

Act March 3, 1825, *section* 28.—Secretaries of Treasury, State, War, Navy, and the Postmaster-General may frank letters and packets on official business prepared in any other public office in the absence of the principal thereof.

Act March 3, 1825, *section* 29.—Printers of newspapers authorized to exchange one paper free of postage, under regulations by Postmaster-General.

Act March 3, 1825, *section* 30.—Newspapers conveyed by mail, 1 cent for any distance not more than 100 miles ; 1½ cents for any greater distance. Single newspapers from one place to another in the same State, 1 cent.

Inclosing or concealing a letter or other thing, or any memorandum in writing, in a newspaper, pamphlet, or magazine, subjects it to single letter postage for each article of which the package is composed.

Size of a sheet defined. When mode of conveyance and size of mail will admit, magazines and pamphlets published periodically may be transported in the mail to subscribers, at 1½ cents a sheet for any distance not exceeding 100 miles, and 2½ cents for any greater distance And such magazines and pamphlets as are not published periodically, if sent in the mail, shall be charged 4 cents on each sheet for any distance not exceeding 100 miles, and 6 cents for any greater distance. (Section 13 of this act defines a sheet to be four folio pages, 8 quarto pages, 16 octavo pages, or 24 duodecimo pages, or pages less than that of a pamphlet size or magazine, whatever be the size of the paper of which it is formed. The surplus pages of any pamphlet or magazine shall also be considered a sheet.)

Act March 3, 1825, *section* 34.—Postmaster-General authorized to make provision for the receipt of letters and packets to be conveyed by any vessel beyond sea, or from one port to another in the United States ; and the postmaster receiving the same at the port to which such vessel shall be bound shall be entitled to a postage of 1 cent on each letter or packet received.

Act March 3, 1825, *section* 36 —Drop or local letters delivered at the post-office, 1 cent each.

Act March 3, 1825, *section* 36.—Authorizes the Postmaster-General to employ letter-carriers at such post-offices as he may designate, for the delivery of letters ; and the carrier may receive from the person to whom the letter is delivered 2 cents.

Act March 3, 1825, *section* 40.—The adjutant-general of the militia of each State and Territory authorized to receive by mail, free of postage, from any major-general or brigadier-general thereof, and to transmit to said generals, any letter or packet relating solely to the militia of such State or Territory, under certain conditions.

Act March 3, 1825, *section* 46.—Repeals all acts and parts of acts which have been passed for the establishment and regulation of the general post-office.

Act March 2, 1827.—Increases the salary of the Postmaster-General $2,000 over the present amount.

Act March 2, 1827, *section* 2.—One cent to be allowed each postmaster for every letter received from any ship or vessel and mailed by him.

Act March 2, 1827, *section* 4.—Authority to frank and receive letters and packets free of postage extended to the commissioners of the navy-board, Adjutant-General, Commissary-General, Inspector-General, Quartermaster-General, Paymaster-General, Secretary of the Senate, Clerk of the House, Superintendent of the Patent-Office.

No other person or officer except those enumerated herein and in the act of March 3, 1825, shall be authorized to frank or receive letters by mail free of postage.

Act March 2, 1827, *section* 5.—One or more pieces of paper mailed as a letter and weighing 1 ounce avoirdupois, shall be charged with quadruple postage, and at the same rate should the weight be greater. Packages containing four pieces of paper, quadruple rates.

Every printed pamphlet or magazine containing more than twenty-four pages on a royal sheet, or any sheet of less dimensions, shall be charged by the sheet ; and small pamphlets printed on a half or quarter sheet of royal, or less size. shall be charged with one-half the amount of postage on a full sheet. Double postage shall be charged, unless there shall be printed or written on one of the outer pages of all pamphlets and magazines the number of sheets they contain.

Act June 30, 1834.—Governors of the several States authorized to transmit by mail, free of postage, all laws and reports, bound or unbound, and all records and documents of their respective States, which may be directed by the several legislatures of the States to be transmitted to the executives of other States.

Act July 2, 1836. *section* 8.—President authorized to appoint an Auditor of the Treasury for the Post-Office Department, who is authorized to frank and receive, free of postage, letters and packets, under regulations provided by law for other officers of the government.

Act July 2, 1836, *section* 8.—All letters or packets to or from the Chief Engineer, which may relate to the business of his office, free of postage.

Act July 2, 1836, *section* 20.—Postmaster-General authorized to employ a Third Assistant Postmaster-General, who may receive and send letters free of postage.

Act July 2, 1836, *section* 36.—No postmaster shall receive free of postage or frank any letter or packet composed of or containing anything other than money or paper.

All letters and packets to and from Dolly P. Madison, relict of the late James Madison, shall be received and conveyed by post free of postage for and during her life

Act July 4, 1836, *section* 1.— Patent-Office established and the Commissioner entitled to receive and send letters and packages by mail relating to the business of his office free of postage.

Act July 7, 1838.—Every railroad built or to be built declared a post-road, over which the Postmaster-General shall cause the mails to be transported, if the cost thereof be not more than 25 per cent. over the cost of similar service in post-coaches. **Railroads declared to be post-roads.**

Act January 25, 1839.—Postmaster General not to allow to any railroad company for carrying the mails more than $300 per mile per annum.

Act September 9, 1841.—All letters and packets carried by post to Mrs. Harrison, relict of the late William Henry Harrison, to be conveyed free of postage during her life.

Act January 20, 1843, *section* 3.—Commissioner of Pensions authorized to send and receive letters and packets by mail free of postage.

Act February 15. 1843, *section* 1.—Authorizes the chief clerk of the office of Secretary of State to frank all public and official documents sent from that office.

Act March 3, 1843.—*Appropriation for testing the capacity and usefulness of the magnetic telegraph by constructing a line of telegraphs between such points as will determine its practicability.* [Under this act a line of telegraphs was constructed by the Government between Washington and Baltimore.] **Magnetic telegraph.**

Act March 3, 1845, *section* 1, *vol.* 5, *page* 732.—After July 1, 1845, Members of Congress and Delegates from Territories may receive letters not exceeding 2 ounces in weight free of postage during the recess of Congress, anything to the contrary in this act notwithstanding; and the same franking privilege which is granted by this act to the members of the two houses of Congress is hereby extended to the Vice-President of the United States.

Postage on letters.—For every single letter in manuscript, or marks and signs by mail, under 300 miles, 5 cents, over 300 miles, 10 cents; double letter, double rates; treble letter, treble rates; quadruple letter, quadruple rates; and every letter or parcel not exceeding one-half ounce in weight shall be deemed a single letter, and every additional weight of one-half ounce or less shall be charged with an additional single postage. Drop or local letters shall be charged a postage rate of 2 cents each.

Act March 3, 1845, *section* 2.— *Postage on newspapers.*— Newspapers of not more than 1,900 square inches in size may be transmitted through the mails by the editors or publishers thereof to subscribers or other persons, within 30 miles of the city, town, or place in which the paper is printed, free of postage. Newspapers of less size, conveyed by mail beyond 30 miles from the place at which they are printed, shall be subject to the rates of postage chargeable under the thirtieth section, act March 3, 1825 Newspapers of greater size than 1,900 square inches subject to same rates of postage as are prescribed by this act on magazines and pamphlets.

Act March 3, 1845, *section* 3.—Printed or lithograph circulars, hand-bills, or advertisements, printed or lithographed on quarto-post or single-cap paper, or paper not larger than single-cap paper, unsealed, shall be charged with postage at the rate of 2 cents for each sheet, without regard to distance. Pamphlets. magazines, periodicals, and all other printed or other matter (except newspapers) unconnected with any writing, shall be charged with postage at the rate of 2½ cents for each copy sent, not exceeding 1 ounce in weight, and 1 cent additional for each additional ounce, without regard to distance; and any fractional excess of not less than one-half ounce above 1 or more ounces shall be charged for as if said excess amounted to a full ounce

Bound books not to be admitted under foregoing provisions.

Act March 3, 1845, *section* 5.— Repeals all acts and parts of acts conferring upon any person the right or privilege to receive and transmit through the mail free of postage letters, packets, newspapers, periodicals, or other matter.

Act March 3, 1845, *section* 6.—All officers of the government of the United States, heretofore having the franking privilege, shall be allowed and paid quarterly all postage on official letters, packages. or other matter received by mail. **New regulations concerning franking.**

Postage upon official letters. packages, or other matter received by the three Assistant Postmasters-General shall be remitted, and they shall be authorized to transmit by mail free of postage official letters, packages, or other matter under certain regulations.

Deputy postmasters allowed all postage which they may have paid or have had charged to them for official letters, packages, or other matters, and they are authorized to send by mail free of postage official letters and packets, under certain regulations.

Act March 3, 1845, *section* 7.—Continues in force act of June 30, 1834, authorizing the governors of the several States to transmit by mail certain books and documents, and authorizes Members and Delegates, Secretary of the Senate and Clerk of the House to transmit by mail free of postage any documents printed by order of either house of Congress.

Act March 3, 1845, *section* 8.—Senators, Members, Delegates, Secretary of Senate, and Clerk of the House, authorized, during each session of Congress and for thirty days before and after every session of Congress, to send and receive through the mail free of postage any letter, newspaper, or packet, not exceeding 2 ounces in weight. Postage charged for excess of weight on official letters, packages, etc., received during any session of Congress, to be paid out of the contingent fund of the house of which the person may be a member. Authorized to frank written letters from themselves during the whole year, etc.

Act March 3, 1845. *section* 13.—Transmission of letters by steamboats, under act of March 3, 1825, section 6, not prohibited : *Provided,* That the requirements of said sixth section shall be strictly complied with by the delivery of all letters so conveyed, not relating to the cargo or some part thereof, to the postmaster or agent of the Post-Office Department at the port to which said letters may be delivered ; and the postmaster or agent shall collect upon all letters or other mailable matter so delivered to him, except newspapers, pamphlets, magazines, and periodicals, the same rates of postage as would have been charged upon said letters had they been transmitted by mail from the port at which they were placed on board the steamboat from which they were received ; weight of packet limited to 3 pounds.

Mailable matter defined.

Act March 3, 1845, *section* 15.—*Mailable matter defined.*—Letters, newspapers, maga- zines and pamphlets periodically published or published in regular series, or in successive numbers, under the same title, though at irregular intervals, and all other written or printed matter, whereof each copy or number shall not exceed eight ounces in weight, except bank- notes sent in packages or bundles, without written letters accompanying them. Bound books not to be included within the meaning of these terms.

Newspapers defined.

Act March 3, 1845, *section* 16.—*Newspapers defined.*—Any printed publication issued in numbers, consisting of not more than two sheets and published at short stated intervals of not more than one month, conveying intelligence of passing events, and bona-fide extras and supplements of any such publication.

Free exchange of newspapers between publishers, as provided for by act of March 3, 1825, section 29. not prohibited.

Act March 3, 1845, *section* 23.—Franking privilege conferred by former acts on the President of the United States when in office, and to all ex-Presidents, and to the widows of the former Presidents, Madison and Harrison, continued in force.

Act March 3. 1845, *section* 19. *volume* 5, *page* 738.—Railroad transporation of the mails divided into three classes, with varying rates of compensation therefor.

Joint resolution of February 20, 1845.—Postmaster-General authorized to contract with railroads for carrying the mails without advertising for bids.

Joint resolution of March 3, 1845.—Provides that act of March 3, 1845, shall go into effect on and after July 1, 1845.

Act May 29, 1846. *section* 3.—Same rates of postage to be charged in Texas as in other States of the United State .

Act June 19, 1846—Appropriation made for defraying expenses of magnetic telegraph from Washington to Baltimore : "*Provided,* That the Postmaster-General be, and he is hereby, authorized to let, for a limited time, the aforesaid telegraph to any person who will keep it in operation for its earnings ; or he may, under the direction of the President of the United States, sell the same."

Telegraph receipts credited to the P. O. Department.

Act August 10, 1846. —"That the proceeds of the telegraph between Washington City and Baltimore be, and the same are hereby, directed to be placed in the Treasury of the United States, for the benefit of the Post-Office Department, in the same manner as other revenues from postages."

Act August 6, 1846, *section* 18 — On and after January 1, 1847, postage shall be paid in gold and silver only, or in Treasury notes of the United States.

Act March 1, 1847, *section* 3.— Members and Delegates in Congress, Vice President of the United States. Secretary of the Senate, and Clerk of the House, to have power to send and receive public documents during their term of office and up to the first Monday of December following the expiration of their term of office.

Act March 1, 1847, *section* 4.—Secretary of the Senate and Clerk of the House to receive and send all letters and packages free of postage during their term of office ; limited to two ounces.

Act March 1, 1847, *section* 5.—Members of Congress to receive and send all letters and packages free of postage, up to the first Monday in December following the expiration of their term of office.

Act March 2, 1847, *section* 1.—Every postmaster whose compensation for the last pre- ceding year did not exceed $200 to send all letters written by himself and receive all addressed to himself, on his private business, free of postage ; limited to one-half ounce in weight.

Act March 3, 1847, *section* 4—Letters, newspapers, and packets, not exceeding one ounce in weight, directed to any officer, musician, or private of the army of the United States in Mexico, or at any place on the frontier of the United States bordering on Mexico, shall be conveyed in the mail free of postage

Act March 3, 1847, *section* 5.—Continues in force section 4 of this act during the present war and three months thereafter.

Act March 3, 1847, *section* 7—Postmaster-General authorized to establish a post- office at Astoria, and other places on the Pacific.

All letters conveyed to or from Chagres 20
All letters conveyed to or from Havana................. ....12½
All letters conveyed to or from Panama 30
All letters conveyed to or from Astoria...40
All letters conveyed to or from any other place on the Pacific....... 40

Act March 3, 1847, section 11 —*Authorizes the Postmaster-General to prepare postage-stamps, which, when attached to any letter or packet, shall be evidence of the payment of postage chargeable therefor.*   **Postage stamps first authorized.**

Act March 3, 1847, section 12.—Repeals so much of section 6 of act March 3, 1845, as requires postage to be paid on free matter from the contingent fund of the two Houses of Congress and the other departments of the government, and in lieu thereof provides for an annual appropriation of $200,000, to be paid to the Post-Office Department.

Act March 3, 1847, section 13.—Newspapers by mail (except exchanges between publishers), except such as are franked by those enjoying the franking privilege, and newspapers not sent from the office of publication, and handbills or circulars printed or lithographed, not exceeding one sheet, shall be subject to 3 cents prepaid postage each. Postmaster-General authorized to pay not exceeding 2 cents each for all letters or packets conveyed in any vessel not employed in carrying the mail from one place to another in the United States, under such regulations as he may provide.

Publications or books published, procured, or purchased by either House of Congress shall be considered public documents and entitled to be franked as such.

Act March 3, 1847, section 14 — Repeals so much of act of March 3, 1845, and of all other acts relating to the Post Office Department, as is inconsistent with this act.

Act March 9, 1848.— Letters and packets by mail to and from Louisa Catherine Adams, widow of the late John Quincy Adams, to be free of postage during her life.

Act May 27, 1848, section 4.—Commissioner of Patents authorized to send by mail free of postage the annual reports of the Patent Office

Act June 27, 1848, section 1.—Postmaster-General authorized to charge and collect upon all letters and other mailable matter carried in foreign packets the same rate of postage which the governments to which such foreign packets belong impose upon letters, etc., carried in American packets.

Act June 27, 1848, section 2 —All letters and other mailable matter conveyed by any foreign ship to or from any port of the United States, to be subject to postage charged 'as in above section, except letters relating to the vessel or cargo.

Act August 14, 1848, section 3.—Postmaster General authorized to establish a post-office at San Diego, Monterey, San Francisco, and other places on the Pacific, in California, and all letters conveyed to or from any of the above places on the Pacific, from or to any place on the Atlantic, to be charged 40 cents postage ; all letters conveyed from one to any other of said places on the Pacific, 12½ cents.

Act March 3, 1849, section 1.—Rates on letters transported under the postal treaty with Great Britain :

Letters not exceeding one-half ounce, one rate of postage.

Letters exceeding one-half ounce avoirdupois, and not exceeding 1 ounce, two rates of postage.

Letters exceeding 1 ounce avoirdupois, and not exceeding 2 ounces, four rates of postage.

Letters exceeding 2 ounces avoirdupois, and not exceeding 3 ounces, six rates of postage.

Letters exceeding 3 ounces avoirdupois, and not exceeding 4 ounces, eight rates of postage.

And in like progression for each additional ounce or fraction of an ounce. Newspapers not sent from the office of publication to be charged with the same rates of postage as other papers ; to be prepaid.

Act January 10, 1850.- Franking privilege granted to Sarah Polk, relict of the late James K. Polk, during her life ; to cover all letters and packages to and from.

Act May 23, 1850, section 17.—Marshals and their assistants authorized to transmit papers and documents relating to the census through the post-office free.

Act March 23, 1850, section 19 —Secretary of the Interior required to appoint a clerk to superintend the census, who shall have the privilege of franking and receiving free of charge all official documents and letters connected therewith.

Act July 18, 1850.—Franking privilege granted to Margaret Smith Taylor, relict of Zachary Taylor, same as granted to widows of deceased Presidents.

Act September 27, 1850.—Third section act of August 14, 1848, extended to Territories of Utah and New Mexico, and Postmaster-General authorized to establish such rates of postage in said Territories as may to him seem proper, not to exceed those authorized in said act.

Act March 3, 1851, section 1.—*Rates of postage on letters.*—From and after June 30, 1851, in lieu of rates of postage now fixed by law, there shall be charged the following rates :   **Reduced rates on prepaid letters.** Every single letter. in writing, marks, or signs, by mails, not exceeding 3,000 miles, prepaid postage, 3 cents ; not prepaid, 5 cents ; for any greater distance, double these rates.

Every single letter or paper conveyed wholly or in part by sea, and to or from a foreign country over 2,500 miles, 20 cents ; under 2,500 miles, 10 cents (excepting rates fixed by postal treaty); double letter, double rates ; triple letter, triple rates ; and every letter or parcel not exceeding one-half ounce in weight shall be deemed a single letter, and every additional weight of one-half ounce or less shall be charged with an additional rate. Drop or local letters, 1 cent each.   Letters uncalled for and advertised, to be charged 1 cent in addition to the regular postage.

Act March 3, 1851, *section* 2.—Newspaper not exceeding 3 ounces in weight sent from the office of publication to bona fide subscribers shall be charged with postage as follows :

Weekly newspapers free, within the county where published ; and for not exceeding 50 miles out of the county where published, 5 cents per quarter ; exceeding 50 miles, and not exceeding 300 miles, 10 cents per quarter ; exceeding 300 miles, and not exceeding 1,000 miles, 15 cents per quarter ; exceeding 1,000 miles, and not exceeding 2,000 miles, 20 cents per quarter ; exceeding 2,000 miles, and not exceeding 4,000 miles, 25 cents per quarter ; exceeding 4,000 miles, 30 cents per quarter.

Newspaper published monthly, sent to bona fide subscribers, one-quarter of the fore-going rates ; published semi-monthly, one-half of the foregoing rates ; published semi-weekly, double the foregoing rates ; published tri-weekly, treble the foregoing rates ; and oftener than tri-weekly, five times the foregoing rates.   On other papers, unsealed circulars, handbills, engravings, pamphlets, periodicals, magazines, books, and all other printed matter, unconnected with written matter, of not more than one ounce in weight, and not exceeding 500 miles, one cent ; and for each additional ounce or fraction thereof, one cent ; exceeding 500 miles, and not exceeding 1,500 miles, double these rates ; exceeding 1,500 miles, and not exceeding 2,500 miles, treble these rates ; exceeding 2,500 miles, and not exceeding 3,500 miles, four times these rates ; exceeding 3,500 miles, five times these rates.

Subscribers to periodicals required to pay one quarter's postage in advance ; postage one half the foregoing rates.

Bound books and parcels of printed matter, not over thirty ounces, made mailable matter.

Postage on printed matter, other than newspapers, and periodicals published at intervals not exceeding three months and sent from office of publication to bona fide subscribers, to be prepaid.

When printed matter on which postage is required by this section to be prepaid, shall be sent without prepayment, the same shall be charged with double the prepaid rate.

Nothing in this act shall subject to postage any matter exempted from postage by existing law.

Publishers of pamphlets, periodicals, magazines, and newspapers which shall not exceed 16 ounces in weight, allowed to interchange their publications free, confined to a single copy of each publication.   Publishers allowed to inclose in their publications bills for subscription without additional postage.   Newspapers not containing more than 300 square inches may be transmitted to bona fide subscribers at one-fourth the rates fixed by this act.

Act March 3, 1851, *section* 8.—Provides for the annual appropriation of $500,000 to the Post-Office Department for mail service for the two houses of Congress, and other depart-ments and officers of the government, in the transportation of free matter.

Act August 30, 1852, *section* 1. *vol.* 10, *page* 38.—*Rates of postage on printed matter.*— From and after September 30, 1852, postage on all printed matter passing by mail, instead of the rates now charged, shall be as follows : Each newspaper, periodical, unsealed circular, or other article of printed matter, not exceeding 3 ounces in weight, to any part of the United States, 1 cent ; and for every additional ounce or fraction thereof 1 cent additional.

Postage on any newspapers or periodicals paid quarterly or yearly in advance at the office of delivery, or at the office of mailing, one-half of said rates only shall be charged.

Newspapers and periodicals not weighing over 1½ ounces, when circulated in the State where published, one-half of the rates before mentioned.

Small newspapers and periodicals, published monthly or oftener, and pamphlets of not more than sixteen octavo pages, sent in single packages weighing at least eight ounces to one address, and prepaid by postage-stamps affixed, only one-half cent for each ounce or fraction of an ounce

Postage on all transient matter shall be prepaid or charged double the rates first above mentioned.

Act August 30, 1852, *section* 2.—*Postage on books.*—Books, bound or unbound, not weighing more than four pounds, will be deemed mailable matter and subject to postage at 1 cent an ounce for all distances under 3,000 miles ; 2 cents for all distances over 3,000 miles ; to which 50 per cent. shall be added unless prepaid.

Publishers of newspapers and periodicals may exchange free of postage one copy of each publication, and may send to actual subscribers, in their publications, bills and receipts for the same free.   Publishers of weekly newspapers may send to each actual subscriber within the county where their papers are printed and published one copy free of postage, under certain conditions.

Act August 30, 1852, *section* 3.—Prescribes certain conditions which if not complied with subject printed matter to letter-postage.

Matter sent by mail from one part of the United States to another, the postage of which is not fixed by this act, shall, unless entitled to be sent free, be charged with letter-postage.

Act August 30, 1852, *section* 5.—Repeals so much of the second section of act of March 3, 1851, as relates to the postage or free circulation of newspapers, periodicals, and other printed matter, and all other provisions of law inconsistent with this act.

Act August 31, 1852, *section* 8, *vol.* 10, *page* 141.—*Postmaster-General authorised to provide stamped letter envelopes.* Letters when inclosed in such envelopes (with stamps thereon equal in amount to the postage to which such letters would be liable if sent by mail) may be sent and delivered otherwise than by mail under certain conditions. **Stamped envelopes authorized.**

Act March 3, 1853, *section* 5.—Assistant Postmasters-General to be in future appointed by President and confirmed by Senate.

Act March 3, 1853.—Increases the salary of the Postmaster-General to $8,000 per annum.

Act February 2, 1854.—The Superintendent of the Coast Survey and the assistant in charge of the Office of the Coast Survey authorized to transmit free of postage, by the mails, all letters and documents in relation to their public duties.

Act March 3, 1855, *section* 1.—In lieu of the rates of postage now fixed by law, there shall be charged the following rates :

For every single letter, in manuscript or paper of any kind, in writing, marks, or signs, conveyed in the mail between places in the United States not exceeding 3,000 miles, 3 cents ; and for any greater distance, 10 cents ; for a double letter, double rates ; treble letter, treble rates ; quadruple letter, quadruple rates ; every letter or parcel not exceeding one-half ounce in weight shall be deemed a single letter, and every additional weight of one-half ounce or less shall be charged an additional rate ; the foregoing rates to be prepaid on domestic letters, except on letters and packages to officers of the Government on official business, and except on letters to or from a foreign country **Compulsory pre-payment of postage.**

Postage on drop or local letters, 1 cent each.

Nothing in this act to alter the laws in relation to the franking privilege.

The foregoing section was the first provision of law making the prepayment of postage on domestic letters compulsory.

Act March 3, 1855, *section* 3.—*Authorizes the Postmaster-General to establish a system for registration of valuable letters, and to require prepayment of postage on such letters, as well as of a registration fee of 5 cents ; the Post-Office Department not to be liable for the loss of such letters or packets.* **First provision for registration.**

Act March 3, 1855, *section* 4.—Franking privilege of Vice-Presidents continued to those who have held or shall hold that office, during life.

Act March 3, 1855, *section* 5.—Books, maps, charts, or other publications, entered by copyright, and which, under act of August 10 1846, are required to be deposited in the Library of Congress and in the Smithsonian Institution, may be sent by mail free of postage, under regulations to be prescribed by the Postmaster-General.

Act January 2, 1857.—Repeals the provision in the act of August 30, 1852, permitting transient printed matter to be sent through the mail without prepayment of postage ; the postage on all such matter shall be paid by stamps or otherwise, as the Postmaster-General may direct.

Act April 3, 1860, *section* 1.—Modifies second clause, section 3, of act August 30, 1852, establishing the rates of postage on printed matter, so as to allow only the name, the date when the subscription expires, and the address of the person to whom sent.

Act April 3. 1860, *section* 2.—Postage on drop or local letters delivered by carriers, 1 cent each.

Act February 27, 1861, *section* 2, *vol.* 12, *page* 167.—*Stamped letter-sheets and newspaper wrappers authorised.* **Stamped letter-sheets and wrappers.**

Act February 27, 1861, *section* 8.— That upon all letters returned from the dead-letter office there shall be paid the usual rate of postage ; to be paid on delivery.

Act February 27, 1861, *section* 9.—That upon every letter or packet brought into the United States, or carried from one port therein to another in any private ship or vessel, 5 cents if delivered at the post-office where the same shall arrive, and if destined to be conveyed by post, 2 cents shall be added to the ordinary postage : *Provided,* That upon all letters or packets conveyed in whole or in part by steamers over any route upon which the mail is regularly conveyed in vessels under contract with the Post-Office Department, the same charge shall be levied, with the addition of 2 cents a letter or packet on the domestic rate.

Act February 27, 1861, *section* 10.—Repeals all acts or parts of acts inconsistent with section 9 of this act.

Act February 27, 1861, *section* 12.—That maps, engravings, lithographs, or photographic prints, on rollers or in paper covers, books, bound or unbound, photographic paper, and letter envelopes, shall be deemed mailable matter, and charged with postage by weight, **Transportation of merchandise in the mails.**

not to exceed 4 pounds, at the rate of 1 cent an ounce, or fraction of an ounce, to any place in the United States under 1,500 miles ; 2 cents an ounce or fraction of an ounce over 1,500 miles, to be prepaid by postage-stamps.

Act February 27, 1861, *section* 13.—That cards, blank or printed, blanks in packages weighing at least 8 ounces, and seeds or cuttings in packages not exceeding 8 ounces, shall also be deemed mailable matter and charged with postage at the rate of 1 cent an ounce, or fraction thereof, to any place in the United States under 1,500 miles, and 2 cents an ounce, or fraction thereof, over 1,500 miles, to be prepaid by postage-stamps.

The foregoing sections were the first provisions of law that authorized the introduction of merchandise into the mails.

Act February 27, 1861, *section* 14.—Modifies the act of March 3, 1855, so as to require the 10-cent rate of postage to be prepaid on letters conveyed in the mail from any point in the United States east of the Rocky Mountains to any State or Territory on the Pacific, and *vice versa.*

Drop-letters shall be prepaid by postage-stamps.

Act February 27, 1861, *section* 16.—The postage over the overland route, between any State or Territory east of the Rocky Mountains to any State or Territory on the Pacific, on each newspaper, periodical, unsealed circular, or other article of printed matter not exceeding 3 ounces in weight, shall be 1 cent, and every additional ounce, or fraction thereof, 1 cent additional.

Act February 27, 1861, *section* 17.—Rate of letter-postage between any State or Territory east of the Rocky Mountains and any State or Territory on the Pacific, 10 cents for every half ounce.

Act March 2, 1861, *section* 9.—Contractors on overland routes to San Francisco required to run a pony-express during the continuance of their contract or until the completion of the overland telegraph, at certain times, carrying for the government free of charge 5 pounds of mail matter, with the liberty of charging the public for transportation of letters by said express, not exceeding $1 for one-half ounce ; to commence before the 25th day of March, 1862, and expire July 1, 1864.

Pony Express.

Act July 22, 1861, *section* 11.—Letters written by soldiers in the service of the United States may be transmitted by mail without prepayment of postage, under regulations of the Post-Office Department ; postage to be paid by the party receiving.

Act July 24, 1861.—Prepaid letters to soldiers in the service of the United States, and directed to a point where they have been stationed, may be forwarded without further charge.

Act January 21, 1862, *section* 1.—Postmaster-General authorized to return all dead letters to writers, except those containing circulars and other worthless matter. Valuable letters to be charged treble, and all others double the ordinary rates of postage, to be collected from the writers.

Provisions of act of July 22, 1861, section 11, extended to sailors and marines in the service of the United States.

Act April 16, 1862, *section* 1.—Postmaster-General authorized to establish branch post-offices in cities, and to charge 1 cent in addition to the regular postage for every letter deposited in them to be forwarded by mail, to be prepaid by stamps ; and 1 cent for every letter delivered at such branch office, to be paid on delivery.

Act May 15, 1862, *section* 1.—Establishes the Department of Agriculture.

Act May 15, 1862, *section* 2.—Provides for the appointment of a Commissioner of Agriculture, and confers franking privilege on said Commissioner to send and receive by mail free of postage all communications and other matter pertaining to the business of his Department ; weight limited to 32 ounces.

Act July 1, 1862, *section* 1.—Creates the office of Commissioner of Internal Revenue and confers on the Commissioner the privilege of franking all letters and documents pertaining to the duties of his office, and of receiving free all such letters and documents.

Act July 5, 1862, *section* 6.— Chiefs of the bureaus of the Navy Department authorized to frank all communications from their respective bureaus, and all communications to their bureaus on the business thereof shall be free of postage.

Postage stamps as currency.

Act July 17, 1862.—Postage stamps to be used as currency in sums less than $5.

Letter carriers.

Act March 3, 1863, *section* 11, *vol.* 12, *page* 703.—*That letter-carriers shall be employed at such post-offices as the Postmaster-General shall direct for the delivery of letters in the places respectively where such post-offices are established ; and for their services they shall severely recive a salary, to be perscribed by the Postmaster-General, not exceeding $800 per annum.*

Act March 3, 1863, *section* 16.—Postmasters of any office where letter-carriers are employed authorized to contract with publishers of newspapers, periodicals, and circulars for delivery by carriers of any such publications not received by mail, at rates and terms to be agreed upon Contracts have no force until approved by the Postmaster-General.

Postmaster-General authorized to provide for delivery by carriers of small packets, other than letters or papers, and not exceeding the maximum weight of mailable packages ; such packages to be prepaid by postage-stamps at the rate of 2 cents for each 4 ounces or fraction thereof.

Act March 3, 1863, *section* 16.—Limits weight to 4 pounds, except books published or circulated by order of Congress.

Act March 3, 1863, *section* 19.—Divides mailable matter into three classes. First class letters ; second class, regular printed matter ; third class, miscellaneous matter.

Act March 3, 1863, *section* 20.—First class embraces all correspondence wholly or partly in writing, except that mentioned in the third class.

Second class embraces all mailable matter exclusively in print and regularly issued at stated periods, without addition by writing, mark, or sign.

Third class embraces all other matter which is or may hereafter be by law declared mailable.

Act March 3, 1863, *section* 21.—Fixes the maximum standard weight for the single rate of letter-postage at one-half ounce avoirdupois.

Act March 3, 1863, *section* 22.—Fixes the rate of postage on domestic letters, not exceeding one-half ounce in weight, at 3 cents, and 3 cents additional for each additional half-ounce or fraction thereof, to be prepaid by postage-stamps affixed. **Uniform rate of postage established.**

This was the first law which established a uniform rate of postage on letters regardless of distance to which matter was to be transmitted.

Act March 3, 1863, *section* 23.—Fixes the rate of postage on drop-letters not exceeding one-half ounce in weight at 2 cents, and 2 cents added for each additional half-ounce or fraction thereof, to be prepaid by postage-stamps affixed ; "but no extra postage or carriers' fee shall hereafter be charged or collected upon letters delivered by carriers, nor upon letters collected by them for mailing or delivery." **Carriers' fees abolished.**

Act March 3, 1863. *section* 24.—Mailable matter wholly or partly in writing, or so marked as to convey further information than is conveyed by the original print in case of printed matter, or sent in violation of law or regulations touching the inclosure of matter which may be sent at less than letter rates, and all matter on which no different rate is provided by law, subject to letter postage : *Provided*, That book-manuscript and corrected proof, passing between author and publisher, may pass at the rate of printed matter : *And provided*, That the publishers of newspapers and periodicals may print or write upon their publications sent to subscribers the address and the date when the subscription expires, and may inclose receipt for payment and bills for subscription.

Act March 3, 1863, *section* 25.—All matter not enumerated as mailable, and to which no specific rates of postage are assigned, subject to letter postage

Act March 3, 1863, *section* 26.—Double rates of postage to be collected on delivery on any matter on which postage is required to be prepaid at the mailing office : *Provided*, Such matter reaches its destination without such prepayment.

Act March 3, 1863, *section* 27.—Postmaster-General authorized to provide for transmitting unpaid and duly-certified letters of soldiers, sailors, and marines, and all other letters which, from accident, appear to have been deposited without prepayment of postage ; but in all cases of letters not prepaid, except certified soldiers' and naval letters, the same shall be charged with double rates of postage, to be collected on delivery.

Act March 3, 1863, *section* 28.—*That when any writer of a letter on which the postage is prepaid shall indorse in writing or in print thereon upon the outside thereof his name and address with the request that the same be returned to him if not called for or delivered within any number of days (not to exceed 30 days), any such letter shall not be advertised nor treated as a dead letter, but shall be returned direct, etc.*

By virtue of this law special-request envelopes were subsequently introduced.

Act March 3, 1863, *section* 29.—Postage on return dead letters, not registered as valuable, 3 cents for the single rate ; registered as valuable, double rates.

Act March 3, 1863, *section* 30.—Letters may be forwarded from office of destination to any other office, with additional charge of postage therefor.

Act March 3, 1863, *section* 31.—Postmaster-General authorized to pay 2 cents each for all letters conveyed in any vessel not employed in carrying the mail from one place to another in the United States. or from any foreign port to any port within the United States and deposited in the post-office at the port of arrival. If for delivery within the United States, double rates of postage.

Act March 3, 1863, *section* 32.—Provides that fee on registered letters shall not exceed 20 cents.

Act March 3. 1863, *section* 33.—Fixes the maximum standard rate for the single rate of postage on printed matter, and also on miscellaneous matter, at 4 ounces avoirdupois, subject to the exception in the next section.

Act March 3, 1863, *section* 34.—The rate of postage on transient matter of the second class, and on miscellaneous matter of the third class (except circulars and books), shall be 2 cents for each 4 ounces or fraction thereof on one package to one address, to be prepaid by stamps affixed ; double these rates for books. Unsealed circulars, not exceeding three in number, 2 cents, adding one rate for three additional circulars or less number to one address.

Act March 3, 1863, *section* 35.—Postage on matter of the second class, issued once a week or more frequently, from a known office of publication, and sent to regular subscribers, shall be as follows ; For newspapers and other periodical publications, not exceeding 4

ounces, and passing through the mails or post offices of the United States, the rate for each quarter shall be, for publications issued once a week, 5 cents ; twice a week, 10 cents ; three times a week, 15 cents ; six times a week, 30 cents ; seven times a week, 35 cents ; and in that proportion, adding one rate for each issue more frequent than one a week. For weight exceeding 4 ounces and not exceeding 8 ounces, an additional rate, and an additional rate for each additional 4 ounces or fraction thereof ; postage to be prepaid for not less than one quarter nor more than one year, at either the office of mailing or delivery, at the option of the subscriber.

Weekly newspapers, to each subscriber within the county where the same are printed and published, one copy free of postage.

Act March 3, 1863, *section* 36.—Postage on mailable matter of the second class, issued less frequently than once a week, from a known office of publication, and sent to subscribers, shall be as follows : Upon newspapers, magazines, and other periodical publications, not exceeding 4 ounces, passing through the mails or post-offices of the United States, the rate for each such paper or periodical shall be 1 cent, and an additional rate of 1 cent for each additional 4 ounces or fraction thereof : *Provided,* That the Postmaster-General may provide for the transportation of *small* newspapers in packages at the same rate by weight when sent to one address ; postage must be prepaid at office of mailing or delivery, at option of subscriber, for not less than one quarter nor more than one year.

Act March 3, 1863, *section* 37.—Publishers may inclose in their publications to subscribers bills for subscription, and may write or print on their publications or their wrappers name and address of subscribers and the date when subscription expires ; but any other inclosure or addition in writing or in print shall subject the same to letter postage.

Act March 3, 1863, *section* 39.—Postmaster-General authorized to prescribe the manner of wrapping all matter not charged with letter postage nor lawfully franked ; if not so wrapped and secured, the same shall be subject to letter postage.

Act March 3, 1863, *section* 42.—Confers the franking privilege upon and limits it to the following persons : President of the United States ; Vice-President of the United States ; **Franking privilege** the chiefs of the several executive departments ; the heads of bureaus or chief clerks of **modified.** executive departments, to be used only for official communications ; Senators. Representatives, and Delegates in Congress, Secretary of the Senate, and Clerk of the House ; to cover correspondence to and from them, and all printed matter issued by authority of Congress, and all speeches, proceedings, and debates in Congress, and all printed matter sent to them ; to commence with the term for which they are elected, and to expire on the first Monday in December following the expiration of such term ; all official communications to any of the executive departments, by an officer responsible to that department, the envelope to be marked '' official,'' with the signature of the officer thereon ; postmasters. for their official communications to other postmasters, the envelope to be marked '' official,'' with the signature of the postmaster thereon.

Petitions to either house of Congress, free.

The franking privilege granted by this act limited to four ounces, except petitions to Congress, congressional or executive documents, and publications or books published, procured, or purchased by order of either house of Congress, or joint resolution of both Houses, which shall be considered as public documents, and entitled to be franked as such ; and except, also, seeds, cuttings, roots, and scions, the weight of packages to be fixed by regulation of the Postmaster-General.

Act March 3, 1863, *section* 43.— Publishers of periodicals, magazines, and newspapers allowed to exchange their publications free of postage ; confined to a single copy, and not to exceed sixteen ounces in weight.

This act to take effect June 30, 1861.

Act March 3, 1863, *section* 45.—Repeals all acts and parts of acts inconsistent with the provisions of this act.

Act January 22, 1864.—Clothing of wool, cotton, or linen. in packages not exceeding two pounds each, addressed to any non-commissioned officer or private in the Army, may be transmitted by mail at the rate of 8 cents for every four ounces or fraction thereof under regulations of the Postmaster-General ; postage to be prepaid.

Act March 16, 1864.—The franking privilege of the President and Vice-President shall extend to and cover all mail-matter sent from or directed to either of them

Act March 25, 1864, *section* 4.—Mailable matter conveyed by mail westward of the western boundary of Kansas, and eastward of the eastern boundary of California, subject to prepaid letter rates, except newspapers sent from a known office of publication to subscribers, not exceeding one copy to each. and franked matter to and from the intermediate points between the boundaries named, which shall be at the usual rate.

Act June 1, 1864.—Official communications to heads of departments or heads of bureaus or chief clerks or one duly authorized by the Postmaster-General to frank official matter, shall be received and conveyed by mail free of postage, without being indorsed, ''official business,'' or with the name of the writer.

Act May 17, 1864, *section* 1.— *Authorizes the Postmaster-General to establish a uniform*

money-order system at such post-offices as he may deem suitable therefor, and which shall be designated as money-order offices.

    Act May 17, 1864, *section* 3.—Provides that no money order shall be issued for less than $1 or more than $30, and that the fees shall be as follows : Upon an order for $1 and not more than $10, 10 cents ; upon an order exceeding $10 and not exceeding $20, 15 cents ; upon an order exceeding $20, 20 cents.

    Act May 17, 1864, *section* 13.—Provides for the appointment of a Superintendent of the Money-Order System.

    Act June 30, 1864, *section* 1.—The franking privilege to the Commissioner of Internal Revenue extended to letters and documents pertaining to the duties of his office and to receiving free of postage all such letters and documents.

    Act June 30, 1864 *section* 3.—Confers on the Deputy Commissioner of Internal Revenue the privilege of franking all letters and documents pertaining to the office of internal revenue.

    Act July 1, 1864, *section* 8.—The rates of postage on letters and other mailable matter addressed to or received from foreign countries and carried by vessels regularly employed in transportation of the mails shall be as follows : Ten cents for one-half ounce or under, on letters ; two cents on each newspaper, and the established domestic rates on pamphlets, periodicals, and other articles of printed matter ; to be prepaid on matter sent, and collected on matter received ; subject to rates established or to be established by international postal convention.

    Act January 20, 1865.—Amends section 4 of act March 25, 1864, so as to insert in the proviso in said section after the word "newspapers," the words,"periodicals, magazines, and exchanges."

    Act March 3, 1865, *section* 1, *vol.* 13, *page* 515.—Chief clerk authorized for each of the Assistant Postmasters-General, at a salary of $2,000 a year.

    Act March 3, 1865, *section* 1, *vol.* 13, *page* 504.—All domestic letters, except those franked and letters of soldiers and sailors, deposited for mailing wholly unpaid, shall be sent to the Dead-Letter Office ; those paid only in part to be forwarded to destination and unpaid rate collected on delivery.

    Act March 3, 1865, *section* 20, *vol.* 13, *page* 487.—Privilege of franking letters and documents pertaining to the duties of the office of internal revenue, and of receiving free of postage all such letters and documents, is extended to the Commissioner of that office.

Postage on drop letters reduced.

    Act March 3, 1865, *section* 15, *vol.* 13, *page* 507.—Fixes the prepaid postage on drop letters, at all offices except free delivery, at 1 cent

    Act March 3, 1865, *section* 15. *vol.* 13, *page* 507.—System of free delivery shall be established at every place having a population of 50,000.

    Act February 10, 1866.—Confers franking privilege on Mary Lincoln, widow of the late Abraham Lincoln, to cover all letters and packets by mail to and from

    Act June 12, 1866, *section* 1.—Provides for the forwarding of prepaid and free letters at the request of the party addressed, from one post-office to another, without additional postage and the return of dead letters to the writers free of postage.

    Act June 12, 1866, *section* 2.—Request letters to be returned to the writers without additional postage.

    Act June 12, 1866, *section* 3.—Forbids the issue of money-orders for any sum over $50 and fixes the following fees : Upon an order for any sum not exceeding $20, 10 cents ; upon an order exceeding $20, 20 cents.

    Act July 13, 1866, *section* 65.—That all official communications made by assessors to collectors, assessors to assessors, collectors to collectors, collectors to assessors, assessors to assistant assessors, assistant assessors to assessors, collectors to their deputies, or deputy collectors to collectors, may be officially franked by the writers thereof and transmitted by mail free of postage.

    Act July 13, 1866, *section* 66.—Authorizes the Secretary of the Treasury to appoint a special commissioner of the revenue ; and all letters and documents to and from said commissioner relating to the duties and business of his office shall be transmitted by mail free of postage.

    Act July 28, 1866, *section* 13.—Establishes the Bureau of Statistics, authorizes the Secretary of the Treasury to appoint a director to superintend the business of said bureau, and provides for the transmission by mail free of postage of all letters and documents to and from him relating to the business of his office.

    Act March 2, 1868.—The adjutants-general of the States and Territories authorized to transmit by mail free of postage any medals, certificates of thanks, or other testimonials awarded or that may be awarded by the legislatures of said States and Territories, to the soldiers thereof, under regulations to be prescribed by the Postmaster-General.

    Act March 9, 1868, *section* 3.—Letters and documents to and from the Congressional Printer relating to the business of his office shall be transmittted by mail free of postage, under regulations to be prescribed by the Postmaster-General.

    Act June 25, 1868.—That the operations of section 4, act of March 25, 1864, shall cease on and after September 30, 1868.

Money order system.

Act July 27, 1868, *section* 1.—Prepaid letters having the name and address of the writer in writing or in print on the outside, after remaining uncalled for at the post-office to which directed 30 days, or the time the writer may direct, shall be returned to the writer without additional postage.

Act July 27, 1868, *section* 2.—Changes the fee on money-orders as follows : For any sum not exceeding $20, 10 cents ; for any sum exceeding $20 and not exceeding $30, 15 cents ; for any sum exceeding $30 and not exceeding $40, 20 cents ; for any sum exceeding $40 and not exceeding $50, 25 cents.

Act July 27, 1868, *section* 8.—Authorizes the Postmaster-General to appoint a superintendent of foreign mails.

Act July 27, 1868, *section* 3.—Weekly newspapers sent to subscribers in the county where printed and published, to be delivered free of postage when deposited in the office nearest the office of publication ; but they shall not be distributed by letter-carriers unless postage is prepaid thereon at the rate of 5 cents per quarter for not less than one quarter nor more than one year, at the office of mailing or delivery, at the option of the subscriber.

Act March 1, 1869.—Requires the franking privilege to be exercised by persons entitled to it by the written autograph signature upon the matter franked ; letters or other mail-matter not thus franked to be charged with postage.

Act July 8, 1870, *section* 8.—Provides that the Commissioner of Patents may send and receive by mail free of postage letters, printed matter, and packages relating to the business of his office, including Patent-Office Reports.

Act July 8, 1870, *section* 95.—Any copyright book or other article may be sent to the Librarian of Congress by mail free of postage : *Provided,* The words "copyright matter" are plainly written or printed on the outside of the package.

Act June 1, 1872, *section* 4.—Repeals section 12, act March 3, 1847, and section 8, act March 3, 1851, so far as said sections provide for specific permanent appropriations for carrying free matter in the mails for the several departments and members of Congress ; hereafter payment for carrying such matter shall be made out of the annual appropriations

Act June 8, 1872, *section* 30.—Authorizes the Postmaster-General to establish a blank agency for the Post-Office Department, to be located at Washington, D. C.

Act June 8, 1872, *section* 99.—The rate of postage on newspapers (excepting weeklies), periodicals not exceeding 2 ounces in weight, and circulars, when deposited in a letter-carrier office for delivery by the office or its carriers, shall be uniform at 1 cent each ; but periodicals weighing more than 2 ounces shall be subject to a postage of 2 cents each ; these rates to be prepaid by stamps.

Act June 8, 1872, *section* 107.—Provides that no money-order shall be issued for more than $50. and establishes the following fees : For any amount not exceeding $10, 5 cents ; for any amount exceeding $10 and not exceeding $20, 10 cents ; for any amount exceeding $20 and not exceeding $30, 15 cents ; for any amount exceeding $30 and not exceeding $40, 20 cents ; for any amount exceeding $40, 25 cents.

Act June 8, 1872, *section* 127.—Letters upon the official business of the Post-Office Department may be registered free of charge and pass by mail free of charge.

Act June 8, 1872, *section* 127.—Provides that the fee for registering valuable letters shall not exceed 20 cents in addition to the regular postage, and must be prepaid. Letters upon official business of the Post-Office Department may be registered free of charge and pass through the mails free of charge.

Three classes of mailable matter. *Act June* 8, 1872, *section* 130.—Divides mailable matter into three classes : First class, letters ; second class, regular printed matter ; third class, miscellaneous matter.

Act June 8, 1872, *section* 131.—Mailable matter of the first class shall embrace all correspondence wholly or partly in writing, except book manuscript and corrected proofs passing between authors and publishers

Act June 8, 1872, *section* 132.—Second class, to embrace all matter exclusively in print and regularly issued at stated periods from a known office of publication, without addition by writing, mark, or sign.

Act June 8, 1872, *section* 133.—Third class, to embrace all other mailable matter.

Matter of this class except books and other printed matter, book-manuscripts, proof-sheets and corrected proof-sheets, shall not exceed 12 ounces in weight. Samples of metals, ores, and mineralogical specimens, limited to 12 ounces.

Act June 8, 1872, *section* 134.—Limits weight of packages to 4 pounds, except books published or circulated by order of Congress.

Act June 8, 1872, *section* 136.—Matter not charged with letter postage, nor lawfully franked. subject to letter postage, unless wrapped in accordance with regulations of the Postmaster-General.

Act June 8, 1872, *section* 141.—Publishers of newspapers or periodicals may print or write upon their publications to regular subscribers the address, the date when the subscription expires, and may inclose therein bills and receipts for subscription, without extra postage.

Act June 8, 1872, *section* 142.—To inclose or conceal any letter, memorandum, or other thing in any mail matter not charged with letter-postage, or to write thereon, subjects such matter to letter-postage.

Act June 8, 1872, *section* 150.—Requires that the postage on all mail-matter, except as hereinafter provided, must be prepaid at the time of mailing.

Act June 8, 1872, *section* 151.—Permits mail-matter on which one full rate has been prepaid to be forwarded to destination, and the unpaid rate collected on delivery.

Act June 8, 1872, *section* 152.—Mail-matter on which postage is required to be pre-paid, reaching its destination, by inadvertence, without such prepayment, shall be subject to double the prepaid rates.

Act June 8, 1872, *section* 156.—That on all matter wholly or partly in writing, except book-manuscripts and corrected proofs passing between author and publisher, and local drop letters ; on all printed matter, so marked as to convey any other information than is conveyed by the original print, except the correction of a mere typographical error ; on all matter sent in violation of law or regulations respecting inclosures ; and on all matter to which no specific rate of postage is assigned, postage shall be 3 cents the half ounce or fraction thereof.

Act June 8, 1872, *section* 157.—Fixes the postage on drop or local letters at letter-carrier offices at 2 cents the half ounce or fraction thereof, and 1 cent the half ounce or fraction thereof at all other offices.

Act June 8, 1872, *section* 158.—Quarterly postage on newspapers and other periodical publications, not exceeding 4 ounces in weight, sent to subscribers, shall be at the following rates : On publications issued less frequently than once a week, 1 cent for each issue ; issued once a week, 5 cents ; and 5 cents additional for each issue more frequent than once a week; an additional rate shall be charged for each additional 4 ounces or fraction thereof.

Act June 8, 1872, *section* 160.—Small newspapers issued less frequently than once a week, in packages to one address, to subscribers, 1 cent for each 4 ounces or fraction thereof.

Act June 8, 1872, *section* 161.—Regular dealers in newspapers and periodicals may receive and transmit by mail such quantities of either as they may require, and pay the post-age as received, at the same rates as subscribers who pay quarterly in advance.

Act June 8, 1872, *section* 163.—Postage on mailable matter of the third class shall be at the rate of 1 cent for each 2 ounces or fraction thereof, except that double these rates shall be charged for books, samples of metals, ores, minerals, and merchandise.

Act June 8, 1864, *section* 164.—Packages of woolen, cotton, or linen clothing, in pack-ages not exceeding 2 pounds, may be sent by mail to any non-commissioned officer or private in the army, if prepaid, 1 cent each ounce or fraction thereof.

Act June 8, 1872, *section* 166.—Letters conveyed in vessels not regularly employed in carrying the mail shall, if for delivery in the United States, be rated with double postage.

Act June 8, 1872, *section* 170 —*Provides for the issue and transmission by mail of postal-cards at 1 cent each.*   Postal cards authorized.

Act June 8, 1872, *section* 180.—Confers the franking privilege upon and limits it to the following named persons :

First.   The President, by himself or private secretary, to cover all mail-matter.

Second.   Vice-President, to cover all mail-matter.

Third.   The chiefs of the several executive departments.

Fourth.   Senators, Representatives, Delegates. Secretary of the Senate, and Clerk of the House—to cover their correspondence, all printed matter issued by authority of Congress, and all speeches, proceedings, and debates in Congress.

Fifth.   Such heads of bureaus or chief clerks as the Postmaster-General may designate, to cover official communications only.

Sixth.   Postmasters, to cover official communications to other postmasters only.

Written autograph signatures, of all persons entitled to frank, required ; mail-matter not thus franked to be charged with postage.

Act June 8, 1872, *section* 181.—The franking privilege of Senators, Representatives, Delegates, Secretary of the Senate, and Clerk of the House, to commence with the term for which they are elected and to expire the first Monday in December following such term.

Act June 8, 1872, *section* 182.—Books or publications procured or published by order of Congress, to be public documents, and may be franked as such.

Act June 8, 1872, *section* 183.—Maximum weight for franked and free matter shall be 4 pounds, except petitions to Congress, congressional and executive public documents, periodical publications interchanged between publishers, and packages of seeds, cuttings, roots, and scions, the weight of which latter may be fixed by the Postmaster-General.

Act June 8, 1872, *section* 184.—*Free mail-matter.*—The following mail-matter shall be allowed to pass free in the mail :

First.   All mail-matter sent to the President or Vice-President.

Second.   Official communications to chiefs, heads of bureaus, chief clerks, or franking-officer of any of the executive departments.

Third.   Letters and printed matter sent to Senators, Representatives, Delegates, Secretary of the Senate, and Clerk of the House.

Fourth.   Petitions to Congress.

Fifth.   Copyright matter to the Librarian of Congress, if marked " copyright mat-ter."

Sixth. Publications sent and received by the Smithsonian Institution, if marked "Smithsonian exchange."

Seventh Newspapers, periodicals, and magazines exchanged between publishers, not exceeding 16 ounces in weight.

Eighth. Weekly newspapers, one copy to each subscriber within the county where the same is printed and published.

Ninth. Notice to the publishers of the refusal or neglect of subscribers to take newspapers, magazines, or other periodicals from the post-office.

Tenth. Dead-letters returned to the writers.

Eleventh. Medals, certificates of thanks, or other testimonials awarded by the legislatures of States and Territories to the soldiers thereof.

Act June 8, 1872, *section* 185.—All mail-matter to or from Mary Lincoln, widow of late President Lincoln.

Act June 8, 1872, *section* 199.—Prepaid and free letters shall be forwarded from one post-office to another at request of the person addressed, without additional charge for postage.

Act January 9, 1873.—Amends section 133 of act of June 8, 1872, so as to authorize the transmission by mail of packages of seeds, cuttings, bulbs, roots. and scions, of any weight. For each package not exceeding 4 pounds, the postage shall be 1 cent for each 2 ounces or fraction of an ounce ; to be prepaid in full.

Act January 31, 1873.—Abolishes the franking privilege from and after July 1, 1873.

Act March 3, 1873.—Repeals, from and after June 30, 1873, all laws and parts of laws permitting the transmission by mail of any free matter whatever.

Official stamps authorized. *Act March* 3, 1873.—*Authorizes the use of official postage stamps and stamped envelopes for payment of postage on official matter of executive departments.*

Act March 3, 1873, *section* 1, *volume* 17, *page* 486.—Salary of the Postmaster-General increased to $10,000 per annum.

Act January 20, 1874.—Reduces the salary of the Postmaster-General to $8,000.

Newspaper and periodical rates. *Act June* 23, 1874, *section* 5.—On and after January 1, 1875, on all newspapers and periodical publications mailed from a known office of publication or news agency, and addressed to regular subscribers or news agents, postage shall be charged at the following rates : On newspapers and periodical publications issued weekly and more frequently, 2 cents a pound or fraction thereof ; and on those issued less frequently than once a week, 3 cents a pound or fraction thereof : *Provided*, That nothing in this act shall be held to change section 99 of the act of June 8, 1872.

Newspaper and periodical stamps were introduced under this act.

Act June 23, 1874, *section* 7.—Newspapers, one copy to each subscriber residing in the county where same are printed in whole or in part, and published, shall go free in the mails ; but they shall not be delivered at letter-carrier offices or be distributed by carriers unless postage is paid thereon.

Act June 23, 1874, *section* 8.—Mailable matter of the third class referred to in section 133 of act of June 8, 1872, may weigh not exceeding 4 pounds to each package, and postage shall be charged thereon at the rate of 1 cent for each 2 ounces or fraction thereof.

Act June 23, 1874, *section* 13 —Fixes the postage on public documents mailed by any member of Congress, the President or head of any executive department, at 10 cents for each bound volume, and unbound documents the same rate as that on newspapers mailed from a known office of publication to subscribers ; and the postage on the daily Congressional Record, mailed from the city of Washington as transient matter, at 1 cent.

Act March 3, 1875, *section* 3.—Extends the provisions of section 13 of act of June 23, 1874, to ex-Members of Congress and ex-Delegates, for nine months after the expiration of their terms; and postage on public documents mailed by them shall be as provided in such section.

Act March 3, 1875, *section* 5.—The Congressional Record, or any part thereof, or speeches or reports therein, shall, under the frank of a Member or Delegate, written by himself, be carried in the mail free of postage ; and public documents printed or ordered to be printed for the use of either house of Congress may pass free by mail upon the frank of any Member or Delegate of the present Congress, written by himself, until the first day of December, 1875.

Act March 3, 1875, *section* 7.—Seeds transmitted by the Commissioner of Agriculture, or by any Member or Delegate receiving them for distribution from said department, together with the Agricultural Reports, shall pass free in the mails under regulations of the Postmaster-General ; and the provisions of this section shall apply to ex-Members and ex-Delegates for the period of nine months after the expiration of their term.

Act March 3, 1875, *volume* 18, *page* 377.—Amends section 8 of act of June 23, 1874, by inserting the word "ounce" in lieu of the words "two ounces."

Act July 12, *section* 15, *volume* 19, *page* 82.—Rates on all printed matter of the third class, except unsealed circulars, fixed at 1 cent for 2 ounces. Permits limited inscriptions and addresses on third-class matter.

Penalty envelopes. *Act March* 3, 1877, *sections* 5 and 6, *volume* 19, *page* 335.—Provides for official penalty envelopes and free transmission of same in mails when sent by executive departments and containing inclosures relating to government business.

Act March 3, 1879, *section* 29, *volume* 20, *page* 362.—The provisions of the preceding act extended to the Smithsonian Institution and to all government officers.

Act March 3, 1879, *sections* 7-27, *volume* 20, *pages* 358-362. — General act repealing all former laws relating to classification of mail-matter and rates of postages. Makes four classes of mail-matter, to wit : First-class, written matter, at 3 cents each half ounce ; second class, periodical publications regularly issued for general information, at 2 cents per pound, including sample copies ; third class, miscellaneous printed matter, at 1 cent for each 2 ounces ; and fourth class, merchandise, all matter not included in the other three classes, at 1 cent each ounce. Liberalizes the provisions of former laws respecting written inscriptions on printed matter, and defines printed matter generally.

Act March 3, 1879, *section* 32, *volume* 20, *page* 362.—Authorizes the Postmaster-General to introduce letter-sheet envelopes and double postal-cards.

Act March 3, 1883, *section* 1, *volume* 22, *page* 455.—Reduces the postage on first-class matter to 2 cents a half ounce on and after October 1, 1883. **Two cent rate on first-class matter.**

Act March 3, 1883, *section* 1, *volume* 22, *page* 526.—The Postmaster-General may authorize postmasters at money order offices to issue money-orders for small sums under $4, without corresponding advices, to be designated as "*postal notes*," the fee therefor to be 3 cents, and the note to be payable to bearer. **Postal notes.**

Act March 3, 1883, *section* 3, *volume* 22, *page* 527.—Forbids the issue of a money-order for more than $100, and fixes the fees as follows : For any sum not exceeding $10, 8 cents ; for any sum exceeding $15, 10 cents ; for any sum exceeding $15 and not exceeding $30, 15 cents ; for any sum exceeding $30 and not exceeding $40, 20 cents ; for any sum exceeding $40 and not exceeding $50, 25 cents ; for any sum exceeding $50 and not exceeding $60, 30 cents ; for any sum exceeding $60 and not exceeding $70, 35 cents ; for any sum exceeding $70 and not exceeding $80, 40 cents ; for any sum exceeding $80 and not exceeding $100, 45 cents.

Act June 9, 1884, *volume* 23, *page* 40 —Rate of postage on newspapers and periodicals sent by other than the publishers fixed at 1 cent for every 4 ounces or fraction thereof.

Act March 3, 1885 *section* 1, *volume* 23, *page* 387.—Reduces postage on first-class matter to 2 cents an ounce or fraction thereof ; the postage on drop letters to be 2 cents an ounce or fraction thereof, including delivery at letter-carrier offices, and 1 cent at non-carrier offices. Reduces the postage on second-class matter sent by publishers to 1 cent a pound or fraction thereof. **Rates reduced.**

Act March 5, 1885, *section* 3, *volume* 23, *page* 387.—*Special-delivery system authorized at all places having a population of 4,000 or more.* Special stamps authorized to secure immediate delivery, which, on arrival of letters at such place, is to be performed by special messengers at a fee of 8 cents for each letter. **Special delivery system authorized.**

Act June 29, 1886, *section* 1, *volume* 24, *page* 86.—Reduces the fee on domestic money-orders for less than $5, from 8 cents to 5 cents.

Act August 4, 1886, *section* 1, *volume* 24, *page* 220 —Special-delivery system extended to all post-offices.

Act January 3, 1887, *section* 1, *volume* 24, *page* 355.—Extends the free-delivery service to all cities having not less than 10,000 inhabitants, or at any post-office the gross annual revenue of which is $10,000.

Act March 3, 1887, *section* 1, *volume* 24, *page* 354.—Authorizes the Postmaster-General to designate other than money-order offices to issue postal-notes for sums under $5, fee 3 cents.

Act July 24, 1888.—Rate of postage on seeds, scions, bulbs, cuttings, roots, and plants reduced to 1 cent for every 2 ounces or fraction thereof.

ADDENDA.

To the bisected stamps of the 1851-55 issue, which are described on pages 70 and 71, another variety must be added. Mr. H. B. Phillips has found a cover bearing three copies of the 3 cent stamp and one-third of another copy, used as 10 cents. The cover is postmarked "Wrentham, Mass., June 4," but the year is missing, as is usual in postmarks of that period. The letter is addressed to a gentleman in San Francisco, from whose correspondence Mr. Phillips obtained it.

1851-55.
Bisected three cent stamps.

On pages 130 and 134, will be found a paragraph referring to the stamps of the Continental Bank Note Co. with the grill. Having obtained some additional information about these stamps, I published a short article in the *American Journal of Philately*, for July, 1901, from which I quote :

1873.
Stamps with the grill.

"A small number of these grilled stamps has recently been found in the possession of a gentleman who obtained them from the Post Office Department at Washington At the same time a few additional facts about the stamps have been learned

In June, 1876, a stamp cleaning case was tried in the courts. It was attended by the usual flurry among officials and a revival of the discussion of preventatives of such frauds. The Continental Bank Note Co., who then held the contract for the manufacture of postage stamps, suggested putting the grill into use once more. They were ordered to prepare 1,000 copies of each value then current. As they had not the requisite machinery for making the grill roller, they entrusted the work to Campbell & Watt, a firm of machinists of New York City. To this we may attribute the small differences between this grill and those of the National Bank Note Co. The order was duly executed and perhaps slightly exceeded, since it included the 2, 7, 12 and 24 cents of the 1873 series, which had ceased to be issued to the public. The grilled stamps were forwarded to Washington and put into circulation ; but the Continental Bank Note Co. did not receive any further orders to apply the patent."

The complete series of these stamps has not yet been found by collectors, but, in addition to the varieties listed on page 137, we now know the following :

May 1st, 1873	10c brown
June, 1875	2c scarlet vermilion
	5c dark blue

1801.
Inverted medallions.   Of the bicolored series, issued in 1901 (described on pages 200 and 201), the one, two and four cents have been found with the central medallion inverted. The five and ten cents are also said to exist in this condition but the report lacks confirmation.

Reprints, etc.
Erroring the sur-
charge.   On page 357 is given a list of official stamps surcharged, in error, " SEPCIMEN " instead of " SPECIMEN." To this list should be added the 10 cents of the Post Office Department.

ERRATA.

Page 66, line 14. For "March 30th, 1855," read : "March 3rd, 1855."

" 67–74, inclusive. The headline should read : "Issues of 1851–55," instead of "Issues of 1851–57."

" 106, line 29. For "1861," read : "1867."

" 194, opposite line 32. Insert the marginal note : "Deliveries to Post-masters."

361, line 40. For "June 16th, 1884," read : "July 16th, 1884."

INDEX.

	PAGE.
Addenda	401
Agriculture, Goddess of	295
" The department of	257, 259
" reprints	357
Alexandria, Va.	12
Allen, Phineas	39
America, Figure of	173, 295, 320
American Bank Note Co.	144
Plates of the	145
Contract awarded to	153
Contract for Columbian series modified	177
Special printing of Official stamps by	357
Annapolis, Va.	13
handstamps	14
Appendix	375
Astraea, Vignette of	295
Automobile	200
Balboa	173
Baloca, R.—" Columbus Announcing his Discovery "	173
Baltimore, Md.	15
Counterfeit	16
Carriers' Stamps	207
Beckman, John C.	215
Stamps of	221
Bisected Stamps :	
1851-57 issue	70, 71, 401
1869 issue	114
1890 issue	165
Post Office department	267
Postage due	341, 342
Books of stamps	187
Boscawen, N. H.	20
Boston Carriers' stamps	211
U. S. Penny Post	211
Penny Post	212
Penny Post Paid	212
Hill's Post	212
Brattleboro, Vt.	21
An eleventh variety of	21
Bridge at Niagara Falls	200
Bridge, Mississippi River	102
Brown & McGill, Stamps of	223
Brozik,—" Columbus Soliciting Aid "	173
Bryan, Daniel	12

	PAGE
Buchanan, James M.	15
Buffalo ", " Indian Hunting	192
Bureau of Engraving and Printing	179
Contract with	179
Canal Locks at Saulte Sainte Marie	200
Capped numerals	164
Carrier service, Local posts and the	202
" " rates	203
" " Review of the	203
" " Cities which had	206
" Carriers' Dispatch " stamps	207, 209
Carriers' stamp, First	9
The Franklin	245
reprints	355
The Eagle	248
reprints	355
Carriers' stamps, issue of 1851	66
origin of the various	202
official and semi-official	206
date of use	206
counterfeits	221
Baltimore	207
Boston	211
Charleston	215
Louisville	222
New York	225
Philadelphia	233
Wells, Fargo & Co.'s Pony Express	238
Reprints :	355
paper	355
color	355
impression	355
quantities sold	356
Cattle in Storm ", " Western	102
Ceres, Vignette of	295
Cerrachi,—Head of Franklin, after bust by	109
Profile bust of Thomas Jefferson	163
Charleston Carriers' stamps :	215
John H. Honour stamps	216
E. J. Kingman "	219
Joseph G. Martin "	220
John F. Steinmeyer "	220
John C. Beckman "	221
Counterfeits	221

	PAGE.
Chubbuck, Thomas	22
City Despatch	230
City Despatch Post, Greig's	225
" " New York	225
" " United States	228
Clay, Henry	122, 163
Clio	296
Cog wheel (Fletcher) punch	134
Collecting, An official view of stamp	171
Collectors, Purchases by stamp dealers and	177
Columbian series, (see also "Issue of 1893")	170
purchases of, by stamp dealers and collectors	177
Columbus	173
"Columbus in Sight of Land"	172
"Landing of	109, 172
"Flagship of	173
"Fleet of	173
Soliciting Aid of Isabella"	173
Welcomed at Barcelona"	173
Restored to Favor"	173
Presenting Natives"	173
Announcing his Discovery"	173
at La Rabida"	173
"Recall of	173
in Chains"	173
Describing Third Voyage"	173
Commerce	296
Continental Bank Note Co.:	144
consolidated with American Bank Note Co.	144
plates of the, used for the 1879 issue	145
Contract awarded to American Bank Note Co.	153
requiring printing by steam	153
with Bureau of Engraving and Printing	179
Counterfeiting grills, Temptations to	105
Counterfeits :	
Baltimore, Md.	16
Providence, R. I.	43
St. Louis, Mo.	50
grills, 1869 issue	117
" 1870 issue	123
two cent stamp, 1894-95 issue	189
Carrier's stamps, Charleston	221
" " Louisville	223
" " New York	230
" " Philadelphia	234
Newspaper stamps, 1865	293
Crawford,—Figure of "America"	295, 320
Criticism on reprinting, Journalistic	343
Cuba, Stamps surcharged for	197
Date of issue ;—see under each issue	
Dead letter office, Seal for letters opened in the	369
"Declaration of Independence"	110
Defective grills, (1870)	123
Degrain, Munoz—"Isabella Pledging her Jewels"	173
Deliveries to postmasters ;—see under each issue	
Delivery stamps, special	250
Department, State	256-288

	PAGE.
Department, Executive	256-288
" Treasury	256-288
" War	256-288
" Navy	256-288
" Post Office	256-288
" Interior	256-288
" Justice	256-288
" Agriculture	256-288
Department stamps	256
" reprints	356
Departments, Deliveries of stamps to	279
Designs ;—see under each issue	
Despatch, City	230
" Post Office	207, 208
Despatch Post, Greig's City	225
" New York City	225
" United States City	228
Destroyed, Plates of all obsolete issues	364
" remainders, 1873-75 issue	143
" stamps, 1867 issue	103
" unsold stamps, 1893 issue	177
Destruction of the grill rollers	124
" of unissued Official stamps	286
Die, Making of	59
Dies, Retouched and re-engraved, 1881-2 issue	147
Dispatch, Carriers'	207, 209
" Government City	209
Distributing stamps to postmasters, methods of, (1847)	62
Dodge,—Portrait of Andrew Jackson by	90
Double paper, Stamps on :	
1869 issue	114
1870 issue	123
1873-75 issue	134, 135
1894-95 issue	182
"Douglas patent" stamps	148
Due stamp, Post Office stamp used as a	267
Due stamps, Postage ;—see Postage Due stamps	
Eagle	222, 223, 249
Eagle Carriers' stamp, The	248
" reprints of	355
Eagle on shield	109, 110
Early postal arrangements	5
" postal laws	6
" rates of postage	6
Eight cents :	
1890	163
1893	172, 173
1898	192
1901	200
Newspaper	295
Newspaper reprint	361
Eighty-four cents :	
Newspaper	295
Newspaper reprint	362
Eleventh variety of Brattleboro, Vt., Discovery of an	25
Emigration", "Hardships of	192
Envelopes, Baltimore	18
" New Haven	29
" New York	36
" Washington	52
" of 1857 not invalid	82
" Official, authorized	257
" Penalty, authorized	277

	PAGE.
Errata	404
Error of surcharge, Official stamps	356, 402
Executive, The	257, 259
special printing of	357
Express, Fast, (train)	200
" stamps, Wells, Fargo & Co.'s Pony	238
"Eye Type" stamps	207
"Farming in the West"	192
"Fast Express"	200
"Fast Lake Navigation"	200
"Fast Ocean Navigation"	200
Ferdinand	173
Find, The Louisville	50
Fifteen cents :	
1861–66, reprint	350
1866	92
1867	102
1867, blackish purple	103
1869	109
1869, types of the	110
1869, inverted medallion	112
1869, reprint	351
1870	122
1873–75, secret mark	132
1873–75, reprint	352
1873–75, reprint of 1880	353
1890	163
1893	173
Fifty cents :	
1893	173
1894–95	181
1898	192
Newspaper, 1895	320
Postage due, 1879	330
Postage due, 1879, special printing	364
Postage due, 1894–95	337
Fifty dollars :	
Newspaper	320
Newspaper, reprint	363
Fireside, Goddess of the	296
First carriers' stamp	9
" local stamp	9
" stamps authorized	59
" " sold	62
Fisher, Maturin L.	54
Five cents :	
1847	60
1847, reprints	346
1851–55	67
1851–57, types of	69
1857, reprints	348
1857–60 types of	76
1861	84, 89
1861, reprint	349
1867, grilled all over	100
1867	101
1873–75	132, 149
1873–75, reprint	352
1873–75, reprint of 1880	353
1882	150
1882, reprint	354
1888	154
1888 on pink paper	155
1890	163
1893	173

	PAGE.
Five cents :	
1898	192
1901	200
Newspaper, 1865	289
Newspaper, 1865, reprints	360
Newspaper, 1895	320
Postage due, 1879	330
Postage due, 1879, reprints	364
Postage due, 1894–95	337
Five dollars :	
1893	173
1894–95	181
State department	259
Newspaper, 1895	320
Newspaper, 1895, reprint	363
"Flagship of Columbus"	173
"Fleet of Columbus"	173
Fletcher punch ("cog wheel')	134
Forty-eight cents :	
Newspaper	295
Newspaper, reprint	362
Forty-eight dollars :	
Newspaper	296
Newspaper, reprint	362
Four cents :	
1883	151
1883, reprint	354
1888	154
1890	162
1893	173
1893, error of color	174
1898	192
1901	200
1901, inverted medallion	402
Newspaper	295
Newspaper, reprint	361
Four dollars :	
1893	173
"Francis" patent	91
Franking	256
" privilege (1845)	57
" " abolished	257
" " Abolition of, causes dissatisfaction	276
" " extended	278
Franklin, Benjamin 60, 66, 76, 83, 109, 121, 153, 166, 244, 290	
Franklin Carriers' stamp, The	244
reprints	355
"Fremont on the Rocky Mountains"	192
Gardner, Col. Chas. K.	52
Garfield, James A.	150, 163
"Garter" stamp	240
" " Counterfeits of the	241
Goddess of Agriculture	295
" of Peace	296
" of the Fireside	296
" of Victory	296
" of Wisdom	296
" of Youth	296
Government Issues	57
Grafflin's local post	207
Grant, U. S.	163
Gravures, Premières, 1861 issue	85
Gray surfaced paper, Post Office department	267

PAGE.

Gregori, Luigi ;—"Columbus presenting
     Natives"   173
Greig's City Despatch Post   225
Greig's Post   9
Grill roller, Process of making the   98
   " rollers, Destruction of the   124
   " Sizes of the, 1869 issue   111
Grilling stamps, Patent for   97
   "   Oddities of   99
Grills, Counterfeit 1870   123
   " counterfeiting, Temptations to   105
   " Defective 1870   123
   " genuine, Characteristics of   106
   " Issue of 1870   123
   " Issue of 1873   133, 401
   " Marginal   99
   " Oddities of   99
   " Points up and points down   99
   " Sizes of   98
Guam, Stamps surcharged for   197, 255
Guide marks, Platemaker's   115
Gum ;—see " Gum " under each issue

Handstamps, Annapolis, Va.   14
Hamilton, Alexander   122
"Hardships of Emigration "   192
Heaton, A. G ,—"Recall of Columbus"   173
         " Hardships of Emigra-
         tion "   192
Hebe   296
Hill's Post   213
Historical Notes   5
Honour, John H.   215
        Stamps of   216
" Horseman " stamps   207
Houdon, Portrait of Washington after
               66, 121, 162

Imperforate and part perforate stamps 71, 78
Imprints ;—see " Plates and Imprints "
     under each issue
" Indian Hunting Buffalo"   192
Indian maiden   296
Initials on stamps, (New York)   34
   "   Platemen's   253
Inman, Portrait of John Marshall by   181
Interior department, The   257, 259
       Special printing   357
Introductory   3
Invalid, Authority to declare stamps   82
     Envelopes of 1857 not declared   82
Inverted medallions, issue of 1869   112
   "   "   issue of 1901   402
   "   "   State department   267
"I. R.", Stamps surcharged   197
Isabella ", " Columbus soliciting aid of 173
" Isabella Pledging her Jewels"   173
Isabella, Portrait of   173
Issue, date of ;—see under each issue
Issue of 1847 :
     contractors   59
     plates   61
     designs   60
     paper   61
     gum   61
     reference list   61
     orders sent to contractors   63
     stamps unsold   63

PAGE.

Reprints of the :   346
     dies and plates   347
     paper   347
     reference list   347
     quantities sold   347
Issue of 1851-57 :   65
     date of issue   66
     carriers' stamps   66
     designs and colors   66
     sizes   67
     types   67
     paper   69
     reference list   70
     bisected stamps   70, 71, 401
     plates   72
     imprints   72
     plate numbers   72
     statistics   73, 74
     remainders   83
Issue of 1857-60 :   75
     first delivery   75
     designs and colors   75
     sizes   76
     paper   76
     reference list   77
     imperforate and part perforate   78
     shades   78
     changelings   78
     plates and imprints   78
     plate numbers   79
     statistics   79
     redemption of the stamps of
       the   81
     invalid, Authority to declare   82
     Reprints of the :   348
       plates   348
       types   348
       paper and perforation   348
       reference list   348
       quantities sold   349
Issues of 1861-66   81
Issue of 1861 :   81
     historical   81
     Announcement of   81
     report of Postmaster General   82
     designs   83
     sizes   85
     premières gravures   85
     alterations in   85
     second series   86
     types of the one cent   86
     "   "   " three cents   86
     "   "   " five cents   87
     "   "   " ten cents   87
     "   "   " twelve cents   87
     "   "   " ninety cents   87
     reference list   88
     color varieties   88, 89
     plates and imprints   91
     plate numbers   92
     statistics   93
     specimen stamps   93
     Reprints of the :   349
       plates   349
       paper   349
       perforation and gum   349
       reference list   349
       quantities sold   350

	PAGE.
Issue of 1863 :	90
design	90
reference list	90, 91
on laid paper	91
" Francis " patent	91
reference list	93
statistics	93, 95
two cents,	90
Issue of 1866 :	91
registration	91
fifteen cents	92
design	92
reference list	92
statistics	94, 96
Issue of 1867 :	97, 118
patent for grilling stamps	97
sizes of grills	98
marginal grills	99
date of issue	100
grilled all over	100
paper	100
reference list	101
statistics	103
stamps destroyed	103
plates	104
plate numbers	104
again brought into use	118
Issue of 1869 :	108
historical	108
date of issue	108
original designs	109
designs and colors	109
sizes	110
types of the fifteen cents	110
sizes of the grill	111
reference list	111
inverted medallions	112
varieties without grill	114
on double paper	115
plate maker's guide marks	115
plates	115
imprints and plate numbers	115
marginal marks	115
plate numbers	116
statistics of manufacture	116
deliveries to postmasters	117
counterfeits	117
Reprints of the :	350
characteristics	350
plates	350
plate numbers	350
reference list	351
one cent stamp on soft paper	351
quantities sold	351
Issue of 1870 :	119
historical	119
announcement of issue	119
date of issue	120
the seven cent stamp	120
designs	121
on double paper	123
gum	123
paper	123
grills	123
counterfeit grills	123
reference list of grills	124
reference list of colors	124

	PAGE.
plates	126
plate numbers	127
statistics of manufacture	127
deliveries to postmasters	128
Reprints of the :	351
dates of delivery	351
characteristics	352
reference list	352
plates	352
printing by American Bank Note Co. (1880)	352
characteristics	353
reference list	353
plates	353
quantities sold	353
Issue of 1873-75 :	130
historical	130
secret marks	130
plates, new	131
secret marks, description of	131
five cent stamp announced	132
three denominations discontinued	133
five cent stamp, design of	133
grills	133, 401
Fletcher, or cog wheel, punch	134
chemical paper	134
double paper	134
starched paper	135
regular papers	135
ribbed paper	136
gum	136
reference list	137
plates	138
plate numbers	139
printings on steam press	139
plates used on steam press	140
statistics of manufacture	140
deliveries to postmasters	141
remainders destroyed	143
Issue of 1879 :	144
reference list	144
Continental B. N. Co.'s plates used	145
American B. N. Co.'s plates	145
plate numbers	145
deliveries to postmasters	156
Issues of 1881-82	147
retouched and re-engraved dies	147
description of altered dies	147
dates of issue	148
" Douglas patent " stamps	148
reference list	148
plate numbers	149
serial letters	149
deliveries to postmasters	156
Issue of April 10th, 1882	149
historical	149
design	150
varieties of the five cents	150
date of issue	150
reference list	151
deliveries to postmasters	157
Reprints of the :	354
quantity sold	354
characteristics	354
plates	354

	PAGE.
Issue of October 1, 1883 :	151
historical	151
designs	151
date of issue	152
reference list	152
plate numbers	152
laid paper	152
specimen stamps	152
deliveries to postmasters	157
Reprints of the :	354
date of delivery	354
characteristics	354
quantities sold	355
Issue of June 15, 1887 :	153
design	153
reference list	154
plate numbers	154
deliveries to postmasters	158
Issue of 1887–88 :	154
changes in colors	154
reference list	154
plate numbers	155
deliveries to postmasters	157
Issue of 1890 :	160
historical	160
sample stamps in the proposed	
colors	161
dates of issue	162
designs and colors	162
paper, etc	163
capped numerals	164
reference list	164
bisected stamps	165
proofs	165
plates	165
plate numbers	165
deliveries to postmasters	167
Issue of 1893 :	170
historical	170
negotiations with the con-	
tractors	171, 177
the eight cent stamp	172
designs and colors	172
paper, gum, etc	173
reference list	173
varieties	174
error of color	174
plates	174
plate numbers	174
deliveries to postmasters	175
proofs	176
purchases by stamp dealers and	
collectors	177
unsold stamps withdrawn and	
destroyed	177
Issue of 1894–95 :	179
history of the contract	179
transfer of stamps	180
transfer of dies, rolls and plates	180
date of issue	180
additions to the designs	180
varieties of the triangle	180
new denominations	181
designs and colors	181
paper	181
watermark	181
laid, double and ribbed paper	181
paper watermarked "U. S. I. R."	181

	PAGE
chemical paper	181
reference list	182
plates	184
imprints and numbers	184
plate numbers	184
books of stamps	187
deliveries to postmasters	188
counterfeit two cent stamp	189
quantities of stamps without	
watermark	189
stamps with various imprints	189
Issue of 1898,—(Trans-Mississippi) :	191
designs and colors	191
reference list	193
plates	193
plate numbers	193
plates not used	194
plates for experimental work	194
deliveries to postmasters	194
specimen stamps	195
Issue of 1898 :	196
changes in colors	196
reference list	196
plate numbers	196
stamps surcharged "I. R."	197
stamps surcharged for Cuba, etc.	197
deliveries to postmasters	197
deliveries to Universal Postal	
Union	198
specimen stamps	199
Issue of 1901,—(Pan American Series) :	200
official description	200
reference list	201
plates and imprints	201
inverted medallions	402
Issues, Government	57
Jackson, Andrew	90, 121, 151, 162
Jefferson, Thomas	67, 84, 122, 163, 181
Jover, Francisco,—"Columbus Restored	
to Favor"	173
"Columbus Describ-	
ing Third Voyage"	173
Justice,—The department of	257, 259
special printing	357
Justice, Vignette of	295
Kingman, E. J.	215
" " stamps of	219
Laid paper, 1863 issue	91
1883 issue	152
1894–95 issue	182
Lamprecht,—"Marquette on the	
Mississippi "	192
La Rabida ", "Columbus at	173
Laws, Early postal	6
Lehman, George T.	38
Leslie James, Article by	6
Letter of Frederick N. Palmer	21
" " Postmaster Morris	35, 36
Letters, Serial	149
Letters opened in the Dead Letter Office,	
Seal for	369
Leutze,—"Columbus in Chains "	173
Liberty, Figure of	173
Lincoln, Abraham	92, 110, 121, 162, 290
Local Post, Grafflin's	207

	PAGE.
Local stamps, First	9
Lockport, N. Y.	26
Locomotive	109
Longacre, John B.,—Portrait of Franklin after the	60
Lotto painting, Portrait of Columbus after the	173
Louisville carriers' stamps :	222
David B. Wharton stamps	222
Brown & McGill "	223
counterfeits	223
Louisville find, The	50
MacWhirter,—"Western Cattle in Storm"	192
Madison, Fla.	55
Madison, James	181
Maiden, Indian	296
Mail, U. S., stamps	231
Manufacture, Statistics of ;—see "Statistics of manufacture" under each issue	
Marginal grills	99
" marks	115
Marks, Marginal	115
" Plate maker's guide	115
" Secret, 1873-75	130
" " " description of	131
" " " purpose of	130
"Marquette on the Mississippi"	192
Marshall, John	181
Martin, Joseph G.	215
" " " stamps of	220
Maso, R.—"Columbus at La Rabida"	173
Medallions, Inverted, 1869 issue	112
" " 1901 issue	402
" " State department	267
Messenger boy	250
Millbury, Mass.	27
Minerva	296
Mining Prospector", "Western	192
Mississippi River bridge	192
Mitchell, E. A.	10, 29
Monson, A. C	34
" Marciana	34
Morris, Robert H.	10, 11 29
Natives ", " Columbus Presenting	173
Navigation ", "Fast Lake	200
" "Fast Ocean	200
Navy department	257, 259
special printing	356, 357
two cents green	266
New Haven, Conn.	29
reprints	30
New Orleans postage cards	56
Newspaper and periodical stamps 289, 294, 303, 318, 320, 359	
Issue of 1865 :	289
Act concerning transportation of newspapers	289
announcement of first newspaper stamps	289
designs	289
manufacture	290
paper	290
reference list	290
plates, imprints, plate numbers	291

	PAGE.
restricted use	291
cancellations	291
specimen stamps	291
use discontinued	292
statistics of manufacture	292
reprints	293, 359
counterfeits	293
Issue of 1875 :	294
system suggested by Postmaster General	294
plan authorized by Congress	294
manner of using the stamps	295
reason for the various denominations	295
cancellation	295
designs and colors	295
paper	297
reference list	297
plates, plate numbers	298
specimen stamps	299
statistics of manufacture	299
deliveries to postmasters	300
reprints	361
Issue of 1879 :	303
change of contractors	303
rates reduced	303
one cent stamp	303
plate, plate numbers	304
reference list	304
suggested destruction of unissued stamps	305
three cent stamp again In use	305
specimen stamps	305
deliveries to postmasters	305
order for special printing	315
purpose of special printing	316
disposition of sheets	316
trouble about stamps	316
nine cents printed by American B N. Co.	316
paper, perforation, colors	316
reference list	317
Issue of 1894 :	318
printings from plates of previous contractors	318
reference list	318
plate numbers	319
deliveries to postmasters	319
Issue of 1895 :	320
official announcement	320
designs	320
paper	321
reference list	321
plates	322
plate numbers	322
plates not used	322
deliveries to postmasters	323
other deliveries	324
sets sold to the general public	324
regulations concerning newspaper and periodical stamps	325
seizure of stamps	325
discontinuance of stamps recommended	326
order discontinuing use	327
stamps returned to the P. O. department	327
number of sets sold to the public	328

	PAGE.
reprints	362
Reprints :	359
Issue of 1865	359
Issue of 1875	361
Issue of 1895	362
Newspapers, Act concerning transportation of	289
New York, N. Y.	32
" " " envelopes	36
" " " Initials on the stamps of	34
" " " used in other cities	10, 11
New York carriers' stamps :	225
City Despatch	230
Greig's City Despatch Post	225
New York City Despatch Post	225
U. S. Mail	231
United States City Despatch Post	228
Niagara Falls, Bridge at	200
Nine cents :	
Newspaper	295
Newspaper, reprint	361
Nine dollars :	
Newspaper	296
Newspaper, reprint	362
Ninety cents :	
1856, imperforate	71
1857–60	76
1857–60, reprint	348
1861	85
1861, ultramarine	89
1861, reprint	350
1867	102
1869	110
1869, inverted medallion	114
1869, reprint	351
1870	122
1873–75, secret mark	132
1873–75, reprint	352
1873–75, " of 1880	353
1888	154
1890	163
Ninety-six cents :	
Newspaper	295
Newspaper, reprint	362
Notes, Historical	5
Numerals, Capped	164
Official circulars :	
Issue of 1861	81
" " 1869	108
" " 1870	119
Special delivery stamps	251
Official stamps	258, 278
Newspaper and periodical stamps	327
Postage due stamps	329
reprints	344, 345
Sale of newspaper and periodical stamps	362
Official seals (see " Seals ", Official)	365
Official stamps :	250
Issue of 1873 :	256
historical	256
franking	256
stamps and envelopes authorized	257
early deliveries	257
official description	258

	PAGE.
designs	258
varieties of the higher values	260
paper	260
reference list	260
Navy department 2 cents green	266
P. O. department bi-sected 6 cents	267
P. O. department gray surfaced paper	267
State department inverted medallions	267
plates	268
imprints and plate numbers	268
statistics of manufacture	271
Issue of 1879 :	274
reference list	274
specimen stamps	276
a possible provisional issue	276
plates	276
" Penalty " envelopes authorized	277
Franking privilege extended	278
the stamps entirely abolished	279
Deliveries to departments	279
Unissued official stamps	285
destruction recommended	286
Reprints :	356
plates	356
colors	356
error in surcharge	357, 402
printing by American B. N. Co. (1881)	357
quantities sold	357
One cent :	
1851–55	66
1851–57, types of	67, 68
1857, reprint	348
1861	83
1861, reprint	349
1867, grilled all over	100
1867	101
1869	109
1869, reprint	352
1869, reprint on soft paper	352
1870	121
1873–75, secret mark	131
1873–75, reprint	352
1873–75, reprint of 1880	353
1881–2	147
1887	153
1890	162
1893	172
1898	192
1901	200
1901, inverted medallion	402
Newspaper, 1875	295
Newspaper, 1879	303
Newspaper, 1895	320
Postage due, 1879	330
Postage due, 1879, special printing	364
Postage due, 1894–95	337
One dollar :	
1893	173
1894–95	181
1898	192
Newspaper, 1895	320

	PAGE.
One dollar and ninety two cents :	
Newspaper, 1875	295
Newspaper, 1879	304
Newspaper, reprint	362
One hundred dollars :	
Newspaper, 1895	320
Newspaper, reprint	363
Packages of stamps sent to postmasters,	
. Seal for	367
Palmer, Frederick N.	21
" " " Letter of	21
Pan American series	200
Paper ;—see " Paper " under each issue	
Paper, Double, 1869	114
1870	123
1873–75	134
1894–95	182
Gray surfaced, Post office	
department	267
Laid, 1863	91
1883	152
1894–95	182
Ribbed, 1873–75	136
1894–95	182
Standard	153
Starched, 1873–75	135
Patent, "Douglas"	148
" for grilling stamps	97
" " Francis"	91
Peace, Goddess of	296
Pemberton, E. L., Remarkable study of	49
" Penalty " envelopes authorized	277
Penny Post	212
Penny Post Paid	212
Perforating, Letter concerning	75
Perforation ;—see various issues	
Periodical stamps ;—see "Newspaper and	
periodical stamps "	
Perry, Commodore O. H.	122, 163, 181
Perry, S J.	55, 56
Philadelphia, Pa.	38
Philadelphia carriers' stamps, The	233
Philippine Islands, Stamps surcharged	
for	197, 255
Pittsfield, Mass.	39
Plate, Making of	60
Plate numbers ;—see "plate numbers "	
under each issue	
Platemen's initials	253
Plates ;—see "plates " under each issue	
" experimental	194
" ordered to be cancelled	287
Points up and points down (grills)	99
Pony Express stamps, Wells, Fargo	
& Co.'s	238
" " " counterfeits of	243
Post, Grafflin's Local	207
Greig's City Despatch	225
Hill's	213
New York City Despatch	225
Paid, Penny	212
Penny	212
United States City Despatch	228
Post horse and rider	109, 240
Post Office department, The	257, 259
stamp used as a	
" due " stamp 267, 341	
	PAGE.
gray surfaced	
paper	267
special printings	
	356, 357, 402
" Post Office Despatch " stamps	207, 208
Postage, Prepayment of	57
" Rates of, 1845	57
Postage due stamps :	329
Issue of 1879 :	329
Act authorizing postage due	
stamps	329
circular announcing issue	329
date of issue	330
designs and colors	330
reference list	331
plates and plate numbers	331
used to pay regular postage	332
special printing	332
specimen stamps	332
deliveries to postmasters	332
Issue of 1894–95 :	336
supposed printings from plates	
of A B. Note Co.	337
announcement of the issue	337
color	337
design	337
paper	337
reference list	338
plates	338
imprints	338
plate numbers	338
deliveries to postmasters	338
deliveries to Universal	
Postal Union	339
Universal Postal Congress	340
specimen stamps	340
Provisional issues :	341
Post Office department	
stamp used	341
ordinary postage stamp	
surcharged	341
bisected stamps	341
stamps bisected and sur-	
charged	342
postage due paid by ordinary	
postage stamps	342
Special printing :	364
characteristics	364
plates	364
quantities sold	364
Postal rates modified	153
Postal Union, Countries in the Universal	132
Postmasters, Deliveries to ; — see under	
each issue	
Postmaster's stamp officially recognized,	
A	10
" stamps, Status of	58
" " The	9
" Post Obitum " stamp	369
Post routes, Streets of cities made	65
Posts, Private	6
Powell, Wm. H.,—" Columbus in Sight	
of Land "	172
Powers, Portrait of Andrew Jackson	
by	121, 162
Premierès gravures, 1861 issue	85
Prepaid letters, Special rate for	65
Prepayment of postage	57

	PAGE.
Presses, steam, Printing on, required by contract	153
" " Printings on	139
Printed matter, Reduction of rates for	66
Printing on steam presses required by contract	153
Printing on steam presses	139
Private posts	6
Proofs, 1890 issue	165
Prospector", "Western Mining	192
Protest against reprinting, No	343
Providence, R. I.	40
counterfeits	43
reprints	42
Providence plate, Discovery of the	41
Provisional postage due stamps	341
Punch, Cog wheel	134
" Fletcher or cog wheel	134
Puerto Rico, Stamps surcharged for	197
Purchases by stamp dealers and collectors (1893 issue)	177
Rates of postage, Early	6
" of postage in 1845	57
" of the carrier service	203
". Postal, modified	153
"Recall of Columbus"	173
Redemption of three and six cent stamps	153
Re-engraved and retouched dies, 1881-2	147
Reference list ;—see under each issue	
Registered letters and packages, Seal for	365
Re-Issues ;—see also "Reprints"	343
" differentiated, Reprints and	345
Remainders, 1857-60 issue	83
" destroyed, 1873-75 issue	143
Remington, Frederick ;—"Troops Guarding Train"	192
"Western Mining Prospector"	192
Reprinting, Journalistic criticism	343
" No protest against	343
" Official circular relating to	344
Reprints 31, 35, 42, 293, 344-365	
" and re-issues differentiated	345
" carriers' stamps	355
" dates of first and last sales of	346
" issue of 1847	346
" issue of 1857	348
" issue of 1861	349
" issue of 1869	350
" issue of 1870	351
" issue of 1882	354
" issue of 1883	354
" New Haven, Conn.	31
" newspaper and periodical stamps	359
" newspaper stamps, 1865	293
" New York, N. Y.	35
" official stamps 356, 402	
" postage due stamps	364
" quantities of	346
" Reasons for making	344
" seals for registered letters	365
" Special treatment for the	346
Retouched and re-engraved dies, 1881-2	147
Revell, Martin F.	13
Ribbed paper, 1873-75	136
1894-95	182

	PAGE.
Rocky Mountains", "Fremont on the	192
Rogers, Randolph ;—"Columbus Welcomed at Barcelona"	173
Roller, grill, Process of making	98
Rollers, grill, Destruction of the	124
Rubricht, Portrait of Franklin after 83, 162	
St. Louis, Mo.	45
counterfeits	50
stamps, Louisville find of	50
Sample stamps	161
Sayles, Welcome B.	40
Scarlet three cents of 1861	90
Scott, Gen. Winfield	122
Scovell, Hezekiah W.	26
Seals, official	365
for registered letters and packages	365
date of issue	365
purpose of the seal	365
design	365
gum and perforation	366
reference list	366
plates	366
reprint	366
for packages of stamps sent to postmasters	367
date of issue	367
first design	367
overprint	367
colors	367
reference list	368
second design	368
varieties	368
reference list	368
for letters opened in Dead Letter Office, etc.	369
"Post Obitum"	369
design	369
plate	369
reference list	369
changes in design	369
date of issue	369
plates and imprints	370
paper	370
reference list	370
another change in the seal	370
method of production	370
distinguishing marks	370
reference list	371
stone	371
historical	371
sheets	372
type-set	372
origin	372
design 372, 373	
changes in design and paper	373
colors	373
rouletting	373
reference list	373
Secret marks, 1873-75	130
" " " description of	131
" " " purpose of	130
Seizure of newspaper and periodical stamps	325
Serial letters	149
Seven cents :	
1870 120, 121	

PAGE.

Seven cents :
    1873–75, secret mark   132
    1873–75, reprint   352
    1873–75, reprint of 1880   353
Seventy-two cents :
    Newspaper, 1875   295
    Newspaper, 1879   304
    Newspaper, reprint   362
Seward, William H.   259
Sherman, Gen. Wm. T.   163
Shield and eagle   109, 110
Signatures on stamps   10
Six cents :
    1869   109
    1869, reprint   351
    1870   121
    1873–75, secret mark   132
    1873–75, reprint   352
    1881–82   147
    1890   163
    1893   173
    Post Office department,
        bi-sected   267
    Newspaper, 1875   295
    Newspaper, 1879   304
    Newspaper, reprint   361
Six dollars :
    Newspaper, 1875   296
    Newspaper, 1879   305
    Newspaper, reprint   362
Sixty cents :
    Newspaper, 1875   295
    Newspaper, 1879   304
    Newspaper, reprint   362
Sixty dollars :
    Newspaper, 1875   296
    Newspaper, 1879   305
    Newspaper, reprint   362
Sizes ;—see under each issue
Special delivery stamps :   250
    design   250
    official circular   251
    change of color   252
    changes in design   253
    platemen's initials   253
    paper and gum   253
    reference list   253
    plates   254
    plate numbers   254
    deliveries to postmasters   255
    specimen stamps   255
    surcharged stamps   255
Special printing of Newspaper stamps,
    Order for   315
    "   "   Postage due stamps of
        1879   332
Special printings (see also " Reprints ")   343
Specimen stamps :
    1861–66   93
    1883   152
    1894–95   189
    1898   195, 199
    Special delivery   255
    Newspaper, 1865   291
    Newspaper, 1875   299
    Newspaper, 1879   305
    Postage due, 1879   332
    Postage due, 1894–95   342

PAGE.

Specimen stamps :
    Official   356, 402
Stamp collecting, An official view of   171
    "   collectors, Purchases by   177
Stamps authorized, First   59
    "   Bisected, 1851–57 issue   70, 401
    "   1863 issue   90
    "   1869 issue, three cents   114
    "   1890 issue   165
    "   Books of   187
    "   Carriers',—see " Carriers' stamps "
    "   destroyed, 1867 issue   103
    "   " Douglas patent "   148
    "   grilling, Patent for   97
    "   invalid, Authority to declare   82
    "   on double paper   114, 123, 134, 182
    "   Postage due,—see " Postage
             due stamps "
    "   Postmasters', The   9
    "   " Sample "   161
    "   " Specimen ",—see " Specimen
             stamps "
    "   Unpaid letter,—see " Unpaid
             letter stamps "
Standard paper   153
Stanton, Edward M.   121
Starched paper, 1873–75   135
State department, The   257, 259
    inverted medallions   267
    special printing   356, 357
Statistics ;—see under each issue
Steam presses, Printings on   139
    Printing on, required by
        contract   153
Steamship   109
Steinmeyer, John F.   215
    Stamps of   220
Streets of cities made post routes   65
Stuart, Gilbert, Portrait of Washington
    after   60, 67, 75, 109
    Portrait of Madison after   181
Surcharged as Postage due stamps,
    Ordinary stamps   341
    "   for Cuba, Stamps   197
    "   " Guam   "   197, 255
    "   " Philippine Islands,
             Stamps   197, 255
    "   " Puerto Rico, Stamps   197, 255
    "   " I. R.", Stamps   197
    "   official stamps, Error of   356, 402
    "   Postage due stamps,
             bisected and   342
Surfaced paper, Gray, Post Office
    department   267

Taylor, Gen. Zachary   133
Ten cents :
    1847   60
    1847, reprint   346
    1851–57   67
    1851–57, reprint   348
    1851–57, types of   69
    1851–57, bisected   71
    1857–60, types of   76
    1861   84
    1861, reprint   349
    1867   102
    1869   109

	PAGE.
Ten cents :	
1869, reprint	351
1870	121
1873–75, secret mark	132
1873–75, reprint	352
1873–75, reprint of 1880	353
1881–82	147
1890	163
1893	173
1898	192
1901	200
Special delivery	250
Newspaper, 1865	289
Newspaper, 1865, reprint	360
Newspaper, 1875	295
Newspaper, 1875, reprint	361
Newspaper, 1879	304
Newspaper, 1895	320
Postage due, 1879	330
Postage due, 1879, special printing	364
Postage due, 1894–95	337
Ten dollars :	
State deparment	259
Newspaper, 1895	320
Newspaper, 1895, reprint	363
Thirty cents :	
1856, imperforate	71
1857–60	76
1857–60, reprint	348
1857–60, the black	78
1861	85
1861, reprint	350
1867, grilled all over	100
1867	101
1869	110
1869, inverted medallion	112
1869, reprint	351
1870	122
1870–73, secret mark	132
1870–73, reprint	352
1870–73, reprint of 1880	353
1888	154
1890	163
1893	173
Postage due, 1879	330
Postage due, 1879, special printing	364
Postage due, 1894–95	337
Thirty-six cents :	
Newspaper, 1875	295
Newspaper, 1879	304
Newspaper, reprint	361
Thirty-six dollars :	
Newspaper, 1875	296
Newspaper, 1879	305
Newspaper, reprint	362
Three cents :	
1851–55	66
1851–57, types of	68, 69
1851–57, bisected	70, 401
1857–60, types of	76
1857, reprint	348
1861	83
1861, scarlet	90
1861, reprint	349
1867	101
1869	109

	PAGE.
Three cents :	
1869, bisected	114
1869, reprint	351
1870	121
1873–75, secret mark	132
1873–75, reprint	352
1873–75, reprint of 1880	353
1881–82	147
1887	154
1890	162
1893	173
Newspaper	295, 305
Newspaper, reprint	361
Postage due, 1879	330
Postage due, 1879, special printing	364
Postage due, 1894–95	337
Three dollars :	
1893	173
Newspaper, 1875	296
Newspaper, 1879	304
Newspaper, reprint	361
Train ", " Troops Guarding	192
Trans-Mississippi series	191
Treasury department, The	257, 259
special printing	356
Triangle, Varieties of	180
" Troops Guarding Train "	192
Trumbull,—Portrait of Washington by	76
" Declaration of Independence " by	110
Twelve cents :	
1851–57	67
1851–57, reprint	348
1851–57, bisected	70
1861	84
1861, reprint	349
1867	102
1869	109
1869, reprint	349
1870	122
1873–75, secret mark	132
1873–75, reprint	352
1873–75, reprint of 1880	353
Newspaper, 1875	295
Newspaper, 1879	304
Newspaper, reprint	361
Twelve dollars :	
Newspaper, 1875	296
Newspaper, 1879	305
Newspaper, reprint	362
Twenty dollars :	
State department	259
Newspaper	320
Newspaper, reprint	363
Twenty-four cents :	
1856, imperforate	71
1857–60	75
1857–60, reprint	348
1861	84
1861, reprint	350
1869	110
1869, inverted medallion	112
1869, reprint	351
1870	122
1873–75, secret mark	132
1873 75, reprint	352
1873–75, reprint of 1880	353

PAGE.

Twenty-four cents :
    Newspaper, 1875   295
    Newspaper, 1879   304
    Newspaper, reprint   361
Twenty-four dollars :
    Newspaper, 1875   296
    Newspaper, 1879   305
    Newspaper, reprint   362
Twenty-five cents :
    Newspaper, 1865   289
    Newspaper, 1895   320
    Newspaper, reprint   360
Two cents :
    1863   90
    1863, bisected   90
    1861, reprint   349
    1867   101
    1869   109
    1869, reprint   351
    1870   121
    1873-75, secret mark   131
    1873-75, reprint   352
    1873-75, reprint of 1880   353
    1883   151
    1883, varieties   151
    1883, reprint   354
    1887   154
    1890   162
    1890, capped numerals   164
    1893   172
    1893, imperforate   174
    1894-95, counterfeit   189
    1898   192
    1901   200
    1901, inverted medallion   402
    Navy department, green   266
    Newspaper   295, 305
    Newspaper, reprint   360
    Newspaper, 1895   320
    Postage due, 1879   330
    Postage due, 1879, special
        printing   364
    Postage due, 1894-95   337
Two dollars :
    1893   173
    1894-95   181
    1898   192
    State department   259
    Newspaper, 1895   320
Type-set seals   372

Union, Universal Postal, Countries in
    the   132
United States City Despatch Post   228
Universal Postal Congress, Stamps
        overprinted for   189

PAGE.

Newspaper stamps
    overprinted for   324
Postage due stamps
    overprinted for   340
Special delivery stamps
    overprinted for   255
Universal Postal Union, Countries in the   132
Postage due stamps
    delivered to   340
Stamps of 1898
    delivered to   198
"U. S. I. R." watermark   182
U. S. Mail (New York Carriers' stamp)   231
"U. S. P. S." watermark   181
Unissued Official stamps, Schedule of   285
Unpaid letter stamps,—see " Postage
        due stamps"

Vanderlyn,—" Landing of Columbus"
    by   109, 172
Vesta   296
Victory, Goddess of   296

War department, The   257, 259
    special printing   357
Washington, D. C.   52
Washington, George (Portrait of)
    27, 32, 60, 66, 67, 75, 76, 83, 84,
    109, 121, 151, 162, 227, 229, 230,
    290.
Washington, General   76
Watermark U. S. I. R.   181
    U. S. P. S.   182
Waters, Asa H.   27
Webster, Daniel   122, 163
Webster, Worcester   20
Wells, Fargo & Co.'s Pony Express
    Stamps :   238
    Overland California Mail   239
    Pony Express   239
    tariff on private corres-
        pondence   240
    " Garter " stamp   240
    counterfeits   241, 243
    reprints   241
West ", " Farming in the   192
" Western Mining Prospector "   192
Wharton, David B , Stamps of   222
Wheel punch, Cog (Fletcher)   134
Wimer, John M.   45
Wisdom, Goddess of (Minerva)   296
Withdrawn, Unsold stamps (1893 or
        Columbian series)   177
Wolcott, Statue of O. H. Perry   163
Worcester, Mass   54

Youth, Goddess of   296

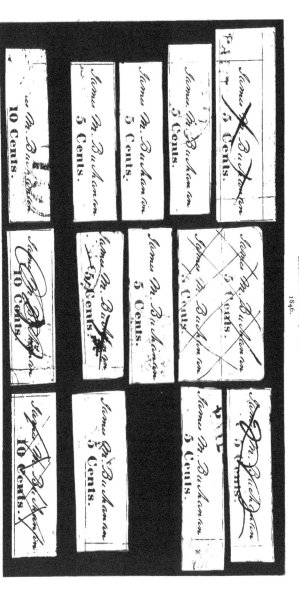

BALTIMORE, Md.
1846.

1849-50.

1849-50.

1851

E. J. KINGMAN.
1851.

1877.

1878.

1888

1889

U. S. Post Office Department.

OFFICIALLY SEALED.

Opened through mistake by

U. S. Post Office Department.

OFFICIALLY SEALED.

Opened through mistake by

U. S. Post Office Department.

OFFICIALLY · SEALED

Opened through mistake by

ImTheStory.com